PATTERNS OF LIFE HISTORY:
The Ecology of Human Individuality

SERIES IN APPLIED PSYCHOLOGY

Edwin A. Fleishman, George Mason University
Series Editor

PATTERNS OF LIFE HISTORY:
The Ecology of Human Individuality

Michael D. Mumford
George Mason University

Garnett S. Stokes
William A. Owens
University of Georgia

LEA LAWRENCE ERLBAUM ASSOCIATES, PUBLISHERS
1990   Hillsdale, New Jersey   Hove and London

155.2
M96p

Lawrence Erlbaum Associates, Inc., Publishers
365 Broadway
Hillsdale, New Jersey 07642

Library of Congress Cataloging-in-Publication Data

Mumford, Michael D.
  Patterns of life history : the ecology of human individuality /
Michael D. Mumford, Garnett S. Stokes, William A. Owens.
    p.   cm.
  Includes index.
  ISBN 0–8058–0225–8
  1. Individuality.   2. Adjustment (Psychology)   I. Stokes,
Garnett S.   II. Owens, William A.   III. Title.
  [DNLM: 1. Adaptation, Psychological.   2. Epidemiological Methods.
3. Individuality.   4. Longitudinal Studies.   BF 697 M962p]
BF697.M82   1989
155.2–dc 19
DNLM/DLC
for Library of Congress   89–1142
                                                                   CIP

Printed in the United States of America
10 9 8 7 6 5 4 3 2 1

Contents

v

Series Foreword

There is a compelling need for innovative approaches to the solution of many pressing problems involving human relationships in today's society. Such approaches are more likely to be successful when they are based on sound research and applications. This *Series in Applied Psychology* offers publications that emphasize state-of-the-art research and its application to important issues of human behavior in a variety of societal settings. The objective is to bridge both academic and applied interests.

Few applied psychologists would dispute the fact that biographical data predicts performance. What we have lacked an explanation for is exactly *why* such background measures predict. Because it is unclear how past behavior conditions future behavior, it has proven virtually impossible to develop a cohesive theoretical approach to background data. This lack of theory has, in turn, stymied growth in what is a promising area.

Some 20 years ago, William Owens started a long-term research program that might, hopefully, solve this problem. His idea was impressively elegant, noting that empirically keyed background data measures define a developmental pattern. He went on to argue that it might be possible to obtain a more general understanding of background data, the manner in which past behavior conditions future behavior, and the nature of developmental patterns, by using subgrouping techniques to define general patterns of differential development. Subsequently, he initiated a longitudinal study intended to elucidate the nature of these general developmental patterns through the application of subgrouping techniques.

This research was a massive undertaking involving the collaboration of many individuals. Michael Mumford and Garnett Stokes, the co-authors of this volume with Dr. Owens, have been among the major contributors. In this volume, these authors focus on the nature and significance of general developmental patterns. The authors first present an argument for the use of such patterns in the description of human individuality. Subsequently, they describe the methods employed and results obtained in a series of studies in which subgrouping techniques were used to define developmental patterns.

Although this research is continuing, this volume illustrates the substantial practical contributions that have already been made. For instance, the conceptual framework for understanding the emergence of the developmental patterns has already proven useful in formulating principles for the construct and content validation of background data measures. In this book, the authors demonstrate, moreover, how subgrouping techniques might be used to address a number of rather trenchant problems facing organizational psychology.

In addition to providing a basis for using subgrouping techniques to address a number of practical problems confronting industrial psychology, this book shows how background data subgroups and the notion of developmental patterns might be used to address a number of different substantive issues. Perhaps most significantly, these developmental patterns provide a vehicle for compromising the extreme ideographic and nomothetic positions. Further, their work suggests some key mechanisms giving rise to the emergence of coherent patterns of behavior, despite the existence of temporal instability.

This is perhaps one of the most intriguing features of this volume of the series. Due to the dedicated efforts of the authors, a measurement technique, which was once derided as atheoretical, has now emerged as one of the most theoretically advanced measurement systems in psychology. As a result, it seems likely that this volume will do much, not only to contribute to the predictive power of background data, but also to our understanding of human individuality.

Edwin A. Fleishman, Editor
Series in Applied Psychology

Preface

The authors of this book are commended for an innovative and imaginative attack on a problem that has thus far given ground only haltingly to some of the most gifted and persistent investigators. Half a century ago, Allport observed that psychology seemed on the verge of losing the individual through the interstices of nomothetic law. Little has changed. The individual case is lawful but not representative whereas an average is both of the foregoing but is, in addition, an abstraction in which individual cases have become blurred and indistinct. To this classical conflict, the authors present not only a philosophical solution but a pragmatic/statistical one as well. Briefly, they suggest a true compromise involving the use of relatively homogeneous subgroups, the means of which are much more stable than an individual case, but across which there is still variation suggestive of the original spread of individuals.

Scored autobiographical data items that cover a number of the major dimensions of development provide a behaviorally based and interpretable vehicle for the subgrouping. Statistical methods they have utilized invoke no preconceptions regarding a number of subgroups to be identified, and "N's" are large. The data permit both longitudinal or sequential and cross-sectional analyses, and not only are both made, but they are followed by a revealing composite analysis as well. Finally, although only biodata responses are utilized in the grouping procedure, a wealth of other data is available in terms of which to characterize the subsets once they are identified. Over time, the authors have found it convenient to refer to the successive test means and other descriptive materials within a given subgroup as constituting or defining a *prototype,* and these prototypes have been found to be conceptually clear, robust, useful in pre-diction, and sensibly related to other variables. Will they bridge the nomothetic–idiographic gap? Perhaps. Meanwhile, the writers have sug-gested some ways of finding out.

ACKNOWLEDGMENTS

The writers recognize that much of what is reported here was accom-plished under the terms of a research grant from the National Institute for Child Health and Human Development (5 R01 Hd04135-10, William A. Owens, principal investigator) and that much more of it was drawn from the theses and dissertations of graduate students, including one by Michael D. Mumford, titled *Individuality and Development: Life History Dimensions and Types Between Age 18 and 30*, The University of Georgia, 1983, and a second by Garnett Stokes Shaffer, titled *A Study of Differential Patterns of Life and Job Satisfaction*, The University of Georgia, 1982.

William A. Owens

Approaches to the Study of Human Individuality: Science and Individuality

The mythology of science describes researchers untangling the complexities of natural phenomena through the objective, dispassionate application of logic and the power of the human mind. Undoubtedly, this myth reflects certain truths concerning the methods and style of scientific research. Yet through long hours and myriad disappointments, what sustains the individual tucked away in the dark bowels of some ancient building is a passionate commitment to some form of knowledge and understanding that transcends pure logic. Although the ensuing discussion presents a variety of logical arguments stemming from an examination of the results obtained in a rather extensive investigation, like most efforts of this sort, it also reflects a nearly compulsive fascination with a particular natural phenomenon; in this case, the development, meaning, and manifold manifestations of human individuality.

This is not an especially novel preoccupation. One of the most obvious facets of human existence is the uniqueness of the individual, and down through the ages the nature of human individuality has been debated by poets, priests, scholars, and peasants. Some of the reasons for this perennial debate are quite easy to identify. From the dawn of culture, mankind has been required to make a variety of decisions concerning the individual. For instance, individuals must be allocated to the available jobs or training programs, selected for leadership positions or public office, chosen as potential friends or mates, and occasionally evaluated by a jury of their peers. Because there is often a lack of other information on which to base these decisions, humanity has found it necessary to analyze the characteristics of the individual and to use this information in selecting a course of action. When this is coupled with the fundamental import and costs of many of these decisions for both the individual and society, it is hardly surprising that the topic of individuality has preoccupied many. Substantial empirical support for the practical importance of basing decisions on the characteristics of the individual may be found in Schmidt, Hunter, McKenzie, and Muldrow's (1979) observation that a failure to employ this information may cost organizations billions of dollars each year, but its true importance may be clarified by considering the possible consequences of placing a paranoid in the Oval Office.

On a more subtle level, the course of history and the quality of our lives may occasionally be influenced by commonly held beliefs concerning the nature of human individuality. An example of this phenomenon may be found in the nature-versus-nurture controversy. Traditionally, some people have believed that an individual's characteristics were the result of ingrained and immutable hereditary predispositions, whereas others have believed that they were the end product of a unique series of past experiences. This latter belief suggests that actions may be taken, by the government or other agents, that will "improve" the individual, whereas the former belief suggests that little can be done to change him or her. When the belief in the nurture argument was dominant in the 1960s and 1970s, a number of actions were taken by the American government in an attempt to induce desirable changes in individuals. Although it continues to be difficult to evaluate the success of these efforts, there is little doubt that the actions associated with this belief, such as affirmative action programs and increased social security benefits, have had a profound effect on American society.

Obviously, this suggests that the nature of human individuality is not a value-free topic. The use of aptitude, ability, and intelligence tests as descriptors of an individual's characteristics and a basis for decisions has been sharply criticized in recent years. Essentially, critics argue that standardized tests yield an inappropriate and artificial description of the individual that is employed in sorting people into the lords, vassels, and serfs of American society. Others argue that such assessments serve an important purpose in a world of limited resources where both the individual and society are benefitted by an optimal allocation of the available talent (Tyler, 1974). Within the context of the present discussion, it is impossible to resolve this conflict, partly because it is a political dispute that involves a tradeoff between equity and equality considerations. Nevertheless, the existence of this conflict and the importance of the decisions that are tied to our conceptions and assessment of human individuality point to the importance of sound scientific investigations of the phenomenon.

Of course, it has often been argued that the scientific study of any topic as nebulous as human individuality represents little more than an exercise in futility. Certainly, any single attempt to study human individuality as an observable natural phenomenon is unlikely to provide answers to many of the questions that mankind has posed in this regard. Moreover, such an effort cannot address the political issues laid out heretofore, nor can it define the essence, soul, or value of a particular person. In our opinion, these matters are best left to philosophers and the courts. Nevertheless, the development of human individuality is a natural occurrence, and so it should be possible to employ the observational logic of science in an attempt to obtain at least a limited, albeit consensual, understanding of the phenomena. Certainly, its conceptional and pragmatic importance would seem to warrant a substantial effort along these lines, even bearing in mind the limitations that are inherent in the scientific method.

INDIVIDUALITY AND PSYCHOLOGY

The importance of human individuality has not been completely ignored in the social sciences, although it has not received the attention it deserves in recent years. Traditionally, the study of human individuality has been the province of psychology. Although definitions of the nature and goals of psychological research differ, general agreement exists that psychology's primary task entails the description, prediction, and understanding of behavior. Behavior may be observed in many forms, and any given behavioral act is a complex event that, in both its conception and expression, is influenced by a variety of factors. Some of the factors underlying a behavioral act may generalize across a number of organisms, whereas others may be specific to a single organism. Yet, in all cases, behavior will be a property of an individual organism. In other words, such variables as physiology, drugs, and social structure may influence behavior, but it is always a single organism that will emit the consequent behaviors.

If behavior is a property of the individual organism, it follows that psychology's attempts to describe, predict, and understand behavior must also be tied to the individual organism. Cognizance of this fact has made the individual the central referent in psychological theory (Vale & Vale, 1969) but not necessarily the central referent in relevant research methods. In its attempt to progress as a science, psychology has been forced to address the issue of what constitutes individuality. Unfortunately, a fundamental question has involved conceptualizing and quantifying individual behavior within a replicable operational methodology.

To date, one of the best descriptions of the parameters within which studies of individuality must operate is Kluckhohn and Murray's (1949) comment that each person's behavior is like the behavior of "all other men, some other men, and no other men" (p. 46). Ideally, psychological research concerned with the nature of human individuality should examine behavior in relation to all three of these levels. Unfortunately, the truly idiosyncratic, or the ways in which a person is like no other person, are beyond the scope of the analytical tools of social science. On the other hand, despite its relevance to understanding individual behavior in the broadest sense, the ways in which a person's behavior is like the behavior of *all* others prevents defining the individual as a separate being with unique behavioral properties. Hence, by default, psychological studies of human individuality have come to focus on the ways in which the individual's behavior is like that of some other persons. Historically, this area of endeavor has been referred to as involving measurement and the psychology of individual differences, and in the remainder of this book an attempt is made to examine individual differences as a natural phenomenon along with psychology's varied attempts to formulate a science of human individuality within the context of differential behavior.

ISSUES IN THE STUDY OF INDIVIDUALITY

At present, the field has not reached any consensus with respect to a single most appropriate methodology for use in attempts to describe, predict, and understand human individuality (Mischel, 1969). The existence of multiple schools of thought has led a number of scholars to suggest that the study of human individuality, like psychology as a whole, remains in a pre-scientific phase of development (Kuhn, 1970). A number of general issues are likely to be important in any effort to study individuality. In the following paragraphs, the general issues are explored, and the various strategies that have been employed in the study of human individuality, along with their relative strengths and weaknesses, are discussed.

As previously stated, studies of human individuality must focus on the ways in which the behavior of the individual is similar to or different from the behavior of others. What, at first glance, seems to be a rather straightforward requirement has been the source of a number of problems. Most problems stem from the fact that individuality will be reflected in *all those behaviors* that different individuals display with different frequency or intensity. In a more technical sense, a legitimate indicator of individuality exists whenever variance among individuals exceeds that attributable to random measurement error. Thus, the sheer number of behaviors that could be legitimate indicators of individuality prohibits a comprehensive description of every person in terms of all their discrete behaviors. Consequently, a perennial problem entails determining how information derived from various indicators of individuality across persons may be summarized in a viable description of the individual. Given the fundamental importance of this issue, it is hardly surprising that it has been a major source of controversy.

All attempts to summarize the differential characteristics of individuals are based on either an explicit or implicit classification of the relevant indicators or persons into categories based on some conception of the similarities and differences between them. These categories then form a basis for formulating a summary description of individuality. Fleishman and Quaintance (1984) have noted that there are a number of different methods that might be employed in classification efforts and a number of different ways in which similarities and differences may be defined. For instance, classification can be made on the basis of inferential logic, deductive logic, or statistical covariation. Similarity may be defined on the basis of the frequency with which a behavior is expressed or its intensity of expression. Given manifold approaches to classification, it is hardly surprising that some disagreement exists concerning the manner in which a summary description of human individuality should be formulated.

Because classification efforts represent a topic beyond the scope of the present discussion, it is not possible to examine the subject in any detail. However, there are certain general points bearing on the description of human individuality that should be noted. Figure 1.1 presents a schematic representation of the strategies that may be employed in classification efforts. It is intended to convey two general notions. First, classification may be carried out either through qualitative observational and theoretical considerations, or through quantitative empirical relationships. Second, the units being classified may be either individuals or their behaviors.

That is, classification and summarization of behavior can be carried out either by assigning individuals to different categories on the basis of

Classification Units	Classification Methods	
	Qualitative	Quantitative
Behaviors	1	2
Persons	3	4

FIG. 1.1.   Classification strategies.

their behaviors or by assigning behaviors to different categories on the basis of their expression by an individual.

Studies of human individuality generally incorporate three specific implementations of these generic strategies. First, differential behaviors are often classified and summarized on the basis of their pragmatic or theoretical significance with respect to a particular phenomena of interest. This strategy falls into cell 1 of Fig. 1.1, and its use is illustrated in numerous experimental studies and in the construction of many tests. For example, in the development of content-valid achievement tests, an attempt is made to identify and combine a set of responses to test items that reflect academic performance in some domain across both persons and situations. A second implementation involves summarizing differential behavior by combining behaviors that display a high degree of overlap across persons. This is accomplished by identifying and combining indicators of differential behavior that give similar descriptions of individuals, as indexed by the extent of their intercorrelations or by the stability with which individuals are ordered in terms of frequency, intensity, or correctness. Summarization attempts of this sort fall into the second cell, and this strategy is often used in the construction of personality tests. Finally, pre-existing groups of observational or theoretical significance, such as males, females, successful salespersons, or schizophrenics, are sometimes used to summarize differential behavior by identification of the behaviors that are characteristic of each of these groups. A statement assigning a person to one of these categories can then be used to summarize a wide variety of differential behaviors. Illustrations of this approach may be found in the procedures employed in the construction of life history keys and vocational interest inventories, and these measures would fall into the third cell of Fig. 1.1.

The preceding procedures for formulating summary descriptions are not necessarily mutually exclusive (Gough, 1957). In fact, most studies employ some combination of both the qualitative and quantitative methods for the classification of behavior. Yet it is also true that most investigations tend to focus on a particular classification strategy, and application of different strategies may yield very different descriptions for the individual. For example, the summary descriptions obtained through application of cell 2 procedures would incorporate a set of manifestly similar or homogenous behaviors, but the summary descriptions obtained through application of cell 3 procedures would incorporate a very diverse set of behavioral indicators. Because these summarization strategies provide the groundwork for any study of human individuality, yet may not yield comparable descriptions of the individual, the selection of an appropriate classification strategy is an important issue that should be based on both the problem at hand and the perceived nature of human individuality. Unfortunately, this topic has not received a great deal of attention, in part because psychology lacks a well-grounded understanding of individuality in behavior (Fiske, 1979).

Assuming that an appropriate method has been selected for summarizing differential indicators, the issue of how much generality should be sought arises; that is, whether a summarization should be applicable to a single individual, a group of individuals, or all human beings. The relative value of the idiographic and nomothetic approaches has been debated at length in the literature (Lamiell, 1981). The distinction becomes blurred if a description is targeted on a limited segment of the population, such as individuals over age 65. Despite this confusion, the choice is an important one because it implies a tradeoff between the descriptive accuracy characterizing the idiographic strategy and the generality, efficiency, and parsimony associated with the nomothetic strategy.

After specifying the indicators and the level of generality needed for application across individuals, the summarization may be operationalized and employed in the description of a particular individual. In operationalization the individual's status on the indicators included in a summary category can be used to obtain a quantitative description of the individual through some subset of psychometric and experimental techniques (Guilford, 1954). However, because there is not likely to be any absolute criterion available for defining individuality, description of a particular individual is generally carried out through a comparative or relativistic strategy. In experimental studies, this is accomplished by comparing the behavior of an experimental group to the behavior of some control group and ascribing differences to all individuals undergoing the experimental treatment. In psychometric studies, the performance of a given individual on the operational summarization is compared to the typical performance of the members of a normative group. In certain cases, the normative comparisons may be replaced by ipsative comparison, in which the individual's performance is assessed in relation to personal performance on other summarizations or in other experimental conditions. The ipsative strategy is most often employed in conjunction with an idiographic approach. Regardless of the particular procedure being employed, the description of the individual must be parsimonious in the sense that the summary categories should be limited to the smallest possible number required to obtain an adequate description, prediction, and understanding of differential behavior.

The meaningfulness or practical significance of the description of individuals derived from a particular summarization of indicators is of substantial importance, because there must be some assurance that a viable summary description has, in fact, been formulated. Scientific and pragmatic concerns have resulted in a two-fold approach to this problem. Initially, it had been incumbent on researchers to establish the reliability or robustness of a particular summary description by demonstrating that it reflected variance among individuals above and beyond that which may be attributed to measurement error or chance expectation. Although some ambiguity exists in determining exactly what constitutes measurement error (Thorndike, 1949), various indices of reliability, along with cross validation and replication efforts, have proven to be of some value. Additionally, researchers should attempt to establish the meaningfulness or validity of a summary description by determining the extent to which (a) the indicators incorporated in a summary description provide an adequate sample of the relevant domain or category of differential behavior (content validity); (b) the description of individuals obtained from the summarization is related to other indicators of differential behavior of some significance (criterion related validity); and (c) the summarization manifests a meaningful pattern of interrelationships with other indicators of individuality (construct validity). Though construct validity subsumes content and criterion related validity (Messick, 1980), the most clearcut evidence of the effectiveness of a summary description of individuality is often provided by focusing on predictive validity.

Differential psychology has expended a great deal of effort on the study of procedures for the operationalization and validation of a summary description of individuality. However, a somewhat more nebulous issue has been the effect of differing assumptions regarding the causal locus of individuality. Some investigations assume that individual differences in behavior can be attributed to the particular sequence of environments and learning experiences to which the individual has been exposed, whereas others assume that they are the result of enduring, perhaps hereditary, predispositions that are properties of the individual rather than the environment. Labels such as nature versus nurture and trait versus state philosophies have often been applied to these divergent perspectives. Although psychologists have not been able to resolve this debate in nearly a century of its cyclical reemergence in the literature, there can be little doubt that the assumptions that investigators make in this regard have had a substantial impact on the methods employed and the results obtained in studies of human individuality.

APPROACHES TO THE STUDY
OF HUMAN INDIVIDUALITY

Over the course of the years, the varied attempts of psychologists to address the foregoing concerns have led to the emergence of four major methodological approaches to the study of human individuality. Experimentation has long been the psychologist's favored vehicle for the study of human behavior as a general phenomenon. Although experimental methodology has tended to be relatively less popular among students of individual differences, the experimental approach has found adherents among those investigators who attribute individual differences to situational influences. This preference may be due to the fact that experimental methods lend themselves to the specification and understanding of situational influences on differential behavior.

Application of the experimental strategy begins with specification and operationalization of a dependent variable reflecting the differential behaviors of interest and an independent variable reflecting a situational influence external to the individual that might affect the expression of this behavior by individuals. Generally, both theoretical and pragmatic considerations enter into the definition and operationalization of the dependent and independent variables. Inferences concerning individual behavior are drawn from significant group differences, indicating that all people exposed to the situational differences manifest in different levels of the independent variable will display similar differences in behavior, other things equal.

Summarization of differential behavior within the experimental paradigm is thus carried out on the basis of nomothetic theory. The meaningfulness of a theory and the results of an investigation derived from it are assessed through internal validity, or contrasting alternative theoretical hypotheses, and external validity, or the realism of manipulations, along with statistical significance and replication of the relevant findings. Because the experimental approach permits investigators to contrast alternative theoretical explanations and manipulate independent variables to examine the effect of these antecedent states on behavior, it provides a powerful test for obtaining a well-founded understanding of differential behavior. However, this advantage of the experimental paradigm is countered by three limitations. First, the lack of realism that is apparent in many psychological experiments limits the utility of this approach. Second, there are many variables relevant to differential behavior that cannot be examined in short-term experimental manipulations, and the ethics of experimentation are open to question in many areas of differential psychology. Finally, although experimental procedures may be useful in providing a nomothetic understanding of certain aspects of individuality, they are not designed to provide a well-organized, global description of a particular individual.

In systematic studies of human individuality, the most popular alternative to experimentation is the trait approach. Broadly speaking, application of the trait model assumes that there are certain enduring characteristics, such as honesty or shyness, that one may use to summarize differential behaviors with constant meaning and accuracy across time, persons, and situations. Although this rather stringent specification of the trait model has been modified in practice such that the possibility of situational influences interacting with traits is often examined (Atkinson, 1981), the model focuses on the description of differential behavior that is, in some fashion, attributed to the influence of certain underlying and enduring characteristics. Moreover, the nomothetic descriptions derived from this approach are designed to define individuals in terms of their differential possession of a limited number of underlying characteristics that summarize a wide variety of differential behaviors.

Implementation of the trait model is consequently based on identifying some construct that provides a legitimate summarization of a number of differential behaviors displayed by individuals. This is accomplished by identifying a subset of differential behaviors through either theory or correlational techniques that each reflect the same underlying construct. These homogenous behaviors are then combined into a measure of the underlying construct or trait. The extent to which the trait measure provides an enduring description of the individual may be determined by retesting individuals at a later point in time. Meaningfulness is established through construct, criterion, or content validation strategies. However, special consideration is often given to the ability of the measure to describe or predict other forms of relevant differential behaviors not directly assessed by the indicators summarized in the trait index.

Because the summary descriptions of differential behavior contained in traits are held to be applicable across persons, time, and situations and to extend to behaviors not directly incorporated in the measure, the trait model can provide an economical and parsimonious description of the individual, which are of value in applied work, such as personnel selection. Yet despite these characteristics, reliance on correlational methods and the inability to establish the antecedents of differential status on a given trait measure have limited the development of understanding of differential behavior (Fiske, 1979; Sontag, 1971). Moreover, in the search for a general, efficient, and parsimonious description of individuals, the model fails to provide an accurate description of a given person and often ignores situational influences on, and qualitative differences among, individuals in the expression of differential behavior. Whenever differential behavior cannot be described in terms of enduring characteristics, or the relevant characteristics are not expressed in the same way by all individuals, the trait model is of limited value due to inappropriate assumptions.

A third approach to the study of human individuality is analogous to the trait model in the sense that it represents a descriptive approach to individuality. However, this alternative methodological approach, which might be conceived of as a type paradigm, emphasizes the classification of persons rather than the classification of behaviors. Essentially, the type strategy holds that some individuals will display systematic similarities in their behavior, and that this type of group of similar individuals will be differentiated from the members of alternative groups or types on one or more indicators of individuality. Summarization of differential behavior is accomplished by assigning an individual to a given type once the differential characteristics of type members have been established. The resulting summarization is neither nomothetic nor idiographic, because each type may be conceived of as a modal individual. Moreover, the similarities and differential characteristics ascribed to type members need not be stable across time, persons, and situations. Provided that the different types continue to manifest internal similarity and external differentiation relative to other types, instability, situational effects, and qualitative differences in the behavioral descriptors of different types are considered both possible and legitimate.

The foregoing discussion suggested that implementation of the typological model must begin by defining a group or groups of individuals who display similarity in their behavior. Although type definition currently may be carried out either empirically or rationally, until recently it could only be carried out on a rational basis. As a result, most typological studies relied on pragmatic and theoretical considerations in type specification and assumed that temporal and situational influences did not affect type status. For example, typologies have been defined on the basis of clinical diagnostic categories, classifications of individuals who have been successful in different occupations, and demographic variables such as age, sex, and race. Differential behaviors characterizing each type can be established on a variety of behavioral indicators through a simple means difference analysis employing a subset of type members. The extent to which a typological summarization represents something beyond measurement error can be determined by assessing the accuracy with which new samples of individuals can be assigned to the different types and by determining whether individuals are consistently assigned to the same types at different points in time or across different indicators. Typically, the validity of a typology is established by examining the meaningfulness of the differential indicators for each type and by the ability of type assignments to yield effective predictions of other related forms of differential behavior *not* employed in assigning individuals to the types.

The use of this paradigm in the study of human individuality has certain advantages. First, the paradigm offers a compromise between the descriptive accuracy obtained in the idiographic strategy and the economy provided by nomothetic efforts. Second, this approach can yield effective prediction and at least limited understanding of differential behavior when linked to experimental designs or antecedent-consequent information that considers type status an independent variable (Tyler, 1965). Unfortunately, the typological strategy has been subject to a number of limitations and criticisms. Because, historically, it has proven difficult to define groups of similar individuals empirically, the relevant categories have often been based on demographic or cultural variables that are not behavioral, are few in number, and do not provide a sufficiently general base for describing human individuality (Kerlinger, 1973; Meehl, 1967). Additionally, it has been argued (a) that the lack of generality suggested by the display of qualitatively different behavioral properties by types leads to a lack of parsimony inappropriate for the formulation of a science of individuality; and (b) that the uniqueness of individuals will effectively prohibit an adequate definition of groups of similar individuals. Yet these criticisms must be approached with some caution because, if such qualitative differences exist, they may be important aspects of human individuality that cannot be derived from a general description of differential behavior, or a trait composite. Moreover, if sufficient similarity exists among individuals to define a type, some generalization is possible. Nevertheless, given the dearth of compelling evidence for this latter viewpoint, both these criticisms deserve some attention.

The fourth major paradigm employed in the study of human individuality represents a pure idiographic model and has been referred to as a clinical approach. The model asserts that each individual is unique and can only be understood in terms of a total pattern of personal behavior and the environment in which it occurs. The emphasis is on the understanding of a particular individual, and, consequently, idiographic or clinical efforts typically emphasize antecedent behaviors and experiences as well as current behavior. Summarization, if it occurs at all, is within the context of the individual. though it is often guided by theoretical considerations of greater generality.

In practice, implementation of this model is relatively straightforward, although it may be expensive and time consuming. Typically, qualitative observations based on discussions with the individual and a review of the available life history data are employed to identify the behaviors and experiences of interest. The information is reviewed and synthesized in an attempt to arrive at a personal understanding of the individual and his or her behavior. The resulting description tends to represent a systematic case study or historical record of the life of a particular individual. After a review by trained psychologists, this amorphous descriptive base may be employed in attempts to predict, understand, and control individual behavior.

Although the classic clinical approach is much maligned in the halls of scientific psychology, the methodology has some valuable attributes. For instance, it can provide an excellent description of a given individual, as well as some understanding of differential behavior through its antecedents. Further, Howe (1982) has noted the flexibility of the approach and its potential for providing a source of viable hypotheses concerning the nature and ontogeny of human individuality.

The problems associated with application of the paradigm are well known. First, prediction and the reliability of the descriptive formulation are highly dependent on the individual investigator and hence do not yield the objectivity, replicability, and consensus considered essential in effective scientific pursuits. Second, the foregoing considerations make it difficult to establish the validity of any description of the individual or of individuality. Third, the model lacks economy because its application is time consuming and requires both detailed descriptions and complex interpretations; thus, it may be of limited value in solving many practical problems. Finally, to some extent, the idiographic model represents a defeatest position with respect to the possibility of formulating a science of individuality because it foregoes the possibility of constructing a replicable and reliable description and understanding of human individuality.

THE EMERGENCE OF "AMEANINGFUL" STUDIES OF INDIVIDUALITY

The preceding discussion presented the four major methodological approaches employed in studies of human individuality. Although each approach has its own assets and liabilities, some overlap exists among them, suggesting that it might be possible to formulate a general paradigm for the study of human individuality that optimizes the strengths and minimizes the weaknesses of other schools of thought. One possibility might entail adopting a paradigm that is analogous to that employed by biologists, where persons would first be classified and behaviors then classified within the resulting subspecies. Of course, other alternatives to the major schools of thought sketched out heretofore also exist. Yet, because integration may be possible, studies investigating a general approach to the phenomenon would be of substantial value.

Given the fundamental importance of the issue, it is rather surprising that so few integrative efforts are found in the literature and that practically no progress along these lines is apparent. The cause of this unfortunate state of affairs in the study of human individuality may be traced to the emergence of methodological empiricism and a modern malady that Koch (1981) has referred to as "ameaningful" thought:

> Decades of inquiry into the inquiry of others, and into germane processes inside my own head, have induced in me a sense of awe at the plentitude of our gift for mismanagement of our own minds. It is perhaps the ultimate genius of our race . . . manifest in part in "ameaningful" thought . . . "Ameaningful" thought or inquiry regards knowledge as the result of processing information rather than discovery. It presumes that knowledge is an almost ultimate result of gimmickry, an assembly line, a methodology. It assumes that inquiry action is so rigidly and fully regulated by rule that in its conception of inquiry it often allows rules to totally displace human users. Presuming as it does that knowledge is generated by processing, its conception of knowledge is fictionalistic, conventionalistic. So strongly does it see knowledge under such aspects that it sometimes seems to suppose the object of inquiry to be an ungainly and annoying irrelevance. The terms and relations of the object of inquiry or problem are seen, as it were, through an inverted telescope: Detail, structure, quiddity are obliterated. Objects of knowledge become caricatures, if not faceless, and thus they lose reality. The world, or any given part of it, is not felt fully or passionately and is perceived as devoid of objective value. Ameaningful thinking tends to rely on crutches: rules, codes, prescriptions, rigid methods. In extreme forms it becomes obsessive and magical. . . . (It tends to) subordinate authentic contextually governed analysis, discovery or invention to blind application of an external method. (pp. 258–260)

The outcome of this mode of thought is stagnation, rigidity, and a lack of substantive progress. Those who doubt the existence of this syndrome among students of human individuality are encouraged to review Cronbach's (1954) "tongue in cheek" presidential address to the Psychonomic Society.

At this point, the question is why "ameaningful" thought emerged at least 40 years ago and why it persists in individual differences research. The underlying reasons may be attributed to the relatively early emergence of a single methodological model as the principal framework for studies of human individuality, relegating the major alternatives to the status of ancillary techniques useful only for certain limited purposes. Combined with the self-supporting nature of "ameaningful" thought and the tendency of victors in academic disputes to rewrite history in their own image, it becomes less surprising that so little progress has been made towards the development of a more general approach to individuality. The reasons for the dominance of a single model, specifically the trait model, are complex and may be based on historical conditions both on the field itself and psychology at large during the early phases of efforts to grapple with the issue of individuality.

Traditionally, the origins of scientific psychology are traced to Wundt's work in the late 1870s and early 1880s. At the time of its conception, psychology was an experimental science concerned with the search for general laws or similarities in the behavior of all individuals. Typically, these early investigations focused, through introspection and reaction-time studies, on the sensory and perceptual processes that were held to underlie mental functioning. Yet, even in these fundamental psychological characteristics, marked individual differences were apparent. Galton (1883) and Cattell (1890) became interested in individual differences in sensory and perceptual characteristics and attempted to formulate measures of them. Their initial studies of individuality had two major outcomes. First, they provided psychology with the basic correlational methodology, which allowed quantitative assessment of reliability, validity, and the similarity between behaviors. Second, although these seminal studies demonstrated the pervasive nature of differential behavior, their findings indicated that measures of sensory and perceptual characteristics were not especially effective predictors of differential behavior in real world situations. For instance, despite their hypothesized relationship to intellectual functioning, the measures did not predict academic performance.

While the limitations of this initial approach were becoming apparent, a second event occurred that gave rise to modern studies of human individuality. The French government had assigned two psychologists, Binet and Simon (1905), the task of devising some means for systematically identifying individuals who were not capable of profitting from the formal educational system. Like Galton and Cattell, they attempted to develop a standardized test to meet this goal. However, they rejected the proposition that effective intellectual functioning was based on sensory and perceptual capacities and attempted to identify more complex and realistic behaviors that might reflect intellect in children. After qualitative observation and case studies of individuals previously classified as mentally unfit, they concluded that a construct labeled intelligence that was held to be manifest in reasoning, judgment, and common sense, could be employed as a basis for classifying individuals as mentally unfit. Subsequently, Binet and Simon (1905) developed a diverse set of higher-order tasks or problems which were intended to reflect typical performance within a given age group. (Examples of such tasks included asking a 3-year-old to give his or her last name and asking a 6-year-old to name four pieces of money and to identify the omission in a drawing.) Because it was held that intelligence increased with age, Binet and Simon described the individual's intelligence by determining that age group to which their problem-solving level was equivalent. These mental age scores were later shown to be capable of identifying the mentally unfit, and with this first successful effort in mental measurement, differential psychology began to grow.

Examination of Binet and Simon's work provides little evidence to suggest the need to employ a particular methodological paradigm in the description of human individuality. In fact, nearly all of the methodological approaches outlined earlier appear to have been used in the course of this seminal effort. Thus, it does not appear that Binet and Simon's work dictated acceptance of the trait model. Instead, the tenor of the times, pragmatic considerations, and the available methodological techniques seem to have forced acceptance of the trait model to the extent that it is implicit in all attempts to conceive of individuality in terms of isolated behavioral traits.

At the outset of the 20th century, democracy and industrial mass production had created marked changes in the established social order and a novel set of social problems. One of these problems involved finding some way of allocating people to social roles in a mass society where much less was known about the individual than in the days of village life. Moreover, it was felt that these decisions must be made democratically, but in such a way as to maximize utilization of the available resources. Consequently, a systematic method for describing large numbers of individuals in terms of similar personal characteristics and for relating these descriptions to real world performance was required. Because the trait model promised an economical and parsimonious description of the general behavioral characteristics of individuals, it presented an attractive alternative.

Despite the fact that the trait model is unusually well suited to simplified mass description, other alternatives might have been capable of meeting this goal. Yet, at roughly the same time, another set of forces arose that provided a powerful argument for application of the trait model. At this time, Darwin's theory of evolution had become an important element in intellectual thought. Essentially, this theory held that evolution functioned through the selective survival and reproduction of those members of the species who were best suited to exploit their environment, and that the characteristics that facilitated the survival of these individuals would be passed on to their offspring through heredity.

As with many other great insights, Darwin's theory of evolution was extended without translation into the world of individuals in the form of Social Darwinism. Social Darwinism has been used for a variety of purposes, some laudable and some nefarious, and three tenets of this theory are of special significance with regard to the emergence of the trait model. First, the philosophy held that an individual's potential for success of achievement was determined by enduring hereditary characteristics. Second, it encouraged overt social selection, an analog of natural selection, to identify the most fit and to place these individuals in leadership positions. Third, it led to the assumption that some ways of living were better or more adaptive than others and that individual differences in behavior had substantial import in this regard.

When the tenets of Social Darwinism were linked to measurement and the psychology of individual differences, it suggested that individual differences were of substantial importance to society and that they were based on stable, enduring characteristics of hereditary character. The former view provided an impetus for Binet and Simon's (1905) work at the same time that the latter view lent itself to acceptance of the trait model with its emphasis on enduring characteristics. Moreover, Social Darwinism provided a logical justification for selection on the basis of traits just as the trait model, with its emphasis on stable general characteristics, provided an efficient mechanism for meeting the pragmatic selection problem facing modern society. Thus, application of the trait model to studies of differential behavior could be "logically" justified. Although this justification may have been sufficient to insure eventual acceptance of the trait concept, additional support was available from other sources. For better or worse, the trait model reflects a highly mechanistic view of differential phenomena, and, hence, it was likely to find some support in the mechanistic conception of natural phenomena that was popular among scientists of the day. Additionally, Binet and Simon's successful measurement of intelligence, or reasoning, judgment, and common sense, reflected a characteristic held to be of great importance in human evolution and so reinforced the foregoing trends.

Although the tenor of the times lent itself to a trait-oriented conception of intelligence and a belief that traits could be advantageously employed, technical considerations and the limited assets of psychological science, when coupled with the demands placed on psychologists, may have been just as important in the ascendance of the trait model. As was noted earlier, industrial societies were faced with a pragmatic problem, in that it was necessary to systematically allocate individuals to function, but the requisite information concerning an individual was not necessarily available to decision makers. As the major avenue to desirable status in industrial societies, this issue first arose within the schools, and psychologists were allocated the task of solving the problem.

In its infancy, psychology had relatively few tools available that could be employed in this effort. Its primary research technique was the experimental method. However, experimentation was incapable of solving this problem, in part because the method was too expensive and time consuming for mass screening efforts, and in part because experimentation could not provide a sufficiently broad description of the individual.

Moreover, the experimental methods of the day could not account for a great deal of the variation among individuals, and the variation around group means was so large that it suggested that individuals were poorly described by general laws or averages. Taken unto themselves, these observations were enough to insure rejection of the experimental paradigm. However, it is also true that the dependent measures employed by the early experimentalists proved to have little utility in solving the problems at hand. The experimentalists, preferring a concern with general behavior, thus displayed little interest in or sympathy with the problems of differential psychology. Consequently, the founders of differential psychology rejected the experimental approach and created a division in psychology that persists to the present day.

Given the progress that had been made by early clinical psychologists, the ancestors of the more recent versions of the idiographic model might also have been employed in this effort. However, certain considerations mitigated against it. Among these were that implementation of the idiographic approach was time consuming and that it did not provide a well-specified, standardized description for mass decision making. Yet the principal objection to application of the clinical model appears to have been rooted in the concern of differential psychologists with developing a general, quantitative description of individuality and the inability of the idiographic approach to provide either one.

Early students of differential psychology appear to have been aware that the typological model might have provided a viable alternative to the trait model, and at the time there was some interest in this approach; however, a combination of influences conspired to ensure that the type strategy would not be employed as the prevailing framework for studies of individuality. The central problem with this approach was methodological. Although empirical quantitative techniques were available for defining similar behaviors, such techniques were not available for defining similar persons. Thus, the type model lost some of its attraction for those attempting to build a science of individuality. Additionally, those types that could be established at that time were necessarily tied to "arm chair" speculations or pre-existing, socially defined classification categories. This approach was deemed unacceptable on the basis of the nonempirical and nonbehavioral nature of the classifications, as well as the fact that a limited number of pre-existing categories could not provide a foundation for a general description of individuality. Further, even when attempts were made to implement the model, it was found that scores on the relevant measures were normally distributed and did not cluster at the tails, leading to the argument that many of the pre-existing categories could be described through a simple linear combination of behavioral variables. Although this outcome might be attributed to a poor classification of persons, in the absence of better techniques it constituted a powerful argument against the type model. Finally, the typological model suggested that differential behavior must be described within a type and general laws built up by observing behavior across the types. However, general laws so built were more time consuming and expensive to construct, and when this was coupled with the possibility that nonconstant measures might be needed for different types, the typological model appeared to provide neither a sufficiently economical and appropriate solution to the mass screening problem nor the speediest road to the development of a general science. As a result of these considerations, the typological model was rejected as a general approach to individuality, although it continued to see use in specific problem areas, such as the measurement of vocational interests or clinical diagnosis.

On the other hand, the trait model possessed a number of advantageous characteristics. Implementation could focus on measures of the actual behaviors of interest, and after Binet and Simon's (1905) work, psychologists had a good idea of the kinds of behaviors and differential indicators that might be of use. The requisite quantitative methodology for the classification of behavior and the assessment of reliability and validity had also become available with Galton and Pearson's derivation of the correlation coefficient, followed by true score theory and the reliability coefficient. Additionally, the possibility of identifying a limited number of central traits promised great parsimony and efficiency in the description of human individuality. When these methodological characteristics were linked to the justification for use of the model and to its utility in solving the problems at hand, there can be little doubt, retrospectively, concerning the field's decision or its wisdom at the time the decision was made.

HISTORICAL PERFORMANCE

As the conceptual background for most attempts to describe, predict, and understand individual differences, trait theory has an impressive history documented by an extensive literature. In the context of the present discussion, it is impossible to review this literature in any detail; however, some of the more salient events and general trends are examined.

One highly significant contribution of the initial studies of intelligence was that they provided psychology with the normative method for scoring trait measures, in which the individual's performance is compared to the average performance of a reference group. However, the individual's performance was established by direct observation of the individual's solutions to problems, making test administration expensive and time consuming. Nevertheless, intelligence testing quickly spread to the United States with Terman's (1916) version of the Stanford Binet, and it was here that the problem of administration was resolved. In order to meet the Army's need to screen a large number of recruits during the First World War, a group of psychologists led by Yerkes assembled a set of objective items intended to measure intelligence that could be administered in a group setting through a paper-and-pencil format. The resulting Army Alpha test provided a solution to the administration problem. Moreover, in the same effort, a general procedure for describing the individual's score was simply compared to those of a letter-graded reference group, thus providing a more simple and flexible scoring procedure than had previously been available.

Having solved these fundamental problems, trait studies of individual differences became a major area of research in American psychology by the end of World War I. The expansion of testing into new areas represented one major trend during the postwar years. Paper-and-pencil tests were developed to measure more specific aptitudes and abilities; traits such as spatial perception and mechanical comprehension were measured employing the methodology developed in intelligence testing. Similarly, attempts were made to use the methodology in the description of noncognitive characteristics or traits, such as sociability and adjustment. Another trend was the widespread application of trait measures in areas outside academics. It was during this period that paper-and-pencil trait measures became commonplace in such diverse areas as personnel selection and attitude measurement.

A third major postwar trend centered on refinement of the methodology that could be employed in the construction of trait measures. A major breakthrough in this regard came with Thurstone's (1931) development of factor analytic procedures. Essentially, factor analysis represents a technique by which the latent variables summarizing the underlying relationships among scores on tests, or test items, can be determined through their intercorrelations. These factors provided psychologists with an empirical, quantitative technique for summary classifications of differential behavior, albeit one that was subject to substantial interpretation and some doubts. It was hoped that the stable summary dimensions or traits identified through this procedure would eventually provide a parsimonious description of differential behaviors and individuality. Aside from factor analysis, substantial progress was made in other methodological areas. For instance, Kuder and Richardson (1937) derived a procedure for estimating reliability through the homogeneity or intercorrelation of test items, while others investigated optimal item parameters and scaling procedures for attitude and ability tests.

The information obtained in application of these new measurement procedures led to a flowering of research concerned with the nature of individual differences. Terman (1925) undertook a large-scale longitudinal study to determine the influence of intelligence on the lives of individuals. Other investigations attempted to determine the degree to which scores on trait measures were actually under the control of hereditary as opposed to environmental influences through studies of identical twins reared apart (Newman, Freeman, & Holzinger, 1937) and studies examining whether individual differences in cognitive abilities increased or decreased with practice (Anastasi, 1934). Yet perhaps the most important trend during this period with respect to the understanding of differential behavior lay in the information accumulated with large-scale application of the various trait measures. It was also at about this time that it was established that well-designed measures of skills, knowledges, and abilities could yield effective short-term prediction of the individual's performance on a variety of real world criteria. Although the magnitude of predictions varied substantially, typical validity coefficients were between .30 and .50 over short periods of time. On the other hand, it was found that trait measures of the noncognitive variety were substantially less effective in predicting differential behaviors (Hartshorne & May, 1928). In fact, the few effective noncognitive measures developed, such as the Strong Vocational Interest Blank, were really based on a qualitative typological approach (Fleishman & Quaintance, 1984).

All of these efforts were not in vain, because psychologists were far better prepared than most for their role in the Second World War. Once again, psychologists were assigned responsibility for mass screening and classification efforts, and this permitted substantial refinement in the procedures that had been developed in earlier years. During this period, more attention was given to the definition of performance on criterion measures to assess the predictive validity of tests, as well as to errors in measurement and their specification. New kinds of trait measures, such as authoritarianism, were developed. Attempts were also made to differentially classify and place individuals on the basis of their aptitudes and abilities, although these efforts were not especially successful due to the substantial intercorrelations characterizing cognitive trait measures.

After the end of World War II, traditional testing procedures were accepted, formalized, and then applied on a truly massive scale with the foundation of the Educational Testing Service and its promotion of formalized achievement testing for college admission. In addition, methods continued to be refined, and three particular advances are worthy of note. First, initial attempts were made to formulate a systematic basis for evaluating the utility or value of selection decisions (Brogden, 1949). Second, with the advent of computers, far more powerful statistical techniques became available, and multivariate statistics were refined and employed in studies of individuality. Third, the concept of construct validity was formulated as a method for validating tests, such as personality tests, that could not be readily evaluated in terms of their prediction of external criterion measures. During this period, investigators developed new measures of personality traits, such as achievement motivation, and a number of new constructs and measures were prepared, though there was little improvement in prediction. Additionally, investigators became interested in and developed procedures for measuring constructs such as creativity, field independence, and other cognitive styles that proved to be of some importance.

In recent years, new issues have arisen in measurement and testing. Once again, an emphasis on the refinement and development of quantitative methodology is evident. Criterion-referenced testing, or testing designed to insure minimal competency, has become an important issue, as has the use of computers and tailor-made testing strategies. Latent trait theory has been developed as a means for avoiding the problems associated with the differential performance of various reference groups on scored tests (Lord, 1980). Tools have also been formulated that would allow the modeling of multivariate relationships among traits via structural equations, and procedures have been developed that would allow examination of the utility of measures and the unbiased predictive power of these measures (Schmidt & Hunter, 1977). However, relatively few new kinds of trait measures have appeared in the literature. On the other hand, new issues have emerged as testing came under serious attack for alleged unfairness to minority groups; that is, government regulation became an important influence on testing, and test bias and the effects of coaching became the subjects of an ongoing debate. Interestingly, a great deal of the more recent work in measurement and differential psychology was instigated principally as a result of the public's criticisms of traditional measurement procedures.

Because the trait model has been the major vehicle for the psychological investigation of human individuality for so long, its general acceptance has been associated with the emergence of ameaningful thought. Consequently, few attempts have been made to assess the value and utility of this approach in the description of human individuality. This is unfortunate, because historical conditions led to prima facie acceptance of the trait model long before we had sufficient scientific data concerning the nature of human individuality to justify its general applicability. Because such data are now available, the successes and failures of the model should be investigated in order to obtain some understanding of its effectiveness.

SUCCESSES AND FAILURES OF THE TRAIT MODEL

The trait model has clearly provided psychology with a highly efficient method for generating summary descriptions of human individuality and differential behavior. More ambiguous is the effectiveness of the resulting summary descriptions. In the cognitive domain of aptitude, ability, and achievement tests, the trait model has yielded adequate predictions of differential behavior over relatively short intervals, especially when various biasing factors have been controlled. However, long-term prediction is much weaker. Moreover, a number of anomalies have appeared in the course of psychology's efforts to investigate cognitive traits. For instance, the trait model argues for highly fractionated, internally homogenous measures of differential behavior that can then be employed in a weighted combination to describe individuality. Yet it has been demonstrated that more complex measures of cognitive characteristics, such as the Stanford Binet, often yield better prediction than a combination of homogenous measures, such as those found among Thurstone's Primary Mental Abilities (Tyler, 1965). This is apparently because the more complex manifestations of individuality cannot be completely described through a simple sum of a limited number of specific components. Cognitive trait measures have enjoyed only limited success in the differential placement of individuals or in addressing the more general issue of moderator effects. The limited success of the model appears to be linked to insensitivity to true situational differences, to the high intercorrelations among trait measures, and to methodological limitations such as linear restraints. Constant methodological refinements have not produced any substantial increase in predictive power in over 40 years, and even a cursory review of the Mental Measurements Yearbook suggests that all these efforts have failed to yield the desired degree of parsimony in the description of individuality.

Conclusions regarding the effectiveness of the trait model are less ambiguous in the noncognitive domain. Sechrest (1974) has noted that with only a few exceptions, such as the California Psychological Inventory, nearly all of the nonintellective trait measures have failed to display either adequate predictive or construct validity. Moreover, measures of personality traits do not display any substantial stability over even relatively brief intervals of 2 to 5 years, and even short-term reliability estimates tend to be poor (Mischel, 1969). Quite often, attempts are made to explain these negative results on the basis of the relatively primitive state of noncognitive trait measures vis-à-vis aptitude, ability, and knowledge measures. Yet nearly 60 years of concentrated effort have been invested in the development of these measures, and the fundamental procedures are identical to those employed in the development of cognitive trait measures. It would seem appropriate to conclude that the trait model may not provide an adequate description of differential behavior in this domain.

General disappointment with the trait model in the noncognitive domain and the various anomalies observed in the cognitive domain suggest that this approach may not have provided psychology with the *ideal* tool for scientific investigations into the nature of human individuality. Certainly, there are some concrete signs of this at a more global level. Despite years of study, the understanding of human individuality and differential behavior has advanced very little (Fiske, 1979). Though the outcome might have been expected given the descriptive, predictive emphasis of the trait model, it constitutes a serious limitation on further progress. A number of major conceptual issues remain unresolved due to this lack of understanding. For instance, little progress has been made towards sorting out the role of hereditary and environmental influences in the ontogeny of differential behavior, while the existence and meaning of group differences continues to be debated.

This lack of understanding of individuality as a phenomenon has resulted in three major trends. First, methodology per se has become a vehicle for pseudo-understanding, and vast amounts of energy are expended on methodological refinement rather than on addressing the more fundamental issues on which methodology is supposed to be contingent. Second, the field seems to have lost sight of the individual as an individual. Rather than conceiving of differential behavior as a result of a dynamic interaction between the individual and the environment that serves certain purposes, the individual is reduced to a collection of static discrete traits represented by a simple linear combination. In other words, individuality has been abstracted from its context in the individual's behavior and environment and compressed through a mechanistic conception of questionable value to a point at which the complexities and ambiguities of life are considered irrelevant. Third, the tendency of investigators to force alternative conceptions of individuality and extraneous sources of information into the trait model has restricted the field's ability to generate fresh ideas and new understandings and led to the assumption that methodology defines understanding rather than allowing understanding to guide methodology. These trends have resulted in what many experts refer to as stagnation. The dearth of new measures and half a century of reliance on the same basic methodology tend to support these conclusions. Some additional support for this statement and many of the foregoing conclusions can be found in Tyler's (1965) comment that:

> Useful as this approach has been, I have found myself questioning more and more whether it is really adequate at this stage in the development of our science. For one thing, it does not *feel* quite right. Most people find it hard to think of themselves as points in N dimensional space. Occasionally, I encounter an unusually articulate student who reacts violently against the whole conception, and I think that at a lower level of awareness many others show a kind of passive resistance to it. For another thing, the system shows signs of becoming completely unworkable in the sense I have defined workability because of the proliferation of dimensions. It looked for a time as though factor analysis would enable us to simplify it, but there are now so many factors, and their relationships with each other are so complex, that factor theory does not really constitute a simplification. But the more important reason I see for questioning the adequacy of this way of looking at things is that we are no longer making the progress with it we have a right to expect. Correlations with criteria significant for theory or for practice are not going up very much. The addition of new dimensions and the increasing refinement in the ways we measure old ones are not "paying off" very well. The possibility is at least worth considering that we are approaching the limit of what can be done with the system. (p. 501)

If one accepts the possibility that our colleagues and the populace have at least some intuitive understanding of individuality, one must wonder whether the trait model and the methodology it employs are sufficiently powerful to allow us to rely on "ameaningful" thought in the study of human individuality and a conception of individuality rooted in historical social problems rather than an understanding of the phenomenon.

DISSENTING OPINIONS

Perhaps the most appropriate conclusion that may be drawn from the preceding discussion is that, although the trait model has served psychology well in limited areas and provided the basis for expansion, it has not provided the consummate model for the description, prediction, and understanding of human individuality. While the emergence of ameaningful thought, following initial acceptance of the trait model, has tended to stymie the search for alternatives, not all students of human individuality fell victim to the syndrome. Primarily concerned with formulating alternative approaches to and conceptions of human individuality, the dissenting literature provides an important source of information with respect to the issues that should be considered in future attempts to examine human individuality and in formulating and evaluating alternative approaches.

Although experimentation remains the single most pervasive methodology in psychology as a whole, it has not been a preferred alternative in the study of human individuality. However, experimental psychologists have occasionally turned their attention to studies of individuality and differential behavior. Their comments have typically been raised as criticisms and do not necessarily represent a unified position. Perhaps the most common approach taken by the experimentalist holds that differential behavior is a cumulative outcome of differential learning experiences deriving from different reinforcements in nonconstant situations. A pungent statement of this conviction may be found in Guthrie's (1944) comment that:

> an individual's . . . past affiliations, political and religious, offer better and more specific prediction of his future than any traits. When we know how men adjust themselves to situations through learning and we know the situations to which they have been exposed . . . we know the men themselves and there is no need to speculate concerning the deeper reaches of the soul until we can explore these with similar knowledge. (p. 66)

Mischel's (1969) criticism of trait theory was based on a similar argument that suggests that the instability of trait measures may be attributed to ongoing learning in different social situations over time. The work of Miller and Dollard (1941) and Staats (1969) represent similar attempts to approach differential behavior through experimentation. Cronbach's (1957b) multimethod concept provides a second alternative to the more traditional implementations of the trait model. Cronbach noted that differential behavior is not solely a function of the individual but, instead, represents an interaction between the individual's characteristics and the situation. In this view, behavior cannot accurately be described, predicted or understood unless both the nature of the situation and the impact of the situation on an individual are considered. This led Cronbach to argue for a wedding of the experimental and trait models by employing trait status as an independent variable in experimental designs. Linking the results to antecedent information bearing on the individual's past behavior and experience could enhance our understanding of differential behavior. Cronbach and Snow (1977) have since demonstrated the feasibility of this approach in studies relating learner characteristics to aspects of the instructional system.

Dissent has also been expressed among adherents to the position that classifying persons may be more appropriate than classifying behaviors.

This position views human individuality as a highly complex composite of characteristics that interact in a systematic fashion yielding groups of similar persons. Though most attempts to implement this approach have been based on gross and poorly specified categories, such as body type (Sheldon, Stevens, and Tucker, 1940), temperament (Jung, 1923), and supposed dominance of the sympathetic, as opposed to the parasympathetic, nervous system (Wagner, 1947), a more sophisticated effort may be found in the work of Toops (1948, 1959). He suggested that individuality could represent a cumulative reflection of a complex interaction between personal characteristics and antecedent behaviors and experiences that are, in part, reflected by the individual's status on various demographic variables, such as age or socioeconomic status. Consequently, cross-classification on these variables might be used to assign individuals to "ulstreths," or subgroups of similar individuals. Despite the limitations of this approach, Toops (1959) believed that one of the most meaningful things that could be said about an individual was reflected in assignment to one of these subgroups or categories. The energy expended by differential psychologists on attempts to study the impact of demographic classification variables on differential behavior lends some support to this conclusion, as does the fact that more limited implementations of this strategy, such as those employed in the development of life history keys (Owens, 1976) and in the Strong Vocational Interest Blank (Strong, 1943), have been shown to be capable of yielding reliable descriptions of substantial predictive power.

Implicit in the assessment center model, which has been widely employed in the industrial setting, is an additional criticism of the trait model as well as a proposed alternative. The assessment-center approach developed because of the need of industrial psychologists to assess the individual's status on a variety of characteristics that the trait model had not been able to describe in a satisfactory fashion. In assessment centers, the individual's performance on a variety of job-related situational exercises is observed and then rated by multiple subject matter experts on dimensions reflecting salient differential characteristics. Ratings on the dimensions, along with data gathered from other sources, such as interviews and trait measures, are used to establish a consensual evaluation of the individual's suitability for a job. The assessment center approach emerged during the Second World War under the guidance of Henry Murray and was employed in the selection of OSS officers (MacKinnon, 1948). In recent years, it has been a popular tool for the description, prediction, and understanding of differential behavior in a series of studies conducted under the auspices of the Bell System and documented by Bray, Campbell, and Grant (1974).

Criticisms of the trait model by assessment center proponents are closely related to ongoing criticisms by clinical and idiographic psychologists, especially when the trait model is applied in the noncognitive domain. The idiographic position holds that the purely nomothetic descriptions derived from the trait model yield poor descriptions of individuals, and thus poor prediction. Moreover, adherents of this position argue that the context, that is the situation and past behaviors and experiences, in which differential behavior occurs is ignored in the trait model, thus losing the significant, purposeful, and patterned activities of the individual. Allport and Vernon's (1930) emphasis on the study of organized patterns of *individual* adaptation across a variety of characteristics reflects one trend in this school of thought. Others, like Bem and Funder (1978), have taken a more quantitative approach, in this case demonstrating that the prediction derived from trait measures may be enhanced when an attempt is made to control for the fact that nomothetic descriptions may not have the same meaning for all individuals.

A variation on the idiographic theme has been voiced by developmental psychologists. In a general sense, developmental psychologists hold that individual behavior develops in a systematic fashion over time through the dynamic ongoing interaction of the individual with an organized environment (Lerner & Busch-Rossnagel, 1981). As a result of these presuppositions, developmentalists often object to the mechanistic orientation of the trait model, its lack of concern with situational influences, and its assumptions that differential indicators have stable meaning at different stages and for different individuals (Haan, 1981). Moreover, according to Livson (1973), there is a quarrel:

> not with nomothetic laws but with nomothetic dimensions. In fact, it is argued that an insistence on a single universal set of dimensions defeats the attainment of truly general laws of individual development. To refuse to dimensionalize personality in ways more fitting the data within detectable subgroups, over time or persons, introduces sheer error. Thus nomothetic laws would seem most probable when dimensions and interrelations are determined in a way which least distorts the structure of the data. (p. 112)

Essentially, this represents an argument for a measurement model that accurately describes the ways individuals develop and live their lives over time, as opposed to a convenient summary description of a hypothetical average individual formulated at a single point in time.

Descriptive accuracy and interactions have also been a concern of one other group of dissenters. Derived from Paterson and his students at the University of Minnesota, this position presents a reaction against attempts to study isolated traits. Instead it is argued that individuals must be described with respect to multiple, interacting characteristics as they relate to behavior in certain situations. Further, it is suggested that differential behavior is determined by multiple differences that must be studied conjointly. Refinements of this viewpoint are provided in Dunnette's (1966) model for personnel selection and Tyler's (1974) directions of development conception. Tyler's viewpoint is especially noteworthy because it argues that individuality must be approached from a developmental perspective in which cross-time relationships, major choice-points in the selection of environments, and environmental influences are considered significant influences on the expression of differential behavior. She suggested that the cumulative impact of these choices, and the resulting experiences, leads to a systematic expression of behavior and individual differences through progressive differentiation in the course of the individual's development.

The foregoing discussion has presented a cursory view of a variety of nontraditional approaches to the description, prediction and understanding of differential behavior and human individuality. Obviously, these alternatives do not represent a unified perspective. Nevertheless, certain recurrent themes do appear. First, there appears to be some consensus that descriptions of differential behavior should be tailored more to the individual than to some hypothetical average person. In other words, completely nomothetic dimensions may not yield effective description of a particular individual, and may thus limit prediction and understanding. Second, individuality should be studied, and described, as it emerges in the course of human development; and antecedent behaviors and experiences should be examined in attempts to describe, predict, and understand current differential behavior. Third, the impact of past and current situations on differential behavior is important and should not be ignored in studies of individuality. Fourth, the complex interrelationships among differential characteristics and situations should be examined, preferably on a cross-time or developmental basis. Fifth, in examining differential behavior, it should be remembered that human beings are purposive, and they organize their behavior and experience in a complex, systematic fashion that may not be adequately described by a mechanistic model and a simple aggregate of fixed trait measures. Sixth, it appears that many of the criticisms leveled against the trait model reflect a demand for a broader, more encompassing, and more holistic description of the individual that cannot be obtained from isolated trait measures or the individual's status on a limited subset of traits. In weaving these threads together, one finds a call for a methodological model that reflects individuality as it is manifest in individual lives, rather than one that forces our conception of human individuality into a pre-existing methodological model chosen out of convenience and pragmatic necessity.

The reader may or may not accept the need for these refinements or the need to revise our approach to the phenomenon of human individuality. Yet in order to develop an alternative, or to evaluate the existing alternatives to the trait model and the appropriateness of the model itself, it is necessary to have some understanding of individuality as a natural phenomenon. Although it is true that only a limited understanding of differential behavior exists, the study reported in the following chapters was undertaken in the hope of obtaining a better understanding of individuality as a natural phenomenon. Among our purposes was to allow an evaluation of both the trait model and its alternatives and, if necessary, encourage the construction of a more general approach to the description, prediction, and understanding of differential behavior.

INDIVIDUALITY AND DEVELOPMENT

Rychlack (1972) has noted that an understanding of natural phenomena is obtained by generating knowledge of their causal underpinnings. Bearing in mind the classic distinction between natural, efficient, formal, and final cause, it is clear that understanding may be obtained in a number of ways. However, in the behavioral sciences, attempts to formulate an understanding of natural phenomena have traditionally focused on a certain kind of causation; that is, efficient cause, related to those antecedent conditions that have brought an observed behavior or behavioral difference into existence. Psychology's preferred tool for establishing such causal antecedents has been the experimental method. Experimentation permits the controlled manipulation of antecedent conditions so that definitive causal statements concerning the antecedent conditions that are necessary and sufficient for the emergence of the behavioral consequent may be generated. Thus, not all antecedents are efficient causes. Despite the conceptual value of the experimental approach in the formation of causal understandings, it has limited utility in attempts to formulate an understanding of individuality, due to the complexity and breadth of human differences, its insensitivity to short-term manipulations, its pre-existing nature, and the ethical considerations entailed in manipulating the behavioral characteristics of an individual.

Nevertheless, one key piece of information provided by the experimental strategy is the systematic linkage of antecedent behaviors or events with their behavioral and experimental consequents, regardless of whether or not these antecedents are in fact necessary and sufficient. Recognition of this fact led Fiske (1979) to suggest that identification of the antecedents of discrete forms of differential behavior might form a basis for the development of at least a preliminary understanding of the nature of human individuality. He suggested that this information might be obtained through longitudinal studies examining antecedents and consequent differential behaviors emerging in the course of individual development. Thus, it would seem appropriate to begin a long trek towards formulating an effective description and understanding of human individuality by examining the various longitudinal studies of differential behavior and the hints they may provide concerning the nature of human individuality.

Studies of Individual Development and their Implications: Methodological Issues

BACKGROUND

The importance of Fiske's (1979) call for studies examining the antecedents of differential behavior cannot be underestimated. Differential psychologists have long recognized that an adequate understanding of human individuality could only be formulated by considering the nature of the phenomenon within a developmental perspective. Over the course of the last century, research into the ontogeny and meaning of inventoried individual differences has been concentrated in three areas: validation studies in applied settings, studies of the hereditability of differential characteristics, and studies concerned with the emergence of differential characteristics across the life span. Due to their specificity and the limited time span involved, validation efforts have been of limited value in attempts to formulate a general understanding of human individuality. Rather than focusing on the unfolding of differential characteristics, heritability studies have been concerned with the extent to which differential characteristics are subject to hereditary determination. Thus, by default, the ensuing discussion must focus on those investigations that have been concerned with the emergence of differential characteristics over the course of the life span.

Initial attempts to examine the unfolding of differential characteristics relied on a cross-sectional methodological approach. Cross-sectional methods provided an economical and relatively straightforward strategy for examining the ontogeny of human individuality. Essentially, this strategy used age-group differences to provide a surrogate indicator of actual developmental change in the characteristics of a given individual.

The most common alternative to the cross-sectional approach to the study of individual development has been the longitudinal design. In longitudinal designs, a single group receives multiple administrations of various measures of individuality, and the resulting data are used to draw inferences concerning the expression of individuality over this time span. Although longitudinal research is expensive and time consuming because individuals must be followed for substantial periods of time before the study is completed, it is sensitive to the dynamics of individuality, because it is capable of tapping sequential influences at the individual rather than the aggregate level (Honzick, 1967).

LONGITUDINAL AND CROSS-SECTIONAL DESIGNS

Discrepant findings regarding the development of intellectual ability using cross-sectional and longitudinal designs (Bayley & Oden, 1955; Jones & Conrad, 1933; Owens, 1953; Vincent, 1952) have stirred a long-running controversy with respect to the relative merits of each design in attempts to delineate the ontogeny of human individuality. The central difficulty in utilizing simple cross-sectional designs lies in its lack of internal validity (Bergman, 1972). In order to draw valid inferences from cross-sectional designs, the differential behavioral characteristics of the various age groups selected for study must be free from the influence of factors not related to age differences. This requirement is difficult to meet, because cultural change may influence the performance of different age groups in a nonconstant manner on both cognitive and noncognitive measures of individuality (Baltes & Nesselroade, 1972; Havighurst, 1971; Rosow, 1978; Schaie & Parham, 1977).

Simple longitudinal designs, on the other hand, do not provide the ultimate vehicle for studies of individual development. The use of a single cohort group to maintain internal validity limits generalizability and external validity because the developmental patterns observed in one cohort group may not extend to other cohorts while ongoing cultural events may interact with individual differences to generate spurious age-related changes (Kuhlen, 1963). The utility of longitudinal designs is also limited by the economic and personal commitment required to follow individuals over a substantial portion of their lives (Bell, 1960). Researchers have often found it difficult to obtain representative samples of sufficient size to permit the derivation of stable and reasonably good conclusions (Rose, 1965). This difficulty is compounded by the possibility that individuals who drop out of a longitudinal study, for whatever reason, may differ in some systematic way from those who remain, generating a potential bias through changes in differential behavior that reflect little more than changing sample composition (Damon, 1965; Labouvie, Bartsch, Nesselroade, & Baltes, 1974; Riegel, Riegel, & Meyers, 1967). Finally, in those longitudinal studies in which the same measures are readministered to sample members as they move through their lives, it is always possible that developmental effects may be confounded with changes that arise solely from repeated testing (Brisson et al., 1974).

COHORT-SEQUENTIAL DESIGNS

Because of problems imposed on developmental investigations by longitudinal and cross-sectional designs, a number of alternative designs have been proposed over the years. Figure 2.1 presents a schematic representation of some of these alternatives. One of the designs presented in this figure is the cohort-sequential approach outlined by Baltes (1968). The

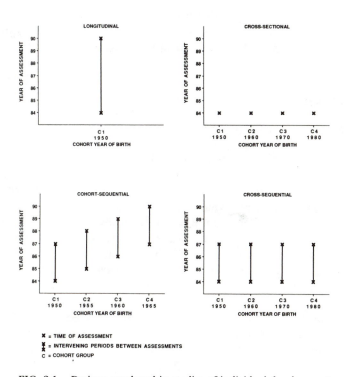

FIG. 2.1.   Designs employed in studies of individual development.

cohort-sequential design requires the investigator to follow members of multiple cohort groups over a specified time period. These cohort groups provide an additional independent variable within a study, and longitudinal results may generalize across cohorts when the cohort grouping variable fails to yield significant effects. Hence, cohort and cohort-by-time confounds are controlled simply by building the cohort variable into the design of the study (Schaie, 1972). There appears to be a general consensus that the cohort-sequential design represents the single most appropriate method for collecting and analyzing data reflecting individual development (Baltes & Schaie, 1973).

Disregarding the generality issue, the cohort-sequential design is subject to the same difficulties associated with conducting longitudinal research. Cognizance of this fact has led to the derivation of a number of alternative designs. One is the cross-sequential design presented in Fig. 2.1, which can be used to ease the burdensome data collection efforts imposed by longitudinal cohort-sequential designs. In the cross-sequential design, the members of different cohorts are followed for a specified period of time as in longitudinal research, but through different phases of their lives, thus shortening the period of time investigators must wait before the data are in final form. Although this alternative has some value in attempts to address specific issues, it also provides an approach of sufficient generality for standard application in studies of individual development.

THE LITERATURE AND ITS IMPLICATIONS

The Impact and Stability of Differential Behavior

Given their enhanced internal validity, longitudinal and cohort sequential designs serve as the principal tools in attempts to understand the ontogeny of differential behavior. As a result of this consideration, studies concerned with the development and expression of human individuality employing these strategies in data collection and analysis are reviewed in this chapter. The literature based on these designs was of an impressive size nearly 40 years ago (Kagan, 1964), and it has expanded rapidly in recent years. Consequently, this review is not exhaustive.

Perhaps the most frequently broached topic in longitudinal studies of differential behavior has been the stability of individual difference characteristics and their long-term implications for later behavior. This concern was one of the driving forces behind a seminal longitudinal study of human individuality. Terman (1925, 1947, 1959) identified some 1,000 preschool and 300 high school students who had intelligence quotients in excess of 140 on the Stanford Binet. Subsequently, he studied these individuals at various points in their lives over the next 30 years by administering further intelligence tests and collecting a variety of psychometric and biographical data describing their lives and personal characteristics. The most clearcut result of this investigation indicated that individuals who displayed high intelligence in childhood continued to manifest substantial intellectual ability throughout their lives. Moreover, these intellectually gifted individuals were unusually successful in the academic setting as indexed by course grades, admission to honor societies, college graduation, and admission to graduate school. Their success was also substantial outside the academic domain, in that these individuals were more likely than the hypothetical average person to obtain upper level jobs and to be successful on their jobs, satisfied with their lives, happy with their marriages, psychologically well adjusted, socially active, and physically adept (Sears, 1977).

A series of longitudinal studies that were conducted in the University of California system also examined the stability of intellectual ability, although the principal concern of these investigations was intellectual growth in a somewhat more representative sample. In a now classic study, Bayley (1949) found that intellectual ability could not be assessed with any accuracy before a child's fifth or sixth year of life. However, after individuals reached their sixth birthday, it was found that differential performance on measures of intelligence was a relatively stable attribute with retest coefficients ranging between .64 and .70 (Jones, 1958; Kangus, 1971). Owens (1953) found similar stability coefficients on the Army Alpha Intelligence Test over a 30- to 40-year interval.

Results regarding intellectual ability provide support for the appropriateness of the stability assumption built into the trait model. There is also some evidence pointing to the stability of differential characteristics in other domains. For instance, Strong (1943) found that after age 20, vocational interests are highly stable attributes yielding retest coefficients near .50 over a 30-year interval. Moreover, in a 10-year longitudinal study employing young adults, Kelly (1955) observed similar stability coefficients for vocational interest measures. Kagan and Pankove (1972) found that creativity was a relatively stable differential characteristic yielding retest coefficients in the middle .80s over a 5-year interval. In a more detailed longitudinal investigation of creativity employing Project Talent data, Torrance (1972) obtained comparable stability coefficients over a somewhat longer interval, and noted that creative adolescents (a) remain creative as adults, (b) tend to become more depressed on measures of creativity as adults, (c) tend to obtain unusual but relevant vocational training, (d) tend to choose and enter unusual occupations, and (e) are more likely to manifest creative achievements in adulthood if they enter the fields of science, medicine, and the arts rather than business.

Finally, in a longitudinal investigation of the stability of cognitive styles between childhood and young adulthood, Witkin, Goodenough, and Karp (1967) found that measures of cognitive style, such as field independence, also displayed substantial stability.

Despite the stability that is apparent in the longitudinal investigations just reviewed, these findings must be approached with caution. Researchers participating in the University of California longitudinal studies, among others, noted that, although intelligence is a fairly stable attribute in terms of the ordering of individuals on this trait, a particular individual's scores on age-normed intelligence measures sometimes shifted by more than half a standard deviation between the ages of 7 and 18 (Bayley, 1957; Hilden, 1949; Schwartz & Cohen, 1975), and there was evidence that most individuals manifest spurts of growth at ages 6 and 9 (Bayley, 1949, 1965). Thus, intelligence does not appear to be a fixed attribute emerging in a continuous mechanistic fashion. The stability coefficients obtained in the foregoing studies only indicate the similarity in the ordering of individuals in their expression of an attribute at two points in time, not the stability of an individual's score. The Torrance (1972) study documented increasing depression of creativity with age. Similarly, Owens (1953) found a statistically significant increase in overall intellectual performance despite maintenance of the initial ordering of individuals.

These findings suggest that the high stability coefficients obtained for some differential characteristics cannot be used as evidence for the stability of differential characteristics in the strictest sense. This troublesome situation is compounded by findings of a number of longitudinal investigations that have failed to support the stability of other traits, even when only the ordering of individuals is considered. Employing information obtained in the University of California longitudinal studies, Tuddenham (1959) noted that on measures of a wide variety of personality characteristics, only aggression and need for power among males, along with social prestige, affiliation, and achievement motivation among females, yielded even moderate correlational stability ($r = .20$) over a 10-year interval. In a similar longitudinal effort examining an individual's status on a wide variety of personality traits between childhood and late adolescence, Kagan and Moss (1961, 1962) found that only achievement motivation, along with aggression among males and passive dependency among females, showed any signs of even moderate correlational stability. Once again, the power of these relationships was unimpressive, particularly when one considers the number of measures at different points in time (Kelly, 1955; Tyler, 1965).

This observation has touched one of the longest running and most intense debates in the recent history of psychological research. After reviewing the stability coefficients obtained in various longitudinal studies of individuality, Mischel (1969) concluded that substantial support did not exist for either the generality of the trait model or the appropriateness of its stability assumption. Based on social learning theory, Mischel argued that differential behavior was solely a function of immediate or cumulative environmental influences. Though Mischel's comments were initially limited to the noncognitive domain, recent investigations into the development of intelligence, reasoning, and problem solving have extended this approach into the cognitive domain (Scandura, 1977; Sternberg, 1982).

Criticisms of the trait model and the conceptual approach on which it is based have not gone without commentary in the literature. One rebuttal holds that inferences drawn from current operationalizations of the trait model presuppose a freedom from psychometric biases, such as range restriction, unreliability, and ceiling effects that act to attenuate the observed magnitude of stability coefficients, regardless of their true magnitude (Alker, 1972). Coupled with our lack of understanding concerning the nature of noncognitive characteristics, sizable stability coefficients cannot be expected. Moreover, obtaining support for the situationalist position by examining differential behavior in a single test item is inappropriate because the resulting measurement error is likely to produce instability (Guilford, 1954).

Although the foregoing technical concerns are important, they do not adequately respond to the situational challenge. A somewhat more powerful response may be found in an impressive, albeit little discussed, longitudinal study. Thomae (1965) followed a group of German children sampled in the aftermath of World War II through adolescence and examined the influence of socialization variables, such as socioeconomic status, maternal employment, bastardy, and immigrant background. Thomae's results indicated that these social-situational variables were no more predictive of inventoried individual differences in adolescence than were traditional measures of individuality obtained in childhood. More evidence contradicting the situationalist position has been obtained from studies indicating that individuals exert some control, through overt selection and action, over the situations to which they are exposed (Buhler, 1968; Precker, 1952; Tyler, 1974). Consequently, an exclusive focus on the situation as the prime mover of differential behavior may represent little more than a spurious causal influence.

SITUATIONAL INFLUENCES

Although Mischel's (1969) conceptions of individual behavior, like those of the differential psychologists, are subject to a number of criticisms, the debate is not likely to fade away. The strategy most commonly employed in attempts to resolve the debate holds that differential behavior emerges as a joint function of the individual and the situation (Bem, 1972; Lerner, 1978). There is at least some limited support for this proposition in the literature. For instance, Atkinson (1981) has used the literature pertaining to situational influences on achievement motivation to develop computer-based simulations for assessing the impact of various situational influences on differential behavior given varying levels of the underlying characteristics and found that such interactive complexity might substantially reduce the predictive power obtained simply from trait measures. A variety of other studies examining laboratory behavior have also indicated that situational influences might have a substantial impact on the nature and expression of differential behaviors (Shaffer, 1988). Yet, despite the intuitive appeal of this position and the existence of an extensive body of supportive empirical findings, the nature of interactive effects and their specific forms in the environment remain unclear. Tobach (1981) proposed that differential behavior emerges as a result of the individual's interaction with his or her current environment in an attempt to further overall adaptation. In this context, the interaction is attributable to the individual's attempt to adapt to the environmental surround. Tobach concluded that these interchanges will always occur in one of four basic forms: (a) passive interactions, or a change in the frequency of behavioral emersion due to a change in the environment; (b) reactive interaction, or a change in the nature of the behavior of the organism due to a change in the environment; (c) interactive interaction, or a change in the nature or frequency of behavior due to a change in the environment and a concommittant change in the environment due to a change in individual behavior, and (d) active interaction, or integrated activities directed toward achieving some specific end, which results in changing the nature of both the individual and the environment. Although the various forms of interaction may occur in isolation or in tandem, these categories have different implications for individual behavior and differential development.

The evidence accrued in a number of longitudinal studies provides some support for the existence of these various forms of interaction between the individual and the situations that constitute his or her current environment. Moreover, the results obtained in these investigations suggest that the nature and content of these interactions may have a substantial impact on the development and expression of later differential behavior. In research efforts along these lines, one variable that has been of substantial interest has been early versus late maturation as indexed by the physical onset of pubertal growth. Employing a sample obtained in the University of California longitudinal study, Mussen and

Jones (1958) determined the time at which puberty began and found that, during adolescence, late maturers manifest negative self-concepts, feelings of rejection, strong affiliative needs, and prolonged dependency needs, whereas early maturers appeared more confident, aggressive, and capable of fulfilling adult social roles than the average adolescent. The results obtained 15 years later suggested that these initial behavior patterns were subject to some radical changes in adulthood. As adults, it was found that later maturers displayed a greater openness to emotions, creativity, and unconventionality, whereas adolescent early maturers were characterized by pronounced social conformity in adulthood (Eichorn, 1973; Peskin, 1967).

These observations indicate a major transformation in the developmental import of this maturation characteristic, and Livson and Peskin (1967) have attributed this transformation to the influence of a complex interchange between the individual and the environment. More specifically, they stated that early maturers are not prepared to handle the emotional upheavals of adolescence, and so they engage in socially sanctioned retreat into the acceptance of adult social roles. This bodes well for the adolescent, because peer cultures value physical and social maturity; however, environmental reinforcement of the coping mechanism results in hyperconformity in adulthood. For later maturers, adolescence is a difficult time due to their low status in the eyes of peers. Yet they fare better in the long run because the delay of puberty provides them with sufficient time to learn how to channel emotions in a constructive fashion. Livson and Peskin have gone on to suggest that the apparent complexity in the early correlates of adult adjustment found by Block and Turula (1963), Brooks and Elliot (1971), and Maas (1968), as well as the apparent instability of this characteristic in longitudinal studies, may be attributed to complex interactive effects of this sort and their impact on the course of individual development.

Another illustration of the fundamental importance of such interactive influences on the ontogeny of differential behavior may be found in the New York longitudinal studies conducted by Thomas and Chess (1977, 1981). In their effort, 133 individuals from middle- and upper middle-class families were followed from 2 to 3 months after birth through the next 16 years and eventually into young adulthood. On the basis of a variety of characteristics indicative of temperament, such as ethnicity, persistence, and attention span, three categories or subgroups of children were identified by specifying common patterns in the expression of these temperamental characteristics through the longitudinal data collected during the first 5 years of the study; these three kinds were the easy child, the difficult child, and the slow-to-warm-up child. Within the context of the present discussion, five findings obtained in followup studies of these subjects and the implications of these three kinds of childhood temperament are of note. First, it was found that the behavioral expression of temperament would oscillate, depending on changes in the situation. Second, the individual's expression of these temperamental patterns might change as a result of environmental feedback and further development. Third, the differential characteristics associated with each temperament pattern and the relationships among these characteristics appeared to shift as a result of environmental feedback. Fourth, different temperamental characteristics led individuals to select or engage in different kinds of situations, and this, in turn, led to further developmental change. Fifth, the developmental outcomes associated with a given pattern of temperament appeared to be highly dependent on the nature of the environment to which an individual was exposed.

An interesting extension of this line of work may be found in a study conducted by Lerner (1980). In this investigation, the temperamental characteristics of junior high school students were assessed, along with the actual and perceived demands made by two school environments. Subsequently, indices of personal and social adjustment, grade point average, self-esteem, and peer evaluations were obtained. A detailed analysis of this data indicated that those individuals whose temperament was most closely matched to their school environment were more likely to display enhanced performance on all of the foregoing measures. Further, it was found that perceived discrepancy was a better predictor of performance on these measures than was actual discrepancy; a finding that seemed to suggest that the individual's own perception and selection of situations had a significant influence on the emergence of differential behaviors.

Another study pointing to the significance of the individual's active and interactive interchanges with the environment may be found in a small-scale cohort sequential investigation concerned with the development of vocational interests. Tyler (1964) obtained 287 individuals between age 6 and age 18 who received repeated administrations of the Strong Vocational Interest Blank. In the course of this effort, she found that the brightest individuals took the longest time to develop well-defined patterns of vocational interests. The development of well-defined vocational preferences was associated with an increase in the proportion of disliked activities reported by the individual. Tyler concluded that vocational interest development is driven by environmental feedback that leads the individual to reject those activities that, for one reason or another, are not expected to be rewarding. Moreover, these findings suggest that the individual's active selection of activities and their associated situations might have a substantial impact on the development and expression of differential behavior, leading to the emergence of qualitative differences among individuals. Additionally, Mumford and Owens (1982) obtained further support for these hypotheses and observed that the apparent stability of vocational interests in the adult population may be based on the anticipated stability of reinforcement contingencies in the adult environment.

Longitudinal studies of actual occupational behavior have also served to underscore the importance of these interactive influences with respect to the development and expression of individuality in adulthood. Bray, Campbell, and Grant (1974) examined the lives of some 200 managers over the course of their first 10 years in the Bell system after collecting a wide variety of descriptive measures at the time of their entry into the organization. It was found that, among individuals of equal assessed capacity for performance, those who had been exposed to a more challenging initial job assignment were far more likely than those who had not had such exposure to be effective performers on later jobs. In addition, the individual who was more successful than expected was, according to Bray, Campbell, and Grant (1974):

> . . . one who places an emphasis on the extension of influence outward into the work and community spheres, seeks expanding responsibilities and is not strongly attached to past ties . . . while the individual who is less successful than expected . . . is not greatly concerned with extending himself into new involvements and responsibilities, he values old ties and tries to deepen them rather than breaking with the past. (pp. 181–182)

These patterns of differential characteristics were present at the time that these individuals entered the organization, but they became more pronounced as time went by. The investigators attributed this finding to conscious preferences on the part of these individuals and subsequent feedback from the environment.

The differential characteristics of the individual and interchange with the environment also may have a substantial impact on intellectual development. For instance, Bayley (1949) identified two stable dimensions of maternal behavior, which she labelled "love versus hostility" and "autonomy versus control." In an investigation employing the sample obtained for the University of California longitudinal study, it was found that, among males, intellectual ability was positively related to mothers' scores on the love-versus-hostility dimension during the child's first 3 years, whereas the autonomy-versus-control dimension yielded similar, albeit weaker, results for females (Bayley, 1965, 1968). Further, studies by Bayley and Jones (1937), Gist and Clark (1938), and Hindley (1962), among others, have seemed to suggest that early exposure to an intellectually rich environment, due to social class or a lack of isolation from the broader society, may also lead to higher capacity at later ages, despite initial similarity. The manner in which the child's own behavior interacts with the environment also appears to be related to patterns of intellectual growth and decline. Using data obtained as part of the Fels Institute Longitudinal Study, Kagan, Sontag, Baker, and Nelson (1958) found that children expressing high achievement needs, competitiveness, assertiveness, and curiosity were likely to manifest relative gains in intelligence test scores during the elementary school years compared to children displaying passive dependent and noncompetitive characteristics. These results may be attributed to the possibility that children displaying the former pattern are more likely to require the skills tapped by intelligence tests in the elementary school environment, whereas the latter pattern is likely to inhibit the acquisition of these skills.

The findings of the longitudinal studies reviewed in the foregoing paragraphs provide substantial support for the capacity of environmental or situational influences to effect the ontogeny, expression, and implications of differential behavior. These results also suggest that all of the various forms of interactions postulated by Tobach (1981) are, in fact, relevant to the development and expression of a wide variety of differential characteristics.

In recent years, some fledgling attempts have been made towards the construction of an integrated and more comprehensive approach to differential development. Riegel (1975) and Lerner (1978), among others, have sketched out a general theoretical approach to individual development that holds that individuals interact with their environment in order to further overall adaptation to the surrounding environment. They noted that, although it provides an important groundwork, human adaptation cannot be adequately measured by hereditary preprogramming, and so interchange with the environment and the appropriate modification of behavior on this basis constitutes a critical aspect of adaptation and provides a basis for effective development.

The organism–environment interchanges are commonly held to be multifaceted in the sense that they may involve one or more of the various classes of interchange denoted by Tobach (1981) occurring in a complex sequence, as specified by multiple environmental demands. Recently, Lewontin and Levens (1982) have summarized a number of important theoretical principles in a series of postulates:

- Organisms select their environments: Organisms actively respond to environmental signals so as to find favorable habitats. However, environmental selection is not a seeking of arbitrary optimal conditions. What is optimal depends on the changing state of the organism and on its developmental history. In addition, different organismic processes have different requirements for optimality; as such, individuals often select habitats that compromise among conflicting needs. Finally, environmental selection with respect to one dimension carries with it other dimensions, due to environmental correlations, and these correlations become factors in selection.

- Organisms modify their environments: Organisms effect their environment by consuming and depleting resources and through the effect of their activities on other organisms.

- Organisms define their environments: Organisms determine what aspects of their environment will be attended to, ignored, combined, or acted on.

- Organisms respond to their environments: Organisms change their behavior in a multifaceted and systematic fashion in order to respond to environmental demands. This implies that identical behaviors may serve different ends, and different behaviors the same ends.

- Organisms respond to their environments in different time scales: Organisms may respond to their environment through immediate adjustments in behavior or through environmental selection and eventual reproductive selection, giving rise to hereditary differences.

- Organisms and their environments are not static: Organisms, in their attempts to adapt, are constantly changing their environment and their behavior in relation to this environment, in search of whatever constitutes optimal conditions, given the immediate and anticipated environmental conditions and personal requirements.

Of course, the framework for understanding organism–environment interactions and their implications for the development and expression of differential behavior is quite broad. Nevertheless, it is based on a solid grounding found in comparative biological theory, and as Lerner and Busch-Rossnagel (1981) have pointed out, it appears to provide the best available explanation for the complex results obtained in longitudinal studies concerned with the development of differential behavior. Hence, at this juncture, it seems appropriate to turn to the implications of this conception and the results obtained in the various longitudinal studies laid out previously for attempts to formulate general summary descriptions of human individuality.

Earlier, it was stated that application of the trait model assumes that the summary of differential behavior manifest in a set of traits and their indicators will describe individuality with similar meaning and accuracy across situations. Unfortunately, both the theoretical conceptions and longitudinal studies of individuality reviewed in the foregoing discussion suggest that this assumption is not well supported. When this assumption is not met, it implies that the traits that provide an adequate and meaningful summary description of individuality in one situation might not do so in others. Moreover, even when the same traits are relevant across situations, there is no assurance that the same indicators of differential behavior will have the same meaning or the same relevance to description of the individual's status on the trait under consideration. Consequently, different situations or environments are likely to require the use of different indicators or traits to obtain an optimal summary description of human individuality; and when this possibility is not considered in the formation of summary descriptions, the accuracy and meaningfulness of the summary description will be reduced. Moreover, ignoring important situational effects may result in misguided theoretical efforts. Thus, it is important to examine alternatives for dealing with the presence of situational influences on individual development.

One strategy that might be employed would entail an effort to identify that subset of all possible trait indicators that are, in some way, applicable across situations. These indicators might then be used to construct a measure of the trait with some cross-situational generality. Unfortunately, regardless of the success of such efforts, to the extent that true situational differences exist that influence the meaning and expression of differential behavior, application of this strategy will result in some loss in the accuracy and predictive power of the resulting summary description. Moreover, the issue of developmental change and instability cannot be addressed through this strategy, because ongoing interchange may lead to shifts in the nature of individuality even when indicators in fact manifest some generality across situations. Traits for which cross-situational indicators can be formulated may not necessarily be exhaustive or provide the most complete and meaningful summary description of individuality in a given situation. Thus, the resulting measurement system may ignore significant components of differential behavior in attempts to describe individuality as it occurs in certain situations or environments.

Alternatively, an attempt might be made to delimit or control the situations in which trait descriptions are formulated and employed. This might be accomplished by specifying a certain subclass of situations and then identifying the relevant traits, along with the meaning and accuracy of the resulting operationalization, through some set of appropriate indicators. As Schmidt and Hunter (1977) have pointed out, this strategy is often successfully employed in applied studies. However, efforts along these lines yield descriptions of limited generality and parsimony, and the concommitant need to formulate and/or reestablish the meaning and accuracy of the measures in different classes of situations makes the trait model somewhat unwieldly. The difficulty is compounded by the fact that a variety of ambiguities arise in attempts to classify situations. Attempts to specify the objective situation, as is common in such classification efforts, will ignore the impact of differential perceptions of the environment, leading to limits on the accuracy and meaningfulness of the resulting descriptions as well as a potentially deficient descriptive system.

Techniques might be devised that would resolve many of the ambiguities associated with these strategies for controlling the impact of situational influences in the description and assessment of human individuality. However, the potential existence of strong interactive effects suggests that attempts to control or delimit the situation or environment apart from the individual expressing it—that is, treating the individual behavior and the situation as two independent variables—is likely to be somewhat misleading and of limited effectiveness. The individual's selection of situations constitutes a significant factor in the development and expression of human individuality. In this case, a failure to consider the individual's selection of situations in attempts to describe human individuality constitutes a serious error. Yet most trait measures and experimental studies continue to focus on overt indicators of immediate differential behavior to the exclusion of the individual's active selection of an interaction with the situation. Although it may well be difficult to examine these active, interactive, and reactive interchanges in the more traditional research strategies, as the longitudinal studies have shown, they may be identified by following the individual's preference for or exposure to various subenvironments over the course of their lives and subsequently assessing the differential behavior occurring within these contexts in a systematic fashion. This strategy is quite similar to a research program proposed by Tyler (1965) more than 20 years ago.

TEMPORAL EFFECTS

The preceding paragraphs have enunciated the fundamental importance of exchanges between the individual and environment with respect to the development and expression of human individuality. The situations to which individuals are exposed change in a systematic fashion over the course of their lives, leading to temporal changes in the nature and expression of individuality. Many of these temporal influences are age-related for, as anthropologists, sociologists, and developmental psychologists have pointed out, society and culture present different options to the members of different age groups. Often coupled with these social demands are biological or motivational factors that influence the individual's resources, capabilities, requirements, and perceptions of the environment. Quite frequently, temporal shifts are quite dramatic and can lead to marked qualitative changes in the nature and expression of individuality. For instance, Benedict (1938) has noted that societies often denote specific times and rituals supporting the individual's movement into a qualitatively new role in the social structure. Further, Neugarten (1964) has noted that society reinforces these changes with specific, normative age-graded behavioral expectations that dictate both the responsibilities and options that will be open to a person. On the other hand, puberty represents a rather dramatic biological change that has marked behavioral implications. Hereditary and environmental influences often work in tandem, in the sense that junior high school is closely timed with respect to the onset of adolescence, and, to some extent, influences of this sort will act to restrict potential individual differences. However, because these influences are rarely completely restrictive in terms of both behavior and situational alternatives and because the previous characteristics of the individual will interact with external influences, it can be expected that differential development will proceed in a rather complex fashion as the individual ages.

The issue of age-related changes in behavior has been addressed in a number of longitudinal studies. One of the most ambitious investigations along these lines may be found in a study conducted by Lehman (1953), concerned with the relationship between age and outstanding occupational achievement. Across occupational areas, it was found that an individual was most likely to make major contributions in his or her early 30s and minor contributions were most likely during the individual's mid-50s to early 60s. The age curve for the frequency of major contributions tended to fall off sharply at the end of young adulthood, but the curve for minor contributions was relatively flat. These curves, and the most likely age of major and minor contributions, tended to shift upward in fields that are highly dependent on training and experience and downward in fields that are highly dependent on native ability. These findings appeared to generalize across at least a limited range of historical periods and cultural conditions.

When first published, Lehman's findings caused some controversy, particularly as they pertained to the ages at which major and minor contributions were most likely to occur. One explanation for these findings was bias introduced by the archival research method (Dennis, 1956, 1958). However, in later studies, Lehman (1960, 1966) successfully refuted many of these criticisms, and thus the issue remaining at this point is why such age-related differences in occupational achievement occur in the first place. Over the years, a variety of hypotheses have been put forth in attempts to account for these findings, including increased social demands on the middle-aged, declines in creativity among the middle-aged, and decrements in physical capacity. Yet, for one reason or another, all these approaches are subject to conceptual flaws.

At present, it appears that these results are best explained on the basis of the developmental tasks facing individuals in young adulthood and middle age (Mumford, 1984). Haan (1981) has pointed out that the tasks facing young adults are bound together by the need to accommodate behavior, goals, values, and so on to the demands of external reality in order to insure adaptation. This accommodating process may occasionally lead talented individuals to formulate new categories of understanding that generate outstanding occupational achievement. On the other hand, during middle age the central task demands for further adaptation involve coming to terms with impending death (Gould, 1978; Roadheaver & Datan, 1981), which leads most individuals to concentrate on control of the remaining portion of their lives and the attainment of discrete, well-defined goals. Perhaps concern with the attainment of limited, well-defined goals lends itself to minor contributions and the extension of known facts and principles. These processes have well-defined sociological underpinnings, which account for the tendency of Lehman's findings to generalize across cultural groups and historical periods. However, these age-related influences also interact with the individual's occupational environment in such a way that the onset of accommodation appears to be delayed in occupational areas that require extensive training and experiences with life.

In a longitudinal study of 247 Harvard undergraduates over a 30-year period, Vaillant and McArthur (1972) also found that age-related changes in environmental demands stimulate a sequence of stage-like behavior in occupational development. For instance, young adults appear to obsessively focus on career goals, but in middle age there is an apparent concern with control, use of power, and the maintenance of success. These findings provide some additional support for Lehman's observations. Moreover, similar results have been obtained in other studies of male career development conducted by Levenson (1978) and Evans and Bartholemew (1981).

Achievement motivation is commonly held to be of substantial importance with respect to occupational achievement, and attempts have been made to investigate age-related changes in achievement motivation in longitudinal studies. Employing data that were obtained as part of the Fels Institute studies, Kagan (1964), Kagan and Moss (1962), and Moss and Kagan (1961) found that achievement motivation was a moderately stable characteristic during childhood, but not between adolescence and young adulthood. Researchers had some difficulty in accounting for such age-related changes in the stability of differential characteristics. However, in a later reanalysis of this data, Crandall (1972) found that this instability could be attributed to differential feedback from the environment that forces the individual to channel general achievement motivation into areas where achievement is most likely to further the overall adaptation of the individual. Thus, the specific expression of achievement motivation was likely to depend on the available options in the environment and the resources and requirements of the individual.

The influence of strong interchanges, or Tobach's (1981) active and interactive categories, on the emergence of differential behavior in various age groups, has also been investigated on both an empirical and theoretical level. In one empirical study, Elkind (1964) found that maturation affects the way in which a child perceives and organizes external stimuli. These temporal changes lead to enhanced performance on some tasks and performance decrements on others. However, changes are most likely to enhance performance on those tasks currently making demands on the members of a given age group. Thus, age-related changes in development may well involve some losses but will act to enhance overall adaptation. Moreover, in an investigation that employed data obtained as part of the University of California longitudinal studies, Haan (1981) found that differences in adult adjustment and moral concerns appear to be a function of changes in preferred cognitive operations and environmental press during adolescence and young adulthood, which result in varying levels of internal conflict with the broader environment, as well as in more advantageous outcomes, in terms of the foregoing criteria, for these individuals who attempt to restructure their self-concepts and the environments in order to reduce conflict.

Another investigation that used the University of California subjects was carried out by Livson (1965), who attempted to examine changes in the structure of anxiety between early childhood, late childhood, early adolescence, and late adolescence. He found that, between early childhood and early adolescence, anxiety was a very general form of differential behavior that was related to a variety of other characteristics and had few well-defined behavioral indicators. However, in late adolescence, anxiety coalesced into a well-defined characteristic associated with the traditional indicators of moodiness, social sensitivity, and nightmares. Additionally, the individual's status on standard measures of anxiety at this point was negatively related to status on measures of this characteristic at earlier periods, although it was positively related to measures of explosive behavior in childhood. The implications are that behavioral characteristics form or crystallize into well-defined categories at different points in time and that the optimal indicators of this characteristic in one age period, given its environmental demands, may not be so in another period. Similar conclusions have been reached by Sternberg (1982), in studies concerned with the ontogeny of intelligence between infancy and young adulthood, as well as by Fleishman and Parker (1962), in studies of motor performance and the influence of differential characteristics and feedback over time.

A number of conclusions may be drawn from the foregoing studies. One is that individual development does not appear to be a simple succession of universal growth followed by a period of decline terminating in death. Rather, it appears to be related to environmental demands, and it may entail both losses and gains. Even more important is the search for genotypic, rather than phenotypic, consistencies in the emergence of individuality over time. Livson (1973) has stated that, to the extent that the meaning and indicators of various differential characteristics shift as individuals move through different stages in the course of their lives, it will be difficult to assume the existence of phenotypic consistency or overt similarity in the meaning and accuracy of differential characteristics over time. Instead, one must search for genotypic consistencies on those aspects of individuality that predict individuality across developmental phases. Phenotypic consistencies are subsumed under the more general concept of genotypic consistencies, yet an emphasis on genotypic consistencies recognizes the fact that, due to ongoing interchange and environmental differences, developmental continuities are likely to be highly complex, rather than phenotypically obvious (Yarrow & Yarrow, 1964). Moreover, the concept of genotypic consistency appears heuristically more appropriate given the strong interactionist conception of human development, while unlike the phenotypic conception, it is capable of incorporating consistencies that may exist in differential behavior despite those qualitative differences in overt expression that may arise as a result of marked changes in the physical and social environments facing the members of various age groups.

One salient, although subtle, implication of the foregoing commentary is that if individuality is to be described in a general sense such that it applies to different age groups and periods within an individual life, it will be necessary to collect data at different time periods and subsequently generate summary descriptions on the basis of this cross-time information. More directly, use of a longitudinal strategy in formulating general summary descriptions makes it possible to incorporate temporal changes and genotypic consistencies. Application of this strategy becomes especially imperative when it is borne in mind that an optimal summary description of individuality in different age phases may require age-tailored indicators and constructs that can be combined only through a longitudinal genotypic approach, as opposed to a cross-sectional phenotypic strategy.

A search for genotypic consistencies enormously complicates the process of formulating summary descriptions, but it does offer certain advantages. First, it is inherently an empirical approach that makes few assumptions about the nature of individuality over time or across age groups, but instead relies on empirically established predictive statements. This strategy appears to be heuristically appropriate given the complex nature of individual development, and it has been shown to be one of the more effective approaches to differential assessment through the development and validation of empirically keyed background data scales and measures, such as the Strong Vocational Interest Blank, where items are selected for use in a measure on the basis of their cross-time predictive power in relation to a specific criterion (Owens, 1976). Second, when utilizing a genotypic strategy, there is no real need to administer the same measures over and over again to participants, avoiding potential biases that are attributable to retest effects. Third, the possibility of temporal shifts in the broader culture in the situations to which individuals are exposed may generate cohort and cohort-by-time effects that need not be viewed exclusively as biasing factors, but may be looked at as an additional source of information concerning individual development. Fourth, the description of individuality can be expanded within the genotypic approach so that the sequential pattern of cross-time relationships might be incorporated in summary descriptions, thus providing a more meaningful and accurate description of individuality when the individual's own activities must be considered relevant and the selection and sequencing of situations might influence the nature and expression of individuality. Finally, in emphasizing the understanding of cross-time predictive relationships among accurate and meaningful indicators of individuality for certain age groups, the genotypic strategy would tend to maximize predictive power and lend itself to the development of a theoretical understanding of human individuality in accordance with the paradigm laid out by Fiske (1979).

PERSON EFFECTS

Of course, temporal effects represent only one potential outcome of an ongoing interchange between the individual and the environment. An additional outcome might be labeled *person effects*. The term *person effects* is intended to convey the fact that the meaning and accuracy of various indicators of individuality and the resulting summary descriptions may differ in a qualitative fashion across individuals. To the extent that such qualitative or intra-individual differences do indeed exist, then fully adequate summary descriptions can be formulated only by employing indicators and characteristics that are tailored to the individual. Moreover, it suggests that the same characteristics or differential indicators might not be equally useful or have similar reliability and predictive power when applied to different individuals.

Over the years, many researchers have objected to measurement systems that argue for an attempt to study qualitative differences of this sort (Fiske, 1971). Typically, they base their objections on the lack of parsimony and generality inherent in this approach. However, this position glosses over the fact that measurement's ultimate concern is the construction of an adequate summary description of human individuality, and thus, the appropriateness of the resulting summary descriptions must be our principal concern. If one grants the truth of this proposition, then the strong interactionist position provides a compelling logic for the examination of person effects of this sort. One of the most obvious facts of human existence is that individuals are not exposed to identical environments. One would expect that exposure to different environments would lead to the emergence of qualitatively different characteristics and indicators of individuality. Further, these differences could be expected to influence the individual's later selection of and interaction with different kinds of subenvironments. The ongoing interchange designed to insure adaptation would eventually lead to a systematic set or organized pattern of qualitative differences that would constitute a critical aspect of human individuality.

Historically speaking, this is not a new argument. Adherents of the ipsative and idiographic approaches to the assessment of human individuality have often argued that different aspects of individuality are of varying importance in determining the behavior of different persons and that human individuality is most clearly seen in the person's unique combination and patterning of their more salient qualities (Lamiell, 1981). Unfortunately, when this argument is extended to its logical extreme by acknowledging that all individuals are exposed to situations or environments that are in some way unique, it implies that we can never formulate a fully adequate description of individuality that applies to more than one individual. On the other hand, Belsky and Tolan (1981), along with a number of others expressing the views of the strong interactionist position, have noted that although they are complex, the environmental forces impinging upon the individual are systematic and emerge in an interdependent fashion over time. Consequently, it should be possible to identify groups of individuals who are more similar to each other than they are to the members of other groups and to investigate meaningful qualitative differences among the members of these groups.

The strategy was used by Bem and Allen (1974) and Bem and Funder (1978) in investigations of the utility of a modified idiographic approach based on assessments specifically designed for a group of similar individuals. The results provided empirical support for the proposition that certain measures are more useful for describing individuality within certain groups of individuals. Moreover, it was found that some measures were more effective predictors of differential behaviors within certain groups of similar individuals. It is of note that similarity in these studies was determined through asking the subjects how relevant they thought the indicators were for describing themselves.

An alternative method that can be used to address this issue by providing a basis for defining groups of similar individuals entails the formation of groups of individuals through the use of demographic classification categories such as age, race, and sex. Meehl (1967) has noted that this methodology will tend to attenuate the effects associated with cross-group differences, because they are not directly based on the differential behaviors and experiences of the individual, they lack a well defined psychological meaning, and they are associated with such a limited number of indicators that subgroup assignments may be of limited reliability. Yet, despite the conservative bias resulting from difficulties of this sort, investigations along these lines have still pointed to the potential significance of person effects.

A limited number of longitudinal studies have attempted to employ a somewhat more sophisticated approach in their attempts to examine person effects in the ontogeny of human individuality. Here, groups of similar individuals are defined through clustering algorithms that group together individuals who display similar patterns of behavior or experiences through statistical methods rather than through the use of pre-existing classification categories. Perhaps the most impressive effort along these lines may be found in Block's (1971) analysis of the data collected as part of the University of California longitudinal study. The sample employed in this study consisted of 84 men and 87 women. Block had rating data, test data, and detailed clinical records, collected for each individual in a number of assessments between childhood and young adulthood, reviewed by a group of trained psychologists. This information was then summarized for each individual by having the psychologists carry out separate Q-sort descriptions for junior high school, high school, and young adulthood after independent reviews of the relevant information. The model Q descriptions received by these males or females during junior high school and young adulthood were then entered into an inverse factor analysis in order to specify subgroups of individuals having similar Q sorts in both of these time periods. As is shown in Table 2.1, this analysis yielded five male subgroups and six female subgroups having similar patterns of differential characteristics at these two points in time.

TABLE 2.1
Block's 11 Subgroups

Males	Females
Ego resilients	Female prototypes
Belated adjusters	Cognitive copers
Vulnerable over-controllers	Hyperfeminine repressors
Anomic extraverts	Dominating narcissists
Unsettled under-controllers	Vulnerable under-controllers
	Lonely independents

Further analyses examining the aggregate characteristics of each of these subgroups of individuals and the ways in which they differed from each other produced a variety of noteworthy results. It was found that each of these subgroups displayed marked differences in their characteristic behavior and experiences on both of the indicators of individuality that were employed in subgroup formation and some additional indicators, such as those obtained in senior high schools, that were not employed in subgroup formation. Moreover, the differential characteristics associated with each subgroup were sufficiently cohesive that they reflected a consistent pattern of development that could be labeled. These subgroups also appeared to provide an adequate description of individuality over these three developmental periods, in the sense that roughly 80% of the males and females had a high probability of belonging to a single subgroup. Some summary dimensions of differential behavior or experiences were more important than others for understanding the current and later behavior of the members of certain subgroups. The organization or interrelationship of various differential characteristics was different for the members of various subgroups and was capable of shifting in a systematic fashion as the individual members of a subgroup moved into new developmental phases. The results also provided strong support for the complex nature of individual development, as well as substantial evidence pointing to the importance of considering the possibility of qualitative differences among individuals in formulating summary descriptions of human individuality. Finally, Block's interpretation of the results obtained for each subgroup and their pattern of development suggested that interchange with the environment and the active selection of environments had a marked impact on the ontogeny of individuality and served both as an impetus to and an expression of these qualitative differences between the members of various subgroups.

Although Block's work represents a carefully conducted study serving to establish the fundamental importance of person effects or intra-individual differences in the development and expression of human individuality, this study's value is limited by a number of specific methodological problems, such as the use of a relatively small, nonrepresentative sample, a reliance on judgmental Q sort data, and the application of one of the less powerful clustering algorithms. Although these problems indicate that the results of Block's (1971) study must be approached with some caution, a limited number of other investigations have served to validate some of the more fundamental findings of this study, as well as the feasibility of this empirical approach to subgroup formation. For instance, Reichard, Livson, and Peterson (1962) obtained ratings of the individual's status on a variety of noncognitive characteristics in a sample of older men between ages 65 and 84. These individuals were then divided into subsamples on the basis of a measure of their overall adjustment to aging, and an inverse factor analysis was used to identify different subgroups of individuals within these subsamples. The resulting subgroups displayed qualitative differences in the nature of their characteristic behaviors and experiences. The particular pattern adopted by an individual appeared to be dependent on the behavior and experience of his past life. An investigation conducted by Neugarten (1964) obtained subgroups and results nearly identical to those of the Reichard et al. (1962) investigation, providing evidence for the reliability of effects of this sort and the need to consider them in attempts to describe human individuality.

A final investigation along these lines may be found in a longitudinal study conducted by Thomas and Chess (1972, 1977, 1981). Measures of children's temperament during the first 5 years of life were obtained for 133 individuals, and subgroups of similar individuals were established through an inverse factor analysis coupled with a qualitative analysis. As was noted earlier, three subgroups of similar individuals were identified: (a) the easy child, characterized by biological regularity, approach responses to new stimuli, quick adaptability to change, and a predominantly positive mood of mild intensity; (b) the difficult child, characterized by biological irregularity, frequent withdraw responses to new stimuli, slow adaptability to change, frequent expression of negative feelings, and high intensity moods; and (c) the slow-to-warm-up child, characterized by frequent withdraw responses to new stimuli, slow adaptability to change, mild intensity of mood expression and mild expression of biological irregularity and negative moods.

A series of analyses focusing on the differential characteristics of these three groups indicated that they responded in a qualitatively different manner to environmental influences. More specifically, the environments associated with good adjustment for the members of one subgroup were different than those for the members of other subgroups.

Moreover, it was found that the developmental importance of differential characteristics varied with subgroup status, and these differences lead to the selection of different subenvironments and marked differences in the feedback received from these environments. For instance, the slow-to-warm-up child's unwillingness to engage in new social situations during the preschool years often induced feelings of insecurity in middle-class parents who value this characteristic and possible adjustment problems for the child, although this did not necessarily hold true during the elementary school years or occur for other subgroups. Finally, the findings of this investigation led the authors to emphasize the importance of genotypic consistencies in the development of a particular subgroup.

The studies cited in the foregoing paragraphs have served to provide substantial support for the emergence of person effects in the course of the ongoing interchange between the individual and the environment, as well as the potential significance of these qualitative differences with respect to the development and expression of human individuality. Obviously, a failure to obtain an adequate description of the individual by incorporating such person effects will lead to theoretical efforts of limited value and empirical observations of questionable utility. The existence of person effects implies that different indicators or constructs may be needed to formulate an adequate description of individuality in different subgroups. Thus, subgroup-specific measures may be required, and it cannot be assumed that identical behaviors will have similar meanings in terms of their development importance, because the meaning of behavior may vary with these qualitative differences. An extension of this principle may be found in the possibility that certain differential characteristics may exert a preponderant control over the behavior of the members of certain subgroups, although they may be irrelevant to describing the behavior of certain subgroups. Pattern differences across subgroups of this sort may well represent a major manifestation of human individuality of great value in the description of differential behavior. Unfortunately, investigators have typically ignored effects of this sort, due to the fact that the trait and experimental models in their exclusive nomothetic focus ignore their potential significance. In fact, these models are incapable of incorporating such pattern differences without a substantial change in their underlying assumptions and goals.

Attention to person effects and their associated moderating influences may yield significant increments in prediction, as well as permit some integration of both the individual differences and experimental paradigms along the lines suggested by Cronbach (1957b). Although researchers in the area of differential psychology stress the importance of moderator effects (Dunnette, 1966), investigators have found it difficult to establish moderator effects on measures of individuality that display any practical significance or tangible stability (Schmidt & Hunter, 1977). However, if these moderator effects are closely tied to person effects, in the sense that the nature and impact of a moderator or differential behavior is dependent on or integrated with other subgroup-specific characteristics or person effects that do not necessarily generalize across a number of subgroups, then one would not expect to find many significant and stable moderator effects in aggregate level studies (Owens, 1978). Owens and Schoenfeldt (1979) have obtained a great deal of evidence that this is, in fact, the case in a series of experimental and correlational studies employing empirically established subgroups. In sum, it appears that the incorporation of person effects in attempts to formulate summary descriptions of human individuality may threaten the more traditional models, but provide a more powerful and general approach by allowing psychology to address phenomena that are currently ignored, providing a basis for interpreting divergent lines of research by conducting experimental studies within well-defined groups of similar individuals and addressing the idiographic criticisms of a pure nomothetic strategy.

VARIATIONS ON THEME

The literature review presented in the foregoing discussion has led to a number of conclusions concerning the development, expression, and assessment of human individuality. Perhaps the most important conclusion reached is that, although the trait model assumes that indicators of individuality and the resulting summary descriptions will have similar meaning and accuracy across time, persons, and situations, these assumptions do not appear to be reasonable ones, because they do not conform to the results obtained in longitudinal studies. In making simplifying assumptions, application of the trait model may have led us to ignore significant aspects of individuality. When individuality is examined within a developmental framework, it becomes apparent that it is highly complex. Consequently, the emphasis placed on parsimony and economy by adherents of the trait model may seriously distort the fundamental nature of development and lead to misguided and empirical efforts.

The evidence presented in the foregoing review, along with the musings of these authors, would suggest that:

1. Individuality must be stretched and defined on a cross-time or developmental basis.

2. Research strategies must search for genotypic consistencies rather than overt behavioral similarity due to developmental transformations in the meaning and expression of differential behavior that result from ongoing interchanges with the environment.

3. Research strategies must acknowledge the importance of the various forms of interchange between the individual and the environment as well as the structure of this environment over the course of the life span in determining the development and expression of individuality.

4. Research strategies must be cognizant of the fact that qualitative differences between individuals may emerge in the course of the organism environment interchange, such that the meaning and accuracy of measures may vary across subgroups of individuals and different age groups.

5. Research strategies must be sensitive to the fact that the individual's selection of situations and the sequencing of activities over time may constitute important aspects of individuality that have a significant influence on the later development and expression of individuality.

6. Research strategies must acknowledge the fact that individuality is manifested in a wide variety of ways and develops through a highly complex process but is manifest as an organized pattern of differential behavior and experiences.

7. Research strategies must be sensitive to the fact that, despite its complex nature, individuality represents an organized and systematic attempt to further the overall adaptation of the individual.

Of course, the preceding comments, as well as much of the foregoing discussion, suggest that the trait model, in its strongest form, cannot provide a fully adequate description of human individuality, due to both assumptional violations and a failure to examine relevant influences. Yet not all investigators have disregarded these considerations. A number of adjustments have been made in implementations of the trait model in attempts to compensate for the potential impact of situational influences. Unfortunately, all of these strategies represent little more than partial solutions to a far larger and more complex set of problems. Additionally, it is unclear whether all these adjustments are capable of solving the problems. Consequently, it appears that we require some viable alternative to the trait model for constructing summary descriptions of human individuality that is capable of incorporating the complex manifestations of individuality. Although it might be possible to employ one of the existing alternatives, as was noted earlier, all of these strategies suffer from certain critical limitations. Moreover, many of the alternatives proposed by the critics of the trait model do not appear to be sufficiently broad or capable of incorporating the significant influences identified in the preceding review of our knowledge of the ontogeny of human individuality. Nevertheless, it is possible that a synthesis of these considerations might give rise to a more general and effective approach to the description of human individuality, and in the following chapter, an attempt is made to lay out the conceptual groundwork for an initial effort along these lines.

3

A Prototype Alternative for the Description of Individuality

THE PROTOTYPE ALTERNATIVE

Taken as a whole, implications of the various longitudinal studies reviewed in the preceding chapter suggest that the trait model is not capable of providing a fully adequate summary description of human individuality. This creates a fundamental problem, because further progress in the description and assessment of human individuality demands a somewhat more sophisticated conceptual and methodological approach that is capable of incorporating the various manifestations of situation, temporal, and person effects. Consideration of the fact that our understanding of individuality as a natural phenomenon is ultimately tied to the descriptive model in use underscores the importance of this problem and the need for a solution.

Perhaps the most obvious way to address this issue would involve replacing the trait model with one of the three traditional alternatives. Unfortunately, the heuristic value of the experimental model is also limited by the operation of situational, temporal, and personal effects. For instance, due to the potential existence of intra-individual or qualitative differences among persons in their reaction to some manipulation, there is no assurance that a nomothetic experimental approach can provide the truly general laws on which applications of this model are based. Moreover, the resulting inflation of the error term, as well as the inability of experimental procedures to examine certain significant aspects of individuality, such as the person's selection and definition of situations, tend to limit the power of this approach. Alternatively, one might attempt to apply the idiographic model. Yet, by implying that each individual is unique, the model precludes accurate summary description that may be applied on a general and reasonably economical basis, limiting the field's ability to formulate the general principles that would constitute a true science of human individuality.

As was noted earlier, the typological model has traditionally provided one of the most appealing alternatives to the trait model, and this holds true even within the context of the present discussion. The issue of intra-individual differences is handled quite readily by assuming that groups of similar individuals, or types, are allowed to differ in a qualitative fashion from the members of other types in terms of their typical behavior and experiences. On the other hand, in its historical formulation, the typological model suffers from certain major flaws, which act to restrict its utility. First, the typological model has traditionally regarded the similarities and differences characterizing types as quite general in the sense that they are held to be maintained across time and situations. Thus, temporal and situational effects are not considered in the definition of individuality, and sufficient attention is not given to the fact that, in any operational system, similarities and differences among individuals are a relative rather than an absolute phenomenon. Second, because of a lack of adequate methodology for defining and validating typological descriptions, many investigators have fallen back on pre-existing demographic categories of limited value, or they have attempted to conceive of types as little more than extremes on some subset of trait dimensions. The resulting proliferation of types and typologies has adversely effected the economy, clarity, and generality of typological descriptions.

Apparently, none of the traditional models are capable of providing a fully adequate description of human individuality as it emerges in the course of a person's development. This suggests the urgent need for a more general model that is capable of taking into account the varied implications of personal, situational, and temporal effects in the summary description of human individuality. Although this may seem a rather monumental undertaking, the differences among individuals are not infinite, and they are channeled by the nature of the environment such that they are expressed in an integrated and systematic fashion that will further adaptation. Assuming this to be true, one might expect that some individuals will be more similar to each other in terms of their behavior and experiences than they are to other individuals. The potential existence of systematic similarities and differences in turn suggests one way in which a more effective and realistic model for the summary description of human individuality might be formulated.

PROTOTYPE AS A MODEL

In an empirical sense, individuality can only be defined by examining the similarities and differences among individuals, regardless of the particular manner in which summary descriptions are formulated. This fundamental consideration in all measurement efforts can be used to form the groundwork for a more general model of human individuality, which has been labeled a *prototypic model* of human individuality. The prototypic model holds that a subgroup of individuals will be more similar to each other than they are to individuals in other subgroups on one or more indicators of individuality. If subgroups of individuals who display similarity in their behavior and experiences can be identified, and the ways in which their typical behavior and experiences differ from those of other groups of individuals can be established, then the subgroups would represent an empirically defined modal pattern in the expression of individuality, which may be referred to as a prototype.

Obviously, the essential requirement for implementation of the prototypic model is that individuals display a meaningful cohesiveness or similarity in their behavior and experiences within a subgroup that serves to differentiate them from the members of other subgroups. Aside from this prosaic consideration, implementation of the prototypic model makes no other assumptions concerning the nature of human individuality. The prototypic model is based on, and focuses on, the ultimate goal of psychological measurement, that is, the classification of individuals and the description of the similarities and differences among them in their behavior and experiences (Binet & Simon, 1905).

When prototypes or subgroups are employed in formulating summary descriptions of individuality, summarization is carried out through the prototypical pattern of the subgroup. All individuals who can be assigned to a prototype would be assumed to display the same behavior and experiences that characterize the prototype as a whole. Once an individual who was not employed in definition of the prototypes has been assigned to a particular prototype, all known characteristics of the prototype may be ascribed to that individual. Thus, assignment to a *prototype* makes it possible to predict the behavior and experiences of the individual and summarize the differential behavior and experiences of a number of individuals. Figure 3.1 presents a hypothetical illustration of four prototypes, where similarity among individuals is related to education and employment level. For all individuals assigned to Prototype 1, high education and employment levels would be predicted, regardless of whether or not these individuals were used in defining the prototype. It should also be noted that individuals might be described through their

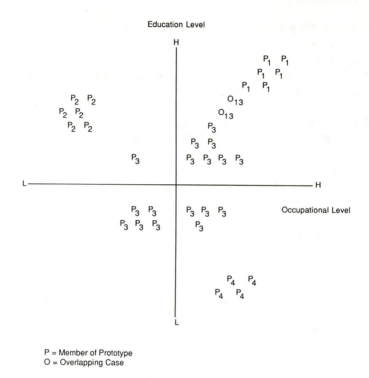

P = Member of Prototype
O = Overlapping Case

FIG. 3.1.   Prototypes in formulating summary descriptions.

relationship to two or more of these modal patterns, as is illustrated in Fig. 3.1.

The core assumptions involved in implementation of the prototype model are (a) that some individuals will display systematic similarities in their behavior and experiences that serve to differentiate them from other individuals, and (b) that the similarities and differences empirically defining a modal pattern can be used to describe individuals who were not used in forming the patterns. These assumptions are not unreasonable if one grants that individuality emerges in a systematic fashion in the course of development.

By focusing on the classification of persons, this approach also offers certain unique advantages. First, as long as individuals manifest systematic similarities and differences over time, there is no need to assume that the behaviors or experiences that define a pattern at one point in their lives are identical to those behaviors and experiences that define a pattern at later points. Thus, the prototype model can incorporate complex genotypic relationships and temporal effects. Second, the similarities and differences in an individual's selection of situations may be employed in defining the patterns, and so situation effects may be directly incorporated into the summary description of individuality. Finally, although the prototypic model does not assume the existence of person effects or qualitative differences among individuals, if such effects represent some aspect of the similarities and differences among individuals on the behavior and experiences employed in defining the prototype, then the effects will be reflected in the resulting modal patterns. Hence, the prototype model is capable of capturing significant aspects of individuality as they emerge in the course of development.

By defining and summarizing individuality through the similarities and differences among individuals in their expression of behavior or experiences, the prototype model offers an additional important advantage. All individuals assigned to a prototype may be treated as a single individual, and their characteristics may be investigated as a unit unto themselves. This approach allows for a variation on the traditional implementation of the idiographic strategy. Some efficiency is afforded, because only a limited number of hypothetical modal patterns need to be investigated rather than treating each individual as unique. Nomothetic laws, on the other hand, may be identified by determining those relationships that hold across prototypes. Consequently, the prototype model provides a viable compromise between the extreme idiographic and extreme nomothetic positions.

The prototype model also bears an interesting relationship to attempts to formulate summary descriptions of individuality through the classification of differential behavior or experiences using the trait model. Disregarding the trait model's assumptions concerning temporal and situational effects, if a given behavior or experience has similar meaning and can be assessed with similar accuracy for all individuals, then individuals can only differ in the extent to which they express the particular behavior or experience. Using the trait approach, a particular individual would be described as being X standard deviations away from the sample mean. Analyzing the prototypic model using the same data, groups of similar individuals might still be identified. However, if prototypes are compared to each other in order to describe individuality, the description obtained for each member of a prototype would be very similar to that obtained from application of the trait model. This relationship is illustrated in Fig. 3.2, and as may be seen, most members of Prototype 3 would be described in much the same way regardless of the particular model in use.

The prototype and trait models offer similar interpretations whenever the indicators being employed in both techniques have similar meaning and accuracy across prototypes. However, when the prototypes differ in this regard, the two models depart, due to the existence of intra-indi-

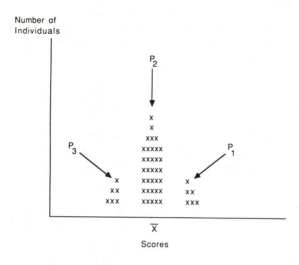

FIG. 3.2.   Relationships among the prototype and trait models.

vidual differences that cannot be examined in the trait model. In addition, unlike the trait model, the prototype model includes temporal and situational effects.

This brings us to a rather interesting issue bearing on the summary description of human individuality. Like the typological model, the prototype model formulates summary descriptions by classifying persons rather than behaviors and experiences. The choice between these two strategies represents a question in psychology that is analogous to the chicken-versus-the-egg riddle. Yet, an answer to this riddle may be found in certain considerations, all of which argue for the primacy of classifying persons. On an elementary level, behavior and experiences are a property of the individual rather than the individual being a property of behavior and experience (Vale & Vale, 1969). Even when behaviors or experiences have been classified, an individual can only be described by contrasting his or her performance with that of some hypothetical average individual. Thus, the classification of persons would appear to be basic and heuristically more appropriate. Moreover, a classification of persons is capable of incorporating both intra-individual, or qualitative, differences and intra-individual, or quantitative, differences, yielding a broader description of the phenomena than could be obtained simply by classifying behaviors or experiences.

The advantages of classifying persons rather than behaviors and experiences are accentuated by the fact that such a classification provides a viable compromise between the extreme idiographic and the extreme nomothetic approaches. It also permits examination of the differences in the organization of behavior and experiences across individuals which may be of great importance in describing individuality. Finally, in any attempt to describe human individuality through empirical methods, one must focus on the ways in which a person is like some other persons. Hence, the classification of persons would seem to provide a more direct solution. Consequently, the prototype model, with its reliance on a classification of persons, provides the most appropriate and effective answer to this riddle in the description of human individuality.

CONSTRUCTING GENERAL PROTOTYPES

Despite the fact that it is logically possible to specify a legitimate prototype on the basis of the similarities and differences obtained on a single indicator, it is unlikely that the resulting classification would display any substantial generality. Thus, attempts to define general prototypes must focus attention on the indicators to be employed for defining the similarities and differences among individuals. The nature of the classification will vary as a function of the indicators selected.

In certain instances, investigators may decide to focus on a limited domain of indicators in order to obtain an optimal classification for some specific purpose (Fleishman & Quaintance, 1984). However, when the central concern of an investigation is the construction of a general classification of persons, selected indicators must meet certain specific criteria.

One step that should be taken to ensure a general description of individuality would entail sampling the more critical or significant indicators of individuality. Viewed from a developmental perspective, a significant indicator is one that is related to a wide variety of later differential behaviors and experiences. Significant indicators are not limited to behavior. Because the individual's interchange with and selection of situations constitute critical elements in the development and expression of human individuality, the indicators employed in formulating general summary descriptions should be capable of examining these critical elements. Additionally, due to the existence of developmental discontinuities and the age grading of behavior, significant indicators of individuality at one point in time may not be so in another, and hence, one would expect that some age-tailoring of the indicators would be required.

It may also be necessary to employ indicators garnered at a number of points in the individual's life. There are three reasons that argue for the use of this strategy. First, the person's sequencing of behavior and experiences may constitute an important manifestation of human individuality. Second, the meaning of a given behavior or experience is difficult to establish in the absence of antecedent information, particularly when such relationships may vary across prototypes. Correspondingly, the availability of information collected at a number of points in an individual's life would allow antecedent and consequent data to be directly incorporated into the definition of similarities and differences, and so should provide a better-specified and more meaningful summary description of individuality. Finally, if the nature of individuality is subject to changes in the course of development due to ongoing interchanges with the environment, then patterns of similarities and differences that will provide a description of individuality that generalizes over developmental periods can be defined only by directly examining cross-time relationships.

Because individuality is manifested in a wide variety of ways, any attempt to formulate a general classification of persons is likely to be forced to employ a fairly large number of significant indicators if an adequate definition of the similarities and differences among individuals is to be obtained. For instance, Fig. 3.3 shows that if only one indicator is used, individual A may be found to be dissimilar to individuals B and C, who belong to a single prototype, yet when six indicators are examined, they may be found to be sufficiently similar to belong to the same prototype. It can usually be expected that the accuracy of the classification will improve as more information concerning the individual becomes available. Fleishman and Quaintance (1984) have underscored the importance of these issues, and they noted that these considerations imply that the definition of the optimal number of classification categories and the assignment of individuals to the categories will always be a matter of relative similarities and differences that are highly dependent on the nature of the indicators in use.

Of course, to the extent that indicators are free from measurement error, one would expect the accuracy of the resulting classification to increase. Hence, an effort should be made to employ reliable indicators in the construction of a general classification. However, unlike reliability as it is traditionally operationalized in psychometrics, indicators do not necessarily need to be stable over time, because stability in indicator scores is irrelevant to the accurate definition of prototypes. Diversity in the nature of the indicators, on the other hand, is likely to enhance the accuracy of prototype definitions by incorporating more unique information concerning similarity in the behavior and experiences of individuals.

In sum, the foregoing discussion has suggested a variety of steps that

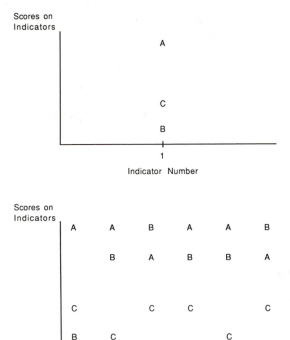

A, B, C = Persons

FIG. 3.3. Prototype definition and number of indicators.

must be taken to formulate a general classification of persons. An attempt should be made to obtain a large and diverse set of reasonably accurate indicators. Moreover, the indicators employed should reflect significant behaviors and experiences and should be collected at a number of points in the individual's life. When indicators have been generated in accordance with these criteria, it should be possible to formulate a general classification of persons through the prototype model. However, despite its importance, indicator content itself does not constitute sufficient evidence to establish the adequacy of a general classification of persons.

ASSESSING THE ADEQUACY
OF GENERAL PROTOTYPES

Unfortunately, the issue of the meaningfulness and accuracy of classifications of persons has not yet received a great deal of attention in the literature. To date, the only comprehensive discussion of the relevant issues may be found in Fleishman and Quaintance (1984). However, in attempts to formulate general summary descriptions of human individuality, investigators will not typically be able to examine and define patterns on all relevant indicators, because the domain of relevant indicators will be incomprehensibly large. Thus, it is critical that an attempt be made to establish the meaningfulness and accuracy of the summary description provided by the classification, regardless of the particular indicators in use. A number of different concerns must be addressed in establishing the adequacy of a classification.

The first concern is the clarity of the classification. Traditionally, the adequacy of a typology or taxonomy has been assessed on the basis of the extent to which the units being classified could be assigned to a single category. Hence, in a perfectly clear solution, each individual should have a probability of 1 of belonging to a single prototype and a probability of 0 of belonging to all other prototypes. This criterion is similar to the simple structure concept employed in factor analysis, and the extent to which it is approximated in a data set provides a basis for assessing the adequacy of the classification.

Although the utility of this criterion is open to question when it is expected that some individuals or units might truly belong to more than one prototype or category (overlapping cases) and that some individuals may not truly belong to any prototype or category (isolates), it is useful in determining whether comprehensive, well-differentiated categories have been established, particularly because it may be expressed in quantitative terms through the aposteriori probabilities obtained from a discriminant analysis. Further, despite the ambiguities introduced by the presence of true overlaps and true isolates, more confidence can be placed in the general summary description derived from a set of prototypes when all individuals can readily be assigned to a single category. Thus, information of this sort is essential in establishing the fact that an adequate classification has been formulated. The use of either the aposteriori probabilities or the number of overlaps and isolates as an objective measure of the need for additional classification categories allows the prototype model to avoid the proliferation problem, which has plagued both traditional implementations of the typological model and modern studies concerned with the classification of behavior through the trait model.

A second concern is the robustness, or generality, of the classification. Similarities and differences that define a given category should be maintained on indicators that were not employed in the initial definition of the classification; that is, for prototypes to be considered robust, the summarization incorporated in them must extend to other relevant indicators not employed in their initial definition. Stronger evidence for robustness is provided if the information obtained from new indicators fits into an interpretable pattern that coincides with the description of the prototypes observed on the initial set of indicators. Once a set of indicators has been specified as defining certain prototypes, the indicators employed in assessing robustness can be designed to allow assessment of the convergent and divergent validity of the prototype descriptions. For example, indicators could be garnered through different measurement formats or collected at different points in an individual's life, and specific hypotheses could be formulated as to the kind of indicators that should either discriminate prototypes from each other or should demonstrate the similarity of the prototypes.

The concept of robustness is closely related to the issue of cross validation in more traditional approaches to the study of human individuality. Consequently, one technique that might be used to assess the robustness of a classification would involve determining the extent to which a sample of individuals not employed in the initial development of the prototypes could be assigned to a single one of these prototypes. If a robust summary description has been obtained, then it should be possible to assign new individuals to the prototypes with little loss in clarity. As a result, a robust classification would be indicated first by demonstrating only a limited increase in the number of overlaps and isolates, and secondly, by a matrix of aposteriori probabilities that approximates the matrix of 0/1 probabilities obtained for individuals who were employed in the initial prototype development. Though somewhat expensive, an alternative strategy would entail developing a second set of indicators independent of the first set. Subsequently, both sets of indicators could be used to formulate two separate classifications. The extent to which similar prototypes emerged in both classifications and to which the same individuals were grouped together within each solution would provide evidence of the robustness of the classification.

A third concern relevant to assessing the adequacy of a classification of persons is the power of the classification. Because a classification of persons is able to incorporate person effects, the demonstration of qualitative or intra-individual differences would suggest that a classification of persons can capture unique information that is not available from a classification of behaviors. The existence of such differences might provide evidence pointing to the power of this approach. One approach to demonstrate the power of the classification would require showing the existence of differences among the members of various prototypes in their organization of behavior or experiences. This might be accomplished through a within-subgroup correlational analysis examining the relationships among either the indicators employed in formulating the classification or the indicators employed in establishing its robustness. Using both sets of indicators to establish the power of the classification of persons provides stronger evidence than either one alone.

Alternatively, the power of a classification might be demonstrated by showing that the developmental implications of a common behavior or experience vary with membership in a given prototype. A demonstration of systematic differences between the members of different prototypes in the meaning or accuracy of differential behavior and experiences would indicate that a classification of persons through the prototype model had greater power than a classification of behavior or experiences through the trait model.

Assessing the reliability of a classification presents a problem with exactly how one defines measurement error. Reliability could be established through an index of the categorization of individuals, but it would be subject to the well-documented forms of rater error. Alternatively, the extent to which individuals are assigned to the same prototype using a short-term test–retest on the relevant indicators could be a solution. However, this strategy should only be employed when the indicators in use are not highly sensitive to retest effects. Finally, it might be possible to employ a technique analogous to a parallel-forms or split-half approach. The total sample of indicators would be divided in half or replicated in such a way as to ensure coverage of the relevant constructs in both sets of indicators. The two sets of indicators would then be applied to the same individuals, and the extent to which the same individuals were assigned to the same categories could be used as evidence bearing on the accuracy of the classification.

As with results obtained from a classification of behavior or experiences, it is also necessary to validate prototypes in order to ensure that a meaningful summary description has been formulated. The validation of prototypes or any classification of persons presents a complex problem. The validation strategies employed in assessing the meaningfulness of more traditional summary descriptions of individuality may be used in attempts to assess the meaningfulness of a classification of persons.

Historically, investigators have preferred to utilize a criterion-related validation strategy in attempts to assess the meaningfulness of a summary description. Meaningfulness is reflected in the extent to which the summary description can predict some future behavior or experience of interest. This approach is effective in establishing the utility of a classification when the concern is the prediction of some measure of behavior or experience that has not yet occurred, such as job performance in personnel selection.

Although the criterion-related strategy provides concrete evidence concerning the validity of a classification, as well as demonstrating its practical utility, it does not provide a fully adequate approach for assessing the meaningfulness of a general classification of persons. Nevertheless, for a general classification of persons formulated through the prototype model to be meaningful, it should be capable of summarizing and predicting for an individual a *number* of different forms of behavior and experience. Thus, if evidence can be obtained that an individual's membership in a given prototype will yield substantial prediction of a broad range of behavior and experience not examined in formulating the prototype (so as to avoid bias), then evidence will have been obtained for its validity as a general description of individuality. The classification as a whole can be validated by establishing this fact for all relevant prototypes.

Two alternative validation strategies exist for assessing the meaningfulness of summary descriptions. The first has been labeled content validity, and it refers to the extent to which the indicators employed in constructing a summary description provide an adequate representation of the domain of relevant behavior or experience. In formulating a general classification of persons, this domain will be extremely large. The value of the content validation strategy is likely to be limited by the ambiguities associated with obtaining an adequate and methodologically feasible sample of the relevant indicators in a domain of this size as well as by the difficulty in specifying in detail the nature of the domain and the relevant indicators. Content validity may have some value as a rough check on indicator development and sensitivity to the relevant phenomena, but it may not provide an ideal approach for assessing the validity of a general classification of persons.

The second alternative to criterion-related validity is construct validity. As defined by Cronbach (1971), construct validity refers to the extent to which the summary description displays a meaningful or conceptually interpretable pattern of relationships with other descriptions of individuality. Because both criterion-related validity and content validity represent specific approaches to establishing the meaningfulness of a descriptive system, construct validity subsumes these strategies. Construct validity may be employed in establishing the meaningfulness of a general classification of persons, as well as establishing the meaningfulness of the summary descriptions incorporated in each prototype. The need to focus on prototypes becomes apparent when it is considered that meaningfulness may not be constant across prototypes and that the description of the individual's behavior and experiences is incorporated in the particular prototype to which a person is assigned.

A variety of techniques might be used to establish the construct validity of a classification of persons and the meaningfulness of the descriptions incorporated in a prototype. For instance, the extent to which the differential behavior and experiences characterizing the members of a given prototype fall into an interpretable and cohesive pattern would provide some evidence for the validity of the summary description incorporated in a prototype, and replication of this result over prototypes would serve to help establish the construct validity of the classification as a whole. More concrete support for the construct validity of the prototype descriptions would be obtained if it were found that the differential characteristics of a prototype could be subsumed under a brief label, particularly if the labels could be extended to incorporate differential characteristics observed on indicators not included in the initial construction of the prototypes. Further evidence supporting the construct validity of a classification of persons would be obtained if it is found that similar prototypes displaying similar differential characteristics were obtained in other studies employing different samples or measurement methods. Such convergence would not only provide strong evidence for the construct validity of a classification of persons, but would also provide evidence pointing to the empirical generality and replicability of the classification scheme as a whole. Finally, evidence of construct validity is provided by demonstrating that the prototype's differential characteristics over time fall into an interpretable pattern with respect to developmental theory.

A variety of other sources of information might also be employed in establishing the construct validity of a classification of persons. The particular evidence marshalled in this regard will depend on the nature of the study at hand. In most cases, construct validity should provide a viable approach to establishing the meaningfulness of a classification of persons and the descriptive information incorporated in the prototypes. This is especially likely to be true when some effort has been made to examine the content and criterion-related validity of the descriptive system. Combining the validation evidence with demonstrations of the reliability, robustness, power, and clarity of the classification should provide a comprehensive and accurate basis for assessing the adequacy of the summary descriptions formulated through the prototype model.

DEFINING SIMILARITY
AND FORMULATING PROTOTYPES

The definition of similarity among individuals and the manner in which similar individuals should be assigned to categories or prototypes represent two discrete methodological issues, and psychologists have had some difficulty in addressing both of them. Similarity among individuals may be defined through either qualitative or quantitative procedures. As armchair rationalizations lacking quantitative empirical indicators, many of the older typologies relied on qualitative methods to define similarity among individuals. However, the present discussion concerns only quantitative procedures, because these would be relied on in any implementation of the empirical prototype model, which examines similarities and differences on objective indicators of individuality. Theologus (1969) has stated that there are basically two approaches, which he has termed the *teleological* and *coassociative* approaches, which might be employed in any attempt to define the empirical similarity among individuals.

The teleological strategy defines similarity on the basis of pre-existing groups, such as males and females, Blacks and Whites, or upper class and lower class. Subsequently, a set of indicators is specified either explicitly or implicitly that defines membership in these categories, and category membership is, in turn, used to specify similarity among individuals. With the teleological strategy, the classification categories define both similarity and how individuals should be assigned to the categories.

This approach to the empirical definition of similarity has been popular in applied settings. Toops' (1948) concept of ulstriths represented an extension of the teleological approach in which individuals were cross-classified in terms of a number of pre-existing categories, and the group characteristics were used to make predictive statements for all individuals assigned to them. The known antecedent characteristics of group members have also been used to develop empirically keyed measures for predicting later group membership. For instance, the Strong Vocational Interest Blank, the Minnesota Multiphasic Personality Inventory, and assorted background data keys have all been developed on this basis and have displayed substantial predictive power.

Despite the popularity and success of the teleological approach, as well as the relative ease of defining similarity among individuals within this framework, it is subject to some substantial problems in attempts to formulate a general classification of persons. First, the categories are not based on the individual's behavior and experiences, and so do not provide a psychologically sound basis for developing prototypes and a classification of persons. Second, the categories are often associated with a limited number of indicators that do not appear to be sufficient in breadth, number, or diversity to be capable of producing a general classification of persons. Finally, there are only a limited number of preexisting groups available, and many of these are so small that it is unlikely that they would have any general relevance. Thus, the teleological strategy for defining similarity does not provide an appropriate basis for implementing the prototype model and formulating a general classification of persons.

If the prototype model cannot be implemented by defining similarity through the teleological strategy, the question is whether it can be implemented through the coassociative approach. With the coassociative approach, the individual's status on each indicator is measured, and a quantitative estimate of the degree of similarity among individuals is obtained in terms of their scores on the indicators. The definition of similarity in the individual's scores on a set of indicators is complex. Cronbach (1957a) noted that when the individual's status on a series of indicators of behavior and experience is related to the status of another individual, a graphic breakdown of the relationship yields three components that are reflected in the elevation, pattern, and scatter of scores on a profile of indicators. Figure 3.4 presents a graphic representation of these three components of similarity. The similarity among individuals can be quantitatively assessed to incorporate all three elements of profile similarity through the d^2 index. The d^2 between any two individuals is calculated via the formula $d^2 = (X_{I,J} - X_{I+1,J})^2$ where X reflects the individual's score on the indicator, I the individual, and J the indicator under consideration. Thus the d^2 index can be used to define the overall similarity between any pairwise combination of individuals on a set of indicators.

Anderberg (1972) presented a variety of alternative measures of similarity and noted that the particular measure of similarity employed in a study will depend on the nature of the question being asked. Anderberg provided an elegant proof that indicates that the d^2 index and the correlation coefficient may be appropriately applied to ordinal data as well as interval and ratio scales, an important consideration in the description of individuality where most of our measures are on an ordinal scale. Second, because the d^2 index is capable of assessing all three elements of profile similarity, and all three are relevant to defining similarity (Hamer & Cunningham, 1981), it appears that the d^2 index provides the most appropriate vehicle for defining similarity in constructing a general classification of persons.

Regardless of how one has obtained a quantitative description of the

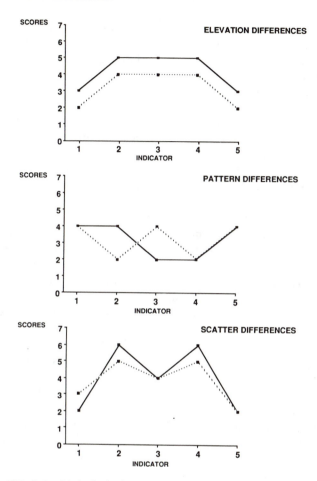

FIG. 3.4. Dissimilarity in profile elevation, pattern, and scatter.

similarity between individuals, the decision rules for defining a cluster of persons must be determined. In large data bases, it is often necessary to formalize the decision rules in the form of a computer based algorithm. Currently, there are a variety of algorithms available that may be employed in classifying individuals. Typically, these algorithms employ one of three kinds of decision rules: complete linkage, single linkage, and average linkage techniques. With the complete linkage technique, the person is described as being most similar to the members of that cluster in which the distance between the person and the most dissimilar individual currently contained in each cluster is minimized. A single linkage decision rule assigns a person to the cluster that contains the individual most similar to the person under consideration. The average linkage technique is somewhat more complex. Using the average linkage technique, the average profile of all individuals currently assigned to a cluster is determined, along with the distance between the average profile of each cluster and the next person to be clustered. The person is then assigned to the cluster associated with the smallest average distance.

Superimposed on these decision models are differences between the algorithms in terms of the manner in which the initial clusters are specified. In a hierarchical algorithm, each person is initially treated as a cluster unto itself, and the clusters are combined in accordance with the foregoing decision rules until all individuals have been combined into a single cluster. At each stage in the sequence, for example, when clusters have just been combined, some index of the similarity of the individuals assigned to each cluster is obtained, and the clusters combined at each stage are determined. The investigator empirically specifies the optimal number of clusters by specifying the smallest possible number of clusters that will still maximize the internal similarity of the individuals assigned to the various clusters. This is often accomplished by plotting the within-cluster similarity at each stage and searching for the inflection point of the resulting curve in a manner that is similar to factor analysis. The tree diagram of the individuals combined at each stage also may be useful as an aid in making these decisions.

When the investigator can specify the categories of interest and their typical profiles before the outset of clustering, a nonhierarchical approach may be employed rather than a hierarchical approach. The principal difference between the hierarchical and nonhierarchical algorithm is that the latter procedure presumes some pre-existing knowledge of the clusters of interest, whereas the former procedure allows the investigation to empirically identify the optimal number of subgroups. In the *initial* construction of prototypes and a general classification of persons, the hierarchical procedure would appear to be most useful because the requisite knowledge for a nonhierarchical analysis is not likely to be available, and definition of the relevant clusters or prototypes will constitute a major concern of the investigation. The nonhierarchical procedure is valuable when sufficient knowledge is available, as in the classification of jobs, particularly because the nonhierarchical procedure is somewhat more accurate in assigning individuals to clusters (Zimmerman, Jacobs, & Farr, 1982). Hierarchical algorithms tend to be slightly less accurate, because the profile of the cluster may drift away from the profile of early assignees. However, this problem may be handled by first identifying the optimal number of clusters and their profiles through a hierarchical algorithm, and then employing a nonhierarchical analysis to reassign individuals to the clusters.

Regardless of the effectiveness of an algorithm and the definition of similarity, it may not be possible to assign all individuals to a single cluster or prototype. This is not necessarily a disadvantage, because individuals may be true isolates or overlaps. However, to the extent that all individuals cannot be assigned to a single cluster, a general classification can be questioned due to lack of clarity.

The foregoing discussion has indicated that a wide variety of clustering algorithms are available for coassociative classification efforts. This is true even when only the variations on the hierarchical procedure are considered. However, one algorithm that appears to be particularly useful in formulating a classification of individuals may be found in the Ward and Hook (1963) procedure. The Ward and Hook algorithm is a hierarchical, average linkage technique that operates in the following fashion. Initially, the similarity between all individuals on a set of indicators is described through a matrix of d^2 values, and each individual is treated as a cluster unto itself. The two most similar individuals are then combined to form a new cluster, their average profile is obtained, and the distance between the new cluster and all other clusters is determined. Subsequently, the two most similar clusters are again combined, and the preceding steps are repeated in an iterative sequence until all individuals have been combined into a single cluster. At each step in this sequence, the average distance among the individuals contained within each cluster is determined. This information is then plotted, and the point preceding the stage where there is a dramatic increase in the dissimilarity of the individuals being assigned to the cluster is used to specify the optimal number of clusters that will maximize within-cluster similarity through the smallest possible number of clusters. The average profile of the clusters obtained in the analysis then forms the basis for a nonhierarchical reassignment of individuals to control for the drift of early assignees. The number of overlaps and isolates is also determined at this point. Generally, if the next nearest subgroup is more than half the distance to the further subgroup, the person is considered an isolate. Thus, individuals are assigned to clusters on the basis of the degree of similarity between their profile and the average profile of cluster members. This assignment can also be carried out through a discriminant analysis once the optimal number of clusters has been specified, and the resulting discriminant function can be used to assign new individuals to the cluster.

As a hierarchical algorithm based on the d^2 index, the Ward and Hook algorithm appears to provide an appropriate basis for the definition of prototypes and the construction of a general classification of persons. At least two other considerations also argue for its appropriateness. In a Monte Carlo study examining the ability of four algorithms to identify the true number of underlying clusters, Blashfield and Morey (1980) and Blashfield (1981) found that, not only was the Ward and Hook procedure capable of consistently identifying the true number of underlying subgroups but, it performed significantly better in this respect than the alternative procedures. This empirical support for application of the Ward and Hook procedure is buttressed by a conceptual consideration. The Ward and Hook procedure essentially acts as an internal analysis of variance that seeks to maximize within-subgroup similarity and between-subgroup differentiation. Because attempts to define an effective general classification of persons demand internal homogeneity within a prototype and differentiation among the prototypes, this characteristic of the algorithm provides a potent argument for its application in the definitions of prototypes. One practical ambiguity exists in interpreting results obtained through the application of any hierarchical algorithm to the problem of defining groups of similar individuals. Because of the high costs of operating algorithms, investigators must often summarize their indicators through principal components analysis. If qualitative differences exist among individuals, these descriptions will be highly approximate and of limited meaningfulness and accuracy. Consequently, even an excellent classification is likely to display substantial variation within a cluster or prototype. The residual variation observed when common summary dimensions are used should not be used to argue against the effectiveness of the classification effort. Rather, it represents our inability to formulate the prototype specific measures called for by the existence of intra-individual differences.

THE PROMISE OF PROTOTYPES

Is there substantial support for the utility of classifying persons rather than behavior? As was noted earlier, much of the work that has been done has relied on a teleological approach. Despite the fact that the teleological approach is less than optimal, it does provide some support for the value of classifying persons. The Strong Vocational Interest Blank (SVIB), the Minnesota Multiphasic Personality Inventory (MMPI), and assorted life history keys have all been constructed through an empirical keying strategy that relies on the differences between members of pre-existing groups to define the indicators of interest and to predict later behavior and experiences. Studies by Strong (1943) and Lefkowitz (1972) have shown the SVIB is an effective predictor of vocational choices, and that it is a better descriptor of vocational interests than the available alternatives. Similarly, reviews by Owens (1976) and Reilly and Chao (1982) have found that empirically keyed background data scales are among the best available predictors of differential job performance and attrition. Although classifications of persons based on the teleological strategy are of limited generality, these classifications of persons can still yield effective prediction.

Although no systematic attempts have been made to formulate a general classification of persons on the basis of the coassociative model, a few studies have attempted to investigate the feasibility and effectiveness of the coassociative strategy in the classification of persons. Most of these efforts have relied on inverse factor analysis and have defined similarity solely on the basis of similarity in the pattern of a profile. Despite this limitation, the results obtained in previous investigations suggest that empirical classifications of persons may display substantial robustness and have a great deal of conceptual value in describing and generating an understanding of human individuality (Neugarten, 1966; Reichard et al., 1962). Further, the Owens and Schoenfeldt (1979) study has served to demonstrate that highly valid classifications of persons can be formulated through the procedures outlined herein and that the resulting prototypes can be differentiated in a variety of ways. Finally, Block's (1971) study has shown that when this approach to the classification of persons is extended to incorporate developmental relationships through the use of indicators obtained at a number of different points in the course of individuals' lives, it can be useful in generating some understanding of individual development.

In sum, although there is not a great deal of data available on the effectiveness and feasibility of classifying persons in attempts to describe individuality, the available evidence provides a strong argument for the utility of this approach. Because it is now possible to implement the prototype model on a systematic basis, an attempt to formulate a general classification of persons would be of substantial value as a means of enhancing our understanding of individuality.

4

Background Data in Formulating Prototypes

LIFE RECORD DATA

A variety of indicators may be employed in defining the similarities and differences among individuals, and the coassociative approach to the definition of prototypes may be implemented regardless of the particular kind of indicators selected. The nature of the most appropriate indicators depends on the particular problem that the investigators are addressing.

Although this suggests that there will be a great deal of ambiguity in the definition of an optimal set of differential indicators for constructing prototypes, when the primary concern of the investigation is the development of a general description of individuality, there are a number of well-defined characteristics that should be displayed by the indicators. For instance, due to the complexity of individuality, the indicators should be numerous and capable of providing a broad and accurate description of the differential behavior and experiences of the individual as they occur across the life span. The indicators must reflect variations in the behavior of individuals in various situations, as these situations occur and are responded to, if a meaningful summary description of individuality is to be formulated through the prototypic model.

Determining the particular kind of indicators that are most capable of meeting this tall order is the next problem. Cattell (1982) has noted that quantifiable observations of human individuality fall into three basic categories: the life record, questionnaires, and objective test formats. All three measurement formats have been employed with some success in studies of individual development. In the Fels Institute studies, Kagan and Moss (1961) relied on a rating approach, and in his classic study of intellectual development, Terman (1959) focused primarily on data collected through objective tests. An illustration of the potential utility of the life-record format may be found in Lehman's (1953) study. Thus, all of these kinds of indicators have some value in attempts to describe individual development.

Although each strategy has been valuable, Livson (1973) has provided a compelling argument that holds that only a life-record format focusing on the behavior and experiences of the individual as they emerge over the life span provides an adequate basis for formulating a general summary description and understanding of human individuality. This conclusion is based on four observations. First, the life-record format allows an investigator to gather data that reflects the way individuals have actually lived their lives, and so it can produce a realistic description of the individual that displays substantial external validity. Second, the life-record format allows the investigator to gather a large number of diverse observations concerning the individual, thus providing the broad, comprehensive information base required to formulate a general classification of individuals. Third, such data tend to be highly sensitive to temporal and situational influences, as well as to person effects. Fourth, life-record data can be collected without making any stringent assumptions concerning the nature of human individuality.

As it is commonly implemented, the life-record format depends on interviews or direct observations of the individual. Unfortunately, reliance on interviews and direct observations creates a variety of difficulties. Both of these data collection methodologies are extremely expensive, and for this reason it is often difficult to obtain a sufficient number of individuals to insure adequate generality in the resulting classification. Additionally, when direct observations or interviews are employed, the investigator is forced to rely on other peoples' judgments concerning the behavior and experiences of the individual, possibly confounding observer characteristics with the characteristics of the subject. Obtaining data that are relevant to important internal states or covert activities is also hindered by the use of these two measurement formats. External observers often do not have enough contact with the individual to insure an adequate sampling of his or her behavior, and the very act of their observation may induce spurious changes in the individual's behavior via the reactive phenomenon. Finally, there is the problem of determining how the massive data record generated by detailed life records can be reduced to provide a comprehensible description of the individual subject that is amenable to quantitative analysis.

Livson (1973) suggested that the data reduction problem might be handled by recording life-record data through the use of a formalized rating strategy. The rating-based evaluation of life-record data has traditionally been quite popular in investigations focusing on the ontogeny of individuality (Block, 1971; Thomas & Chess, 1977). However, this rating strategy does not solve the economy, reactance, observational error, and observational opportunities problems noted previously. Moreover, employing a fixed set of rating scales tends to force the information into a pre-existing format, limiting the range of differential behavior and experiences that may be examined. Thus, the use of rating summarization techniques serves to eliminate the flexibility, breadth, and realism that constitute three principal advantages of using life-record data in construction of a general classification of persons.

BACKGROUND DATA

An alternative to the interview and observation methods of collecting life-record data is the use of background data questionnaires. Background data, or life history items, measure life records through the use of a paper-and-pencil self-report technique. The items present the individual with discrete questions concerning the nature of his or her *past* behavior and experiences, and the individual is asked to recall his or her past behavior and experiences and choose the most appropriate of several response options (usually five). Background data questionnaires represent an outgrowth of the use of interviews and application blanks for personnel selection in the industrial setting. Broadly speaking, the same questions may be asked through background data items that might be asked in an interview. By relying on self-reports of prior behavior and experiences, background data items avoid the problems associated with the use of external observers. Because the format is paper and pencil, the person's life record can be obtained through group testing sessions or mail-out questionnaires. Thus, the history of the lives of a large number of individuals can be studied far more economically than with other strategies used in the collection of life-record data.

Background data items have been utilized in personnel selection and placement since the turn of the century (Owens, 1976), and so a great deal of information is available concerning their psychometric characteristics. French, Lewis, and Long (1976) and Owens and Henry (1966) have found that the individual's responses to background data items tend to be relatively free from the influence of response sets, such as social desirability and acquiescence, and that individuals are less likely to fake responses to background data items than alternative item formats. Further, the information obtained from background data items appears to be quite accurate. Shaffer, Saunders, and Owens (1986) had a sample of individuals complete a background data inventory in adolescence and requested that their parents independently complete portions of the same form in a manner that would best describe their child's behavior and experiences during adolescence. It was found that adolescents' responses to objective biographical data items were correlated in the low .60s with their parents' descriptions of them. In a similar study, Bronson, Katten and Livson (1959) found that individuals' self-reports of behavior and experiences during childhood and adolescence were correlated between .40 and .80 with observations made during interviews conducted during childhood and adolescence. Mumford and Stokes (1981) examined the overlap between the relationships obtained through background data items and those obtained in experimental studies of the same phenomena, and found that there was roughly 80% agreement in the content and direction of the observed relationships. Finally, studies examining the relationship between self-report data and verified background data in the industrial setting have found substantial agreement (Cascio, 1975; Mosel & Cozan, 1952). This relationship may be moderated by threat or strong inducements to be perceived favorably (Goldstein, 1971; Schrader & Osburn, 1977).

Taken as a whole, the findings suggest that the responses obtained from background data items yield a fairly accurate picture of the individual's life history. Most individuals have little reason to distort reports of past behavior and experiences in which the emphasis is on discrete behaviors and experiences with few clear-cut evaluative connotations.

This advantage of background data items finds support in additional studies bearing on the psychometric properties of such items. An individual's responses to background data items display item retest coefficients ranging from the low .70s to low .90s over periods as long as 5 years (Shaffer, Saunders, & Owens, 1986). There is also compelling support for the meaningfulness or validity of biographical data in the literature. In a review of the alternatives to standardized testing, Reilly and Chao (1982) noted that only empirically keyed background data items and peer evaluations yielded validity coefficients of sufficient magnitude against job performance criteria to allow their widespread application. Similar conclusions have been reached in literature reviews conducted by Asher (1972) and Owens (1976). Background data items have been demonstrated to predict a broad range of rather ambiguous criteria, including tenure, interest, academic performance, clinical syndromes, and drug abuse. Also, as noted by Newstad and Schuster (1958) and Owens and Schoenfeldt (1979), the descriptions obtained from background data items predict differential behavior in the noncognitive domain more effectively than the available alternatives.

The fact that background data items have been shown to provide an accurate and meaningful description of the individual suggests that they might be useful in attempts to formulate a general classification of persons through the prototype model. Some support for this conclusion is provided by findings that demonstrate that background data items have been highly useful in implementing the teleological strategy in personnel selection through the use of empirical keys. Correspondingly, background data might have some value in classifying individuals through the coassociative approach.

Additional characteristics of background data argue for their appropriateness in formulating a general classification of persons. The demonstrated independence of background data items (Owens, 1976) is an advantage, because the lack of redundancy in the information suggests that relatively few such items would be required to obtain a broad description of the individual's behavior and experiences. Further, background data items can be designed to examine a wide variety of the individual's prior behavior and experiences, ranging from parental and sibling relations to television viewing habits and occupational activities. Moreover, they can examine the significant behaviors and experiences that occur in a given developmental period.

The ability of background data items to examine the significant behavior and experiences occurring within a given developmental period is supplemented by an additional advantage. As mentioned previously, in responding to background data items, individuals must employ a retrospective strategy that often requires administering age-related background data items at the end of the relevant developmental period. However, there is no reason that the items administered to an individual cannot examine significant behavior and experiences occurring in earlier developmental periods. For instance, an individual at the close of young adulthood might be asked to respond to questions pertaining to childhood and adolescence as well as to young adulthood. This characteristic of background data items increases the breadth of the description of the individual and his or her life that may be generated through this item format.

UNDERSTANDING INDIVIDUALITY

To this point, the discussion has provided a basic description of background data items and established that they might have value in attempts to formulate a general classification of persons. It was also noted that these items provide a realistic life-record description of the discrete past behaviors and experiences of the individual. Background data may also provide a powerful tool for generating an understanding of the nature and ontogeny of human individuality. Fiske (1979) noted that some understanding of individuality can be obtained only by examining discrete antecedent behaviors and experiences, and linking these to their consequent behavior and experiences. Background data items, in fact, explicitly examine discrete antecedent behaviors and experiences. Consequently, they would appear to have substantial value in attempts to gain some understanding of human individuality. Mumford and Owens (1982), Chaney and Owens (1964), and Roe (1956) have all examined the feasibility of this strategy in attempts to formulate an understanding of vocational interests, and they've documented that background data items are very useful in this regard.

In the context of the prototype model and attempts to construct a general summary description of human individuality, background data can provide a powerful and extremely efficient basis for formulating a general understanding of human individuality. If a valid, truly general classification of persons has been formulated on the basis of the similarities and differences manifested by individuals on an extensive set of background data items collected at different points in their lives, then the individuals assigned to a prototype will also have manifested a similar pattern of development in terms of their behavior and experiences. If the background data items that distinguish the members of one prototype from the members of other prototypes at different points in their lives can be identified, the discrete antecedent behaviors and experiences associated with the items would be linked to the consequent expression of a modal pattern of individuality. The antecedent information obtained from these background data items should, in turn, provide a basis for generating some understanding of why individuals manifest these general patterns of similarities and differences. Hence, inspection of the background data items related to the expression of the modal patterns of individuality might provide a sound basis for formulating a general understanding of individuality and individual development. Thus, background data seems to provide an excellent tool for understanding differential development and formulating a general classification of persons.

General Methods and Bias Checks

THE GENERAL DESIGN

Having addressed some of the broader issues involved in constructing a classification of persons, we now turn to our specific implementation of this approach. Because it provides a comprehensive basis for collecting data concerned with individual development, the cohort-sequential design was employed as the principal vehicle for data collection.

Figure 5.1 presents a schematic overview of the cohort-sequential design that was used in the present investigation. Five cohort groups were examined between 1968 and 1973. As can be seen in Fig. 5.1, the members of each cohort group participated in an initial questionnaire at the time they entered the study, and the members of all but one of the cohorts were assessed a second time on a second questionnaire 4 years later. A third questionnaire was administered 2 to 8 years after the second assessment. Some cohorts received the third questionnaire only once, and some a number of times. In all, the members of the various cohort groups were followed from between 6 and 12 years of their lives.

During the course of the three assessments, cohort groups were described on a wide variety of indicators. The primary measurement instrument employed in each assessment was an age-tailored background data form. The ensuing discussion describes the samples, information collected, and the procedures employed in defining and describing the prototypes.

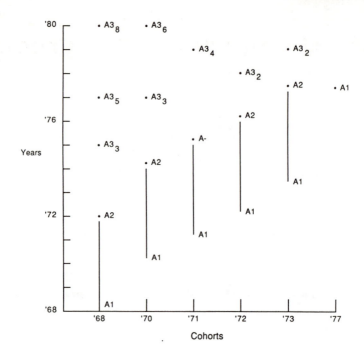

A1 = Assessment 1
A2 = Assessment 2
A3 = Assessment 3
A- = Assessment 2 not conducted
A3 - Subscripts = Years since Graduation on Assessment 3

FIG. 5.1.   Design of the cohort-sequential study..

SAMPLES AND MEASURES:
ASSESSMENT ONE

Because participation in later phases of this investigation was contingent on participation in the initial measurement, the individuals sampled for this phase of the project provided the basic subject pool. In all, 4,852 males and 4,808 females were included. These individuals were contacted as freshmen entering a large southeastern university during the falls of 1968, 1970, 1971, 1972, and 1973. These entering classes formed the cohort groups examined in the present study, and each cohort group provided roughly 1,000 males and 1,000 females. Although participation in the study was nominally voluntary, nearly all members of the five entering classes agreed to participate.

The modal age of cohort members at the time of the initial assessment was 18. The subjects' academic ability, as indexed by SAT scores, was roughly a half a standard deviation above the national average for entering freshmen. The urban–rural composition of the sample was typical of large state universities. However, most sample members had grown up in the southeast. Correspondingly, they appeared to be somewhat more traditional than may have been typical of the national college population during this time period. A review of the ethnic and social class background of sample members indicated a preponderance of middle-class, White Protestants. Yet, within the constraints set by these general characteristics of the sample, it should be noted that there was substantial variability in the abilities, interests, activities, and sociological backgrounds of sample members. Hence, this sample seemed to provide an adequate basis for formulating a general classification of persons.

The principal measure administered to sample members during the initial assessment was a background data inventory that has been labeled the Biographical Questionnaire (BQ). The items contained in the BQ were designed to describe significant aspects of the individual's life history during childhood and adolescence. On the basis of observational considerations and a review of the relevant literature, item content was developed under two major topical headings: (a) significant prior experiences and (b) significant prior behaviors.

Item specifications falling under the first category requested information about general experiences and the individual's reactions to them. In this class, item content attempted to examine, among other influences and experiences, parental beliefs and values, parental warmth and supportiveness, parental control, reactions to parents, the nature of parent–child interactions, number of siblings, the nature of sibling interactions, teachers' behavior, friends' behavior, intellectual environment, community size, and socioeconomic status. A typical item in this class was, "How many books were around your house when you were growing up?"

Items in the second category concerned with significant prior behaviors requested information bearing on the individual's overt and covert activities in a variety of situations. Item content examined behaviors such as social activities, athletic activities, dating, interactions with friends, reading preferences, school grades, academic attitudes and preferences, religious involvement, independence, achievement, and personal values. A typical item in this class asked, "During high school, how many times a month did you go out on a date?"

Eventually, some 2,000 item specifications were generated under the two topical headings. The item specifications were screened with respect to apparent overlap in item content and lack of clarity, reducing the number of items to 654. The number of items was further reduced by administering them in a group testing session to 1,700 male freshmen entering a large midwestern university. Those items that yielded aberrant response distributions or failed to produce a loading above .30 on at least one of the dimensions obtained in an iterative principal components analysis were eliminated. At this juncture, a few additional items of established developmental or predictive significance not clearly covered in the item pool were added to the list of tryout items. These additions resulted in a final pool of 389 items examining significant behaviors and experiences occurring during childhood and adolescence.

Subsequently, the 389-item questionnaire was administered to the 1,037 males and 897 females in the 1968 freshmen class who were members of the first cohort group. Because computer limitations dictated that a single matrix of item intercorrelatives could be no larger than 275 by 275, the item pool was reduced by eliminating items that (a) yielded poor response distributions, (b) covered more unlikely behavior and experiences, and (c) appeared to be somewhat redundant. Male and female responses to the reduced item set were then subjected to principal component analyses by sex. Orthogonal rotations indicated that 13 dimensions in the male subsample and 15 dimensions in the female subsample, accounting for 29.7% and 31.3% of the total variance in item responses, respectively, were both sizable and interpretable. Of the 275 items subjected to this analysis, those items that yielded at least one loading above .30 on any one of the dimensions obtained in the male and female subsample were used to construct the final 118-item version of the BQ. This instrument constituted the principal background data measure from which information concerning the individual was obtained during the first assessment.

In addition to the BQ, a set of traditional psychometric inventories were employed in part of the initial assessment. These inventories were either standard psychometric measures or "in-house" scales constructed especially for the study. Referred to as reference measures, the indices were included in the initial assessment in order to enhance the breadth of the characterization of the prototypes formulated through the background data measures and to provide a basis for assessing the robustness and construct validity of the resulting classification. A listing of the various reference measures can be found in Table 5.1.

The in-house scales were constructed because standard tests were not available to appropriately measure the constructs. The Purdue Values Inventory was patterned after the Allport, Vernon, and Lindzey (1960) study of values, and it was designed to assess the extent to which adolescents valued cognitive, economic, or social accomplishments. The Inventory of Emotional Reactions assessed whether an adolescent reacted to ambiguous or frustrating situations by inhibiting emotions or by displaying a positive or negative emotional reaction. An attempt was also

TABLE 5.1
List of Variables

Standard Measures	In-House Measures	No. of Items	r_{xx}
1. Strong Vocational Interest Blank	1. Purdue Values Inventory		
a. 58 occupational scales	a. Cognitive values	10	.86
b. 22 basic interest scales	b. Social religious	9	.81
2. Academic Achievement	c. Economic values	9	.66
a. high school GPA	2. Inventory of Personal Goals		
b. SAT verbal	a. Physical goals	7	.81
c. SAT math	b. Short-term goals	7	.84
d. SAT linguistic	c. Long-term goals		
e. SAT total	3. Inventory of Emotional Reactions		
3. Inventory of Social Attitudes	a. Positive emotionality	28	.83
a. Radical vs. conservative	b. Negative emotionality	28	.88
b. Tender vs. tough minded	c. Inhibition	7	.82
4. Personal Reaction Inventory (F Scale)	d. Exposure	7	.47
a. Direct F			
b. Reverse F			
c. Total F			
5. Crown-Marlowe			
a. Social desirability			
6. Rotter's Locus of Control			
7. General Outlook Inventory			
a. Integrative complexity			
b. Conceptual simplicity			
c. Hierarchical complexity			
8. Maudsley Personality Inventory			
a. Extraversion			
b. Neuroticism			

made to assess the extent to which an individual had been exposed to emotionally arousing situations. Finally, the tendency of individuals to display long-term, short-term, and athletic goals was assessed through the Inventory of Personal Goals. Except for the economic values (r_{xx} = .66) and emotional exposure (r_{xx} = .44) scales, the various in-house scales yielded internal consistency reliability estimates in excess of .80.

Administration of all the measures was carried out in the following manner. Members of the 1968 cohort were mailed the Strong Vocational Interest Blank (SVIB) along with certain preregistration materials, and they were asked to complete the inventory at home and return it to the principal investigator in a stamped, self-addressed envelope. Nearly all freshmen completed copies of the SVIB. Subsequently, they were asked to complete the 389-item version of the BQ and all reference measures, except for those obtained from the registrar's office (High School GPA and SAT scores) in a 3-hour test session conducted during freshman orientation. Members of the four later cohorts were administered only the 118-item version of the BQ in a 1-hour test session conducted during freshmen orientation. Thus, reference measure data were not available for these individuals.

ASSESSMENT TWO

The sample employed in the second assessment consisted of those members of the 1968, 1970, 1972, and 1973 cohorts who went on to graduate from the university 4 years after their initial assessment. This second assessment was conducted during the final quarter of the subjects' senior year at the university. It entailed mailing a short questionnaire, titled the College Experience Inventory (CEI), to the residences that the cohort members had listed with the university's registrar at the outset of the quarter. The questionnaire was to be completed and returned to the principal investigator in a stamped, self-addressed envelope. No inducements were offered for participation, although confidentiality was assured. The return rate was rather low, averaging roughly 60% of those mailed across the four cohort groups. Eventually, completed questionnaires were returned by 1,266 males and 1,232 females. Each cohort group provided roughly 800 respondents. Although these figures are rather low given the size of the initial sample, roughly 50% of the entering freshmen leave the university prior to their senior year. Thus, the subject pool was substantially restricted by limiting questionnaire administration to graduating seniors who had taken part in the initial assessment. The modal age of the subjects at the time of this second assessment was 22.

The CEI was the sole measure administered to cohort members as graduating seniors. The background data items contained in the CEI were designed to provide information describing significant aspects of the individual's life history during the college years. Item specifications were developed under the two major topical headings of "significant prior behaviors" and "significant prior experiences" on the basis of observational considerations and a review of the relevant literature.

Although the particular items included in the CEI varied from year to year, 55 items were administered to all the cohort groups, and these items constituted the core instrument, which was the primary concern of the present investigation. The content of 55 items was designed to cover a variety of significant behaviors and experiences occurring during the college years, including academic activities, academic preferences, academic performance, extracurricular activities, leisure activities, reading preferences, reactions to college life, work experiences, health, athletics, dating, social activities, political involvement, and religious activities.

All items of the CEI were presented in a multiple-choice format that could be scored along an ordinal continuum. In developing the CEI items, the apparent theoretical significance of item content with respect to the description of individuality during the college years was given great weight. Correspondingly, no attempt was made to ensure any overlap between the content of the CEI and BQ items beyond that which appeared necessary to obtain an adequate description of the significant behavior and experiences occurring during this developmental period.

ASSESSMENT THREE

The sample employed in the third assessment consisted of those members of the 1968, 1970, 1971, 1972, and 1973 cohorts who graduated from the university and had participated in the initial assessment during their freshman year. The third assessment was carried out through a mail-out questionnaire that was sent to the most recent address cohort members had listed with the university's alumni office. Each questionnaire was mailed with a nominal reimbursement of one dollar, along with a letter soliciting the subject's cooperation and ensuring confidentiality. If the questionnaire had not been returned within 3 months, a reminder card was sent to the same address. Completed questionnaires were to be returned in a stamped, self-addressed envelope to the principal investigator.

The first administration of this mail-out questionnaire was conducted in 1975, 3 years after members of the 1968 cohorts had graduated. Whereas members of the 1968 and 1970 cohorts received this questionnaire a number of times, members of the 1971, 1972, and 1973 cohorts were contacted only once. Overall, the longest interval associated with assessment of the 1968 cohort was 8 years after graduation, when the subjects' modal age was 30. The shortest interval occurred in assessment of the 1972 and 1973 cohorts at the modal age of 24, 2 years after their graduation from the university. Across all cohorts and times of administration, the average return rate for the various mailouts of the questionnaires was 75%, a relatively high figure that may be attributed to the use of monetary inducements and follow-up reminders. In all, 1933 males and 1955 females responded to at least one questionnaire, and each cohort group provided roughly 1,000 respondents. Recall that these numbers reflect the restriction implied by the requirement that all participants must have graduated from the university and taken part in the initial assessment.

The only measure administered to cohort members participating in the third assessment was a background data questionnaire called the Post College Experience Inventory (PCEI). The PCEI contained 115 background data items designed to assess significant aspects of the individual's life history during the first 10 years following college graduation. Item specifications were again developed under the two major topical headings of significant prior behaviors and significant prior experiences on the basis of observational considerations and a review of the literature pertaining to significant aspects of individuality and individual development during young adulthood. The content of these items covered a variety of significant behaviors and experiences occurring during young adulthood, including job activities, pay, promotions, job satisfaction, job search activities, marriage and marital satisfaction, reactions to current environment, use of spare time, social activities, leisure activities, reading materials, religious activities, and evaluation of college experiences.

The PCEI response options were presented in a multiple-choice format that could be scored along an ordinal continuum. As was true with development of the CEI, the theoretical significance of item content with respect to the description of individuality during young adulthood was given great weight. Correspondingly, no attempt was made to ensure overlap between the content of the PCEI and that of the BQ and the CEI.

LONGITUDINAL SAMPLE

The sampling procedures described in the foregoing paragraphs provided the longitudinal data base used in the present investigation. The data base consisted of the BQ, CEI, and PCEI item responses of the 417 males and 355 females drawn from the 1968 and 1970 cohorts who had participated in the initial assessment, the assessment conducted at the time of their graduation from the university, and the assessment conducted 6 to 8 years later in the spring of 1980. These individuals were chosen for special examination because construction of a general classification of persons required a description of behavior and experiences over the longest possible time interval.

Despite the severe restriction in sample size imposed by the techniques used to select these subjects, the aggregate characteristics of these individuals were virtually identical to those that characterized the members of all cohorts during each of the three assessments. Reference measure data was available for only the 228 male and 176 female members of the longitudinal sample who were also members of the 1968 cohort. Moreover, PCEI data for the first 2 to 4 years following college graduation was available for only 237 males and 253 females who had returned the PCEI questionnaires mailed out 2 to 4 years following their graduation. The early PCEI data and the reference measure data were used to establish the robustness and construct validity of the prototypic summary description.

ANALYSES

Cross-Sectional Analyses

Basic Methods. The first set of analyses carried out in our attempt to implement the prototype model represented a preliminary step designed to accomplish three objectives. First, a summary description of individuality within each developmental period was generated through both a classification of persons and a classification of behavior and experiences, so that the information might be used to describe the nature and implications of the prototypes based on a cross-time classification of persons. Second, summarization of the data collected in each assessment was required to assess the potential impact of biasing influences, such as cohort effects and selective survival, on any conclusions generated by the investigation. Third, the feasibility of constructing a valid and robust summary description of individuality through the prototype model was established before proceeding to the longitudinal analyses, which were the central concern of the investigation. A series of cross-sectional analyses were conducted to achieve these three objectives.

The basic analytic procedure employed in the cross-sectional analyses were virtually identical across all three assessments. Initially, the background data items administered in each assessment were subjected to a principal components analysis in order to obtain an appropriate summarization of the item response data, which was more amenable to statistical analysis. The principal-components analyses were carried out separately for males and females. Inspection of the resulting eigenvalue plots, reflecting the percentage of total variance accounted for by each factor, was then used to specify optimal solutions. A scree test was used to determine at which point the addition of new summary dimensions yielded a relatively small increment in the percentage of total variance accounted for. The procedure generally served to identify two or three potentially optimal solutions.

Following definition of the potential solutions, the dimensions obtained were subjected to a varimax orthogonal rotation in order to obtain simple structure and enhance the clarity and interpretability of the summary dimensions. An orthogonal solution was employed, despite the generally greater interpretability of oblique rotations, because the two techniques have been shown to yield effectively identical solutions when applied to background data (Owens, 1976), and orthogonal dimensions are associated with a number of advantages, statistically, by virtue of their independence. Subsequently, the loadings of the items on each of the rotated dimensions were obtained. The content and pattern of the items yielding significant loadings ($r > .30$) on each of the rotated dimensions obtained in a given solution were reviewed by three to five trained psychologists. The solution that, in the judgment of the staff, yielded the most interpretable summary dimensions was retained. The judges reached a consensus decision concerning the descriptive labels applied to each of the summary dimensions. A scoring coefficient matrix was generated, and subjects were assigned scores on each of the relevant summary dimensions obtained in a given assessment.

Scores on the summary dimensions served as a basis for formulating a classification of persons through use of the Ward and Hook (1963) algorithm. This was accomplished through the following steps. Within each sex group, the subject's scores on each of the summary dimensions obtained in a single assessment were used to form a profile. The similarity of a subject's profile to the profiles of all other members of his or her group participating in the assessment at hand was then established through Cronbach's d^2 measure of profile similarity. The resulting matrix of similarity data was then subjected, by sex, to a Ward and Hook cluster analysis.

Inspection of the resulting plot of the within cluster sums of squares obtained at each step in the iterative sequence was used to specify the optimal clustering solution. The potentially optimal solutions were identified by finding those points on the plot where the elimination of an additional cluster led to a marked increase in the within-cluster variation.

This modified scree test typically resulted in the identification of two or three solutions that might yield an optimal summary description.

Each potential solution was then entered into the affirmation subroutine, and the assignment of individuals was carried out once again, with a specified number of clusters. The results of the affirmation subroutine indicated the number of individuals who could be assigned to a single cluster (good fits), the number of individuals who could be assigned to two or more clusters (overlaps), and the number of individuals who could not be assigned to any cluster (isolates). The information regarding fit provided one index of the clarity of each of the alternative classification structures.

To obtain information bearing on the interpretability of the structure, mean scores of all cluster members on the background data items and summary dimensions were contrasted with the mean for the overall group, and all differences in excess of half a standard deviation were identified. The number, content, and magnitude of the items and summary dimensions yielding significant differences for each cluster were then reviewed by at least three trained psychologists who reached a consensus decision concerning the label that would best summarize the differences. The alternative solution that, in the judgment of the staff, yielded the clearest and most interpretable classification of persons was retained.

Once the clustering solution had been selected, two additional steps were carried out. First, a discriminant analysis was conducted, employing cluster membership as the criterion category and scores on the relevant summary dimensions as predictors, using only good fits as subjects. The resulting discriminant function allowed new individuals to be assigned to the clusters on the basis of their scores on the relevant summary dimensions. Second, on the basis of the discriminant functions, the aposteriori probabilities reflecting each individual's likelihood of membership in each of the relevant clusters were obtained. The probabilities were used to construct a metric of prototype fit for all individuals against all of the clusters obtained in a given assessment.

Specific Modifications. Although the global procedures just laid out were employed as the basis for all of the cross-sectional analyses, perhaps the most extensive modifications in the basic analytic framework occurred in the analysis of the male and female responses to the BQ. In this instance, the total male and female subsamples were not used to identify the relevant summary dimensions and clusters of similar individuals. Rather, the 1037 males and 897 females who were members of the 1968 cohort were administered the 389-item version of the BQ. The reduced 275-item version of the BQ was then used to identify the male and female summary dimensions and clusters within each of the subsamples. A scoring coefficient matrix was generated based on the 118 items that formed the final version of the BQ, and members of the later cohorts were assigned dimension scores using the scoring matrix. The dimension scores in the 1968 cohort were also used to formulate a discriminant function for assigning members of the later cohorts to the relevant clusters. The degree of shrinkage observed in applying these equations in new cohorts, as indexed by the percentage of cohort members who could be assigned to a single cluster, was held to provide one index of the stability of the classification categories.

The foregoing modification of the basic analytic procedures permitted the construction of an initial set of prototypes far earlier in the study than would otherwise have been feasible. The need to shorten the time lag was based on the fact that it was necessary to demonstrate the clarity, robustness, and power of the prototype approach through an extensive series of feedback studies. In the feedback studies, the extent to which the members of a given prototype could be differentiated from the members of other prototypes in terms of their behavior and experiences was investigated. The studies conducted ranged from investigations of interests and motivation to learning and memory. In all, 44 such studies were conducted. The feedback studies provided a rich source of information concerning the differential characteristics of the prototypes. The feedback studies, along with information obtained from the reference measures, provided information regarding the robustness and predictive validity of the prototype descriptions obtained from the BQ.

Although the CEI administrations required no modifications from the basic analytic framework, certain modifications were made in the course of assessing the PCEI data. Because the PCEI had been collected at different intervals, there was the possibility of time effects. Using scoring coefficient matrices generated from a principal components analyses of the 1975 PCEI administration, scores on the summary dimensions were generated for all PCEI administrations. For men and women, mean scores on each of the dimensions were employed as dependent variables in a series of cohort-by-time analyses conducted through an analysis of variance. Although no significant cohort and cohort-by-time effects were obtained, there were a number of significant time effects. Employing Scheffe's test indicated that significant mean differences were most likely to arise in comparing data collected 2, 3, and 4 years following graduation with data collected 6 and 8 years following graduation. The data collected 5 years after graduation did not clearly fall in either of these groupings.

Time-related differences of this sort could arise from either a change in the level of dimensional scores or through a change in the underlying structure of the summary dimensions. Given the importance of the second possibility, prudence argued for conducting separate sets of analyses on the PCEI data collected 2, 3, and 4 years following graduation and the PCEI data collected 6 and 8 years following graduation. To ensure statistical independence, nonoverlapping samples of subjects were employed. The data provided by the 1968 and 1970 cohorts were used in analyzing the PCEI data collected 6 to 8 years after graduation (PCEI 6/8) and the data provided by the 1971 and 1972 cohorts were used in analyzing the PCEI data collected 2 to 4 years after graduation (PCEI 2/4). The PCEI 2/4 analyses were conducted using the 985 male and 1232 female members of the 1971 and 1972 cohorts, and the PCEI 6/8 analyses were conducted using the 686 male and 596 female members of the 1968 and 1970 cohorts. The item data derived in these two samples was then employed in constructing the PCEI 2/4 and PCEI 6/8 summary dimensions and prototypes according to the procedure outlined earlier. However, once the summary dimensions and prototypes had been formulated for the PCEI 2/4 data, summary dimensions scores and prototype studies were established for male and female members of the 1968, 1970, and 1973 cohorts who had returned PCEI questions 2, 3, or 4 years after their graduation from the university through application of the relevant scoring coefficient matrices and discriminant functions.

Sequential Analyses

Having formulated summary descriptions of individuality at four time periods, the first set of longitudinal analyses could be conducted. The sequential analyses were conducted to investigate the extent to which summary descriptions of individuality formulated at one point in the course of an individual's life had implications for the summary descriptions formulated at later points.

In order to address this issue, two separate sets of analyses were carried out. The first set of analyses was designed to provide information concerning the extent to which the behaviors and experiences incorporated under a summary dimension at one point in an individual's life would serve to predict the individual's status on the summary dimensions obtained at a later point. Scores of the 417 male and 358 female members of the longitudinal sample on the BQ, the CEI, the PCEI 2/4, and the PCEI 6/8 summary dimensions were intercorrelated to determine the magnitude of the relationship between the summary dimensions formulated in the different developmental periods. It was anticipated that this analysis would provide information concerning the emergence of differential behavior and experiences over time as well as the construct validity of the descriptions of individuality formulated through the summary dimensions and the labels applied to them.

The second set of analyses determined the extent to which membership in a prototype established in one phase of an individual's development had systematic implications for the individual's membership in prototypes established in later phases of development. (Only those individuals who could clearly be assigned to a single prototype in a given developmental period were used.) Once these individuals had been identified across all cohorts within the male and female subsamples, (a) the percentage of the members of each BQ prototype entering each CEI prototype was determined, (b) the percentage of the members of each CEI prototype was determined, and (c) the percentage of the members of each PCEI 2/4 prototype was determined. It is of note that these analyses employed the 687 males and 756 females for whom both CEI and PCEI 2/4 data were available and the 390 males and 390 females for whom PCEI 2/4 and PCEI 6/8 data were available. Once these probabilities had been obtained in each of the two subsamples, significant relationships indicating nonchance movement from one of the earlier prototypes to any one of the prototypes obtained in the subsequent developmental period were established through a modified analysis designed to control for empty cells. An overall, modified test examining the existence of significant systematic relationships in the BQ to CEI, CEI to PCEI 2/4, and PCEI 2/4 to PCEI 6/8 matrices was also obtained for each subsample. Supplemental analyses served as a quasi-cross-validation of the results.

Composite Analyses

The systematic patterns of behaviors and experiences reflected in the sequential analyses clearly provided important information concerning the nature of individuality as it emerges over time, but it was not assumed that the information would provide a general summary description of human individuality. The possibility existed that the similarities and differences that define individuality at a particular point in time may not be those that define individuality over time, as it emerges in the course of individuals' lives. In order to address the issue and to formulate the prototypes required to address the fundamental concerns of the present investigation, a series of composite longitudinal analyses were conducted.

In carrying out this effort, it was assumed that the similarities and differences among individuals should be defined through descriptive information obtained over the largest possible time period. Correspondingly, the responses of the 417 male and 358 female members of the longitudinal sample to the final versions of the BQ, CEI, and PCEI 6/8 questionnaires were used to form two separate supramatrices of cross-time item response data. The male and female matrices of item responses were entered into a principal components analysis carried out in accordance with the procedures outlined earlier in our discussion of the general analytic framework employed in the cross-sectional analyses. Once the potential solutions had been specified on the basis of eigenvalue plots, and the rotated dimensions had been reviewed for interpretability and labels had been assigned, the solutions to be retained in the male and female subsamples were established. Subsequently, scoring coefficient matrices were generated, and the male and female members of the longitudinal sample were assigned scores on each of the relevant composite components.

Once the composite summary dimensions had been defined, composite prototypes were identified. Scores on the composite summary dimensions were used to form a profile, and the similarity of each of the 417 male and 355 female members of the longitudinal sample to all other members of their respective groups was then established through Cronbach's d^2 measure of profile similarity. The resulting matrices of similarity data then formed the basis for a Ward and Hook clustering, which was carried out in accordance with the procedures described earlier in discussions of the general analytic framework for the cross-sectional analyses. After an optimal solution had been identified, a discriminant analysis was carried out, in which scores on the composite dimensions served as predictors of prototype membership, and the resulting aposteriori probabilities describing each individual's likelihood of membership in all of the relevant composite prototypes were then used to formulate a metric of subgroup fit. Through a series of further analyses, the composite prototypes were evaluated for robustness, clarity, and validity. Their unique contribution to understanding differential development beyond the information obtained in the sequential analyses was also evaluated.

BIAS CHECKS

The appropriateness of any conclusions drawn in the course of the foregoing analyses are contingent on the freedom of the individual's responses to the background data items from any significant biasing influences. As a result, a number of supplemental analyses were conducted to identify and control the influence of potential biasing influences on the conclusions that might be drawn in this investigation.

Perhaps the most obvious limitation on the generality of the conclusions that might be drawn in the longitudinal analyses may be found in the possibility that cohort effects or historical change would moderate any observed relationships. However, comparison of the mean scores of the participating cohort members on the BQ, CEI, PCEI 2/4, and PCEI 6/8 summary dimensions indicated that in no case did the cohort groups display differences that reached even marginal significance levels ($p \leq$ .05), nor were any mean differences in excess of one quarter of a standard deviation observed. Further, significant cohort and cohort-by-time effects were not obtained in the analyses of the exploratory PCEI summary dimensions formulated for members of the 1968 cohort 3 years after their graduation from the university. Thus, it appears that cohort or historical effects were not likely to restrict the generality of the conclusions drawn in the research effort. Some additional support for these conclusions may be found in the observation that the classification structures derived for members of the 1968 cohort on the BQ and the members of the 1971 and 1972 cohorts on the PCEI 2/4 could be applied in the description of the members of other cohorts with little shrinkage. Of course, the lack of significant cohort effects may be attributed in part to the limited time frame examined in the present investigation and in part to the use of a sample drawn from a southeastern university, which was rather removed from the major historical trends occurring during the period. Yet, it should also be noted that the weakness of these effects could be attributed to the fact that the background data items in use could reasonably be applied in almost any cohort since the turn of the century. Regardless of the reasons underlying these observations, the dearth of significant cohort effects provides some evidence pointing to the generality of the conclusions that might be drawn in the investigation.

A second biasing factor that might limit the value of the present research effort was the possibility that selective survival and selective dropout induced some sampling bias and lead to change on the composition and characteristics of the later CEI, PCEI 2/4, and PCEI 6/8 samples. In order to examine this issue, all respondents to the CEI, the PCEI 2/4, and the PCEI 6/8 questionnaires were contrasted with nonrespondents in terms of scores on the original BQ summary dimensions. Examination of the results obtained in the analyses indicated that there were no mean differences between respondents and nonrespondents in excess of half a standard deviation on the BQ summary dimensions obtained in both subsamples. However, mean differences in excess of one quarter of a standard deviation between respondents and nonrespondents were obtained on the BQ academic achievement dimension in both the male and female CEI, PCEI 2/4, and PCEI 6/8 analyses. This was the only significant difference obtained in the series of analyses, and respondents scored higher on the dimension. Additional comparisons of respondents and nonrespondents to various combination of questionnaires were also made, but no bias was detected in any of the analyses.

Given the fact that the central criterion for participation in the later assessments was graduation from the university, it is not especially surprising that significant differences were observed between respondents and nonrespondents on the BQ academic achievement dimension. What is surprising is that these differences were not larger and did not extend to the other summary dimensions, although this finding might be due to the many and varied reasons that lead an entering freshman to leave a large state university. Further, the many reasons for either responding or not responding to mail-out questionnaires may underlie the apparent freedom of the longitudinal sample and subsamples from any substantial sampling bias. Of course, no analysis can be conducted that can completely rule out the potential impact of sampling bias. Nevertheless, the foregoing results provide at least some preliminary evidence indicating that the samples obtained in the later assessments were not particularly biased.

A third limitation on the conclusions that might be drawn in the course of the present investigation may be found in the possibility that item responses were markedly influenced by response biases or measurement error. Turning first to the issue of response bias, scores on the Crown-Marlowe social desirability scale and scores on an acquiescence measure derived from responses to the California F scale were correlated with scores on the BQ, CEI, PCEI 2/4, and PCEI 6/8 items and summary dimensions. It was found that acquiescence was not significantly related to scores on the background data items and summary dimensions, and that, although social desirability yielded a number of marginal relationships with the background data items, it was not significantly related to summary dimension scores. Thus, it appears that responses to the background data items and scores on the summary dimensions employed in constructing the prototypes were not substantially distorted by psychometric response styles. This conclusion was validated in a study conducted by French, Lewis, and Long (1976), cited earlier.

The accuracy of responses to background data items has been assessed in two studies. In a 6-month retest study employing a subsample of 200 males and 228 females, it was found that the reliabilities of scores on the BQ summary dimensions were typically in the low .90s. These findings indicate substantial consistency in the recall of past behavior and experiences. Somewhat more detailed evidence in this regard may be found in a study conducted by Shaffer, Saunders, and Owens (1986), who read-ministered the 118-item version of the BQ to a sample of 124 males and 113 females 5 years after their graduation from the university. They found that there was substantial consistency in item responses, with dimension reliability coefficients typically in the .80s. Moreover, when the parents of these individuals were asked to respond to a subset of the same background data items in the way they felt would best describe their sons or daughters during adolescence, it was found that the correlation between parents' responses and their child's responses were in the low .60s on concrete items and in the mid .40s for the moderately subjective items. The high degree of interrater agreement in item responses provides compelling evidence for both the accuracy of responses to background data items as well as the objectivity or reality of item responses. In sum, it seemed reasonable to assume that the conclusions that might be drawn in the course of the present investigation would not be greatly distorted by response styles, undue influence of random error, or self-presentation bias.

A final phenomenon that might limit the generality of the conclusions drawn in the present investigation may be found in the potential instability of these results across other samples. In one study along these lines, Anderson (1973) obtained freshmen samples from three different universities located in different regions and replicated the initial BQ analyses within each of these samples. The results obtained indicated that the same summary dimensions and prototypes were obtained in each sample, although the number of individuals assigned to each prototype varied in a systematic fashion. This finding has been substantiated in a similar study conducted at a large northeastern technical university (Owens & Schoenfeldt, 1979). Another study employing a sample of freshmen drawn from a large midwestern state university supported the stability of the male but not the female summary dimensions and prototypes (Eberhardt & Muchinsky, 1982). However, Lautenschlager and Shaffer (1987) further analyzed the female factor dimensions and documented their stability. Finally, it should be noted that a pilot study cited by Owens (1976) indicated that the BQ summary dimensions and prototypes displayed some stability in a sample of freshmen drawn from a primarily Black university. Of course, the value of all these investigations is, to some extent, diminished by virtue of the fact that they have only examined replicability of the BQ summary dimensions and prototypes in samples of college-level freshmen, and it is quite possible that in non-college-level samples or in later developmental periods, evidence pointing to the stability and replicability of these summary descriptions might not be obtained. Nevertheless, at least in a limited sense, it would seem that the foregoing studies have provided substantial evidence pointing to the stability and generality of the summary descriptions obtained from this methodology, and thus provided some evidential groundwork for drawing general conclusions concerning the nature of human individuality and the ontogeny of individuality.

6

Cross-Sectional Results

Having provided a detailed review of the methodology used to construct a general classification of persons through the prototype model, the discussion now focuses on the results obtained in the cross-sectional analyses of the data collected in each assessment. A great deal of data were generated, so the discussion concentrates on a selective set of major findings.

CROSS-SECTIONAL ANALYSES

Assessment One

The first step in the various cross-sectional analyses involved a set of principal components analyses of the 389-item version of the BQ to the male and female members of the 1968 cohort. Inspection of the eigenvalue plots indicated that no more than 19 summary dimensions should be retained within each subsample. Orthogonal rotations indicated that only 13 dimensions in the male subsample and 15 dimensions in the female subsample were interpretable and associated with sizable eigenvalues. The two retained solutions accounted for 29.7% and 32.6% of the total variance in the male and female subsamples, respectively. Although the percentage figures might seem small, the background data items in use were relatively heterogeneous. Further, because item data were in use, a sizable proportion of the total variance would probably reflect random error, which, quite appropriately, would not be captured in a principal components analysis.

Table 6.1 presents the labels assigned to the male and female summary dimensions along with the number of items yielding significant loadings and the percentage of total variance accounted for by each dimension. As can be seen in the labels assigned, the summary dimensions covered a wide range of past behavior and experiences. Table 6.2 provides an example of one dimension, presenting the content of the items yielding significant loadings on the Positive Academic Attitudes factor for women. The items reflect prior behavior and experiences related to an individual's involvement in and enjoyment of high school academic activities. A review of Table 6.1 indicates that there was some overlap in the nature of the summary dimensions identified in the male and female subsamples. However, there were some differences across the sex groups in the content and magnitude of the items yielding significant loadings on each of these dimensions. The Social Leadership, Feeling of Social Inadequacy, Social Maturity, and Interest in the Opposite Sex dimensions were unique to the female subsample, and their content suggested that social interaction might be more critical to females than males during childhood and adolescence.

Once scores on the relevant summary dimensions had been generated for members of the 1968 cohort, the BQ prototypes were constructed. Examination of the plot of within-cluster sums of squares, along with the clarity of the alternative clustering solutions, suggested that 23 male and 15 female prototypes should be retained. A review of the classification rate associated with these solutions indicated that roughly 73% of the male and female members of the 1968 cohort could be assigned to a single prototype, 20% could be assigned to two or more of the relevant prototypes (overlaps), and 7% of these individuals could not be assigned to any one of the relevant prototypes (isolates). As a result, it was concluded that the BQ prototypes provided an adequate set of categories for description of the members of the 1968 cohort. Additionally, the summary descriptions appeared to be reasonably robust in that roughly 65% of the male and female members of the four later cohorts could be assigned to a single prototype through use of discriminant analysis. The relatively small shrinkage (8%) obtained in this analysis provides evidence for the stability and generality of this classification structure when it is applied to independent samples.

Once the prototypes were identified, it was necessary to establish that the prototypes formulated on the basis of an empirical clustering of responses to background data items would display differential characteristics on measures not employed in subgroup formation. Members of the male and female prototypes were examined using the reference mea-

TABLE 6.1
Description of the Male and Female BQ Summary Dimensions

Males (N = 1,031)			Females (N = 897)		
Dimension Name	Variance Accounted	Items Loading	Dimension Name	Variance Accounted	Items Loading
1 Warmth of parental relationship	3.5	13	1 Warmth of maternal relationship	4.3	14
2 Academic achievement	3.1	16	2 Social leadership	3.2	14
3 Social introversion	3.1	13	3 Academic achievement	3.1	13
4 Intellectualism	2.3	10	4 Socioeconomic status	2.6	11
5 Aggressiveness/independence	2.2	10	5 Parental control vs. freedom	2.4	11
6 Socioeconomic status	2.1	10	6 Cultural/literary interests	2.0	5
7 Parental warmth vs. freedom	2.0	9	7 Athletic participation	1.9	9
8 Athletic interests	2.0	11	8 Scientific interests	1.8	13
9 Social desirability	1.9	10	9 Feeling of social inadequacy	1.8	4
10 Scientific interest	1.8	12	10 Adjustment	1.8	5
11 Positive academic attitude	1.5	8	11 Expressive of negative emotions	1.7	4
12 Religious activity	1.3	6	12 Popularity with opposite sex	1.6	4
13 Sibling friction	1.1	5	13 Social maturity	1.6	2
			14 Positive academic attitude	1.5	8
			15 Warmth of paternal relationship	1.3	8
Cumulative	29.7		Cumulative	32.6	

TABLE 6.2
Items Loading on the Female Positive Academic Attitudes Dimension

Item Content	Loading
How successful were your teachers in arousing your academic interests?	.51
In your high school classes, how much class participation and discussion was allowed?	.48
In general, how much did you like your high school teachers?	.47
How often did your high school teachers stress the importance of students thinking for themselves and applying the knowledge they acquired?	.45
How much did you like school?	.37
On the average, how many hours of homework did you do a week in high school?	.36
During high school, how often did you try to become like a teacher or a coach?	.35
How much were you influenced to choose your field of study or to continue your education by a teacher, principal, or counselor?	.32
How adequate do you feel your high school education was?	.32

sures. Significant mean differences ($p \leq .01$) among the prototypes were obtained on all but two of the reference measures. In the male subgroups, the reference measures that failed to yield significant differentiation were the internal control and emotional inhibition scales. In the female subsample, the direct and reverse F scales failed to differentiate between the groups. It was found that roughly one sixth of the significant differences were in excess of half a standard deviation in the male subsample. Results were similar, though somewhat weaker, for the female prototypes. When the magnitude and consistency of the differences across the male and female prototypes are considered, along with the observation that the power of these differences was comparable to that observed on the original background data measures, the results provide evidence for the robustness, generality, and validity of the summary descriptions of individuality formulated through the prototypic model.

Further evidence of the effectiveness of the prototype model is provided by the results obtained in the 44 major feedback studies conducted. A brief overview of each of these feedback studies is presented in Table 6.3. The feedback studies were conducted across a number of domains, but of particular importance are those of a methodological nature. Anderson (1973) used the BQ at three major universities and investigated the similarity of the dimensions and subgrouping. He found that the structure of the summary dimensions and prototypes was relatively stable across universities, but that the number of individuals assigned to particular prototypes shifted in an interpretable fashion given

TABLE 6.3
A Summary of Feedback Studies by Area

Author/Title	Problem	Subject/Task	Instruments [a]	Analyses	Results
			Perception		
Frazier (1971): Differential perception of individuals subgrouped on the basis of biodata responses.	To determine if biodata subgroups differ in responses to ambiguous stimuli.	80 male students viewed and interpreted 10 slides of the group Rorschach.	Multiple choice Rorschach response materials.	Two-way ANOVA with repeated measures between subgroups and all 10 inkblots. χ^2 analysis between subgroups and each inkblot.	Subgroups showed significant differences in their responses to five of the blots; were marginal on a sixth.
Leifer (1971): An investigation of the validity of subjective frames of reference on a life-history questionnaire.	To examine the correspondence between subjective estimates of biodata scores and the actual scores.	337 males and 421 females completed self-ratings on scales similar to the biodata factor scales.	Self-ratings on scales dealing with areas of prior experience.	High and low accuracy groups were selected based on D^2 similarity of estimated and obtained profiles. ANOVA was employed to compare these across biodata factors. χ^2 was employed to evaluate D^2 differences by biodata subgroups.	The superiority of high accuracy subjects extended across all biodata factor dimensions. Biodata subgroups did not differ significantly in accuracy.

(Continued)

TABLE 6.3
(continued)

Author/Title	Problem	Subject/Task	Instruments[a]	Analyses	Results
		Cognition, Creativity, Decision Making			
Eberhard and Owens (1975): Word association as a function of biodata subgrouping.	To examine performance on a word association test as a function of biodata subgroup membership.	110 female students selected from four biodata subgroups completed a word association test.	The Kent-Rosanoff Word Association Test of 100 stimulus words: responses were scored on reaction time, commonality, and four idio-dynamic response sets (6 scores).	An overall MANOVA (protocols by subgroups) followed by ANOVAS and Scheffé tests to evaluate subgroup differences on each of the protocols.	There were significant differences in subgroup behaviors according to each of the six protocols; results were also highly congruent with hypotheses.
French (1974): Biographical correlates of writing ability.	To examine performance on an essay exam as a function of both biodata factor scores and biodata subgroup membership.	2,572 students who completed 60 quarter hours took the Language Skills Essay Exam (LSEE).	The LSEE (taken by all rising juniors) requires a 30-minute essay on a given topic. Three of over 300 participating faculty independently rate each essay on a 1 (fail) to 4 (high pass) scale.	Regression of biodata factor scores on essay score. ANOVAS followed by post mortem pair-wise comparisons seeking subgroup differences on the essay.	Rs of .27 (males) and .24 (females) between LSEE score and biodata factor scores with Academic Achievement contributing the most. Both ANOVAS were significant, although no pairwise differences were found.

Halpin (1973): A study of the life histories and creative abilities of potential teachers.	To determine the relationships between biodata factors and creative thinking abilities of future teachers.	65 male and 164 female students completed the Torrance Tests of Creative Thinking.	The Torrance test yields scores on figural elaboration and verbal and figural fluency, flexibility, and originality.	Canonical and Pearson's rs between biodata factor scores and creative abilities.	Some significant relationships (rs) between biodata factors and creative abilities; significant female subgroup differences on verbal fluency.
Klein (1973): Personality characteristics of discrepant academic achievers.	To identify characteristics of students with deviate GPAs in relation to aptitude measures.	2,347 males and 2,087 females who had completed 45 credit hours and for whom GPA and SAT scores were available.	Selected subjects completed Rotter's I–E scale and Alpert and Habor's Achievement Anxiety Test (ATT).	One-way ANOVAS and post hoc comparisons to determine differences between over- and underachieving groups on biodata factors and other measures.	There was a significant differential affinity of biodata subgroups for academic achievement. The under- and over-achieving groups were characterized in terms of biodata factor scores and supplementary measures.
Milner (1970): Biodata correlates of decision making.	To compare the decision-making styles of two biodata subgroups.	20 male students from two contrasting biodata subgroups participated in a modified poker dice game.	Poker dice game, preceded by questionnaire on gambling style and attitude toward games of chance, and followed by postexperimental interview.	Mann-Whitney U test comparing the groups on conservatism of style and propensity for extreme risks.	As hypothesized, Subgroup 3 was characterized by a more conservative and consistent style of play (decision-making behavior) than Subgroup 11.

(Continued)

TABLE 6.3
(continued)

Author/Title	Problem	Subject/Task	Instruments[a]	Analyses	Results
Nutt (1975): An examination of student attrition using life experience subgroups	To examine biodata subgroup differences with respect to five areas of academic attrition.	417 (55% response) males and females from the entering classes of 1968 and 1970, who had dropped out as of spring 1973 and who had subsequently responded to a questionnaire.	Postcard questionnaire on reasons for dropping out and subsequent experiences.	ANOVAS comparing subgroup differences on each questionnaire item. Categorical scaling to reveal biodata subgroup differences in reason for dropping out.	Male and female biodata groups differed in drop out rate (by a 3:1 ratio). Only female subgroups differed in reason for leaving.
Robbins (1975): Biographical correlates of job changing behavior.	Relationship between number of jobs held by college graduates and five biographical questions.	275 males and 277 females who were administered the Post-College Experience Inventory (PCEI) three years after graduation.	The PCEI is a questionnaire concerning the major dimensions of experiences during the early postcollege years.	χ^2 tests of association between number of jobs held and five PCEI items.	For males, number of jobs held related to marital status, extent to which they knew and found desired employment, and their need for a job. For females, number of jobs related to extent to which they knew and found desired employment, and their need for a job. Type of em-

Schoenfeldt (1974): Utilization of manpower; development and evaluation of an assessment-classification model for matching individuals with jobs.	Biodata subgroup differences with respect to academic-curricular data were examined.	1,934 males and females, 1,450 of whom had completed (at least) 90 quarter hours 4 years later, were included in the study.	Academic criteria, such as dean's list, probations, and GPA, plus patterns of course taking were obtained from transcripts of record.	ANOVAS comparing biodata groups on academic criteria. Categorical scaling to study biodata subgroup differences in patterns of course taking.	Subgroups differed significantly with respect to data collected four years later and covering both academic criteria and curricular paths walked.
Wright (1973): Some biodata subgroup differences in reading comprehension.	To determine whether selected pairs of biodata subgroups are differentially disturbed by *pied* vs. *nonpied* reading examinations.	68 males from four subgroups were equally divided between experimental and control conditions. All subjects read 13 paragraphs. The experimental group responded to 13 sets of questions in random order, whereas the control group responded immediately after reading the pertinent paragraph.	Paragraphs were about 100 words in length. Total test reliability (split-halves) was .83.	A two-way ANOVA was used to test effects due to condition, subgroup, and an interaction.	Effects due to condition were significant at the 5% level, and those due to subgroups at the 10% level and in conformance with hypothesis. The interaction was not significant.

(Continued)

TABLE 6.3
(continued)

Author/Title	Problem	Subject/Task	Instruments[a]	Analyses	Results
		Learning and Memory			
Helms (1972): Bio-data subgroup differences in recall and clustering of interest area stimulus words.	To examine differential performance of subgroups on two word tasks.	64 males selected from six subgroups participated in a free recall and free association word task.	Three lists of seven words each, selected to reflect major interest areas of the subjects.	ANOVAS seeking trial by subgroup differences followed by t tests evaluating high vs. low interest subgroups for recall, clustering, and associations.	Significant subgroup differences in mean number of words recalled on Trial 1 by high vs. low interest groups; no significant differences in clustering or associations.
Hughes (1971): Bio-data subgroup differences in serial verbal learning.	To examine differential subgroup performance in learning words from a serial list.	32 males from two subgroups were asked to associate each item from a stimulus list with the subsequent item.	Four lists of nine 2-syllable adjectives presented on a memory drum.	ANOVAS involving Subgroup × Meaningfulness × Frequency of Usage × Trials or Position.	A significant interaction effect of subgroup by usage for percentage of correct responses over first 15 trials.
O'Neill (1973): Stylistic differences in human maze learning.	To examine differential styles and performance for subgroup members learning a T maze.	69 males and 52 females drawn from seven subgroups who participated in a maze-learning task.	A multiple T maze and a self-report questionnaire describing experiences while learning maze.	Principal components analysis to determine the dimensions of maze performance followed by ANOVAS examining subgroup differences.	Subgroups differed significantly in persistence with the motor method.

Pace (1974): Prior experience as a mediating variable in the reproduction of random shapes in the presence and absence of verbal labels.	To examine subgroup differences in the redrawing of shapes as a function of treatment conditions.	58 females from two subgroups who viewed and redrew four simple shapes with or without selecting one of four verbal associates.	Slides of four 8-sided figures. Three judges rated these for similarity to stimulus shapes; three others rated redrawings as more or less like stimulus word than originals.	ANOVAS for paired and unpaired conditions and ANOVAS for each subgroup. Correlations between pairs of verbal labels for shapes.	No subgroup main effects. Conditions found effective for word, but not for shape, similarity for one subgroup; reverse true for other.

Interests, Attitudes, Values, and Motives

Bell (1974): Life history antecedents and attitudes toward death.	To investigate differential responses to two frequently employed measures of death attitudes.	273 males completed Lester's Fear and Death Scale (FDS) and the Death Anxiety Scale (DAS) of Templer.	A questionnaire containing 21 randomized FDS items and 15 randomized DAS items.	Canonical correlation and regressions of biodata factor scores on FDS and DAS. ANOVAS and MANOVA seeking subgroup differences on FDS and DAS.	Canonical resulted in one significant root and Rs of .328 (DAS) and .266 (FDS). No pairwise differences were found.
Brush (1974): Predicting major field of college concentration with biographical and vocational interest	To compare biodata and interest scores as predictors of broad and specific curricular choices, to examine bio-	414 males and 325 females completed the Strong Vocational Interest Blank (SVIB) as freshmen and	22 basic interest scales of the SVIB. Majors grouped into Holland's six broad areas and 13 ra-	Discriminant analysis using biodata and SVIB to differentiate college majors. Categorical scaling to	Biodata predicted broad major as well as SVIB; SVIB was superior or with specific areas. Biodata

(Continued)

TABLE 6.3
(*continued*)

Author/Title	Problem	Subject/Task	Instruments[a]	Analyses	Results
data: a longitudinal study.	data subgroup differences in curricular choice.	provided data on major curriculum as seniors.	tionally formed specific areas.	study the biodata subgroup vs. college major relationship.	groups were related to major, although small cell sizes reduced confidence.
Feild (1975): Subgroups and individual differences in the quasi-actuarial assessment of behavior: A longitudinal study.	To study biographical correlates of, and subgroup differences in, longitudinal patterns of experience through the college years.	743 freshmen (416 males and 327 females) of 1968 who completed an 88-item questionnaire as seniors in 1972.	An 88-item College Experience Inventory (CEI) measuring 12 dimensions of non-academic and academic experience.	Biodata subgroup vs. college path matrices were constructed and tested using categorical scaling and canonical correlation procedures.	Longitudinal patterns of college experience (paths) were identified, and it was established that these pathways have differential affinities for both biodata factor and biodata subgroup.
Geisinger (1974): Prayer, biographical background, and college students.	To find which biographical developmental factors are related to an intrinsic orientation toward religion, as measured by frequency of prayer.	738 freshmen of 1968 (412 males and 326 females) completed the College Experience Inventory (CEI) in 1972.	One criterion item from the CEI dichotomized group into those who pray (362) and those who do not (379).	χ^2 analysis (Prayer Dichotomy × Biodata Subgroup); one-way ANOVAS on biodata factor scores by prayer dichotomy.	χ^2 was significant for both males and females; seven male and eight female biodata factors discriminated the prayer groups.
Golembiewski, Billingsley, & Munzenrider (1970): Electoral choice and indi-	To examine voting behavior as a function of biodata subgroup membership.	445 male students completed a political questionnaire (PQ) during 1970.	PQ sought reports on voting intention and performance and on political attitudes.	χ^2 on voting intention (Dem., Rep., and Other) vs. subgroup membership.	Overall χ^2 was significant at approximately the .05 level. Reported percentages of ac-

Reference	Purpose	Sample	Measure	Analysis	Results
vidual characteristics: Toward a biodata approach.					tual voting, by subgroup, ranged from 47% to 100%.
Jones (1970): The affinity of subgroups for vocational interests.	To determine how well SVIB scores can (a) be predicted from biodata and (b) differentiate biodata subgroups.	895 males who completed the SVIB in 1968.	As indicated.	R of SVIB scores on biodata factor scores and one-way ANOVAs comparing subgroups on the SVIB.	All Rs were in the range of .40–.60, and were significant. Biodata groups could be coherently characterized in terms of the SVIB.
Speed (1970): Differential influence of monetary incentive on performance on the College Qualifications Test (CQT).	To examine differential motivation in response to a monetary incentive as a function of biodata subgroup.	60 subjects from three subgroups completed the CQT, and were subsequently retested with reward contingent on amount of gain.	The CQT is a 75-item, multiple choice, synonym–antonym test.	One-tailed t tests to assess differential subgroup gain. ANOVA to assess Subgroup × Gains interaction.	Significant differential motivation in response to a monetary incentive as a function of biodata subgroup.
Walton (1976): Prediction of individual and subgroup behavior via quasi-actuarial assessment: A cross-validation.	To cross validate the biodata subgroup–college group–college paths relationships observed by Feild (1973, 1975).	710 students who entered college in 1970 and completed a questionnaire as seniors in 1974.	An 88-tem CEI, which measured 12 dimensions of experience.	Biodata subgroup–college path matrices were constructed and the present and Feild's cell values were compared.	The major subgroup differences in longitudinal patterns of experience previously observed were cross validated.
White (1974): Moral judgment in college students; the development of	To examine the relationships between biodata subgroup mem-	186 students from five selected subgroups responded to an essay form	Moral dilemmas and questions objectively scorable and yielding an eval-	3 × 5 ANOVAs on subgroup differences in mean moral maturity	Subgroups 7 and 13 stood relatively low in moral judgment and Sub-

(Continued)

TABLE 6.3
(continued)

Author/Title	Problem	Subject/Task	Instruments [a]	Analyses	Results
an objective measure and its relationship to life experience dimensions.	bership, scale scores, and a measure of moral judgment.	of the Kohlberg moral dilemma.	uation in terms of five stages of moral judgment.	score (range: only 3 stages). Stepwise R on relationships between biodata scale score and moral maturity.	group 16 relatively high.

Personality

| Geisinger (1977): Differential self-concepts among prior experience subgroups. | To examine differences among selected biodata subgroups in the acceptability of personal descriptors. | 99 females from three subgroups Q sorted 40 descriptors (20 favorable and 20 unfavorable) in terms of felt applicability to themselves. | Materials for Q-sorting and instructions. | ANOVAs by subgroup, on mean ranks of descriptors; χ^2 test for association of Q-type factors and biodata subgroups; discriminant analysis on descriptors vs. subgroups. | 8 descriptors significantly discriminated subgroups; Q-factors and subgroups are associated; classification of subjects to subgroups 25% > chance. |
| Lewis (1973): Life experience characteristics of homosexual activists. | To compare homosexual with heterosexual and heterosexual-activist males on biodata factors and biodata subgroup membership. | 42 members of the Gay Education Committee were compared to three groups of heterosexual controls ($N > 3,000$) and a group of activists. | Intermediaries who identified groups but not individuals. | t tests comparing homosexuals to controls on biodata factors. Comparison of observed vs. expected frequencies in each biodata subgroup. | Homosexuals differed from controls on 8 of 19 factors, 5 of which also characterized activists in general. Three of 23 subgroups contained 76% of homosexuals. |

Study	Purpose	Sample	Measures	Analysis	Results
Markos (1976): Self-reported personality difference among female subgroups with similar biographical profiles.	To test for biodata subgroup differences on self-reported personality factor scores.	212 females from 11 subgroups completed Gough's Adjective Check List (ACL).	24 original ACL scales were factorially reduced to the three dimensions used in this study, good adjustment, assertiveness, and capriciousness. Biodata only.	One-way ANOVAS comparing 11 biodata groups on the ACL factors.	The groups differed significantly on assertiveness and capriciousness.
Spool (1973): Life experience differences between Black and White college students as assessed with a biographical questionnaire.	To examine the degree to which biodata factors and subgroups developed on a largely White population are generalizable to Blacks.	31 Black males and 56 Black females who completed the biodata questionnaire were compared to controls both matched for SES and unmatched.		t tests to compare Blacks and White on biodata factors. χ² to compare the subgroup structures of the two race groups.	Blacks differed significantly from Whites on the biodata dimensions, the largest differences being on the SES factor. The subgroup structure seemed applicable to the Black sample.
Strimbu & Schoenfeldt (1973): Life-history subgroups in the prediction of drug usage patterns and attitudes.	To examine the extent to which biodata subgroups differ in their use of 12 drugs.	425 college males (42% sample) who responded to a drug usage survey.	A postcard survey of drug use with biodata subgroup precoded so that responses could be treated anonymously.	χ² comparison of biodata subgroups by users vs. nonusers.	Subgroups differed significantly with drug usage percents ranging from 0 to 80.
Strimbu (1973): A quasi-actuarial approach to the	To examine biodata subgroup differences with re-	1,840 students (from a statewide sample of 14,000) who	A 112-item Drug Attitude Survey, which included 45	ANOVAS and discriminant comparisons of	The 17 biodata groups significantly differed in

(Continued)

TABLE 6.3
(continued)

Author/Title	Problem	Subject/Task	Instruments [a]	Analyses	Results
identification of college student drug users.	spect to patterns of drug usage.	completed a survey questionnaire.	biodata items and 9 on drug usage.	biodata subgroup differences in drug usage.	their usage of all nine substances. The substances formed four discriminant functions in differentiating the subgroups.
		Social Processes			
Boardman, Calhoun, & Schiel (1974): Life experience patterns and development of college leadership roles.	To determine whether campus leadership has differential affinity for biodata subgroups.	1,037 males and 897 females from the entering class of 1968.	Number of offices held by these students in 253 campus organizations was determined from college records.	The χ^2 test was employed to determine the independence of a given subgroup from all remaining groups.	Among males (only), 5 of the 23 subgroups (less than 22% of the grouped subjects) contained over 59% of the campus leaders.
Hatcher (1973): Differential persuasibility; subgrouping on the basis of experiential data.	To determine if subgroups differ in persuasibility and comprehension as affected by five differing appeals.	58 males from each of three subgroups were administered an opinionnaire, pretest and test, plus five persuasive communications.	Persuasibility score—shift in opinion in treatment-favored direction; comprehension score—percent correct recall of communications.	One-way ANOVAS of subgroup means on persuasibility and comprehension.	Significant subgroup differences were found for fear arousal–persuasibility and for hedonistic appeal–comprehension.
Jones (1971): The relationships	Relationships among biodata similarity	636 freshmen (300 males and 336	The RCQ measures the perceived sim-	Stepwise multiple regression to suc-	Biographical similarity significantly

Study	Purpose	Sample	Measure	Analysis	Results
among biographical similarity, perceived similarity, and attraction in the roommate situation.	and roommate ratings of similarity and attractiveness.	females) who completed a 25-item roommate compatibility questionnaire (RCQ).	ilarity of roommates and their mutual attraction.	cessively predict RCQ scores for roommate similarity and attraction from their biodata factor score differences.	predicted attraction.
Kupke (1974): Interpersonal attraction as a function of emitted verbal reinforcement, physical attractiveness, and background similarity.	To relate verbal reinforcement, physical attractiveness, and biodata similarity to three measures of attraction.	105 heterosexual dyads were observed in 15-minute laboratory interactions.	Biodata similarity within dyads was the sum of differences across the factors.	Stepwise R of all predictor variables on attraction to dyad partner.	No significant relationship was found between biographical similarity and attraction for either sex.
Lewis, Hornsby, & Brady (1973): Behavioral correlates of biodata subgroup membership.	To describe differential subgroup behavior in a complex interpersonal situation.	Groups of six females—two from each of three subgroups—participated in 30-minute discussion groups.	Each subject's interpersonal behavior was recorded via Borgotta's Behavioral Scores system (BBS).	MANOVA across the three subgroups on the four major BBS categories.	Members of Subgroup 12 were most receptive to the comments of others, and their comments in turn were most kindly received.
Long (1976): Individual differences in mood-mediated helping.	To test subgroups as mediators of the effects of observed behavior on subsequent affective and behavioral response.	70 females from three subgroups heard recording of helping or nonhelping act, filled out a mood questionnaire, and had	20-item adjective rating scale on mood; positive and negative items yielded two scores; number of pages sorted as	Three way ANOVAs on positive and negative mood scores and helping score. Compared correlations of mood and	No significant subgroup effects on helping or a priori mood scales. However, post hoc tests on 20 mood items re-

(Continued)

TABLE 6.3
(continued)

Author/Title	Problem	Subject/Task	Instruments[a]	Analyses	Results
				helping for each subgroup.	vealed significant subgroup differences on an activity dimension.

Physical and Physiological

Author/Title	Problem	Subject/Task	Instruments[a]	Analyses	Results
Long (1975): Birth-order differences on developmental interest factors.	To assess factor score differences and subgroup affiliation among subjects of different birth order.	2,031 males and 1,954 females were classified by family size and birth order.	Biodata only.	Separate MANOVAS on 13 male and 15 female factors for each Sex × Family Size group, followed by univariate ANOVAS.	First-borns scored higher on parental control and on academic interest, but not achievement factors. There were no meaningful differences on social factors.
Mendoza (1972): Emotional response and biodata subgroup.	To examine GSR responses to a loud buzzer by contrasting biodata subgroups.	30 females from two subgroups who were exposed to a series of 40 loud buzzes at irregular intervals.	GSR apparatus and buzzer.	t tests on mean differences in trials to adaption, response latency, and reactivity.	No subgroup differences were significant.
Piacentini (1974): Physical correlates of prior behavior pattern.	To determine the relationship of subgroup membership to weight, height/weight ratio, and weight change during college.	300 males and 236 females responded to a CEI during their senior year.	CEI items dealing with height and weight at college entrance and graduation.	One-way ANOVAS of subgroups on weight, height/weight ratio, and weight change.	Only significant F was for weight among males; post hoc tests revealed no significant differences between mean pairs.

Methodology

Study	Purpose	Sample	Instrument/Variables	Analysis	Results
Anderson (1973): An interinstitutional comparion on dimension of student development: a step toward the goal of a comprehensive developmental-integrative model of human behavior.	To examine the interinstitutional generalizability of the biodata factors and subgroups.	5,370 students from three major universities, all of whom completed a core of 356 biographical items.	246 of the 356 biographical items were selected for analysis. In addition, sex and institution were included as dummy variables.	Factor analysis of the biographical items and subgrouping on the basis of factor score profiles.	No significant institutional variance was found among the 18 biodata factors. 58 biodata subgroups were identified across the three schools and two sexes; one northern vs. two southern schools were differently distributed across these.
Feild, Lissitz, & Schoenfeldt (1975): The utility of homogeneous subgroups and individual information in prediction.	To examine empirically the utility of subgrouping vs. individual information in prediction.	509 students from the 1968 entering class who completed a questionnaire as seniors in 1972.	An 88-item CEI, which measured 12 dimensions of experience.	Canonical correlations to relate biodata scores vs. dummy coded subgroup information to 12 CEI scores.	Prediction of 4 of 24 criteria (12 CEI scores for two sexes) was significantly enhanced when subgroup information was added to biodata scores.
French, Lewis, & Long (1976): Development and validation of a methodology to assess social desir-	To assess susceptibility of biodata items to a social desirability response set.	212 females and 147 males took the biodata questionnaire under conditions to either maximize or mini-	Biodata form with instruction intended to produce either "fake good" or honest sets.	rs between item social desirability ratings and mean item response on each Sex × Treatment group.	Correlations were only moderate, resulting in the conclusion that biodata items are largely immune to

(Continued)

TABLE 6.3
(continued)

Author/Title	Problem	Subject/Task	Instruments [a]	Analyses	Results
ability responding in a multiple choice biographical questionnaire.		mize a social desirability response set.			social desirability response tendency.
Gordon (1976): Logical incongruities contained within the biographical inventory blank.	To develop an index to discriminate biodata questionnaires filled out in a careless fashion.	500 of 10,000 who completed biodata questionnaire and had one or more response errors.	Error responses to biodata questionnaire, including nonexistent options and incongruous question pairs.	χ^2 comparisons.	There were significant differences in carelessness of response among both male and female subgroups.
Lissitz & Schoenfeldt (1974): Moderator subgroups for the estimation of educational performance: A comparison of prediction models.	To compare four moderator subgroup prediction procedures to the overall least-squares method in predicting GPA.	1,855 students entering in 1968 comprised the validation sample; 1,987 students from 1970 were used for cross validation.	GPA was obtained on all subjects three quarters after enrollment.	Four regression procedures that used biodata subgroups as collateral information were compared to the overall regression for all the subjects.	Although the biodata regressions were not statistically superior to the overall, they offered the possibility of increased specificity in prediction.

Note: ANOVA = analysis of variance; MANOVA = multivariate analysis of variance; GPA = grade point average; SAT = Scholastic Aptitude Test.

[a] All subjects completed University of Georgia Biographical Questionnaire.

the nature of the student body at each university. This evidence for the stability or generality of the classification structure is complemented by a study conducted by Feild, Lissitz, and Schoenfeldt (1975), which concluded that prototype status enhances the prediction of multiple criteria obtained 4 years later beyond that obtained from the BQ summary dimensions alone. Results obtained from the methodological feedback studies suggest that the BQ prototypes yield a powerful, valid, stable, and accurate summary description of individuality. Table 6.4 presents a summarization of the results obtained in the feedback studies broken down by content area. Overall, 80% of the feedback studies yielded significant mean differences among the prototypes. However, when broken down by content area, a trend in the results becomes apparent—that is, the prototypes were most likely to yield significant differences in the areas of personality, social interaction, interests, cognition, and learning, rather than perception and physiology. Apparently, prototypes formulated on the basis of life-history data are most sensitive to phenomena tied to individual development rather than to phenomena with a constant, possibly hereditary, organismic basis. These findings suggest that the prototypes are most effective in describing individuality as it is related to ontogeny and life history.

Evaluating the results obtained in the various feedback studies provides support for a number of conclusions. First, the studies provide evidence that the descriptions of individuality obtained from the BQ summary dimensions and prototypes are reasonably stable across samples and cohorts. Second, the prototypes are capable of yielding sizable predictive validity coefficients against a wide range of criteria. Third, the robustness and generality of these summary descriptions was empirically demonstrated in the feedback studies that indicated that members of the various BQ prototypes displayed significant differences in studies exam-

TABLE 6.4
Differential Subgroup Behaviors by Domain

Domain	Of Studies	WSI	Positive	% Positive
Personality	6	5	5	100
Interests, attitudes, values, and motives	9	9	8	89
Cognition, creativity, and decision making	9	8	7	87
Social processes	6	6	5	83
Learning and memory	4	4	3	75
Perception	2	2	1	50
Physical-physiological	3	3	1	33
Methodology	5	4	3	75

Note: WSI = with subgroup implications.

ining phenomena in a number of different domains employing different samples, measures, and methods. The feedback studies have provided substantial evidence supporting the feasibility of constructing a general classification of persons based on the prototype model.

Table 6.5 presents the significant differential characteristics of the male and female prototypes on the background data, reference measures, and feedback study measures. Labels assigned to each prototype in an attempt to summarize their differential characteristics are provided, along with the number of members of the 1968 cohort that could be assigned to each prototype. As can be seen in Table 6.5, the differential characteristics of each prototype was sufficiently cohesive and meaningful to allow each prototype to be described in terms of a brief summary label satisfactory to a number of trained psychologists. Moreover,

TABLE 6.5

Subgroups Based on Biographical Questionnaire Factors—
Females and Males

	Females	
Group	*Subgroup*	*Description*
Well-adjusted achievers	Biodata	(*H*) adjustment[2]; (*L*) athletic participation[2]
	Reference	(*H*) HS grade point,[2] reverse F,[2] social service and business detail interests (Strong); (*L*) emotional exposure,[2] physically active and artistic interests (Strong)
	Feedback	(*H*) education and speech pathology,** speech and journalism*[2] majors; CGPA = 3.16
Extraverted, materialistic authoritarians	Biodata	(*H*) maternal warmth,[1] popularity with opposite sex[2]; (*L*) cultural-literary interests,[1] warmth of paternal relationship[2]
	Reference	(*H*) California F scale,[1] social-religious conformity,[2] economic values,[1] short-term goals,[1] extraversion,[1] business detail and sales interests (Strong); (*L*) HS grade point,[2] SAT,[2] inhibition, human science and academic-literary interests (Strong)
	Feedback	(*H*) business,[1] education and speech pathology*[2] majors; (*L*) dean's list, creativity; CGPA = 2.83
Conservative athletes	Biodata	(*H*) athletic participation[2]; (*L*) maternal warmth[2]
	Reference	(*H*) HS grade point; physically active and business detail interests (Strong); (*L*) radicalism,[1] long-term goals,[1] cognitive values[2] and complexity,[2] personal service and administrative interests (Strong)

TABLE 6.5
(*continued*)

Group	Subgroup	Females Description
	Feedback	(H) health and physical education,*[1] education and speech pathology; business,[2] pharmacy[2] majors*; (L) verbal fluency; CGPA = 3.13
Active, conventional, social leaders	Biodata	(H) social leadership,[2] athletic participation; (L) negative emotions[2]
	Reference	(H) tender-minded,[2] social-religious conformity,[2] physical goals,[2] extraversion,[2] social service and sales-managerial interests (Strong); (L) externalization,[1] human and "hard" science interests (Strong)
	Feedback	(H) education and speech pathology,** health and physical education[2] majors; CGPA = 3.08
Unpopular, cognitively simple, introverts	Biodata	(L) scientific interest,[2] popularity with opposite sex,[1] social maturity[2]
	Reference	(H) printer and accountant (Strong); (L) social desirability,[1] physical goals,[1] long-term goals,[2] positive emotionality,[1] cognitive complexity,[1] extraversion[2]
	Feedback	(H) music,[2] dramatic arts majors; CGPA = 3.06
Dependent, poorly adjusted dropouts	Biodata	(H) parental control,[2] feelings of social inadequacy,[2] warmth of paternal relationship[1]; (L) academic achievement,[1] adjustment[2]
	Reference	(H) reverse F,[1] negative emotionality,[2] emotional exposure,[1] short-term goals,[2] tender-minded, neuroticism,[2] mortician (Strong); (L) HS grade point[1]
	Feedback	(H) music,*[1] language[1] majors; ultimate transfers and dropouts; CGPA = 2.85
Retiring, action-oriented science majors	Biodata	(L) social leadership,[1] feelings of social inadequacy,[2] popularity with the opposite sex[2]
	Reference	(H) social desirability,[2] professional-scientific and action-oriented interests (Strong); (L) positive[2] and negative[1] emotionality, emotional exposure,[1] social service and business-oriented interests (Strong)
	Feedback	(H) physical science,*[2] social science,[2] veterinary medicine,**[1] medicine[1] majors; academic motivation; CGPA = 3.03

(*continued*)

TABLE 6.5
(*continued*)

	Females	
Group	*Subgroup*	*Description*
Mature, socially oriented low achievers	Biodata	(*H*) cultural-literary interests,[2] social maturity[1]; (*L*) academic achievement,[2] parental control,[2] expression of negative emotions,[1] warmth of paternal relationship[1]
	Reference	(*H*) social desirability,[1] inhibition,[2] cognitive complexity[2]; (*L*) HS grade point, F scale,[2] economic values,[2] externalization,[2] negative emotionality,[2] conceptual simplicity, neuroticism,[1] author-journalist (Strong)
	Feedback	(*H*) social science,[1] social work*[1] majors; transfers to other schools; CGPA = 2.85
Unconventional achievers	Biodata	(*H*) cultural-literary interest,[1] scientific interest,[1] expression of negative emotions[2]; (*L*) feelings of social inadequacy,[1] positive academic attitude[1]
	Reference	(*H*) radical,[1] cognitive values,[1] inhibition,[1] cognitive complexity,[1] SAT, human science and administrative interests (Strong); (*L*) tender-minded,[1] F scale,[1] social-religious conformity,[1] short-term goals,[1] business interests (Strong)
	Feedback	(*H*) speech and journalism,**[1] agriculture,**[2] humanities[2] majors; innovators; CGPA = 3.15
Cognitively simple, emotional dropouts	Biodata	(*H*) adjustment,[1] scientific interest,[2] expression of negative emotions[1]; (*L*) SES,[1] social maturity[1]
	Reference	(*H*) positive emotionality,[2] negative emotionality,[1] economic values,[2] conceptual simplicity,[1] veterinarian, carpenter, and farmer (Strong); (*L*) HS grade point, SAT,[1] radicalism,[2] cognitive values,[2] tender-minded,[2] social welfare interests, CPA owner, occupational level (Strong)
	Feedback	(*H*) home economics,[1] language,[2] agriculture[2] social work[2] majors; careless on BQ, tend to leave the university; CGPA = 2.62
Mature, liberal humanists	Biodata	(*H*) SES,[2] maternal warmth,[2] warmth of paternal relationship,[2] social maturity[2]; (*L*) academic attitude[2]
	Reference	(*H*) SAT (M),[2] positive emotionality,[1] minister, librarian, musician (Strong); (*L*) F scale,[1] economic values[1]; math-science teacher, policeman, business detail (Strong)
	Feedback	(*H*) dramatic arts,*[1] humanities,*[1] law[2] majors; "creative personalities"; CGPA = 3.11

TABLE 6.5
(*continued*)

		Females
Group	*Subgroup*	*Description*
Scholarly bookworms	Biodata	(*H*) academic achievement,[1] positive academic attitude,[1] (*L*) social leadership,[2] SES,[2] athletic participation,[1] adjustment[1]
	Reference	(*H*) HS grade point,[1] SAT,[1] cognitive values,[2] long-term goals,[2] neuroticism,[1]; human sciences, "hard" sciences, artist and musician, specialization level, and academic achievement (Strong); (*L*) social desirability,[2] short-term goals,[2] extraversion,[1] reverse F[2]; social service, business detail, verbal-sales, administration (Strong)
	Feedback	(*H*) dramatic arts,[2] physical science,[1] law[1] majors; underachievers, conscientious in filling out BQ, may leave university with personal problems; CGPA = 3.28
Cognitively complex achievers	Biodata	(*H*) academic achievement,[2] SES[1]
	Reference	(*H*) HS grade point, SAT,[2] cognitive complexity,[1] occupational level (Strong)
	Feedback	(*H*) medicine,[2] biological science majors; conscientious on BQ; CGPA = 3.22
Liberated women	Biodata	(*H*) parental control[1], popularity with opposite sex,[1] positive academic attitude[1]; (*L*) maternal warmth[1]
	Reference	(*H*) radicalism,[2] externalization,[1] social service occupations and promotional-verbal occupations (Strong); (*L*) social-religious conformity,[2] physical goals,[2] conceptual simplicity,[2] scientific and physically active occupations (Strong)
	Feedback	(*H*) biological science,[1] pharmacy,[1] dramatic arts, language majors; (*L*) probations; CGPA = 3.15
Goal-oriented social leaders	Biodata	(*H*) social leadership,[1] feelings of social inadequacy[1]; (*L*) parental control,[1] cultural-literary interests[2]
	Reference	(*H*) tender-minded,[1] F scale,[2] physical and long-term goals,[1] emotional exposure,[2] cognitive complexity,[2] externalization,[2] conceptual simplicity[2]; YWCA secretary, sales manager, administrator (Strong); (*L*) SAT, dentist (Strong)
	Feedback	(*H*) education and speech pathology,[1] home economics[2] majors; CGPA = 3.12

(*continued*)

TABLE 6.5
(continued)

Males

Group	Subgroup	Description
Indifferent low-achieving artists	Biodata	(H) SES: (L) pseudointellectualism,[1] scientific and athletic interest
	Reference	(H) music teacher (Strong); (L) long-term goals,[1] cognitive values[2]
	Feedback	(H) music majors, drug users; CGPA = 2.73
Traditional, science-oriented, achieving leaders	Biodata	(H) academic achievement[1]; (L) social introversion[2]
	Reference	(H) social-religious conformity,[2] HS grade point, Reverse F[2]; (L) inhibition[2]
	Feedback	(H) biological science,*[1] physical science* majors, campus leaders; CGPA = 3.08
Cognitively simple, non-achieving business majors	Biodata	(H) pseudointellectualism[1]; (L) aggressiveness-independence[2]
	Reference	(H) negative emotionality,[2] conceptual simplicity[2]; (L) SAT[2]
	Feedback	(H) business,** law,[1] health and physical education[2] majors, careless in completion of BQ; CGPA = 2.55
Unconventional, overachieving, self-directed leaders	Biodata	(H) academic achievement; (L) religious activity[1]
	Reference	(H) radicalism,[2] advertising man, psychiatrist, librarian (Strong); (L) tender-minded,[1] F scale,[2] externalization,[1] social-religious conformity,[2] negative emotionality,[1] conceptual simplicity,[1] neuroticism[1]
	Feedback	(H) law[2] majors, campus leaders, drug users, overachievers, homosexuals; CGPA = 3.07
Analytical independents	Biodata	(H) scientific interest[2]; (L) parental control[2]
	Reference	(H) emotional exposure,[2] cognitive complexity, long-term goals
	Feedback	(H) speech pathology and education,[1] biological science[2] majors, probations, drug-users; CGPA = 2.81
Cognitively complex religious converters	Biodata	(H) aggressiveness-independence,[2] academic attitude,[2] religious activity[1]; (L) social introversion,[1] scientific interest[1]
	Reference	(H) F scale,[1] social-religious conformity,[1] long-term goals,[2] emotional exposure,[1] cognitive complexity,[1] extraversion,[1] neuroticism,[2] occupational level (Strong); (L) computer programmer and osteopath (Strong)
	Feedback	(H) music,[1] speech and journalism,[1] social science[2] majors, careful in completing BQ; CGPA = 3.04

TABLE 6.5
(*continued*)

Group	Subgroup	Description
		Males
"Eggheaded" leaders	Biodata	(*H*) social introversion,[1] positive adjustment response bias[2]; (*L*) parental control,[1] athletic interest[2]
	Reference	(*H*) HS grade point,[2] SAT,[1] printer (Strong); (*L*) physical goals,[2] positive emotionality[2] and emotional exposure,[2] extraversion,[1] life insurance salesman and chamber of commerce executive (Strong)
	Feedback	(*H*) language,[2] physical science,[2] agriculture,[2] dramatic arts, pharmacy majors, leaders; CGPA = 3.16
Business-oriented "Fraternity Joe"	Biodata	(*H*) academic attitude,[1] SES[2]
	Reference	(*H*) economic values,[2] physical goals,[2] extraversion[2]; community recreation director, chamber of commerce executive, credit manager (Strong); (*L*) physicist, dentist, artist (Strong)
	Feedback	(*H*) business,** humanities[1] majors; CGPA = 2.79
Emotional nonachievers	Biodata	(*H*) pseudointellectualism[2]
	Reference	(*H*) F scale,[2] economic values,[1] short-term goals,[1] positive emotionality,[1] negative emotionality,[2] conceptual simplicity[1]; community recreation director, chamber of commerce executive, credit manager, life insurance salesman (Strong); (*L*) SAT,[1] reverse F,[1] physicist (Strong)
	Feedback	(*H*) business**[1] majors, homosexuals, assertive, careless on BQ, academic probations; CGPA = 2.65
Authoritarian dropouts	Biodata	(*H*) parental warmth,[2] sibling friction[2]; (*L*) scientific interest[2]
	Reference	(*H*) F scale[1]; (*L*) integrative complexity,[2] inhibition[1]
	Feedback	(*H*) business,**[2] speech and journalism,** health and physical education majors, academic dropouts; CGPA = 2.76
Competent, independent aesthetes	Biodata	(*H*) aggressiveness-independence,[1] sibling friction[1]; (*L*) academic attitudes[1]
	Reference	(*H*) SAT, integrative complexity,[1] inhibition[1]; minister, music teacher, lawyer (Strong); (*L*) reverse F,[2] economic values,[1] short-term goals,[1] externalization,[2] conceptual

(*continued*)

TABLE 6.5
(continued)

Group	Subgroup	Description
		simplicity[2]; dentist, production manager, pharmacist, osteopath, senior certified public accountant (Strong)
	Feedback	(H) dramatic arts,[2] speech pathology and education,[2] speech and journalism majors, aesthetic-personal interests; CGPA = 2.99
"Jocks"	Biodata	(H) athletic interest[2]
	Reference	(H) life insurance salesman; (L) physicist, psychiatrist (Strong)
	Feedback	(H) veterinary medicine,[2] health and physical education**[1] majors, underachievers, drug users; CGPA = 2.92
"Farm boy"	Biodata	(L) SES,[1] positive adjustment response bias[2]
	Reference	(L) radicalism,[2] long-term goals,[1] positive emotionality,[1] SAT, cognitive values and complexity
	Feedback	(H) agriculture**[1] majors, probations, dropouts; CGPA = 2.86
Nonathletic scientists	Biodata	(L) sibling friction,[2] athletic interest[1]
	Reference	(H) long-term goals[1]; physicist, minister, computer programmer (Strong); (L) physical goals[1]; community recreation director, credit manager, purchasing agent, life insurance salesman (Strong)
	Feedback	(H) physical science* majors, impersonal and unstructured interests, drug users, homosexuals; CGPA = 3.03
Athletically oriented science majors	Biodata	(H) scientific interest,[1] athletic interest[1]; (L) SES[2]
	Reference	(H) cognitive values,[2] physical goals,[1] short-term goals,[2] Air Force officer (Strong); (L) life insurance salesman (Strong)
	Feedback	(H) physical science,*[1] pharmacy,*[1] medicine[2] majors, careless on BQ; CGPA = 2.84
Service-oriented or humanitarian underachievers	Biodata	(H) parental warmth,[1] social introversion,[2] religious activity[2]; (L) positive adjustment response bias[1]
	Reference	(H) SAT, tender-minded,[2] cognitive values[1]; physicist, dentist, minister, math-science teacher (Strong); (L) negative emotionality,[2] managerial interests (Strong)
	Feedback	(H) veterinary medicine,*[1] music,[2] home economics[1] majors, campus leaders, underachievers; CGPA = 2.89

TABLE 6.5
(*continued*)

	Males	
Group	*Subgroup*	*Description*
Bright, achieving leaders	Biodata	(*H*) academic achievement,[1] SES[1]
	Reference	(*H*) HS grade point,[1] SAT (verbal,[1] mathematics[2]); librarian, minister, music teacher (Strong); (*L*) emotional exposure,[1] production manager (Strong)
	Feedback	(*H*) language, agriculture majors, overachievers, leaders; CGPA = 3.37
Poorly adjusted business majors	Biodata	(*L*) positive adjustment response bias[1]
	Reference	(*H*) SAT,[2] externalization,[1] neuroticism[1]; (*L*) social desirability[1]
	Feedback	(*H*) business* majors, probations; CGPA = 2.84
Approval-seeking humanitarian	Biodata	(*H*) parental control[2]; (*L*) parental warmth,[2] sibling friction[1]
	Reference	(*H*) tender-minded,[1] positive emotionality,[1] social desirability[2]; physicist, artist, minister, music teacher, advertising man, lawyer, psychiatrist (Strong); (*L*) economic values,[2] neuroticism[1]; community recreation director, credit manger, purchasing agent, math-science teacher, printer (Strong)
	Feedback	(*H*) social science,[1] medicine,[1] pharmacy[2] majors, interest in "things", cognitive-abstract interest, politically republican; CGPA = 2.94
Concretely oriented underachievers	Biodata	(*L*) pseudointellectualism,[2] academic achievement[2]
	Reference	(*H*) hierarchical complexity,[2] dentist and osteopath (Strong); (*L*) HS grade point[2]; music teacher and occupational level (Strong)
	Feedback	(*H*) business,** dramatic arts[1] majors, academic probations, underachievers, careful completing BQ; CGPA = 2.60
Conservative, achieving introverts	Biodata	(*L*) aggressiveness-independence[1]
	Reference	(*H*) HS grade point; physicist, dentist, math-science teacher, osteopath (Strong); (*L*) radicalism,[1] short-term goals,[1] integrative[1] and hierarchical[2] complexity, extraversion,[2] community recreation director and credit manager (Strong)
	Feedback	(*H*) biological science and pharmacy majors,

(*continued*)

TABLE 6.5
(*continued*)

| | *Males* | |
Group	Subgroup	Description
		interest in "things," political undecideds; (L) Rorschach adjustment; CGPA = 3.08
Rebellious nonachievers	Biodata	(H) SES, parental control[1]; (L) parental warmth[1]
	Reference	(L) HS grade point, social-religious conformity
	Feedback	(H) dramatic arts, social work[2] majors, drug users, academic probations; CGPA = 2.67
Nonconformist dropouts	Biodata	(L) academic achievement,[1] religious activity[2]
	Reference	(H) SAT (verbal), radicalism,[1] externalization,[2] inhibition,[2] printer (Strong); (L) HS grade point,[1] F scale,[2] social desirability,[2] cognitive values,[1] social-religious conformity,[1] hierarchical complexity[1]; community recreation director, Air Force officer, psychiatrist (Strong)
	Feedback	(H) speech and journalism,* language,[1] humanities,[2] social work[1] majors, dropouts; CGPA = 2.71

Note: H = high, *L* = low. 1 = highest, or lowest; 2 = second highest or second lowest. HS = high school, CGPA = college grade point average, BQ = biographical questionnaire, SES = socioeconomic status, SAT = Scholastic Aptitude Test, CPA = certified public accountant.
     Females:
  *Significantly different from base rate at $p < .05$.
 **Significantly different from base rate at $p < .01$.
     Males:
  *Significantly different from base rate at $p < .01$.
 **Significantly different from base rate at $p > .05$.

these interpretable patterns were maintained even on the feedback study and reference measures that were not employed in defining the BQ prototypes.

Examination of the differential characteristics of each prototype suggested that prototype membership was associated with a diverse set of characteristics. Interestingly, the patterns reflected differential concerns with leadership, achievement, social interaction, and relationships to adult society, all major themes of childhood and adolescence. Of course, these prototypical descriptions are not, in any sense, intended to be written in stone. For instance, it is quite possible that more divergent prototypes might be identified in other populations, particularly non-college-level populations. Thus, it is possible that the power of the fore-going results and the number of prototypes would increase with further studies. Moreover, because the prototypes were developed based on a limited developmental time span, they cannot reflect ongoing develop-ment that might lead to divergence in the individual's prototype status. Such a possibility suggests that this cross-sectional methodology has probably not provided the most general possible description of indi-viduality. Nevertheless, the results obtained in this initial investigation provide powerful preliminary evidence supporting the feasibility of for-mulating a valid and adequate summary description of human indi-viduality through the prototype model.

Assessment Two

The principal background data measures employed in the second assess-ment was the 58-item College Experience Inventory (CEI). Analyses of the CEI data began with a set of male and female principal components analyses. Inspection of the resulting eigenvalue plots as well as the in-terpretability of the rotated components indicated that ten dimensions should be retained for both men and women. The retained solutions accounted for 41.1% of the total variance in male item responses and 38.4% of the total variance in the females item responses. Table 6.6 presents the labels assigned to these summary dimensions along with the percentage of total variance accounted for and number of items yielding significant loadings on each of these summary dimensions. The retained solution provided good coverage of the item base. The large variance figures for the CEI compared to the BQ might be attributed to the use of a smaller and more homogeneous item base.

As can be seen in Table 6.7, which presents the items yielding signifi-cant loadings ($r \geq .30$) on the male Bohemianism dimension, the content of the items incorporated under each of the summary dimensions, as was the case with the BQ, reflected common patterns of person behaviors and experiences. Although common dimensions were obtained in the male and female subsamples, some sex differences were again observed in the content and magnitude of the specific items yielding significant loadings on these summary dimensions. The results suggest a continua-tion of the trend observed in the BQ analyses, in which personal social interchange appeared somewhat more important to females than to males during this developmental period. Intellectual pursuits and in-volvement in both formal and informal organizations appeared to be of greater significance to males during this developmental period.

When scores of these summary dimensions were generated, and men

TABLE 6.6
Description of the Male and Female CEI Summary Dimensions

Males (N = 1,131)			Females (N = 1,226)		
Dimension Name	Variance Accounted	Items Loading	Dimension Name	Variance Accounted	Items Loading
1 Literary pursuits	7.2	6	1 Dating activity	5.4	5
2 Sociability	7.0	13	2 Liberal activism	6.5	9
3 Religious involvement	5.1	4	3 Religious involvement	4.8	5
4 Positive college experience	4.1	8	4 Athletic participation	3.7	6
5 Health	3.4	4	5 Positive college experience	3.5	5
6 Marital status	3.3	4	6 Health	3.4	4
7 Activity in organizations	3.0	6	7 Traditional social involvement	3.2	8
8 Athletic pursuits	2.8	7	8 Self-support	2.9	3
9 Self-support	2.7	3	9 Sociability	2.6	11
10 Bohemianism	2.5	9	10 Leisure reading	2.4	5
Cumulative	41.1		Cumulative	38.4	

TABLE 6.7
Items Loading on the Male Bohemianism Dimension

Item Content	Loading
Approximately how many musical events did you attend each year?	.57
Approximately how many cultural affairs programs did you attend each year?	.55
Have your political views been described as liberal?	.50
How many times have you publicly demonstrated for or against any political or social cause?	.44
To what extent have you been involved in a musical group or club?	.41
Have you planned to get a job or enter graduate or professional school after graduation?	−.39
Have you ever lived with a person of the opposite sex?	.39
Have you every been a member of a fraternity or sorority?	−.37
How many football, basketball, baseball, tennis, track meets, or other sporting events have you attended each year?	−.33

and women were clustered in accordance with the procedures outlined earlier, a review of the resulting incremental sums of squares plots, along with the clarity of the assignments produced by the alternative solutions, indicated that the 13-cluster solution should be retained for the men, and the 12-cluster solution should be retained for the women. Roughly 80% of the members of both the male and female subsamples, drawn from all four cohorts, could be assigned to a single one of the resulting prototypes. Very few isolates were obtained in either solution, suggesting that the retained solutions provided classification structures of adequate clarity. Table 6.8 presents the cluster results for men and women, including the labels assigned to the clusters and definitive summary dimensions. As may be seen in both the content of the descriptive labels and the nature of the summary dimensions yielding significant differences for each prototype, different prototypical patterns of prior behavior and experience were identified in the male and female subsamples. Further, the content and nature of the prototypes was clearly tied to patterns of life history during the college years, a finding illustrated by the labels Fraternity Members, Adjusted Academics, and Traditional Daters. To some extent, both trends were apparent among the BQ prototypes; however, the nature of the BQ prototypes was less clearly tied to the particular developmental period for two reasons. First, the BQ items examined both childhood and adolescence, and the CEI items focused exclusively on behavior and experiences during the college years. Second, the CEI items examined a narrower range of behaviors and experiences as a result of the subjects' exposure to a common environment. Examination of the content of the CEI prototypes in relation to the college environ-

TABLE 6.8
CEI Subgroup Names and Characterization

| | | Males | | |
Cluster	Name	High Dimensions	Low Dimensions	N_S
1	Dependent womanizers	2	10, 4	93
2	Adjusted academics	4, 5	10	146
3	Constrained young marrieds	6, 10	7	119
4	Ineffective isolates		1, 6, 8, 4	91
5	Unrestricted working students	8, 10	6	80
6	Born-again christians	3, 8	4	66
7	Maladjusted drifters	2, 9	8, 10, 5	43
8	Health-restricted individuals		5, 2, 9	81
9	Bohemians	1, 2, 10	8	129
10	Fraternity members	2	1	134
11	Realistic intellectuals	9, 10, 7	3, 4	39
12	Spiritual thinkers	3, 9, 4		69
13	Organizational activists	7, 10		24

| | | Females | | |
Cluster	Name	High Dimensions	Low Dimensions	N_S
1	Traditional daters	1, 5	9	229
2	Effective intellectuals	2, 7	1, 4	85
3	Fashionable liberals	9	8, 3, 7	142
4	Fragile flirts	5		107
5	Self-supporting women	8	7	135
6	"Married" students		10, 9	132
7	Dependent isolates	4, 7, 2		63
8	Introverted escapists	10, 5	1, 8	115
9	Christians	3	7	78
10	Athletes		6	70
11	Aggressive joiners	9, 8, 4, 3, 7	1, 10, 6, 5, 2	9
12	Sorority sisters	4, 9, 7	2, 1	63

Note: Dimension scores were standardized with a $\bar{X} = 0$, and $\sigma = 1$; thus, a "high" score is .5 or above, and a "low" score is $-.5$ or below.
For males: $N_T = 1,131$ Overlaps = 246   Fits = 884   Isolates = 1
For females: $N_T = 1,226$ Overlaps = 212   Fits = 1,014   Isolates = 0

ment provides additional evidence for the validity and meaningfulness of these summary descriptions. However, the CEI and BQ prototypes are dissimilar, indicating that similar prototypes may not emerge in different developmental periods. However, this does not preclude the possibility that prototype status would be systematically interrelated across developmental periods.

Assessment Three

Analysis of the PCEI was conducted based on data collected 2 to 4 and 6 to 8 years following graduation from the university. In the principal components analyses of the PCEI 2/4 data for members of the 1971 and 1972 cohorts, inspection of the eigenvalue plots along with the interpretability of the rotated dimensions indicated that the eight-dimension solution should be retained in the male subsample, and the nine-dimension solution should be retained in the female subsample. These solutions accounted for 29.3% and 31.1% of the total variance in the male and female subsamples, respectively. Table 6.9 provides a description of the summary dimensions and labels assigned to them. Given the amount of heterogeneity in the item pool, the retained solutions provided good coverage of the item base.

Inspection of the content of the PCEI 2/4 summary dimensions indicated that occupational and career-related aspects of an individual's life were of substantial importance. Items loading on the male Early Occupational Success dimension are provided in Table 6.10. This is not an especially surprising finding, because entry into the occupational world is perhaps the most important developmental task facing individuals during this period of their lives. Nevertheless, these observations point to the validity of these summary descriptions as well as their specificity to the developmental period.

Sex differences in the summary dimensions suggest differences in the career development process occurring in the two groups. For example, based on demographic trends during the 1970s, it is not especially surprising that the Rudimentary, People-Oriented Jobs would emerge in the female subsample. The absence of an Occupational Initiative and Upward Occupational Mobility dimension in the male subsample may be due to range restriction resulting in weak differentiation and intercorrelation. The PCEI 2/4 dimensions overall reflect primarily the occupational focus of individuals during this time period rather than reflecting adulthood as it is typically conceived.

When the scores generated on these dimensions were subjected to a Ward and Hook clustering, inspection of the incremental sums of squares plots, as well as the clarity of the assignments resulting from alternative classification structures, indicated that the 11-cluster solution should be retained in the male subsample, and the 13-cluster solution should be retained in the female subsample. Approximately 83% of the male and female members of the 1971 and 1972 could be assigned to a single prototype, and only 2% were considered isolate cases. When men and women of the 1968, 1970, and 1973 cohorts were assigned to the

TABLE 6.9
Description of the Male and Female PCEI 2/4 Summary Dimensions

Males (N = 985)

Dimension Name	Variance Accounted	Items Loading
1 Job satisfaction	4.7	18
2 Extra-occupational satisfaction	3.6	9
3 Early occupational success	3.2	10
4 Entry level occupational tasks	3.0	10
5 Vocational direction	2.7	10
6 Religious involvement	2.6	7
7 General reading	2.3	7
8 College-moderated social development	2.2	11
Cumulative	29.3	

Females (N = 1232)

Dimension Name	Variance Accounted	Items Loading
1 Job appropriateness	8.3	17
2 Extra-occupational satisfaction	4.3	9
3 Job satisfaction	3.6	12
4 Intellectual leisure reading	3.1	8
5 Upward occupational mobility	2.6	11
6 Occupational initiative	2.6	12
7 Religious beliefs	2.4	6
8 Collegiate personal development	2.2	6
9 Rudimentary, people-oriented jobs	2.0	7
Cumulative	31.1	

TABLE 6.10
Items Loading on the Male Early Occupational Success Dimension

Item Content	Loading
What is your approximate gross monthly income?	.64
How important has managing and supervision been on your job?	.49
After expenses, how much of your income do you assign to investments?	.46
Are you employed full-time?	.44
How many substantial salary increases have you had since graduation?	.42
How important was opportunity for advancement in selecting your first job?	.41
How important has computational work been on your job?	.37
How important has sales work been on your job?	.35
How important have organizing activities been on your job?	.34
After expenses, how much of your income have you assigned to savings?	.34

prototypes through the appropriate discriminant functions, there was a 5% drop in the number of individuals who could be assigned to a single prototype and a corresponding increase in the number of overlaps. These findings suggest that the PCEI 2/4 prototypes and classification structures were capable of describing most individuals in an unambiguous fashion. The small amount of shrinkage in the number of good fits obtained when the classification was applied in the description of individuals who were not employed in initial derivation of the prototypes and summary dimensions argues for the generalizability of the classification. Table 6.11 presents the prototype descriptions for the PCEI 2/4 analysis.

Thus, it appears that the prototypes provided meaningful summary descriptions of individuality during this developmental period. The content of the life-history pattern identified during the developmental period were clearly tied to career behavior and experiences. As might have been expected on the basis of the summary dimension results, this trend was more pronounced in the male subsample. This finding is illustrated in labels such as Graduate Students, Concrete Careerists, Young Entrepreneurs, and Newly-Married Careerists. The content of some of the female prototypes reflected involvement in establishing a somewhat more traditional family life.

Principal components analysis of the PCEI data collected from members of the 1968 and 1970 cohorts 6 to 8 years after their graduation resulted in identifying eight dimensions for men and nine dimensions for women. These solutions accounted for 29.3% and 31.8% of the total item variance in the male and female subsamples, respectively. Table

TABLE 6.11
PCEI 2/4 Subgroup Names and Characterization

		Males		
Cluster	Name	High Dimensions	Low Dimensions	N_S
1	Graduate students	7, 8	1	94
2	Religious dogmatics	6	8	71
3	Traditional achievers	3, 5	4	89
4	Good ole boys		3, 6, 7	111
5	Disillusioned occupational idealists	3, 4, 8	1, 6	34
6	Young entrepreneurs	1, 4		64
7	Alienated occupational successes	3, 4	1, 8	29
8	Intellectual unconventionals	7	3, 6, 8	106
9	Socially maladapted individuals		2	78
10	Early maturers	3, 1	4, 5	82
11	Disappointed laborers		1, 3, 4, 5	53

		Females		
Cluster	Name	High Dimensions	Low Dimensions	N_S
1	Concrete careerists	4, 5	8, 9	82
2	Immature escapists		4, 7, 8	99
3	Religious copers	7		118
4	Effective adapters	3, 8	1, 9	51
5	Self-developers	2, 5, 8	4	88
6	Unaspiring workers	3, 9	7	58
7	Satisfied conventional females	1, 2, 4, 6	5	83
8	Self-defeating passives	9	1, 2, 6	40
9	"Schoolmarms"	1	2, 5, 7, 9	69
10	Homebodies	6, 9	5, 8	28
11	Unprepared underemployeds		1, 3, 6	66
12	Young professionals	5, 6	2, 3, 4	32
13	Newly married careerists	4, 5, 9	3	46

Note: Dimension scores were standardized with a $\bar{X} = 0$, and $\sigma = 1$; thus, a "high" score is .5 or above, and a "low" score is $-.5$ or below.

For males: $N_T = 985$ Overlaps = 169   Fits = 854   Isolates = 22
For females: $N_T = 1,232$ Overlaps = 195   Fits = 1,042   Isolates = 25

6.12 presents the pertinent data along with the percentage of total variance accounted for by each dimension and the labels assigned to them.

As was apparent in the PCEI 2/4 summary dimensions, the PCEI 6/8 summary dimensions again tended to focus on career-related issues in both the male and female subsamples. Nevertheless, the content of the summary dimensions obtained on the PCEI 6/8 analyses did display some substantial differences from those obtained in the PCEI 2/4 analyses. For instance, neither of the PCEI 2/4 summary dimensions labeled Entry Level Occupational Tasks or Rudimentary, People-Oriented Jobs

TABLE 6.12
Description of the Male and Female PCEI 6/8 Summary Dimensions

Males (N = 741)			Females (N = 771)		
Dimension Name	Variance Accounted	Items Loading	Dimension Name	Variance Accounted	Items Loading
1 Job satisfaction	8.6	12	1 Job determinants	7.3	15
2 Job channelling	3.8	15	2 Job satisfaction	4.9	9
3 Religious morality	3.5	9	3 Extra-occupational satisfaction	4.0	9
4 Extra-occupational satisfaction	3.1	8	4 Asocial job activities	3.6	7
5 Cognitive orientation	2.9	11	5 Collegiate social maturation	2.8	10
6 Semi-skilled labor	2.8	7	6 Perceived occupational status	2.5	12
7 Occupational status	2.4	9	7 Religious community involvement	2.4	12
8 Social adjustment	2.2	11	8 Intellectual reading	2.2	9
			9 Occupational initiative	2.1	8
Cumulative	29.3		Cumulative	31.8	

were replicated in the PCEI 6/8 analyses, and the Occupational Status dimensions were unique to the PCEI 6/8 analyses. Moreover, even on those dimensions assigned similar labels in the two time periods, differences were manifest in the content and magnitude of the specific items yielding significant loadings on these dimensions. Thus, it appears that the separate analyses of the PCEI 2/4 and PCEI 6/8 data were justified by virtue of the fact that these two time periods were associated with qualitatively different patternings of life history. The content of the PCEI 6/8 summary dimensions suggests that these individuals have moved into young adulthood as it has been traditionally conceived. Table 6.13 describes the items loading in the female Religious-Community Involvement dimension.

Some differences were observed among the PCEI 6/8 summary dimensions obtained in the male and female subsamples. The emergence of the Semi-Skilled Labor dimension in the male subsample and the Religious-Community Involvement dimension in the female subsample suggests that these differences are linked to overall sex-role expectations in young adulthood. Further, based on both the PCEI 2/4 and PCEI 6/8 dimensions, it is tempting to speculate that these trends might become more pronounced as individuals move from the postcollege phase into young adulthood and its commitments of marriage and childrearing.

Once scores on these summary dimensions had been obtained, and the similarity among individuals defined, the Ward and Hook clustering procedure was conducted. A review of the within-cluster sums-of-squares plots, along with the clarity of the potential solutions identified through this technique, indicated that the 11-cluster solution should be

TABLE 6.13

Items Loading on the Female Religious-Community Involvement Dimension

Item Content	Loading
About how many times a month do you attend church?	.67
After expenses, how much of your income do you devote to charity?	.64
How often do you attend mid-week activities at your church?	.59
Are you Protestant?	.49
How many social clubs do you belong to?	.41
How satisfied are you with the community you live in?	.40
How satisfied are you with your standard of living?	.38
How satisfied are you with your living quarters?	.37
How satisfied are you with your friends and acquaintances?	.37
In the community you live in, how many of your close friends are of the same sex?	.31
About how much of your spare time do you spend on TV viewing or listening to the radio or stereo?	−.31

retained in the male subsample, and the 14-cluster solution should be retained in the female subsample. Roughly 83% of the males and females could be labeled good fits within a single prototype, and 2% were considered isolate cases. These classification rates suggested that the retained solutions provided a reasonably effective summary description of individuality during these time periods.

Table 6.14 presents the results of the cluster procedure. A review of the content of these prototypes indicated that, 6 to 8 years following

TABLE 6.14
PCEI 6/8 Subgroup Names and Characterization

		Males		
Cluster	Name	High Dimensions	Low Dimensions	N_S
1	Unambitious townsmen	2, 3	5, 7	68
2	Unhappy isolates		4	68
3	Underemployed malcontents	4, 6	1, 8	36
4	OMIT ($N = 2$)			2
5	Successful occupational misfits	7, 8	1	47
6	Impoverished ineffective men		1, 2, 7	34
7	Country boys	5, 6, 8	3	60
8	Contented affluent conservatives	3, 7, 8	2	69
9	Born-again believers	3, 4	6, 8	50
10	Areligious careerists	1, 5	3, 6	97
11	Enterprising intellectuals	2, 4	5	114

		Females		
Cluster	Name	High Dimensions	Low Dimensions	N_S
1	Professionals	3, 6	4, 5	71
2	Disillusioned capitalists	5, 6, 9	2, 4	32
3	Adapted conventionalists	4, 7		56
4	Community-directed housewives	3, 7	6	58
5	Realistically mature adults	1, 2, 5		72
6	Inactive, vocationally uncommitted females	4	1, 8, 9	16
7	Underemployed intellectuals	5	1, 7	31
8	Vocationally adjusted expressives	1, 2, 3, 4, 9	7	40
9	Asocial, occupationally focused women		7, 8	39
10	Presently devastated women	2, 9	3, 5, 6, 8	8
11	Occupational defensives	6, 7	1, 3	41
12	Occupationally disaffected women	8, 9	2, 3, 6	18
13	Downtrodden passives		3, 4, 7, 9	35
14	Family focused women	3	2, 9	33

Note: Dimension scores were standardized with a $\bar{X} = 0$, and $\sigma = 1$; thus, a "high" score is .5 or above, and a "low" score is $-.5$ or below.

For males: $N_T = 741$ Overlaps = 110   Fits = 621   Isolates = 10
For females: $N_T = 771$ Overlaps = 129   Fits = 233   Isolates = 11

graduation, patterns of individuality were not as clearly tied to occupational activity as they had been in the preceding period. Further, patterns of differential effectiveness in adulthood appeared to be emerging. These patterns were somewhat different for males and females. The female prototypes often appeared to be differentiated in terms of the extent to which they chose to concentrate their energies on a career or a family. This is not especially surprising when the pressures brought to bear on females at this point in their lives are considered.

SUMMARY OF THE CROSS-SECTIONAL RESULTS

Taken as a whole, the results obtained in the various cross-sectional analyses have provided compelling evidence for the feasibility of employing the prototype model in attempts to formulate a general summary description of human individuality. Within each developmental period, it was found that most individuals could be described through their assignment to a single prototype, and that these prototypes were associated with a cohesive and meaningful pattern of differential behavior and experiences that could be incorporated in a consensual label derived by trained psychologists.

Moreover, the adequacy of these summary descriptions were not restricted to the particular sample employed in their construction, because the resulting classification could be employed on other samples with little shrinkage in the number of good fits. Of somewhat greater importance were the results obtained in examination of the BQ prototypes with respect to differences on the reference measures and feedback studies. Here, the results indicated that the summary description of individuality could be extended to measures not employed in prototype formation and collected through different formats.

Finally, it appears that the prototypical descriptions of individuality could be applied in a number of developmental periods. As a result of these considerations, it seems reasonable to conclude that prototypical descriptions of individuality have substantial value and that the extension of these principles to data gathered on a cross-time basis might provide a viable means for meeting the central goals of the present investigation and for generating some general conclusions concerning the nature and ontogeny of human individuality.

7

Sequential Results

with Kenneth E. Jackson

Historically, investigations of individual development have relied on the sequential analytic paradigm. In sequential analyses, descriptions of individuality formulated at a single point in an individual's life are related to descriptions of individuality formulated at a later point in the course of an individual's life. Typically, researchers who rely on this approach employ a particular implementation of the more general analytic paradigm. Here, trait descriptions intended to reflect individuality in general are constructed and administered to a sample of individuals at different points in their lives in order to assess the stability of trait differences or the nature of developmental change in trait expression.

Of course, the sequential strategy has been widely used in both longitudinal and cross-sectional studies of human individuality. Examples of investigations employing the sequential paradigm may be found in the stability studies reviewed in chapter 2 as well as the impressive cohort-sequential study conducted by Baltes and Nesselroade (1972). For reasons that are made apparent as the present discussion proceeds, we do not believe that the sequential strategy provides the most viable procedure for delineating the nature of human individuality and individual development. Nevertheless, application of the sequential analytic paradigm may have substantial value in studies of human individuality. First, it provides relatively clear-cut information pertaining to what individuality at one point in people's lives means for later points in their lives. Second, it provides some useful baseline data for describing the nature and implications of individuality over time. Finally, the information obtained from sequential analyses provides evidence that points to the systematic characteristics of individual development, particularly as it relates to the issues of genotypic and phenotypic consistencies.

Because information of the sort lined out here seemed to have substantial value within the context of the present investigation, it was decided that a series of sequential analyses would be carried out relating the descriptions of individuality generated in the various cross-sectional analyses. The cross-sectional analysis provided two kinds of descriptions of human individuality: the summary dimension scores and the prototype assignments. In chapter 5, the specific methods for analyzing both sources of descriptive information within the sequential analytic framework were described. Hence, the ensuing discussion provides the results obtained in these analyses as well as their more general implications. Given the large number of summary dimensions and prototypes identified in the cross-sectional analyses, it seemed necessary to control for spurious findings by establishing a relatively conservative significance level ($p < .01$). Consequently, presentation of the results obtained in the sequential analyses focuses on the significant relationships identified.

SUMMARY DIMENSION RESULTS

Intercorrelation of the Summary Dimensions

The most appropriate starting point for a review of the results obtained in the sequential analysis entails examining the significant relationships identified by intercorrelating scores on the summary dimensions derived in the various cross-sectional analyses. Scores on the BQ, CEI, PCEI 2/4, and PCEI 6/8 dimensions, respectively, were intercorrelated using only the members of the longitudinal sample, to insure that orthogonality was maintained in the more restricted longitudinal sample. In all analyses, coefficients larger than .10 and significant at the .05 level were not observed any more frequently than would be expected by chance. Hence, it seems reasonable to conclude that the orthogonality of the summary dimensions was maintained and that the characteristics of the longitudinal sample did not display any marked departure from the characteristics of the total sample.

Relationships with the BQ Summary Dimensions

The significant relationships obtained in correlating scores on the summary dimensions formulated in different developmental periods were next determined. In examining the correlations among BQ and CEI summary dimensions within the male subsample, six significant coefficients were obtained. Continuity of prior behaviors and experiences was evident in the correlations of the BQ Social Introversion, Religious Activity, and Athletic Interests dimensions with the CEI Activity in Organization ($r = .20$), Religious Involvement ($r = .33$), and Athletic Pursuits ($r = .41$) dimensions, respectively. Familial Socioeconomic Status was negatively related to collegiate Bohemianism ($r = .33$), a result that may reflect the conservative nature of upper-class families. The collegiate Sociability dimension was correlated with the BQ Athletic Interests ($r = .31$) dimension. This relationship may reflect the highly social nature of adolescent athletics and its role in developing social skills. A similar developmental trend appears to include the negative coefficient obtained in correlating scores on the BQ Religious Activities dimension with scores on the CEI Literary Pursuits dimension ($r = -.40$). Apparently, highly religious families and religious values do not foster an interest in literature and culture.

When the relationships among the BQ and CEI summary dimensions were evaluated within the female subsample, 13 significant coefficients emerged. A maintenance of prior patterns of behavior and experiences was manifest in the relationships between collegiate Dating Activity and Popularity with the Opposite Sex ($r = .32$) during adolescence. However, the CEI Dating Activity dimension was also related to the BQ Social Leadership ($r = .24$), Athletic Participation ($r = .20$), and Expression of Negative Emotions ($r = -.20$) dimensions. This pattern of intercorrelations suggests that a pleasant, optimistic, socially active pattern of adolescent behavior facilitates later dating activity. It was also found that collegiate Sociability was positively related to scores on the BQ Cultural/Literary Interests ($r = .20$) and Scientific Interests ($r = .21$) dimensions. Although certain ambiguities arise in interpreting these relationships, it is possible that such antecedent activities provide a basis for later social contact in the college environment and reflect a tendency towards an active engagement in both social and intellectual pursuits. Some support for the foregoing hypotheses may be found in the positive relationship between collegiate Social Activism and adolescent Cultural/Literary Interests ($r = .30$). In correlating scores on the CEI Religious Involvement dimension with scores on the BQ Feelings of Social Inadequacy ($r = .23$) and Parental Warmth ($r = .20$) dimensions, significant positive coefficients were obtained. This suggests that, among females, religious involvement is linked to an earlier acceptance of the traditional feminine role and its religious connotations as well as identification with parental morality. Collegiate Athletic Participation was negatively related to the BQ Warmth of Maternal Relationship ($r = -.23$) and Academic Achievement ($r = -.23$) dimensions. These relationships suggest that female athletic involvement in college may be contingent on an earlier rejection of inhibitions such as a concern with academic achievement or a desire for traditional maternal approval. Finally, it was found that Self-Support during the college years was negatively related to Parental Socioeconomic Status ($r = -.31$). This result appears to reflect the tendency of upper-class families not to force substantial financial responsibility on their daughters.

In correlating scores on the BQ summary dimensions with scores on the PCEI 2/4 summary dimensions, eight significant coefficients were obtained for men. Extra-Occupational Satisfaction in the period immediately following college graduation proved to be related to the BQ Social Introversion ($r = -.21$) and Independence ($r = .20$) dimensions. These relationships seem to reflect the fact that an independent, socially outgoing disposition is likely to facilitate the development of a satisfactory social life once the individual has been removed from the confines of academics. The PCEI 2/4 dimension labeled Entry Level Job Tasks yielded a negative correlation with the BQ Social Introversion ($r = -.20$) dimension and a positive correlation with the BQ Athletic Interests ($r = .23$) dimension. Apparently, introverts are not attached to the lower-level jobs obtained by college graduates where social contact is a salient influence, while individuals manifest athletic interests perhaps because of the social conditions. Job Satisfaction during this period was related to earlier Parental Warmth ($r = .21$). This result may reflect the importance of parental warmth on the emergence of the confidence and self-esteem necessary to cope with the ambiguous, and often rather difficult, process of occupational entry. Given the nature of the foregoing relationships, it was not especially surprising that scores on the PCEI 2/4 Religious Involvement dimension were correlated with scores on the BQ Athletic Interest ($r = .20$) and Independence ($r = -.23$) dimensions. It appears that, in the ambivalent social environment following college graduation, dependence and the conservative social orientation reflected in athletic participation encouraged individuals to employ religion as a social support mechanism.

When the relationships between the BQ and PCEI 2/4 summary dimensions were examined in the female subsample, eight significant relationships were obtained. The positive relationship between scores on the PCEI 2/4 Collegiate Personal Development dimensions and scores on the BQ Warmth of Maternal Relationship ($r = .27$), Social Leadership ($r = .23$), and Social Desirability ($r = .21$) dimensions suggests that favorable outcomes from college experiences are related to an early emergence of social confidence and social skills, perhaps because of the salience of social influences in the lives of many women. It was also found that the PCEI 2/4 Religious Beliefs dimension was related to the BQ Social Leadership ($r = -.22$), Cultural/Literary Interests ($r = -.30$),

Expression of Negative Emotions ($r = .21$), and Positive Academic Attitudes ($r = .21$) dimensions. Although this is a rather complex pattern of correlates, it appears that an unassertive, nonintellectual pattern in adolescence leads to religious involvement in the novel postcollege environment because religious groups provide a source of stability and social contact. It should also be noted that the PCEI 2/4 Job Appropriateness dimension yielded a positive correlation with the BQ Academic Achievement ($r = .20$) dimension. This result might be attributed to the fact that high-ability females are more likely than most to have definitive career plans.

In correlating the BQ summary dimensions with the PCEI 6/8 summary dimensions within the male subsample, five significant relationships emerged. The PCEI 6/8 Job Channeling dimension was positively related to the BQ Academic Achievement ($r = .25$) dimension. Again, this result may be attributed to the tendency of high-ability males to have better-defined career plans and a better chance of carrying out these plans than most other members of their group. It was also found that Religious Morality 6 to 8 years after graduating was directly related to the BQ Warmth of Parental Relationship ($r = .20$) and Religious Activity ($r = .28$) dimensions. These results seem to suggest that, once males have established a reasonably stable adult life, religious morality is a function of a warm, religious family background that would facilitate the acquisition of religious values via identification and learning, despite the fact that these values may be dormant during the turbulence and self-definition of the college and postcollege years. Finally, it was found that the PCEI 6/8 Cognitive Orientation dimension was negatively related to both the BQ Religious Activity ($r = .28$) and Athletic Interest ($r = -.23$) dimensions. Once again, it seems that adolescent religious involvement is not likely to facilitate later intellectual interests, and adolescent athletics and the associated social emphasis is likely to militate against the later emergence of an interest in intellectual pursuits.

Only one significant relationship was obtained in correlating scores on the BQ summary dimensions with scores on the PCEI 6/8 summary dimensions among members of the female subsample. Here, it was found that the PCEI 6/8 Intellectual Reading dimension was positively related to the BQ Cultural/Literary Interests dimension. Of course, this relationship seems to reflect an apparent maintenance of prior behavior patterns.

Relationships With the CEI Summary Dimensions

In correlating scores on the CEI summary dimensions with scores on the PCEI 2/4 summary dimensions, seven significant relationships emerged within the male subsample. The PCEI 2/4 Religious Involvement dimension was negatively related to the CEI Sociability ($r = -.20$) and Self-Support ($r = -.43$) dimensions. These relationships are rather similar to those obtained in relating the BQ summary dimensions to the PCEI 2/4 Religious Involvement dimension. Again, it appears that in the difficult and ambivalent postcollege environment, nonindependent individuals lacking social facility employed religion as a coping mechanism. It was also found that the PCEI 2/4 General Reading dimension yielded negative coefficients when correlated with the CEI Religious Involvement ($r = .31$) and Health ($r = -.21$) dimensions. Of course, religious involvement during the college years is not likely to foster or reinforce an interest in intellectual pursuits such as general reading, whereas poor health may encourage the use of reading as a spare-time activity because it makes few physical demands. Following graduation, Extra-Occupational Satisfaction was related to scores on the CEI Literary Pursuits ($r = .25$) dimension, a result that may reflect the fact that the development of literary interests during college may provide a basis for leisure activities and social contacts in the postcollege years. The CEI Literary Pursuits ($r = .37$) and Religious Involvement ($r = .32$) dimensions were also related to the PCEI 2/4 dimension labeled Entry Level Occupational Tasks. These results might be attributed to the tendency of individuals focusing on concerns of religion and intellectual matters to fail to prepare themselves for the occupational world leading to a lower probability of attending graduate or professional schools and forced acceptance of lower level jobs.

In correlating scores on the CEI and PCEI 2/4 summary dimensions within the female subsample, six significant relationships were observed. CEI Dating Activity was positively related to the PCEI 2/4 Extra-Occupational Satisfaction ($r = .21$) and Collegiate Personal Development ($r = .38$) dimensions. These relationships seem to reflect the fact that collegiate dating may serve as a basis for the development of social skills and contact with the opposite sex and so lead to a satisfying social life and favorable evaluation of college experiences. Occupational Initiative following graduation yielded a negative correlation with the CEI Religious Involvement ($r = -.54$) dimension, a finding that may reflect the powerful influence of traditional role behavior on female occupational commitment. It was also found that Religious Involvement following graduation was negatively related to collegiate Liberal Activism ($r = -.31$), Sociability ($r = -.30$), and Health ($r = -.27$). Although this is a complex pattern of correlates, it appears that conservative, introverted females of poor health may employ religion as a source of security and social contact in the turbulent college environment.

When males' scores on the CEI summary dimensions were correlated with their scores on the PCEI 6/8 summary dimensions, five significant relationships emerged. Maintenance of prior behaviors was apparent in the positive relationship between the PCEI 6/8 Religious Morality dimension and the CEI Religious Involvement dimension (r = .45). Religious Morality 6 to 8 years after graduation was also related to the CEI Sociability (r = .21) dimension. This relationship may be due to the highly social nature of religious morality and the fact that religious organizations provide a major outlet for adult sociability. The PCEI 6/8 Cognitive Orientation dimension was related to both the CEI Sociability (r = −.27) and Self-Support (r = −.36) dimensions. It is possible that an introverted, somewhat protected college life might facilitate the development of an interest in intellectual activities by providing the time and financial support for successful engagement in these activities during the college years. Interestingly, the collegiate Literary Pursuits dimension was positively related to Social Adjustment (r = .34) in young adulthood. This relationship might be attributed to the tendency of intellectual explanation to enhance social development and provide a basis for engagement in the adult world.

Within the female subsample, four significant relationships were obtained in correlating the CEI and PCEI 6/8 summary dimension scores. Continuity of prior behaviors and experiences was again exhibited in the positive relationship between the CEI Religions Involvement dimension and the PCEI 6/8 Religious-Community Involvement dimension (r = .33). A translation of collegiate intellectual and liberal social concerns into more controversial channels seems to underlie the positive correlation between the CEI Liberal Activism dimension and the PCEI 6/8 Intellectual Reading (r = .31) dimension. The positive relationship between Perceived Occupational Status and collegiate Dating Activity (r = .32) may be attributed to the influence of social effectiveness and skill in interacting with males on female occupational success. Finally, it should be noted that collegiate Athletic Participation was negatively related to the PCEI 6/8 Job Determinants (r = −.24) dimension. This result might be attributed to the limited academic concerns of many student athletes and the importance of academics in the earlier phases of an individual's career development.

Relationships With the PCEI 2/4 Summary Dimensions

In correlating scores on the PCEI 2/4 and PCEI 6/8 summary dimensions, 12 significant relationships were obtained in the male subsample. Five of the significant coefficients reflected a maintenance of prior patterns of behavior and experience. These maintenance relationships were apparent in the coefficients obtained in correlating the PCEI 6/8 Job

Satisfaction, Extra-Occupational Satisfaction, Religious Morality, Occupational Status, and Social Adjustment dimensions with the PCEI 2/4 Job Satisfaction ($r = .32$), Extra-Occupational Satisfaction ($r = .25$), Religious Involvement ($r = .48$), Early Occupational Success ($r = .43$), and College-Moderated Social Development ($r = .50$) dimensions, respectively. Job Channeling 6 to 8 years following graduation was directly related to earlier Job Satisfaction ($r = .25$), General Reading ($r = .29$), and Social Adjustment ($r = .29$). This pattern of relationships suggests that later occupational commitment is facilitated by reinforcing initial job experiences as well as by an active intellectual and social life that allows the individual to satisfy nonoccupational needs and to maintain and support initial vocational choices. The PCEI 6/8 Religious Morality dimensions was positively related to the PCEI 2/4 Entry Level Occupational Tasks ($r = .31$) dimension, a result that may reflect the effects of a religious-family orientation on male occupational success. Interestingly, expression of a Cognitive Orientation 6 to 8 years after college graduation was related to Occupational Success ($r = .27$) 2 to 4 years after graduation. This result seems to suggest that the intellectual challenge involved in an initial upper-level job may lead to general expansion of intellectual interests when it is accompanied by occupational success. Finally, the salience of career adjustment to male psychological well-being seems to be reflected in the positive relationship between the PCEI 6/8 Social Adjustment dimension and the PCEI 2/4 Job Satisfaction ($r = .22$) dimension.

When the same set of analyses was carried out within the female subsample, 11 significant relationships were obtained. Again, the maintenance of prior patterns of behavior and experiences was apparent in a number of these relationships, including the positive coefficients obtained in correlating the PCEI 6/8 Job Determinants, Job Satisfaction, Extra-Occupational Satisfaction, Collegiate Social Development, Religious-Community Involvement, and Occupational Initiative dimensions with the PCEI 2/4 Job Appropriateness ($r = .74$), Job Satisfaction ($r = .28$), Extra-Occupational Satisfaction ($r = .30$), Collegiate Personal Development ($r = .35$), Religious Beliefs ($r = .61$), and Occupational Initiative ($r = .23$) dimensions, respectively. Asocial Job Activities 6 to 8 years following graduation were related to earlier Upward Occupational Mobility ($r = .41$), a result suggesting that occupational mobility leads families out of stereotypical lower-level, social-contact jobs and into more independent, cognitively oriented work. Scores on the PCEI 2/4 Extra-Occupational Satisfaction were related to the PCEI 6/8 Collegiate Social Maturation ($r = .32$) dimension. This relationship seems to reflect the fact that the social outcomes associated with an individual's college experiences are, to some extent, dependent on the earlier maintenance of social contacts. The tendency of intellectual activities to facilitate occupational success may be seen in the positive relationship between the PCEI 6/8 Perceived Occupational Status and Intellectual Reading dimensions and the PCEI 2/4 Leisure Reading ($r = .36$) and Occupational Initiative ($r = .23$) dimensions, respectively. Finally, it should be pointed out that the PCEI 6/8 Religious Community Involvement dimension yielded a negative correlation with the PCEI 2/4 Occupational Initiative ($r = -.47$) dimension. This result, once again, seems to reflect the restrictions that a religious-family orientation places on the effort expended and value placed on occupational success by an individual as well as the fact that females not concerned with occupational success are likely to focus on a traditional family life.

SUMMARY DIMENSION CONCLUSIONS

The foregoing discussion has indicated that the relationship among summary dimensions derived in different developmental periods could be interpreted with little difficulty. To the extent that the observed relationships fall into a meaningful or interpretable pattern, the summary dimensions obtained in the various cross-sectional analyses can be said to display some construct validity. Thus, one conclusion that may be drawn from the sequential analyses of summary dimension interrelationships is that the cross-sectional dimensions have some validity in the descriptions of human individuality.

It is of some importance that the differential descriptions obtained from the cross-sectional dimensions displayed validity in the sequential analyses because it provides the requisite groundwork for any other conclusions to be drawn on the basis of these findings. One of these conclusions is concerned with the nature of the antecedent dimensions that will yield significant prediction across developmental periods. Table 7.1 presents a listing of the significant relationships obtained in the sequential summary dimension analyses. It is apparent from reviewing the table that some dimensions were far more likely than others to be of predictive significance. More specifically, those dimensions concerned with religion, athletics, intellectual activities, independence, and social relationships accounted for the majority of the significant relationships observed in the sequential analyses. Interestingly, these dimensions were not necessarily the ones that yielded the most powerful description within a single developmental period, and the relatively small cross-sectional eigenvalues associated with these dimensions do not appear to be the

TABLE 7.1
Significant Sequential Dimensional Relationships

Males

BQ	CEI	BQ	PCEI2/4
Social introversion	Activity in organizations (r = -.20)	Social introversion	Extra-occupational satisfaction (r = -.21)
Religious activity	Religious involvement (r = .33)	Social introversion	Entry level job tasks (r = -.20)
Athletic interests	Athletic pursuits (r = .41)	Independence	Extra-occupational satisfaction (r = .20)
Socioeconomic status	Bohemianism (r = -.33)	Independence	Religious involvement (r = -.23)
Athletic interests	Sociability (r = .31)	Athletic interests	Entry level job tasks (r = .23)
Religious activity	Literary pursuits (r = -.40)	Religious activity	General reading (r = -.24)
		Parental warmth	Job satisfaction (r = .21)

Females

BQ	CEI	BQ	PCEI2/4
Popularity with the opposite sex	Dating activity (r = .30)	Warmth of maternal relationship	Collegiate personal development (r = .27)
Social leadership	Dating activity (r = .24)	Social leadership	Collegiate personal development (r = .23)
Athletic participation	Dating activity (r = .20)	Social desirability	Collegiate personal development (r = .21)
Expression of negative emotions	Dating activity (r = -.20)	Social leadership	Religious beliefs (r = -.22)
Cultural/literary interests	Social activism (r = .30)	Cultural/literary interests	Religious beliefs (r = -.30)
Feelings of social inadequacy	Religious involvement (r = .23)	Expression of negative emotion	Religious beliefs (r = .21)
Paternal warmth	Religious involvement (r = .20)	Positive academic attitudes	Religious beliefs (r = .21)
Warmth of maternal relationship	Athletic participation	Academic achievement	Job appropriateness (r = .20)
Academic achievement	Athletic participation (r = .23)		
Socioeconomic status	Self-support (r = -.30)		
Cultural/literary interests	Sociability (r = .20)		
Scientific/interests	Sociability (r = .21)		

Males

BQ	PCEI6/8	CEI	PCEI2/4
Academic achievement	Job channelling ($r = .25$)	Literary pursuits	Extra-occupational satisfaction ($r = .25$)
Parental warmth	Religious morality ($r = .20$)		
Religious activity	Religious morality ($r = .28$)	Literary pursuits	Entry level occupational tasks ($r = .37$)
Religious activity	Cognitive orientation ($r = -.28$)	Religious involvement	Entry level occupational tasks ($r = .32$)
Athletic interests	Cognitive orientation ($r = -.23$)	Religious involvement	General reading ($r = -.31$)
		Health	General reading ($r = .21$)
		Sociability	Religious involvement ($r = -.20$)
		Self-support	Religious involvement ($r = -.43$)

Females

BQ	PCEI6/8	CEI	PCEI2/4
Cultural/literary interests	Intellectual reading ($r = .34$)	Dating activity	Extra-occupational satisfaction ($r = .21$)
		Dating activity	Collegiate personal development ($r = .38$)
		Social activism	Religious involvement ($r = -.31$)
		Sociability	Religious involvement ($r = -.30$)
		Health	Religious involvement ($r = -.27$)
		Religious involvement	Occupational initiative ($r = -.54$)

(Continued)

TABLE 7.1
(continued)

Males

CEI	PCEI6/8	PCEI2/4	PCEI6/8
Literary pursuits	Social adjustment ($r = .34$)	Job satisfaction	Job satisfaction ($r = .32$)
Self-support	Cognitive orientation ($r = -.36$)	Extra-occupational satisfaction	Extra-occupational satisfaction ($r = .25$)
Sociability	Cognitive orientation ($r = -.27$)	Religious involvement	Religious morality ($r = .45$)
		Early occupational success	Occupational status ($r = .43$)
Sociability	Religious morality ($r = .21$)	College moderated social development	Social adjustment ($r = .50$)
Religious involvement	Religious morality ($r = .45$)	Job satisfaction	Job channelling ($r = .25$)
		General reading	Job channelling ($r = .29$)
		College moderated social development	Job channelling ($r = .29$)
		Entry level occupational tasks	Religious morality ($r = .31$)
		Job channelling	Semi—skilled labor ($r = .38$)
		Early occupational success	Cognitive orientation ($r = .27$)
		Job satisfaction	Social adjustment ($r = .22$)

Females

CEI	PCEI6/8	PCEI2/4	PCEI6/8
Athletic participation	Job determinants ($r = -.24$)	Job appropriateness	Job determinants ($r = .74$)
Dating activity	Perceived occupational status ($r = .36$)	Job satisfaction	Job satisfaction ($r = .28$)
		Extra-occupational satisfaction	Extra-occupational satisfaction ($r = .30$)
Social activism	Intellectual reading ($r = .33$)		Collegiate social maturation ($r = .35$)
Religious involvement	Religious community involvement ($r = .33$)	Collegiate personal development	Religious community involvement ($r = .61$)
		Religious beliefs	Occupational initiative ($r = .23$)
		Occupational initiative	Asocial job activities ($r = .41$)
		Upward occupational mobility	College social maturation ($r = .32$)
		Extra-occupational satisfaction	Perceived occupational status ($r = .36$)
		Intellectual leisure reading	Intellectual reading ($r = .23$)
		Occupational initiative	Religious community involvement ($r = -.47$)
		Occupational initiative	

result of the number of relevant items contained in the cross-sectional data bases. Of course, this suggests that the dimensions that best summarize differential behaviors and experiences over time are not necessarily the ones that best summarize differential behaviors and experiences at a single point in time.

The question is: Why do these particular dimensions yield significant relationships? In examining the content of these predictive dimensions, there does appear to be one thread binding them together. The religion, intellectual activities, independence, and social relationships dimensions all reflect various means by which individuals relate themselves to and engage their environmental surround. For instance, independence in dealing with others or introversion reflect rather broad, complex processes by which the individual attempts to adapt to the surrounding physical and social environment and the opportunities and limitations presented. Thus, it appears that the summary dimensions of tangible cross-time significance are those that are tied to the processes used by individuals in attempts to adapt to their environmental surround. It is tempting to speculate, in this regard, that the significance of such dimensions lies in either their relationship to or their control over choices among alternative action in later environments. Although it is speculative, this interpretation provides a basis for interpreting the complex nature of the later developmental correlates of these dimensions, in that changing environments across developmental periods might open up a new set of choices that are influenced by these dimensions, despite the lack of overt, direct continuity in prior behavior and experiences.

Although these process-oriented dimensions appear to have substantial significance with respect to the description of individual development, that does not imply that dimensions of this sort have stable predictive or developmental implications. The relationships associated with these process-oriented dimensions displayed a great deal of complexity across developmental periods. For instance, Dating Activity was related to Extra-Occupational Satisfaction immediately following graduation but not 6 to 8 years later, although it was related to Perceived Occupational Status among females. Similarly, although collegiate religious involvement was related to postcollege religious involvement for females, male collegiate religious involvement was related to Entry Level Occupational Tasks and General Reading, but not religious involvement 2 to 4 years after graduation. This same complexity was manifest even among the dimensions that were less likely to yield significant relationships, and the complexity of these relationships argues for the importance of genotypic, rather than phenotypic, consistencies in the nature of individual development.

Some support for this conclusion may be found in the nature of the maintenance relationships obtained in the sequential analyses. Even bearing in mind the fact that the instruments employed in this study were not explicitly designed to focus on stability or phenotypic consistency, a number of similar dimensions were obtained in the various developmental periods that did permit some examination of the possibility of direct continuity. Yet, with the exception of the PCEI 2/4 and PCEI 6/8 relationships, very few maintenance relationships were observed, even when the dimensions were nearly identical, such as was the case in female adolescent and collegiate Athletic Participation dimensions. Moreover, even when significant maintenance relationships were obtained, they were not generally of any great power. For instance, the female PCEI 2/4 and PCEI 6/8 Occupational Initiative dimensions were correlated in the low .20s, and Job Satisfaction for males and females across these two developmental periods yielded correlations in the low .30s or high .20s. Thus, it seems reasonable to conclude that continuities in individuality across developmental periods are likely to reflect complex genotypic consistencies rather than a simple maintenance of prior patterns of behavior and experience.

The foregoing conclusion has at least two important implications. First, although the observation does not necessarily negate the ancient axiom that the best predictor of future behavior is past behavior, it does suggest that researchers should not assume that there is an isomorphic relationship between past and future behavior. The reason that such a limitation on the conventional wisdom employed in psychological assessment is necessary has been richly illustrated in the results obtained in the sequential analysis. For instance, as was apparent in the lack of a significant relationship between female adolescent and collegiate Athletic Participation, even nearly identical dimensions examining nearly identical lists of behavior in adjacent developmental periods may not yield significant predictive relationships. Further, it appears that the meaning of identical lists of behavior may shift across developmental periods. The case in point may be found in the fact that the meaning of male religious involvement 2 to 4 years after graduation, as indexed by its pattern of antecedent and consequent correlates, was different than that observed in earlier and later developmental periods. Apparently, religious involvement in the period immediately following graduation may not reflect religious values as much as a means for independent, socially unskilled individuals to adapt to the turbulent postcollege environment. This does not hold true in either earlier or later developmental periods. Obviously, these derivations suggest that, in attempts to describe individual development, it is necessary to search for signs of future behavior in the individual's past instead of assuming simple continuity.

The second implication is concerned with the reasons that the more parsimonious assumption of direct continuity does not apply. Based on the interpretations used in explaining the relationships obtained in the sequential analyses, it appears that the meaning of differential behavior and experiences shifts over time in response to changes in the broader environment and the influence of ongoing individual development. The ability of environmental influences to produce such changes is illustrated by the change in the meaning of male religious involvement across developmental periods, and the influence of ongoing development on individuality is illustrated by the relationship between Early Occupational Success and the later emergence of a Cognitive Orientation, despite the fact that the Cognitive Orientation was not related to an earlier interest in intellectual pursuits. These observations lead to the conclusion that individuality may change over time as a result of ongoing development. Such changes may occur in a complex, albeit systematic fashion, based on the individual's prior pattern of behavior and experiences.

The influence of a complex, yet systematic pattern of individual development on predictive relationships may account for two other phenomena observed in the sequential analysis. First, there was no clear-cut tendency for the number of significant relationships to decrease as the time between assessments increased, although there was a slight trend in this direction. However, this result might be expected if systematic changes are related to the *total pattern* of the individual's past behavior and experiences. Second, the magnitude of even the significant relationships obtained in this analysis was not overwhelming. The observed coefficients rarely exceeded .40 and typically lay in the mid .20s to mid .30s. Further, when the number of computations carried out in these analyses is considered, the power of these relationships becomes even less impressive, because a number of marginally significant relationships and a few major relationships might be expected to change. The rather weak relationships are typical of longitudinal studies of this type. Such effects might be attributed to the moderating influence of ongoing developmental change that serves to limit the magnitude of correlational relationships. Yet the statement does not imply that developmental change precludes adequate prediction, in part because many of the dimensions identified in the cross-sectional analysis may not be those of developmental or predictive significance, and in part because the limited number of significant interpretable relationships identified in this analysis suggests that some prediction, albeit complex in nature, is possible.

Given the nature of the foregoing observations, it seems reasonable to conclude that there are some complex systematic relationships between the differential behavior and experiences observed at different points in the course of an individual's life. However, these relationships are neither of the power nor the consistency that would be anticipated within the more traditional models of individuality and individual development, particularly those employing a trait-oriented behavioristic conception of the phenomena. This suggests that it may be necessary to employ a somewhat different approach in attempts to describe individuality and individual development. Although it is not clear exactly how this issue should be approached, the foregoing data argues for the need to describe individuality with respect to the more complex genotypic relationships. In the following section, some further evidence along these lines is presented that tends to confirm these conclusions and suggests a particular solution to the problem this data poses for the summary description of human individuality and individual development.

PROTOTYPE RESULTS

In the preceding chapter, evidence was presented that suggested that the prototypes formulated in the various cross-sectional analyses could provide a meaningful summary description of human individuality. As a result, it is possible that the relationships between assignments in the cross-sectional prototypes obtained at different points in an individual's life might have some value in attempts to describe individuality. Because memberships in the cross-sectional prototypes appear to reflect cohesive patterns of prior behavior and experiences, this approach promises to be especially fruitful. In essence, an analysis of this sort permits us, first, to determine the extent to which a given pattern of prior history determines future patterns of behavior and experiences, and second, where and when changes occur in these patterns for a certain type of individual.

Although this analysis was described in some detail in chapter 5, it is briefly reviewed here. Individuals responding to any given pair of instruments who could be fitted to a single prototype were employed as subjects. Subsequently, the probability of any male or female who could be assigned to single BQ prototype moving into any one of the CEI, PCEI 2/4, and PCEI 6/8 prototypes was determined, along with the probability of those individuals moving into a given CEI or PCEI 2/4 or 6/8 prototype. The significance of these relationships was then established in a modified X^2 analysis designed to control for cells containing less than five individuals, and the significant patterns of movement were then laid out. Additionally, a series of analyses examining the patterns of movement of individuals who were assigned to a single CEI prototype into the PCEI 2/4 and PCEI 6/8 prototypes, as well as individuals who were assigned to a single PCEI 2/4 prototype into the PCEI 6/8 prototypes, were carried out in an attempt to insure the stability of the results obtained in the initial BQ analyses.

PROBABILITY ANALYSIS RESULTS

Relationships Among the Male Prototypes

Figure 7.1 presents a schematic overview of the significant relationships among the male prototypes obtained in the course of the BQ-based probability analyses. This table presents the original BQ prototype and the percentage of prototype members moving to each of the CEI, PCEI 2/4, and PCEI 6/8 prototypes, along with the percentage of prototype members traveling from a CEI or PCEI 2/4 prototype to a PCEI 2/4 or PCEI 6/8 prototype. Only relationships indicating more frequent, as opposed to less frequent, movement are presented in this table, and no relationship was tabled unless it exceeded chance at $p \leq .01$ level. A brief review of the figure indicates that not all of the male BQ prototypes followed a predictable pattern of movement into the CEI, PCEI 2/4, and PCEI 6/8 prototypes. In fact, an overall chi square analyses indicated that only 14 out of the 23 male BQ prototypes followed any non-random patterns of movement into the later CEI, PCEI 2/4, and PCEI 6/8 prototypes.

In examining the significant chi squares indicating more frequent than expected movement among the individual prototypes, it was found that an interpretable pattern of movement emerged among the predictable prototypes. Members of the BQ prototype labeled Traditional Science-Oriented Achieving Leaders tended to flow into the Adjusted Academics and Fraternity Members prototypes during the college years. Each of these CEI prototypes seemed to reflect a differential emphasis of past trends that were apparent in the lives of these individuals; the adjusted Academics prototype reflected the orientation towards academic achievement characteristic of this BQ prototype, whereas the Fraternity Members prototype reflected the orientation towards traditional social achievement that was also apparent in the earlier behavior and experiences of these individuals. Movement into the Fraternity Members prototype led to only one systematic outcome for Traditional Science-Oriented Achieving Leaders; that is, movement into the PCEI 6/8 Areligious Careerists prototype, a result that seems to reflect a continued emphasis on traditional social achievement. On the other hand, the individuals entering the Adjusted Academics prototype tended to enter either the Graduate Students or Good Ole Boys prototypes 2 to 4 years

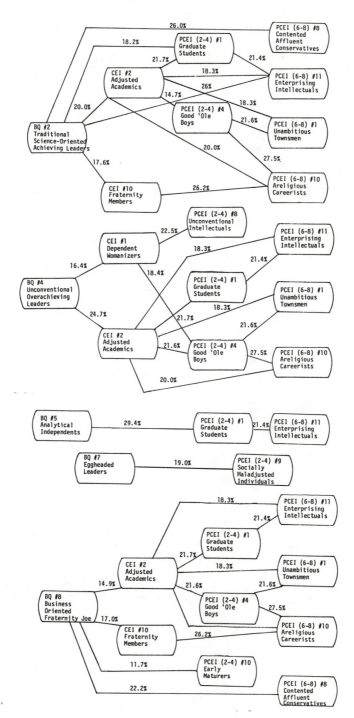

FIG. 7.1. Life history pathways—males

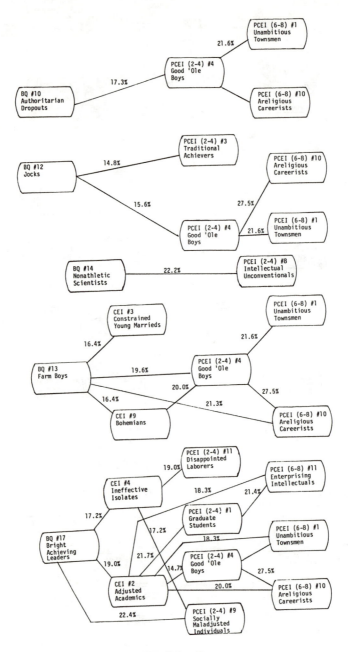

FIG. 7.1.   Cont.

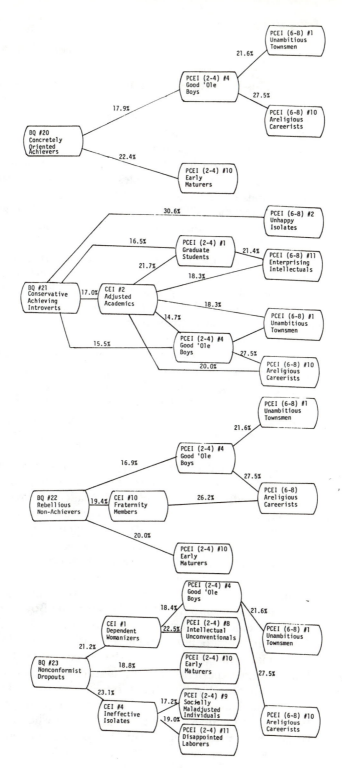

FIG. 7.1. Cont.

after graduation. This dichotomy seems to reflect the outcomes of a decision to continue an academic, intellectual orientation or return to the social orientation that's characteristic of the Good Ole Boys prototype. Individuals who entered the Good Ole Boys prototype after graduation tended to enter the Areligious Careerists or Unambitious Townsmen PCEI 6/8 prototypes, as might have been expected on the basis of their renewed concern with traditional social roles and achievement through these roles. Individuals entering the PCEI 2/4 Graduate Students prototype tended to enter the PCEI 6/8 Enterprising Intellectuals prototype, reflecting some continuity in their orientation towards intellectual achievement. Irrespective of movement into the CEI Adjusted Academics prototype, a number of Traditional Science-Oriented Achieving Leaders tended to enter the PCEI 6/8 Enterprising Intellectuals and Contented Affluent Conservatives prototypes. These relationships seem to reflect a continuation of earlier trends that were apparent in adolescence. However, the fact that individuals entering the Fraternity Members prototype did not enter either of these PCEI 6/8 prototypes suggests that fraternity involvement may have an impact on the developmental paths followed by members of this BQ prototype.

Members of the BQ prototype labeled Unconventional Overachieving Leaders also tended to enter the CEI Adjusted Academics prototype. This relationship might be attributed to the tendency of prototype members to focus on independent intellectual achievement, and this orientation would seem to account for their tendency to flow directly into the PCEI 6/8 Enterprising Intellectuals prototype without intervening prototype membership or enter the Enterprising Intellectuals prototype after movement into either the CEI Adjusted Academics prototype or the CEI Adjusted Academics and PCEI 2/4 Graduate Students prototypes. However, this maintenance of an independent, intellectual achievement did not hold for all members of this BQ prototype. Some members of the Unconventional Overachieving Leaders prototype who entered the CEI Adjusted Academics prototype also entered the PCEI 6/8 Unambitious Townsmen and Areligious Careerists prototypes either directly or after movement into the PCEI 2/4 Good Ole Boys prototype. This pattern of movement suggests a change in some individuals from an orientation towards independent intellectual achievement to a more mundane traditional social orientation, perhaps because of differential college and postcollege experiences or because their original orientation towards independence and achievement reflected a somewhat bitter search for approval. Some support for this latter hypothesis may be found in the fact that members of this BQ prototype who entered the highly social and rather nonindependent CEI Dependent Womanizer prototype also tended to enter the PCEI 2/4 Good Ole Boys prototype and from there move to the PCEI 6/8 Unambitious Townsmen and Areligious Careerists prototypes. The members of this prototype who entered the CEI Dependent Womanizers prototype, but did not follow this pattern of movement, tended to return to a precollege pattern of behavior by movement into the PCEI 2/4 Unconventional Intellectuals prototype. Apparently, some members of this prototype appear to learn how to manage their concern with independent achievement and others do not, leading to two rather different patterns of movement through the cross-sectional prototypes.

The patterns of movement followed by members of the BQ prototype labeled Authoritarian Dropouts are also presented in the figure. As may be seen, these individuals did not systematically flow into any collegiate prototype. However, their tendency to enter the PCEI 2/4 Good Ole Boys prototype may be viewed as reflecting a maintenance or reassertion of their unmotivated, authoritarian, social orientation in the years following graduation. This traditional pattern of social engagement, in turn, seems to have led prototype members to enter either the Unambitious Townsmen or the Areligious Careerists prototypes 6 to 8 years after graduation. These observations suggest a change towards a more traditional social orientation in the postcollege years and less alienation but in a manner that is congruent with the earlier authoritarian trends.

It was not especially surprising that the pattern of movement followed by members of the BQ Jocks prototype was rather similar to that which characterized members of the Authoritarian Dropouts prototype. These individuals did not systematically enter any CEI prototype. However, they did tend to enter the PCEI 2/4 Good Ole Boys prototype and from their move into the PCEI 6/8 Unambitious Townsmen and Areligious Careerists prototypes. It seems reasonable to conclude that this pattern reflects the maintenance of the traditional social orientation that is characteristic of male adolescent attitudes with some transformations in later developmental periods. It is interesting to note that the alternative to the foregoing pattern was entry into the PCEI 2/4 Traditional Achievers prototype, which was followed by a nonsystematic pattern of movement into the PCEI 6/8 prototypes. It is tempting to speculate in this regard that initial success in the postcollege environment served to disrupt prior patterns and lead to a lack of further predictability. Additionally, it appears that for both the Jocks and the Authoritarian Dropouts, postcollege patterns of behavior and experiences are of far greater importance to later development than collegiate behavior and experiences.

A somewhat more complex pattern of movement through the prototypes was obtained for members of the BQ Farm Boys prototype. These individuals tended to enter the PCEI 2/4 Good Ole Boys prototype either directly or after a period of rebellion as evidenced by movement into the CEI Bohemians prototype. From the Good Ole Boys prototype, these individuals tended to move into either the Unambitious Townsmen or Areligious Careerists prototypes. However, a number of prototype members tended to enter the Areligious Careerists prototype directly without any intervening PCEI 2/4 or CEI prototype membership. This pattern of movement suggests that members of this prototype displayed the traditional social orientation and lack of concern with occupational achievement that might be expected on the basis of their background, with the exception of a brief period of collegiate rebellion by some individuals. The only alternative to this pattern was tied to a single event, more specifically, early marriage. Members of this prototype who entered the CEI Constrained Young Marrieds prototype did not follow the foregoing movements; rather, they distributed themselves randomly among the PCEI 2/4 and PCEI 6/8 prototypes in later years. Although it seems likely that the background of these individuals predisposed them towards early marriage, the foregoing results suggest that this event and the outcomes associated with it has a profound impact on their later lives.

Only one significant relationship was obtained for those males originally assigned to the BQ Nonathletic Scientists prototype. It was found that some of these individuals tended to enter the PCEI 2/4 prototype labeled Unconventional Intellectuals. This result seems to reflect a maintenance or re-emergence of their earlier nontraditional nonsocial intellectual orientation in the years immediately following college graduation. Yet, because this trend did not have any systematic implications for later development, it may reflect a temporary regression to prior patterns of behavior and experiences as a means for adapting to the turbulent postcollege environment.

The BQ prototype labeled Bright Achieving Leaders yielded a rather interesting pattern of movement through the later prototypes. Apparently, the future well-being of members of this prototype was highly contingent on their adjustment to and success in college. Those individuals *who did not* move into the collegiate Adjusted Academics prototype either moved directly into the PCEI 2/4 prototype labeled Socially Maladjusted Individuals or into the collegiate Ineffective Isolates prototype and from this into the PCEI 2/4 Disappointed Laborers and Socially Maladjusted Individuals prototypes. Afterwards, individuals who followed this pattern of movement distributed themselves randomly among the PCEI 6/8 prototypes. The members of this BQ prototype who entered the CEI Adjusted Academics prototype seemed to follow one of two general patterns of movement derived from their prior pattern of behavior and experiences. First, they might have moved directly into the PCEI 6/8 Enterprising Intellectuals prototype or moved into this

PCEI 6/8 prototype after entering the PCEI 2/4 Graduate Students prototype. This pattern seems to reflect an accentuation of their earlier concern with intellectual achievement. Second, members of this prototype might have moved into the PCEI 6/8 Unambitious Townsmen or Areligious Careerists prototypes either directly from the Adjusted Academics prototype or after movement through the PCEI 2/4 Good Ole Boys prototype. Apparently, Bright Achieving Leaders who decided to emphasize social relations after a successful college experience de-emphasize their former intellectual orientation and emphasize their former social skills, leading them to enter socially oriented, rather than traditional, male prototypes in young adulthood. In examining the nature of the significant relationships obtained for this prototype, it appears that an inability to maintain their previous pattern of intellectual and social success in college leads to a difficult collegiate and postcollege experience for these individuals as they try to adjust to this change. However, when their collegiate experiences were successful, they appeared to choose to emphasize either one of the trends that were apparent in their earlier patterns, which led to relatively favorable, although divergent, outcomes.

The importance of a successful collegiate experience was also apparent in the patterns of movement that were exhibited by members of the BQ Conservative Achieving Introverts prototype. Members of this prototype who did not display some signs of collegiate academic and social success, as indexed by their entry into the CEI Adjusted Academic prototype or the PCEI 2/4 Graduate Students prototype, tended to enter the Unhappy Isolates prototype 6 to 8 years after graduation, perhaps because they failed to develop the social skills required for a satisfying adult life or because they failed to obtain the academic background required for a reasonably satisfying introverted life in adulthood. This hypothesis finds some support in the fact that those individuals who did not enter the Adjusted Academics, but did develop a more pronounced social orientation by virtue of their entry into the PCEI 2/4 Good Ole Boys prototype, tended to enter the Unambitious Townsmen and Areligious Careerists prototypes 6 to 8 years after graduation. Those individuals who were socially and academically successful in college were most likely to flow from the CEI Adjusted Academics prototype to the PCEI 2/4 Graduate Students prototype and, from there, move to the PCEI 6/8 Enterprising Intellectuals prototype, a trend that seems to reflect a maintenance of their earlier trend towards introversion and achievement, extended to the occupation domain. Some individuals who had entered the Adjusted Academics prototype moved into the PCEI 6/8 Enterprising Intellectuals prototype without the intervening Graduate Student status. However, some members of this prototype, flowing through the

Adjusted Academics prototype but not the Graduate Students prototype, also entered the Unambitious Townsmen prototype, either directly or after entry into the PCEI 2/4 Good Ole Boys prototype. Alternatively, these individuals might have entered the Good Ole Boys prototype and, from there, moved into the Areligious Careerists prototype. Although these later patterns of movement after entry into the CEI Adjusted Academics prototype again appear to reflect the development of a traditional social orientation, perhaps as a result of favorable college experiences, it is also clear that further postgraduation schooling had a strong effect on these individuals, ensuring entry into the Enterprising Intellectuals prototype, which might or might not have occurred without this experience.

Members of the BQ Rebellious Nonachievers prototype tended to flow into the CEI Fraternity Member prototype, and individuals having this college experience tended to enter the PCEI 6/8 Areligious Careerists prototype. This is a rather surprising pattern of movement that reflects a transformation of a previous rebellious pattern into a pattern of traditional social behavior with college entry, and this pattern appears to be maintained in young adulthood. Although it is rather difficult to tease apart these relationships in a way that will allow a clear-cut specification of the underlying cause of the transformation, it seems reasonable to conclude that the earlier rebellion might have reflected a search for attention that was fulfilled by fraternity membership in a conservative college environment or rebellion against overbearing parents. Although members of the Rebellious Nonachievers prototype did not flow into any other CEI prototype, they did tend to directly enter the PCEI 2/4 Good Ole Boys and Early Maturers prototypes. Both of these relationships reflect movement into traditionally socially oriented prototypes in a later developmental period, favoring the attention explanation because these individuals would have been removed from direct parental control for some time. Individuals entering the Good Ole Boys prototype tended to enter the PCEI 6/8 Unambitious Townsmen prototype, reflecting a maintenance of a traditional social orientation and a lack of concern with achievement. On the other hand, individuals entering the Early Maturers prototype did not systematically enter any PCEI 6/8 prototype, perhaps because the emergence of the achievement orientation characteristics of this prototype led to sufficient change to make further prediction difficult. Interestingly, it appears that the emergence of a traditional social orientation among members of this prototype during different developmental periods led to different long-term outcomes in terms of membership in the PCEI 6/8 prototypes.

Those individuals who were initially assigned to the male BQ prototype labeled Concretely Oriented Achievers followed a pattern that was similar to the Rebellious Nonachievers. Membership in this prototype was not systematically related to membership in any of the CEI prototypes. However, members of this prototype did tend to enter the PCEI 2/4 Early Maturers prototype, as might have been expected given the fact that a concern with concrete achievement should lead to early movement into young adulthood. The loss of this advantage as the members of other prototypes adapted the pragmatic views of adulthood may account for the fact that these individuals did not systematically enter any PCEI 6/8 prototype. However, members of this prototype who followed an alternative developmental path tended to enter the PCEI 2/4 Good Ole Boys prototype and, from there, flow into the PCEI 6/8 Unambitious Townsmen and Areligious Careerists prototypes. This result appears to reflect the emergence of a more traditional social orientation and a corresponding de-emphasis of achievement concerns among individuals who followed this pattern.

The final male prototype that yielded significant relationships was the BQ prototype labeled Nonconformist Dropouts. These individuals appeared to follow one of three major patterns of movement through the later prototypes. In the first of these, individuals did not enter any particular collegiate prototype, but did move directly into the PCEI 2/4 Early Maturers prototypes and then distributed themselves among the PCEI 6/8 prototypes. This result might be attributed to the tendency of an independent, somewhat rebellious individual to see more of the world and grow up more rapidly than peers. Individuals who followed the second major pathway had a rather negative college experience, entering the Ineffective Isolates prototype in college, perhaps due to the maintenance of their prior pattern of nonconformity and withdrawal. These individuals, in turn, had rather negative postcollege experiences, as indexed by their movement into the PCEI 2/4 Socially Maladjusted Individuals and Disappointed Laborers prototypes and their subsequent entry into the PCEI 6/8 prototypes in a non-systematic fashion. Apparently, these difficult college experiences and the continued withdrawal and rebellion of prototype members left them poorly prepared to deal with the occupational world, and although this pattern eventually changed under the pressure of the demands to adapt to the requirements of young adulthood, such changes did not occur in a systematic fashion. In the third general pattern, members of the BQ prototype entered the Dependent Womanizer CEI prototype and, from this, moved into the PCEI 2/4 prototypes labeled Unconventional Intellectuals and Good Ole Boys. Whereas the individuals who entered the Unconventional Intellectuals prototype did not enter any particular PCEI 6/8 prototype, individuals who entered the Good Ole Boys prototype tended to enter the PCEI 6/8 prototypes labeled Unambitious

Townsmen and Areligious Careerists. It appears that individuals who followed this pattern began to develop a somewhat more traditional social orientation in college by virtue of contact with the opposite sex. If this pattern was maintained in the postcollege years, they tended to flow through the more traditional socially oriented prototypes; otherwise they returned to their precollege behavior pattern and changed thereafter in an apparently unsystematic fashion.

Relationships Among the Female Prototypes

Figure 7.2 presents a schematic overview of the significant relationships among the prototypes obtained in the BQ-based probability analysis. The nature of the results presented in this table are identical to those presented in Fig. 7.1 in the sense that they reflect relationships significant at the $p \leq .01$ level and positive transition probabilities originating from a single BQ prototype. As may be seen in Fig. 7.2, not all of the female BQ prototypes were associated with a systematic pattern of movement through the later prototypes. However, significant relationships were obtained for 13 of the 15 female prototypes, and, in the ensuing discussion, an attempt is made to lay out the content and meaning of these relationships.

In this analysis, it was found that members of the female BQ prototype labeled Well-Adjusted Achievers tended to follow one of two major developmental pathways. Members of this BQ prototype tended to enter the PCEI 6/8 Realistic Mature Adults and the PCEI 2/4 Religious Copers prototypes. Whereas the former relationship may be viewed as reflecting a maintenance of past trends, the latter relationship seems to reflect a transformation, perhaps attributable to the inability of these females to adjust to the difficulties that are inherent in the postcollege environment and their use of religion as a coping mechanism. Those females who followed the second major pathway tended to enter the CEI Married Students prototype during college. Subsequently, these individuals moved into either the Unprepared Underemployeds or the Religious Copers PCEI 2/4 prototypes and distributed themselves randomly among the PCEI 6/8 prototypes. Apparently, early marriage has some impact on the developmental paths followed by members of this BQ prototype.

Members of the BQ Extraverted Materialistic Authoritarians prototype tended to enter the CEI Traditional Daters prototype, as might have been expected given their earlier focus on social success and interest in the opposite sex. From here, these individuals were likely to move into the PCEI 6/8 Community-Directed Housewives and Realistic

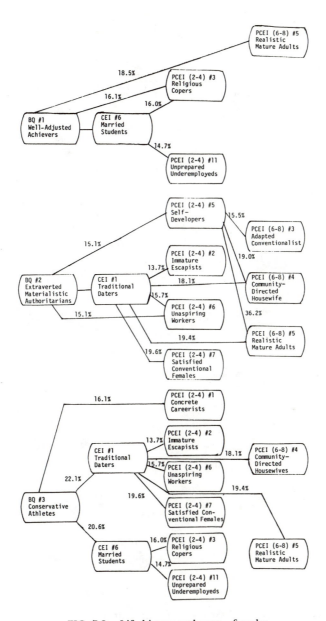

FIG. 7.2. Life history pathways—females

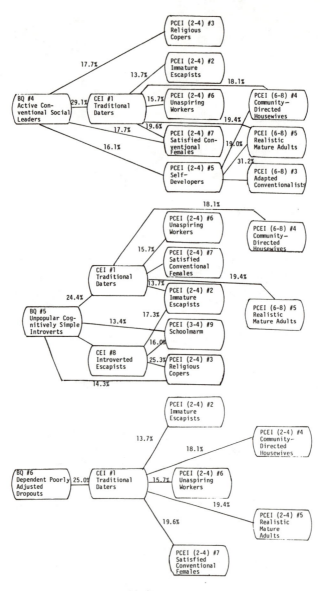

FIG. 7.2. Cont.

Mature Adults PCEI 6/8 prototype, without any intervening PCEI 2/4 prototype membership, a result that reflects the same traditional social orientation. Members of this BQ prototype who entered the CEI Traditional Daters prototype also tended to flow into the PCEI 2/4 Immature Escapists, Unaspiring Workers, and Satisfied Conventional Females pro-

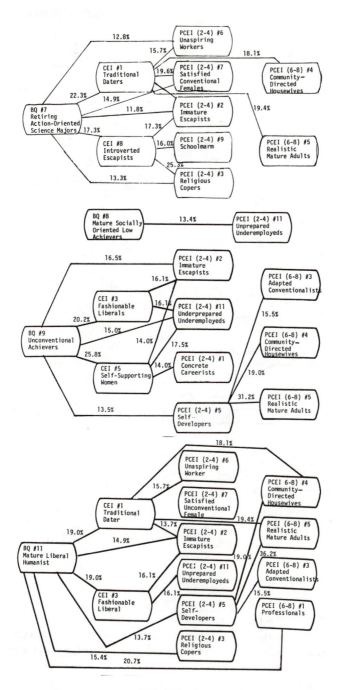

FIG. 7.2. Cont.

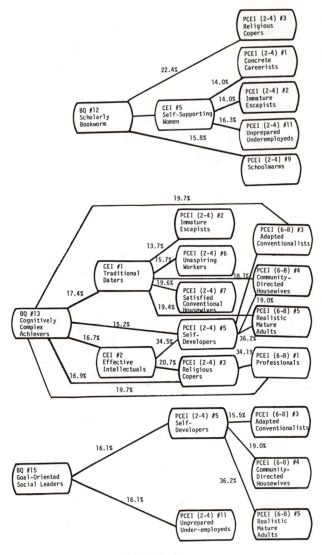

FIG. 7.2.   Cont.

totypes, and then distribute themselves randomly among the PCEI 6/8
prototypes. This pattern of movement reflects the maintenance of their
collegiate traditional dating orientation in the postcollege environment
and its potential consequences during movement into the adult world.
The Extraverted Materialistic Authoritarians who did not enter the CEI
Traditional Daters prototype tended to enter the PCEI 2/4 Self-Developers prototype and, from there, move into the PCEI 6/8 Adapted Con-

ventionalists, Community-Directed Housewives, and Realistic Mature Adults prototypes, reflecting a maintenance of their earlier traditional and rather concrete social orientation. Apparently, membership in the Traditional Daters prototype could bode well or poorly for these females, depending on their ability to move past the orientation in the postcollege environment, and when they expanded themselves in the postcollege years, the long-term outcomes were especially likely to be favorable.

Members of the BQ prototype labeled Conservative Athletes tended to follow one of three distinct patterns of movement through the later prototypes, all of which appeared to center around different kinds of contact with males. First, a number of these females entered the Married Students prototype in college. Subsequently, they moved into the PCEI 2/4 Religious Copers and Unprepared Underemployeds PCEI 2/4 prototypes and then scattered themselves among the PCEI 6/8 prototype. Again, this pattern seems to reflect the outcomes of early marriage for rather traditional females. In the second pathway, instead of early marriage, members of this prototype tended to enter the CEI Traditional Daters prototype. Six to 8 years after graduation, this traditional social orientation led them to enter the Community-Directed Housewives and Realistic Mature Adults prototype. Those individuals entering the CEI Traditional Daters prototype also tended to enter the PCEI 2/4 Immature Escapists, Unaspiring Workers, and Satisfied Conventional Females prototypes and, from there, distribute themselves randomly among the PCEI 6/8 prototypes. This latter pattern of movement from the Traditional Daters prototype seems to reflect the outcomes associated with an attempt to rigidly maintain this hyperfeminine pattern in the difficult postcollege years. Finally, the females who did not enter the CEI prototypes moved directly into the PCEI 2/4 Constrained Careerists prototype and then distributed themselves randomly among the PCEI 6/8 prototypes.

Members of the Active Conventional Social Leaders BQ prototype were likely to enter CEI Traditional Daters prototype. These individuals then tended to move into either the PCEI 6/8 Community-Directed Housewives and Realistic Mature Adults prototype or the PCEI 2/4 Immature Escapists, Unaspiring Workers, and Satisfied Conventional Females prototypes. Although this pattern of movement seems to reflect an orientation towards traditional social behavior, once again there appeared to be some females who could successfully employ this pattern in the postcollege years and some females whom it led into difficulty in the period immediately following graduation. Members of this prototype who did not enter the Traditional Daters prototype were not characterized by any particular pattern of behaviors and experiences during the college years. However, in the postcollege years, they appeared to follow one of two contrasting pathways. In the first of these, prototype members capitalized on the energy and social skills they had exhibited earlier and entered the PCEI 2/4 Self-Developers prototype. From here, they moved into the PCEI 6/8 Community-Directed Housewives, Realistic Mature Adults, and Adapted Conventionalists prototypes, reflecting a maintenance of their orientation towards traditional social enjoyment. In the alternative pathway, some prototype members moved directly into the PCEI 2/4 Religious Copers prototype and then distributed themselves among the PCEI 6/8 prototypes. Although the reasons for this pattern of movement are unclear, it is possible that it reflects some difficulty in adapting to the demands of the postcollege environment and the use of religion as a coping mechanism, rather than as a means of self-development.

The individuals who had been assigned to the BQ prototype labeled Unpopular Cognitively Simple Introverts tended to follow one of two major pathways. A number of members of this prototype maintained their prior pattern of behavior and experiences during the college years, as indexed by their entry into the CEI Introverted Escapists prototype. This rather negative and limiting set of experiences led these females to enter the PCEI 2/4 Immature Escapists, Schoolmarms, and Religious Copers prototypes and distribute themselves in an unsystematic fashion among the PCEI 6/8 prototypes. Apparently, the maintenance of this initial pattern led to some difficulties in the lives of these individuals. Alternatively, some females changed their initial pattern during the college years and entered the CEI Traditional Daters prototype. This emergence of a traditional social orientation had some long-term effects, as was apparent in the tendency of these individuals to enter the PCEI 6/8 Community-Directed Housewives and Realistic Mature Adults prototypes.

A similar set of pathways was obtained for those females assigned to the BQ Dependent Poorly Adjusted Dropouts prototype. These individuals did not systematically enter any CEI prototypes except the CEI Traditional Daters prototype. This emergence of a traditional social orientation, in turn, led a number of prototype members to enter the PCEI 6/8 Community-Directed Housewives and Realistic Mature Adults prototypes. Otherwise, these individuals tended to enter the PCEI 2/4 Immature Escapists, Unaspiring Workers, and Satisfied Conventional Female prototypes and distribute themselves randomly among the PCEI 6/8 prototypes. Again, it appears that if this emergent social orientation could not be adjusted to the demands of the post college environment, it led to some difficulties.

Members of the BQ Retiring Action-Oriented Science Majors prototype followed a somewhat more complex set of pathways through the later prototypes. A number of these individuals tended to enter the CEI Introverted Escapists prototype. Subsequently, they moved into the PCEI 2/4 Immature Escapists, Schoolmarms, and Religious Copers prototypes, although they did not systematically enter any PCEI 6/8 prototype. Thus, this introverted pattern apparently led to some difficulty during the college and postcollege years and later lack of predictability. Moreover, a maintenance of introverted tendencies and their impact on postcollege prototype membership may account for the tendency of some members of the BQ prototype to directly enter the PCEI 2/4 Immature Escapists and Religious Copers prototypes. On the other hand, those females who developed a more traditional social orientation in college, as evidenced by their entry into the CEI Traditional Daters prototype, tended to follow a rather different set of pathways. Either the newly emergent social orientation was effectively employed following graduation, leading to entry into the PCEI 6/8 Community-Directed Housewives and Realistic Mature Adults prototypes, or they had some difficulty in adjusting the orientation to the demands of the postcollege environment and entered the PCEI 2/4 Immature Escapists, Unaspiring Workers, and Satisfied Conventional Females prototypes. Apparently, collegiate social enjoyment had a powerful effect on the developmental pathways that might be followed by these individuals.

The BQ Mature Socially Oriented Low Achievers prototype yielded only one significant relationship. Some members of this prototype tended to enter the PCEI 2/4 prototype labeled Unprepared Underemployeds. This relationship seems to reflect little more than a natural outcome of their earlier lack of concern with academic and occupational achievement and its implication for initial job opportunities.

Members of the BQ Unconventional Achievers prototype followed a much more complex set of pathways. Some of these individuals did not enter any particular CEI prototype but flowed directly into the PCEI 2/4 Self-Developers prototype, which reflected a continuation of the earlier pattern of behavior and experiences in a manner that was congruent with the concrete social demands of the postcollege period. This change in emphasis, in turn, led prototype members to enter the traditional socially oriented PCEI 6/8 Adapted Conventionalists, Community-Directed Housewives, and Realistic Mature Adults prototype. Alternatively, these females entered the CEI Fashionable Liberals and Self-Supporting Women prototypes. Both of these relationships seem to reflect a continuation of their earlier active independent lifestyle, one emphasizing work and the other social involvement. Some individuals who employed work during this period continued this trend, as indexed by their exclusion entry into the PCEI 2/4 Constrained Careerists prototype. On the other hand, others entered the PCEI 2/4 Unprepared Under-employeds and Immature Escapists prototypes along with those individuals flowing through the CEI Fashionable Liberals prototype and a number of Unconventional Achievers who did not enter any particular CEI prototype. Apparently, members of this BQ prototype who remained nontraditional and did not emphasize work had some difficulty in adjusting to the demands of the postcollege environment.

A complex pattern of pathways was also obtained for members of the BQ Mature Liberal Humanists prototype. Members of this prototype who did not adopt any particular pattern of collegiate behavior and experiences tended to enter the PCEI 2/4 Immature Escapists and Religious Copers prototypes and then distribute themselves among the PCEI 6/8 prototypes, suggesting that these individuals had some difficulty in adapting to the demands of the postcollege environment, particularly demands made by occupations. Mature Liberal Humanists who did not enter a CEI prototype also entered the PCEI 6/8 Professionals prototype and the PCEI 2/4 Self-Developers prototype. From the Self-Developers prototype, the individuals tended to enter the PCEI 6/8 Community Directed Housewives, Realistic Mature Adults, and Adapted Conventionalists prototype. Apparently, the emergence of a traditional social orientation following college led these females to enter analogous prototypes 6 to 8 years after graduation, and if this trend did not emerge, it was possible for these females to move into the Professional prototype, which appeared to reflect a likely outcome of their earlier intellectual orientation. Members of this BQ prototype tended to enter the CEI Fashionable Liberals and Traditional Daters prototypes. The former pathway led to negative postcollege outcomes, as indexed by their tendency to enter the PCEI 2/4 Immature Escapists and Unprepared Underemployeds prototypes, perhaps because this trend did not facilitate entry into the occupational world. Those females entering the Traditional Daters prototype tended to enter either the PCEI 6/8 Community-Directed Housewives and Realistic Mature Adults prototype or the PCEI 2/4 Immature Escapists, Satisfied Conventional Females, and Unaspiring Workers prototypes. This pattern seems to reflect the acceptance of a traditional feminine role that was either effectively maintained and modified to fit the demands of young adulthood or that led to some difficulty when the passivity and dependency inherent in this orientation had to be adapted to the demands of the occupational arena in the postcollege period.

Members of the BQ Scholarly Bookworms prototype who did not enter any particular CEI prototype tended to enter the PCEI 2/4 Religious Copers and Schoolmarms prototypes. This result seems to reflect a continuation of their previous rather passive and introverted intellectual orientation. This pattern did not appear especially enduring, because it was not systematically related to entry into any of the PCEI 6/8 prototypes. The members of this BQ prototype who entered a discrete CEI prototype tended to become Self-Supporting Women. This pattern of collegiate life had a marked impact on the later behavior and experiences of these individuals, in the sense that they tended to enter the PCEI 2/4 Concrete Careerists, Immature Escapists, and Unprepared Underemployed prototypes, rather than the PCEI 2/4 Religious Copers and Schoolmarms prototypes. However, membership in these groups did not predict pathways into the PCEI 6/8 prototypes. Thus, it appears that it is difficult to predict the status of these females in young adulthood.

The BQ Cognitively Complex Achievers who did not enter any of the CEI prototypes tended to enter the PCEI 6/8 Adapted Conventionalists and Professionals prototypes. Whereas the latter relationship reflects a likely outcome of their emphasis on intellectual achievement, the former seems to reflect a modification of this earlier trend, perhaps as a result of their acceptance of the traditional feminine role. Some support for this hypothesis may be found in the tendency of the Cognitively Complex Achievers to enter two rather contrasting collegiate prototypes: the CEI Traditional Daters and Effective Intellectuals prototypes. The individuals who adapted a traditional feminine role pattern and more social orientation tended to flow into the PCEI 6/8 Community-Directed Housewives and Realistic Mature Adults prototypes, suggesting an effective accommodation of this pattern to the demands of adulthood. Other individuals who entered the Traditional Daters prototype tended to flow into the PCEI 2/4 Immature Escapists, Unaspiring Workers, and Satisfied Conventional Females prototypes. Again, it appears that these individuals had some difficulty in incorporating this traditional role orientation into the demands of the postcollege years, and so it is not surprising that they did not systematically enter any PCEI 6/8 prototype. Members of this BQ prototype who entered the CEI Effective Intellectuals prototype tended to flow into the PCEI 2/4 Self-Developers and Religious Copers prototypes. Movement into the Self-Developers prototype apparently reflected a belated, and perhaps better-timed, emergence of a traditional social orientation, and it was associated with movement into the PCEI 6/8 Adapted Conventionalists, Community-Directed Housewives, and Realistic Mature Adults prototypes. However, those females who moved from the Effective Intellectuals to the Religious Copers prototype tended to enter the PCEI 6/8 Professionals prototype. This pattern of movement suggests some conflict in the postcollege years between intellectual concerns and a traditional role orientation in which religion served as an intervening coping mechanism followed by reassertion of their intellectual concerns and movement into professional occupations.

The last female BQ prototype that yielded significant relationships in the chi-square analysis was labeled Goal-Oriented Social Leaders. Members of this BQ prototype tended to follow one of two divergent pathways. The individuals did not systematically enter any CEI prototype, but tended to flow directly into either the PCEI 2/4 Self-Developers prototype or the PCEI 2/4 Unprepared Underemployed prototype. The reaffirmation of the earlier traditional social orientation apparent in entry into the Self-Developers prototype led them to enter the PCEI 6/8 Adapted Conventionalists, Community-Directed Housewives, and Realistic Mature Adults prototypes. Individuals who entered the Unprepared Underemployed prototype appeared to have lost their initial goal orientation to social concerns, leading to some difficulty in the postcollege years and random movement into the PCEI 6/8 prototypes.

Follow-Up Analyses

After having reviewed the results obtained in these initial chi-square analyses, it seemed necessary to conduct two sets of follow-up analyses to confirm and extend the findings obtained in this phase of the study. One of these analyses entailed extending the basic chi-square procedure by following the movement of the members of each CEI prototype through the PCEI 2/4 and PCEI 6/8 prototypes, and the movement of the members of each PCEI 2/4 prototype through the PCEI 6/8 prototypes. This analysis was carried out in the hope of obtaining some additional evidence pointing to the stability of the relationships identified in the BQ-based chi-square analyses. Neither time nor space permits a detailed review of the results obtained in this adjunct analysis. Nevertheless, it should be noted that the results obtained in this analysis did tend to confirm the general pattern of movement identified in the BQ-based chi-square analysis. Although, of course, some differences were observed, as might be expected given the use of different samples and starting points, on the whole there was sufficient overlap to argue for the stability and validity of the foregoing relationship and, especially, the more general conclusions drawn from these relationships.

Having obtained some evidence of the stability and meaningfulness of the results produced by the initial chi-square analyses, it becomes appropriate to ask a second question in the follow-up analysis; that is: Were there any systematic differences between the members of the prototypes who did and did not follow predictable paths of individual development. To answer this question, four sets of two criterion group discriminant analyses were conducted for the members of each sex group, in which the prototypes that displayed significant ($p \leq .01$) systematic patterns of movement in the chi-square analyses examining adjacent developmental periods were contrasted with the prototypes that did not display significant patterns of movement. The first such analyses employed scores on the BQ summary dimensions as predictors of membership in the BQ prototypes that did and did not systematically enter the CEI prototypes, and the second set of these analyses employed scores on the marker variables as predictors of membership on the BQ prototypes that did and did not systematically enter the CEI prototypes. In the third set of discriminant analyses, the CEI summary dimensions served as predictors of membership in the CEI prototypes that did and did not systematically enter at least one PCEI 2/4 prototype. The final set of discriminant analyses contrasted the PCEI 2/4 prototypes that did and did not display significant patterns of movement into at least one PCEI 6/8 prototype in terms of their scores on the PCEI 2/4 summary dimensions. The discriminant analyses were based on a stepwise procedure. Further, because of the substantial statistical power afforded by the number of subjects available for each of these analyses, cut points for the inclusion of predictors were established on the basis of the inflection point of the F value resulting from the stepwise discriminant analyses.

Among the males, the results of the first discriminant analyses indicated that eight dimensions should be retained as discriminating the 4,565 predictable and 1,061 unpredictable prototype members. It was found that the predictable individuals were discriminated from the unpredictable, in order of entry, by having higher Religious Activity, more Positive Academic Attitudes, greater tendencies toward Social Desirability, lower Sibling Friction, higher Athletic Interest, higher Academic Achievement, lower Social Introversion, and lower Intellectualism. Among the marker variables, five scales were retained as discriminating among the 647 predictable and 328 unpredictable prototype members for whom the information was available. In order of entry, it was found that predictable males were differentiated from the unpredictable by a lack of Negative Emotionality, better high school GPAs, more pronounced trends towards Extroversion, less frequent expression of Cognitive Goals, and less Conceptual Simplicity. In sum, the foregoing results suggest that members of the BQ prototypes who followed predictable developmental pathways tended to be bright, socially constrained, outgoing individuals who were not especially inclined towards purely intellectual pursuits.

Comparison of the 838 members of the CEI prototypes who followed predictable paths into the PCEI 2/4 prototypes with the 427 members of the CEI prototypes who did not follow predictable paths indicated that three dimensions should be retained as having substantial discriminating power. On the male CEI summary dimensions, it was found that predictable, as opposed to unpredictable, individuals tended to be healthy, sociable, and conservative. In contrasting the 1,057 members of the PCEI 2/4 prototypes who flowed into at least one PCEI 6/8 prototype with 417 males who were members of prototypes that did not yield significant relationships, three dimensions were retained. The results of this analysis indicated that predictable as opposed to unpredictable males were higher on College-Moderated Social Development, Extra-Occupational Satisfaction, and Early Occupational Success. Apparently, predictable males in these later developmental periods were conservative, healthy, and socially and occupationally effective individuals.

In contrasting the 4,203 females who followed predictable pathways from the BQ to the CEI prototypes with 152 females who were members of nonpredictable prototypes in terms of their scores on the BQ summary dimension, it was found that eight dimensions should be retained. On these dimensions, it was found that predictable, as opposed to unpredictable, females tended to display greater Warmth of Maternal Relationships, lower Socioeconomic Status, lower Popularity with the Opposite Sex, lower Social Maturity, higher Warmth of Parental Relationships, lower Scientific Interests, higher Athletic Participation, and higher Parental Control. On the marker variables, it was found that seven scales differentiated the 832 females who were members of prototypes following predictable pathways from the 68 females who were members of prototypes not following significant pathways from the BQ and CEI prototypes. The predictable females were distinguished from the unpredictable females by higher scores on Socioreligious Conformity, lower SAT-Math scores, lower Scientific Interest, higher Teaching Interest, lower scores on Negative Emotionality, and lower scores of Neuroticism. Overall, these results suggest that predictable females during this period are well-adjusted adolescents from warm, protective families that have encouraged their daughters to accept a traditional feminine role.

Comparison of the 825 members of the CEI prototypes who displayed predictable patterns of movement into the PCEI 2/4 prototypes with the 379 females who were members of prototypes that did not yield significant pathways yielded four discriminating dimensions. Further inspection of the data indicated that predictable, as opposed to unpredictable, females tended to have more Positive College Experiences, higher Religious Involvement, better Health, and lower Athletic Participation. In examining the PCEI 2/4 summary dimensions that discriminated the 1,163 females who were members of prototypes that followed predictable pathways from the 198 females who were members of prototypes that did not follow a predictable pattern of movement from the PCEI 2/4 to the PCEI 6/8 prototype, two dimensions yielded meaningful discrimination. It was found that predictable, as opposed to unpredictable, females had lower scores on the Rudimentary People-Oriented Jobs dimension and higher scores on the College-Moderated Social Development dimension. Thus, predictable females in these later developmental periods appeared more likely to have favorable college experiences, display good health, and display a religious and rather traditional pattern of behavior.

The results laid out heretofore led to two general conclusions. First, it appears that more dimensions emerged in contrasting predictable and unpredictable individuals across the BQ and CEI periods than in the later developmental periods. Second, across developmental periods, a rather consistent picture of the predictable male and female emerged. Apparently, predictable males and females came from warm, relatively secure family backgrounds, were well adjusted, and socially and occupationally effective. They also appeared to be conservative individuals who accepted traditional roles, and although they were bright and outgoing, they were not markedly concerned with intellectual matters in adolescence and college. In sum, they appeared to be rather traditional, well-adjusted individuals. This conclusion is consistent with results obtained in Block's (1971) study of changers and nonchangers, which indicated that better-adjusted individuals were less likely to change over time. It should also be noted that the general conclusion bears a close correspondence to the results obtained in the chi-square analyses and the interpretations applied to them. It confirms the earlier finding that individuals who had some difficulty in adjusting to the demands made by the environment in a developmental period often changed in a nonsystematic fashion, limiting later predictability. Finally, these results suggest that an early acceptance of traditional social norms, along with a favorable family background that encourages the acceptance of these norms, may be an important factor in determining the stability of an individual's developmental trajectory.

PROTOTYPE CONCLUSIONS

Perhaps the most straightforward conclusion that may be drawn from the results obtained in the sequential analyses of prototype membership pertains to the validity of the prototypical descriptions of individuality. Typically, the movement of the BQ prototypes through the CEI, PCEI 2/4, and PCEI 6/8 prototypes was readily interpretable. This suggests that the prototypes provided a meaningful description of individuality, and so may be said to display some construct validity. Some additional evidence that points to the validity of these descriptions of individuality may be found in the content of the significant relationships observed in the chi-square analyses that employed the CEI and PCEI 2/4 prototypes as points of origin.

The significant relationships observed in these analyses lead to a number of general conclusions. Across the various BQ prototypes, certain consistent patterns of movement appeared to emerge in two or more different BQ prototypes. The existence of these overriding patterns suggests that there might be systematic differences between the predictable and unpredictable prototypes in various developmental periods. However, the most important implication of the results is that they indicate that individual development occurs in a systematic fashion.

Support for the two preceding conclusions was obtained in the discriminant analyses that contrasted the members of predictable and unpredictable prototypes across adjacent developmental periods in terms of their scores on the relevant summary dimensions and marker variables. It appears that predictable individuals are effective and well adjusted and that unpredictability and nonsystematic change occurs when adjustment and effectiveness are not maintained in a given developmental period. In the chi-square analyses, random movement among the later prototypes was often associated with difficulties in the preceding developmental period. Although the limitations of the cross-sectional dimensions for reflecting aspects of individuality of developmental significance must be considered in evaluating this conclusion, it appears that predictability is not an absolute phenomenon, but one that is contingent on further developmental experiences. Apparently, certain kinds of individuals are predictable between certain points in their lives, depending on the nature of their current and prior patterns of behavior and experiences and their consequences in a given environment.

To this point in the discussion, we have focused on elucidating certain general trends in the sequential results, and this may have led to the impression that the relationships obtained in these analyses were relatively straightforward and consistent across individuals. Although it is clear that some generalities exist, it is also true that the most striking conclusion that emerged from the sequential analysis is that the systematic patterns of movement through the prototypes were such that an individual's status at one time does not clearly determine his or her status at a later time. Rather, it appears that movement through the prototypes, and individual development as it is indexed by movement through the prototypes, reflects a systematic change in and maintenance of prior differential characteristics. This is to say that behavior and experiences in later developmental periods across the prototypes are not selected nor do they occur at random; instead, they reflect a particular kind of individual's attempt to relate past patterns to his or her current situation. However, the current situation has its own effects on the nature of individuality, leading to change as well as complex genotypic consistencies in the course of individual development.

This rather broad overview of the results obtained in the sequential analyses of prototype membership has some interesting implications. First, it suggests that individual development is a complex event in which different starting points may lead to the same end points, and different end points may be arrived at from a common origin, depending on the intervening pattern of behavior and experiences. This conclusion was illustrated by the results obtained in the various chi-square analyses. For instance, the females assigned to the BQ prototype labeled Bright Cognitively Complex Achievers could arrive at such different end points as the PCEI 6/8 Professionals and Community-Directed Housewives prototypes, due to different intervening patterns of behavior and experiences. Second, the foregoing conclusions suggest that an individual's pattern of behaviors and experiences during a given developmental period, when coupled with earlier characteristics, will selectively open and close further avenues of potential development. Again, this conclusion was illustrated by the results obtained in the chi-square analyses, and a case in point may be found in the BQ Bright Achieving Leaders prototype. The males assigned to this prototype who did not enter into the PCEI Adjusted Academics prototype did not enter the PCEI 6/8 prototype labeled Enterprising Intellectuals. Third, the specific later effects of even common patterns of behavior or experiences appeared to be dependent on the particular pattern of past behavior and experiences possessed by the individual. An example may be found in the paths of the Mature Liberal Humanities and the Cognitively Complex Achievers. The former who became Traditional Daters in college might enter the PCEI 6/8 Community-Directed Housewives and Realistic Mature Adults, whereas the latter who became Traditional Daters in college might enter the Community-Directed Housewives, Realistic Mature Adults, and Adapted Conventionalists PCEI 6/8 prototypes.

It was also apparent that the behavior and experiences that occurred in some developmental periods were more important to the development of individuality in some prototype members than others. For instance, continued academic and social success in college, indexed by membership in the Adjusted Academic CEI prototype, was critical to favorable developmental outcomes for members of the BQ Bright Achieving Leaders prototype, and a poor college experience, as indexed by membership in the Ineffective Isolates CEI prototype, led to rather negative outcomes, such as membership in the PCEI 2/4 Disappointed Laborers and Socially Maladjusted Individuals prototypes. On the other hand, collegiate behaviors and experiences appeared to have little impact on the development paths followed by members of the BQ Traditional Science-Oriented Achieving Leaders and Analytical Adapters prototypes. These observations suggest that there may be certain sensitive periods during which developmental change is likely to occur and in which certain types of behavior and experiences can have profound impact on the future course of an individual's life. However, the nature of these periods and the relevant behavior and experiences appears to be dependent on the particular kind of individual under consideration. Finally, the outcomes of a particular pattern of behavior or experience also appear to vary with the individual's current stage of development, due to differences in prior patterns. A case in point may be found in the fact that the emergence of a traditional social orientation among members of the BQ Rebellious Nonachievers prototype led to membership in different PCEI 6/8 prototypes, depending on whether it first became apparent during college or in the postcollege years.

Another outcome of the sequential analysis was the conclusion that individual development is a multipotential phenomenon. One aspect of this multipotentiality is that a variety of different pathways may be followed to the same end point even by members of the same initial prototype. An example of this phenomenon may be found in the fact that the Traditional Science-Oriented Achieving Leaders might enter the PCEI 6/8 Areligious Careerists prototype through either the Adjusted Academics or Fraternity Members CEI prototype. A second aspect of this multipotentiality is apparent in that the developmental change can occur by individuals employing one or another pre-existing trend in a new environment. The tendency of some female Unconventional Achievers to emphasize independence and some liberal social involvement during college reflects a selective utilization of pre-existing characteristics that led to highly divergent outcomes. A third aspect of this multipotentiality may be found in the tendency of certain events, which are sometimes beyond the individual's control, to have a marked, systematic effect on individual development in some prototypes during some developmental periods. The apparent effect of early marriage on the female Conservative Athletes and male Farm Boys prototypes provides an example of this kind of change, as does the importance of an unsuccessful collegiate career on the lives of the Bright Achieving Leaders.

In sum, the results obtained in the sequential analyses of prototype membership indicate that, in attempting to describe individuality and individual development, one must be cognizant of the existence and importance of developmental change and the ongoing nature of individual development. However, ample evidence has been provided in the preceding discussion that suggests that such changes occur in a systematic fashion, contingent on the individual's prior pattern of behavior and experiences. The existence and pervasiveness of these complex, yet optimistic, modifications in the nature of individuality and individual development argue for a more sophisticated conception of the phenomenon that is capable of capturing genotypic consistencies. The importance of genotypic consistencies suggests that cross-sectional summary descriptions and sequential analyses are not ideal tools for the summary description of individuality and individual development for two reasons. First, they do not incorporate cross-time genotypic consistencies into the summary description, and second, they may ignore important qualitative differences in the nature of systematic transformations over time. Moreover, cross-sectional analyses may not identify or give appropriate weight to the dimensions that best describe individuality over time. As a result of these considerations, a fully adequate summary description of individuality and individual development will require an alternative methodology to that employed in the cross-sectional and sequential analyses.

8

The Composite Summary Dimensions

Although a variety of conclusions concerning the nature of individuality and individual development were formulated on the basis of the results obtained in the sequential study, three of these conclusions were particularly important. First, the summary descriptions that most aptly describe individuality at a single point in time are not necessarily those that provide the most effective description of individuality over time. Second, individuality appears to emerge in a complex fashion over the course of a person's development. More specifically, change occurs in a systematic and integrated fashion that is specific to particular kinds of individuals and the environmental conditions to which they were exposed. Finally, it appears that the systematic patterns of genotypic transformation that are tied to the nature of a given prototype are not especially amenable to assessment through the more traditional approaches to describing human individuality. This brings us to the question of how summary descriptions of human individuality that are capable of capturing the complex, ongoing interchange might be constructed. It has been pointed out that a variety of models are available that might be used in attempts to describe human individuality. Further, some evidence was offered that suggested that the prototype model might have particular value in an effort along these lines, but it has not received a great deal of attention in the developmental literature. The prototype model makes relatively few assumptions concerning the nature of individuality and individual development. Instead, a general description of individuality is formulated by grouping together individuals who display similar patterns of behavior and experiences and by assigning individuals through their profiles to a particular modal pattern of differential behavior and experiences. Of course, the behavior and experiences incorporated in defining the modal patterns could be collected in different developmental periods, and so the prototype model could be extended to provide a summary description of individuality in development.

A wide variety of considerations argue for the utility of the composite prototypes, constructed on the basis of longitudinal data measuring prior behaviors and experiences over time, in attempts to characterize human individuality and individual development. For instance, composite prototypes can yield a valid description of individuality only to the extent that there are some significant and systematic similarities and differences among individuals at various points in their lives. Moreover, the evidence reviewed in the preceding chapters, which points to the systematic nature of individual development, provided substantial support for the appropriateness of this assumption and the potential utility of the composite prototypes. Moreover, the approach appears to be capable of summarizing systematic changes that occur over time and the multipotentiality induced by these changes. When descriptive information has been collected at a number of points in an individual's life, it is clear that any changes in the nature of the individual's behavior and experiences will be considered in defining the similarities and differences among individuals, and so these systematic transformations will be explicitly incorporated into the definition of individuality. Taken as a whole, the preceding comments suggest that composite prototypes might, in fact, be capable of capturing the significant empirical phenomena that characterize individual development.

The composite extension of the general prototype model offers two additional advantages that support its application in the summary description of human individuality. One of these is specifically concerned with the summary description that best describes individuality over time. Because cross-time relationships are explicitly considered in constructing the composite prototypes, it can be expected that the summary descriptions of individuality that they provide will also be those that yield better cross-time prediction. Further, by formulating prototypes on the basis of cross-time relationships, it can be expected that the summary descriptions will reflect the genotypic relationships that are of substantial importance in the systematic unfolding of individuality over time. When these observations are considered in light of the foregoing discussion, as well as the fact that the prototype model is capable of providing a reasonably general description of human individuality given the availability of the descriptive information provided by the background data measures, it would seem that a composite analysis of the descriptive information provided by the BQ, CEI, PCEI 2/4, and PCEI 6/8 background data items would provide a viable basis for formulating a general summary description of individuality and individual development through the prototype model.

A number of alternative methodological strategies might be employed in an attempt to formulate composite prototypes. Yet, for reasons described earlier, it appears that this is best accomplished by an initial principal components analysis of the descriptive information obtained from the BQ, CEI, and PCEI 6/8 items, followed by a Ward and Hook (1963) clustering of the subjects' profiles on the resulting summary dimensions. Because these composite summary dimensions provide the principal groundwork for the description of individuality through the composite prototypes, the ensuing discussion focuses on the definition of the composite summary dimensions.

DEFINITION OF THE COMPOSITE SUMMARY DIMENSIONS: OVERALL RESULTS

In order to obtain a viable summarization of the behavior and experiences of individuals at various points in their lives, the responses of the 415 males and 358 female members of the longitudinal sample to the BQ, CEI, and PCEI 6/8 items were combined to form two supramatrices. Subsequently, the complete set of male and female item responses were subjected to a principal components analysis. An inspection of the plot of eigenvalues for the components indicated that either 5 or 12 dimensions would be likely to yield an effective summarization of the item data within the male subsample, and retention of either 10 or 14 dimensions would be likely to yield an effective summarization of the item data within the female subsample.

Once these potential solutions had been identified on the basis of their ability to yield an adequate description of item responses with the smallest possible number of summary dimensions, the alternative solutions obtained for each subsample were subjected to a varimax rotation to enhance the clarity and interpretability of the items loading on each dimension. Subsequently, the content of the items that yielded significant loadings on the related dimensions obtained for the alternative solutions in each subsample were identified. Three psychologists reviewed the data and concluded that, among the males, the 12-dimensions solution yielded the most meaningful and interpretable summarization of item responses; among the females, the 14-dimension solution yielded the most meaningful and interpretable summarization of item responses. Consequently, the 12-dimension solution was retained within the male subsample, and the 14-dimension solution was retained within the female subsample.

Tables 8.1 and 8.2 present an overview of the characteristics of the male 12-dimension solution and the female 14-dimension solution. More specifically, these tables represent the percentage of the total variance in item response accounted for by each dimension, the number of items yielding significant loadings ($\geq$ .30) on each dimension, the label eventually assigned to each dimension on the basis of the content of the items yielding significant loadings, and the percentage of the total variance in item responses accounted for by all of the summary dimensions identified in the retained solutions. As may be seen in Table 8.1, the summary dimensions in the male solution accounted for 33.2% of the total variance in item responses. When it is borne in mind that this percentage is based on a principal components analysis of item data, and that the resulting error variance would serve to limit the percentage of the total variance in item responses that could be accounted for under any conditions, it seems reasonable to conclude that the solution provided an adequate summarization of the item data. Some support for this conclusion may be found in the observation that less than 20% of the BQ, CEI, and PCEI 6/8 items yielded significant loadings on more than one summary dimension and that 213 of the 291 items (74%) employed in the analysis yielded significant loadings on at least one of the retained summary dimensions. Thus, it appears that the male summary dimensions provided good coverage of the item response domain.

TABLE 8.1
Male Composite Dimensions

Factor Name	% Variance Accounted For	Items Loading
1 Parental warmth and social adjustment	11.1	82
2 Professional occupational orientation	4.0	25
3 Traditional masculine role	2.6	18
4 Religious involvement	2.4	11
5 Academic achievement	2.1	18
6 Intellectual pursuits	1.9	13
7 Sociability	1.7	16
8 Socioeconomic status	1.6	10
9 Satisfaction with social life	1.5	10
10 Family conflict	1.4	10
11 Scientific/engineering interests	1.4	9
12 Occupational satisfaction	1.3	11

$N_T = 417$ Cum. 33.2

TABLE 8.2
Female Composite Dimensions

Factor Name	% Variance Accounted For	Items Loading
1 Traditional social adjustment	13.3	74
2 Job channelling	3.3	18
3 Occupational success and satisfaction	2.8	19
4 Self-esteem	2.6	13
5 Sociability	2.1	21
6 Intellectual pursuits	1.8	18
7 Scientific interests	1.7	10
8 Religious involvement	1.6	12
9 Negative parent/child conflict	1.5	8
10 Paternal identification	1.5	12
11 Socioeconomic status	1.4	10
12 Life satisfaction	1.4	11
13 Athletic interests	1.3	9
14 Sibling friction	1.2	6

$N_T = 358$ Cum. 38.6

In the female subsample, the summary dimensions incorporated in the 14-dimension solution accounted for 38.6% of the total variance in item responses. Again, it appears that the percentage is of sufficient magnitude to argue that good summarization was obtained from the 14-dimension solution within the female subsample. Significant loadings on at least one dimension were obtained for 226 of the 291 (78%) of the items involved in this analysis. Further, the finding that less than 20% of these items yielded significant loadings on more than one dimension indicates that the retained solution displayed some clarity and so might provide a valid taxonomic structure.

Aside from the statistical information pointing to the overall effectiveness of the summarization of male and female item responses accounted with the retained solutions, there are certain additional characteristics of these solutions that should be laid out. As frequently occurs with principal components analysis, the first dimension extracted in both the male and female solutions accounted for a very large share of the total item variance. The first dimension extracted in the male subsample accounted for 11.1% of the total variance, and the first dimension extracted in the female subsample accounted for 13.3% of the total variance. These dimensions were also associated with a relatively large number of significant item loadings. In the male subsample, 82 items yielded significant loadings on the first summary dimension, and in the female subsample, 74 items yielded significant loadings on the first summary dimension. Of course, these large variances accounted for figures, and the large number of items yielding significant loadings indicate the emergence of a highly complex, rather general summary dimension. Nevertheless, it should be noted that the content of the items that produced significant loadings on these dimensions were sufficiently cohesive and interpretable to allow them to be assigned brief descriptive labels. The remaining male and female summary dimensions accounted for between 1.2% to 4.0% of the variance in item responses, and 6 to 25 items produced significant loadings on any one of these remaining dimensions.

CONTENT OF THE MALE SUMMARY DIMENSIONS

Having described the overall characteristics of the solutions retained in our attempt to generate an effective summarization of the subjects' responses to the BQ, CEI, and PCEI 6/8 items, it now seems appropriate to examine the nature of these summarizations. As a result, the following section reviews the content of the items yielding significant loadings on each dimension and their implications for our understanding of these summarizations. In the course of the discussion, an attempt is made to evaluate the consistencies that emerged in the pattern of item loadings, as well as their implications for the labels eventually assigned to the various male and female summary dimensions.

The first male summary dimension derived in the principal components analysis contained 82 items drawn primarily from the BQ. Because the large number of items made it difficult to identify the underlying pattern, only those items with loadings above .60 were examined during the initial phases of the effort to describe the nature of the summary dimension. A review of the content of the items indicated that they were rather heterogeneous. However, a number of items yielding sizable loadings were found to reflect effectiveness in social and institutional settings as well as parental warmth. These suggested that the summary dimension reflected the behaviors and experiences described from a warm, secure family environment. Consequently, the dimension was labelled Parental Warmth and Social Adjustment. Subsequently, it was found that the label provided an adequate explanation for the items that yielded loadings between .30 and .54. As a result, it was decided that this label was likely to provide an adequate description of the content of the first summary dimension.

The majority of the items loading on the second dimension were drawn from the PCEI 6/8, although a few CEI items also produced significant loadings. These items reflected an early emergence of concern with achievement, job channeling, academic and occupational success, and movement into intellectually demanding upper-level jobs. Overall, the items seem to reflect the developmental processes that lead males to enter professional occupations, as well as the behaviors and experiences associated with professional status. As a result of these considerations, the summary dimension was labelled Professional Occupational Orientation.

Nearly all of the items loading on the third component were drawn from the BQ. A number of items reflected effectiveness or an enjoyment of athletic pursuits. However, other items that were incorporated reflected early and frequent dating activity along with high school popularity. When these two trends are combined with the tendency of individuals receiving high scores to reject intellectual pursuits and try to be like their fathers, it seems reasonable to conclude that scores on this dimension reflected an orientation towards an acceptance of the masculine role in adolescence with its associated athletic prowess, peer acceptance, and success with the opposite sex, leading to the decision to label this dimension Traditional Masculine Role.

Unlike the foregoing dimensions, the item content of the fourth summary dimension was relatively homogeneous. The majority of the items indicated rather direct involvement in religious activities or the concommittants of religious values, such as devoting income to charity. The staff concluded that the dimension should be labelled Religious Involvement. In a southeastern sample, it was not especially surprising that scores on this dimension were related to a Protestant background.

All of the 15 items yielding significant loadings on the fifth male summary dimension were drawn from the BQ. High scores on this dimension were related to involvement in extracurricular activities and an interest and success in academic pursuits. In addition, some of the items suggested that scores on the dimension might be related to the development of achievement motivation. If it is granted that both academic success and involvement in student groups reflect an underlying concern with achievement, it appears that this rather diverse set of items incorporated under this summary dimension may be subsumed under the label Academic Achievement.

A review of the content of the items incorporated under the sixth dimension indicated that scores were strongly related to the amount of reading done by an individual during and after college. Further, it appeared that individuals receiving high scores were likely to be involved in cultural and literary activities, to express liberal political views in college, and to dislike sports. Taken as a whole, the diverse content and nature of the items suggested that this dimension reflected a liberal intellectual orientation and it was labelled Intellectual Pursuits.

The majority of the items loading on the seventh dimension indicated involvement in a variety of group social activities, close relationships with members of the opposite sex, time spent with friends of the same sex, and limited studying during the college years. After college, individuals with high scores on this dimension were likely to report that the university helped them make life-long friendships and learn how to get along with people. These individuals were also likely to indicate that personality helped them find their first jobs. Because this diverse set of items appeared to be bound together by an involvement with other individuals and engagements in social activities, it was decided that this dimension should be labelled Sociability.

The eighth summary dimension identified in the male principal components analyses was derived from the BQ. The item content reflected parental education, income, and involvement with organizations. Items concerned with parental occupational level and social class produced somewhat smaller loadings than did attitudes towards parents' achievements and attending summer camp. On the whole, it is clear that these items reflect various aspects of parental socioeconomic status. However, the tendency of traditional measures of socioeconomic status (such as self-reports of social class or parental occupational level) to produce smaller loadings than items concerned with parental education, income, and organizational activity, may be because it is these latter aspects of social class that are most likely to have long-term implications for individual development. Given the hypothesis, it appeared that the dimension could be appropriately assigned the label Socioeconomic Status.

Some 10 items from the PCEI 6/8 produced significant loadings on the ninth male summary dimension. The majority of the items indicated satisfaction with friends, family, social activities, and leisure activities. Individuals with high scores on this dimension were likely to report being satisfied with their standard of living, having received a number of raises, and devoting income to recreation. This latter trend reflects the economic background and personal preferences required for an active and satisfying social life, whereas the former trend reflects the consequences of an active and satisfying social life. As a result of these considerations, this dimension was labelled Satisfaction with Social Life.

All 10 items yielding significant loadings on the tenth dimension were from the BQ. Scores on this dimension were directly related to items indicating conflict with parents, such as parental anger, parental criticism, and disagreement with parents, as well as conflict with siblings. A few items reflected likely outcomes of family conflict, such as depression, frustration, and daydreaming. Because all of these trends seem tied together by their reflection of the manifestation and outcomes of conflict in the home, this summary dimension was labelled Family Conflict.

Items on the eleventh summary dimension were directly related to engagement in and enjoyment of science courses and activities. It was also found that individuals with high scores on this dimension were likely to have built things or repaired electrical and mechanical devices. Clearly, both the foregoing trends are closely related, and they appear best subsumed under the label Scientific/Engineering Interests.

The final dimension extracted in the male composite component analysis was derived from the PCEI 6/8. In one way or another, these items were all concerned with job satisfaction. For example, it was found that scores on this summary dimension were positively related to items indicating satisfaction with the nature of work, type of work, opportunities for advancement, and opportunities for individual action, as well as willingness to re-enter the same type of work. Rather than labelling the dimension Job Satisfaction, it was assigned the label Occupational Satisfaction, due to the emphasis on satisfaction with the nature of the work and work-related opportunities rather than specific working conditions.

CONTENT OF THE
FEMALE SUMMARY DIMENSIONS

Because the male summary dimensions provided an interpretable summarization of the individual responses to the BQ, CEI, and PCEI 6/8 background data items, there was reason to believe that the same trend would be apparent in the female subsample. On the first summary dimension extracted, 74 BQ items had significant loadings, and consequently, only those items with loadings above .60 were examined in the attempt to label this dimension. Although the content of these high loading items was quite diverse, three trends were apparent. First, scores were negatively related to items concerned with traditional male activities, such as shop work, business, and craft hobbies. Second, females with high scores were likely to be effective in interpersonal and academic situations, as well as to be somewhat conservative. Finally, high scores on this dimension were directly related to a warm, supportive family background that encouraged achievement but not financial independence. The first two of the foregoing trends indicated that this dimension represented effective social adjustment within the traditional feminine role, and the latter trend reflected a family background that would encourage and highly maintain both role acceptance and adjustment. In part because female social adjustment has been tied to acceptance of the traditional feminine role (Tyler, 1964), this dimension was labelled Traditional Social Adjustment.

The second summary dimension was drawn from the CEI and PCEI

6/8. High-scoring individuals had performed well during their college years in an area in which they were interested and in a manner that formulated movement into the kind of job they wanted after graduation. Although quite diverse, items loading on this component seemed to reflect the antecedents, outcomes, and processes entailed in a highly effective job search. Because this search process was not closely tied to any particular kind of job or occupational level, it seemed appropriate to label this summary dimension Job Channelling.

Some 18 PCEI 6/8 items yielded significant loadings on the third summary dimension. High scores reflected two trends. The first was satisfaction with the nature of work, willingness to continue in it, satisfaction with job conditions, and satisfaction with co-workers. The second trend included items indicating upper-level occupational success and early salary increases. Apparently, occupational success is closely related to occupational satisfaction, and so this summary dimension was labelled Occupational Success and Satisfaction.

The fourth summary dimension was made up of 12 BQ items. Scores on this dimension were related to a lack of popularity and success with males. Individuals with high scores were likely to expect failure, to feel downcast, to daydream, and to report that they were not effective in social situations. Taken as a whole, these relationships served to reflect the outcomes and antecedents of low self-esteem among adolescent females where a great deal of value is placed on social success and success with the opposite sex. Consequently, it appeared that this rather diverse item set could be labelled Self-Esteem.

High scores on the fifth dimension were directly related to sorority memberships, involvement with dating activities, engagement in group social activities, and time spent in the cultivation and maintenance of friendships. All these items indicated a concern with participation and effectiveness in a variety of social activities, and so this dimension was labelled Sociability.

The sixth dimension indicated that, during college, individuals receiving high scores were likely to be involved in cultural activities, to spend time reading, to display liberal political views, and to be active in student government or volunteer work. Six to 8 years after college graduation, individuals with high scores were likely to spend a great deal of their time in serious reading. As a whole, these relationships appear to reflect a general liberal orientation, which is further supported by item loadings that indicated limited television viewing, a non-Protestant background, and a desire to become more socially acceptable. As a result of these considerations, the dimension was labelled Intellectual Orientation.

The BQ contained 19 items that produced significant loadings on the seventh summary dimension. Unlike the foregoing dimensions, the content of this dimension was not especially complex. The majority of the items indicated success in physical science and biology courses, as well as a tendency to obtain good grades in these courses and to make the honor role. Because items concerned with conducting experiments and building or repairing things did not yield significant loadings on this dimension (unlike one of the male composite dimensions), it was labelled Scientific Pursuits.

The eighth summary dimension indicated a relatively homogeneous pattern that reflected involvement in religious organizations. For instance, individuals with high scores reported being Protestant and were likely to attend religious services during college and 6 to 8 years after graduation. They were also likely to devote income to charity, spend little time reading men's and women's entertainment magazines, and to not cut classes. Consequently, the dimension was labelled Religious Involvement.

Conflict with parents characterized the items loading on dimension nine, including parental anger, parental esteem, and overt disagreements. Scores were also directly related to items reflecting the outcome of ongoing conflict, as indexed by feelings of frustration and a desire to become more socially acceptable. This set of items seemed aptly described by the label Parent/Child Conflict.

High scores on the tenth summary dimension were directly related to a close, warm relationship between daughters and their parents, particularly their fathers. Women with high scores on this dimension were also likely to report that they tried to become like their fathers, and like their fathers, they tended to be active in organizations and to read sports magazines. Because these relationships seem to reflect the antecedents, concomitants, and outcomes of a daughter's attempt to be like her father, this summary dimension was labelled Paternal Identification.

On the 11th summary dimension, high scores were related to parental education, parental income, and parental involvement in organizations. Those items that yielded smaller, but significant, positive loadings were indicative of parental intellectual activities, father's occupational level, and self-reported social class. As was true with the parallel male component, both of these sets of item loadings seemed to reflect those aspects of socioeconomic status that are likely to have the most powerful impact on individual development. As a result, this dimension was assigned the label Socioeconomic Status.

Scores on the twelfth summary dimension included a rather homogeneous set of items that indicated satisfaction with family, friends, social activities, standard of living, and living quarters. High scores were also related to the intention to marry, as well as having a number of friends of the same sex. Although this dimension was similar to its counterpart in the male analysis, the somewhat broader focus indicated by such concerns as satisfaction with living quarters suggested that this dimension should be labelled Life Satisfaction.

The thirteenth summary dimension also included a rather homogeneous item set. The significant loadings obtained for this dimension reflected engagement in, enjoyment of, and success in athletic pursuits. For instance, it was found that high scores on this dimension were related to involvement in team sports, membership in athletic organizations, and watching sports on television. Correspondingly, this dimension was assigned the relatively straightforward label of Athletic Interests.

Significant loadings for the final summary dimension indicated that high scores were directly related to items reflecting fighting and competition among siblings. High scores on this dimension were related to being a younger child in a small family, a condition that would be likely to induce conflict with older brothers and sisters. These observations indicated that this summary dimension could be appropriately described by the label Sibling Friction.

DISCUSSION OF DIMENSION CONTENT

The foregoing discussion has presented a variety of results bearing on the nature of the composite summary dimensions. Perhaps the most obvious and important results obtained in the composite components analyses were concerned with the effectiveness of the summary descriptions of item responses. Evidence for the effectiveness of the summarizations of the background data items included the adequate coverage of the item base provided by the components, and the clarity of the solutions. The fact that all of the composite summary dimensions could be assigned brief labels acceptable to staff psychologists suggested that they provided a valid and meaningful summary description of the item responses. Moreover, the composite component analysis identified summary dimensions that were likely to have developmental significance, and so produced results in accordance with theoretical expectations.

The summary dimensions that best described individuality at a point in time were not necessarily those that best described individuality over time, arguing for the need for the composite analyses in the description of individual development. Even those dimensions assigned similar labels in both the composite and cross-sectional analyses, such as Socioeconomic Status, displayed certain differences that would enhance the cross-time or developmental impact of the composite dimension. For instance, whereas the cross-sectional Socioeconomic Status dimensions reflected the traditional measure of income, education, housing, and overt class status, the composite Socioeconomic Status dimensions were more heavily weighted toward parental income and education, which are the aspects of family socioeconomic status that are most likely to influence the course of individual development.

Finally, evidence pointing to the meaningfulness of the summarization of item responses was found in relating the content of the composite summary dimensions to the dimension identified in studies in the broader psychological literature. Among the male dimensions, it should be noted that Bayley (1968) has obtained evidence in the University of California longitudinal studies that indicates that parental warmth is closely related to later male social adjustment and effectiveness. Levenson (1978) and Shien (1980) have noted that, for males, the emergence of a professional occupational orientation is an important differential developmental process. The Bray, Campbell, and Grant (1974) longitudinal study has also indicated that achievement, religious values, intellectual pursuits, sociability, and satisfaction with social relationships may all be of substantial significance to the developmental behavior and experiences of men. Studies employing the University of California longitudinal data have indicated that family conflict (Block, 1971) and an orientation towards the traditional masculine role (Livson & Peskin, 1967) in adolescence may have a marked impact on the later behavior and experiences of males, although the outcomes associated with these characteristics are quite complex. Finally, the longitudinal studies conducted by Strong (1943) have served to underscore the cross-time significance of occupational satisfaction and scientific interests.

Although the longitudinal literature concerned with significant behavior and experiences in the lives of females is less extensive than the male literature, it nevertheless provides some support for the significance of the summary dimensions identified in the female composite component analysis. For example, in Block's (1971) analysis of the University of California longitudinal data, he found that a daughter's relationship to her father had a far greater impact on later development than had previously been recognized, and that acceptance of the traditional feminine role as well as social effectiveness were important to later female adjustment. Thus, the results obtained in this study provide some support for the Traditional Social Adjustment, Paternal Identification, and Sociability composite summary dimensions. The nature of the female Job Channelling and Occupational Success and Satisfaction composite dimensions suggest that female career development is less explicitly tied to occupational level than is the case for males. As a result, it is not surprising that Job Channelling and Occupational Success and Satisfaction would emerge as separate composite summary dimensions. On a broader level, the work of Block (1971) has served to establish the developmental components of religious involvement, intellectual pursuits, sibling conflict, and parent/child conflict in the lives of females. This abbreviated review of the literature indicates that the content and nature of both the male and female composite summary dimensions have some support in the broader longitudinal literature, providing additional evidence that points to the meaningfulness and validity of the cross-time summarization of behavior and experience obtained through the composite summary dimensions.

MALE–FEMALE COMPARISONS ON COMPOSITE DIMENSIONS

In comparing the content of the summary dimensions obtained in the cross-time components analysis of male and female item responses, certain similarities and differences were apparent. Four dimensions emerged in both analyses that were sufficiently similar to warrant identical labels: Religious Involvement, Intellectual Pursuits, Sociability, and Socioeconomic Status. Despite the overt similarity of the interpretation applied to these dimensions, there were differences in the magnitude and the content of the items yielding significant loadings. Three other dimensional pairs obtained in the cross-time analyses displayed limited similarity in the two subsamples. The male Satisfaction with Social Life, Scientific/Engineering Interests, and Traditional Masculine Role dimensions bore some similarity to the Life Satisfaction, Scientific Interest, and Athletic Activities dimensions obtained within the female subsample. However, differences in the content of the high loading items led to the application of different labels. These differences appeared to reflect the operation of sex-role influences. For instance, the failure of the female Scientific Interests dimension to incorporate engineering or mechanical activities may be attributed to the cultural restrictions placed on female involvement in these pursuits. On the other hand, the female Life Satisfaction dimension was somewhat broader than the Satisfaction with Social Life dimension obtained within the male subsample. This difference was due to the addition of items that focused on satisfaction with community and living arrangements. It seems likely that this addition reflects the fact that the social role of married females emphasizes home and community whereas these aspects of the extra-occupational environment are given less weight by males. Finally, the Traditional Masculine Role dimension displayed some overlap with the female Athletic Activities dimension. However, in the male sample, there was an additional social component that may reflect the high social value placed on male athletic pursuits and their importance for traditional concepts of masculinity, a concept that bears little relevance to female athletic involvement.

Although the remaining dimensions displayed some overlap, their differences were far more marked than their similarities. Nevertheless, the nature of the differences is of some interest. Clearly, the male Professional Occupational Orientation and Occupational Satisfaction dimensions overlapped in terms of item content with the female Job Channelling and Occupational Success and Satisfaction dimensions. Yet these dimensions displayed clearcut content differences that appeared to reflect sex differences in occupational socialization. Among males, occupational success is associated with early channelling that directs the individual to a high-status professional job. Moreover, the career orientation of males is likely to lead to a differentiation of success in achieving professional status and satisfaction with a given job. The male Family Conflict dimension contained elements of both the Negative Parent/Child Conflict and Sibling Friction dimensions obtained in the female subsample. Although the relatively weak predictive power of these dimensions may have created a situation in which the split reflects little more than an artifact of the number of dimensions retained in these analyses, it is also possible that these dimensions may not be well differentiated among males and that the pattern and impact of familial interaction differ for the two sex groups. Finally, the male Academic Achievement and Parental Warmth and Social Adjustment dimensions, along with the female Self-Esteem, Paternal Identification, and Traditional Social Adjustment dimensions appeared to be highly specific in terms of item content. Explanation of this specificity is difficult; however, three points should be noted in this regard. First, paternal identification may have special significance for differential female behavior, because it may serve as an impetus for either confinement to or an extension of a restrictive female role. Second, the salience of academic achievement for males may lie in the more pronounced differential implication of manifest achievement and achievement motivation within this sex group. Third, social adjustment and self-esteem may have markedly different implications within the two sex groups, as well as somewhat different antecedents and consequents, perhaps due to the salience of social success and traditional social behavior for females.

COMPARISON OF THE COMPOSITE AND SEQUENTIAL DIMENSIONS

Chapter 7 presented the findings associated with correlating the various sequential dimension analyses with each other. Overall, the prediction was relatively poor. The composite components analyses appear to present a viable alternative to the sequential dimensions for describing individuals over time. Within both the male and female subsamples, the composite components analyses accounted for a large proportion of the variance in item responses collected over a 12-year period. In fact, this summarization was more effective than that typically obtained in the sequential analysis, despite the increased heterogeneity of item content. Moreover, the composite dimensions displayed both empirical and conceptual temporal characteristics. The foregoing considerations suggest that the composite components analysis is an effective, and perhaps a more effective, means for describing individuality over time. However, this leads to the questions of (a) whether the cross-time composite dimensions manifest their temporal nature by incorporating information from a number of points in time and (b) whether they provide unique information that emerges only when relationships are observed over time.

Some qualitative information in this regard may be acquired by examining the correlation between scores on the sequential dimensions and the composite dimensions. In examining the results obtained within the male subsample, the composite Parental Warmth and Social Adjustment dimension yielded only one coefficient in excess of .20. This relationship was with the PCEI 2/4 Early Occupational Success ($r = .27$) dimension. Apparently, one outcome of adolescent parental warmth and social adjustment is early occupational success, perhaps because it generates the self-confidence necessary for occupational success.

The Professional Occupational Orientation dimension yielded by the male composite analysis was defined primarily on the basis of CEI and PCEI items. However, this dimension was related to a wide variety of sequential dimensions, including the BQ Warmth of Parental Relationship ($r = .20$) and Academic Achievement ($r = .27$) dimensions; the CEI Literary Pursuits ($r = -.22$) and Positive College Experience ($r = .33$) dimensions; the PCEI 2/4 Job Satisfaction ($r = .32$), Entry Level Occupational Tasks ($r = .20$), General Reading ($r = .35$), and College-Moderated Social Development ($r = .32$) dimensions; and the PCEI 6/8 Job Channelling ($r = .84$) and Occupational Status ($r = .36$) dimensions. This pattern of correlates serves to validate the labelling of the composite dimension, in that this dimension was related to both Job Channelling and Occupational Level 6 to 8 years following graduation from the university. Moreover, these results suggest that the warm parent/child relationships that serve to build confidence and achievement motivation, along with the requisite academic achievement, are also relevant to the development of a professional occupational orientation. The finding that individuals with high scores on this dimension were not especially likely to engage in literary pursuits or enjoy college may be attributed to their study habits and occupational focus. Nevertheless, the attainment of occupational goals upon graduation appears to generate satisfaction with university experiences as well as with the job. Preparation for professional jobs is manifested in the negative relationship obtained for the Entry Level Occupational Tasks dimension while continuing preparation after graduation may underlie the coefficient yielded by the PCEI 2/4 General Reading dimension.

The Traditional Masculine Role dimension obtained in the cross-time analysis was defined solely on the basis of BQ items. However, as the differing labels suggest, this dimension yielded only a weak positive relationship with the BQ Athletic Participation dimension ($r = .15$). The only major relationship observed for this dimension was yielded by the PCEI 2/4 Extra-Occupational Satisfaction ($r = -.24$) dimension, a result that suggests that the traditional masculine role may be somewhat inappropriate for establishing social relationships in the postcollege environment.

In the composite analysis, the male Religious Involvement dimension was composed primarily of CEI item responses and PCEI item responses collected 6 to 8 years following graduation. However, scores on this summary dimension yielded a number of major correlations with scores on dimensions derived at a number of points in time, including the BQ Academic Achievement ($r = .22$) and Religious Activities ($r = .36$) dimensions; the CEI Religious Involvement ($r = .79$) and Activity in Organizations ($r = -.31$) dimensions; the PCEI 2/4 Extra-Occupational Satisfaction ($r = .21$), Entry-Level Occupational Tasks ($r = .36$), Vocational Direction ($r = -.21$), and Religious Involvement ($r = .39$) dimensions; and the PCEI 6/8 Religious Morality ($r = .64$) and Occupational Status ($r = .26$) dimensions. Overall, the results obtained in this analysis validate the label assigned to this composite summary dimension. Moreover, they demonstrate that the composite dimension was a more effective description of religious involvement over time than the chaining of the sequential dimensions, regardless of whether the items drawn from an instrument helped define the dimension or were included in the components analysis. The results for the BQ Academic Achievement dimension may reflect the greater acceptance of authority and institutions, which would result in enhanced academic performance. A concern with religious matters apparently limits interest in the occupational world, and the subsequent lack of vocational direction apparently results in low occupational status. The negative relationships obtained for the Activity in Organizations and postcollege Extra-Occupational Satisfaction dimensions may reflect an inward or introverted component of male religiosity that would tend to make it difficult to form contacts in new environments and stymie involvement in nonreligious organization.

The Academic Achievement dimension obtained in the composite analysis was composed primarily of BQ items. This dimension yielded only a weak relationship with the BQ Academic Achievement ($r = .16$) dimension, due to its additional extracurricular content. No other major coefficients were obtained for this cross-time dimension.

The composite Intellectual Pursuits dimension was defined on the basis of CEI and PCEI items. A number of major relationships were observed when the dimension was correlated with the various sequential dimensions. Major relationships were obtained for the BQ Aggressiveness/Independence ($r = .31$) and Athletic Interests ($r = -.26$) dimensions; the CEI Literary Pursuits ($r = .56$), Health ($r = -.23$), Activity in Organizations ($r = .21$), Athletic Pursuits ($r = -.20$), and Self-Support ($r = .20$) dimensions; the PCEI 2/4 General Reading ($r = .63$) dimension, and the PCEI 6/8 Cognitive Orientation ($r = .64$) dimension. These results serve to validate the label assigned to this dimension and indicate that the dimension was an effective summarization of individual differences in intellectual behaviors, even when the relevant indicators were not used in the definition or formation of the dimension. It is of interest to note that these relationships manifest the young intellectuals' typical disdain for athletics. The relationship of the Self-Support, Independence, and Activity in Organizations dimensions with this dimension suggests that an independent, financially responsible pattern of behavior may limit the time that can be devoted to organizations as well as their attractiveness. Moreover, independence and responsibility may well be qualities that facilitate an interest in solitary, often demanding, intellectual pursuits. Finally, it seems likely that poor health in college may buttress or facilitate the development of intellectual interests, such as reading, because they demand relatively little physical exertion.

The Sociability dimension obtained in the composite analysis was defined on the basis of CEI items within the male subsample. However, it was related to summary dimensions derived at a number of other points in time, including the BQ Athletic interests ($r = .20$) dimension; the CEI Sociability ($r = .74$), Health ($r = -.24$), and Activity in Organizations ($r = -.29$) dimensions; the PCEI 2/4 Extra-Occupational Satisfaction ($r = .23$) and Entry Level Occupational tasks ($r = .50$) dimensions; and the PCEI 6/8 Occupational Status ($r = .29$) and Social Adjustment ($r = .56$) dimensions. The results obtained for the Sociability and Social Adjustment dimensions support the nature of the label applied to this dimension and indicate that it describes sociability over time and on items not used in defining the summary dimension. It is of note that the adolescent Athletic Interests dimension may reflect an antecedent expression of sociability, and the relationship obtained for the Extra-Occupational Satisfaction dimension may reflect a consequence of this characteristic because highly social individuals should have an easier time establishing a satisfying social life in the novel postcollege environment. The coefficients yielded by the Activity in Organizations and Health dimensions would appear to reflect the side effects of social activity in terms of the required time and energy. Apparently, individuals with high scores on this dimension are likely to choose highly social, entry-level jobs, such as sales, and they are eventually successful in these jobs, perhaps due to the match between job demands and personal characteristics.

BQ items defined the Socioeconomic Status dimension obtained in the composite analysis. The dimension did not yield any major relationships with the sequential summary dimensions, although weak relationships were obtained for the BQ Socioeconomic Status ($r = .18$) and Social Desirability ($r = .15$) dimensions. The pattern of relationships may reflect the heavy behavioral components of the composite Socioeconomic Status dimension.

As defined in the male composite components analysis, the Scientific/Engineering Interest dimension was also composed primarily of BQ items. This dimension yielded only one major relationship that was reflected in its correlation with the BQ Scientific Interest ($r = .21$) dimension. Although this relationship validates the label assigned to this dimension, the magnitude of this relationship may be attributed to the inclusion of a powerful engineering element in the composite dimension that was not manifest in the BQ dimension.

The Family Conflict dimension obtained in the composite analysis was also defined on the basis of BQ items. The only major relationship obtained for this dimension was with the PCEI 6/8 Religious Morality ($r = -.20$) dimension, a result that seems to reflect the fact that families that manifest substantial conflict are likely to lack the warmth and closeness that tends to engender later religiosity through processes described earlier.

The composite Satisfaction with Social Life dimension was defined primarily on the basis of PCEI items administered 6 to 8 years following graduation from the university. Nevertheless, this dimension was related to a number of the dimensions derived in the sequential analysis, including the CEI Health ($r = .30$), Marital Status ($r = .22$), and Activity in Organizations ($r = .26$) dimensions; the PCEI 2/4 Extra-Occupational Satisfaction ($r = .29$) dimension; and the PCEI 6/8 Extra-Occupational Satisfaction ($r = .77$) dimension. This pattern of results serves to validate the label assigned to the summary dimension. It is of note that the relationships obtained for the Marital Status and Activity in Organizations dimensions may represent an early establishment of adult social behavior and, thus, a more satisfactory adaptation to adult social life. The results obtained for the Health dimension apparently indicate the importance of good health as a prerequisite for an active and satisfying social life.

Like the preceding dimension, the composite Occupational Satisfaction dimension was defined on the basis of PCEI items administered 6 to 8 years following graduation and was cross-related to a number of sequential dimensions, including the CEI Positive College Experiences ($r = .20$) and Bohemian ($r = .28$) dimensions; the PCEI 2/4 Job Satisfaction ($r = .21$) dimension; and the PCEI 6/8 Job Satisfaction ($r = .71$) dimension. The job satisfaction relationships indicate that this composite dimension was capable of indicating job satisfaction over time. Moreover, the cross-time nature of this dimension helps justify use of the occupational satisfaction label. The relationship obtained for the Positive College Experiences dimension may reflect the importance of a generally sanguine disposition for job satisfaction. Apparently, the social expansion and exploration that are inherent in the Bohemianism dimension also influence satisfaction, perhaps by contributing to the definition of more realistic goals.

The Traditional Social Adjustment dimension obtained in the composite analysis of female item responses was defined principally on the basis of BQ items. The only major relationship observed for this dimension was the positive correlation yielded by the BQ Academic Achievement ($r = .20$) dimension. This result may be attributed to the fact that achievement in academic situations is one aspect of traditional feminine adjustment.

The Job Channelling dimension yielded by the female composite analysis was defined principally on the basis of PCEI items administered 6 to 8 years following graduation. Nevertheless, this dimension was related to a number of sequential dimensions including the PCEI 2/4 Job Appropriateness ($r = .63$) and Intellectual Reading ($r = .21$) dimensions, and the PCEI 6/8 Job Determinants ($r = .86$) dimension. The relationship observed for the Intellectual Reading dimension may reflect the fact that Job Channelling is more likely among females with a cognitive interest in the external world during the period following graduation because this interest might extend to occupational concerns.

Like the Job Channelling dimension, the composite Occupational Success and Satisfaction dimension was composed of PCEI items administered 6 to 8 years following graduation and was related to a number of sequential summary dimensions, including the CEI Positive College Experience ($r = .20$), Health ($r = -.30$), and Self-Support ($r = .20$) dimensions; the PCEI 2/4 Job Satisfaction ($r = .33$) dimension; and the PCEI 6/8 Job Satisfaction ($r = .81$) dimension. Again, the coefficient associated with the Positive College Experience dimension indicates the importance of a generally sanguine disposition for job satisfaction. The results obtained for the Self-Support dimension suggest that financial responsibility may influence female job satisfaction by tying them more closely to the job.

Sociability, as defined in the composite components analysis, was composed primarily of CEI items and PCEI items administered 6 to 8 years following graduation. This dimension was related to a wide variety of sequential dimensions. Among them were the BQ Warmth of Maternal Relationship ($r = .25$), Social Leadership ($r = .25$), and Popularity with the Opposite Sex ($r = .20$) dimensions; the CEI Dating Activity ($r = .65$), Traditional Social Involvement ($r = .43$), Sociability ($r = .33$), and Health ($r = -.28$) dimensions; the PCEI 2/4 Extra-Occupational Satisfaction ($r = .28$) and Collegiate Social Development ($r = .51$) dimensions; and the PCEI 6/8 Extra-Occupational Satisfaction ($r = .21$) and Collegiate Social Maturation ($r = .59$) dimensions. The results obtained for the Extra-Occupational Satisfaction and Collegiate Social Development dimensions may reflect the influence of sociability in establishing a satisfactory postcollege social life, as well as reinforcing and acting as a pre-requisite for attaining satisfactory social outcomes from college experiences.

Like the Sociability dimension, the composite Intellectual Pursuits dimension was defined principally on the basis of CEI items and PCEI items administered 6 to 8 years following graduation from the university, and was related to a variety of sequential summary dimensions, including the BQ Cultural/Literary Interests ($r = .21$) and Parental Freedom vs. Control ($r = .36$) dimensions; the CEI Liberal Activism ($r = .48$), Leisure Reading ($r = .66$), and Health ($r = -.27$) dimensions; the PCEI 2/4 Intellectual Leisure Reading ($r = .49$) dimension; and the PCEI 6/8 Intellectual Reading dimension. Overall, these results serve to validate the label applied to this dimension, in the sense that they reflect the same liberal intellectual trend, although it is often manifested in reading. It seems likely that the influence of a lack of parental control on female intellectual interests is due to the fact that controlling parental behaviors would tend to discourage the independent thought necessary for these activities. On the other hand, poor health may encourage involvement in intellectual activities, because these pursuits do not require any substantial physical effort.

The Scientific Interests dimension obtained in the composite components analysis was composed exclusively of BQ items. As the label assigned to this dimension leads one to expect, this dimension was related to the BQ Scientific Interests ($r = .29$) dimension. The CEI Liberal Activism dimension also yielded a significant relationship ($r = -.20$), a result that may reflect a somewhat introverted conservative trend on the part of females interested in science.

As it was defined in the composite components analysis, the Religious

Involvement dimension contained only CEI items and PCEI items administered 6 to 8 years following graduation from the university. This dimension yielded major relationships with the BQ Expression of Negative Emotions ($r = .25$) dimension; the CEI Religious Involvement ($r = .73$) and Athletic Participation ($r = -.25$) dimensions; the PCEI 2/4 Religious Beliefs ($r = .51$) and the PCEI 6/8 Religious Community Involvement ($r = .57$) and Perceived Occupational Status ($r = -.40$) dimensions. The failure of the BQ Religious Activities dimension to yield a significant relationship may be attributed to moderating familial influences. On the other hand, the relationship obtained for the Perceived Occupational Status dimension may reflect the results of the restrictions that religious and community involvement places on occupational concerns. The positive coefficients produced by the Expression of Negative Emotions and the negative relationship with Athletic Participation may simply reflect conformity to traditional values as they apply to females.

The Negative Parent/Child Conflict dimension obtained in the composite analysis was composed of items drawn from the BQ. This dimension's only major relationship was with the PCEI 6/8 Asocial Job Activities ($r = .22$) dimension. Apparently, this early difficulty in social situations leads to later withdrawal from such situations when they involve substantial personal investment. Like the Negative Parent/Child Conflict dimension, the composite Sibling Friction dimension was defined on the basis of BQ items. The sole major relationship obtained for this dimension was with the CEI Positive College Experience ($r = -.28$) dimension. However, the meaning of this relationship is unclear. The composite Athletic Activities dimension was also defined on the basis of BQ items, yet this dimension failed to yield a major relationship with the BQ Athletic Participation dimension, perhaps because the composite dimension reflected interest as much as participation and success in athletics. No other major relationships were obtained for this dimension. BQ items also defined the composite Paternal Identification. No major relationships were obtained, but the failure of the dimension to yield a significant relationship with the BQ Paternal Warmth dimension tends to support the assignment of a unique label. The composite Socioeconomic Status dimension was also formed on the basis of BQ items, but because of the highly social nature of the composite dimension, it did not yield a major relationship with the more economically oriented BQ Socioeconomic Status dimension. On the other hand, major relationships were obtained for the PCEI 2/4 Intellectual Leisure Reading ($r = -.21$) dimension, and the PCEI 6/8 Intellectual Reading ($r = -.30$) and Perceived Occupational Status ($r = -.30$) dimensions. Apparently, upper-class females are less likely to engage in serious reading or hold upper-level jobs. This result may reflect the outcomes of a protected, secure family environment that would tend not to demand use of intellectual skills or force employment, although these relationships may also reflect heightened expectations.

As it was defined in the composite analysis, the Life Satisfaction dimension was composed primarily of PCEI items administered 6 to 8 years following graduation. This dimension yielded major relationships with a number of sequential summary dimensions, including the CEI Sociability ($r = .21$) dimension; the PCEI 2/4 Extra-Occupational Satisfaction ($r = .38$) dimension; and the PCEI 6/8 Extra-Occupational Satisfaction ($r = .85$) and Religious Community Involvement ($r = .33$) dimensions. Overall, these relationships support the nature of the label assigned to this summary dimension. The relationship obtained for the Religious Community Involvement dimension seems to reflect the importance of these activities for a full social life among adult females.

Consideration of the results presented in the preceding paragraphs leads to a number of general conclusions that are of some importance in discussions revolving around the nature of the composite summary dimensions. First, a variety of dimensions failed to yield major correlations with the sequential summary dimensions. Included here were the male Parental Warmth and Social Adjustment, Traditional Masculine Role, Academic Achievement, Socioeconomic Status, Family Conflict, and Scientific/Engineering Interest dimensions, as well as the female Traditional Social Adjustment, Self-Esteem, Scientific Interest, Paternal Identification, Athletic Activities, and Sibling Friction dimensions. In the sense that these composite dimensions were not well predicted by the sequential dimensions, they may be said to be unique dimensions that reflect individuality over time but not at a point in time. To the extent that the composite component analyses yields such unique results, it seems that it may be viewed as a qualitatively different solution that produced at least some novel dimensions. Second, the results obtained for the non-unique composite dimensions served to validate the labels assigned to these summary dimensions. They also indicated that the composite dimensions provided an effective summarization of individuality over time within a given content area. Moreover, the results obtained for the PCEI 2/4 dimensions indicated that these summarizations were robust in the sense that they incorporated relevant information that was not utilized in derivation of the cross-time dimensions. Third, a variety of results obtained from the non-unique dimensions showed that even when a composite component was defined on the basis of items drawn from a limited subset of instruments, it would yield logically consistent and interpretable relationships with the summary dimensions derived from other instruments. This implies that a dimension may have cross-time implications even though it is defined on the basis of a single instrument. Fourth, although the major relationships were generally highly interpretable, it was also obvious that they were often of a complex genotypic variety and that their interpretation was, to some extent, contingent on ongoing events. This observation tends to support the earlier statement that the cross-time dimensions were of a genotypic process-oriented variety. Finally, it should be noted that the entire preceding discussion has concentrated on major relationships. However, *all* of the composite summary dimensions produced at least five correlations with the sequential dimensions that exceeded marginal significance levels. Because these relationships were spread across a number of instruments, this finding argues for the temporal nature of the composite dimensions. Moreover, when the prediction manifest in the number of marginal and major relationships obtained for the composite analysis is compared to that obtained in the chaining of sequential dimensions, it is clear that the composite dimensions yield a better summarization of individuality over time. Of course, this result may be attributed to spurious overlap. However, because the difference in predictive efficiency was maintained on the PCEI 2/4 summary dimensions, which did not include information utilized in formation of the composite dimensions, spurious overlap alone cannot account for the enhanced prediction obtained from the cross-time analysis.

REGRESSION ANALYSES

Although the results produced by the preceding analyses provide a strong argument for the cross-time predictive utility of the component analyses, there are certain problems with this approach when the uniqueness and temporal implications of the dimensions are being examined. Somewhat more direct information with regard to the temporal and unique characteristics of the composite dimensions may be obtained by examining the regression equations derived for the cross-time components. Tables 8.3 and 8.4 present the results of these analyses within the male and female subsamples. Within both subsamples, the pattern of standardized regression weights were similar to that which would be expected given the correlational results presented earlier. Hence, the content of the significant predictions are not elaborated at any length here. What is of note with regard to these regression weights is that all of the composite dimensions were associated with significant independent prediction from dimensions contained in at least two of the four component analyses carried out on the basis of data collected at a single point in time. This result provides strong support for the conclusion that the composite summary dimensions incorporated temporal considerations

TABLE 8.3
Regression of the BQ, CEI, PCEI 2/4, and PCEI 6/8
Sequential Dimensions on the Composite Dimensions for Males

Factor	R^2	R	Y	Variables and Standardized Weights
1	.28	.53	2.50	−.25 BQ 3 + −.21 BQ 9 + .25 P2/4 3 + −.31 P2/4 4 + −.18 P2/4 8 + .15 P6/8 5
2	.90	.94	.00	−.13 CEI 4 + .13 P2/4 1 + .18 P2/4 2 + .13 P2/4 3 + .28 P2/4 7 + .16 P6/8 8
3	.10	.31	−1.00	.20 BQ 8 + −.25 P2/4 3
4	.87	.93	−.03	.57 CEI 3 + −.14 CEI 4 + −.28 CEI 7 + .38 P6/8 3 + −.21 P6/8 7 + −.11 P6/8 8
5	.11	.33	−1.30	.22 BQ 4 + −.12 CEI 1 + .13 CEI 5 + −.16 CEI 10
6	.85	.92	−.05	.44 CEI 1 + −.15 CEI 5 + −.12 CEI 6 + −.16 CEI 7 + .46 CEI 9 + .36 P6/8 5
7	.84	.91	.08	.63 CEI 2 + −.21 CEI 5 + −.28 CEI 7 + .21 CEI 8 + .19 P6/8 5 + −.30 P6/8 8
8	.06	.26	1.60	.15 BQ 6 + .17 BQ 5 + .14 P6/8 3
9	.86	.92	.00	.13 CEI 5 + .21 CEI 7 + .60 P6/8 1 + .81 P6/8 4 + .15 P6/8 8
10	.19	.44	.85	−.16 BQ 9 + .16 CEI 2 + −.22 CEI 4 + −.15 P6/8 5 + −.19 P6/8 3 + −.20 P6/8 8
11	.18	.43	−.51	.14 BQ 4 + −.14 BQ 3 + .24 BQ 10 + −.12 BQ 13 + −.17 P2/4 1 + −.15 P6/8 3
12	.81	.90	.05	−.16 CEI 8 + −.11 CEI 9 + −.14 CEI 10 + .53 P6/8 1 + .12 P6/8 6 + −.16 P6/8 7
Overall Mean	.43	.66		

R^2 = Variance Accounted For

R = Multiple Correlation

Y = Intercept

$N = 415$

TABLE 8.4
Regression of the BQ, CEI, PCEI 2/4, and PCEI 6/8 Sequential Dimensions on the Composite Dimensions for Females

Factor	R^2	R	Y	Variables and Standardized Weights
1	.52	.72	-.56	-.13 BQ 3 + .12 BQ 14 + .10 P2/4 4 + -.11 P2/4 6 + -.63 P2/4 9
2	.83	.91	.00	-.14 CEI 4 + .15 CEI 6 + .10 P2/4 4 + .81 P6/8 1 + .12 P6/8 5 + .07 P6/8 6
3	.92	.96	-.04	.13 CEI 5 + -.17 CEI 6 + .12 CEI 8 + .76 P6/8 2 + .45 P6/8 6
4	.22	.47	.00	.22 CEI 1 + .14 P2/4 4 + -.17 P6/8 1 + .21 P6/8 4 + .45 P6/8 5
5	.88	.94	-.02	.57 CEI 1 + -.15 CEI 4 + -.27 CEI 6 + .33 CEI 7 + .26 CEI 9 + .28 P6/8 5
6	.87	.93	.01	.32 CEI 2 + -.22 CEI 5 + .12 CEI 7 + .55 CEI 10 + .10 CEI 9 + .34 P6/8 8
7	.20	.45	-1.20	.23 BQ 8 + -.16 CEI 2 + -.16 CEI 9 + -.16 P6/8 2 + .20 P6/8 6 + .18 P6/8 9
8	.84	.92	-.04	.58 CEI 3 + -.15 CEI 4 + .16 CEI 6 + .20 CEI 10 + .32 P6/8 7 + -.32 P6/8 6
9	.26	.51	1.00	-.16 BQ 9 + .17 CEI 5 + -.22 CEI 6 + -.17 P6/8 2 + .33 P6/8 4
10	.14	.38	.63	-.11 BQ 3 + .13 CEI 1 + .12 CEI 7 + .14 P2/4 1 + .18 P6/8 2 + -.17 P6/8 6
11	.29	.54	-.93	.14 BQ 3 + -.14 BQ 5 + -.16 BQ 4 + -.29 P6/8 6 + -.29 P6/8 7 + -.12 P6/8 8
12	.90	.95	-.01	.13 CEI 3 + -.12 CEI 9 + .84 P6/8 3 + .13 P6/8 5 + .36 P6/8 7 + -.10 P6/8 9
13	.10	.32	-.03	.18 CEI 6 + .17 CEI 7 + .23 P6/8 5
14	.21	.45	.60	-.28 CEI 5 + -.20 CEI 10 + -.18 P6/8 5 + .16 P6/8 6 + .14 P6/8 7
Overall Mean	.44	.69		

R^2 = Variance Accounted For

R = Multiple Correlation

Y = Intercept

$N = 358$

into the description of individuality regardless of whether or not these dimensions were defined on the basis of item data collected at a single point in time.

The second result yielded by this analysis that deserves some consideration is the magnitude of the multiple R and R^2 obtained for each composite dimension on the basis of the prediction yielded by the dimensions contained in the sequential analysis. Within the male subsample, multiple Rs above .90 were observed for six of the composite dimensions, including the Professional Occupational Orientation, Religious Involvement, Intellectual Pursuits, Sociability, Satisfaction with Social Life and Occupational Satisfaction dimensions. Multiple Rs of similar magnitude were associated with the female Job Channelling, Occupational Level and Satisfaction, Sociability, Intellectual Pursuits, Religious Involvement, and Social Satisfaction dimensions. The magnitude of these multiple Rs indicates that, although these dimensions display a temporal component, they do not appear to be unique to the composite analysis because they were well predicted by some combination of sequential dimensions. On the other hand, the Parental Warmth and Social Adjustment, Traditional Masculine Role, Academic Achievement, Socioeconomic Status, Family Conflict, and Scientific/Engineering Interests dimensions obtained in the male composite component analyses did not yield any multiple R in excess of .53 or below .28. In the female subsample, the Traditional Social Adjustment, Self-Esteem, Scientific Interests, Negative Parent/Child Conflict, Socioeconomic Status, Athletic Interests, and Sibling Friction dimensions were associated with multiple Rs below .72 and accounted for less than half of the variance in scores on the composite components. When it is remembered that these regression analyses were carried out using techniques that led to an inflationary bias in multiple Rs, and these multiple Rs account for less than half of the variance in scores on the reliable composite components, then it appears that this second set of composite summary dimensions provides unique information not garnered by the components analysis of data collected at a single point in time. This leads to the conclusion that the composite components analysis yields a novel, temporally bound description of individuality that is not replicated by the point-in-time sequential analyses.

The foregoing discussion has served to demonstrate the construct validity of the composite components, as well as their conceptual clarity and temporal characteristics. When these observations are considered, along with the percentage of total variance accounted for in these component analyses, then it is clear that they provide a valid, effective summarization of individual differences in behavior and experiences over a 12-year period. Summary dimensions that yield such an effective description of individuality over time are likely to provide a solid foundation for the definition of cross-time similarities among individuals in their behaviors and experiences. This suggests that scores on these dimensions will be adequate base data for the formation of composite subgroups. Additionally, the breadth and robustness of these dimensions indicates that the resulting subgroups might be nontrivial and might display the differential characteristics necessary for construction of an acceptable developmental typology.

9

Description of the Composite Prototypes

Having established the ability of the composite dimensions to provide an effective summarization of the individual's behavior and experiences over time, we now examine the results obtained when the information was employed to formulate a description of individuality through the prototype model. As previously indicated, in attempts to formulate a general summary description through this model, it is necessary to employ a set of indicators that themselves are capable of providing a meaningful and accurate description of a broad range of significant past behaviors and experiences. The process-oriented dimensions identified in the composite component analysis might provide such a basis for constructing such a classification.

GENERAL RESULTS

In constructing the composite prototypes, the scores of 417 male and 355 female members of the longitudinal sample on the composite summary dimension were obtained. The Ward and Hook cluster analysis procedure was applied to the matrices of similarity data identified through Cronbach's d^2 measure. The plots of within-cluster incremental sums of squares were examined to identify the smallest possible number of clusters that would serve to minimize the differences among the individuals assigned to the various prototypes. For men, it was found that either the 10- or the 15-cluster solution appeared as possible, whereas for women, the 10-, 14-, and 17-cluster solutions were identified.

Each of the potential male and female solutions were entered into the affirmation subroutine to identify the number of good fits, overlaps, and isolates associated with each solution. Because the number of good fits, overlaps, and isolates reflects the clarity with which individuals could be assigned to a single taxonomic category or prototype, this information was used as a criterion for establishing the relative effectiveness of alternative solutions. In the female subsample, the 14- and 17-cluster solutions yielded roughly 11% more good fits and 10% fewer overlaps than did the 10-cluster solution. However, there was no discernible difference between the 14- and 17-cluster solutions. Within the male subsample, nearly identical numbers of good fits, overlaps, and isolates were also obtained for the 10- and 15-cluster solutions.

The choice among the remaining alternative solutions was based on an examination of the differential characteristics of the male and female prototypes associated with each solution. The mean differences between the average dimension score of all individuals assigned to a cluster and the sample (by sex) as a whole were established for each solution. Mean differences in excess of $\frac{1}{2}$ standard deviation were defined as significantly differentiating the prototypes from all other prototypes within each solution. The prototypes were then reviewed by five staff members for interpretability and psychology meaningfulness. In the male subsample, the 15-cluster solution produced more significant mean differences per prototype on the composite summary dimensions than the 10-cluster solution. Examination of the results by the staff psychologists led to a consensus decision that the 15-cluster solution produced a more interpretable pattern of prototype differentiation. Within the female subsample, it was found that the 17-cluster solution produced more significant mean differences per prototype on the composite summary dimensions than the 14-cluster solution, and a review by staff psychologists indicated that the 17-cluster solution appeared to provide a more cohesive and interpretable description of individuality than the 14-cluster solution.

An examination of the number of individuals who could be described through the modal patterns of behavior and experiences manifest in the composite prototypes provided some strong support for the potential value of the retained solutions. Overall, 360 of the 417 males (88%) were assigned to a single prototype, whereas only 57 of the 417 males (12%) were overlaps. None of the members of the male longitudinal sample were found to be isolates. In the female subsample, 300 of the 358 females (84%) could be assigned to a single prototype; the remaining 58 were classified as overlaps. Again, no isolate cases were identified among the female prototypes. Because most individuals could be adequately described through their assignment to a single prototype, the retained solutions appeared to be of sufficient clarity to argue for the value of the taxonomic structures identified in the male and female cluster analyses.

The foregoing conclusion finds substantial support in the results obtained in a review of the aposteriori probabilities reflecting the likelihood

TABLE 9.1
Aposteriori Probability of Prototype Membership for 25 Males

Subject #	Prototype #														
	1	2	3	4	5	6	7	8	9	10	11	12	13	14	15
1	.00	.00	.00	.00	.00	.00	.00	.00	.00	.00	.00	.00	.00	.00	.00
2	.00	.00	.00	.00	.00	.00	.00	.00	.00	.00	1.00	.00	.00	.00	.00
3	.00	.00	.00	.00	.00	1.00	.00	.00	.00	.00	.00	.00	.00	.92	.00
4	.00	.00	.00	.00	.00	.00	.00	.00	.00	.00	.00	.00	.07	.00	.00
5	.00	.00	.00	.00	.00	.00	.00	.00	.00	.99	.00	.00	.00	.99	.00
6	.00	.00	.00	.00	.00	.00	.00	.00	.00	.00	.00	.00	.07	.92	.00
7	.00	.00	.00	.00	.00	.00	.00	.00	.00	.00	.00	.00	.00	.97	.00
8	.00	.08	.89	.00	.00	.00	.00	.00	.00	.00	.00	.00	.00	.00	.34
9	.00	.00	.00	.00	.00	.00	.00	.00	.00	.00	.00	.08	.52	.00	.00
10	.00	.00	.00	.03	.00	.00	.00	.00	.00	.00	.00	.00	.00	.00	.00
11	.00	.00	.00	.00	.00	.00	.00	.97	.00	.00	.99	.00	.00	.00	.00
12	.00	.00	.00	.00	.00	.00	.00	.00	.00	.00	.98	.00	.00	.00	.00
13	.00	.00	.08	.00	.00	.00	.00	.00	.00	.00	.00	.00	.00	.00	.00
14	.00	.08	.00	.00	.00	.00	.00	.00	.00	.00	.00	.00	.00	.00	.00
15	.00	.08	.00	.00	1.00	.97	.00	.00	.00	.00	.02	.00	.00	.00	.00
16	.00	.00	.00	.00	.00	.00	.00	.00	.00	.00	.00	.00	.00	.00	.99
17	.00	.00	.00	.00	.00	.00	.00	.00	.00	.00	.00	.00	.96	.00	.00
18	.00	.00	.00	.00	.00	.99	.00	.00	.00	.00	.00	.00	.00	.00	.00
19	.00	.00	.00	.99	.00	.00	.00	.01	.00	.00	.00	.00	.00	.00	.00
20	.00	.00	.00	.00	.00	.99	.00	.00	.00	.00	.00	.00	.00	.00	.00
21	.00	.00	.00	.00	.00	.00	.00	.99	.00	.00	.00	.00	.00	.00	.00
22	.00	.00	.00	.00	.00	.00	.00	.00	.00	.00	.00	.00	.00	.00	.00
23	.06	.00	.00	.00	.00	.00	.00	.00	.00	.00	.00	.00	.00	.00	.00
24	.00	.00	.00	.00	.00	.00	.00	.00	.00	.00	.00	.07	.00	.00	.92
25	1.00	.00	.00	.00	.00	.00	.00	.00	.00	.00	.00	.00	.00	.00	.00

TABLE 9.2
Aposteriori Probability of Prototype Membership for 25 Females

Subject #	Prototype #																
	1	2	3	4	5	6	7	8	9	10	11	12	13	14	15	16	17
1	.00	.00	.00	.00	.00	.00	.00	.00	.00	.00	.00	.00	.00	.00	.00	.00	.00
2	.00	.00	.00	.00	.00	.00	.00	.00	.00	.00	.30	.00	.00	.00	.00	.00	.00
3	.00	.00	.04	.00	.00	.00	.00	.00	.00	.00	.00	.62	.00	.00	.00	.00	.00
4	.99	.00	.00	.00	.00	.00	.00	.00	.00	.00	.00	.00	.00	.00	.00	.00	.00
5	.00	.00	.00	.00	.00	.92	.77	.00	.08	.00	.00	.00	.00	.00	.00	.00	.00
6	.00	.00	.00	.00	.00	.00	.00	.00	.00	.00	.00	.21	.22	.00	.00	.00	.18
7	.56	.00	.00	.00	.09	.00	.00	.00	.00	.00	.00	.00	.85	.00	.00	.00	.00
8	.10	.00	.95	.00	.00	.00	.00	.00	.00	.00	.00	.00	.00	.00	.00	.00	.00
9	.00	.00	.00	.00	.00	.00	.00	.00	.00	.00	.00	.00	.64	.00	.00	.00	.00
10	.00	.00	.00	.00	.00	.00	.75	.00	.00	.00	.32	.00	.00	.00	.00	.00	.06
11	.00	.00	.00	.00	.00	.00	.09	.00	.00	.00	.00	.00	.33	.47	.00	.00	.00
12	.06	.00	.00	.00	.00	.00	.04	.00	.68	.00	.00	.08	.00	.00	.00	.00	.02
13	.00	.00	.95	.00	.00	.00	.01	.00	.00	.00	.00	.00	.00	.00	.00	.00	.00
14	.00	.00	.00	.00	.00	.00	.00	.00	.99	.00	.00	.02	.00	.00	.00	.00	.00
15	.99	.00	.00	.00	.00	.00	.00	.00	.00	.00	.00	.00	.00	.00	.00	.00	.00
16	.00	.00	.00	.00	.00	.00	.02	.00	.00	.00	.00	.00	.96	.00	.00	.00	.08
17	.01	.00	.00	.00	.00	.00	.00	.00	.00	.00	.00	.00	.65	.00	.00	.00	.00
18	.00	.00	.00	.82	.00	.00	.04	.00	.00	.00	.00	.00	.00	.00	.00	.00	.00
19	.32	.00	.00	.00	.00	.00	.00	.00	.00	.00	.94	.00	.00	.00	.00	.00	.00
20	.00	.00	.00	.66	.00	.00	.00	.00	.00	.00	.00	.96	.00	.00	.00	.00	.00
21	.00	.00	.00	.00	.00	.00	.00	.00	.00	.00	.00	.98	.00	.00	.00	.00	.00
22	.00	.00	.00	.00	.00	.00	.84	.00	.00	.00	.00	.03	.00	.00	.00	.00	.00
23	.00	.00	.00	.00	.00	.00	.00	.00	.00	.00	.00	.00	.00	.00	.00	.00	.96
24	.00	.00	.00	.00	.00	.00	.00	.00	.00	.00	.00	.00	.00	.00	.00	.00	.00
25	.00	.00	.00	.00	.00	.00	.00	.00	.85	.00	.00	.10	.00	.00	.00	.00	.00

TABLE 9.3
Intercorrelations of the Composite Prototypes for Males

Composite Prototypes

	1	2	3	4	5	6	7	8	9	10	11	12	13	14	15
1	1.00	-.08	-.07	-.11	-.10	-.06	-.06	-.10	-.06	-.07	-.05	-.08	-.14	-.09	-.08
2		1.00	-.09	-.09	-.06	-.05	-.05	-.08	-.04	-.05	-.04	-.06	-.11	-.07	-.08
3			1.00	-.08	-.08	-.05	-.05	-.09	-.05	-.06	-.04	-.08	-.13	-.08	-.09
4				1.00	-.08	-.06	-.06	-.05	-.06	-.06	-.04	-.08	-.14	-.09	-.07
5					1.00	-.06	-.05	-.07	-.05	-.06	-.04	-.07	-.12	-.07	-.09
6						1.00	-.03	-.06	-.03	-.04	-.04	-.03	-.05	-.05	-.06
7							1.00	-.05	-.03	-.02	-.02	-.04	-.07	-.04	-.05
8								1.00	-.02	-.06	-.04	-.05	-.06	-.06	-.08
9									1.00	-.03	-.04	-.04	-.06	-.04	-.04
10										1.00	-.02	-.04	-.07	-.05	-.05
11											1.00	-.03	-.05	-.03	-.04
12												1.00	-.07	-.05	-.06
13													1.00	-.08	-.07
14														1.00	-.06
15															1.00

Note: $N = 415$ $p < .05 = .095$

227

TABLE 9.4
Intercorrelations of the Composite Prototypes for Females

Composite Prototypes

	1	2	3	4	5	6	7	8	9	10	11	12	13	14	15	16	17
1	1.0	-.05	-.14	-.05	-.07	-.08	-.19	-.11	-.19	-.04	-.12	-.19	-.05	-.11	-.06	-.05	-.09
2		1.0	-.04	-.03	-.02	-.02	-.02	-.06	-.03	-.06	-.01	-.04	-.05	-.04	-.02	-.01	-.03
3			1.0	-.05	-.05	-.02	-.05	-.05	-.06	-.02	-.07	-.06	-.09	-.06	-.03	-.02	-.06
4				1.0	-.05	-.03	-.06	-.00	-.08	-.02	-.05	-.07	-.04	-.05	-.02	-.02	-.05
5					1.0	-.00	-.08	-.01	-.06	-.02	-.05	-.07	-.06	-.05	-.02	-.02	-.05
6						1.0	-.05	-.01	-.03	-.01	-.04	-.05	-.06	-.04	-.02	-.01	-.04
7							1.0	-.07	-.10	-.03	-.02	-.05	-.06	-.09	-.04	-.04	-.08
8								1.0	-.01	-.01	-.04	-.07	-.07	-.05	-.02	-.02	-.05
9									1.0	-.03	-.07	-.08	-.13	-.09	-.04	-.04	-.09
10										1.0	-.02	-.03	-.03	-.02	-.01	-.02	-.02
11											1.0	-.01	-.06	-.06	-.03	-.03	-.06
12												1.0	-.13	-.08	-.04	-.02	-.09
13													1.0	-.06	-.04	-.02	-.07
14														1.0	-.02	-.01	-.04
15															1.0	-.01	-.02
16																1.0	-.03
17																	1.0

Note: N = 358 $p < .05 = .10$

of an individual's membership in each of the composite prototypes. The probabilities were derived by employing summary dimension scores as predictors of prototype membership in a discriminant analysis. In an ideal solution, each individual has a probability of one of being assigned to a single prototype and a zero probability of being assigned to all other prototypes. Tables 9.1 and 9.2 present the probabilities obtained for 25 randomly selected male and female members of the longitudinal sample, respectively.

Most of the male and female probabilities were either quite large or quite small. In fact, only 41 (5%) of the 800 probability statements examined in this analyses were above .10 and below .90. Thus, it appears that the retained male and female solutions provided a surprisingly close approximation to the ideal 0/1 matrix of probability data that would have been produced by a perfectly clear classification of individuals. These results provide some substantial evidence pointing to the clarity of the taxonomic structures manifest in the composite prototypes.

Also derived from the discriminant analysis was information on the degree of the interrelationships among the prototypes as an index of the amount of redundancy in these descriptions. The aposteriori probabilities were intercorrelated, and results are presented in Tables 9.3 and 9.4. Once again, an unusually large number of weak negative relationships were observed. This was not especially surprising, because membership in one prototype tends to preclude membership in the remaining prototypes when assignment probabilities have been obtained through a discriminant analysis. Nevertheless, even a cursory review of the tables indicates that the likelihood of an individual's membership is one composite prototype was essentially independent of his or her membership in another composite prototype. No coefficients in excess of .15 were obtained within the male subsample. Only three coefficients larger than .15 but less than .20 were obtained within the female subsample. Apparently, membership in the composite prototypes was relatively independent, and there was little redundancy inherent in the resulting prototypical descriptions of individuality. Moreover, with the minor exceptions noted previously it appears that the description of individuals is parsimonious.

PROTOTYPE DESCRIPTIONS

Overview

The foregoing discussion has provided a broad overview of the characteristics of the composite prototypes as well as evidence pointing to the effectiveness of the summary descriptions obtained from the composite prototypes. In the following section, the differential characteristics of the

composite prototypes and the extent to which they fell into an interpretable and cohesive pattern are described.

The differential characteristics of the composite prototypes were established in the following manner. The mean scores of prototype members on the composite summary dimensions, the BQ, CEI, PCEI 2/4, and
PCEI 6/8 items and summary dimensions, and the reference measures
were contrasted with the mean scores of all male and female members of
the longitudinal sample. Mean differences larger than half of the longitudinal subsample's standard deviation on the measure were considered
significant and were used as a basis for describing the prototypes' differential characteristics. Subsequently, scores on all measures yielding significant differentiation were correlated with the aposteriori probabilities
reflecting the individual's likelihood of membership in the various composite prototypes to generate an overall index reflecting the ability of the
measure to differentiate prototype members from the subsample as a
whole. Additionally, correlations reflecting the relationship between likelihood of membership in the various composite prototypes and the likelihood of membership in the sequential BQ, CEI, PCEI 2/4, and PCEI
6/8 prototypes were obtained, although they were not explicitly examined in the initial description of the composite prototypes.

Obviously, these analyses generated numerous results, which could
not be reviewed in detail for all prototypes. Tables 9.5 and 9.6 present a
brief overview of the results. What follows is an interpretative overview
of the more salient results obtained for each composite prototype.

Male Composite Prototypes

Prototype 1. Of the total longitudinal sample, consisting of 417
males, 35 individuals were assigned to the first prototype extracted in the
composite cluster analyses. Prototype members were likely to receive
high scores on the Parental Warmth and Social Adjustment, Socioeconomic Status, and Academic Achievement composite summary dimensions
as well as low scores on the composite Family Conflict and Sociability
dimensions. At the time of the first assessment, the reference measures
indicated that prototype members were likely to be interested in practical, business-oriented occupations, such as production managers, and
to dislike highly social or intellectual jobs, such as social worker or artist.
The reference measures also indicated that these individuals were not
likely to be extroverted, integratively complex, or to have been exposed
to emotionally arousing situations. They were likely to receive good
grades in high school.

Unsurprisingly, the scores on the BQ summary dimensions indicated
high Academic Achievement, high Social Introversion, low Intellec-

TABLE 9.5
Composite Prototypes—Males

Prototype	Differential Characteristics
Channelled Concrete Achievers Prototype #1 $N = 35$	*Composite Dimensions:* parental warmth and adjustment ($r = .34$); socioeconomic status ($r = .24$); family conflict ($r = -.21$); academic achievement ($r = .20$); sociability ($r = -.21$) *Sequential Dimensions:* BQ—intellectualism ($r = -.15$); academic achievement ($r = .16$); social introversion ($r = .17$); parental control ($r = -.18$); CEI—literary pursuits ($r = -.17$); health ($r = .13$); PCEI 2/4—general reading ($r = -.22$); entry-level occupational tasks ($r = -.32$); PCEI 6/8—job channelling ($r = .13$); cognitive orientation ($r = -.15$); religious morality ($r = .25$); social adjustment ($r = .16$) *Sequential Prototypes:* BQ—traditional science-oriented leaders ($r = .16$); conservative achieving leaders ($r = .13$); PCEI 2/4—graduate students ($r = .21$); PCEI 6/8—enterprising intellectuals ($r = .25$) *Reference Measures:* high school grades ($r = .23$); college grades ($r = .28$); introversion ($r = .23$); integrative complexity ($r = -.30$); banker ($r = .28$); production manager ($r = .16$); social worker ($r = -.27$); minister ($r = -.24$) *Prototype Description:* These individuals came from warm, supportive, upper-class families which were traditional and engendered achievement motivation. Their sons were somewhat introverted and worked hard to achieve within traditional areas on a rather materialistic level. They also manifested substantial concern with family–community considerations.
Upwardly Mobile Individuals Prototype #2 $N = 27$	*Composite Dimensions:* parental warmth and social adjustment ($r = .32$); socioeconomic status ($r = .32$); family conflict ($r = -.30$); satisfaction with social life ($r = -.16$); occupational satisfaction ($r = .26$) *Sequential Dimensions:* BQ—warmth of parental relationship ($r = .14$); parental control ($r = -.11$); sibling friction ($r = -.14$); socioeconomic status ($r = .10$); CEI—positive college experience ($r = -.11$); bohemianism ($r = -.13$); PCEI 6/8—job satisfaction ($r = .19$) *Sequential Prototypes:* BQ—unconventional self-directed achieving leaders ($r = .16$); PCEI 2/4—unconventional intellectuals ($r = .15$) *Reference Measures:* social desirability ($r = .18$); neuroticism ($r = -.16$) *Prototype Description:* These individuals came from warm, highly cohesive, entrepreneurial families. Members of this prototype manifested some achievement motivation and social leadership in high school. They were also somewhat independent. This pattern of independent social leadership was apparent in the college and postcollege years. However, they eventually found satisfactory jobs and concentrated their efforts on achievement in this domain, apparently through social leadership.

(Continued)

TABLE 9.5
(continued)

Prototype	Differential Characteristics
Unrealistic Independents Prototype #3 $N = 27$	*Composite Dimensions:* Parental warmth and social adjustment ($r = .27$); professional occupational orientation ($r = -.29$); academic achievement ($r = -.44$); religious involvement ($r = -.17$); satisfaction with social life ($r = -.14$) *Sequential Dimensions:* BQ—warmth of parental relationship ($r = .13$); intellectualism ($r = -.18$); CEI—religious involvement ($r = -.11$); athletic pursuits ($r = -.16$); PCEI 2/4—general reading ($r = -.32$); PCEI 6/8—job channelling ($r = -.29$); religious involvement ($r = -.16$) *Sequential Prototypes:* PCEI 2/4—graduate students ($r = -.14$); traditional achievers ($r = -.30$); PCEI 6/8—impoverished ineffective men ($r = .17$); areligious careerists ($r = -.18$) *Reference Measures:* high school grades ($r = -.20$); college grades ($r = -.21$); socio-religious conformity ($r = -.22$); architecture ($r = .21$); chemistry ($r = .18$); engineering ($r = .16$); school superintendent ($r = -.19$); credit manager ($r = -.20$); business education teacher ($r = -.23$) *Prototype Description:* These individuals came from warm supportive families which encouraged independence. Prototype members manifested substantial independence from social institutions and a lack of academic ability. They obtained a sample-typical level of job success but remained dissatisfied with their jobs and unwilling to merge into adult social institutions.
Virile Extraverts Prototype #4 $N = 36$	*Composite Dimensions:* parental warmth and adjustment ($r = .27$); traditional masculine role ($r = .36$); sociability ($r = .17$); satisfaction with social life ($r = .29$) *Sequential Dimensions:* BQ—social introversion ($r = -.24$); social desirability ($r = .22$); CEI—literary pursuits ($r = -.18$); religious involvement ($r = .15$); PCEI 2/4—entry level occupational tasks ($r = .13$); social adjustment ($r = .14$) *Sequential Prototypes:* CEI—fraternity members ($r = .16$); PCEI 6/8—contented affluent conservatives ($r = .18$) *Reference Measures:* masculinity ($r = .25$); physical goals ($r = .31$); economic values ($r = .16$); liberalism ($r = -.19$); academic achievement ($r = -.20$); sales ($r = .20$); military ($r = .22$); community recreation director ($r = .22$); mathematics ($r = -.30$); psychology ($r = -.34$); journalism ($r = -.23$) *Prototype Description:* These individuals came from traditional families in which they were close to their warm, supportive fathers. They were highly athletic and highly social in both high school and college. Involvement with traditional social institutions was especially likely among these males. They obtained jobs in line with their interests, which led to some degree of occupational success in adulthood. Their continued athletic and social involvement apparently led to an active and satisfying social life.

Analytical Adapters
Prototype #5
N = 23

Composite Dimensions: parental warmth and social adjustment ($r = .23$); socioeconomic status ($r = .12$); family conflict ($r = .12$); scientific/engineering interests ($r = .41$).

Sequential Dimensions: BQ—parental control ($r = -.14$); academic achievement ($r = .17$); PCEI 2/4—college-moderated social development ($r = .11$)

Sequential Prototypes: BQ—traditional science-oriented achieving leaders ($r = .18$); athletically oriented science majors ($r = .28$); PCEI 6/8—enterprising intellectuals ($r = .16$)

Reference Measures: cognitive values ($r = .22$); integrative complexity ($r = .18$); academic achievement ($r = .19$); science ($r = .31$); mathematics ($r = .21$); computer programming ($r = .24$); Air Force officer ($r = .19$)

Prototype Description: These individuals displayed a marked interest in scientific and engineering pursuits as well as some degree of social success in high school. Members of this prototype were rather typical in college. In adulthood, they tended to enter scientific or technically oriented professions. They also formed successful marriages and were somewhat religious.

Withdrawn
Effeminates
Prototype #6
N = 16

Composite Dimensions: parental warmth and social adjustment ($r = .21$); traditional masculine role ($r = -.22$); intellectual pursuits ($r = .23$); scientific/engineering interests ($r = -.28$); family conflict ($r = .17$)

Sequential Dimensions: BQ—sibling friction ($r = .14$); scientific interests ($r = -.25$); social desirability ($r = -.27$); CEI—marital status ($r = -.43$); self-support ($r = -.16$); athletic pursuits ($r = -.19$); PCEI 2/4—religious involvement ($r = -.11$); job satisfaction ($r = .11$); PCEI 6/8—cognitive orientation ($r = .21$)

Sequential Prototypes: BQ—competent independent aesthetes ($r = .18$); CEI—maladjusted drifters ($r = .21$); PCEI 2/4—graduate students ($r = .15$); PCEI 6/8—enterprising intellectuals ($r = .16$)

Reference Measures: masculinity ($r = .23$); economic values ($r = -.16$); physical goals ($r = -.25$); minister ($r = .34$); social worker ($r = .26$); lawyer ($r = .33$); author/journalist ($r = .27$); librarian ($r = .38$); teacher ($r = .28$); forest service ($r = -.26$); engineering ($r = -.25$); chemistry ($r = -.18$)

Prototype Description: These individuals came from upper-class families in which they were especially close to their warm, supportive, and somewhat protective mothers. In high school, these males were somewhat withdrawn and active in intellectual and artistic pursuits. This pattern was maintained in college. They eventually obtained jobs in line with their interests and they continued to devote spare time to solitary intellectual pursuits. These males tended to marry late or not at all. They displayed little interest in community affairs and religion.

(Continued)

TABLE 9.5
(continued)

Prototype	Differential Characteristics
Insecure Socialites Prototype #7 $N = 15$	*Composite Dimensions:* sociability ($r = .16$); intellectual pursuits ($r = .15$); scientific/engineering interests ($r = -.11$); occupational satisfaction ($r = -.37$); satisfaction with social life ($r = -.25$) *Sequential Dimensions:* BQ—parental warmth ($r = .09$); academic achievement ($r = .11$); scientific interests ($r = -.11$); CEI—literary pursuits ($r = .09$); activity in organizations ($r = .23$); bohemianism ($r = .15$); PCEI 2/4—extra-occupational satisfaction ($r = -.07$); job satisfaction ($r = -.14$); PCEI 6/8—job satisfaction ($r = -.36$); extra-occupational satisfaction ($r = -.15$); occupational status ($r = .09$); social adjustment ($r = -.09$) *Sequential Prototypes:* CEI—dependent womanizers ($r = .23$); organizational activists ($r = .20$); PCEI 6/8—unhappy isolates ($r = .15$); successful occupational misfits ($r = .42$) *Reference Measures:* high school grades ($r = .10$); SAT scores ($r = .15$); liberalism ($r = .11$); conceptual simplicity ($r = .10$); engineering ($r = -.12$); production manager ($r = -.15$); YMCA secretary ($r = .12$); community recreation director ($r = .10$) *Prototype Description:* These individuals had parents who allowed them some independence, and they were close to their fathers. In high school, they were active in athletics and intellectual pursuits, and they were socially active. However, they displayed little social confidence. In college, they were highly involved with the opposite sex and a variety of extracurricular activities. After graduation, they took jobs which were not in line with their interests and apparently had some difficulty in establishing an independent social life. Consequently, they displayed marked social and occupational dissatisfaction which became more pronounced over time due to their unwillingness to take action to change the situation.
Constrained Careerists Prototype #8 $N = 30$	*Composite Dimensions:* parental warmth and social adjustment ($r = -.24$); professional occupational orientation ($r = -.17$); religious involvement ($r = -.19$); academic achievement ($r = -.24$); intellectual pursuits ($r = -.17$); scientific/engineering interests ($r = -.11$); socioeconomic status ($r = -.20$); occupational satisfaction ($r = .26$) *Sequential Dimensions:* BQ—socioeconomic status ($r = -.14$); athletic interests ($r = -.11$); social desirability ($r = -.14$); CEI—sociability ($r = .25$); religious involvement ($r = -.14$); PCEI 2/4—general reading ($r = -.26$); religious involvement ($r = .10$); PCEI 6/8—job satisfaction ($r = .20$); occupational status ($r = -.16$); religious morality ($r = -.19$) *Sequential Prototypes:* PCEI 2/4—traditional achievers ($r = .23$); alienated occupational successes ($r = .23$); early maturers ($r = .26$)

| Ineffectual Authoritarians Prototype #9 N = 11 | *Reference Measures:* high school grades ($r = -.15$); college grades ($r = -.09$); cognitive values ($r = -.09$); conceptual simplicity ($r = .13$); liberalism ($r = -.08$); tendermindedness ($r = .08$); introversion ($r = .07$); sales ($r = .14$); merchandising ($r = .20$); office practices ($r = .15$). SAT scores ($r = -.14$); cognitive

Prototype Description: These individuals were raised in a strict, lower-class family environment. In high school, they were likely to engage in stereotypic activities, such as athletics and building things. During college, these males adopted a rather bohemian, highly social lifestyle. While not especially successful occupationally, due to their intellectual limitations, they invested themselves in their jobs and were satisfied with them.

Composite Dimensions: parental warmth and social adjustment ($r = .17$); traditional masculine role ($r = .23$); religious involvement ($r = .14$); professional occupational orientation ($r = -.14$); intellectual pursuits ($r = -.25$); sociability ($r = -.10$); family conflict ($r = -.18$)

Sequential Dimensions: BQ—warmth of parental relationship ($r = .15$); parental control ($r = .14$); social desirability ($r = .19$); religious activity ($r = .13$); CEI—self support ($r = .14$); sociability ($r = .18$); religious involvement ($r = .14$); PCEI 2/4—early occupational success ($r = -.24$); job satisfaction ($r = -.18$); PCEI 6/8—job channelling ($r = -.13$); occupational status ($r = -.12$); cognitive orientation ($r = .14$); social adjustment ($r = -.17$)

Sequential Prototypes: CEI—bohemians ($r = -.18$); PCEI 2/4—early maturers ($r = .15$)

Reference Measures: None |
| Religious Copers Prototype #10 N = 17 | *Prototype Description:* These individuals were raised in a harsh, controlling, lower-class family in which they tried to be like their father. In high school they engaged in athletics, dating, and traditional social activities. During college, they engaged in few social or athletic activities; rather, they retreated into religion and manifested conservative political views. Members of this prototype failed to prepare themselves for the occupational world and subsequently they obtained lower-level jobs, often clerical in nature, which they were dissatisfied with. They dropped their religious involvement and failed to establish a satisfying marital and social life, although they tended to marry early in adulthood.

Composite Dimensions: religious involvement ($r = .34$); satisfaction with social life ($r = .18$); professional occupational orientation ($r = -.19$)

Sequential Dimensions: BQ—athletic interests ($r = .13$); CEI—religious involvement ($r = .39$); activity in organizations ($r = .11$); PCEI 2/4—vocational direction ($r = .21$); general reading ($r = .13$); PCEI 6/8—job channelling ($r = .15$); job satisfaction ($r = .15$); extra-occupational satisfaction ($r = .11$); religious morality ($r = .22$) |

(Continued)

TABLE 9.5
(continued)

Prototype	Differential Characteristics
	Sequential Prototypes: CEI—born again believers ($r = .28$); spiritual thinkers ($r = .20$); PCEI 2/4—religious dogmatics ($r = .14$); PCEI 6/8—born again believers ($r = .24$)
	Reference Measures: high school grades ($r = -.15$); SAT scores ($r = -.16$; cognitive values ($r = -.10$); hierarchical complexity ($r = -.10$); integrative complexity ($r = -.12$); conceptual simplicity ($r = .10$); introversion ($r = .16$); carpentry ($r = .08$); printing ($r = .09$); medicine ($r = -.10$); chemistry ($r = -.09$); law ($r = -.21$); recreational leadership ($r = .13$)
	Prototype Description: These individuals were not especially social or religious in high school, although they were active in athletics and a variety of hobbies. They were somewhat simple, protected, and lacking in intellectual abilities. In college, they dealt with these limitations by an involvement in religious groups. Prototype members did not prepare themselves for an occupation and obtained rather poor jobs. However, they were not especially dissatisfied and continued to focus their activities on religious and community involvement.
	Composite Dimensions: parental warmth and social adjustment ($r = -.11$); religious involvement ($r = .14$); sociability ($r = .25$); academic achievement ($r = .17$); intellectual pursuits ($r = .11$)
	Sequential Dimensions: BQ—warmth of parental relationship ($r = -.10$); intellectualism ($r = .08$); CEI—literary pursuits ($r = .13$); sociability ($r = .17$); activity in organizations ($r = .34$); PCEI 2/4—entry-level occupational tasks ($r = .09$); college-moderated social development ($r = .10$); PCEI 6/8—extra-occupational satisfaction ($r = .09$); social adjustment ($r = .08$)
Expansive Compensators Prototype #11 $N = 7$	*Sequential Prototypes:* BQ—cognitively complex religious converters ($r = .17$); jocks ($r = .16$); CEI—organizational activists ($r = .33$)
	Reference Measures: None
	Prototype Description: These individuals were raised in a turbulent, somewhat restrictive family environment in which they were the youngest child. In high school, they were socially withdrawn and involved in solitary intellectual pursuits. During college, these males became highly active in a variety of organizations; they also spent time reading and in holding jobs. After graduation, they obtained entry-level business jobs, and they were sufficiently successful to eventually attain upper-level managerial jobs. They continued to engage in substantial intellectual reading and social activities, and they eventually formed happy marriages on the basis of shared interests.

Fortunate Approval Seekers
Prototype #12
$N = 21$

Composite Dimensions: parental warmth and social adjustment ($r = .21$); traditional masculine role ($r = -.28$); sociability ($r = .27$); professional occupational orientation ($r = -.15$); academic achievement ($r = .14$); intellectual pursuits ($r = -.26$); socioeconomic status ($r = .19$)

Sequential Dimensions: BQ—social desirability ($r = .22$); parental control ($r = .08$); intellectualism ($r = -.07$); scientific interests ($r = -.07$); CEI—literary pursuits ($r = -.25$); sociability ($r = .07$); marital status ($r = -.07$); athletic pursuits ($r = .18$); self-support ($r = -.18$); PCEI 2/4—religious involvement ($r = -.30$); entry-level occupational tasks ($r = .13$); PCEI 6/8—job channelling ($r = -.13$); cognitive orientation ($r = -.14$)

Sequential Prototypes: CEI—fraternity members ($r = .20$); PCEI 2/4—good old boys ($r = .29$)

Reference Measures: None

Prototype Description: These individuals were raised by strict, distant, apparently upper-class individuals. In high school, they were withdrawn and spent their spare time on solitary hobbies. Nevertheless, they manifested a desire for social approval. In college, they joined a fraternity and became socially active and involved in athletics. They found satisfactory jobs after graduation and established an active, albeit limited, social life. During this time, they displayed little interest in intellectual pursuits, although they were involved with athletics.

Adjustive Successes
Prototype #13
$N = 42$

Composite Dimensions: parental warmth and social adjustment ($r = -.40$); traditional masculine role ($r = -.25$); academic achievement ($r = .12$); professional occupational orientation ($r = .20$); religious involvement ($r = -.17$); socioeconomic status ($r = -.14$)

Sequential Dimensions: BQ—socioeconomic status ($r = -.18$); social desirability ($r = .17$); PCEI 2/4—entry level occupational tasks ($r = -.21$)

Sequential Prototypes: BQ—analytical independents ($r = .15$); approval seeking humanitarians ($r = .15$); PCEI 6/8—areligious careerists ($r = .16$)

Reference Measures: None

Prototype Description: These individuals were raised in a harsh, restrictive, lower-class family. They disliked high school but worked hard and did well in academics, although they were somewhat withdrawn socially, and spare time was spent on individual sports or solitary intellectual activities. In college, they continued to work hard but were otherwise typical undergraduates. They channelled themselves into upper-level business-oriented jobs which paid well. Since this was in line with their desires, they were satisfied with their jobs. Aside from establishing satisfactory marriages, they were otherwise rather typical adults.

(Continued)

237

(continued)

Prototype	Differential Characteristics
Premature Conformists Prototype #14 $N = 22$	*Composite Dimensions:* parental warmth and social adjustment ($r = -.16$); traditional masculine role ($r = .17$); religious involvement ($r = .14$); sociability ($r = .14$); socioeconomic status ($r = -.30$); family conflict ($r = .14$); academic achievement ($r = .12$); scientific/engineering interests ($r = .12$); occupational satisfaction ($r = -.12$); satisfaction with social life ($r = -.11$) *Sequential Dimensions:* BQ—social introversion ($r = -.26$); athletic interests ($r = .12$); sibling friction ($r = .12$); CEI—literary pursuits ($r = -.28$); activity in organizations ($r = .19$); marital status ($r = .10$); PCEI 2/4—job satisfaction ($r = -.19$); extra-occupational satisfaction ($r = -.26$); college-moderated social development ($r = -.12$); PCEI 6/8—job satisfaction ($r = -.18$); religious morality ($r = -.12$); social adjustment ($r = -.11$) *Sequential Prototypes:* BQ—nonconformist dropouts ($r = .20$); CEI—ineffective isolates ($r = .39$); PCEI 2/4—socially maladapted individuals ($r = .22$); early maturers ($r = .20$) *Reference Measures:* None *Prototype Description:* These individuals were raised in a somewhat harsh, lower-class family environment; however, they were close to their fathers. In high school, they appeared to adopt the traditional masculine role, being active in athletics and extracurricular activities. They were also active with the opposite sex. Moreover, these males began dating early and were likely to be married at the time of college entry. In college, they were active in a variety of organizations but were somewhat isolated socially. They took a job immediately after graduation. However, as a result of trying to establish a marriage and career, they became dissatisfied with both. Although these effects diminished with the passage of time, some after-effects were apparent 6 to 8 years after graduation.
Bourgeois Outliers Prototype #15 $N = 30$	*Composite Dimensions:* parental warmth and social adjustment ($r = -.35$); socioeconomic status ($r = .14$); professional occupational orientation ($r = -.26$); religious involvement ($r = .13$); academic achievement ($r = .22$); satisfaction with social life ($r = -.21$) *Sequential Dimensions:* BQ—academic achievement ($r = -.24$); scientific interests ($r = -.15$); social introversion ($r = -.11$); CEI—literary pursuits ($r = .15$); positive college experience ($r = -.22$); PCEI 2/4—early occupational success ($r = -.13$); college moderated social development ($r = .16$); PCEI 6/8—job channelling ($r = .27$); religious morality ($r = .14$); extra-occupational satisfaction ($r = -.20$) *Sequential Prototypes:* PCEI 2/4—graduate students ($r = .27$); PCEI 6/8—unambitious townsmen ($r = .21$); unhappy isolates ($r = .15$) *Reference Measures:* None *Prototype Description:* These individuals were raised in relatively wealthy homes in which the parents displayed little concern with their son's activities. While doing well in school, these males were apparently somewhat rebellious, rejecting traditional social activities for solitary intellectual pursuits. In college, this rebellion and liberal intellectual orientation became more pronounced. This trend was also apparent in their postcollege years. They obtained upper-level social service jobs. These males were likely to avoid adult social institutions

TABLE 9.6
Composite Prototypes—Females

Prototype	Differential Characteristics
Unscathed Adjusters Prototype #1 $N = 46$	*Composite Dimensions:* traditional social adjustment ($r = .56$); negative parent/child conflict ($r = -.12$); sibling friction ($r = -.21$); sociability ($r = .10$); job channelling ($r = .26$); intellectual pursuits ($r = -.15$); life satisfaction ($r = .20$)
	Sequential Dimensions: BQ—feelings of social inadequacy ($r = .18$); CEI—self support ($r = -.15$); PCEI 2/4—religious beliefs ($r = .14$); rudimentary people-oriented jobs ($r = .34$); job determinants ($r = .24$); PCEI 6/8—job determinants ($r = .24$); perceived occupational status ($r = -.18$); extra-occupational satisfaction ($r = .36$)
	Sequential Prototypes: BQ—well-adjusted achievers ($r = .18$); CEI—traditional daters ($r = .23$); PCEI 2/4—concrete careerists ($r = .49$); immature escapists ($r = -.16$); effective adapters ($r = .23$); PCEI 6/8—realistically mature adults ($r = .38$)
	Reference Measures: socioreligious conformity ($r = .26$); extroversion ($r = .25$)
	Prototype Description: These individuals were reared in warm, supportive, somewhat traditional families. In high school, they were active and attempted to achieve in those areas open to females, while they avoided achievement in traditional male areas, such as science and athletics, even when they had the requisite abilities. These females were socially active in college and dated frequently. They did not marry immediately after graduation but were likely to be married 6 to 8 years after graduation. These marriages were happy and somewhat traditional, and these women appeared to maintain the social service jobs that had prepared themselves for.
Competent Nurturers Prototype #2 $N = 9$	*Composite Dimensions:* traditional social adjustment ($r = .20$); religious involvement ($r = .42$); self esteem ($r = .12$); intellectual pursuits ($r = .08$); socioeconomic status ($r = .11$); negative parent/child conflict ($r = -.08$); sibling friction ($r = .07$); life satisfaction ($r = .04$)
	Sequential Dimensions: BQ—academic achievement ($r = .10$); expression of negative emotions ($r = -.11$); athletic participation ($r = -.11$); feelings of social inadequacy ($r = .10$); popularity with the opposite sex ($r = .16$); CEI—religious involvement ($r = .40$); PCEI 2/4—religious beliefs ($r = .21$); extra-occupational satisfaction ($r = .11$); occupational initiative ($r = -.10$); upward occupational mobility ($r = -.08$); rudimentary people-oriented jobs ($r = .17$); PCEI 6/8—religious-community involvement ($r = .20$); intellectual reading ($r = -.07$); job satisfaction ($r = .08$); perceived occupational status ($r = -.18$)

(Continued)

239

TABLE 9.6
(continued)

Prototype	Differential Characteristics
	Sequential Prototypes: CEI—Christians ($r = .46$); joiners ($r = -.24$); PCEI 2/4—newly married careerists ($r = .30$); PCEI 6/8—community-directed housewives ($r = .28$)
	Reference Measures: high school grades ($r = .14$); college grades ($r = .11$); SAT scores ($r = .17$); academic achievement ($r = .24$); femininity ($r = .13$); liberalism ($r = -.22$); introversion ($r = .10$); physician ($r = .13$); biologist ($r = .16$); religion ($r = .22$); teaching ($r = .12$); music ($r = .25$); merchandizing ($r = -.11$); military pursuits ($r = -.22$); technical work ($r = -.09$)
	Prototype Description: These individuals were reared in a warm, religious, upper-class family in which the mother was socially active. They displayed substantial intellectual ability and a rather nurturant pattern of activities. While somewhat introverted in high school, they were socially active and effective. In college, they became more involved with religion and less concerned with academics. They tended to acquire social service jobs after graduation. However, their successful marriages, religious activities, and community activities seemed to be the focus of their lives.
Unconventional Successes Prototype #3 $N = 20$	*Composite Dimensions:* traditional social adjustment ($r = -.24$); sociability ($r = -.21$); religious involvement ($r = -.16$); socioeconomic status ($r = -.23$); occupational level and satisfaction ($r = .10$); intellectual pursuits ($r = .31$); life satisfaction ($r = .12$)
	Sequential Dimensions: BQ—cultural/literary interests ($r = .28$); socioeconomic status ($r = -.14$); popularity with the opposite sex ($r = -.08$); CEI—liberal activism ($r = .20$); sociability ($r = .18$); religious involvement ($r = -.18$); PCEI 2/4—religious beliefs ($r = -.22$); occupational initiative ($r = -.13$); rudimentary people-oriented jobs ($r = .16$); PCEI 6/8—intellectual reading ($r = .30$); extra-occupational satisfaction ($r = .16$); religious-community involvement ($r = -.15$)
	Sequential Prototypes: BQ—unconventional achievers ($r = .22$); CEI—traditional daters ($r = -.16$); fashionable liberals ($r = .17$); PCEI 2/4—unaspiring workers ($r = -.19$); unambitious passives ($r = .16$); PCEI 6/8—vocationally adjusted expressives ($r = .17$)
	Reference Measures: SAT mathematics ($r = -.08$); SAT verbal ($r = .11$); academic achievement ($r = .06$); femininity ($r = .11$); hierarchical complexity ($r = -.08$); introversion ($r = .09$); tendermindedness ($r = .10$); authoritarianism ($r = -.08$); emotional exposure ($r = .13$); emotional inhibition ($r = .08$); expression of negative emotions ($r = .11$); music ($r = .07$); arts ($r = .08$); writing ($r = .10$); science ($r = .10$); mathematics ($r = -.09$); mechanics ($r = -.11$); sales manager ($r = -.09$); Chamber of Commerce executive ($r = -.10$)

Prototype Description: These individuals were raised in a relatively harsh, lower-class environment. In high school, these females were somewhat withdrawn and spent their spare time in solitary intellectual pursuits. During college, they were rather rebellious and manifested a liberal intellectual lifestyle. There was also an expansion of social contact, particularly with males. After college, they channelled themselves into the cultural/social service jobs they desired, and they were eventually successful on these jobs. They continued to display an independent intellectual orientation, and they appeared to have established an active, satisfying, somewhat nontraditional social life.

Frustrated Incompetents Prototype #4 N = 15

Composite Dimensions: job channelling ($r = -.25$); intellectual pursuits ($r = -.12$); self-esteem ($r = -.30$); sociability ($r = -.33$); negative parent child conflict ($r = .16$)

Sequential Dimensions: BQ—parental control ($r = .12$); adjustment ($r = .08$); CEI—religious involvement ($r = -.14$); positive college experience ($r = -.16$); PCEI 2/4—job satisfaction ($r = -.15$); PCEI 6/8—job appropriateness ($r = -.15$); collegiate social maturation ($r = -.31$); intellectual reading ($r = -.08$)

Sequential Prototypes: PCEI 2/4—unprepared underemployeds ($r = .20$)

Reference Measures: high school grades ($r = -.16$); college grades ($r = -.18$); SAT scores ($r = -.16$); external control ($r = .11$); economic values ($r = .12$); acquiescence ($r = .14$); occupational level ($r = -.22$); specialization level ($r = -.13$); real estate sales ($r = .26$); office work ($r = .18$); purchasing agent ($r = .21$); science ($r = -.24$); mechanics ($r = -.19$)

Prototype Description: These individuals were raised in middle-class families. They were not intellectually gifted. In high school, they were socially active although not especially self-confident. During both high school and college they did poorly academically. When this was coupled with a lack of occupational preparation, they obtained poor jobs. They were dissatisfied with these jobs and despite focusing their activities in this area, they were not able to change the situation. These females also had trouble establishing an independent social life, and this led to further dissatisfaction.

Social Manipulators Prototype #5 N = 16

Composite Dimensions: self-esteem ($r = .18$); sociability ($r = .22$); religious involvement ($r = .14$); sibling friction ($r = .14$); intellectual pursuits ($r = .38$); life satisfaction ($r = -.16$)

Sequential Dimensions: BQ—parental control ($r = .12$); cultural/literary interests ($r = -.12$); expression of negative emotions ($r = -.08$); parental warmth ($r = -.09$); CEI—liberal activism ($r = .13$); religious involvement ($r = .12$); sociability ($r = .12$); leisure reading ($r = .12$); PCEI 2/4—intellectual leisure reading ($r = .13$); PCEI 6/8—intellectual reading ($r = .10$)

Sequential Prototypes: CEI—effective intellectuals ($r = .26$); PCEI 2/4—"schoolmarms" ($r = .21$)

Reference Measures: high school grades ($r = -.19$); SAT mathematics ($r = .10$); academic achievement ($r = -.23$); integrative complexity ($r = .23$); conceptual simplicity ($r = .20$); cognitive values ($r = .12$);

(Continued)

TABLE 9.6
(continued)

Prototype	Differential Characteristics
	extraversion ($r = .10$); neuroticism ($r = .23$); social desirability ($r = .27$); occupational level ($r = .09$); specialization level ($r = .21$); personnel director ($r = .25$); public administrator ($r = .20$); school superintendent ($r = .12$); veterinarian ($r = -.20$); psychologist ($r = -.13$); carpentry ($r = -.16$); farming ($r = -.24$)
	Prototype Description: These individuals came from warm, supportive families which engendered a sense of achievement motivation. They in turn manifested substantial achievement motivation; however, it appeared to be focused in the social domain where they were highly active and effective. This pattern was maintained during their college years. However, they also displayed the then fashionable liberal intellectual orientation. Nevertheless, they carefully prepared themselves for jobs in line with their interests which entailed social control. They eventually obtained these jobs and were successful at them. Members of this type also formed a superficially successful social life, although this appeared to deepen problems, and they remained active in intellectual pursuits.
Paternal Reactives Prototype #6 $N = 8$	*Composite Dimensions:* traditional social adjustment ($r = -.11$); job channelling ($r = -.21$); occupational level and satisfaction ($r = -.18$); sociability ($r = -.08$); intellectual pursuits ($r = .20$); religious involvement ($r = -.18$); paternal identification ($r = .26$); negative parent/child conflict ($r = -.15$); sibling friction ($r = -.09$) *Sequential Dimensions:* BQ—warmth of maternal relationship ($r = -.21$); paternal warmth ($r = .10$); positive academic attitudes ($r = -.14$); CEI—religious involvement ($r = .11$); athletic participation ($r = -.19$); health ($r = -.10$); sociability ($r = .17$); traditional social involvement ($r = .18$); PCEI 2/4—intellectual leisure reading ($r = .15$); occupational initiative ($r = -.10$); religious beliefs ($r = -.20$); rudimentary people-oriented jobs ($r = .10$); PCEI 6/8—job determinants ($r = -.12$); job satisfaction ($r = -.15$); religious-community involvement ($r = -.16$); intellectual reading ($r = .16$) *Sequential Prototypes:* CEI—fashionable liberals ($r = .18$); dependent isolates ($r = .38$); PCEI 2/4—unaspiring workers ($r = .23$); PCEI 6/8—underemployed intellectuals ($r = .18$) *Reference Measures:* None *Prototype Description:* These individuals came from a harsh, restrictive family environment in which they were closer to their fathers than their mothers, perhaps because of the former's relatively more positive behavior. In high school, this environment led to poor adjustment, dependency, social withdrawal, and a preference for athletic and solitary intellectual pursuits. In college, they rebelled against this environment, becoming social

and political radicals. Some expansion of social and intellectual interests was also apparent. However, they failed to prepare themselves for the occupational world and could not form satisfying social relationships, especially with men. They subsequently had marital and occupational difficulties which were worsened by their continued rebellion. These females remained interested in intellectual pursuits.

Restricted Socializers Prototype #7 $N = 28$	*Composite Dimensions:* traditional social adjustment ($r = -.29$); job channelling ($r = -.17$); occupational level and satisfaction ($r = .16$); sociability ($r = .27$); religious involvement ($r = -.19$); negative parent/child conflict ($r = -.23$); paternal identification ($r = .22$); socioeconomic status ($r = -.11$); sibling friction ($r = .28$) *Sequential Dimensions:* BQ—social leadership ($r = -.16$); socioeconomic status ($r = -.08$); CEI—dating activity ($r = .23$); religious involvement ($r = -.18$); PCEI 2/4—job appropriateness ($r = -.17$); PCEI 6/8—job determinants ($r = -.16$); job satisfaction ($r = .18$); collegiate social maturation ($r = .16$); perceived occupational status ($r = .17$) *Sequential Prototypes:* BQ—extraverted materialistic authoritarians ($r = .29$); CEI—fragile flirts ($r = .23$); PCEI 2/4—self-defeating passives ($r = .15$) *Reference Measures:* high school grades ($r = -.14$); academic achievement ($r = -.16$); integrative complexity ($r = -.12$); long-term goals ($r = -.15$); social desirability ($r = .09$); socioreligious conformity ($r = .11$); authoritarianism ($r = .14$); positive emotionality ($r = .09$); negative emotionality ($r = -.13$); introversion ($r = .10$); occupational level ($r = -.16$); osteopath ($r = -.06$); CPA owner ($r = .09$); minister ($r = -.07$); nature ($r = .12$); technical responsibility ($r = .11$); agriculture ($r = .15$) *Prototype Description:* These individuals came from a strict, cold, lower-class family. In high school, they were not strongly motivated to achieve in academic situations. They were conformists, and while they expressed a desire for social approval, they were not especially socially effective. In college, they joined a sorority but apparently for friendship and contact with the opposite sex. Their social effectiveness increased during this period. They failed to plan for a specific job but eventually obtained sales jobs on which they were moderately successful. These females continued to manifest an interest in the opposite sex, and they centered their social lives around their husbands.
Discontented Male Dependents Prototype #8 $N = 10$	*Composite Dimensions:* traditional social adjustment ($r = -.19$); self-esteem ($r = -.11$); sociability ($r = -.14$); scientific interests ($r = -.07$); religious involvement ($r = .22$); negative parent/child conflict ($r = -.09$); paternal identification ($r = .09$); life satisfaction ($r = -.27$); athletic activities ($r = .30$) *Sequential Dimensions:* BQ—warmth of maternal relationship ($r = -.12$); social leadership ($r = .11$); feelings of social inadequacy ($r = .11$); popularity with the opposite sex ($r = .17$); athletic participation ($r = .27$); academic achievement ($r = -.13$); CEI—dating activity ($r = -.15$); religious involvement ($r = .23$);

(Continued)

243

TABLE 9.6
(continued)

Prototype	Differential Characteristics
	traditional social involvement ($r = .13$); sociability ($r = .13$); PCEI 2/4—occupational initiative ($r = .22$); rudimentary people-oriented jobs ($r = .16$); upward occupational mobility ($r = -.13$); intellectual leisure reading ($r = -.19$); extra-occupational satisfaction ($r = -.16$); PCEI 6/8—extra-occupational satisfaction ($r = -.27$); perceived occupational status ($r = -.15$); collegiate social maturation ($r = -.10$) *Sequential Prototypes:* BQ—unpopular, cognitively simple introverts ($r = .29$); scholarly bookworms ($r = .29$); CEI—Christians ($r = .26$); PCEI 2/4—self-defeating passives ($r = .15$); PCEI 6/8—presently devastated women ($r = .30$); family-focused women ($r = .15$) *Reference Measures:* None *Prototype Description:* These individuals were raised in harsh, restrictive, nonreligious middle-class families. In high school, they were concerned with achievement and effective in the social and extracurricular domains. However, this did not carry over into college. Here, they withdrew into religion and traditional social roles while failing to prepare themselves for the occupational world. This withdrawal seemed to be based on the same desire for security which was apparent in their early marriages. In their dependency on their husbands these females failed to establish a satisfactory, social, marital, or occupational life.
Defensive Conformists Prototype #9 $N = 23$	*Composite Dimensions:* traditional social adjustment ($r = -.36$); job channelling ($r = .29$); self-esteem ($r = .15$); sociability ($r = -.28$); intellectual pursuits ($r = -.23$); scientific interests ($r = .17$); socioeconomic status ($r = -.20$) *Sequential Dimensions:* BQ—social leadership ($r = .16$); CEI—liberal activism ($r = -.23$); leisure reading ($r = -.17$); sociability ($r = -.15$); health ($r = .15$); PCEI 2/4—job appropriateness ($r = .20$); rudimentary people-oriented jobs ($r = .29$); upward occupational mobility ($r = -.21$); religious beliefs ($r = -.20$); PCEI 6/8—job determinants ($r = .26$); job satisfaction ($r = -.17$) *Sequential Prototypes:* CEI—married students ($r = -.22$); PCEI 2/4—immature escapists ($r = .54$); PCEI 6/8—family-focused women ($r = .15$) *Reference Measures:* None *Prototype Description:* These females were raised in an extremely harsh, lower-class family environment in which they were criticized, pushed for achievement, and allowed little independence. In high school they were highly conformist, socially isolated, desiring of power and structure, and academically ineffective. Their spare time was spent on solitary intellectual pursuits. They remained conformist and socially introverted in college. Their activities seemed to be focused on going steady. They also channelled themselves into the teaching jobs

"Orphaned" Adapters
Prototype #10
N = 3

they apparently desired. Throughout this time period, they displayed little interest in religious or intellectual pursuits. Otherwise, their adult behavior was sample-typical.

Composite Dimensions: traditional social adjustment ($r = -.10$); self-esteem ($r = -.10$); sociability ($r = .11$); negative parent/child conflict ($r = .26$); socioeconomic status ($r = -.10$); athletic interests ($r = -.16$)

Sequential Dimensions: BQ—social leadership ($r = -.11$); feelings of social inadequacy ($r = -.07$); socioeconomic status ($r = .04$); CEI—traditional social involvement ($r = -.10$); leisure reading ($r = .11$); self-support ($r = -.09$); PCEI 2/4—job satisfaction ($r = .09$); intellectual leisure reading ($r = .09$); upward occupational mobility ($r = -.10$); occupational initiative ($r = .09$); rudimentary people-oriented jobs ($r = .09$); religious beliefs ($r = -.10$); PCEI 6/8—social job activities ($r = -.17$); perceived occupational status ($r = .10$); collegiate social maturation ($r = .10$); religious-community involvement ($r = .09$)

Sequential Prototypes: PCEI 6/8—disillusioned capitalists ($r = .26$)

Reference Measures: None

Prototype Description: These individuals were raised in relatively entrepreneurial families in which the parents displayed little overt concern for or warmth toward their daughters, although they did encourage independence. In high school, they appeared to be somewhat independent, socially withdrawn, socially immature, and emotionally flat. They also tended to dislike and do poorly in school. In college, these females were likely to join a sorority and this served as a basis for an expansion of social skills. After graduation, they capitalized on these newly developed skills and their family background to obtain managerial jobs at which they were quite successful, although a concern with advancement led to some dissatisfaction. They were also successful in establishing a satisfactory social life and marriage which allowed them some independence.

Unambitious Passives
Prototype #11
N = 17

Composite Dimensions: traditional social adjustment ($r = -.17$); occupational level and satisfaction ($r = -.36$); life satisfaction ($r = .11$); religious involvement ($r = .20$); scientific interests ($r = .17$); socioeconomic status ($r = -.17$); sibling friction ($r = -.18$)

Sequential Dimensions: BQ—positive academic attitude ($r = -.08$); PCEI 2/4—job appropriateness ($r = -.20$); upward occupational mobility ($r = -.14$); occupational initiative ($r = -.17$); extra-occupational satisfaction ($r = .08$); PCEI 6/8—job determinants ($r = -.28$); religious-community involvement ($r = -.19$)

Sequential Prototypes: CEI—athletes ($r = .22$); PCEI 6/8—community directed housewives ($r = .29$)

Reference Measures: SAT scores ($r = .09$); social desirability ($r = .16$); authoritarianism ($r = -.07$); integrative complexity ($r = .12$); occupational level ($r = -.11$); dentistry ($r = .16$); physical therapist ($r = .19$); forest service ($r = .24$); carpentry ($r = .12$); real estate sales ($r = -.15$); advertising ($r = .19$)

Prototype Description: These individuals tended to be a younger daughter in a rather typical middle-class family. In high school, they were unassertive and somewhat withdrawn socially. Their spare time was spent on

(Continued)

245

TABLE 9.6
(continued)

Prototype	Differential Characteristics
	solitary intellectual pursuits while their academic and extracurricular performance was sample-typical. This same general pattern was apparent in their college behavior where they seemed to retreat into the student role. The failed to prepare themselves for or to take an active approach to the occupational world and so they obtained rather poor jobs which were not in line with their interests or abilities. However, they were not especially unhappy due to their merger into the protective social institutions of marriage and religion.
Social Copers	*Composite Dimensions:* traditional social adjustment ($r = -.40$); self-esteem ($r = -.17$); sociability ($r = .33$); intellectual pursuits ($r = -.12$); religious involvement ($r = .15$); negative parent/child conflict ($r = .24$); paternal identification ($r = -.19$); athletic interests ($r = -.12$); life satisfaction ($r = .12$)
Prototype #12	*Sequential Dimensions:* BQ—warmth of maternal relationship ($r = -.18$); parental control ($r = .08$); socioeconomic status ($r = .12$); social leadership ($r = .15$); academic achievement ($r = .12$); athletic participation ($r = -.21$); CEI—dating activity ($r = .18$); traditional social involvement ($r = .21$); athletic participation ($r = -.17$); PCEI 2/4—extra-occupational satisfaction ($r = .20$); collegiate social development ($r = .10$); rudimentary people-oriented jobs ($r = .26$); PCEI 6/8—collegiate social maturation ($r = .15$)
$N = 26$	*Sequential Prototypes:* CEI—traditional daters ($r = .17$); PCEI 2/4—immature escapists ($r = .17$)
	Reference Measures: None
	Prototype Description: These individuals were raised by controlling, rather cold mothers who pushed their daughters for achievement. In high school, they appeared to desire social approval and attempted to achieve through social leadership. However, they were not especially socially effective and tended to be somewhat withdrawn and maladjusted. In college, they joined a sorority and this served as a basis for the development of social skills and self-esteem. They also dropped their previous intellectual and academic interests and expressed the role congruent with a conservative religious orientation. Subsequently, these females channelled themselves into jobs where their social skills would be of use. However, they concentrated their energy on marital and community areas and were apparently successful in these areas, perhaps because of their social skills and concern with social achievements.

Channelled
Extraverts
Prototype #13
N = 13

Composite Dimensions: traditional social adjustment (r = .35); self-esteem (r = .35); religious involvement (r = −.22); job channelling (r = −.15); scientific interests (r = −.15); negative parent/child conflict (r = .25); socioeconomic status (r = .20); sibling friction (r = .14); athletic activities (r = .21); life satisfaction (r = −.10)

Sequential Dimensions: BQ—social leadership (r = .13); scientific interests (r = .15); expression of negative emotions (r = −.22); CEI—dating activity (r = .21); religious involvement (r = −.13); PCEI 6/8—extra-occupational satisfaction (r = −.10); perceived occupational status (r = .12)

Sequential Prototypes: PCEI 2/4—homebodies (r = .18); PCEI 6/8—community-directed housewives (r = .15)

Reference Measures: extraversion (r = .29); Air Force officer (r = .19); recreational leadership (r = .22); printer (r = −.14); librarian (r = −.24)

Prototype Description: These individuals were raised in a warm, supportive upper-class environment which instilled a sense of social confidence, a concern with appropriate social behavior and achievement. In high school and college, these females attempted to achieve in both athletic and social activities, and they were generally quite successful in this attempt. However, in college, these females seemed to be especially concerned about achievement with the opposite sex and in traditional areas. They eventually fell into the managerial jobs which were in line with their concerns, and they were relatively successful in them. Members of this subgroup also established an active social life and married relatively early, but the apparent superficial nature of many of these relationships led to some difficulties.

Isolated Intellectuals
Prototype #14
N = 17

Composite Dimensions: traditional social adjustment (r = −.09); sociability (r = −.37); athletic activities (r = −.30); self-esteem (r = −.10); paternal identification (r = −.26); sibling friction (r = .14); scientific interests (r = .14); occupational level and satisfaction (r = .08)

Sequential Dimensions: BQ—warmth of maternal relationship (r = −.21); academic achievement (r = .17); scientific interests (r = .09); athletic interests (r = −.20); expression of negative emotions (r = −.15); cultural/literary interests (r = −.15); popularity with the opposite sex (r = −.10); CEI—dating activity (r = −.37); leisure reading (r = −.15); health (r = .12); PCEI 2/4—extra-occupational satisfaction (r = −.10); collegiate personal development (r = −.28); rudimentary people-oriented jobs (r = −.19; PCEI 6/8—collegiate social maturation (r = −.24); occupational initiative (r = −.13)

Sequential Prototypes: BQ—scholarly bookworms (r = .15); CEI—introverted escapists (r = .19); PCEI 2/4—satisfied conventional females (r = .31); homebodies (r = −.21); PCEI 6/8—professionals (r = .22); realistically mature adults (r = .21)

Reference Measures: high school grades (r = .22); college grades (r = .22); SAT scores (r = .32); emotional exposure (r = −.24); introversion (r = .34); integrative complexity (r = −.24); physical goals (r = −.20);

(Continued)

TABLE 9.6
(continued)

Prototype	Differential Characteristics
	mathematics ($r = .36$); physicist ($r = .36$); engineer ($r = .33$); psychologist ($r = .23$); YMCA secretary ($r = -.45$); social worker ($r = -.26$); credit manager ($r = -.29$) *Prototype Description:* These individuals were raised in a warm, supportive family environment in which they were close to their intellectual fathers, but not their mothers. Their parents pushed for achievement and their daughters attempted to and did develop adequate intellectual skills, were somewhat introverted, and tended to live a rather restricted "academic" life. They had little difficulty in finding a job but did not attain one in line with their interests or abilities. However, they were reasonably successful on their jobs and were satisfied with them. They tended to marry late and live a limited but satisfying social life within the traditional feminine role.
Independent Achievers Prototype #15 $N = 5$	*Composite Dimensions:* traditional social adjustment ($r = .09$); self-esteem ($r = -.08$); intellectual pursuits ($r = .17$); scientific interests ($r = .17$); athletic activities ($r = .15$); negative parent/child conflict ($r = .10$); paternal identification ($r = -.16$); socioeconomic status ($r = -.17$); sibling friction ($r = .18$) *Sequential Dimensions:* BQ—academic achievement ($r = .09$); scientific interests ($r = .04$); socioeconomic status ($r = -.09$); popularity with the opposite sex ($r = -.08$); positive academic attitudes ($r = .17$); paternal warmth ($r = -.06$); CEI—dating activity ($r = .04$); health ($r = .09$); self-support ($r = .13$); sociability ($r = .16$); leisure reading ($r = .07$); positive college experience ($r = .12$); PCEI 2/4—occupational initiative ($r = -.16$); job appropriateness ($r = -.12$); extraoccupational satisfaction ($r = -.07$); religious beliefs ($r = -.08$); PCEI 6/8—job satisfaction ($r = -.10$); religious-community involvement ($r = -.15$); intellectual reading ($r = .08$); occupational initiative ($r = .11$) *Sequential Prototypes:* CEI—fashionable liberals ($r = .24$); PCEI 2/4—satisfied conventional females ($r = .18$); PCEI 6/8—occupationally disaffected women ($r = .17$) *Reference Measures:* SAT scores ($r = .15$); college grades ($r = .32$); cognitive values ($r = .11$); long-term goals ($r = .32$); hierarchical complexity ($r = .09$); emotional exposure ($r = .16$); emotional inhibition ($r = .13$); positive emotionality ($r = -.13$); physical goals ($r = -.10$); economic values ($r = -.11$); liberalism ($r = -.08$); socioreligious conformity ($r = .11$); internal control ($r = .07$); femininity ($r = .08$); secretary ($r = -.20$); banker ($r = -.14$); accountant ($r = -.12$); carpentry ($r = -.08$); art ($r = .16$); writing ($r = .14$); religion ($r = .08$)

Prototype Description: These individuals were raised in a warm, supportive, lower-class family. In high school, they were somewhat independent, academically effective, and socially mature and effective. During college, they developed an interest in intellectual pursuits. They planned for and found jobs in the business world and were eventually quite successful at these jobs, although they were somewhat dissatisfied with them. These females maintained their intellectual interests and independence. They eventually formed satisfactory social lives outside the established adult social institutions.

Composite Dimensions: traditional social adjustment ($r = .11$); self-esteem ($r = .16$); intellectual pursuits ($r = .12$); athletic activities ($r = .14$); negative parent/child conflict ($r = .16$); paternal identification ($r = .08$); socioeconomic status ($r = .14$)

Sequential Dimensions: BQ—warmth of maternal relationship ($r = .08$); academic achievement ($r = -.10$); cultural/literary interests ($r = .12$); scientific interests ($r = -.06$); adjustment ($r = .13$); positive academic attitudes ($r = .07$); paternal warmth ($r = .05$); CEI—liberal activism ($r = .10$); sociability ($r = .23$); traditional social involvement ($r = -.07$), religious involvement ($r = -.10$); PCEI 2/4—upward occupational mobility ($r = -.10$); occupational initiative ($r = -.16$); rudimentary people-oriented jobs ($r = -.12$); religious beliefs ($r = -.08$); PCEI 6/8—asocial job activities ($r = .11$); collegiate social maturation ($r = .11$); intellectual reading ($r = .16$)

Sequential Prototypes: CEI—fashionable liberals ($r = .29$); PCEI 2/4—satisfied conventional females ($r = -.21$); PCEI 6/8—downtrodden passives ($r = .25$)

Reference Measures: SAT scores ($r = .04$); high school grades ($r = -.08$); tendermindedness ($r = .10$); authoritarianism ($r = .25$); internal control ($r = -.13$); conceptual simplicity ($r = .11$); integrative complexity ($r = .09$); hierarchical complexity ($r = .17$); emotional exposure ($r = .17$); emotional inhibition ($r = .09$); law ($r = .10$); author/journalist ($r = .08$); social work ($r = .05$); accounting ($r = -.09$)

Prototype Description: These individuals were raised in a warm, supportive, upper-class family which valued independence. In high school they were somewhat rebellious, socially active, and rather mature and conformed to peer norms. In college, they became highly rebellious and adopted a liberal bohemian lifestyle. They failed to prepare themselves for the occupational world and so had some early difficulties. In adulthood, they remained socially active but failed to merge into adult social institutions due to their continuing rebellion. This resulted in both marital and occupational difficulties.

Insecure Bohemians
Prototype #16
$N = 4$

(Continued)

(continued)

TABLE 9.6

Prototype	Differential Characteristics
Female Eunuchs Prototype #17 N = 20	*Composite Dimensions:* traditional social adjustment ($r = .13$); self-esteem ($r = -.34$); life satisfaction ($r = -.38$); athletic activities ($r = -.20$); socioeconomic status ($r = .11$); sibling friction ($r = -.13$) *Sequential Dimensions:* CEI—traditional social involvement ($r = .16$); PCEI 2/4—occupational initiative ($r = -.11$); PCEI 6/8—extra-occupational satisfaction ($r = -.33$); religious-community involvement ($r = -.19$); intellectual reading ($r = -.16$) *Sequential Prototypes:* BQ—unpopular, cognitively simple introverts ($r = .20$); CEI—introverted escapists ($r = -.19$); PCEI 6/8—innovative vocationally uncommitted women ($r = .15$) *Reference Measures:* introversion ($r = .42$); emotional exposure ($r = -.11$); hierarchical complexity ($r = -.14$); personnel director ($r = -.14$); arts ($r = -.20$); music ($r = -.13$); painter ($r = .26$); carpenter ($r = .26$); farmer ($r = .16$) *Prototype Description:* These individuals were raised in rather protective, middle-class families. In high school, they were rather introverted and socially inactive. They also tended to avoid traditionally male activities, such as science and athletics, despite having some ability in these areas. These females also displayed a lack of self-confidence. In college, they engaged in traditional feminine activities but remained somewhat withdrawn. They tended to enter clerical jobs after graduation. Their introversion, inflexible role behavior, and simplicity made it difficult for them to establish a satisfying marriage and social life in adulthood.

tualism, and low Parental Control. Members of this composite prototype were likely to be assigned to the Traditional Science-Oriented Achieving Leaders and Conservative Achieving Leaders BQ prototypes. Inspection of the BQ background data items yielding significant differences indicated that prototype members came from well-educated, religious, upper-class, protected families in which they were an older son. They had warm parents who were interested in their activities and to whom they were close. However, their parents were not controlling and harsh, nor were they likely to push for achievement. However, their sons tried to achieve, especially in academic situations, and they were successful at and interested in their high school classes. Involvement in athletics and extracurricular activities was common among these males. Although they were independent, these prototype members reported that they felt guilty when they violated external standards, were conventional, and wished to become more socially acceptable. However, they were not especially active socially.

During college, these prototype members were likely to receive good grades as well as high scores on the CEI Health dimension and low scores on the Literary Pursuits dimension. The item data indicated that they were not likely to join political groups or participate in intellectual activities. They reported taking friends home, although they had few friends of the same and opposite sex. They attended church, studied hard, and reported good health.

Immediately after graduation, composite prototype members tended to enter the PCEI 2/4 Graduate Students prototype and receive low scores on the PCEI 2/4 General Reading and Entry-Level Occupational Tasks summary dimensions. A review of the item data suggested that they had little trouble in finding their first job and that college majors and undergraduate grades influenced their being hired. They chose their first jobs on the basis of pay, security, and opportunities for advancement. Relatively little of their income was devoted to recreation, and they spent little time on light reading. Those individuals who were married reported that their marriages were happy. They were likely to attend church.

Six to 8 years after graduation, composite prototype members were likely to enter the PCEI 6/8 Enterprising Intellectuals prototype and to receive high scores on the PCEI 6/8 Religious Morality, Social Adjustment, and Job Channelling dimensions as well as low scores on the Cognitive Orientation dimension. The PCEI 6/8 item data indicated that those individuals who were married were happy in their marriages and were satisfied with companionship in them. It is of note that those individuals who were not married planned to marry in the near future. They continued to attend church and did not read entertainment or cultural magazines. At this point, their jobs were likely to involve management and provide a high income. Prototype members were likely to be willing to continue in this work.

In reviewing the differential characteristics of the prototype, it appears that they came from a warm, traditional, rather protected background. They appeared to identify with their background, and it seemed to foster a concern with academic and occupational achievement. When this was coupled with their academic ability, it led to academic and occupational success. Nevertheless, these males manifested the traditional social values and religiosity that was apparent in their family backgrounds throughout their lives and displayed little interest in intellectual pursuits or casual social relationships. Consequently, they tended to prefer and enter traditional, nonintellectual and pragmatic managerial jobs. Further, in adulthood, they settled into the traditional religious-family orientation that was characteristic of their early years. As a result of their manifest academic and occupational success, concern with concrete achievement, traditional social values, and their successful attainment of this traditional lifestyle through family and career, members of this prototype seemed best described as Channelled Concrete Achievers.

Prototype 2. The second prototype identified in the male composite cluster analyses contained 27 individuals. Prototype membership tended to be directly related to scores on the composite Parental Warmth and Social Adjustment, Socioeconomic Status, and Occupational Satisfaction dimensions and negatively related to scores on the composite Family Conflict and Satisfaction with Social Life dimensions. On the reference measures, it was found that prototype members displayed signs of social desirability but not neuroticism; no other significant differences were obtained.

Membership in this composite prototype was associated with high scores on the BQ Warmth of Parental Relationships and Socioeconomic Status summary dimensions as well as low scores on the Parental Control and Sibling Friction BQ summary dimensions. They tended to enter the BQ prototype labeled Unconventional Overachieving Leaders. The BQ item data indicated that prototype members came from a poorly educated but financially successful family. They were close to their parents, who were warm, supportive, and interested in their activities, but did not push for achievement. Members of this prototype reported trying to achieve and being competitive. Generally, they liked school and did well in their courses, although not strikingly so. These males were not especially interested in athletic and intellectual activities. However, they were socially successful in high school despite their tendency not to form close social relationships and to display some independence.

In college, composite prototype membership was not systematically related to membership in any CEI prototype, although prototype members did tend to receive low scores on the CEI Bohemian and Positive College Experience summary dimensions. During this time, they were not especially remarkable in terms of their CEI item responses. However, they were likely to display a limited concern with classwork, limited financial responsibility for college, good health, aggressiveness with the opposite sex, and little concern for religion. They tended to dislike university-based job preparation. Members of the composite prototype were likely to enter the PCEI 2/4 Unconventional Intellectuals prototype. Although they did not receive particularly high or low scores on any PCEI 2/4 summary dimension, the item data indicated that they were not especially well prepared for their first jobs and that independence and type of work were not important considerations in selecting their first job. These males had close friends of the opposite sex, but were not likely to have friends of the same sex. They were not likely to be married. Little time was spent by prototype members on casual conversation, but a great deal of time was spent reading news and general-interest magazines. Six to 8 years after graduation, prototype members were likely to receive high scores on the PCEI 6/8 Job Satisfaction summary dimension. The PCEI 6/8 item data indicated that they were particularly likely to be satisfied with opportunities for advancement and individual action in their work. By this time, they had committed to high status jobs that involved reading professional journals and produced a high income. Now they believed that they had fallen into their first job through luck or sex. Prototype members spent their spare time reading books and reported that the university had helped them make life-long friendships.

The preceding findings indicate that these prototype members come from warm, successful, traditional families that allowed them some independence. This upwardly mobile background instilled a concern with both independent achievement and social success, particularly with the opposite sex. In high school and college, they were highly successful socially but on a somewhat superficial level. During college, they remained socially active, especially with females, and displayed little interest in academics or assuming financial responsibilities. This lack of academic preparation led to some difficulties in their initial job search. However, in response to these demands, they began independent reading, and while maintaining their interest in the opposite sex, they committed themselves to occupational success. Six to 8 years after graduation, they were successful and happy in their jobs. Thus, the early social desirability of these males, attributed to their family background, led to some difficulties. However, their independence and desire for age-appropriate achievement led them to expand themselves and eventually obtain jobs that they were successful at. Due to the influence of their upwardly mobile family in the development of this pattern—particularly, age-appropriate achievement concerns, their early social focus and job and academic difficulties, and their later occupational success, these males seemed aptly described by the label Upwardly Mobile Individuals.

Prototype 3.   The third prototype identified in the male composite cluster analysis contained 27 individuals who were likely to receive high scores on the Parental Warmth and Social Adjustment composite summary dimensions and low scores on the composite Professional Occupation Orientation, Academic Achievement, Religious Involvement, and Satisfaction with Social Life composite summary dimensions. On the reference measures, it was found that these males were likely to be interested in creative, technically oriented, professional occupations, such as engineering or architecture, whereas they disliked social service or business occupations. They were also found to display little socioreligious conformity and they received low high school grades.

Although members of this composite prototype did not systematically enter any BQ prototype, they tended to receive high scores on the BQ Warmth of Parental Relationship and Intellectualism dimensions. A review of the BQ item data indicated that these males tended to be an elder child in an economically well-off family that encouraged independence. Although they reported that their parents were warm, supportive, and interested in their lives, they were not especially close to them. Prototype members reported that they were independent and unconventional. They were not likely to participate in extracurricular activities or team sports, although they did take part in individual sports. Although these males liked school, teachers, and science courses, they did not do especially well academically. Prototype members were popular and had friends in high school, but they did not date or attend parties.

During college, these males tended to receive low scores on the CEI Religious Involvement and Athletic Pursuits dimensions. A review of the CEI item data indicated that prototype members did not participate in extracurricular, athletic, and religious activities during college. They were likely to be in good health. These males also tended to receive low grades and report some disaffection with their college experiences.

Two to 4 years after graduation, composite prototype members were not likely to be assigned to the PCEI 2/4 Graduate Students and Traditional Achiever prototypes, and they tended to receive low scores on the PCEI 2/4 General Reading summary dimension. The PCEI 2/4 items suggested that, immediately after graduation, these males were not academically prepared for the occupational world and had some difficulty in finding their first jobs. Prototype members were not likely to belong to professional organizations or to read professional journals during this period. Six to 8 years after graduation, composite prototype members were likely to receive low scores on the Job Channelling and Religious Involvement PCEI 6/8 summary dimensions. These males were likely to be assigned to the PCEI 6/8 prototype labelled Impoverished Ineffective Men but not the PCEI 6/8 Constrained Careerists prototype. On the PCEI 6/8 item data, it was found that these individuals were not especially dissatisfied with their jobs, but would not go into the same type of work again. They did not read professional journals or belong to professional organizations. Prototype members displayed a marked dissatisfaction with their standard of living, social contacts, and living arrangements and were not likely to be involved with religious groups or adult social organizations.

Members of this prototype came from a warm, supportive family that encouraged independence and achievement. It appears that these males were highly independent individuals who desired upper-level technical jobs. Unfortunately, they did not perform well academically and failed to prepare themselves for the adult social and occupational world during college. As a result, they did not obtain the kinds of jobs they desired, and although they achieved sample-typical levels of success, they were dissatisfied with their jobs, income, and social lives. In part, this trend might be traced to their independence and rejection of established institutions. Further, throughout their lives they appeared to withdraw from organized social activity, as might be expected given their independence. When this trend is coupled with the nature of their occupational preferences and their failure to obtain these jobs, it appeared appropriate to describe these males as Unrealistic Independents.

Prototype 4. The fourth male prototype contained 36 individuals who tended to receive high scores on the Parental Warmth and Social Adjustment, Traditional Masculine Role, Sociability, and Satisfaction with Social Life composite summary dimensions. On the reference measures, it was found that prototype members preferred social contact jobs, such as sales and the military, and that they disliked scientific and literary occupations, such as mathematics and journalism. These males tended to display a masculine pattern of interests, including physical goals, economic values and socioreligious conformity.

Prototype membership was directly related to scores on the BQ Social Desirability summary dimension and negatively related to scores on the Social Introversion dimension. A review of the BQ item data indicated that these males were likely to be the oldest child in a warm, religious, middle-class family. Their parents were close to their sons, interested in their activities, and they encouraged achievement and independence. Their sons were conservative, religious, and were not especially independent. Generally, these males liked school but displayed little interest in scientific and intellectual pursuits. Although they were competitive in academic situations, they received sample-typical grades. Members of this prototype were involved in a variety of extracurricular activities, and they were highly active socially and were socially successful in high school. These males also enjoyed, and were highly successful in, student athletics.

During college, members of this composite prototype were likely to enter the CEI Fraternity Members prototype while receiving high scores on the CEI Religious Involvement summary dimension and low scores on the CEI Literary Pursuits dimensions. The CEI item data indicated that prototype members were highly active socially and that they spent a great deal of time with the opposite sex. These males remained interested and involved in student athletics. They tended to be somewhat religious and politically conservative. Immediately after graduation, prototype members did not systematically enter any PCEI 2/4 prototype; however, they did receive high scores on the PCEI 2/4 Entry-Level Occupational Tasks summary dimension. On the PCEI 2/4 items, it was found that they were likely to be employed full time and feel that the university had provided adequate vocational training. Prototype members reported that they had received a number of salary increases, were satisfied with their jobs, and devoted income to recreation. They were likely to be happily married at this point in their lives and satisfied with social activities. These males continued to display an interest in athletics and the opposite sex as well as some involvement with religious organizations.

Six to 8 years after graduation, these composite prototype members were likely to be assigned to the Contented Affluent Conservative PCEI 6/8 prototype and to receive high scores on the Extra-Occupational Satisfaction and Social Adjustment PCEI 6/8 summary dimensions. The PCEI 6/8 item data indicated that they remained satisfied with their jobs and had received a number of salary increases. They felt that the university had helped them establish life-long friendships and a happy family life. These males were happily married and were satisfied with various aspects of their marriages. Prototype members were also satisfied with friends, community, and living arrangements. They had a number of male friends whom they and their wives socialized with. Although they continued to be interested and involved in athletics, they were not especially religious at this point in their lives.

In reviewing the foregoing data, it is clear that these males came from warm, conservative, middle-class families that engendered some achievement motivation. They appeared to identify with their family background, displaying conservative values and an acceptance of the traditional masculine role. When this trend was coupled with their manifest extraversion and physical ability, it led to an interest and success in adolescent athletics and social pursuits. As might be expected, these males married early and established happy marriages and adult social lives. Further, these males appeared to be reasonably successful in satisfying jobs. When this limited job success is considered along with their extroversion, early marriage, interest in the opposite sex, social satisfaction, and traditional masculinity, this group was described as Virile Extraverts.

Prototype 5. The 15 males assigned to the fifth composite prototype tended to receive high scores on the composite Parental Warmth and Social Adjustment, Socioeconomic Status, Family Conflict, and Scientific/Engineering Interests summary dimensions. On the reference measures, it was found that prototype membership was directly related to scores on the cognitive values and integrative complexity scales. These males tended to express an interest in technical and scientific occupations such as chemist and computer programmer.

In the first assessment, composite prototype members were likely to be assigned to the BQ prototypes labelled Traditional Science-Oriented Achieving Leaders and Athletically Oriented Science Majors. Prototype membership was directly related to scores on the BQ Academic Achievement dimension and negatively related to scores on the BQ Parental Control dimension. The BQ item data indicated that prototype members came from a relatively warm, somewhat religious, non-Protestant family. Their parents were well educated and somewhat intellectual, although their income and social status was sample-typical. The parents of these males were warm, supportive, and flexible, and they allowed their sons substantial independence. Prototype members reported being independent of others. However, they were likely to have a number of close and casual friends and to feel that they had met the demands of social situations. These males were likely to assume social leadership positions. Prototype members also appeared to be somewhat religious. They tried to achieve, expected to be successful on academic tasks, and enjoyed school, particularly discussion courses and courses where they could question teachers. Their most salient characteristic during this period was that they enjoyed and did well in science courses and activities.

During college, these males displayed a sample-typical pattern of behavior and experiences. Their only defining characteristic on the CEI items was manifest in their tendency to pay for their education through loans. Following graduation, prototype members were likely to receive high scores on the College-Moderated Social Development PCEI 2/4 summary dimension. The PCEI 2/4 item data indicated that they felt that the university had helped them make friendships, and they were somewhat more religious than most. Six to 8 years after graduation, members of this composite prototype tended to be assigned to the PCEI 6/8 Enterprising Intellectuals prototype. A review of the PCEI 6/8 item data indicated that their jobs tended to involve research or computational work and that they read professional journals and belonged to professional organizations. They indicated that type of work was important in choosing their first job and that they were hired on the basis of special skills. They were satisfied with companionship and social activities and remained somewhat religious during this period.

The members of this prototype clearly displayed an early interest in scientific or technical jobs, which they prepared themselves for and eventually obtained. They also appeared to be socially mature and effective in both adolescence and young adulthood. Their family backgrounds appear to have instilled an independent intellectual orientation, apparent in their high school behavior, as well as a moralistic, religious, and not especially rebellious set of social attitudes. These background trends appeared to facilitate the development of their occupational preferences and social effectiveness. Given the fact that these males successfully employed this orientation toward independent thought in both their social and occupational lives, and this same trend was apparent in their family background, these males seemed aptly described by the label Analytical Adaptors.

Prototype 6.   Of the 417 male members of the longitudinal sample, 16 were assigned to the sixth prototype extracted in the composite cluster analyses. Prototype membership was associated with high scores on the Parental Warmth and Social Adjustment, Intellectual Pursuits, and Family Conflict composite summary dimensions and with low scores on the Traditional Masculine Role and Scientific/Engineering Interests composite summary dimensions. On the reference measures, it was found that these males tended to display a rather feminine pattern of interests and a dislike for traditional masculine, adventurous, and scientific occupations, such as engineering, the military, and chemistry. They tended to be interested in jobs that involved social science or verbal intellectual pursuits, such as minister, librarian, or lawyer. It was also found that these prototype members were not likely to display economic values or physical goals.

At the time of the first assessment, composite prototype members tended to be assigned to the BQ Competent Independent Aesthetes prototype while receiving high scores on the BQ Sibling Friction summary dimension and low scores on the Scientific Interests summary dimension. The BQ item data indicated that members of this composite prototype were likely to be a younger son in a small family in which they did not get along with their siblings. Their fathers were well educated and well paid, and there were a number of books in the house. The parents of these males were warm and interested in their sons activities, but did not allow them a great deal of independence and often criticized and punished them. Prototype members reported being close to their mothers but not to their fathers. Generally, these males liked school, especially English and civics courses; however, they did not like, or do well in, scientific and athletic pursuits. Although they were somewhat introverted and not especially likely to engage in group activities, they reported having a number of friends. These males also indicated that they wished to become more socially acceptable and were not self-confident in social situations. In high school they were somewhat religious and read a great deal.

During college, members of this composite prototype tended to enter the CEI Maladjusted Drifters prototype and receive low scores on the Marital Status, Self-Support, and Athletics Pursuits CEI summary dimensions. A review of the items yielding significant differences indicated that prototype members continued to spend a great deal of time reading and were likely to be involved in political organizations and religious fraternities. They displayed little interest in the opposite sex or in athletics. After graduation, these males were likely to enter the PCEI 2/4 Graduate Students prototype while receiving high scores on the PCEI 2/4 Job Satisfaction dimensions and low scores on the PCEI 2/4 Religious Involvement dimensions. Their responses to the PCEI 2/4 items indicated that they had prepared themselves for their first job in college and had obtained the kind of jobs they wanted. Although they were satisfied with the nature of the work, they were not satisfied with immediate working conditions. These prototype members continued to do a great deal of intellectual reading and to display little interest in athletics. Most were not married at this point in their lives and did not plan to marry in the near future.

Six to 8 years after graduation, membership in this composite prototype was directly related to membership in the PCEI 6/8 Enterprising Intellectual prototype and scores on the PCEI 6/8 Cognitive Orientation summary dimensions. The PCEI 6/8 item data indicated that prototype members were likely to be satisfied with the nature of the work and coworkers, and were likely to consider their jobs an important part of their lives. However, they were not satisfied with opportunities for advancement and had received few salary increases. They had close friends of the same sex and were likely to devote time to casual conversation rather than TV viewing. Prototype members continued to do a great deal of intellectual reading. Although they were less likely than most to be married at this point in their lives, those who were married tended to be unhappy with them.

Generally, these males displayed a highly feminine pattern of behavior, which was apparent in their rejection of the traditional masculine role, their occupational interests, and their dislike of science and athletics. This pattern may be traced to their warm but turbulent and critical family background, in which they were close to their mothers. The family background, when coupled with the foregoing trends, also led to an abiding interest in intellectual pursuits. Although they were concerned with social acceptance, able to establish friendships, and willing to engage in social service work, these males were not likely to be active in social groups, nor were they particularly active with the opposite sex. They appeared to withdraw from social contact into intellectual reading, and displayed substantial insecurity in social situations, especially those involving contact with the opposite sex. Further, this trend appeared rooted in their early family environment and led to later and difficult marriages. As a result of this social withdrawal and insecurity, their closeness to their mothers, and their feminine pattern of interests and activities, members of this prototype were described as Withdrawn Effeminates.

Prototype 7. The seventh composite prototype contained 15 individuals who were likely to receive high scores on the Sociability and Intellectual Pursuits composite summary dimensions and low scores on the Scientific/Engineering Interests, Satisfaction with Social Life, and Occupational Satisfaction summary dimensions. Strong scores on the reference measures indicated that prototype members disliked technical and scientific occupations, such as engineering, and preferred social service occupations, such as YMCA secretary. Although they were somewhat conceptually simplistic, members of this prototype were likely to receive good grades in high school and high SAT scores.

At the time of the first assessment, prototype membership was related to low scores on the BQ Parental Warmth, Scientific Interests, and Academic Achievement summary dimensions. A review of the BQ item data indicated that these males had warm, concerned fathers who allowed them some independence. They were likely to be close to and spend time with their fathers. Prototype members were concerned about academic achievement, and they did well in their classes. However, they did not especially like school and displayed little interest in intellectual pursuits. These males were likely to enjoy and do well in athletics. However, they were not especially likely to be socially active or effective, reporting that they did not meet the demands of social situations, were self-conscious, did not attend parties, and were difficult to get to know.

During college, membership in this composite prototype was directly related to membership in the CEI Dependent Womanizer prototype and to scores on the CEI Sociability summary dimension and negatively related to scores on the CEI Religious Involvement summary dimension. The CEI item data indicated that these males became involved in a variety of extracurricular activities during college, attended concerts, demonstrated for causes, and began dating quite frequently. However, their academic performance was sample-typical. Following graduation, prototype members tended to receive low scores on the PCEI 2/4 Job Satisfaction and Extra-Occupational Satisfaction summary dimensions. A review of the item data suggested that they had not prepared themselves for jobs in terms of grades or special skills, and they were not likely to employ any of the standard job-search activities. Consequently, they obtained poorly paying jobs that they were dissatisfied with and planned to leave in the near future. A number of prototype members either had married or planned to get married at this point. Those individuals who were married tended to be unhappy and dissatisfied with various aspects of their marriages. They were also likely to be dissatisfied with community, living quarters, family size, and friends. Prototype members socialized with their spouse's friends, spent spare time reading, and did not attend church.

Six to 8 years after graduation, composite prototype members were likely to be assigned to the PCEI 6/8 Unhappy Isolates or Successful Occupational Misfits prototypes. These males tended to receive high scores on the PCEI 6/8 Occupational Status summary dimension and low scores on the Job Satisfaction, Extra-Occupational Satisfaction, and Social Adjustment summary dimensions. The PCEI 6/8 item data indicated that, although they did not hold lower-level jobs, neither did they hold professional jobs. Prototype members did not like their jobs, did not intend to remain in them and were dissatisfied with various aspects of their jobs. Although their income was sample-typical, they were dissatisfied with their standard of living, and they devoted income to savings. These individuals continued to be dissatisfied with various aspects of their marriages. Prototype members did not belong to social clubs, and they spent their spare time reading.

Members of this prototype were bright, athletic individuals who came from warm families in which they were close to their fathers and somewhat dependent on them. Although they were academically successful in high school, they were not especially socially secure or effective, although they appeared to desire social success. In an attempt to become socially successful in college, they became active in a variety of organizations, made friends, and dated frequently. However, their academic performance suffered, and they tended to marry early. It appears that their dependence on their fathers was translated to a dependence on wives and good friends. After marriage, they became less social and more involved in solitary intellectual pursuits. Their dependence and poor academic preparation led them to find jobs that they were not happy with, that did not pay well, and that were not in line with their abilities. When this was accompanied by early marriage, it led to substantial dissatisfaction that was still apparent 6 to 8 years after graduation. Due to the negative influence of their dependence and desire for social approval on the course of their lives, as well as their sociability in college, it seemed appropriate to describe these prototype members as Restricted Socializers.

Prototype 8. The eighth prototype identified in the male composite cluster analysis contained 30 individuals who tended to receive high scores on the Occupational Satisfaction composite summary dimension and low scores on the Parental Warmth and Social Adjustment, Professional Occupational Orientation, Religious Involvement, Academic Achievement, Intellectual Pursuits, Scientific/Engineering Interests, and Socioeconomic Status composite summary dimensions. Prototype members' performance on the reference measures indicated that they preferred business and social service occupations, such as sales or personnel director, whereas they disliked scientific and technical occupations, such as physics or chemistry. These males were likely to be tenderminded, introverted, conservative, conformist, and to display socially desirable tendencies. They were also likely to display conceptual and hierarchical simplicity and a lack of cognitive values. These prototype members were characterized by low high school grades and SAT scores.

In the first assessment, it was found that prototype membership was related to low scores on the BQ Socioeconomic Status, Athletic Interests, and Social Desirability summary dimensions. The BQ item data indicated that prototype members were likely to be an older child in a lower-class family in which the parents were socially active, strict, and allowed their sons little independence. Their parents were not especially warm or supportive, and their sons often disagreed with them. Prototype members did not enjoy or do well in their high school classes. They were likely to participate in athletics and various hobby groups. Although they attended parties and had female friends, they reported that they often wished to be alone.

During college, membership in this composite prototype was related to high scores on the CEI Sociability dimension and low scores on the

Religious Involvement dimension. A review of the CEI item data suggested that these males did not study, and they obtained poor grades in college. They were likely to join a fraternity, date frequently, live with a person of the opposite sex, attend musical events, and espouse liberal political views. They displayed little interest in athletics and religious pursuits. In the period following graduation, composite prototype members were likely to be assigned to the PCEI 2/4 Traditional Achievers, Alienated Occupational Successes, and Early Maturers prototypes and to receive low scores on the PCEI 2/4 General Reading summary dimension. The PCEI 2/4 item data indicated that these males found the transition from college life easy. Prototype members began looking for a job early and were employed full time. They felt that initiative and personal contacts had helped them find their first job, but not grades or university training. Salary, type of work, and opportunities for advancement were important in choosing their first job, and they badly needed the job when they found it. Their job involved lower-level business tasks such as sales, computational work, mechanical work, and unskilled labor. Although their pay was low and they had received few salary increases, they were satisfied with the work and working conditions. These males had a number of close friends of the opposite sex and spent spare time in casual conversation or listening to music or radio. Six to 8 years after graduation, these prototype members were likely to receive high scores on the PCEI 6/8 Life Satisfaction summary dimension and low scores on the Religious Morality and Occupational Status dimensions. The PCEI 6/8 item data indicated that they had a low income and had received few salary increases. Nevertheless, they had not changed jobs frequently and were satisfied with both the nature of the work and the organization.

These males came from a rather harsh, socially oriented lower–middle-class background that engendered a conservative social orientation and social withdrawal during high school. However, once removed from this difficult family environment, they became highly social and entered a period of rebellion, both trends that may be traced to their family background. Nevertheless, these males were sufficiently realistic and conservative to begin their job search early and obtain the business contacts and lower-level managerial jobs in line with their earlier interests. Although they were not highly successful on their jobs, they were satisfied with them. Their lack of occupational success was not especially surprising, because these males were intellectually and academically limited and not highly achievement-oriented. Thus, it appears that, although they were constrained by motivation, intellectual ability, and family background, these males effectively channelled themselves with the business contact jobs they desired. As a result of these considerations, these prototype members were described as Constrained Careerists.

Prototype 9. Membership in the ninth male prototype was associated with high scores on the Traditional Masculine Role and Religious Involvement composite summary dimensions, along with low scores on the Parental Warmth and Social Adjustment, Professional Occupational Orientation, Intellectual Pursuits, Sociability, and Family Conflict composite summary dimensions. Although no significant differences were obtained on the reference measures, it was found that prototype members tended to receive high scores on the BQ Warmth of Parental Relationships, Parental Contact, Social Desirability, and Religious Activity summary dimensions. Examination of the BQ items yielding significant differences indicated that prototype members came from nonintellectual, religious, lower-class homes in which the parents were harsh disciplinarians who pushed for achievement. Although their parents displayed little interest in them, they spent time with, talked to, and tried to be like their fathers. These males were not independent, unconventional, or socially assertive. They were involved in a variety of extracurricular activities and enjoyed and did well in athletics. Prototype members were somewhat extroverted and socially active; attending parties, having casual friends, and dating frequently. However, they displayed signs of social immaturity, in that they took things out on others, did not help friends, and had few close female friends. These males worked hard in school but did not like school, particularly civics and discussion courses, and they tended to receive typical grades.

These composite prototype members were not likely to enter the CEI Bohemian prototype, and they were likely to receive high scores on the CEI Self-Support, Sociability, and Religious Involvement summary dimensions. The CEI item data indicated that these males continued to be involved with religious activities and athletics during college. A lack of sociability was apparent in their reports that they did not date frequently, had few close friends, and did not join fraternities. Spare time was devoted to musical events, sports events, television viewing, and radio. Prototype members held jobs and exhibited conservative political attitudes. They did not evaluate their university experiences favorably.

Following college graduation, these males tended to enter the PCEI 2/4 Early Maturers prototype and to receive low scores on the Early Occupational Success and Job Satisfaction PCEI 2/4 summary dimensions. Examination of the PCEI 2/4 items suggested that prototype members began looking for a job early, badly needed a job, and took some time to find one, eventually finding one by luck. Their jobs did not pay well and were likely to involve unskilled, rather than managerial or professional, labor. Prototype members were dissatisfied with and felt they were overqualified for their jobs. Those individuals who were married were unhappy in their marriages. At this point, they were not interested in sports, and they spent their spare time reading books but not news, professional, or sports periodicals.

Six to 8 years after graduation, prototype membership was directly related to scores on the PCEI 6/8 Cognitive Orientation summary dimension and negatively related to scores on the Job Channelling, Occupational Status, and Social Adjustment summary dimensions. Their PCEI 6/8 item responses indicated that prototype members felt that the university had not prepared them for life. At this point, their jobs tended to involve clerical but not professional or managerial labor, and they were dissatisfied with them. They had a low income and had received few salary increases. What income they had was devoted to savings. Most prototype members were married at this point or planned to marry in the near future. Those who were married were somewhat dissatisfied with their marriages, but they tended to socialize with their wives' friends. Prototype members spent their spare time reading books, and they displayed little interest in athletics. They were satisfied with their community, and they attended church.

It appears that the harsh, controlling lower-class family background of these prototype members generated a conservative, nonassertive, dependent conformity in an attempt to gain approval. They tried to be like their fathers and adopted the traditional masculine role in adolescence, being active with the opposite sex, involved in athletics, and likely to participate in group social activities. However, they had some difficulty in close personal relationships, perhaps because of family influences, and appeared to prefer structured activities. In college, these prototype members became less socially involved and appeared to retreat into religion as a mechanism for structuring their lives. They displayed conservative political views, but failed to prepare themselves for the occupational world. Consequently, they obtained poor jobs that they were dissatisfied with. Yet they did little to improve this situation and eventually obtained clerical jobs in line with their need for structure. During this period, they dropped their earlier interests in religion and athletics and spent their spare time reading. Moreover, their social and marital lives did not appear to be satisfying. Given the rather negative life outcomes of these prototype members, their conformist authoritarian orientation, and harsh family background, they seemed appropriately described by the label Ineffectual Authoritarians.

Prototype 10. The 17 individuals who were assigned to the 10th male prototype tended to receive high scores on the Religious Involvement and Satisfaction with Social Life composite summary dimensions and low scores on the Professional Occupational Orientation composite summary dimension. On the reference measures, it was found that prototype members were likely to dislike scientific and professional occupations, such as law and chemistry, and display an interest in social service occupations, such as minister or teacher. They were also likely to display a feminine pattern of interests, inhibit the expression of negative emotions, lack short-term goals, and be introverted. Prototype members were likely to be low in conceptual and hierarchical complexity and cognitive values. These males tended to have low high school grades and receive low SAT scores.

Scores on the BQ Athletic summary dimension were directly related to prototype membership, and the BQ item data indicated that these males came from strict, middle-class families that were Protestant but not especially religious. Although these males often disagreed with their parents, they tried to be like them. A lack of social effectiveness was apparent in their reports that they did not meet the demands of social situations and were difficult to get to know. Prototype members did not like or do well in high school, particularly in science courses. Although they were not involved in sports, they did participate in extracurricular activities.

During college, membership in this composite prototype was directly related to membership in the CEI Born-Again Believers and Spiritual Thinkers prototypes as well as scores on the CEI Religious Involvement and Activity in Organizations summary dimensions. The item data indicated that prototype members were highly involved in religious groups and were likely to display conservative religious values. They remained somewhat introverted socially, having few friends and not joining fraternities. These males tended to receive poor grades in college.

After college graduation, prototype membership was associated with assignment to the PCEI 2/4 Religious Dogmatics prototype as well as high scores on the Vocational Direction and General Reading PCEI 2/4 summary dimensions. A review of the items yielding significant differences indicated that personal contacts did not help them find their first job. They chose their first job on the basis of security, location, and type of work, and they felt that the university had not prepared them for the work place. Their jobs involved management, organization, unskilled labor, and training, rather than research or consulting. These jobs provided a relatively high income and were an important part of their lives, and they were satisfied with them. Most of these prototype members were happily married at this point in their lives and were satisfied with various aspects of their marriages. They were highly involved in religious groups, and they devoted spare time to reading and athletics.

Six to 8 years after graduation, prototype members tended to be assigned to the Born-Again Believers PCEI 6/8 prototype and to receive high scores on the PCEI 6/8 Job Channelling, Job Satisfaction, Extra-

Occupational Satisfaction, and Religious Morality summary dimensions. The PCEI 6/8 item data indicated that they remained highly religious and happily married. Spare time was devoted to television and radio but not to reading professional journals. These males tended to socialize with their wives' friends and have a number of friends of the opposite sex. Although their jobs did not involve professional or technical labor, their income was sample-typical, and they were satisfied with most aspects of their jobs.

The most striking characteristic of prototype members was their limited intellectual ability and high religiosity, despite the fact that they did not come from a highly religious family. Their family background was sufficiently harsh and restrictive to generate a lack of independence and social withdrawal in high school. In high school, prototype members attempted to cope with their problems by avoiding different courses and concentrating on athletics. However, in the more demanding college environment, their strategy was no longer successful. Consequently, these males seemed to retreat into religion as a coping mechanism. They maintained this strategy when faced with the demands of the occupational world, and they appeared to have established satisfying marital and social lives within the religious framework. As a result of these considerations, it seemed appropriate to label members of this prototype Religious Copers.

Prototype 11. The seven members of the 11th prototype extracted in the male composite component analysis tended to receive high scores on the Religious Involvement, Academic Achievement, Sociability, and Intellectual Pursuits composite summary dimensions and low scores on the Parental Warmth and Social Adjustment composite summary dimensions. Although no reference-measure data were available for members of this prototype, it was found that prototype members tended to be assigned to the BQ Cognitively Complex Achievers and Jocks prototypes and to receive high scores on the BQ Intellectualism dimension and low scores on the Parental Warmth dimension. Inspection of the BQ item data indicated that prototype members came from large, lower-class families in which they were a younger child and did not get along well with their siblings. Their parents were neither religious nor intellectual, and although they were strict, they provided little warmth or emotional support. These males were not particularly achievement-oriented, reporting that they did not try to achieve or set difficult goals. Although they worked hard in high school, they did not do especially well, although they liked science courses. Socially, these males were withdrawn and insecure, reporting that they did not date, did not attend parties, and did not participate in extracurricular activities. Despite this pattern, prototype members did not wish to be alone and felt guilty when they violated social standards.

In college, members of this composite prototype were likely to be assigned to the CEI Organizational Activists prototype and to receive high scores on the CEI Sociability, Activity in Organizations, and Literary Pursuits summary dimensions. An examination of the CEI item data indicated that these males were highly involved in a variety of extracurricular activities and religious groups. They became aggressive with the opposite sex and acquired a number of female friends. These prototype members attended musical events, sports events, and movies. They spent their spare time in casual conversation and reading and were involved in cultural activities. These males were likely to be satisfied with their grades and college experiences.

Following graduation, members of this prototype were likely to receive high scores on the PCEI 2/4 College Mediated Social Development and Entry Level Occupational Tasks summary dimensions. The PCEI 2/4 item data indicated that they felt that their university experiences had helped prepare them for adult social life. Personality, undergraduate grades, and special skills influenced their being hired for their first job, which they selected on the basis of location and opportunities for individual action and advancement. Their jobs involved sales, design, training, and organizing, but not professional or unskilled labor. Although their jobs paid well and were an important part of their lives, they did not plan to remain in them. Prototype members remained socially active, joining clubs and civics groups and reportedly having a number of female friends. They were likely to be satisfied with friends, community, and standard of living. Spare time was devoted to reading books, literary, sports, and home magazines, but not professional journals. They were not likely to be involved with religious groups at this point.

Six to 8 years after graduation, these prototype members were likely to receive high scores on the PCEI 6/8 Extra-Occupational Satisfaction and Social Adjustment summary dimensions. In examining their item responses, it was found that their jobs were likely to involve sales and consulting work. They had a high income, had received a number of salary increases, and were satisfied with the nature of the work and benefits. These prototype members were likely to have a number of male friends, and those who were married were satisfied with various aspects of their marriages. These males continued to read cultural and home and fashion magazines.

Clearly, members of this prototype came from a poor family background in which they were allowed little independence or warmth. In high school this led to social withdrawal, a desire for social approval, and a lack of achievement motivation. However, when removed from this environment by college entry, their desire for social approval led them to become highly active in a variety of social organizations. Further, they appeared to develop newly found interests in the opposite sex and intellectual pursuits. They felt their experiences helped them develop, and they employed their newly developed social skills to obtain good jobs that involved social contact. Prototype members were successful in their jobs and were highly achievement-oriented. They also established satisfying adult lives. Because much of this activity reflects a need for social approval that stems from a harsh early background, and the resulting self-expansion led to favorable outcomes, these males were described as Expansive Compensators.

Prototype 12. The 21 males assigned to the 12th prototype identified in the composite clustering tended to receive high scores on the Socioeconomic Status, Sociability, and Academic Achievement composite summary dimensions, as well as low scores on the Professional Occupational Orientation, Traditional Masculine Role, Parental Warmth and Social Adjustment, and Intellectual Pursuits composite summary dimensions. Although no significant differences were obtained on the reference measures administered in the first assessment, it was found that composite prototype membership was positively related to scores on the BQ Social Desirability and Parental Control summary dimensions, and negatively related to scores on the BQ Intellectualism and Scientific Pursuits summary dimensions. The BQ items yielding significant differences indicated that prototype members tended to be a younger child in a nonreligious, upper-class family. Their parents provided little warmth and were not interested in their activities, but they were strict and pushed for achievement. Nevertheless, these males tended to spend time with and talk things over with their parents. Prototype members were not independent or unconventional, and they appeared to desire social approval, reporting that they wished to become more socially acceptable and did not wish to be alone. They took part in a variety of extracurricular activities, but were not popular, had few friends, did not date, did not attend parties, and did not lead others. Prototype members did not enjoy or do well in science courses and athletics. Although they displayed some interest in intellectual activities and in reading or watching public television, they did not like or do well in school and were not competitive in academic situations.

These composite prototype members were likely to enter the CEI Fraternity Members prototype while receiving high scores on the CEI

Sociability summary dimension and low scores on the CEI Literary Pursuits dimension. A review of the item data indicated that prototype members were likely to join a fraternity, become aggressive with the opposite sex, date a number of different people, and have a number of friends. They began attending athletic events and exercising, although their health was not good. Prototype members were likely to display conservative political views and display little interest in intellectual activities.

Following college graduation, these males were likely to enter the CEI Good Ole Boys prototype while receiving high scores on the PCEI 2/4 Entry Level Occupational Tasks summary dimension and low scores on the PCEI 2/4 Religious Involvement summary dimension. The PCEI 2/4 item data indicated that the university had helped them prepare for the adult social and occupational world. They were likely to be employed full time. Job search began early and these males believed that grades, personality, gender, and luck influenced their being hired. Salary, security, location, opportunities for advancement, and individual action were important in selecting their first jobs. They tended to be satisfied with working conditions, standard of living, and friends. Most were married at this point in their lives and were satisfied with various aspects of their marriages. Prototype members continued to be interested in sports and to do little intellectual reading. Six to 8 years after graduation, composite prototype membership was associated with low scores on the PCEI 6/8 Job Channelling and Cognitive Orientation summary dimensions. The PCEI 6/8 item data indicated that they were satisfied with most aspects of their jobs, continued to be interested in athletics, and did little intellectual reading. However, for the most part, their item responses were sample-typical.

Although these males came from a privileged family background, it was not a particularly warm one, and this led to a lack of achievement motivation, social withdrawal, and insecurity. They also displayed a strong desire for social approval from both their parents and others. This desire for social approval led them to join fraternities in college, and they actively conformed to the demands of fraternity life. Correspondingly, they became highly active, socially, within the traditional fraternity stereotype. This was apparent in their diminishing intellectual interests, new interest in athletics, and high interest in the opposite sex. This emergent sociability and athletic orientation was maintained in later years and led to a satisfying social life and early, remarkably happy marriages. Moreover, these males appear to have capitalized on these newly developed social skills in the occupational world. Because entry into a fraternity environment on the basis of their desire for social approval affected the lives of these males in a positive manner, they were assigned the label Fortunate Approval Seekers.

Prototype 13. The 42 members of the 13th male prototype tended to receive high scores on the Academic Achievement, Professional Occupational Orientation, and Satisfaction with Social Life composite summary dimensions and low scores on the Parental Warmth and Social Adjustment, Religious Involvement, Traditional Masculine Role, and Socioeconomic Status composite summary dimensions. Although no significant differences on the reference measures were obtained for this prototype, it was found that prototype membership was directly related to scores on the BQ Social Desirability dimension and inversely related to scores on the BQ Parental Warmth dimension. A review of the items yielding significant differentiation indicated that prototype members were likely to be an older child in a nonreligious, lower-class family. Their parents displayed little warmth towards, or interest in, their sons. They allowed them little independence and often punished them. Although their sons did not like school and were not competitive in academic situations, they studied hard, received good grades, and obtained scholarships. Involvement in school publications, hobby clubs, and intellectual pursuits, such as reading and scientific activities, was common. These males did not like or do well in athletics. They were not popular, had few friends, were not effective in social situations, and did not assume leadership positions. Nevertheless, they desired social approval, did not want to be alone, and were often depressed.

During college, prototype members were not especially remarkable, although the CEI item data indicated that they dropped their intellectual interests and began to display some interest in athletics. Following graduation, these prototype members were likely to receive low scores on the PCEI 2/4 Entry Level Occupational Task summary dimension. The PCEI 2/4 item data indicated that they began looking for a job early, and it did not take them long to find one. They chose their first job on the basis of pay, type of work, and opportunities for advancement. The jobs they obtained were likely to involve research work and consulting but not unskilled labor. Their jobs paid well, they had received a number of salary increases, and they were satisfied with their jobs. Those individuals who were married were satisfied with various aspects of their marriages. Spare time was devoted to reading magazines, and they were satisfied with recreational and leisure activities. Six to 8 years after graduation, these males were likely to enter the PCEI 6/8 Areligious Careerists prototype. On the PCEI 6/8 items, it was found that they held similar jobs to those described earlier, had a high income, and were not especially religious.

In reviewing the characteristics of these males, it is clear that they came from a difficult family environment, which led to social withdrawal and insecurity in high school. Despite disliking school, they worked hard and were reasonably successful in academic and extracurricular activities, apparently in an attempt to improve themselves and obtain social approval. Prototype members channelled themselves into the well-paying jobs that they desired and had successfully prepared themselves for in college. They concentrated a great deal of energy on their jobs and appeared to use them as a basis for establishing a satisfying social and family life. Because these males employed work, career, and career success as a means for extricating themselves from a difficult background, they were described as Adjustive Successes.

Prototype 14.   The 22 members of the 14th male prototype were likely to receive high scores on the Traditional Masculine Role, Family Conflict, Academic Achievement, Socioeconomic Status, and Scientific/Engineering composite summary dimensions and low scores on the Parental Warmth and Social Adjustment, Sociability, Satisfaction with Social Life, and Occupational Satisfaction composite summary dimensions. These prototype members did not produce any significant differences on the reference measures; however, it was found that these individuals tended to enter the BQ Nonconformist Dropouts prototype while receiving high scores on the BQ Sibling Friction summary dimension and low scores on the BQ Social Introversion and Athletic Interests summary dimensions. On the BQ items, it was found that prototype members tended to be a younger child in a poorly educated middle-class family. Their parents were harsh disciplinarians who allowed them little independence and pushed for achievement but displayed little warmth towards or interest in them. Nevertheless, prototype members spent time with and tried to be like their fathers and reported that their mothers provided emotional support. Although these males did not try to achieve, they were involved in a variety of extracurricular activities. They began dating at a young age, attended parties, dated frequently, and led group activities. However, they also took things out on friends and did not help them, suggesting a shallow sociability. In line with their extraverted traditional role behavior, prototype members were conformists, were not independent, and did not wish to be alone. Finally, although they liked building things and working with their hands, they displayed little interest in either science or athletics.

During college, members of this composite prototype tended to enter the CEI Ineffective Isolates prototype while receiving high scores on the CEI Activity in Organizations and Marital Status summary dimensions and low scores on the CEI Literary Pursuits summary dimension. The CEI item data indicated that prototype members continued to be involved in a variety of extracurricular activities. However, they also studied hard, did not cut classes, and did not demonstrate for political or social causes. These males were not especially socially active at this point, reporting that they did not date, did not join fraternities, did not spend time with friends, and did not attend cultural or sporting events.

Immediately after graduation, these males were likely to enter the PCEI 2/4 Early Maturers and Socially Maladapted Individuals prototypes. It was found that prototype membership was related to low scores on the Job Satisfaction, Extra Occupational Satisfaction, and College-Moderated Social Development summary dimensions. On the PCEI 2/4 item data, it was found that most were married soon after graduation, apparently to someone not at the university. They had some difficulty in finding a job and badly needed the job that they found through family or an employment agency. These males believed that they were hired on the basis of luck rather than special skills. Their pay was low, and they had received few salary increases. Prototype members were highly dissatisfied with their jobs, marriages, living arrangements, and university preparation. They socialized with their wives' friends and spent spare time reading books and literary magazines. Six to 8 years after graduation, composite prototype membership was related to low scores on the PCEI 6/8 Job Satisfaction, Social Adjustment, and Religious Morality summary dimensions. The PCEI 6/8 item data indicated that, although their income was now sample-typical, they remained very dissatisfied with their jobs. These males were somewhat dissatisfied with their marriages. They had few close friends of either sex and were not involved with religion. Spare time was devoted to radio and television.

The difficult family environment of these males appeared to engender a desire for parental approval. They identified with their fathers and adopted a conservative social orientation and the traditional masculine role. Moreover, when these trends were coupled with the harsh controlling nature of their parents, they led to conformity and a lack of independence. These trends also led to an extroverted pattern of social behavior in high school and early dating, which appeared to provide a source of approval. These males worked hard in college and were active in a variety of organizations. However, they married early and had some difficulty in finding a good job. This resulted in substantial dissatisfaction with their social and occupational lives immediately after graduation. Although they obtained better jobs in later years, they remained dissatisfied with their jobs and marriages and spent spare time in passive activities. Thus, their conformity to the traditional masculine role and early movement into adult social roles led to substantial difficulties for these males and so they were described as Premature Conformists.

Prototype 15. The final male prototype contained 30 individuals who received high scores on the Academic Achievement and Socioeconomic Status composite summary dimensions, and low scores on the Parental Warmth and Social Adjustment, Professional Occupational Orientation, Religious Involvement, and Satisfaction with Social Life composite summary dimensions. Although these males did not produce any significant differences on the reference measures, prototype membership was negatively related to scores on the BQ Academic Achievement, Social Introversion, and Scientific Interests dimensions. A review of the BQ items yielding significant differences indicated that these prototype members were likely to be an older child in a nonintellectual upper-class family in which religion was considered important. Their parents were warm, supportive, and interested in their activities. However, they allowed their sons little independence, were strict, criticized them, and pushed for achievement. Nevertheless, these males were close to their mothers and siblings. They tended to take things out on parents and friends. These males reported that they were somewhat conventional, did not wish to be alone, and were not independent. They were somewhat withdrawn socially because they had few casual friends, did not attend parties, and did not participate in extracurricular activities. Prototype members did not like school and did not do well academically, especially in science classes. They did not try to achieve and reported that they were not competitive in academic situations. Spare time was devoted to solitary intellectual pursuits, such as reading or watching public television, and building or repairing things.

Composite prototype membership during the college years was directly related to scores on the CEI Literary Pursuits summary dimension and inversely related to scores on the CEI Religious Involvement summary dimension. Surprisingly, the CEI item data indicated that prototype members studied hard and obtained satisfactory grades, although they did not make honorary societies. They displayed liberal social attitudes, demonstrated for causes, and had lived with a person of the opposite sex. Spare time was devoted to reading and cultural and musical events. Following graduation, these males were likely to enter the PCEI 2/4 Graduate Students prototype, while receiving high scores on the PCEI 2/4 College Moderated Social Development dimension and low scores on the PCEI 2/4 Early Occupational Success summary dimension. The PCEI 2/4 item data indicated that they were not employed full time, but knew exactly what kind of job they wanted. They obtained their jobs on the basis of recommendations, grades, major, and special skills. Their jobs did not involve sales, unskilled, or semiskilled labor, and they paid relatively little. They were satisfied with the nature of the work and most aspects of their jobs.

Six to 8 years after graduation, these males were likely to be assigned to the PCEI 6/8 Unhappy Isolates or Unambitious Townsmen prototypes, while receiving high scores on the PCEI 6/8 Job Channelling and Religious Morality summary dimensions and low scores on the PCEI 6/8 Extra-Occupational Satisfaction summary dimensions. An examination of the PCEI 6/8 item data indicated that their jobs involved specialized professional labor, but not sales work. They read professional journals, had received few salary increases and their pay was low. Although they considered their jobs an important part of their lives and were satisfied with the nature of the work, they were dissatisfied with a number of aspects of the job environment. These males were also dissatisfied with friends and living arrangements, and they read sports and hobby magazines.

These males came from a relatively wealthy but cold and strict family environment in which they were pushed for achievement. In high school, this resulted in social withdrawal, social immaturity, and a retreat into solitary intellectual pursuits. Through their dislike of school and unwillingness to compete, these males displayed an implicit rebellion that became an overt rebellion when they entered college. They adopted liberal political orientations and rejected established institutions but studied hard and maintained their intellectual interests. Eventually, they entered graduate school in nontechnical areas and had a clear idea of the kind of jobs they wanted. Subsequently, they obtained low-paying professional jobs that they were satisfied with. Given their upper-class background and rebellion against it, and their satisfaction of achievement needs and a rejection of their environment by obtaining marginal professional jobs, it seemed appropriate to describe these males as Bourgeois Outliers.

Female Composite Prototypes

Prototype 1. The 46 females assigned to the first prototype extracted in this composite analysis tended to receive high scores on the Traditional Social Adjustment, Job Channelling, Sociability, Life Satisfaction, and Sibling Friction composite summary dimensions, and low scores on the Intellectual Pursuits and Negative Parent/Child Conflict composite summary dimensions. On the reference measures, it was found that prototype membership was directly related to scores on the socioreligious conformity and extroversion scales. In the first assessment, composite prototype members tended to be assigned to the Well-Adjusted Achievers prototype and to receive high scores on the BQ Adjustment and Feelings of Social Inadequacy summary dimension. A review of the BQ item data indicated that these females tended to be an older child in a somewhat religious middle-class family. Their parents were warm, supportive, and interested in their activities, but allowed them some independence and did not push for achievement. Prototype members reported that they were close to their parents and tried to achieve. They liked school and did well in their coursework. Despite their success in science courses and athletics, they displayed little independent interest in either. Prototype members also displayed little interest in intellectual pursuits, such as reading. They were both socially active and effective, reporting that they adopted leadership positions, dated frequently, were popular, and had a number of close and casual friends.

During college, these females tended to enter the CEI Traditional Daters prototype and to receive low scores on the CEI Self-Support summary dimension. The CEI item data indicated that they dated frequently, but did not live with a member of the opposite sex. Otherwise, their college behaviors and experiences were sample-typical. Immediately after graduation, composite prototype members were likely to be assigned to the PCEI 2/4 Concrete Careerists and Effective Adaptors prototypes, but not the Immature Escapist prototype. They also tended to receive high scores on the PCEI 2/4 Rudimentary, People-Oriented Jobs, Job Determinants, and Religious Beliefs summary dimensions. A review of the PCEI 2/4 items indicated that prototype members began looking for a job early and had little difficulty in finding one. Their jobs paid relatively well and were selected on the basis of type of work, security, and opportunities for individual action. Their jobs were likely to involve working with people. They were satisfied with their supervisors and opportunities for individual action. Although most of these females were not married at this point in their lives, they planned to marry in the near future. Prototype members read home and fashion magazines and were satisfied with the university's preparation for family life. They tended to be somewhat religious.

Six to 8 years after graduation, composite prototype members were likely to be assigned to the PCEI 6/8 prototype labelled Realistically Mature Adults. These females were likely to receive high scores on the Extra-Occupational Satisfaction and Job Determinants PCEI 6/8 summary dimensions and low scores on the Perceived Occupational Status summary dimension. Most prototype members were happily married at this point in their lives and were satisfied with the family and intellectual stimulation provided by their marriages. They continued to read home and fashion magazines, and they socialized with their husbands' friends. They felt that the university had helped them make life-long friendships and prepare them for family life. Their employment characteristics were sample-typical except that they held low-status jobs that did not involve sales work.

These women came from a warm, supportive family background that encouraged the acceptance of traditional values and led to the emergence of a traditional role orientation. When this was coupled with their concern for achievement, it led them to focus on social success and display little interest in masculine and intellectual pursuits. They were, in fact, highly successful and effective socially, and they obtained jobs that employed their social skills. However, their primary concern appeared to be establishing a satisfying family life within the traditional structure, and after frequent dating, they eventually established a satisfying family and social life. Because their family background facilitated their adaptation of this pattern, and they successfully employed their femininity and social skills in establishing a satisfying life within the traditional feminine role, these females were described as Unscathed Adjustors.

Prototype 2. The nine members of the second female prototype tended to receive high scores on the Traditional Social Adjustment, Religious Involvement, Intellectual Pursuits, Self-Esteem, Socioeconomic Status, Life Satisfaction, and Sibling Friction composite summary dimensions. On the reference measures, it was found that prototype members preferred jobs in the life sciences or social services, such as a biologist or nurse, whereas they disliked business and mechanical occupations. They also tended to display an interest in a high occupational level and academic achievement. Prototype members tended to be somewhat more feminine, conservative, and introverted than was typical of the sample as a whole. These females tended to obtain good grades in high school and high SAT scores.

Membership in this composite prototype was directly related to scores on the BQ Academic Achievement, Feelings of Social Inadequacy, and Popularity with the Opposite Sex summary dimensions, and negatively related to scores on the Athletic Participation summary dimension. A review of the BQ item data indicated that these prototype members came from religious, middle-class homes in which the mothers were socially active. Their parents were warm, supportive, and interested in their daughter's activities, and they rarely argued with or criticized them. These females were achievement-oriented and did extremely well in their courses, particularly biology courses. Prototype members reported that they were conventional, but independent and introverted. They were not likely to be involved in extracurricular activities or to attend parties. Nevertheless, they appeared to be socially mature and effective, reporting that they helped friends, gave advice, did not take things out on friends, had a number of close and casual friends, and dated frequently. These prototype members tended not to engage in masculine pursuits, such as athletics and building things, and they also displayed little interest in intellectual pursuits.

During college, composite prototype members tended to be assigned to the CEI Christians prototype and receive high scores on the CEI Religious Involvement summary dimension. The CEI item data indicated that they studied hard, did not cut classes, and had not changed majors. They were likely to obtain good grades, but did little leisure reading. These females tended to be active in religious groups and service organizations. Spare time was spent on television and radio, and they did not work over the summer.

Two to 4 years after graduation, prototype members were likely to receive high scores on the Extra-Occupational Satisfaction and Religious Beliefs PCEI 2/4 summary dimensions, and low scores on the Upward Occupational Mobility summary dimension. Composite prototype members were likely to be assigned to the PCEI 2/4 Newly Married Careerist prototype. The PCEI 2/4 item data indicated that they began looking for a job early and had little difficulty in finding one they wanted. Family and trade publications did not help them find this job, and salary and opportunities for advancement were important in choosing it. Their income was sample-typical, and they were satisfied with the nature of their work, but not with their coworkers. Prototype members were also satisfied with their standard of living, living quarters, family size, and friends. Those who were married at this point were happy in their marriages and satisfied with various aspects of them. Those who were not already married planned to marry in the near future. They socialized with their husbands' friends, read home and fashion magazines, but did little serious reading. Prototype members were highly involved in religious groups and devoted income to charity.

Six to 8 years after graduation, these females were likely to be assigned to the PCEI 6/8 Community-Directed Housewives prototype. Composite prototype membership was directly related to scores on the PCEI 6/8 Religious-Community Involvement and Job Satisfaction summary dimensions and negatively related to scores on the Perceived Occupational Status and Intellectual Reading summary dimensions. Their jobs tended to involve clerical work or unskilled labor, but not consulting or operating machinery. Although their pay was low, they were satisfied with opportunities for advancement and the reputation of the organization. Most were happily married at this point in their lives and were satisfied with various aspects of their marriages and living arrangements. They did little reading, and they had a number of female friends whom they and their husbands socialized with. Prototype members remained highly religious and were active in religious organizations.

These females were intellectually gifted individuals who had been brought up in a warm, supportive, conservative, and traditional religious family in which the mother was socially active. They appeared to identify with their mother and adopted a conservative, traditional religious orientation that they maintained throughout their lives. These females also appeared to be rather nurturant in both their occupational preferences, social behavior, and religious values. This trend led them to deemphasize occupational success and focus on the nurturant activities of home, religion, family, and community, in line with their traditional role orientation. They employed their intellectual ability and social skills to establish a satisfying family life and were active in community affairs. In order to capture their intellect, social skills, nurturant values, and satisfaction with their lives, these females were described as Competent Nurturers.

Prototype 3. The 20 members of the third female prototype tended to receive high scores on the Occupational Success and Satisfaction, Life Satisfaction, and Intellectual Pursuits composite summary dimensions, and low scores on the Traditional Social Adjustment, Sociability, Religious Involvement, Scientific Interests, and Socioeconomic Status composite summary dimensions. Their scores on the reference measures indicated that they were cognitively complex, introverted, tenderminded, and nonauthoritarian. Although they had been exposed to emotionally arousing situations, they tended to inhibit emotional expression. Strong scores indicated a masculine pattern of interests and an interest in academic achievement among prototype members. They indicated an interest in cultural work, such as writing, music, and art, and a distaste for business and technical occupations such as sales, merchandising, and mathematics. These females tended to obtain high verbal and low mathematical scores on the SAT.

Composite prototype members were likely to be assigned to the BQ Unconventional Achievers prototype, while receiving high scores on the BQ Cultural/Literary Interests dimension, and low scores on the BQ Socioeconomic Status and Popularity with the Opposite Sex summary dimensions. Examination of the content of the BQ items yielding significant differences indicated that these females came from non-intellectual, lower-class homes in which the parents were not socially active. Their parents were not warm, supportive, or interested in their daughters' activities, although they were strict and pushed for achievement. Prototype members did not get along well with their parents, and did not try to achieve or expect to be successful in academic situations. These females did not like school or do especially well academically. Further, they were socially withdrawn and ineffective, reporting that they had few friends, did not date, were not popular, and were not involved in extracurricular activities. Spare time was spent in solitary intellectual pursuits, such as reading or watching public television.

During college, these females were likely to be assigned to the CEI Fashionable Liberals prototype, but not the Traditional Daters prototype. Composite prototype membership was directly related to scores on the CEI Sociability and Liberal Activism summary dimensions and negatively related to scores on the CEI Religious Involvement summary dimension. The CEI item data indicated that prototype members were not likely to join a sorority, and tended to express liberal political views. They dated frequently and had lived with a member of the opposite sex. A great deal of their time was spent reading books and literary and news magazines, and they were likely to attend musical and cultural events. They displayed little interest in either religion or athletics.

Immediately after graduation, these females were likely to be assigned to the PCEI 2/4 Unambitious Passives prototype rather than the Unaspiring Worker prototype. Membership in this composite prototype was directly related to scores on the Rudimentary People-Oriented Jobs PCEI 2/4 summary dimension and inversely related to scores on the Occupational Initiative and Religious Beliefs PCEI 2/4 summary dimensions. The PCEI 2/4 item data indicated that prototype members knew what kind of job they wanted and that they eventually obtained this job. Security and opportunities for advancement did not lead them to choose this job, and they were hired on the basis of special skills. Although their jobs did not pay well, they tended to entail research work. What little spare income they had was devoted to charity and investments. Although they continued to read extensively, they did not read home and fashion magazines, and they displayed little interest in religion.

Six to 8 years after graduation, these females were likely to be assigned to the Vocationally Adjusted Expressives PCEI 6/8 prototype and to receive high scores on the PCEI 6/8 Extra-Occupational Satisfaction and Intellectual Reading summary dimensions, while receiving low scores on the PCEI 6/8 Religious-Community Involvement summary dimension. The PCEI 6/8 item data indicated that their income was now sample-typical. They were satisfied with the nature of the work and opportunities for individual action. Prototype members were likely to belong to clubs, devote income to recreation, and be satisfied with friends, community, and family size. Prototype members continued to devote a great deal of time to serious reading and to display little interest in religion.

One of the more striking characteristics of this prototype was its harsh, lower-class family background. This difficult early environment appeared to lead to social withdrawal and a retreat into solitary intellectual pursuits, which their substantial verbal abilities had prepared them for. Once removed from the environment by college entry, they appeared to rebel by adopting a liberal behavior lifestyle in line with their earlier intellectual interests. Their rebellion entailed a rejection of both religion and a traditional feminine role and the development of newly found social skills. These females prepared themselves for, and eventually obtained, jobs that were in line with their liberal social orientations, intellectual orientation, and earlier vocational interests. They were satisfied with these jobs and successful in them. Prototype members appeared to employ their social skills and intellectual orientation to establish a satisfying personal life in adulthood, although they continued to reject religion and the family. In order to incorporate their rebellion, satisfying occupational and social lives, and the distance they had travelled to create these lives, prototype members were described as Unconventional Successes.

Prototype 4. The 15 females assigned to the fourth prototype identified in the composite cluster analysis were likely to receive low scores on the Job Channelling, Self-Esteem, Intellectual Pursuits, and Sociability composite summary dimensions and high scores on the Negative Parent/Child Conflict composite summary dimension. Scores on the reference measures indicated that members of this prototype were likely to prefer social contact jobs, such as sales and merchandising, and dislike scientific, technical, and outdoor occupations. Their interests reflected a preference for a low occupational and specialization level. These prototype members were likely to feel externally controlled, be acquiescent, and manifest economic values. They tended to receive low grades and SAT scores in high school.

In the first assessment, it was found that membership in this prototype was related to low scores on the BQ Parental Freedom and Adjustment summary dimensions. A review of the BQ item data indicated that prototype members came from middle-class, religious homes in which the parents were relatively strict. Correspondingly, they reported that they were religious and somewhat conservative. These females did not do well academically, had a low class standing, and did not make the honor role. They were especially likely to dislike, and do poorly in, science courses. These prototype members were socially active, reporting that they were popular, had a number of friends, and were active in student politics. However, low self-esteem was apparent in their sensitivity to criticism and feeling that they bored others.

During college, composite prototype members tended to receive low scores on the CEI Religious Involvement and Positive College Experience dimensions. The CEI item data indicated that they were likely to be healthy and to express conservative political views, although they were not active in student politics, service groups, or religious groups. Their college grades were poor, and they were dissatisfied with most aspects of their college experiences. Immediately after graduation, these females were likely to be assigned to the PCEI 2/4 Unprepared Underemployeds prototype and to receive low scores on the PCEI 2/4 Job Satisfaction dimension. Inspection of the PCEI 2/4 items indicated that special skills and grades did not influence their being hired for their first job and that salary, type of work, and security were not important in selecting their jobs. Their jobs involved unskilled or semiskilled labor, but not consulting or specialized professional labor. Pay was low, and they were dissatisfied with most aspects of the work, reporting that they would not go into the same type of work again. Prototype members had few female friends and devoted their spare time to hobbies.

Six to 8 years after graduation, prototype membership was negatively related to scores on the Job Appropriateness, Collegiate Social Maturation, and Intellectual Reading summary dimensions. The PCEI 6/8 item data indicated that these females had held a number of jobs but were not likely to be employed full time. Although they were no longer likely to holds jobs involving unskilled and semiskilled labor, they were not likely to perform professional work. Although their income was sample-typical, they were dissatisfied with their pay. They had few female friends, did little reading, and were not involved in religious activities. Those individuals who were married were not satisfied with recreational and leisure activities in the marriage.

Members of this prototype came from families that encouraged a conservative, nonindependent orientation. Although they were intellectually limited, they were socially active and successful in high school. However, they found this particular pattern of social activity difficult to maintain in the more complex college environment. When this was coupled with their low self-esteem and their desire for social success, it led to some difficulty in establishing social relationships and to dissatisfaction throughout their adult lives. Despite their interest in business contact jobs and their desire for occupational success, these females did not prepare themselves for the occupational world, and they obtained poor jobs that were not in line with their interests or desires for a high income. Although they eventually obtained better jobs, they remained dissatisfied. In order to incorporate their desire for concrete social and occupational success, their limited intellectual ability, and dissatisfaction resulting from their failure to meet these goals, these prototype members were described as Frustrated Incompetents.

Prototype 5. The 11 members of the fifth composite prototype tended to receive high scores on the Self-Esteem, Sociability, Intellectual Pursuits, Religious Involvement, Life Satisfaction, and Sibling Friction composite summary dimensions. Their Strong scores indicated that they preferred jobs that involved social administration, such as public administration or personnel director, but disliked social service and outdoor jobs. It was also found that prototype members were likely to engage in socially desirable behavior, not to be neurotic or introverted, and to express both cognitive values and conceptual and integrative complexity. They tended to have low high school grades but high scores on the mathematics section of the SAT.

Membership in this prototype was negatively related to scores on the BQ Parental Control, Parental Warmth, Cultural/Literary Interests, and Expression of Negative Emotions summary dimensions. An examination of the content of the items yielding significant differences indicated that prototype members came from middle class homes in which they did not get along well with their siblings. Their parents provided emotional support, allowed them some independence, and praised them when they did things well. Although these prototype members were not close to their parents, they were achievement oriented, reporting that they tried to achieve, set difficult goals, and were competitive. Their achievement motivation seemed to be focused on social activities, and they appeared to be socially active and effective. Prototype members guided group activities, were popular, had a number of casual friends, went to parties, and dated. However, the extroverted social activity did not extend to helping friends or having a number of close friends. These females were athletic and likely to be engaged in intellectual activities, such as reading or watching public television. Although they did not do well academically, they enjoyed and did relatively well in science courses.

During college, composite prototype members were likely to enter the CEI Effective Intellectuals prototype and to receive high scores on the CEI Liberal Activism, Religious Involvement, Sociability, and Leisure Reading summary dimensions. The CEI item data indicated that prototype members were likely to engage in a variety of cultural and intellectual activities, such as reading, attending cultural and musical events, and joining literary groups. These prototype members also displayed an interest in sports. Although they dated frequently and had a number of male friends, they did not live with a member of the opposite sex. These females displayed liberal political views and demonstrated for causes. They had not changed their major and were satisfied with their college experiences.

Immediately after graduation, composite prototype members were likely to be assigned to the PCEI 2/4 Schoolmarms prototype and receive high scores on the PCEI 2/4 Intellectual Leisure Reading summary dimension. The PCEI 2/4 item data indicated that they were likely to be employed full time after graduation, and that they found their first job through their own initiative rather than an employment agency. Apparently, they had prepared themselves for the job, because they were hired on the basis of their major, special skills, and personality. Their jobs were chosen on the basis of security and opportunities for advancement and individual action. Their jobs were likely to involve consulting, organizing, games, literary and research work, but not unskilled or specialized professional labor. They considered their jobs an important part of their lives and were satisfied with most aspects of it; however, they did not plan to remain in it. Although their income was sample-typical, they were not satisfied with their standard of living or acquaintances. Spare time was devoted to reading professional, literary, and sports magazines, but they were not involved in religious activities. Most were not married at this point in their lives, and those who were were dissatisfied with social activities.

Six to 8 years after graduation, prototype members were likely to receive high scores on the PCEI 6/8 Intellectual Reading summary dimension. The PCEI 6/8 item data indicated that their marriage characteristics were sample-typical. Prototype members continued to read books and magazines, especially literary and women's entertainment periodicals. They had a number of male friends and displayed little interest in religion. Their jobs involved organizing, advising, managing, and literary or artistic work, but not specialized professional labor.

In examining the characteristics of these females, it appears that their family background instilled self-confidence and achievement motivation. This achievement motivation and self-confidence were channelled into extroverted social activities. These females were highly socially active throughout their lives and quite interested in the opposite sex, and they displayed an enduring concern with social control, which was reflected in both their interests and overt behavior. They prepared themselves for and obtained jobs in line with their interest in social control and apparently were successful in them. These females also established satisfying adult social lives based on their social skills and intellectual interests. However, given the fact that they have few close female friends and had difficulties with their siblings throughout their lives, it appears that this emphasis on control led to some difficulties in close social relationships. When this observation is coupled with their occupational performance, concern with social achievement and extraversion, and interest in the opposite sex, these females seem described best by the label Social Manipulators.

Prototype 6. The eight females assigned to the sixth prototype tended to receive high scores on the Paternal Identification and Intellectual Pursuits composite summary dimensions as well as low scores on the Traditional Social Adjustment, Job Channelling, Occupational Success and Satisfaction, Sociability, Religious Involvement, and Negative Parent/Child Conflict composite summary dimensions. Although no significant differences were observed in the reference measures for prototype members, it was found that composite prototype membership was directly related to scores on the BQ Paternal Warmth summary dimension and inversely related to scores on the BQ Warmth of Maternal Relationship and Positive Academic Attitudes summary dimension. Examination of the content of the items yielding significant differences indicated that members of this prototype came from nonreligious, middle-class families that were not intellectually oriented. The parents of prototype members were strict, pushed for achievement, and were not especially interested in their daughter's activities. However, these females did not disagree with their parents, and they were close to, spent time with, and tried to be like their fathers. They displayed little achievement motivation, reporting that they did not try to achieve or set difficult goals. Although they worked hard in school, they did not obtain good grades, although they liked civics and discussion courses. During high school, these females appeared to be introverted and socially ineffective, reporting that they did not assume leadership positions, did not attend parties, and were difficult to get to know. These females also indicated that they did not say what they felt, were sensitive to criticism, bored others, and were often depressed. Spare time was spent on solitary intellectual activities, such as reading or watching public television.

During college, composite prototype members were likely to be assigned to the CEI Fashionable Liberal and Dependent Isolates prototypes. It was also found that composite prototype membership was directly related to scores on the CEI Traditional Social Involvement, Sociability, and Religious Involvement summary dimensions while being inversely related to scores on the CEI Athletic Participation and Health summary dimensions. The CEI item data indicated that these females attended classes regularly, but did not study in college. Although they did not join a sorority, they became active in a variety of extracurricular activities. Prototype members displayed an interest in sports and attended cultural events, musical events, and movies. Although they were not aggressive with the opposite sex, they dated frequently, had male friends, and had lived with a member of the opposite sex. They became active in liberal politics during college and displayed little interest in religion. These prototype members spent their spare time reading.

Immediately after graduation, these prototype members were likely to be assigned to the PCEI 2/4 Unaspiring Workers prototype while receiving high scores in the Rudimentary, People-Oriented Jobs and Intellectual Leisure Reading PCEI 2/4 summary dimensions and low scores on the Occupational Initiative and Religious Beliefs PCEI 2/4 summary dimensions. The PCEI 2/4 item data indicated that it took prototype members some time to find a job and that they found their jobs through personal contacts, rather than through university interviews or an employment agency. Their first job was their only means of employment, and salary and opportunities for advancement, rather than opportunities for individual responsibility, were important in choosing this job. Their jobs were not likely to involve technical or professional labor. Their pay was low, they felt overqualified, and they did not plan to remain in their current positions. They were also dissatisfied with most aspects of their jobs. Most were not married at this point in their lives, but they planned to get married in the near future. Frequent diverse reading and casual conversation occupied their spare time, and these prototype members continued to display little interest in religion.

Six to 8 years after graduation, these females were likely to be assigned to the Underemployed Intellectuals PCEI 6/8 prototype while receiving low scores on the Job Determinants and Religious-Community Involvement PCEI 6/8 summary dimensions and high scores on the Intellectual Reading summary dimension. A review of the PCEI 6/8 item data indicated that prototype members continued to display little interest in religion and to read extensively, particularly books and women's entertainment magazines, but not home and fashion magazines. Most were married at this point in their lives; however, they were dissatisfied with most aspects of their marriage. Their jobs did not involve management, research, or training. They had received few salary increases, felt overqualified for their jobs, and would not go into the same work again.

Members of this prototype came from a relatively harsh, restrictive family environment in which they were close to their fathers but not their mothers. In high school, their family background led to low self-esteem, poor adjustment, a lack of achievement motivation, limited social effectiveness, and a withdrawal into solitary intellectual pursuits. In college, these prototype members appeared to rebel against their background, adopting a liberal bohemian life style, dropping their early interest in athletics and rejecting traditional institutions such as religion, college sororities, and careers. However, they also became highly active socially and maintained their earlier intellectual interests. This rebellion continued in the postcollege years and, when coupled with a lack of preparation, it led to poor jobs that they were dissatisfied with as well as a rejection of jobs, religion, family, and community and some marital difficulties. Given the significance of this continuing rebellion against a family background in which their fathers were a central element, it seemed appropriate to describe these females as Paternal Reactives.

Prototype 7. The 25 females assigned to the seventh prototype tended to receive low scores on the Traditional Social Adjustment, Job Channelling, Religious Involvement, Socioeconomic Status, and Negative Parent/Child Conflict composite summary dimensions and high scores on the Occupational Success and Satisfaction, Sociability, and Sibling Friction composite summary dimensions. On the reference measures, it was found that prototype members disliked social and medical science occupations such as teacher, minister, or osteopath, and preferred technical outdoor occupations, such as agriculture. Their interest pattern indicated a low occupational level and low academic achievement. It was also found that they tended to be conformist, authoritarian, and to display socially desirable behaviors. Long-term goals and integrative complexity were low and prototype members tended to receive poor grades in high school.

At the time of the first assessment, these females were likely to be assigned to the BQ Extraverted Materialistic Authoritarians prototype and to receive low scores on the BQ Social Leadership and Socioeconomic Status summary dimensions. A review of the items yielding significant differences indicated that these prototype members were likely to be a younger child in a nonintellectual lower-class family. Their parents provided little warmth or emotional support, but were strict and pushed for achievement. Prototype members spent time with their fathers and did not disagree with their parents. These females tended to be conformist and in need of social approval, reporting that they wished to become more socially acceptable, conventional, did not wish to be alone, and felt guilty when they violated external standards. Nevertheless, prototype members were neither active nor effective socially, reporting that they had not met the demands of social situations, were not popular, had few friends, and were not involved in extracurricular activities. These females began dating early and frequently. Spare time was devoted to solitary intellectual pursuits, such as reading or building things. They disliked school and received poor grades.

During college, these females tended to be assigned to the CEI Fragile Flirts prototype, while receiving high scores in the Dating Activity CEI summary dimension and low scores on the CEI Religious Involvement summary dimension. The CEI item data indicated that prototype members did not study and frequently cut classes. They were likely to join a sorority and date a number of different individuals frequently. However, they did not display any interest in religion or social science groups.

Following graduation, these composite prototype members were likely to be assigned to the PCEI 2/4 Self-Defeating Passives prototype and to receive low scores on the Job Appropriateness PCEI 2/4 summary dimension. The PCEI 2/4 item data indicated that, although they did not know what kind of work they wanted, they tended to obtain sales jobs. Although their pay was low, they had received a number of pay increases and were satisfied with most aspects of their jobs. These prototype members read women's entertainment magazines and were not likely to be involved in religious groups. In the final assessment, these prototype members tended to receive high scores on the PCEI 6/8 Job Satisfaction, Collegiate Social Maturation, and Perceived Occupational Status summary dimensions and low scores on the PCEI 6/8 Job Determinants summary dimension. They continued to hold sales jobs, and their pay was now sample-typical. These prototype members were satisfied with their supervisors and co-workers. Their marital characteristics were sample-typical, and they continued to read women's entertainment magazines.

Prototype members came from a harsh, restrictive lower-class family background that engendered a conservative orientation and a desire for social approval. As a result of their difficult family environment, these females displayed signs of poor adjustment and withdrew from social contact into the solace of solitary intellectual pursuits and dating. In college, they joined a sorority in an attempt to satisfy their desire for approval and continued to date frequently. They became socially active at this time and eventually obtained jobs in line with their newly developed social skills and original interests in which they were successful and satisfied. Moreover, these females remained social and interested in the opposite sex during their postcollege years. Because of the significance of their family background, the use of sororities as a means for social development, their desire for social approval, and their occupational interests, these females were described as Restricted Socializers.

Prototype 8.   The 10 members of the eighth female prototype tended to receive high scores on the Paternal Identification, Athletic Interests, and Religious Involvement composite summary dimensions and low scores on the Traditional Social Adjustment, Self Esteem, Sociability, Scientific Interests, Life Satisfaction, and Negative Parent/Child Conflict summary dimensions. Although no reference measures data were available for these individuals, it was found that composite prototype members were likely to be assigned to the BQ Unpopular Cognitively Simple Introverts and Scholarly Bookworms prototypes. It was also found that composite prototype membership was directly related to scores on the BQ Social Leadership, Feelings of Social Inadequacy, Popularity with the Opposite Sex, and Athletic Interests summary dimensions while being inversely related to scores on the Warmth of Maternal Relationship and Academic Achievement BQ summary dimensions. The BQ item data indicated that these prototype members were likely to be an older child in a nonreligious middle-class family. Their parents were strict, allowed them little independence, and displayed little interest in their activities. While prototype members were not close to their cold mothers, they were close to, spent time with, and tried to be like their fathers. These females did not try to achieve and were not competitive in academic situations. They did not like school and were likely to perform poorly academically. Prototype members were conventional and likely to engage in socially desirable behaviors. They reported that they were popular, went to parties, dated frequently, and were active in student politics and extracurricular activities. Although they enjoyed and did well in athletics, they disliked intellectual pursuits, such as reading.

During college, these females were likely to be assigned to the CEI Christians prototype and to receive high scores on the CEI Religious Involvement, Traditional Social Involvement, and Sociability summary dimensions as well as low scores on the CEI Dating Activity summary dimension. The CEI item data indicated that these prototype members were not likely to join a sorority or participate in extracurricular activities during college. They did not date frequently or date the same person, and they were likely to drop their earlier interests in athletics. Prototype members were highly involved in religious activities and were dissatisfied with their grades.

Following graduation, members of this composite prototype were likely to be assigned to the PCEI 2/4 Self-Defeating Passives prototype. Composite prototype membership was directly related to scores on the PCEI 2/4 Occupational Initiative and Rudimentary, People-Oriented Jobs summary dimensions and inversely related to scores on the Upward Occupational Mobility, Intellectual Leisure Reading, and Extra-Occupational Satisfaction dimensions. Examination of the PCEI 2/4 items indicated that prototype members did not feel that the university had prepared them for the adult social and vocational world. These females began looking for a job early and reported that recommendations, rather than luck or sex, influenced their being hired for their first job. Their jobs involved lower-level social tasks, but not technical, managerial, or professional work. These jobs were not an important part of their lives. Most prototype members were married at this point, yet were dissatisfied with living quarters and family size. Spare time was spent on athletics and reading cultural and entertainment magazines. Religion was not an important part of their lives.

Six to 8 years after graduation, these individuals were likely to be assigned to the PCEI 6/8 prototypes labelled Presently Devastated Women and Family-Focused Women and to receive low scores on the PCEI 6/8 Extra-Occupational Satisfaction, Perceived Occupational Status, and

Collegiate Social Maturation summary dimensions. The PCEI 6/8 item data indicated that most of these prototype members were married at this point in their lives or planned to get married in the near future. They were unhappy in their marriages and dissatisfied with most aspects of them. These females tended to socialize with their husbands' friends, but they had few male friends. Prototype members did not belong to clubs, and they were dissatisfied with living quarters and family size. Spare time was spent on sports, casual conversations, and reading literary and entertainment magazines. They were not religious and did not devote income to recreation or investments. Their income was now sample-typical and their jobs involved advising and organizing but not unskilled labor.

Members of this prototype appeared to grow up in a harsh, restrictive environment in which their fathers were a major source of comfort and their mothers were especially distant. They appeared to identify with their fathers, being active in sports and adopting leadership positions. Although they were socially outgoing and effective in high school, they were not concerned with academic achievement. When removed from their fathers' support in college, they appeared to employ religion as a means for structuring their lives, despite the fact that their families were not especially religious. They dropped their early pattern of social involvement and athletic interests during this period. These females married early and remained married, despite being unhappy and dissatisfied with their marriages. Prototype members dropped their religious interests and apparently depended on their husbands to structure their lives and provide social contact. Correspondingly, they were not highly committed to their jobs. When this dependence on male support is coupled with their family background and close relationship with their fathers, as well as with their dissatisfaction with their lives, it seemed appropriate to describe these females as Discontented Male Dependents.

Prototype 9. The 23 members of the ninth female prototype tended to receive high scores on the Scientific Interests and Job Channelling composite summary dimensions and low scores on the Traditional Social Adjustment, Self-Esteem, Sociability, and Socioeconomic Status composite summary dimensions. Significant differences on the reference measures were not obtained for this prototype, although it was found that composite prototype membership was directly related to scores on the BQ Social Leadership summary dimension. The BQ item data indicated that prototype members were likely to be an older child from a nonreligious, middle-class home. Their parents were strict and pushed for achievement but did not provide attention and emotional support. Although prototype members were not close to their mothers, they spent time with and tried to be like their fathers. They reported that their parents were often angry at and critical of them, and they were frustrated with the rules of their homes. These females did not try to achieve in academic situations, did not like school, and did not perform well academically, particularly in civics and discussion courses. Prototype members appeared to be socially withdrawn and ineffective, reporting that they did not attend parties, had few friends, took things out on friends, and did not help them. Spare time was devoted to extracurricular activities and solitary intellectual pursuits, such as reading or watching public television.

During college, these females were likely to be assigned to the CEI Married Status prototype, and they were likely to receive low scores on the CEI Liberal Activism, Leisure Reading, Sociability, and Health summary dimensions. A review of the pertinent item data indicated that these prototype members were not likely to engage in intellectual activities, reading, or extracurricular activities. They were likely to be politically conservative, date only one person, have few friends of the opposite sex, and they did not go out with any female friends. These prototype members were not satisfied with their grades.

Following graduation, these prototype members were likely to be assigned to the PCEI 2/4 Immature Escapists prototype. They tended to receive low scores on the PCEI 2/4 Upward Occupational Mobility and Religious Beliefs summary dimensions and high scores on the PCEI 2/4 Job Appropriateness and Rudimentary People-Oriented Jobs summary dimensions. The PCEI 2/4 item data indicated that they felt that the university had not prepared them for their first jobs and that grades and undergraduate major influenced their being hired. These prototype members knew what kind of work they wanted and reported that the type of work and security were important in choosing their first jobs. Their jobs were likely to involve teaching. They were satisfied with coworkers and the nature of their work, and they planned to remain in it. Six to 8 years after graduation, these females were likely to be assigned to the PCEI 6/8 prototype labelled Family-Focused Women, receiving high scores on the PCEI 6/8 Job Determinants dimension and low scores on the PCEI 6/8 Job Satisfaction summary dimension. The PCEI 6/8 item data indicated that prototype members had remained on their initial jobs, which they were somewhat dissatisfied with. They read literary magazines and were somewhat religious. Otherwise, their characteristics were sample-typical.

In examining the differential characteristics of this prototype, it is clear that they came from a cold, harsh, lower-class background in which they were criticized and pushed for achievement. It appears that they did not rebel, but attempted to mitigate these circumstances by imitating their fathers and conforming to their parents' wishes. They also tended to withdraw from social contact. This same trend towards social withdrawal and overt conformity was apparent during their college years. However, they established a commitment to one male and prepared themselves for the traditional feminine occupation of teaching. They eventually obtained these jobs and were reasonably satisfied with them. As a result of their tendency to use conformity as a means for adapting to a difficult family background, and their maintenance of this pattern in their later lives, these females were described as Defensive Conformists.

Prototype 10. The three females assigned to the 10th prototype were likely to receive low scores on the Traditional Social Adjustment, Self-Esteem, Negative Parent/Child Conflict, Athletic Interests, and Socioeconomic Status composite summary dimensions, as well as high scores on the Sociability composite summary dimension. Although no reference measure data were available for members of this prototype, it was found that prototype membership was directly related to scores on the BQ Socioeconomic Status summary dimension and negatively related to scores on the Parental Control, Social Leadership, Feelings of Social Inadequacy, Expression of Negative Emotions, Scientific Interests, and Cultural/Literary Interests BQ summary dimensions. Examination of the items yielding significant mean differences indicated that prototype members were likely to be an older child in a closely spaced family where siblings did not get along and did compete with each other. Their parents were not likely to be well educated or religious, although they held jobs that generated a high income. Prototype members reported that their parents did not provide attention, warmth, or support; neither did they become angry at, criticize, or push their daughters for achievement, allowing them some independence. Although prototype members were not close to their parents, they did discuss important matters with their fathers. These females did not try to achieve or set difficult goals. They were not competitive in academic situations, did not like school, and did poorly in their coursework. Prototype members also disliked athletics and scientific and intellectual activities. Social immaturity and ineffectiveness were apparent in the fact that they had few female friends, did not help friends, and had not met the demands of social situations. However, a desire for social approval was apparent in their dislike of being alone and their unwillingness to say what they felt. A lack of adjustment was apparent in their tendency to daydream, become depressed, and take things out on others. They also indicated that they were independent, unconventional, and did not try to be like friends.

During college, membership in this prototype was inversely related to scores on the CEI Liberal Activism, Self-Support, and Religious Involvement summary dimensions and directly related to scores on the Traditional Social Involvement and Leisure Reading CEI summary dimensions. The CEI item data indicated that prototype members were not likely to work or join religious and service groups. However, they did join sororities and became highly active socially, attending sports events and going out with their female friends. These females dated a number of different males and had a number of male friends. They tended to be politically conservative and spend their spare time reading books.

Immediately after graduation, prototype membership was directly related to scores on the PCEI 2/4 Job Satisfaction, Rudimentary, People-Oriented Jobs, Occupational Initiative, and Intellectual Leisure Reading summary dimensions and inversely related to scores on the PCEI 2/4 Upward Occupational Mobility and Religious Beliefs summary dimensions. Examination of the item data indicated that prototype members felt that the university had helped them develop socially, and had prepared them for the adult social and vocational world. They found the transition from undergraduate studies easy. Prototype members reported that they knew what kind of job they wanted and that family, personal interests, and university interviews helped them find their jobs. Luck and personality, rather than grades, influenced their being hired, and their jobs were likely to involve sales, training, managing, and organizing. Satisfied with most aspects of their jobs, prototype members planned to remain on them. They reported being satisfied with friends and living conditions. Spare time was spent in reading or casual conversation, but not athletics. Most were not married at this point in their lives, but planned to marry in the near future.

Six to 8 years after graduation, composite prototype members were likely to be assigned to the PCEI 6/8 Disillusioned Capitalists prototype, and they tended to receive high scores on the PCEI 6/8 Perceived Occupational Status, Collegiate Social Maturation, and Religious-Community Involvement summary dimensions and low scores on the Asocial Job Activities summary dimension. The PCEI 6/8 item data indicated that these prototype members were employed full time and had been on their current jobs for some time. Although they were satisfied with their jobs, they would not go into the same type of work again. Prototype members had received a number of salary increases and had a high income, which was devoted in part to savings and charity. They were satisfied with living quarters, community, and family size. Most were happily married at this point in their lives and were satisfied with various aspects of their marriages. Spare time was devoted to reading news and financial magazines, along with involvement in religious organizations.

Prototype members appeared to come from successful business families that engendered self-confidence, independence, and achievement motivation. However, their parents were not especially warm or supportive, and this led to poor adjustment, social withdrawal, social immaturity, a desire for social approval, and poor academic performance in high school. In college, they joined a sorority in an attempt to obtain social approval, and sorority membership served as a source of social support and a basis for successfully expanding their social and intellectual lives. After graduation, these prototype members capitalized on their business background and newly developed social skills to obtain managerial and business contact jobs that they were quite successful in, given their independence and achievement motivation. Although they were not completely happy with these jobs, they established full and satisfying social and family lives and continued to expand their intellectual interests. When their isolation from their parents is considered, as well as its effect on their lives, the importance of sorority membership and their effective capitalization on this experience, and the influence of their family background in establishing their careers, this group of females was described as "Orphaned" Adaptors.

Prototype 11.   The 17 females assigned to the 11th prototype tended to receive high scores on the Religious Involvement, Life Satisfaction, and Scientific Interests composite summary dimensions, as well as low scores on the Traditional Social Adjustment, Occupational Success and Satisfaction, Sibling Friction, and Socioeconomic Status composite summary dimensions. Their scores on the reference measures indicated that these prototype members were likely to prefer medical service and outdoor occupations, such as dentist, physical therapist, and forestry officer, and to dislike mechanical and business contact occupations, such as carpentry or real estate sales. Although they had low-level occupational interests, these prototype members were cognitively complex and likely to display socially desirable behavior. These females tended to receive low SAT scores.

On the BQ summary dimensions, it was found that prototype membership was negatively related to Positive Academic Attitudes. Examination of the content of the items producing significant mean differences indicated that prototype members tended to be a younger child in a middle-class family in which they got along with their siblings. These females were not socially assertive, reporting that they did not lead others or try to make others see their point of view, nor did they take part in student politics. They were not popular, had few casual friends, and were difficult to get to know. Despite their linguistic ability, these prototype members disliked English and civics courses. Spare time was devoted to independent scientific and engineering pursuits such as experiments and building things.

During college, these females tended to be assigned to the CEI Athletes prototype. A review of the CEI item data indicated that prototype members were not likely to be involved in student politics. They had few casual friends, did not go out with their friends, and did not date different people. They read a great deal and felt that the university had not met their expectations. Immediately after graduation, prototype membership was related to low scores on the PCEI 2/4 Job Appropriateness, Upward Occupational Mobility, and Occupational Initiative summary dimensions. Their first job was their only means of employment, but they did not badly need it. Undergraduate grades and recommendations did not influence their being hired, and university-sponsored interviews, teachers, employment agencies and trade publications did not help them find their jobs. Their jobs involved managing, organizing, and unskilled labor, but not research. These females had received few salary increases and were dissatisfied with opportunities for advancement. Most were married at this point in their lives and were satisfied with recreational and leisure activities in their marriages. They attended church, and spare time was spent on sports and reading news and general interest magazines.

Six to 8 years after graduation, these females were likely to be assigned to the PCEI 6/8 Community-Directed Housewives prototype, receiving high scores on the PCEI 6/8 Religious-Community Involvement summary dimension and low scores on the Job Appropriateness summary dimension. The PCEI 6/8 item data indicated that their jobs were diverse, but did not involve training. They were satisfied with their standard of living, and they devoted income to charity and attended church. Spare time was devoted to television and radio and reading sports magazines. Prototype members were likely to have a number of close female friends.

The differential characteristics of these prototype members indicated that they were not assertive, extroverted, or particularly ambitious in either high school or college. These females did not actively prepare themselves for the occupational world or display a concern with occupational achievement. Instead, they focused on establishing a satisfying marital and family life. They were happily married at a young age and became involved in religious groups. Moreover, they appeared to establish satisfying social lives within this traditional feminine role. Although they continued to read and display interest in athletics throughout this period, they tended to read light material and spent time on passive forms of entertainment. To incorporate their lack of ambition and assertiveness, as well as their passivity and acceptance of the traditional feminine role, these females were described as Unambitious Passives.

Prototype 12. The 26 females assigned to the 12th composite prototype were likely to receive high scores on the Self-Esteem, Religious Involvement, Negative Parent/Child Conflict, and Life Satisfaction composite summary dimensions, and low scores on the Traditional Social Adjustment, Intellectual Pursuits, Athletic Interests, and Paternal Identification composite summary dimensions. No significant differences were obtained on the reference measures, but it was found that composite prototype membership was directly related to scores on the BQ Social Leadership, Socioeconomic Status, and Academic Achievement summary dimensions and inversely related to scores on the Warmth of Maternal Relationship, Parental Freedom, and Athletic Participation summary dimensions. Examination of the BQ items yielding significant differences indicated that prototype members were likely to be a younger child in a nonintellectual, nonreligious, middle-class family in which there was competition with siblings. Their fathers appeared to hold business jobs in which they received a good salary. Their parents were strict, allowed their daughters little independence, and provided little support and warmth. They also pushed for achievement and criticized their daughters. Their daughters were not close to them, disagreed with them, and were frustrated by their rules. Prototype members did not try to achieve, set difficult goals, or compete in academic situations. They did not like school or perform well academically, particularly in science courses. These females were withdrawn and ineffective in social situations, reporting that they had few friends, were not popular, did not assume leadership positions, did not try to make others see their point of view, did not help friends, and took things out on friends. Spare time was spent in solitary intellectual pursuits, such as reading or watching public television.

During college, these females were likely to be assigned to the CEI Traditional Daters prototype and to receive high scores on the CEI Dating Activity and Traditional Social Involvement summary dimensions and low scores on the CEI Athletic Participation summary dimension. The CEI item data indicated that prototype members were likely to join a sorority and begin dating a number of individuals in college. They dated frequently, developed a number of close friendships, and frequently went out with their friends. Members of this prototype were likely to express conservative religious and social views and to become involved with religious groups.

Following college graduation, these females were likely to be assigned to the PCEI 2/4 Immature Escapists prototype and receive high scores on the PCEI 2/4 Extra-Occupational Satisfaction, Collegiate Social Development, and Rudimentary People-Oriented Job summary dimensions. On the PCEI 2/4 item data, prototype members indicated that they felt the university had helped them make life-long friendships. They reported that special skills, personality, and luck influenced their being hired for their first jobs. Their jobs were likely to involve training and sales. Their pay was low, but they had received a number of salary increases. Satisfaction with standard of living, living quarters, community, and friends characterized these individuals. They were likely to have a number of friends of both sexes. Spare time was devoted to sports, and they displayed little interest in religion. Although they were not unusually likely to be married, those who were married were happily so.

Six to 8 years after graduation, these females were likely to receive high scores on the PCEI 6/8 College-Moderated Social Development summary dimension. The PCEI 6/8 item data indicated that they felt that the university had helped prepare them for adult social and family life. Prototype members were satisfied with their standard of living, family size, and marital companionship. They read home and fashion magazines.

The differential characteristics of this prototype suggested that they came from entrepreneurial families where the parents were not warm, but demanded achievement. Their negative family background led them to withdraw from social activities into solitary intellectual pursuits during high school. Once removed from this environment, the desire for approval that it had instilled led these females to join a sorority. They became highly socially active and effective as a result of this experience. After college, they appeared to maintain this social orientation and obtain jobs where their newly developed social skills would be of use. Although they were successful on these jobs, their conservative, conformist orientation and acceptance of the traditional feminine role led them to focus on establishing a traditional marriage and family life that they found satisfying. Because their social life was of great importance and represented a way of overcoming a difficult adolescence and family background, these females were described as Social Copers.

Prototype 13. The 13 females assigned to the 13th prototype tended to receive high scores on the Traditional Social Adjustment, Self-Esteem, Scientific Interests, Negative Parent/Child Conflict, Socioeconomic Status, Sibling Friction, and Athletic Activities composite summary dimensions and low scores on the Job Channelling, Religious Involvement, and Life Satisfaction composite summary dimensions. On the reference measures, prototype members were likely to receive high scores on the extraversion scale. Strong scores indicated a preference for adventurous, social occupations, such as army officer, and a distaste for more scholarly occupations, such as librarian. Membership in this composite prototype was found to be directly related to scores on the BQ Social Leadership and Athletic Interest summary dimensions and inversely related to scores on the BQ Expression of Negative Emotions summary dimension. The BQ item data indicated that prototype members were likely to be an older daughter in a rather religious, somewhat intellectual, upper-class family where they got along well with their siblings. Their parents were not strict, allowed their daughters some independence, and did not push for achievement. Prototype members set difficult goals, tried to achieve, and were competitive. Although they were good athletes, they were not greatly interested in athletics. These prototype members were high social, socially effective, and socially secure, reporting that they were not self-conscious, said what they felt, were popular, dated frequently, and had a number of friends. They were conventional and wished to become more socially acceptable. Prototype members read frequently and extensively in adolescence.

During college, these females tended to receive high scores on the CEI Dating Activity summary dimension and low scores on the CEI Religious Involvement summary dimension. A review of the CEI item data indicated that they were aggressive with the opposite sex and dated a number of different individuals regularly. Spare time was devoted to sports and musical events, but they displayed little interest in religious or musical groups. Following graduation, composite prototype members were likely to be assigned to the PCEI 2/4 Homebodies prototype and to receive low scores on the PCEI 2/4 Religious Involvement summary dimension. The PCEI 2/4 item data indicated that they had nondescript, well-paying jobs on which they were satisfied with coworkers. They displayed little interest in religion and read women's entertainment magazines. Six to 8 years after graduation, composite prototype members were likely to be assigned to the PCEI 6/8 Community-Directed Housewives prototype while receiving high scores on the PCEI 6/8 Perceived Occupational Status summary dimension and low scores on the PCEI Extra-Occupational Satisfaction summary dimension. The PCEI 6/8 item data indicated that their jobs involved managing, organizing, and advising. They devoted spare time to sports, but did not attend church. Those individuals who were married tended to be unhappy in their marriages.

These females came from a secure, upper-class family that instilled a sense of self-confidence, independence, and a concern with appropriate social behavior. Prototype members were highly social and socially successful in high school. They appeared to be consumed with social achievement and were quite extraverted. This pattern was maintained in college but centered on contact with males. Their interest in the opposite sex was maintained in later years, and they eventually obtained socially oriented business jobs, which they were successful in. Despite these favorable outcomes, this extraverted pattern of social activity led to a certain shallowness, a lack of close relationships with peers, and marital difficulties. In order to describe this extraverted pattern of social activity and the fact that these females came from a background that would encourage such behavior, prototype members were ascribed the label Channelled Extroverts.

Prototype 14.   The 17 females assigned to the 14th prototype tended to receive high scores on the Traditional Social Adjustment, Occupational Success and Satisfaction, Self-Esteem, Scientific Interests, and Sibling Friction composite summary dimensions, along with low scores on the Parental Identification, Athletic Interests, and Sociability composite summary dimensions. Their scores on the reference measures indicated that they preferred technical, professional occupations, such as physicist or engineer, and disliked social contact jobs, such as social worker or credit manager. Prototype members did not have physical goals, had not been exposed to emotionally arousing situations, and were not integratively complex. Nevertheless, they obtained good grades in high school and were likely to do well on the mathematics subsection of the SAT.

At the time of the first assessment, these females were likely to be assigned to the BQ Scholarly Bookworm prototype. Prototype membership was directly related to scores on the BQ Academic Achievement and Scientific Interests summary dimension and negatively related to scores on the BQ Warmth of Maternal Relationship, Athletic Participation, Expression of Negative Emotions, Popularity with the Opposite Sex, and Cultural/Literary Interests summary dimensions. A review of the BQ items yielding significant differences indicated that prototype members came from intellectual, middle-class families in which the parents were warm, supportive, and interested in their daughters' activities. Although their parents were not strict and allowed them some independence, they pushed for achievement. Prototype members spent time with their fathers, but did not try to be like them. However, they tried to achieve, were competitive in academic situations, and expected to be successful in academics. These females liked school and did extremely well academically. Prototype members did especially well in science courses, and they conducted independent experiments and built or repaired things. A dislike of athletics and poor athletic performance characterized these females. They also appeared socially insecure and introverted, reporting that they were self conscious, sensitive to criticism, attended few parties, and did not participate in extracurricular activities. However, they tried to help friends and did not take things out on them.

During college, these females were likely to be assigned to the Introverted Escapists CEI prototype and to receive low scores on the CEI Dating Activity and Leisure Reading summary dimensions. The CEI item data indicted that they were socially withdrawn in college, reporting that they had few friends of the same sex, did not go out with friends, did not join a sorority, did not spend spare time in conversation, did not take friends home, and did not attend musical and sports events. These females did not join cultural or literary groups, and they felt that the university had not facilitated their social development. These prototype members did not cut classes, and they received good grades in college.

Following graduation, these females were most likely to be assigned to the PCEI 2/4 prototypes labelled Satisfied Conventional Females and Homebodies. They tended to receive low scores on the PCEI 2/4 Extra-Occupational Satisfaction, Collegiate Personal Development, and Rudimentary People-Oriented Jobs summary dimensions. The PCEI 2/4 item data indicated that it did not take prototype members long to find a job, and initiative, employment agencies, and newspapers did not help them find the job. Type of work and salary were important in choosing this job. Their jobs were diverse in content and low-paying. Although they had received few salary increases, they planned to remain on their jobs. Prototype members were dissatisfied with their standard of living, living quarters, and community. They had few friends of the same sex and were not likely to belong to civic or professional groups. Spare time was spent reading cultural and home and fashion magazines, rather than on sports and religion.

Six to 8 years after graduation, prototype members were likely to be assigned to the PCEI 6/8 Professionals and Realistic Mature Adults prototypes. Prototype membership was related to low scores on the Collegiate Social Maturation and Occupational Initiative PCEI 6/8 summary dimensions. The PCEI 6/8 item data indicated that these prototype members had managed to avoid jobs involving tasks such as sales, sports, and mechanics, which they had little interest in. Their income was sample-typical, and they indicated that they would prefer a more complex job. Most were happily married at this point in their lives and were satisfied with marital companionship. They tended to socialize with their husbands' friends and to have few close friends of the same sex. These prototype members were not likely to belong to social clubs and tended to be dissatisfied with their friends.

Members of this prototype appeared to come from warm, secure, intellectual families that fostered independence and pushed for achievement, especially in academics. In fact, in both high school and college, these females were competitive in academic situations and highly successful. However, this was accomplished to the exclusion of a satisfying social life, because throughout this period prototype members appeared introverted, socially isolated, and socially ineffective. This trend led to some dissatisfaction. Moreover, these prototype members were not as successful in the occupational world as might have been expected on the basis of their academic performance. These females also displayed little interest in intellectual pursuits for their own sake aside from academic achievement, and they did not seem especially concerned with occupational achievement. In order to capture the social withdrawal, academic achievement, dissatisfaction, and restricted intellectual lives, these females were assigned the label Isolated Intellectuals.

Prototype 15. The five females assigned to the 15th female prototype tended to receive high scores on the Traditional Social Adjustment, Intellectual Pursuits, Scientific Interests, Negative Parent/Child Conflict, Athletic Interests, and Sibling Friction composite summary dimensions and low scores on the Self-Esteem, Socioeconomic Status, and Paternal Identification composite summary dimensions. On the reference measures, it was found that these prototype members disliked business and outdoor occupations, such as accountant or farmer, and preferred verbal or artistic jobs involving writing or public speaking. Prototype members expressed a feminine, specialized pattern of interests. Although they were acquiescent and conformist, they did not display economic and physical goals. These females tended to be internally controlled, independent, and oriented towards long-term goals and cognitive values. They were hierarchically complex and tended to receive high SAT scores.

Composite prototype membership was directly related to scores on the BQ Academic Achievement, Scientific Interests, and Positive Academic Attitudes summary dimensions and negatively related to scores on the BQ Socioeconomic Status, Popularity with the Opposite Sex, and Paternal Warmth summary dimensions. A review of the BQ items yielding significant differences indicated that prototype members came from non-Protestant, lower-class families in which the parents were not intellectual, religious, or socially active. Their parents were warm, supportive, and interested in their activities, and prototype members were close to their mothers, but did not spend time with or try to be like their fathers. Although their parents were not especially strict, they found the rules of their home frustrating and often disagreed with them. Prototype members tried to achieve and set difficult goals. They liked school and did extremely well academically, especially in civics courses. However, they displayed little interest in independent intellectual pursuits or extracurricular activities. Instead, they were more concerned with athletics, which they enjoyed and did well in. These females were independent and assertive, reporting that they said what they felt, were independent, spent time alone, tried to make others see their point of view, and guided group activities. Signs of social maturity and effectiveness were apparent in the fact that they attended parties, had a number of close and casual friends, began dating early, and did not take things out on others.

During college, these females were likely to be assigned to the CEI Fashionable Liberals prototype and to receive high scores on the CEI Dating Activity, Health, Self-Support, Sociability, and Positive College Experience summary dimensions. The CEI item data indicated that they worked, paid for their education, and received good grades. They had close friends of both sexes and attended cultural and musical events. Prototype members displayed liberal political views and little interest in religion.

Following graduation, these females were likely to receive low scores on the PCEI 2/4 Job Appropriateness, Extra-Occupational Satisfaction, and Religious Beliefs summary dimensions, and they were not likely to be assigned to the PCEI 2/4 prototype labelled Satisfied Conventional Females. The PCEI 2/4 item data indicated that prototype members began looking for a job early and found one primarily through their own initiative, rather than through teachers, contacts, or an employment agency. Personality, gender, and grades led them to be hired for their first job, which they chose on the basis of location, type of work, and opportunities for advancement and individual action. They badly needed a job, found the kind of job they wanted, and were satisfied with most aspects of it. Although their income was sample-typical, they were not satisfied with their standard of living, living quarters, or community. Most were not married at this point in their lives and did not plan to marry in the near future. Those individuals who were married were unhappy in their marriages and dissatisfied with various aspects of them. Spare time was spent in casual conversation and reading literary or news magazines, rather than on television and radio.

Six to 8 years after graduation, these females were likely to be assigned to the PCEI 6/8 prototype labelled Occupationally Disaffected Women. Composite prototype membership was directly related to scores on the PCEI 6/8 Intellectual Reading and Occupational Initiative summary dimensions and negatively related to scores on the Job Determinants, Job Satisfaction, and Religious-Community Involvement summary dimensions. The PCEI 6/8 item data indicated that their jobs involved management, but not design or training. They desired a more complex job, were dissatisfied with opportunities for advancement, and planned to change jobs. Prototype members were also dissatisfied with their standard of living, community, and family size. Although they had friends of the same sex, they did not belong to civic and social organizations and were dissatisfied with their friends. They were likely to be single. Spare time was devoted to casual conversation and reading literary magazines, rather than to religion and reading home and fashion magazines.

Prototype members were clearly bright, independent women from a disadvantaged but warm and supportive family background. They appeared to dislike their fathers' failure and strongly desired achievement and overt success. These females were highly successful academically and socially, and they managed to maintain this success as they worked their way through college. During college, they were somewhat rebellious, and they adopted a liberal intellectual orientation, which they maintained throughout their lives. Although these females obtained the jobs they wanted and did reasonably well on them, they were dissatisfied with them. They tended not to marry, perhaps due to their extreme independence and rebelliousness, and they appeared to have some difficulty in merging into adult social institutions. In order to describe their independence, rebellion, desire for achievement and success, as well as the distance they had come on their own relative to their family background, these females were described as Independent Achievers.

Prototype 16. The four females assigned to the sixteenth prototype tended to receive high scores on the Traditional Social Adjustment, Intellectual Pursuits, Negative Parent/Child Conflict, Parental Identification, Socioeconomic Status, and Athletic Interests composite summary dimensions. On the reference measures, it was found that prototype members tended to prefer literary and social science occupations and to dislike business occupations. These prototype members were likely to be tenderminded, nonauthoritarian, and externally controlled. They were conceptually and integratively simple, but displayed hierarchical complexity. These females tended to receive high scores on the linguistic subsection of the SAT and poor grades in high school.

Composite prototype membership was directly related to scores on the BQ Warmth of Maternal Relationship, Cultural/Literary Interests, Socioeconomic Status, Positive Academic Attitudes, and Paternal Warmth summary dimensions, and inversely related to scores on the BQ Academic Achievement, Scientific Interest, and Adjustment summary dimensions. Examination of the content of the items yielding significant differences indicated that prototype members came from somewhat religious and intellectual, upper-class families where the parents were warm, supportive, and interested in their daughters' activities. Their parents were not strict and did not push for achievement. Their daughters were close to their parents and tried to be like their fathers. However, they took things out on their parents and did not get along with their siblings. Prototype members were independent and somewhat maladjusted, reporting that they were not traditional, were independent, were unconventional, were depressed, often daydreamed, and wished to be alone. They did not participate in religious groups or extracurricular activities. Although they began dating early and had a number of close and casual friends, they did not assume leadership positions. These females disliked school and did not do well academically, although they did relatively well in English and civics courses and did relatively poorly in science courses. They enjoyed and did well in athletics.

During college, these females were likely to be assigned to the CEI Fashionable Liberals prototype. Composite prototype membership was directly related to scores on the Liberal Activism and Sociability CEI summary dimensions, and inversely related to scores on the Traditional Social Involvement, Religious Involvement, and Health CEI summary dimensions. The CEI item data indicated that prototype members adopted a liberal, bohemian lifestyle in college. They were active in liberal politics, dated a number of different individuals, lived with a member of the opposite sex, attended cultural and musical events, and devoted spare time to intellectual reading and cultural groups. Prototype members displayed a distaste for traditional social activities and collegiate institutions, such as athletics, sororities, and religious groups. They were not likely to be married and paid for relatively little of their education.

After college graduation, these females were likely to receive low scores on the PCEI 2/4 Upward Occupational Mobility, Occupational Initiative, Religious Beliefs, and Rudimentary People-Oriented Jobs dimensions. They were not likely to be assigned to the PCEI 2/4 prototype labelled Satisfied Conventional Females. The PCEI 2/4 item data indicated that they were likely to be satisfied with their university experiences and to believe that their experiences had helped them develop socially. Prototype members began looking for a job early, had some difficulty in finding one, and badly needed their jobs when they found them. Luck, major, and sex, rather than grades, influenced their being hired for these jobs. They found their jobs through family and teachers, rather than an employment agency or trade publications. Their income was low, they had received few salary increases, and they planned to leave their job in the near future. Prototype members were dissatisfied with their standard of living and living quarters. Spare time was spent reading books, but not home and fashion magazines. They displayed little interest in religion.

Six to 8 years after graduation, these females were likely to be assigned to the PCEI 6/8 Downtrodden Passives prototype and receive high scores on the PCEI 6/8 Asocial Job Activities, Intellectual Reading, and Collegiate Social Maturation summary dimensions. The PCEI 6/8 item data indicated that they felt that the university had helped prepare them for the adult social world. Their jobs were likely to involve artistic, consulting, and research work rather than sales, training, computational, and specialized professional labor. Although they were satisfied with the nature of the work and would go into it again, they were dissatisfied with working conditions and opportunities for advancement and individual action. Their income was sample-typical, but they were dissatisfied with their standard of living, living quarters, and community. Prototype members had a number of friends of both sexes, and they belonged to clubs and social groups. Spare time was devoted to intellectual reading rather than to sports, hobbies, or reading home and fashion magazines. They displayed little interest in religion. Most were not married at this point in their lives, and those who were indicated that they were unhappy in their marriages.

Prototype members came from a warm, secure, upper-class background. However, they had a difficult adolescence, displaying signs of poor adjustment while rejecting school and religion, and fighting with their families. Nevertheless, they were independent and socially active and effective. In college, they adopted a liberal bohemian lifestyle and continued to reject established institutions. They maintained this orientation in adulthood as well. Although they displayed some concern with occupational achievement and eventually obtained jobs in line with their interests, they tended to be dissatisfied with them. These females also tended to be dissatisfied with their social lives, despite a high degree of social activity and an average income. This disaffection, when coupled with their bohemian lifestyle and poor high school adjustment, led these females to be described as Insecure Bohemians.

Prototype 17. The 20 members of the 17th prototype tended to receive high scores on the Traditional Social Adjustment and Socioeconomic Status composite summary dimensions and low scores on the Self-Esteem, Life Satisfaction, Athletic Interests, and Sibling Friction composite summary dimensions. Their scores on the reference measures indicated that prototype members tended to be introverts who had not been exposed to emotionally arousing situations and were hierarchically simple. Strong scores suggested that these females preferred masculine, outdoor occupations such as carpenter and farmer, and that they disliked artistic and social contact jobs, such as writer or personnel director. It was found that these females tended to be assigned to the BQ Unpopular Cognitively Simple Introverts prototype. The BQ item data indicated that prototype members were an older child in an upper-class family where their parents were not strict, but allowed them little independence. They had a difficult adolescence, reporting that they were depressed, self-conscious, and often wished to be alone. Prototype members were difficult to get to know, were not popular, did not attend parties, and began dating late. Despite their masculine interests, they did not build or repair things, and did not like or do well in sports, scientific activities, or civics courses.

During college, these females tended to be assigned to the CEI Introverted Escapists prototype and to receive high scores on the Traditional Social Involvement summary dimension. The CEI item data indicated that they remained introverted and did not join service groups, volunteer groups, or sororities. They were satisfied with their grades, but felt that the university had not enhanced their social development. Immediately after graduation, these females were likely to receive low scores on the PCEI 2/4 Occupational Initiative summary dimension. The PCEI 2/4 item data indicated that they did not find their first jobs through personal contacts or trade publications and were not hired on the basis of their major or recommendations from others. Their first jobs were their only means of employment and they had badly needed the jobs when they found them. These jobs were likely to involve clerical or computational work but not sales, unskilled, or professional labor. Although pay and promotions were sample-typical, they would not go into the same work again. They were not likely to spend time on serious reading, and they displayed little interest in religion.

Six to 8 years after graduation, prototype members were likely to be assigned to the PCEI 6/8 prototype labelled Introverted Vocationally Uncommitted Women and to receive low scores on the PCEI 6/8 Extra-Occupational Satisfaction, Religious-Community Involvement, and Intellectual Reading PCEI 6/8 summary dimensions. The PCEI 6/8 item data indicated that prototype members were likely to hold jobs involving clerical tasks rather than professional labor. Their income was low, and they were not likely to devote income to charity or savings. These females were dissatisfied with their standard of living, living quarters, community, family size, and friends. The social disaffection of prototype members was accompanied by a lack of involvement in civic and social organizations. Prototype members did not read professional or news magazines. Those individuals who were married reported that they were unhappy in their marriages and were dissatisfied with various aspects of them.

Apparently, prototype members came from a warm, upper-class family background in which they were protected and were close to their mothers. When this background was coupled with their introversion, dependence, and conformity, it led prototype members to accept the traditional feminine role and reject masculine activities, such as athletics and science, despite their interest in these areas. As a result, they eventually entered the clerical jobs that were traditionally the domain of females, and they were dissatisfied with them. Further, their dependence, introversion, and conformity led to a poor social life in adolescence, college, and young adulthood. Moreover, these same trends appear to have led to poor marriages. Because their family background appeared to have thwarted these females in relation to sex role stereotypes and led to negative outcomes when accompanied by introversion, it seemed appropriate to describe prototype members as Female Eunuchs.

CONCLUSIONS

The preceding paragraphs have reviewed the differential characteristics of the various male and female composite prototypes. Perhaps the most important implication of these data is that the composite prototypes provided a summary description of individuality and individual development by virtue of their ability to capture differential behavior and experiences at multiple points in the course of an individual's life. These differences did not appear to occur in a random fashion. The foregoing discussion has served to demonstrate that the composite prototypes were associated with a cohesive pattern of differential behavior and experiences that appeared to reflect an unfolding of individuality over time. Moreover, these cohesive patterns appeared to be amenable to psychological interpretation and have some substantive meaning. Consequently, it appears that the composite prototypes provided a meaningful description of individuality and individual development. The next step was a formal evaluation of the validity of the composite prototypes and the prototype model in the description of individuality and individual development.

10

Evaluation of Composite Prototypes

Chapter 9 presented a good deal of information concerning the nature of the composite prototypes and the likely behavior and experiences of prototype members over a 12-year interval. The information indicated that the composite prototypes were capable of capturing a variety of differential behaviors and experiences over time. Further, the nature and content of these differences as they emerge over the course of individuals' lives have important implications for conceptions of individuality and individual development. Yet, before this can be addressed, the validity of the summary descriptions obtained from the composite prototypes, as well as the utility of the prototypical model in constructing general summary descriptions of human individuality, should be established.

Any attempt to provide evidence for the validity of a general prototypical description of individuality must be a multifaceted effort. For instance, it was noted that the indicators in use must be of sufficient breadth and significance to provide the content base required for the derivation of general prototypical descriptions. An additional source of information pertaining to the value of prototypical summary descriptions may be found in the clarity of and completeness by which individuals are described by a set of taxonomic categories. Further, it should be robust in the sense that it is capable of capturing differences in behavior and experiences over time and measurement formats and on indicators not employed in the initial formation of the prototypes. Of course, these differences should also fall into a cohesive and interpretable pattern that displays some overlap with the pattern obtained in other attempts to describe individuality and individual development through the prototype model. However, if the prototype model is to provide some descriptive information that is not available by other means, it should also be capable of capturing any qualitative differences in the organization of behavior and experiences that are manifest in the course of individual development.

In the ensuing discussion, an attempt is made to outline the evidence obtained with respect to each of the foregoing points. Once evidence for the validity and cross-time nature of the summary descriptions incorporated in the composite prototypes has been established, attention turns to some of the more important implications of the composite prototypes' patterns of differential development.

PROTOTYPE CONTENT

For the prototype model to provide a general summary description of individuality, the prototypes must be based on indicators that provide a comprehensive description of individuals' behaviors and experiences over the course of their lives. The previous discussion has noted that the content of the BQ, CEI, and PCEI items was specifically designed so as to be capable of examining significant behaviors and experiences that occur during adolescence, the college years, and young adulthood. Further, by employing the retrospective characteristics of background data items, it proved possible to examine certain significant behaviors and experiences that occur prior to adolescence, such as socioeconomic status and sibling relations. Evidence presented earlier indicates that these items were capable of providing a highly accurate or reliable description of the individual's behaviors and experiences, given the limitations that are inherent in all item data, and that these items responses were not generally distorted by any of the more common biasing influences. Consequently, these items appear to be of sufficient accuracy to insure an adequate description of the individual and so an appropriate implementation of the prototype model. Second, it is clear that the BQ, CEI, and PCEI items covered a broad range of significant behaviors and experiences, suggesting that the indicators were of sufficient breadth to permit the construction of a general classification of persons, particularly given the relative independence of background data and the uniqueness of the descriptive information contained in the individuals' responses to each of these items.

Of course, the composite prototypes were formulated on the basis of the composite summary dimensions, and so any discussion of the content validity of the composite prototypes must also consider the appropriateness of the descriptive information. As was noted earlier, within the constraints imposed by the use of a principal components analysis and an item base of limited, albeit relatively substantial, reliability, the composite components appeared to be capable of providing an excellent summarization of the total variance in the BQ, CEI, and PCEI 6/8 item responses. As a result, it appears that the requisite breadth and accuracy in the coverage of significant behaviors and experiences was not lost in the course of summarization. The evidence presented in the preceding chapters also suggested that the composite summary dimensions were capable of describing and summarizing the individual's behaviors and experiences over time or in different developmental periods. Moreover, the composite summary dimensions were found to be more effective predictors of differential behaviors and experiences over time than were the various cross-sectional dimensions. This was true when the PCEI 2/4 data that were not employed in defining the composite prototypes were examined. Because the composite summary dimensions appeared to be capable of describing a variety of differential behavior and experiences over time, they seemed to provide an appropriate basis for the description of individual development through the prototype model.

Some additional support for the appropriateness of the composite summary dimensions and their content validity may be found in the meaningfulness of the summarization obtained from the composite summary dimensions. It has been noted that the composite summary dimensions displayed an interpretable pattern of item content that allowed them to be assigned consensual labels. Moreover, the labels assigned to these dimensions were in line with the composite dimension's pattern of correlations with scores on the cross-sectional summary dimensions. This evidence for the meaningfulness of the composite summary dimensions was borne out in the fact that the content of the composite summary dimensions differed from the cross-sectional dimensions in a manner that would enhance their cross-time and developmental significance. The nature and content of the composite summary dimensions themselves found substantial support in the developmental literature.

Of course, relative to the cross-sectional summary dimensions, the composite summary dimensions provided some unique information that was relevant to the description of individuality over time. However, this would be expected if an effective cross-time summarization was generated, and the dimensions that best summarize an individual's behavior and experiences over time are not necessarily those that do so at a point in time. It was also suggested that the uniqueness of the composite summary dimensions and their ability to provide an effective summarization of a wide variety of behaviors and experiences over time could be traced to the fact that they reflected complex, genotype processes emerging over time that are expressed in a variety of ways. Nevertheless, broad, process-oriented dimensions of this sort seem to provide a nearly ideal backdrop for the definition of general prototypes capable of describing individuality.

CLARITY

One criterion that may be employed in assessing the meaningfulness and validity of any taxonomic description is the clarity of the resulting classification structure. The evaluation criterion is analogous to Thurstone's concept of simple structure. When the concern at hand is the classification of individuals on the basis of their behavior and experiences, the concept implies that a valid, fully adequate classification structure is one that will allow each individual to be exclusively assigned to a single prototype. Of course, it should be noted that the application of a simple structure criterion is subject to certain ambiguities because the "true" pattern of behavior and experiences might lead some individuals to be legitimately assigned to two or more prototypes, whereas other individuals might not be assigned to any prototype. Although this ambiguity is of substantial importance, it is nonetheless true that the simple structure criterion provides a viable method for assessing the validity of prototype descriptions in terms of the clarity of the resulting classification.

In the present study, information pertaining to the clarity of the summary description produced by the composite prototypes was available from two sources: (a) the percentage of good fits, overlaps, and isolates associated with the retained male and female solutions; and (b) the extent to which the derivative male and female matrices of aposteriori probabilities approached the ideal of 0/1 matrix in which the individual had a probability of 1 of being assigned to a single prototype and a 0 probability of being assigned to all other prototypes. These two sources of information provided some compelling evidence for the clarity of the retained prototypical descriptions, and their results are briefly reviewed in the following discussion.

An examination of the aposterior probabilities reflecting 25 randomly selected males' and 25 randomly selected females' likelihood of membership in each composite prototype provided some striking evidence for the clarity of the summary descriptions produced by the composite prototypes. The vast majority, roughly 94% of the aposteriori probabilities obtained for these individuals, were above .90 or below .10. Consequently, the data indicate that the likelihood of individuals' assignments to the relevant composite prototypes provided a close approximation of the ideal 0/1 matrix that would be produced by solutions of perfect clarity. The results obtained in determining the number of good fits, overlaps, and isolates produced by each of the retained solutions also provided some substantial support for the clarity of the model. Overall, 88% of the males and 84% of the females could be thought of as belonging to a single prototype. The remaining 12% of males and 16% of the females were overlapping cases who might legitimately be assigned to two or more prototypes, given the distance criterion in use. Effectively, no isolates were obtained in the male and female composite clustering solutions. Taken as a whole, the classification rates and the aposteriori probabilities provide some substantial support for the clarity and validity of the summary descriptions obtained from the composite prototypes, as well as the comprehensiveness of the descriptive system and its value, even given the existence of continuing within prototype variation.

The classification rates are also of interest in a comparative sense, because classification rates employing the same specifications for defining overlaps, isolates, and good fits were obtained for the BQ, CEI, PCEI 2/4, and PCEI 6/8 cross-sectional prototypes. As was noted earlier, roughly 70–75% of the males and females participating in a given assessment could be assigned to a single cross-sectional prototype. In the cross-sectional analyses, roughly 5–10% of the sample members were found to be isolates. Because no isolates and approximately 10–15% more good fits were obtained in the composite analysis, this suggests that the composite prototypes yielded a clearer and more comprehensive description of individuality than could be obtained from the point-in-time, cross-sectional description of individuality through the prototype model.

The enhanced effectiveness of the summary descriptions obtained from the composite prototypes cannot readily be tied to any single underlying cause. The enhanced effectiveness of the composite prototypes might be attributed to the more effective summarization of behavior and experiences obtained from the composites as opposed to the cross-sectional summary dimensions. Moreover, the use of a larger and more comprehensive descriptive item base in the derivation of the composite prototypes and summary dimensions might have provided a stronger and more extensive foundation for prototype definition than could be employed in the more limited cross-sectional analyses and data bases. Alternatively, the greater predictive value of the composites, as opposed to the cross-sectional summary dimensions, as well as the ability of the composite summary dimensions to capture significant aspects of individuality and complex genotype relationships that could not be identified with cross-sectional analyses might account for the tendency of the composite prototypes to yield a description of greater clarity. Obviously, all of these alternatives are somewhat interdependent. As a result, it seems reasonable to hypothesize that all of these trends might have contributed to the enhanced clarity of the summary descriptions obtained from the composite, as opposed to the cross-sectional prototypes.

Although the foregoing discussion has provided substantial evidence supporting the clarity and comprehensiveness of the summary descriptions obtained from the composite prototypes, there are two restrictions on the strength of this evidence that should be noted. Due to limitations on the sample size available for the composite analyses, it was not possible to cross-validate the classification rates associated with the composite solution in an independent sample. It can be expected that once this has been accomplished, some shrinkage in the proportion of good fits will occur. However, based on results obtained in the earlier phases of this investigation, it is likely that the observed shrinkage will be roughly between 5% and 15% in comparable samples and that this shrinkage will apply to both the composite and cross-sectional prototypes. Thus, it appears that this shrinkage will not be sufficient to invalidate any of the foregoing conclusions. Nevertheless, this stability cannot be expected to extend to widely divergent samples, because the prototypes identified in the present study reflect individuals in middle-class culture. In highly divergent samples, it seems likely that some novel prototypes may be required to provide an adequate description of individuality. Although, at present, the number and nature of the additional prototypes that might be required under these conditions is unclear, some of these prototypes might be quite stable, and only a few new prototypes might be required to insure adequate descriptions of new populations.

The comprehensiveness and clarity of the summary descriptions obtained from the composite prototypes are of substantial conceptual importance with respect to the appropriateness of the prototype model. At the outset of this book, it was noted that one of the fundamental criticisms that led to the rejection of the typological model was that most individuals could not be unambiguously assigned to the various categories of persons proposed in the early taxonomic efforts. Rather, most individuals were found to fall between categories and distribute themselves more or less on a normal continuum. However, the evidence presented heretofore with respect to the classification rates and the aposteriori probabilities of prototype membership indicate that it is possible to unambiguously assign individuals to the empirically defined categories of persons that constitute the prototype model. Thus, these results invalidate one of the major criticisms initially leveled against attempts to classify persons, rather than behavior, and they argue for the appropriateness of the prototype model and the validity and utility of the summary descriptions obtained from the composite prototypes.

ROBUSTNESS

Taxonomic descriptions of either people or their behaviors may be either very broad or very narrow in focus. When a rather narrow taxonomy has been constructed for some discrete purpose, one can not legitimately expect the resulting categories to provide a broad-ranging summarization of behavior, experiences, or people. However, if the classification effort is intended to describe individuality and individual development in a general sense, it is clear that the resulting summarization must be applicable over a wide range of behaviors and experiences. The robustness of the classification categories in the description of individual behavior and experiences over time may legitimately be employed as a means for establishing the validity or meaningfulness of the composite prototypes as a basis for formulating a general summarization of human individuality.

An attempt to assess the robustness of the summary descriptions obtained from the composite prototypes formulated in the present investigation must address a number of discrete causes. First, because the composite prototypes are intended to reflect individuality in development, it is obvious that they must be capable of summarizing significant differential behavior and experiences at different points in a person's life. Second, the cross-time summarization must extend to indicators of differential behavior and experiences that were not employed in the initial construction of the prototypes if the generality of the summarization is to be demonstrated. Third, a consistent pattern of differences should be observed on indicators of similar differential behaviors and experiences obtained through different measurement formats, so that we may have some assurance that the resulting summary descriptions are not specific to a particular methodology. The data pertinent to addressing each of these issues, at least in a preliminary sense, have been presented in Tables 9.7 and 9.8, which display the significant differences obtained from the various male and female composite prototypes on the items, summary dimensions, and reference measures across the four major developmental periods.

Even a cursory review of this data indicates that the members of the 15 male and 17 female composite prototypes were differentiated on a wide variety of indicators. In fact, the members of all of the composite prototypes displayed significant differences on the BQ, CEI, and PCEI 6/8 items and summary dimensions, as well as in the likelihood of membership in the relevant cross-sectional prototypes. Further, the descriptive information derived from these various kinds of indicators was relatively consistent for the members of a given prototype. For instance, members of the female composite prototype labeled Competent Nurturers tended to receive high scores on the CEI and PCEI 6/8 Religious Beliefs and Religious-Community Involvement summary dimensions and be assigned to the CEI Christians and PCEI 6/8 Community-Directed Housewives. Similarly, those individuals who were members of the male composite prototype labeled Virile Extraverts were found to produce lower scores on the BQ Social Introversion and Social Desirability summary dimensions and be assigned to the CEI Fraternity Members and the PCEI 6/8 Contented Affluent Conservatives prototypes. Although other examples might be provided, the foregoing examples serve to underscore the point that memberships in the composite prototypes summarized significant differences in behavior and experiences on a number of indicators and summary descriptions obtained in the course of analyzing the BQ, CEI, and PCEI 6/8 item data. This, in turn, suggests that the composite prototypes provided a robust summary description of individuality and individual development, in the sense that they captured differential behavior and experiences over time and on different forms of summary descriptions in a consistent and interpretable fashion.

Yet it should also be noted that not all of the composite prototypes were equally well differentiated from the sample as a whole on the BQ, CEI, and PCEI 6/8 indices, either at a single point in time or over time. An excellent example of this phenomenon may be found in the female composite prototype labelled Defensive Conformists. Relatively few significant differences were obtained for members of this composite prototype on the PCEI 6/8 items, summary dimensions, and prototypes. Nevertheless, it should be pointed out that this weak pattern of differentiation might be expected on the basis of the label that was eventually assigned to this composite prototype, because conformity should lead to sample-typical behavior and experiences in adulthood. Because the patterns of particularly good and poor differentiation of prototype members typically followed the broader pattern of the prototypes' differential characteristics, the existence of this variation in the frequency and power of differentiation cannot be said to reflect negatively on the foregoing conclusions, and, in fact, they provide some support for their meaningfulness and validity.

If it is granted that the composite prototypes displayed a significant and internally consistent pattern of differences on the BQ, CEI, and PCEI 6/8 indices, indicating that the composite prototypes were capable of summarizing differential behavior and experience over time, the next question that comes to fore is whether or not these differences were maintained with similar power on indicators that were not employed in the construction of the prototypes, were collected at different points in the course of an individual's life, and were collected through different measurement formats. Because the reference measures and PCEI 2/4 items were not employed in the initial construction of the composite prototypes, were collected 6 to 8 years apart, and were collected through different measurement formats, the existence and nature of the significant differences observed on the reference measures and PCEI 2/4 items summary dimensions and prototypes provide an excellent tool for addressing these issues.

All of the composite prototypes produced at least some significant differences on the reference measures on PCEI 2/4 items, summary dimensions, and prototypes. Significant results were not obtained for all the reference measures on PCEI 2/4 indicators for each and every composite prototype, but this should not be expected, because these indices may or may not have been relevant to the description of a given composite prototype's differential behaviors and experiences. Yet, it is of note that roughly 75% of the composite prototypes produced significant differences on one or more of the reference measures, and 66% of the composite prototypes produced significant differences on the PCEI 2/4 summary dimensions.

Although the mere existence of these significant differences provides substantial evidence pointing to the robustness or generality of the summary descriptions formulated through the composite prototypes, it is important to note that the nature of these differences was congruent with the broader pattern of the prototypes' differential behaviors and experiences. For instance, members of the female composite prototype labelled Effective Social Manipulators were likely to express a preference for, and obtain jobs involving, the control of others and extensive social interaction. Moreover, on the BQ, CEI, and PCEI 6/8 items, they were likely to be socially active, assume leadership positions, and display continued success on their jobs. Similarly, members of the male composite prototype labeled Analytical Adapters expressed an interest in scientific and behavioral jobs in the reference measures as well as cognitive values and complexity. Two to 4 years after graduation, they were found to have obtained jobs of this sort. Further, these males were likely to be assigned to either of the BQ Scientists prototypes and then assigned to the PCEI 6/8 Enterprising Intellectuals prototype while expressing an interest and involvement with scientific pursuits on the BQ items. Although a number of other examples of this sort might be laid out, it is clear that the composite prototypes' differential characteristics on the reference measures and PCEI 2/4 indicators were conceptually consistent with the broader pattern of differential characteristics observed on the BQ, CEI, and PCEI 6/8 indices.

In this point in the discussion of robustness, little attention has been given to the magnitude of these differences and the ability of composite prototypes' status to predict status on these external indices. Perhaps the most important point in this regard is that the number and magnitude of the significant differences obtained for the various composite prototypes in the reference measures, as well as the PCEI 2/4 items, summary dimensions, and composite prototypes, were comparable to those obtained in the BQ, CEI, and PCEI 6/8 measures. Additionally, the magnitude of the correlations between the individual's likelihood of membership in the composite prototype and scores on both the internal and external measures were again similar in magnitude. When these observations are considered in light of the fact that no differences on any indices were held to be half a standard deviation, it is clear that prototype status was associated with some sizable differences in behavior and experiences that were maintained on the reference measures and PCEI 2/4 indices.

Of course, this conclusion might be criticized on the basis of the fact that, even when associated with highly significant mean differences, the composite prototypes generally produced coefficients lying between .08 and .50, when the likelihood of composite prototype memberships were correlated with scores on the various measures. This indicates that a knowledge of the individual's membership in a given prototype could not completely predict the individual's status on either the reference measures or the BQ, CEI, PCEI 2/4, and PCEI 6/8 items, summary dimensions, and prototypes. However, in evaluating this information, certain additional considerations should be borne in mind. First, it was expected that composite prototype membership could not be completely defined by the individual's scores on any single indicator, because general prototypical descriptions should summarize behavior and experiences on a wide range of indicators. Second, because multiple prototypes may obtain either high or low scores on any single nomothetic dimension, correlational discrimination of the members of a given prototype from the sample as a whole would be limited by this legitimate convergence on any single measure. Third, the preceding conclusion finds some support in the fact that all of the coefficients were associated with mean differences in excess of half a standard deviation, as indexed by the subsample variance. Thus, it appears that the magnitude of these univariate coefficients per se can not be said to reflect negatively on the robustness and magnitude of the differentiation associated with the composite prototypes.

Some additional evidence along these lines may be found in an in-house study conducted by Mumford (1983). Here, the ability of SAT scores, the likelihood of membership in the BQ prototypes, and the likelihood of membership in the composite prototypes to predict freshmen grade point average (GPA) were examined separately for each sex in a series of stepwise regression analyses. It was found that an optimal *combination* of the composite prototypes predicted freshmen GPA better than an optimal combination of the BQ prototypes in both the male and female subsamples, an impressive result when it was borne in mind that a larger percentage of the information contained in the BQ prototypes was specifically concerned with academic achievement than was the case for the composite prototypes. Further, in both of these subsamples, it was found that an optimal combination of the composite prototypes predicted freshmen GPA ($R = .50$) as well as SAT scores and that a knowledge of composite prototype status produced significant increments in the prediction obtained from SAT scores ($R = .65$). Consequently, it appears that when status on normative measures is evaluated in terms of multiple composite prototypes, the composite prototypes can be highly predictive, despite the fact that they were not specifically designed to predict status on a normative measure of this sort. In addition to the support that this provides for the predictive power, validity, and robustness of the composite prototypes, the analyses also serve to suggest that they might be more effective in this regard than the cross-sectional prototypes.

Comparison of the magnitude and percentage of the total domain of items and summary dimensions that produced significant differences for the composite and cross-sectional prototypes also indicated the relatively greater robustness of the summary descriptions obtained from the composite prototypes. Even with the number of comparisons controlled for, on the average, it was found that the male and female composite prototypes were likely to produce roughly 25% more significant differences than the cross-sectional prototypes. The magnitude of the mean differences obtained for the composite prototypes also tended to be larger than those obtained for the cross-sectional prototypes. Additionally, the composite prototypes, on the average, yielded a larger number of more sizable mean differences on the reference measures than did the BQ prototypes, indicating that the superior differentiation associated with the composite prototypes was not specific to the information employed in constructing the composite and cross-sectional prototypes. As a result, it seems reasonable to conclude that the composite prototypes produced a more robust description of individuality than did the cross-sectional prototypes.

In sum, the evidence just laid out suggests that the composite prototypes provided a robust description of individuality and individual development. Composite prototype membership was found to be associated with a variety of significant differences on measures obtained at a number of points in the individuals life. The differentiation was maintained in an interpretable fashion on measures that were not employed in defining the composite prototypes and that were based on different measurement formats and collected at different points in time. Thus, the composite prototypes appeared to be capable of summarizing a variety of differential behaviors and experiences over time and to be sufficiently robust to produce a general summary description of individuality and individual development. Moreover, the magnitude of these differences was sufficient to suggest that they produced a nontrivial summary description of the phenomena. Finally, it appears that the composite prototypes provided a more robust and general description of the phenomena than did the various cross-sectional prototypes.

RELATIONSHIPS BETWEEN THE COMPOSITE AND CROSS-SECTIONAL PROTOTYPES

The foregoing discussion has examined the specific nature of the relationship between the composite and cross-sectional prototypes only as it pertained to the enhanced clarity and robustness of the composite prototypes. However, in evaluating the nature of the composite prototypes, their relationship to the various cross-sectional prototypes is of some interest in its own right for three reasons. First, the nature of the relationships between the composite and cross-sectional prototypes might serve to support the meaningfulness or validity of the composite prototypes, because this information was not considered in the initial labeling of the prototypes. Second, comparison of these relationships with those obtained in the sequential analyses of cross-sectional prototype interrelationships might provide some evidence bearing on whether the composite prototypes provided a more effective summary description of individuality over time than did the cross-sectional prototypes. Finally, these relationships might provide some evidence pertaining to whether the composite prototypes provided some unique information concerning the nature of individuality. In order to address these issues, the aposteriori probabilities reflecting the likelihood of membership in each of the relevant composite prototypes were obtained for the male and female members of the longitudinal sample, and they were correlated with the probabilities of membership in each of the relevant BQ, CEI, PCEI 2/4, and PCEI 6/8 prototypes. Subsequently, the males' and females' probabilities of membership in each of the relevant composite prototypes were regressed on these probabilities of membership in the various BQ, CEI, PCEI 2/4, and PCEI 6/8 prototypes through a stepwise procedure in which the six best predictors expressing a .10 tolerance level were retained. From the results obtained in correlating the likelihood of composite and cross-sectional prototype membership within the male and female subsamples, certain general conclusions emerged.

From the standpoint of the meaningfulness of validity of the summary descriptions, some support was obtained for the appropriateness of the labels assigned to the composite prototypes. This conclusion is justified by the fact that the vast majority of the relationships between the composite and cross-sectional prototypes were readily interpretable, given a knowledge of the composite prototypes' differential characteristics on the reference measures, items, and summary dimensions. Moreover, this was true despite the fact that the correlation between the composite and cross-sectional prototypes were not explicitly considered in the labelling of the composite prototypes. These interpretable relationships with a set of external indices in turn argue for the psychological meaningfulness or construct validity of the composite prototypes.

Not only did this analysis serve to indicate the meaningfulness of the composite summary descriptions, it also served to argue for its predictive efficiency. In comparing the number and magnitude of the significant relationships observed between the composite and cross-sectional prototypes with those obtained in the sequential analyses of cross-sectional prototype interrelationships, it was found that the composite analyses yielded a larger number of significant ($r \geq .15$) and sizable relationships than did the sequential analyses, controlling for the absolute number of potential comparisons. Although this result might be attributed to spurious overlap, it should be noted that these findings held for the PCEI 2/4 prototypes, even though they were based on information that was not employed in constructing the composite prototypes. Thus, it seems reasonable to conclude that the composite prototypes provided a more effective summary description of individuality over time than did the cross-sectional prototypes.

In this regard, it should be pointed out that the magnitude of the coefficients obtained when correlating the composite and cross-sectional prototypes was not overwhelming. Typically, the significant ($r \geq .15$) coefficients were around .25. The limited magnitude of the coefficients could be because a number of different composite prototypes were related to the same cross-sectional prototype and a number of different cross-sectional prototypes were assigned to the same composite prototype. Because this intermingling would limit the clarity of the relationships in prototype membership, it would tend to limit the magnitude of the observed relationships.

In reviewing the patterns of movement of composite prototype members through the cross-sectional prototypes, it was clear that there was not a high degree of overlap between these patterns of relationships and those defined in the sequential analyses of interrelationships among the cross-sectional summary dimensions. This result may reflect the fact that the composite prototypes were formulated on the basis of summary dimensions containing unique information. Nevertheless, it also underscores the preceding conclusion that the composite analyses and the sequential analyses of the relationships among the cross-sectional prototypes did not yield identical descriptions of individuality in development.

Despite the possibility that the composite prototypes might contain some unique information concerning the nature of individuality and individual development, some strong support for the cross-time nature of the composite prototypes was obtained in examining the relationships between the composite and cross-sectional prototypes. Clearly, almost all of the composite prototypes produced significant relationships with cross-sectional prototypes identified in the analyses of data collected on at least two different developmental periods. This result provides some concrete evidence, in addition to that obtained from the item and summary dimension data, which indicated that the composite prototypes did in fact describe individuality in a developmental context.

REGRESSION ANALYSES

Of course, the conclusion that the composite prototypes summarized the descriptive information contained in the cross-sectional prototypes over time and simultaneously provided a somewhat unique description of individuality might be questioned on the basis of at least two considerations. First, the apparent cross-time nature of the composite prototypes might reflect little more than the intrinsic relationship among the cross-sectional prototypes identified in different developmental periods. Second, the composite prototypes might appear to provide some unique descriptive information concerning individuality only because the combined predictive power of the cross-sectional prototypes has not been examined. The stepwise regression analyses examining the ability of cross-sectional prototype status to predict composite prototype status were carried out in an attempt to address these issues.

Tables 10.1 and 10.2 present the results obtained in regressing the probabilities of membership in the male and female composite prototypes on the probabilities of membership in the various cross-sectional prototypes within the longitudinal sample. As may be seen, all of the composite prototypes were associated with significant independent increments in predictions obtained from cross-sectional prototypes derived in at least two separate developmental periods. Because these results allow us to discount the possibility that the extreme relationships among the cross-sectional prototypes lead to the apparent cross-time nature of the composite prototypes, this result provides some rather powerful sup-

TABLE 10.1
Regression of the Male Composite Prototypes on the Male Cross-Sectional Prototypes

Subgroup	R^2	R	Y	Variables and Standardized Weights
1	.35	.59	.03	.18 BQ 7 + .20 BQ 17 + .19 BQ 21 + .37 P2/4 1 + .30 P2/4 11
2	.13	.37	.03	.21 BQ 4 + .24 P6/8 6 + .17 P6/8 9
3	.32	.57	−.02	.18 CEI 8 + .17 CEI 9 + −.38 P2/4 3 + .32 P6/8 6 + .30 P6/8 10
4	.23	.48	.04	.20 BQ 6 + .10 BQ 9 + .35 CEI 11 + .15 P6/8 7
5	.16	.40	.02	.24 BQ 2 + .15 BQ 9 + −.22 BQ 15 + .12 BQ 16 + .12 P6/8 10
6	.19	.43	−.00	.17 BQ 1 + .14 BQ 7 + .27 BQ 11 + .14 BQ 8 + .13 CEI 7 + .17 P6/8 10
7	.30	.55	−.02	.14 BQ 3 + .30 BQ 10 + .25 CEI 1 + .14 CEI 13 + .26 P6/8 2 + .15 P6/8 4
8	.23	.48	−.03	.20 BQ 3 + .14 BQ 9 + .25 P2/4 3 + .26 P2/4 7 + .23 P2/4 10 + .12 P6/8 3
9	.16	.40	−.01	−.13 BQ 19 + −.17 BQ 23 + −.29 CEI 12 + .18 P6/8 3
10	.30	.55	−.01	.14 BQ 16 + .17 BQ 17 + .37 CEI 6 + .21 CEI 12 + .13 P2/4 2 + .14 P6/8 9
11	.33	.57	−.00	.14 BQ 12 + .13 BQ 7 + .48 CEI 13 + .15 P2/4 10
12	.20	.44	−.02	.32 CEI 10 + .25 P2/4 4 + .13 P6/8 8
13	.13	.36	.02	.26 BQ 5 + .16 BQ 14 + .13 CEI 10 + .19 P6/8 4
14	.35	.59	−.04	.13 BQ 7 + .17 BQ 19 + .25 BQ 23 + .13 CEI 2 + .38 CEI 4 + .16 P2/4 9
15	.24	.49	−.04	.23 CEI 5 + .23 P2/4 1 + .29 P6/8 1 + .15 P6/8 2
Overall Mean	.23	.48		

Note: R^2 = Variance Accounted For; R = Multiple Correlation; Y = Intercept; N = 358

TABLE 10.2

Regression of the Female Composite Prototypes on the Female Cross-Sectional Prototypes

Subgroup	R^2	R	Y	Variables and Standardized Weights
1	.46	.68	.09	.41 P2/4 1 + .22 P2/4 4 + .16 P6/8 4 + .30 P6/8 5
2	.37	.60	-.01	.32 CEI 9 + -.32 CEI 11 + .25 P2/4 13 + .14 P6/8 4
3	.17	.41	.00	.15 BQ 11 + .26 BQ 13 + -.14 CEI 1 + .20 P2/4 6 + .19 P2/4 8
4	.08	.29	.02	.21 P2/4 11 + .17 P6/8 6 + .12 P6/8 10
5	.19	.44	-.01	.34 CEI 2 + .13 CEI 9 + .18 P2/4 9 + .11 P6/8 2 + .15 P6/8 11
6	.23	.48	-.02	.16 BQ 15 + .13 CEI 4 + .30 CEI 7 + .20 P2/4 6 + .12 P2/4 12 + .10 P6/8 7
7	.13	.37	.05	.24 BQ 2 + .15 BQ 8 + .16 P2/4 8 + .14 P6/8 7
8	.39	.62	-.02	.22 BQ 5 + .28 BQ 12 + .16 CEI 9 + .30 P2/4 12 + .18 P6/8 10 + .13 P6/8 13
9	.36	.60	.04	.11 BQ 12 + .58 P2/4 2 + .17 P6/8 3
10	.11	.33	-.01	.16 BQ 11 + .12 CEI 4 + .17 P2/4 4 + .21 P6/8 2
11	.22	.47	.00	.14 BQ 6 + .25 CEI 10 + .23 CEI 11 + .21 CEI 12 + -.14 P2/4 1 + .19 P6/8 4
12	.23	.48	.00	.23 CEI 1 + .34 CEI 10 + -.13 P2/4 1 + .14 P2/4 2 + .15 P2/4 12 + .16 P6/8 3
13	.17	.41	.02	.13 BQ 4 + .14 BQ 6 + .26 BQ 9 + .12 BQ 15 + .14 P2/4 10 + .17 P6/8 8
14	.32	.57	-.03	.14 BQ 14 + .13 CEI 6 + .24 P2/4 7 + -.18 P2/4 10 + .25 P6/8 1 + .28 P6/8 6
15	.15	.39	-.02	.17 BQ 6 + .14 BQ 9 + .16 P2/4 6 + -.19 P2/4 7 + .13 P6/8 8 + .20 P6/8 12
16	.29	.54	-.03	.34 CEI 3 + .11 CEI 7 + .16 P2/4 5 + .16 P2/4 7 + .13 P6/8 3 + .26 P6/8 12
17	.17	.42	.01	.22 BQ 5 + .16 BQ 14 + .13 P6/8 6 + .18 P6/8 7 + .15 P6/8 9 + .14 P6/8 12
Overall Mean	.22	.47		

Note: R^2 = Variance Accounted For; R = Multiple Correlation; Y = Intercept; N = 415

port for the conclusion that the composite prototypes provided a cross-time description of individuality. It is also of note that the beta weights associated with the significant cross-sectional predictions were readily interpretable, given a knowledge of the composite and cross-sectional prototypes differential characteristics.

As examination of the multiple Rs obtained in this analysis indicated that the composite prototypes provided some unique information concerning the nature of individuality and individual development. Within the male subsample, the average multiple R obtained for the composite prototypes was .48, and no multiple Rs in excess of .59 or below .40 were observed. In the female subsample, the multiple Rs obtained for the composite prototypes ranged between .68 and .29, and the average multiple R was .40. It is clear that all of the male and female composite prototypes contained at least some unique descriptive information concerning individuality that could not be reflected by an optimal combination of cross-sectional prototypes. Although this result might have been expected, based on the fact that the composite summary dimensions contained some unique descriptive information, it is nonetheless true that the composite prototypes provided a description of individuality that could not be completely replicated by the cross-sectional prototypes, although there were some significant and systematic relationships. Thus, the results of the regression and correlational analyses relating the composite and cross-sectional prototypes suggest that the composite prototypes provided a somewhat unique, cross-time description of individuality that displayed some validity and appeared to be more effective than a combination of the cross-sectional summary dimensions.

COMPOSITE PROTOTYPE INTERRELATIONSHIPS

Although parsimony in a summarization may not necessarily be a desirable characteristic if it entails an inappropriate cost in terms of descriptive accuracy, an optimal summarization should yield a comprehensive description of individuals with as little redundancy as possible. An index of the redundancy of the descriptive system incorporated in the composite prototypes may be obtained by examining the intercorrelations among the male and female members of the longitudinal sample's probabilities of membership in the composite prototypes.

The findings in the present study indicated that the probabilities of an individual's assignment to the various male and female composite prototypes were essentially independent. No coefficient in excess of .15 was obtained within the male subsample. In the female subsample, only three coefficients in excess of an absolute value of .15 were observed. The preponderance of weak negative relationships observed within both the male and female subgroups may be because individual membership in a given composite prototype to some extent precluded membership in the remaining composite prototypes in a discriminant analyses. Taken as a whole, these results suggest that there was little redundancy in the summary descriptions of individuals provided by the taxonomic system manifest in the composite prototypes.

Although a correlational analysis of this sort is of some value in examining the relative independence of the prototypical descriptions of individuals, the data do not necessarily suggest the absence of relationships among the average pattern of prototype scores on the composite summary dimension in euclidian space. Tables 10.3 and 10.4 present the distances between the male and female composite prototypes with respect to the scores of prototype members on the composite summary dimensions.

A review of Table 10.3 indicates that, within the male subsample, the mean profiles of the Channelled Concrete Achievers, Upwardly Mobile Individuals, Unrealistic Independents, Virile Extroverts, Analytical Adaptors, and Withdrawn Effeminates lay close together in Euclidean space, but were relatively distant from the remaining male composite prototypes. The similarity among these prototypes may be traced to the high probability of prototype members having a warm, secure, and supportive family background and reasonably good adjustment in adolescence, characteristics that are not shared by the remaining prototypes. The Constrained Careerists, Fortunate Approval Seekers, Adjustive Successes, Premature Conformists, and Burgeois Outliers all lay close together in Euclidean space but quite distant from the foregoing prototypes. These prototypes seem to be bound together and differentiated from the foregoing prototypes by their different family backgrounds and adjustment problems and social withdrawal during adolescence. The Upwardly Mobile Individuals prototype was also found to be relatively close to the composite Expansive Compensators prototype, a result that may reflect their mutual business orientation and late emergence of a concern with achievement. Finally, the Insecure Socialites, Ineffective Authoritarians, Religious Copers, and Expansive Compensators did not lie close to each other or to either of the two major clusters sketched out previously. These results may reflect the relatively small size of these prototypes and their relatively unique patterns of individual development.

In the female subsample, it was found that the Unscathed Adjustors, Frustrated Incompetents, Social Manipulators, Restricted Socializers, Channelled Extroverts, Isolated Intellectuals, and Female Eunuchs all

TABLE 10.3
Generalized Intersubgroup Distances for Male Composite Prototypes

							Subgroup #								
	1	2	3	4	5	6	7	8	9	10	11	12	13	14	15
1	−5.1	24.8	10.4	19.6	24.7	10.6	66.1	77.9	7282.1	62.8	849.6	344.1	120.6	41.3	184.3
2	6.2	−4.6	12.4	11.7	8.9	25.0	72.9	53.4	10406.2	85.5	12.7	305.3	101.4	65.7	133.7
3	11.7	29.5	−3.5	9.8	21.2	18.6	63.0	41.1	9317.6	60.5	12644.2	257.3	125.4	35.8	177.2
4	9.9	15.3	8.0	−6.2	21.0	11.1	63.4	56.2	11134.5	35.9	363.4	268.7	94.1	40.1	109.1
5	15.0	17.6	9.3	4.8	−4.2	17.1	37.7	31.0	7588.8	123.9	1508.7	284.9	97.9	23.3	107.7
6	16.9	48.3	20.2	18.7	23.0	−4.0	41.6	51.5	9888.8	132.0	14150.5	347.4	141.2	79.3	127.4
7	31.9	49.4	21.6	23.6	40.2	15.0	−3.9	42.4	6371.7	37.0	1885.7	285.0	97.7	56.0	138.6
8	123.6	42.2	50.6	59.1	25.6	105.1	68.1	−3.5	140.5	56.8	7246.7	18.3	7.1	16.7	27.3
9	173.2	90.0	62.7	107.1	49.1	152.6	88.2	16.4	−6.2	105.4	8902.3	69.0	31.9	42.7	53.0
10	51.5	61.0	26.0	43.6	35.9	81.5	52.4	35.8	2608.8	−7.0	248.8	75.4	37.8	51.2	42.4
11	89.9	46.2	38.9	51.4	30.2	82.2	82.9	24.2	3274.1	103.9	−4.2	55.3	32.2	61.0	42.6
12	108.1	47.1	49.9	56.4	30.3	175.9	101.1	36.4	1230.6	47.4	32.0	−7.3	8.6	20.9	20.2
13	102.1	58.4	49.1	44.8	16.4	123.8	45.5	8.6	345.1	56.8	907.3	18.8	−7.4	14.9	18.4
14	120.0	68.3	70.0	56.2	25.9	95.6	66.3	14.4	73.0	123.6	188.2	24.9	10.0	−3.2	21.9
15	124.1	94.3	52.7	72.5	40.3	134.1	58.0	14.5	158.5	77.6	11414.9	32.3	7.1	11.4	−5.4

TABLE 10.4
Generalized Intersubgroup Distances for Female Composite Prototypes

Subgroup #

	1	2	3	4	5	6	7	8	9	10	11	12	13	14	15	16	17
1	3.6	24.0	22.9	19.5	22.7	37.0	32.2	29.7	21.9	73.3	26.7	28.3	13.7	26.1	41.0	37.1	18.0
2	20.2	7.3	38.0	39.3	26.1	53.3	33.5	39.9	35.2	73.7	28.9	32.2	33.4	29.5	40.9	48.6	25.8
3	21.1	40.0	5.4	22.9	25.0	25.8	16.6	28.4	18.4	65.3	24.6	20.9	25.9	27.9	37.0	41.8	24.9
4	17.0	40.6	22.2	6.0	33.9	35.3	21.2	24.2	22.9	68.5	24.4	27.3	19.6	31.9	51.6	54.8	25.9
5	20.1	27.3	24.2	33.7	6.2	28.6	25.6	25.1	25.8	66.9	25.8	31.8	22.9	35.3	30.6	36.7	24.2
6	33.0	53.0	23.6	33.8	27.2	7.6	22.4	26.5	25.3	73.9	32.9	41.3	37.5	46.4	57.6	52.5	33.6
7	22.2	36.5	17.6	22.8	27.4	25.5	4.4	26.2	18.0	50.1	16.5	15.2	23.4	31.1	43.6	56.6	23.8
8	26.7	40.7	27.2	23.6	24.8	27.5	24.0	6.6	15.7	70.8	25.6	29.9	29.6	45.5	58.0	56.2	30.7
9	21.0	38.1	19.4	24.5	27.5	28.5	17.9	17.9	4.4	59.6	19.9	17.9	25.5	28.1	51.8	55.8	26.6
10	67.3	71.5	61.1	65.0	63.5	71.9	44.9	67.9	54.6	9.5	43.3	43.6	79.4	60.6	93.1	129.5	68.7
11	24.5	30.5	24.2	24.8	26.3	34.7	15.1	26.4	18.6	47.2	5.7	15.3	24.2	28.3	46.6	53.3	26.1
12	27.1	34.9	21.5	28.6	33.2	44.1	14.8	31.7	17.5	48.3	16.2	4.8	31.6	39.2	46.5	59.6	26.1
13	12.4	35.9	26.4	20.4	24.0	40.2	23.0	31.3	25.1	84.1	25.1	31.5	4.8	25.8	30.4	32.0	20.5
14	23.7	30.9	27.3	32.0	35.5	48.0	29.5	46.2	26.6	64.2	28.1	33.0	24.7	5.9	31.4	54.9	19.1
15	36.1	39.7	33.8	49.2	30.3	56.7	39.5	56.0	47.7	94.2	43.8	42.8	26.8	28.8	8.5	43.8	30.0
16	31.7	47.0	38.2	51.9	34.0	51.1	52.0	53.8	51.3	130.1	50.1	55.5	27.9	51.9	43.4	8.9	35.0
17	16.0	27.6	24.7	26.4	24.9	35.6	22.7	31.8	25.5	72.7	26.3	25.4	19.8	19.5	32.9	38.4	5.5

lay close together in Euclidean space. These composite prototypes all appear to be bound together by their warm family background, conservative nature, and the centrality of conformity to the traditional female role in their lives. Unsurprisingly, these prototypes were quite distant from a set of composite prototypes that were bound together by their lack of traditional social adjustment and introversion in adolescence, along with a difficult family background. The composite prototypes that were included in this group were the Unconventional Successes, Paternal Reactives, Discontented Male Dependents, Defensive Conformists, Unambitious Passives, and Social Copers. Although the Competent Nurturers lay close to both the Unscathed Adjustors and the Female Eunuchs, due to their traditional role orientation and family background, the composite prototypes did not clearly fall into the first cluster, perhaps because of their religious involvement and intellectual ability. Otherwise, the Competent Nurturers, Orphaned Adaptors, Independent Achievers, and Insecure Bohemians were all isolated in Euclidean space because of their relatively small size and rather unique pattern of development.

Three conclusions emerge in examining the nature of the foregoing relationships. First, warmth of family background and adolescent social adjustment seem to be of substantial importance in differentiating both the male and female composite prototypes. However, in the female subsample, traditional sex role orientation appears to be of special importance. The added significance of this characteristic may account for the emergence of a greater number of female composite prototypes and the tendency of a large number to channel themselves through prototypes that lie in the first overriding cluster. Second, the two male and two female overriding clusters display some overlap with a general developmental trend observed in the sequential analyses of movement through the cross-sectional prototypes. Here, we refer to the fact that traditional, well-adjusted individuals were found to follow predictable patterns of movement through the cross-sectional prototypes, whereas nontraditional, poorly adjusted individuals were not found to be predictable. When coupled with the excellent classification rates obtained for the composite prototypes, this observation suggests that individuals who are not necessarily predictable on the basis of point-in-time information may follow a consistent pattern of development when individuality is defined on a cross-time basis. Further, this suggests that predictability and patterns of development may not be adequately described by summary descriptions on the basis of data that is gathered at a single point in time. Finally, because the interrelationships among the composite prototypes in Euclidean space appeared to be interpretable and meaningful, given a knowledge of the descriptive label assigned to the composite prototype and the differential characteristics over time, the foregoing discussion seems to provide some additional support for the validity and meaningfulness of the summary descriptions incorporated on the composite prototypes.

POWER

Earlier, it was pointed out that prototypical descriptions of individuality will yield descriptive information concerning the nature of individuality above and beyond that which may be obtained through a simple amalgamation of trait measures only when there are qualitative differences among the members of the various prototypes with respect to their organization of behavior and experiences. To the extent that these qualitative differences do exist, they provide evidence pertaining to the unique value or power of the prototypic model in the description of individuality. In order to search for qualitative differences, scores on the composite summary dimensions, which were orthogonal within the total male and female longitudinal subsamples, were intercorrelated, using as subjects only those individuals who could be assigned to a single composite prototype. Although it was recognized that this information would be of little value in the less popular composite prototypes, it was hoped that the evidence obtained from some of the larger composite prototypes would serve to indicate both the existence of qualitative differences and the power of the prototype model.

Because a sizable number of correlation matrices were generated in the course of this analyses, it is not possible to display all of the results obtained for each and every composite prototype. As a result, evidence derived from a conservative test of this proposition is presented for two of the larger male and female composite prototypes that lay relatively close together in Euclidean space. Tables 10.5 a and b and 10.6 a and b present this data for the male Channelled Concrete Achievers (upper diagonal) and Upwardly Mobile Individuals (lower diagonal) composite prototypes as well as the female Unscathed Adjusters (upper diagonal) and Channelled Extroverts (lower diagonal) composite prototypes. These male and female composite prototypes contained 35 and 27 individuals, respectively, and the two female prototypes contained 46 and 23 individuals, respectively.

A review of Table 10.5 indicates that the male Channelled Concrete Achievers prototype produced nine correlations among the composite summary dimensions that were larger than .29 and significant at the .05 level. In examining the content of the coefficients in excess of .40, it was found that Parental Warmth and Social Adjustment was related to Academic Achievement ($r = .61$); Religious Involvement was negatively related to Academic Achievement ($r = -.40$); and Traditional Masculine Role was negatively related to Intellectual Pursuits ($r = -.49$). The male Upwardly Mobile Individuals composite prototype produced 12 coefficients larger than .32 and significant at the .05 level. Inspection of the content of the coefficients larger than .40 indicated that Parental Warmth and Social Adjustment was negatively related to both Academic Achievement ($r = -.57$) and Religious Involvement ($r = -.49$); Academic Achievement was related to both Professional Occupational Orientation ($r = .44$) and to Religious Involvement ($r = -.45$); and Scientific/Engineering Interests were negatively related to Traditional Masculine Role ($r = .45$), and were directly related to Intellectual Pursuits ($r = .41$).

Within the female subsample, 15 coefficients larger than .25 and significant at the .05 level were obtained for the Unscathed Adjustor composite prototype. When the coefficients in excess of .40 were examined, it was found that Traditional Social Adjustment was related to Self-Esteem ($r = .58$), Sociability ($r = .49$), and Paternal Identification ($r = .58$); Occupational Success and Satisfaction was negatively related to Negative Parent/Child Conflict ($r = -.41$); and Scientific Interests were related to Satisfaction With Social Life ($r = .40$). In the Channelled Extroverts composite prototype, 11 coefficients in excess of .31 and significant at the .05 level were obtained. A review of the coefficients larger than .40 indicated that Traditional Social Adjustment was related to Self-Esteem ($r = .47$) and Job Channelling ($r = .47$); Self-Esteem was directly related to Athletic Interests ($r = .42$); and Intellectual Pursuits were negatively related to Scientific Interests ($r = -.43$).

The coefficients larger than .40 obtained in the analyses were, for the most part, interpretable. Because athletics and traditional social adjustment would provide a basis for social contact among extroverts, it was not surprising that Self-Esteem would be directly related to Traditional Social Adjustment and Athletics among the Channelled Extroverts who were highly concerned with social effectiveness. Further, Traditional Social Adjustment would be expected to enhance Job Channelling, because it would lead to acceptance of, and success in, the social service jobs preferred by these females. Because these prototype members were not especially intellectually oriented, time investment would tend to induce a negative relationship between Intellectual Pursuits and Scientific Interests.

It was not especially surprising that the Traditional Social Adjustment dimension yielded a number of sizable coefficients within the Unscathed Adjustors prototype, because these prototype members appeared to organize much of their lives around adjustment to the traditional Femi-

TABLE 10.5a
Composite Summary Dimension Intercorrelations
Within Two Male Composite Prototypes (Upper Diagonal)

Factor #

	1	2	3	4	5	6	7	8	9	10	11	12
1	1.0	.06	-.34	.27	.61	.34	-.18	-.11	-.29	.22	-.13	-.20
2		1.0	-.05	-.20	.00	.09	.27	-.03	-.37	.23	.01	-.21
3			1.0	-.06	-.22	-.49	.14	.12	.25	-.14	-.03	.13
4				1.0	-.40	-.06	.20	-.20	-.07	-.08	.37	-.04
5					1.0	.15	-.14	-.06	-.08	.11	-.22	-.11
6						1.0	-.08	-.05	-.06	.20	.21	-.06
7							1.0	.08	-.15	-.07	.00	-.09
8								1.0	-.03	.21	.16	.11
9									1.0	-.33	-.21	.12
10										1.0	-.01	.03
11											1.0	.15
12												1.0

Note: N = 35 $p < .05 = .29$

TABLE 10.5b
Cross-Time Dimension Score Correlations Within Male Subgroup 2
(Lower Diagonal)

	1	2	3	4	5	6	7	8	9	10	11	12
1	1.0											
2	.34	1.0										
3	-.27	.17	1.0									
4	-.44	-.13	-.10	1.0								
5	-.57	-.44	.05	.45	1.0							
6	.33	-.02	-.50	.05	.02	1.0						
7	-.18	.20	.12	-.17	-.23	.05	1.0					
8	.30	.09	.04	-.25	.12	.19	.06	1.0				
9	.09	-.11	.09	-.10	.24	.07	-.30	-.26	1.0			
10	.29	.00	-.14	-.23	.31	.04	-.16	-.26	.25	1.0		
11	.34	-.35	-.45	-.05	-.03	.43	-.17	-.09	.25	.34	1.0	
12	-.10	-.25	-.10	.15	.07	.03	-.37	.07	.33	.14	.05	1.0

Note: $N = 27$ $p < .05 = .32$

TABLE 10.6a
Composite Summary Dimension Intercorrelations
Within Two Female Composite Prototypes (Upper Diagonal)

	1	2	3	4	5	6	7	8	9	10	11	12	13	14
								Factor #						
1	1.00	.34	.06	-.57	.49	.06	.22	.23	.23	.53	.05	.13	-.29	.11
2		1.00	.17	-.25	.19	.22	.10	.24	.13	.37	.00	-.06	-.11	-.05
3			1.00	-.06	-.03	-.13	-.01	.12	-.41	.21	.19	-.12	.10	.08
4				1.00	-.28	-.15	-.00	-.29	-.10	-.19	.01	.07	.08	-.14
5					1.00	.12	-.03	.05	.31	.39	-.22	.18	.05	-.05
6						1.00	.13	.34	.26	.03	-.30	.31	-.11	.06
7							1.00	.01	.09	.06	.19	.40	.10	-.22
8								1.00	.01	-.12	-.10	-.14	.00	-.03
9									1.00	.06	-.19	.17	-.00	-.20
10										1.00	-.02	.08	-.08	-.07
11											1.00	.01	-.08	.06
12												1.00	-.01	-.19
13													1.00	-.08
14														1.00

Note: N = 46 $p < .05 = .25$

TABLE 10.6b
Cross-Time Dimension Score Correlations
Within Female Subgroup 13 (Lower Diagonal)

Factor #

	1	2	3	4	5	6	7	8	9	10	11	12	13	14
1	1.00													
2	.47	1.00												
3	-.15	.15	1.00											
4	-.45	-.32	.18	1.00										
5	.00	-.35	-.10	.03	1.00									
6	.06	-.04	.08	.22	-.24	1.00								
7	.23	-.09	.07	.11	.11	-.43	1.00							
8	.02	.00	.17	-.35	-.05	-.17	.00	1.00						
9	-.11	-.10	-.28	.23	-.09	.15	-.28	.10	1.00					
10	-.25	-.29	.11	.20	.23	.05	.03	-.10	.17	1.00				
11	.26	.04	.11	-.05	.17	-.27	.52	.10	-.01	-.00	1.00			
12	-.05	.29	-.02	-.26	-.34	-.12	.02	.15	-.10	.00	-.09	1.00		
13	-.13	-.21	.00	.42	-.11	.09	.08	.15	.02	-.03	-.39	.04	1.00	
14	-.09	.16	-.10	-.07	-.37	-.13	-.06	.14	-.05	-.19	-.11	.38	.33	1.00

Note: $N = 23$ $p < .05 = .31$

335

nine Role. Moreover, Traditional Social Adjustment should facilitate sociability among conservative, moderately social females, and paternal identification in a warm family environment should facilitate the emergence of traditional Social Adjustment. However, given their highly constrained and protected family background, it is not surprising that high levels of traditional Social Adjustment would be negatively related to Self-Esteem, because it might limit the growth of self-confidence. The positive relationship between Scientific Interests and Life Satisfaction may reflect the positive influence of some growth beyond the traditional feminine role for these females, whereas the inverse relationship between Occupational Success and Satisfaction and Negative Parent/Child Conflict may reflect the fact that these females need parental support to enter and commit themselves to the occupational world.

The finding that, among the Upwardly Mobile Individuals, high scores on the Parental Warmth and Social Adjustment dimensions were negatively related to Academic Achievement and Religious Involvement may reflect that extreme closeness to parents enhanced the trend towards adolescent rebellion that is apparent in this prototype. Similarly, a lack of independence in adolescence and its potential impact on the later development of achievement motivation may underlie the negative relationship between Academic Achievement and a Professional Occupational Orientation. Lack of independence may also explain the positive relationship between Academic Achievement and Religious Involvement. Finally, the verbal, social orientation of these males may underlie the positive relationship of Scientific/Engineering Interests with Intellectual Pursuits as well as its negative relationship to the traditional Masculine role.

On the other hand, the sizable coefficients obtained within the Channelled Concrete Achievers prototype indicated that Parental Warmth and Social Adjustment was directly related to Academic Achievement. However, the finding is not particularly surprising when it is borne in mind that the warm, supportive family background of these males provided a basis for their academic achievement. Similarly, given their conservative, athletic orientation, it is not surprising that involvement in Intellectual Pursuits would be negatively related to acceptance of the traditional Masculine role. Finally, the tendency of these males to accept authority may explain the negative relationship between Religious Involvement and Academic Achievement within the composite prototype.

The preceding discussion of the significant relationships observed in correlating scores on the composite dimensions within the male and female composite prototypes serves to underscore two points. First, the relationships among the summary dimensions within a composite prototype were readily interpretable, given a knowledge of the prototypes' other differential characteristics. Consequently, the results of this analysis provide additional support for the meaningfulness and validity of the summary descriptions incorporated in the composite prototypes. Second, because the sizable coefficients obtained in this analysis were subject to reasonable interpretation, there is little reason to expect that these differences were purely the result of chance.

The nonchance nature of the results obtained in these intercorrelational analyses and the orthogonality in the major longitudinal subsamples of the composite summary dimensions provide an unambiguous demonstration of the existence of qualitative differences in the organization of behavior and experiences across the composite prototypes. Further, these qualitative differences were observed among even those male and female prototypes lying relatively close together in Euclidean space. A powerful demonstration of this point may be found in the observation that Academic Achievement was positively related to Parental Warmth and Social Adjustment within the male Channelled Concrete Achiever composite prototype but negatively related to the same factor within the Upwardly Mobile Individuals composite prototype. These correlational results were quite sizable and become even more impressive when it is noted that, by considering only the members of a given composite prototype in this analysis, some degree of range restriction was induced. All of the foregoing conclusions were confirmed in intercorrelating scores on the summary dimensions within all of the remaining composite prototypes containing 20 or more individuals. Because these organizational differences were significant, sizable, interpretable, and capable of enhancing understanding of the composite prototypes differential behavior and experiences, it seems that these qualitative differences in the organization of behavior and experience reflect significant aspects of individuality that can be captured in the prototype and should not be ignored in attempts to formulate a general and accurate summary description of individuality and individual development.

The existence of these qualitative differences has two important implications; one methodological and one conceptual. Turning first to the methodological implication, the pervasive and systematic loss of the composite summary dimensions orthogonality within the various composite prototypes indicates that the composite summary dimensions provided a highly approximate description of individuality. The possibility of this phenomenon was noted earlier, and it would seem to restrict the absolute accuracy of both the composite summary dimensions and prototypes. This problem could be solved through a clustering technology that would allow for the simultaneous definition of summary dimensions and prototypes. In lieu of a clustering technique of this sort, it appears that we must live with some error and the approximate strategy employed in the present investigation. Nevertheless, the observation also indicates that the composite summary dimensions should not be approached as absolute descriptions of the individual. This consideration, in part, lead to the use of both the item data and the summary dimension data in the description of the composite prototypes differential characteristics.

On the conceptual side, investigators have traditionally preferred to assume that individuals did not manifest qualitative differences in the meaning of their behavior and experiences. The failure of previous attempts to provide a convincing demonstration of the existence and significance of these organizational differences was a major reason for the early rejection of the typological model and its empirical descendant, the prototype model. However, the results obtained in the present investigation demonstrate such qualitative differences exist and can be empirically identified, providing some justification for use of the prototype model by demonstrating its ability to capture organizational differences beyond the reach of the trait model.

Overall, the foregoing analyses provide additional evidence for the meaningfulness and validity of the summary descriptions incorporated in the composite prototype. They have also provided some evidence pointing to the theoretical appropriateness and meaningfulness of the prototype model as well as its ability to capture significant organizational differences in the meaning of differential behavior and experiences. This suggests that the composite prototypes displayed the power necessary for their use in the summary descriptions of individuality and individual development.

INTERPRETATION

Regardless of whether or not the composite prototypes provide a clear, robust, and powerful summary description of individuals' differential behaviors and experiences over time, before they can be said to provide a meaningful summary description of individuality and individual development, it must be demonstrated that the differential data incorporated with the prototypes' summary descriptions form an interpretable, cohesive pattern that is conceptually meaningful. This is a difficult issue to address in any single fashion, because one person's meaning may be another's confusion. Despite such ambiguities, this issue is of sufficient importance to warrant some attention. In an attempt to address this issue, five staff psychologists reviewed the differential characteristics of each composite prototype and attempted to formulate a brief, consensual label that they felt summarized the prototype's differential characteristics.

These labels and the logic underlying their derivation were presented in chapter 9. A review of chapter 9 indicates that all of the composite prototypes could be assigned brief descriptive labels that appeared to summarize their differential characteristics. Moreover, the results obtained in correlating the males' and females' likelihood of membership in the relevant composite prototype with their likelihood of membership in the various cross-sectional prototypes provided some independent support for the appropriateness of these descriptive labels, because this information was not employed in the initial labeling of the composite prototypes.

In sum, the preceding paragraphs suggest that the composite prototypes were associated with a cohesive, interpretable, and meaningful pattern of differential behavior and experiences over time that permitted the prototypes' differential characteristics to be summarized in terms of a brief descriptive label. A number of additional analyses, such as the distance between the composite prototypes in Euclidean space and their relationship with the cross-sectional prototypes, have provided evidence for the meaningfulness and cross-time nature of these summary descriptions. In light of the findings obtained in the previous sections with respect to clarity, robustness, and power of the composite prototypes, it seems reasonable to conclude that the composite prototypes provided a valid and highly effective summary description of individuality and individual development. Of course, one limitation on the appropriateness of this conclusion is that it is completely dependent on information obtained in the course of the present investigation. However, in the ensuing discussion, an attempt is made to remedy this situation and extend support for the validity of the composite prototypes.

COMPARISON WITH BLOCK'S PROTOTYPES

Block (1971) also attempted to construct a set of composite prototypes as part of an effort to summarize the data collected in the California longitudinal studies during junior high school, high school, and young adulthood. These composite prototypes were identified through an inverse factoring of Q sort data collected during the 1950s and 1960s describing the observed characteristics of each subject during junior high school and young adulthood. In the course of this analysis, five male and six female composite prototypes were identified and assigned brief descriptive labels. Because these composite prototypes were constructed over a development period similar to that in the present investigation, one might expect some convergence between the composite prototypes identified in Block's study and those identified in the present study if the composite prototypes provided a stable and meaningful summary description of individuality and individual development.

Because Block's investigation used a different cohort, clustering technique, and item base from that employed in the present investigation, substantial convergence in the nature of the composite prototypes identified in these two investigations would provide compelling evidence for the stability and convergent, construct validity of the summary descriptions of individuality incorporated in the composite prototypes. Unfortunately, these same differences in methodology and design made it impossible to carry out this comparison in any direct, quantitative fashion. As a result, this comparison was made through a qualitative review of the differential characteristics shared by Block's composite prototypes and those established in the present study.

In contrasting the differential characteristics of Block's prototypes with the differential characteristics of the composite prototypes identified in the present investigation, it was found that all five of Block's male prototypes had analogs among the composite prototypes identified in the present investigation, and three clear-cut analogs could be identified. The Channelled Concrete Achiever prototype established in the present study displayed a marked similarity to Block's Ego Resiliants in terms of their favorable family backgrounds, achievement motivation, conservative, somewhat introverted, social orientation, occupational preference, and eventual occupational success. Block's Belated Adjustors were characterized by a withdrawn and difficult adolescence, a harsh family background, limited general intellectual ability, and the eventual attainment of a satisfying, if somewhat limited, family, occupational, and social life. This pattern displays a marked similarity to the one that was found to characterize the Constrained Careerists composite prototype established in the present study. The composite prototype labelled Burgeois Outliers in the study at hand displayed strong similarities to Block's Vulnerable Undercontrollers in terms of family background, rebelliousness, occupational preference, and downward mobility.

The Virile Extroverts composite prototype displayed some similarity to the Anomie Extroverts prototype identified in Block's study with respect to the athletic interests, acceptance of the traditional masculine role, sociability, conservative social orientation, and occupation preferences. Nevertheless, this must be considered an ambiguous match, because the Virile Extroverts manifested a higher degree of occupational and social success than did the Anomie Extroverts. Similar ambiguities arose in matching Block's Vulnerable Over-Controllers to the Premature

Conformists prototype established in the present study. Although both prototypes displayed signs of early maturation and adjustment difficulties in adulthood, along with similar family backgrounds, the Premature Conformists prototype established in the present study appeared to have a more pronounced set of difficulties and lower occupational success.

As was the case with the males, all six of Block's female prototypes had analogs among the prototypes identified in the current effort. However, only five of these six matchings could be made with little ambiguity. The Unscathed Adjustors prototype established in the present study was, for all purposes, identical to Block's Feminine Prototypes with respect to family background, traditional social adjustment, social skills, and occupational and family characteristics in young adulthood. Similarly, the composite prototype labelled Unconventional Successes in the current investigation was a good match for Block's Cognitive Coper prototype. The similarity was manifest in their difficult adolescence, movement toward psychological health, independence, verbal intellectual orientation, and occupational behavior. Although it is true that the females assigned to the Unconventional Successes prototype were somewhat more rebellious and career-oriented than Block's prototypes, these differences may be attributed to the broader cultural shifts occurring between the inception of these studies and the sensitivity of prototype members to the broadening effects of these changes.

The members of Block's Dominating Narcissists prototype were described as self-absorbed women who were socially constrained and employed aggressive social manipulation to obtain their desires. When this description is coupled with similarities in family background, adolescent behavior, occupational preferences, and marital characteristics, it is clear that these females are quite similar to the Social Manipulator prototype identified in the present study. With respect to their family background, high intelligence, vocational aspirations, social isolation, and adult social and family lives, it appears that Block's Lonely Independents provided a good match for the present study's Isolated Intellectuals. Block's Vulnerable Fantasizers were also found to have a clear-cut analog in the Restricted Socializers prototype identified in the present study in terms of their family background, adolescent activities, desire for social approval, and their intellectual and social limitations.

The Hyperfeminine Repressor was the only female prototype identified by Block that did not have a clear-cut analog among the composite prototypes identified in the study at hand. Members of Block's prototype apparently restricted themselves to the traditional feminine role, were not especially socially active or effective, tended to be downwardly mobile, dissatisfied with their adult lives, and incapable of establishing satisfying marriages. This general pattern seems to fit either the Female

Eunuch or the Disgruntled Male Dependents composite prototypes. However, the Disgruntled Male Dependents prototype appears to provide a slightly better match, given the tendency toward paternal identification and the closeness to father exhibited by Block's prototype.

It must be concluded that the foregoing discussion has reviewed some very complex data and carried out a number of complex comparisons in a rather cursory fashion. Nevertheless, this discussion has served its purpose in the sense that it has provided some limited evidence indicating that there is a high degree of similarity between the prototypes identified in Block's study and those established in the present investigation. In fact, of Block's 11 prototypes, 8 had clear-cut analogs among the composite prototypes established in the present investigation, whereas the remaining were somewhat more ambivalent analogs. Given that these two studies employed different measures, cohorts, and clustering techniques in establishing their composite prototypes, this represents a surprisingly high degree of overlap.

Of course, it is also true that a larger number of composite prototypes were established in the present investigation than in Block's study. However, this result may reflect little more than the use of a more sensitive clustering technique and a larger, more diverse sample in the present study, because these influences would tend to facilitate the identification of a larger number of composite prototypes. This conclusion finds some support in the observation that Block's prototypes tended to replicate the larger or more populous prototypes identified in the present investigation. Given these considerations, it seems reasonable to conclude that the results obtained in this comparative effort argue for the replicability, stability, and construct validity of the summary descriptions of individuality and individual development formulated in both these investigations, at least within the middle-class populations that were the focus of these investigations.

CONCLUSIONS

The preceding discussion has reviewed a variety of facts and observations that are relevant to evaluating the effectiveness of the summary descriptions of individuality and individual development produced by the composite prototypes. Perhaps the most significant result to emerge in the course of this review concerns the legitimacy of employing the prototype model in the description of human individuality. Earlier, it was noted that three major empirical observations lead to the rejection of the typological model in the summary description of human individuality. First, it was found that individuals could not be unambiguously assigned to a taxonomic category but tended to fall between these categories. Second, qualitative differences among the individuals assigned to different types in their organization of behavior and experiences could not be empirically demonstrated. Third, meaningful general typologies or classifications of persons could not be established empirically. However, the foregoing discussion has shown that individuals can be unambiguously assigned to membership in a single composite prototype, and that members of these prototypes display qualitative differences in their organization of behaviors and experiences. Further, much of the foregoing discussion has served to suggest that the composite prototypes could be empirically identified and provide a general, valid, and highly meaningful summary description of the individual's behavior and experiences over time that was subject to replication. Thus, it appears that many of the criticisms initially leveled at the typological model cannot be applied to its empirical derivative in the prototypic model.

The composite prototypes appeared to provide a more effective summary description of individuality than did the various cross-sectional prototypes. The enhanced effectiveness of the composite prototypes in the description of individuality appears to be based on their unique ability to capture significant cross-time developmental relationships and genotypic consistencies in patterns of individual development. When this enhanced effectiveness of the summary descriptions of individuality and individual development incorporated in the composite prototypes is considered in light of the meaningfulness of these summary descriptions, it appears that they provide a general base for gaining some understanding of the nature of individuality and individual development.

11

Comparative Findings

In any attempt to generate an understanding of individuality and individual development within the framework provided by the prototype model, there can be little doubt that the information presented in chapter 10 is of great importance. Obviously, if the prototype model could not be both efficiently and legitimately employed, the summary description of individuality incorporated in the composite prototypes would have little value in an attempt to formulate an understanding of human individuality through its unfolding over time. However, it has been shown that the prototype model can provide a clear and comprehensive description of individuality by virtue of the fact that most individuals can be described through their assignment to a single prototype. Moreover, the composite prototypes seemed to be capable of capturing qualitative differences in the organization of behavior and experiences. Consequently, a review of the composite prototypes might provide some unique information concerning the emergence of individuality over time.

Although the comprehensiveness and uniqueness of the descriptive information contained in the composite prototypes argues for the potential value of this descriptive data in studies of human individuality, there can be little doubt that this information would be of limited utility if the composite prototypes did not provide a valued or meaningful summary description of differential behavioral experiences. In chapter 10, this issue was addressed in some detail. Generally, the results obtained in this phase of the present investigation provided strong evidence for the validity of the summary descriptions incorporated in the composite prototypes. Some compelling evidence for the validity of these summary descriptions was provided by the cohesiveness and conceptual interpretability of the composite prototypes' differential characteristics. Moreover, these differential characteristics were sufficiently cohesive and meaningful to allow brief descriptive labels that summarize the composite prototypes' differential characteristics to be formulated. Additional evidence for the meaningfulness of these summary descriptions, as well as their replicability, stability, and generality, was obtained by comparing the differential characteristics of the composite prototypes generated in the present study with those constructed by Block (1971).

If the composite prototypes are to be employed as a vehicle for understanding individuality in a developmental context, they must be capable of capturing not only a broad range of differential behaviors and experiences, but also of capturing differential behaviors and experiences as they emerge over the course of an individual's life. Fortunately, the data presented in the foregoing chapters indicated that the composite prototypes did summarize differential behaviors and experiences at a number of points in the individual's development. The ability of the composite prototypes to describe the individual's likely behaviors and experiences at different points is critical to the effective and appropriate use of the composite prototypes in an attempt to obtain a general understanding of human individuality.

One piece of information that may be used to enhance understanding of individuality as a natural phenomenon may be found in the identification and analysis of the relationship between antecedent and consequent events. Because the composite prototypes describe the differential behaviors and experiences of prototypes members at different points in their lives, this antecedent consequent information may be extracted from the composite prototypes, by revising and contrasting prototypes member's typical status on a variety of earlier and later indicators. Moreover, the background data items provide discrete and reasonably accurate descriptions of antecedents and consequents and so generate the information that Fiske (1979) has shown to be of particular value in establishing antecedent–consequent relationships for theoretical analyses. As a result, the differential characteristics of the composite prototypes on the background data items obtained in different developmental periods provide the basic information required in an attempt to formulate at least a preliminary understanding of the nature and ontogeny of human individuality.

By examining the emergence of prototype members' differential behaviors and experiences over the course of their lives and comparing this antecedent–consequent information with the characteristic behaviors and experiences of other composite prototypes, it should be possible to obtain the differential antecedent–consequent information required to generate some understanding of individuality and individual development. Subsequently, the basic phenomena observed in this comparative effort might serve as a groundwork for theory development. The appropriateness and effectiveness of this strategy is enhanced by qualities of the descriptive data employed, but there are certain limitations inherent in this strategy of which the reader should be aware. Obviously, the information obtained in contrasting the differential characteristics of the composite prototypes can not provide an unambiguous demonstration of causality in the antecedent–consequent relationships. Moreover, because the differential characteristics of the composite prototypes were defined on an extensive set of background data items, it was not possible to carry out all possible comparisons of the composite prototypes' differential characteristics. Thus, these comparisons were carried out in a selective fashion, although an attempt was made to guide this comparative effort by focusing on certain major content areas and theoretical constructs. Finally, this guided comparative effort was necessarily based on little more than a qualitative review and comparison of the differences and experiences yielding significant differentiation. As a result, a certain element of subjectivity necessarily pervades the resulting comparisons. Although the authors do not denigrate the importance of these limitations and do hope that the reader will bear them in mind, it nevertheless appeared that the information obtained in this comparative effort would be of great importance with respect to our understanding of the nature and ontogeny of human individuality.

CONTENT COMPARISON

Because they were grounded in the content of the background data items per se, comparison of the composite prototypes with respect to certain discrete categories of antecedent behavior and experiences and their developmental outcomes presented a relatively straightforward task. Additionally, the content-oriented approach provided an especially appropriate implementation of Fiske's (1979) general framework. Due to the nature of the data base in use, these comparisons were subsumed under three broad headings, which have been labeled Family Influences, Individual Influences, and Social Influences. In the ensuing discussion, an attempt is made to examine some of the more interesting comparative findings obtained in each of these areas.

Family Influences

A number of items that appeared in the initial background data questionnaire examined the characteristics of the individual family environment. It has long been postulated that the individual's early family environment may have a profound impact on the nature of individual development. One comparison of this sort that leads to some interesting observations was gleaned from a review of the relationship between family background and the adolescent characteristics of the composite prototypes. The early family environments of a large number of the composite prototypes could be characterized by a differential syndrome of environmental stimuli that might be thought of as a "good" or "bad" family environment. These syndromes were defined by systematic differences on a complex set of indicators, including parental warmth, positive parental behaviors, closeness to parents, and a lack of parent–child conflict. In adolescence, the members of composite prototypes that were characterized by a good family environment, such as the Unscathed Adjustors and Channelled Concrete Achievers, tended to be socially active, socially effective, well adjusted, and concerned with achievement. However, members of composite prototypes that were characterized by a bad family environment, including the Expansive Compensators and Defensive Conformists, among others, tended to be poorly adjusted and socially ineffective during adolescence. Further, these individuals displayed little concern with achievement and devoted their spare time to solitary activities.

Although these syndromes of family influences lead to a unitary set of outcomes in adolescence, these patterns of differential behavior were not necessarily maintained in later developmental periods, once prototype members had been removed from their family environments. Instead, the consequences in later developmental periods seemed to depend on a complex interaction between individuals' existing characteristics and the situations to which they were subsequently exposed. For instance, the Unconventional Successes were withdrawn and socially ineffective in adolescence, as might be expected for individuals raised in a bad family environment. However, their intellectual interests, social attitudes, and verbal ability led them to adopt a liberal bohemian lifestyle in college, which led to self-expansion and heightened social activity. On the other hand, the limited ability and high expectations of the Unrealistic Independents led to social and occupational difficulties in adulthood, despite their favorable pattern of adolescent behavior and family background. These observations suggest that, although some developmental experiences may have unitary effects in one developmental period, these effects may not be maintained in a consistent fashion across prototypes in later developmental periods, as a result of ongoing development based in a continuing organism–environment interchange. Moreover, the nature of these effects and the resulting changes seemed dependent on the characteristics that the individual brought to his or her ongoing interchange.

Although not explicitly considered part of the "good" or "bad" syndrome, the extent to which parents do or do not push their children for achievement represents a closely related phenomenon in a conceptual sense. However, the tendency of parents to push for achievement was apparent in composite prototypes from both good and bad family backgrounds. Across the composite prototypes, it was found that when parents pushed for achievement in a bad family environment, composite prototype members were especially unlikely to try to achieve in adolescence. However, when this trend was accompanied by a good family environment and at least some ability, composite prototypes members tried to achieve in adolescence. This effect was manifest in the differential characteristics of the Isolated Intellectuals. Nevertheless, under both these conditions, it was found that when the parents of prototype members pushed for achievement, their children were likely to have some difficulties in their adult careers and social relationships, indicated by a tendency to display lower degrees of satisfaction and success in these areas.

In a more positive area, it was found that a syndrome of early environmental influences, including parental warmth, independence training, and emotional reinforcement for achievement—which the literature emphasizes as underlying the later emergence of achievement motivation—characterized 12 of the composite prototypes. Among them were the Channelled Concrete Achievers, the Virile Extroverts, the Competent Nurturers, and the Social Manipulators. As might be expected given the literature along with the content of the foregoing discussion, all these composite prototypes displayed some signs of overt achievement and achievement motivation in adolescence and later developmental periods. However, the specific way in which these achievement concerns were expressed appeared to be specific to the particular composite prototype. For instance, the Virile Extroverts appeared to focus on social and athletic achievement, whereas the Isolated Intellectuals focused on academic achievement. These differences seemed tied to the fact that other characteristics of the composite prototypes led satisfaction of achievement concerns to be more likely in some areas than in others, which, when coupled with environmental feedback, led to the selective expression of these characteristics.

On the other hand, it should be noted that this was not the only syndrome of environmental influences that led to the expression of achievement motivation in adulthood. Members of four composite prototypes, including the Expansive Compensators, Orphaned Adaptors, Adaptive Successes, and Unconventional Successes, displayed substantial achievement motivation in adulthood, but not necessarily in adolescence, despite the fact that they were not exposed to the supposedly requisite developmental syndrome and were raised in bad family environments where parental warmth and reinforcement were not likely to be forthcoming. In these cases, achievement motivation appeared to emerge in a form of Adlerian compensation that was tied to a desire for social approval or acceptance. This result implies two obvious, but often overlooked, facts. First, a given form of differential behavior may develop through more than one avenue, and population-based statements may fail to identify these significant, yet less common, patterns of development. Second, differential characteristics may emerge at different times for different individuals, depending on the developmental avenues that are in use.

Parental warmth appeared to play an important role in the emergence and acceptance of traditional values, as well as in the expression of achievement motivation. The composite prototypes whose members reported that they had a warm relationship with their parents nearly always adopted traditional sex roles and displayed traditional values, which lead to the satisfying acceptance of traditional life styles in young adulthood. Excellent examples of this phenomenon may be found in the differential characteristics of the Competent Nurturers, Unscathed Adjustors, Channelled Extraverts, Virile Extraverts, and Channeled Concrete Achievers composite prototypes. The implication is that the reinforcement and identification tied to parental warmth is likely to spawn the acceptance of traditional values and reduce stress by enhancing the individual's acceptance of later social demands.

Nevertheless, it should be recognized that the apparent inverse of this process did not hold. Composite prototypes who were exposed to cold parents, such as the Defensive Conformists, Fortunate Approval Seekers, Ineffectual Authoritarians, Bourgeois Outliers, and Unconventional Successes, might or might not display acceptance of traditional values and role behaviors in later years. The differences between these composite prototypes seemed to be linked to whether they did or did not attempt to gain approval from their parents. Almost universally across the composite prototypes, individuals exposed to a cold, harsh family environment expressed a desire for social approval. However, members of some composite prototypes, such as the Defensive Conformists and the Ineffectual Authoritarians, attempted to obtain this approval through conformance to their parents demands. Typically, these individuals were likely to display overt conformity to traditional values and roles in young adulthood, yet at the same time they appeared to have some difficulty in adjusting to these roles and were likely to find them unsatisfying. However, those individuals who came from this background and rebelled in college or sought approval from external sources after they left home tended to be more satisfied with their adult lives, although they might or might not display traditional values and role behaviors, depending on the nature of their rebellion and the sources they employed in an attempt to gain approval. Examples of this phenomenon may be found in the differential characteristics of the Constrained Careerists and the Unconventional Successes. When these trends are considered in light of the preceeding observations, they suggest that overtly similar behavior may have very different implications, depending on the distal backdrop of developmental experiences it occurs in.

Another modification of the basic pattern that was laid out in the foregoing paragraph may be found in the issue of identification with the cross-sex parent. In the case of the male Withdrawn Effeminates and the female Paternal Reactives and Discontented Male Dependents, composite prototype members appeared to be far closer to the cross-sex than the same-sex parent, due to their greater warmth or reduced abrasiveness. This was apparent in self-reports of closeness to and time spent with their parents. Consequently, these individuals appeared to reject the traditional patterning of sex roles and display cross-sex interests. Provided that these individuals were placed in environments that would accept this nontraditional orientation, they fared relatively well in terms of overall adjustment even though this trend was maintained into young adulthood. However, as was the case with the Withdrawn Effeminates during their undergraduate years, when these individuals were placed in an environment that would not accept these differences, they appeared to have some difficulties. This observation suggests that the outcome of social processes, such as identification, may be closely tied to the demands of later social roles, and favorable outcomes may require a delicately orchestrated developmental background.

The background data items provided a number of indicators of parental socioeconomic status that were somewhat complex in the sense that they reflected both monetary income and parental education. Across the composite prototypes, it was found that individuals who came from high-socioeconomic-status backgrounds, in either sense, generally fared better in young adulthood than did individuals who came from lower-class backgrounds. However, it should be noted that this trend was not a *constant.* This fact is illustrated in the many difficulties of the Bourgeois Outliers in young adulthood and the success of the Unconventional Successes. The prototypes who came from a lower-class background and displayed a high degree of later social and occupational success typically displayed a higher degree of independence and achievement motivation, particularly during the college years, than did other individuals from this background. Similarly, the individuals who came from upper-class families and had problems in later years often had some difficulty in adapting to the demands of young adulthood due to other problems in their family background, as may be seen in the Bourgeois Outliers. It was also found that individuals from educated families are likely to report greater parental warmth and a more pronounced concern with educational achievement during adolescence, although this trend was not necessarily maintained in adulthood. These results suggest that more general aspects of the individual's family background may have a significant impact on development, although the eventual impact of such influences may be moderated by other characteristics of the individual and the family situation.

Another aspect of the composite prototypes' family background that yielded some interesting results was manifest in the extent to which parents attempted to protect their children. Parental protectiveness did not lead to any effects that appeared to generalize across the composite prototypes. Yet this influence did appear to have some significant outcomes attached to it when coupled with certain characteristics of the individual, particularly intellectual simplicity. Among composite prototypes, such as the Female Eunuchs and the Religious Copers, it was found that individuals who were raised in a protective family environment and were intellectually limited or simplistic were likely to have some difficulty after they left their families, unless they could find substitute institutions. Thus, it appears that the long-term outcomes associated with their background depended not only on the individuals' characteristics but also the environments to which they were later exposed.

A final aspect of family background that produced some interesting comparative results was found in the birth-order positions of prototype members. Across the composite prototypes, males and females who were younger children reported a higher degree of conflict with siblings than did those individuals who were members of prototypes that tended to be composed predominately of older children. This finding might be attributed to competition with siblings and disadvantaged position of the younger child in this competition. However, when older children, such as the Social Manipulators, reported sibling conflict, it often had profound implications for their later social behavior, though this was not the case for younger children. Apparently, the developmental implications of a pattern of differential behavior may be modified by some rather subtle aspects of the individual's family background.

Individual Influences

The background data items incorporated in the instruments that were administered during the various developmental periods made it possible to examine a wide variety of differential characteristics in the various developmental periods as well as their implications for the later behaviors and experiences of the individual. Some of these differential characteristics represented traditional psychometric constructs, whereas others appeared to reflect somewhat more novel aspects of individuality that were relevant to the emergence of individuality over time.

One of these differential characteristics that is clearly tied to the nature of individual development may be found in early or late maturation. The members of certain composite prototypes, such as the Premature Conformists and the Insecure Bohemians, appeared to move into adult social roles or aspects of these roles earlier than would be expected via the age grading of behavior, thus resulting in early maturation as defined within the context of the present study. Typically, it was found that early maturation did not bode well in terms of later development. Members of these composite prototypes often displayed signs of poor adjustment and a lack of social and occupational success in the periods of young adulthood following this acceleration. Apparently, this early movement into adult roles led to a lack of preparation for coping with the role demands. In contrast, slow social maturation or movement into adult roles did not appear to be associated with any noticeable negative outcomes. For instance, members of the male prototype labeled Upwardly Mobile Individuals experienced an extended period of youth during their postcollege years, yet they had a rather successful young adulthood. These results indicate the importance of adequate preparation in the course of individual development.

Rebelliousness, as indexed by independence, unconventionality, radical political involvement, and liberal sexual attitudes during college also appeared to be of some importance in differentiating the developmental paths followed by the members of different composite prototypes. The developmental implications of rebelliousness appeared to vary with the nature of the composite prototype at hand and the nature of this rebellion. Generally, the members of composite prototypes such as the Constrained Careerists and Unconventional Successes, who were raised in restrictive family environments and subsequently rebelled during college, fared well with respect to their long-term outcomes in adulthood. On the other hand, the members of some other composite prototypes, such as the Unrealistic Independents or Insecure Bohemians, who rebelled during adolescence or their college years despite the fact that they come from warm, supportive family backgrounds, tended to maintain their rebellion in later years and encounter some difficulties in their jobs, marriages, and social lives. This suggests that the developmental implications and meaning of certain differential characteristics may be dependent on the individual's broader pattern of development.

Unlike rebelliousness or maturation, the constructs of independence and conformity have received a great deal of attention in the psychometric literature. A review of the differential characteristics of the composite prototypes with respect to these constructs produced several interesting findings. First, it was apparent that qualities such as conformity or independence might have very different meanings, depending on when and how they were manifested. Some composite prototypes exhibiting conformist social behavior clearly evidenced these behaviors as a result of their earlier acceptance of traditional roles and values. Example of conformist patterns of this sort may be found in the differential characteristics of the Unscathed Adjustors, where their acceptance and effective utilization of the traditional feminine role led to conformity to role expectations. However, other composite prototypes, such as the Ineffectual Authoritarians, did not base their conformity on value acceptance. This latter type of conformity typically led to negative developmental outcomes in terms of marital, social, and job satisfaction, whereas the former trend led to positive outcomes. For the members of certain composite prototypes who desired social approval and were somewhat insecure and ineffective socially during adolescence, conformity to the social expectations of collegiate fraternities and sororities could be quite beneficial. The fraternity involvement of the male Insecure Socialities and the sorority involvement of the female Social Copers and Orphaned Adapters led them to develop social skills that they lacked in adolescence and could employ in constructing reasonably effective lives in adulthood.

Independence also seemed to have both favorable and unfavorable implications, depending on the particular composite prototype under consideration. The differential implications of the independence among the composite prototypes seemed to be traceable to a destinction between independent thought and action and independence through the rejection of group social activities. The former trend was manifest in the differential characteristics of the composite Analytical Adapters and Upwardly Mobile Individuals, whereas the latter trend was manifest in the differential characteristics of the Unrealistic Independents and Bourgeois Outliers. Apparently, independence in thought and action led to personally satisfying occupational and social lives, whereas the rejection of social activities led to dissatisfaction and isolation in young adulthood. When these results are considered in light of the preceding discussion and the fact that both these forms of independence could be manifested in similar ways during certain developmental periods, it seems reasonable to conclude that the meaning of differential behavior may vary with the broader pattern of an individual's behavior and experiences.

The topic of psychological adjustment has received a great deal of attention in the literature. A number of interesting findings also emerged when the differential characteristics of the composite prototypes were reviewed with respect to their implications for adjustment.

One of the more optimistic findings to emerge in the course of this effort may be found in the pervasiveness of adequate adjustment. Roughly 75% of the sample proved to be members of composite prototypes that followed developmental paths that could be characterized as being reasonably well adjusted in the sense that the individuals lived reasonably productive lives that they found satisfying overall. Unsurprisingly, many of these composite prototypes were characterized earlier as being accepting of, and reasonably effective at, working in traditional jobs and institutions, such as the Channeled Concrete Achievers, Virile Extraverts, Channelled Extraverts, and Unscathed Adjusters prototypes. This result seems to reflect the fact that adjustment in any society is likely to be facilitated by acceptance of, and a capacity for, working within the dominant social roles. Nevertheless, members of the Unconventional Successes lived active and satisfying lives after adolescence, despite their rejection of traditional roles.

In nearly all instances, effective adjustment appeared to be tied to an alignment between prototype members' desires and capabilities and the demands of the general environment in which they were placed. Of course, adjustment is more likely to be evident among individuals who are able to function in the roles made available by this culture. However, if these roles are not able to satisfy their desires, adjustment can not be expected. An excellent example of this point may be found in the maladjustment of the Female Eunuchs, who disregarded their masculine pattern of interests in order to conform to the traditional feminine role and consequently were dissatisfied and poorly adjusted throughout the interval that was examined in the present study. This implies that exactly what is required for adjustment depends on the particular kind of individual at hand and the nature of their current environment.

It should also be pointed out that satisfactory adjustment in one or more developmental periods might not necessarily be beneficial to the individuals long-run adaptation. For instance, the Insecure Socialites appeared to be relatively well adjusted during the college years, yet this was accompanied by a continuing dependence on others and lack of direction. When this well-adjusted behavior pattern in college was coupled with a concommittant failure to prepare themselves for the occupational world or to develop an independent social orientation, it led to difficulties in young adulthood and poor adjustment during this period. This suggests that immediate adjustment should not be confused with long-run adaptation and that poor adjustment might, under certain conditions, facilitate eventual adaptation. The latter hypothesis finds some support in the differential characteristics of the Adjustive Successes, whose long-run adaptation and adjustment was facilitated by a lack of adjustment in adolescence as they prepared themselves to exploit later environments. Further, adjustment can not be arbitrarily expected to be a stable characteristic. Rather, it depends on the characteristics of the individual, the situations to which he or she is exposed, and their implications for further development. Substantial support for this viewpoint may be found in the changes in the Orphaned Adapters' level of overall adjustment as they moved through different developmental periods.

In examining the differential characteristics of the composite prototypes, it appears that long-run adaptation was tied to the individuals' ability to employ personal resources in a satisfying manner by preparing themselves to exploit appropriate aspects of the environment. An excellent example of the phenomenon may be found in the differential characteristics of the Constrained Careerists. These males carefully sought out and prepared themselves for jobs that were in line with their interests and abilities and, in the long run, lived happy and satisfying lives despite their limited intellectual capacity. Similarly, the adaptation of the Analytical Adapters and the Orphaned Adapters appeared to be tied to the fact that they sought out and prepared themselves for later activities that were in line with their desires and personal abilities. This suggests that, although the specific content of adaptation may vary, underlying it is a general process that is particularly tied to the individual's active influence over the course of his or her own developmental paths.

The statement also suggests that the individual's goals, values, and interests may play an important role in guiding the course of individual development. Substantial support for this proposition was obtained in reviewing the differential characteristics of the composite prototypes. The importance of realistic goals was underscored by the high expectations of the Unrealistic Independents and the disaffection that was associated with their failure to attain these goals due to their limited ability and their rebelliousness. Although not all of the composite prototypes expressed strong vocational interests, those who did and failed to obtain jobs that were in line with their interests tended to be dissatisfied with their jobs. These results suggest that, like goals, interests may be of some importance in understanding individual development. Values were also found to have some significance in controlling the course of individual development. The composite prototypes who expressed cognitive values, such as the Analytical Adapters, Unconventional Successes, and Withdrawn Effeminates, typically engaged in activities that were likely to provide rewards in this area. However, as was the case with interests, the manner in which the common value patterns was expressed seemed to depend on the broader characteristics of the composite prototype under consideration. For instance, the Analytical Adapters were likely to express their cognitive values through their involvement with scientific pursuits, whereas the Withdrawn Effeminates were likely to focus on intellectual and artistic activities. These examples also suggest that values, goals, and interests influence individual development by controlling the individual's selection of activities and defining the outcome desired from these activities. Even though this occurs in a manner that is congruent with the broader pattern of a prototype's differential characteristics, it suggests that overt conscious selections of activities are an important manifestation of individuality and may influence the course of individual development.

Interestingly, inspection of the composite prototype's differential characteristics indicated that, even in adolescence, the various prototypes who manifested signs of achievement motivation expressed this characteristic only in a select set of activities. Examples of this phenomenon may be found in the fact that the Social Manipulators appeared to focus on social activities, the Virile Extraverts on athletic and social activities, and the Isolated Intellectuals and Channeled Concrete Achievers an academic activities. A review of the differential characteristics of the composite prototypes indicated that these focus differences arose as a result of background, aptitude, and personality differences that led the identification of achievement needs to be more likely in some areas than others during adolescence. Crandall (1972) obtained similar results in a reanalysis of the Fels Institute data and noted that this selection of the activities that achievement motivation will be expressed in may be linked to environmental feedback, leading the satisfaction of the need to be more likely in some areas than others. The existence of this phenomenon suggests an important conclusion; that is, even a common differential characteristic may be selectively expressed in the manner that is most favorable to the individual, given current environmental constraints.

The close tie between the development and expression of differential characteristics and the situations to which individuals are exposed suggests that the individual's selection of environments to meet his or her needs may exert a profound effect on the nature of the observed differential characteristics. Some support for this hypothesis may be obtained by examining the emergence of social skills. Quite often, the members of composite prototypes who had been raised in a bad family environment expressed a desire for the social approval that had not been forthcoming in their early years. The Fortunate Approval Seekers, Orphaned Adapters, and Social Copers all displayed this trend. Their desires, in turn, led them to search out and become involved with collegiate social groups, and these experiences led them to develop and maintain a newfound set of social skills that they employed in establishing satisfying social and occupational lives.

In examining the differential characteristics of the composite prototypes, some additional results of interest emerged in considering the implications of effective social behavior on social skills. One important implication that was alluded to in the preceeding paragraph concerned the timing involved in the emergence of these skills. Members of composite prototypes, such as the Fortunate Approval Seekers and Orphaned Adapters, who came from a difficult or bad family environment, tended to be withdrawn in adolescence and to manifest few social skills of any sort. Yet, in college, their involvement with social organizations led to the emergence of a new set of social skills and pronounced sociability. What is of note here is that these differential characteristics emerged relatively late in comparison with the Virile Extraverts and Social Manipulators, who came from good family environments and displayed sociality and social skills in adolescence. This implies that differential characteristics may develop at different rates or at different times for different kinds of individuals. Moreover, this suggests that the presence or absence of a characteristic in one developmental period may not preclude its chances to emerge in later periods.

Academic ability has often been held to be an important determinant of the individual's scholastic performance. In examining the differential characteristics of the composite prototypes, it was found that the members of prototypes having high SAT scores tended to do relatively well academically in both high school and college. However, it also appeared that this relationship might be moderated by other considerations. Certain composite prototypes, such as the Channelled Concrete Achievers and the Isolated Intellectuals, tended to perform better academically than might have been expected only on the basis of their SAT scores. On the other hand, it was found that members of composite prototypes such as the Unconventional Successes and the Fortunate Approval Seekers performed less well in high school academics than their SAT scores would lead one to expect. This result appeared to stem from a difficult adolescence and social withdrawal, which limited their committment to and concern with academic achievement. As the collegiate characteristics of the Unconventional Successes and the Expansive Compensators suggest, the trend was not necessarily maintained in college, due to a broader pattern of change.

The importance of choice in the utilization of intellectual abilities was also apparent in the differential characteristics of the composite prototypes. For instance, it was found that the Bourgeois Outliers performed poorly in high school, despite their later academic success, in part because academic failure appeared to be an integral part of their adolescent rebellion. Similarly, the Competent Nurturers were far less successful in the occupational world than their substantial intellectual ability would lead one to expect, due to their concern with establishing a home and family. In contrast, the Adjustive Successes displayed little motivation or interest in academia. Nevertheless, they worked hard in school and did well despite average ability.

Social Influences

The foregoing discussion has examined some of the differential characteristics of the composite prototypes with respect to the expression and development of human individuality. In the course of this discussion, it was apparent that both the nature and the impact of these differential characteristics were closely tied to the situations to which individuals were exposed. The social environment subsumes a variety of the critical developmental situations. Some of the more salient implications of the present study with respect to the importance of these social influences of the differential behaviors and experiences of prototype members are evaluated in the ensuing discussion. Perhaps the most obvious conclusion that may be drawn in this regard is concerned with the nature and importance of the postcollege years. Until the time of college graduation, prototype members were clustered in the academic world. After college graduation, they were thrust into the adult social and occupational world. It appears that, during this period, they began sorting themselves into adult roles and preparing themselves for the central tasks of adulthood, including establishing a career and family. Consequently, the immediate postcollege years seemed to reflect a period of metamorphosis, and there was not necessarily a high degree of overlap between the composite prototypes' differential behaviors and experiences on the PCEI 2/4 and PCEI 6/8 measures. An excellent example of this phenomenon may be found in the differential characteristics of the Competent Nurturers. During their initial postcollege period, they held jobs and were planning to marry; however, their family orientation did not become apparent until 6 to 8 years after their graduation. Another example of his phenomenon may be found in the fact that a number of certain composite prototypes, such as the Constrained Careerists, appeared to do relatively well occupationally during the first few years following graduation, in part because the members of other composite prototypes who would later become more successful were pursuing further education. This suggests that the initial postcollege years represent a unique developmental period associated with certain differential characteristics bound up in society's age-grading of behaviors and experiences.

Religious involvement has, at times, been viewed as a differential characteristic and, at times, as a social influence. Although there seems to be some truth in both these viewpoints, the present discussion focuses on religion as a social influence. A number of the composite prototypes were involved with religious organizations at different points in their lives. Yet, the reason for this involvement seemed to vary from prototype to prototype. Members of the Religious Copers prototype did not come from an especially religious background, but they became highly religious during their college years and maintained their religious involvement in their later lives as a means for adapting to a complex social world for which their background and personal characteristics had not prepared them. The Ineffectual Authoritarians became highly involved with religious organizations during college apparently as a mechanism for structuring their lives in the ambivalent college environment. However, they dropped their involvement in later years. The Competent Nurturers came from a religious family background and remained religious because such involvement was conjoint with a traditional nurturant orientation. These observations suggest that different kinds of individuals may become involved with the same activity for very different reasons and that the timing, nature, and consequences of this involvement will be tied to the unique characteristics of the individuals and their needs at their current stage of development.

Another illustration of this phenomenon may be found in collegiate fraternity and sorority involvement. It was found that both the Virile Extraverts and Fortunate Approval Seekers exhibited the stereotypical pattern of collegiate behaviors and experiences among fraternity members, an observation that was confirmed by the tendency of members of both these composite prototypes to be assigned to the CEI Fraternity Member prototype. Yet fraternity membership for the Virile Extraverts seemed to be a natural extension of their earlier pattern of extraverted social engagement and did not involve any substantial changes in their general pattern of behaviors and experiences. However, the Fortunate Approval Seekers were withdrawn and socially ineffective individuals in adolescence who joined fraternities in a search for approval. This active conformity to the demands of the college environment eventually led to a marked change and a new social orientation that was maintained in later years. Thus, it appears that the influence of institutional involvement on the course of an individual's life depends on the characteristics and concerns brought to this situation in the first place.

Some substantial support for this hypotheses may be obtained by examining the influence of the broader collegiate environment on the differential characteristics of the composite prototypes both before and after college. Generally, it was found that members of composite prototypes who came from good family environments were not markedly effected by their collegiate experiences in the sense that they resulted in a pronounced shift in their earlier pattern of differential characteristics. These individuals, including the Unscathed Adjusters, Channelled Concrete Achievers, Competent Nurturers, and Virile Extraverts, among others, seemed to be on a stable developmental trajectory during this period, and college served only as a vehicle for fulfilling the goals, plans, and patterns that had been laid out earlier. Among individuals who came from a "bad" or difficult family environment, however, college experiences exerted a profound effect on the course of their later lives and resulted in marked changes. These changes might be for either better or worse, and they appeared to occur in one of two ways. First, a number of these individuals became involved with one or more social organizations or relationships and employed them as mechanism for adaptation to their current environment. Second, some composite prototypes went through a period of rebellion that was associated with substantial self-expansion and led to some enduring changes in their differential characteristics.

One of the more significant institutions in the adult social world is marriage. Perhaps the most compelling illustration of the potential effects of marriage may be found in the differential characteristics of the Premature Conformists. These males married early as part of their accelerated movement into adult social roles, and when the pressure of early marriages was combined with a difficult early career, it led to extreme dissatisfaction with their marriages, jobs, and general situations. The members of composite prototypes manifesting traditional values who tended to marry late, such as the Unscathed Adjustors, Channelled Concrete Achievers, and Virile Extraverts, were more likely to be happy in their marriages. These results suggest that a lack of preparation for engagement in complex social situations may lead to negative outcomes.

Another common thread running through the composite prototypes may be found in the individual's apparent reasons for marriage and their implications for later family life. Examination of the composite prototypes' differential characteristics suggested that certain kinds of individuals attempted to employ marriage as means for coping with life. For instance, the Discontented Male Dependents appeared to enter marriage as a source of security, whereas the Ineffectual Authoritarians seemed to employ marriage as a means for structuring their lives within traditional role demands. Typically, the members of composite prototypes who married for reasons of this sort tended to find their marriages unsatisfying. Another source of marital difficulties appeared to stem from the nature of the individual's early family background. It was noted earlier that the members of certain composite prototypes, including the Withdrawn Effeminates and the Paternal Reactives, identified with the cross-sex parent. Unsurprisingly, it was found that members of these composite prototypes tended to marry late or not at all and to report that they tended to be unhappy in their marriages if they had married. On the other hand, it was found that the members of composite prototypes who had accepted traditional sex roles, such as the Virile Extraverts, Competent Nurturers, and Unscathed Adjustors, tended to choose a partner who expressed similar characteristics and indicated that they were satisfied with their marriages. These results suggest that early experiences may play an important role in preparing the individual for future social activities by influencing the emergence of the relevant skills, and that social structuring of early development may have a powerful impact on the course of individual development and later developmental outcomes.

One of the major social institutions that individuals must cope with in adulthood may be found in the domain of vocational endeavors. Because a number of PCEI items examined areas such as vocational choice, job satisfaction, and job success, it became possible to review the differential characteristics of the composite prototypes in order to draw some comparative conclusions in this regard. One of the more straightforward implications of this data was that individuals were likely to employ job-search strategies that were congruent with their broader pattern of differential characteristics. For instance, the Social Copers indicated that personal contacts helped them find their first jobs, whereas the Isolated Intellectuals indicated that they used university-sponsored job-search activities. Moreover, the reasons that individuals chose their first jobs also appeared to be dependent on the composite prototypes' broader pattern of differential behavior and experiences. This point is illustrated by the fact that the Ineffectual Authoritarians considered security an important consideration in choosing their first jobs, whereas members of the Upwardly Mobile Individuals prototype chose their first jobs on the basis of opportunities for advancement. Taken as a whole, these two trends suggest that individuals will tend to employ environmental resources in the manner that is most likely to be effective, given their previous developmental histories, resulting in a directed and selective job search.

In examining the differential characteristics of the composite prototypes, it was also found that a variety of considerations influenced occupational success. Perhaps the most central of these influences are manifest in the fact that individuals who had a clear idea of the kind of jobs they wanted and had prepared themselves for those jobs tended to be more successful on their jobs in terms of income and promotion rates than those who had not displayed these characteristics. The differential characteristics of the Social Manipulators and Channeled Concrete Achievers provide an excellent illustration of this phenomenon. However, clear-cut goals and preparations appeared more important for individuals entering complex technical and professional occupations. Prototypes such as the Virile Extraverts and the Upwardly Mobile Individuals did not explicitly prepare themselves for the world of work. However, they eventually fell into business jobs that were in line with their interests and abilities, and they were quite successful in them. Not only did the importance of explicit preparation vary with occupation field, but the requisite abilities and skills for job success appeared to vary by field. For instance, it was found that social skills were important to the occupational success of composite prototypes such as the Virile Extraverts or the Expansive Compensators entering business occupations. However, the performance of the Unconventional Successes on their professional jobs seemed linked to their verbal abilities, whereas the success of the Analytical Adaptors in science seemed tied to their predisposition towards independent thought and their careful development of scientific skills. This suggests that the amount of preparation and the specific nature of the skills that the individual must develop for occupational success varied with the particular nature of the field that the individuals selected.

Occupational success appeared to be closely tied to motivational factors. Both the Expansive Compensators and the Orphaned Adaptors were highly successful in their careers. However, they also displayed a high degree of career motivation in their reports that, despite being satisfied with their initial jobs, they planned to leave them in the near future. A similar phenomenon was evidenced in the differential characteristics of the Competent Nurturers. Despite their substantial intellectual ability and despite having found jobs for which they had prepared, these females were not highly successful occupationally, apparently due to their focus on establishing a traditional family life rather than career accomplishment. In the case of a number of other composite prototypes, such as the Unscathed Adjustors, it was also evident that career motivation and success was limited by an overriding concern with family matters. These results suggest that differential career success is, to some extent, dependent on the individual's values and conscious choices, which are in turn determined to some extent by the individual's background.

Unsurprisingly, it was found that composite prototypes whose members were likely to focus on family concerns were more likely to be satisfied with lower-level jobs. This phenomenon was apparent in the differential characteristics of the Religious Copers and the Competent Nurturers. Among the composite prototypes concerned with occupational success, it appeared necessary to maintain a clear distinction between job and occupational satisfaction. The differential characteristics of the composite prototypes, including the Premature Conformists, Female Eunuchs, Analytical Adaptors, and Unconventional Successes, indicated that dissatisfaction with occupation was likely to have a far greater negative impact on the course of an individual's life than dissatisfaction with immediate working conditions. This result suggests that broader, more nebulous environmental characteristics that are capable of influencing the individual's future may be as important, if not more important, than specific situational exposure with respect to the course of individual development. Although it is unclear exactly what kind of processes would give rise to this phenomenon, the preceeding hypothesis does find some support in the fact that the effects of occupational dissatisfaction, particularly among composite prototypes concerned with occupational success, appeared to be quite diffuse and capable of affecting a number of different aspects of their adult lives, although this did not hold for job dissatisfaction.

CONCEPTUAL COMPARISONS

The preceding section has examined the differential characteristics of the composite prototypes with respect to a limited number of content areas. Although the results obtained in this analysis are of some importance in their own right, there can be little doubt that they also have a number of conceptual or theoretical implications. Unfortunately, these results do not allow any systematic examination of these theoretical issues. In order to address some of the more important conceptual areas that have arisen in the course of the present investigation, an attempt was made to review the differential characteristics with respect to a limited set of critical theoretical questions. Broadly speaking, an attempt was made to carry out the review with respect to three general theoretical topics: (a) the implication of the organism–environment interchange; (b) the emergence of individuality over time, and (c) the nature of continuity and change in the course of individual development. In the ensuing discussion an attempt will be made to review each of these content areas in turn.

Organism–Environment Interchanges

In examining the differential characteristics of the composite prototypes, it rapidly became apparent that the nature of individuality and individual development was bound up in an interchange between the individual and the environment. Because various aspects of this interchange are of some importance to our conceptions of the nature of individuality, it seems germane to examine this interchange in terms of the differential characteristics of the composite prototypes.

Broadly speaking, by stating that the nature of human individuality is dependent on an ongoing, multifaceted interchange between the characteristics of the individual and the environment, it is implied that the nature, expression, and meaning of human individuality will be modified by the environment, and that the activities of the individual will, in turn, modify the environment. Moreover, the ongoing progressive nature of this interchange should lead to a systematic, though complex, pattern of differential development. The value of these principles in understanding the ontogeny of the composite prototypes and the emergence of differential characteristics over time is aptly illustrated in the development of the Unconventional Successes. Members of this composite prototype came from the cold, harsh background characteristics of a "bad" family environment. Correspondingly, they displayed the social withdrawal and lack of motivation that are characteristics of individuals exposed to this environment. However, when this withdrawal was coupled with tendermindedness, cognitive values, and verbal ability, it led to an involvement in solitary intellectual pursuits, which led to the emergence of a powerful verbal intellectual orientation. During college, this verbal intellectual orientation and rebellion against their family background led these females to adopt a Bohemian lifestyle, which encouraged self-expansion and the emergence of social skills and served to reinforce their verbal intellectual orientation. Subsequently, these experiences formed the basis for the active intellectual lifestyle that these females effectively employed in young adulthood. Similarly, members of the male Fortunate Approval Seekers prototype were raised in a harsh family environment, although it was one that encouraged a conservative orientation and a desire for social approval. As a result, they entered fraternities and actively conformed to the demands of the environment by exercising and socializing, trends that were not apparent during adolescence. These experiences led to the emergence of a new set of interests and social skills, which were maintained in their later lives and provided a basis for many activities. Although other examples of this sort could be cited, the foregoing examples do provide evidence that indicates that individual development proceeds as a result of an ongoing interchange between the characteristics of the individual and the broader environment.

The importance of the ongoing, multifaceted interchange in the emergence of human individuality has a number of salient implications for our conception of the phenomenon, which was borne out in the differential characteristics of the composite prototypes. One of these implications is concerned with the nature of differential experiences. Because the development of individuality is contingent on both the nature of the individuals and the nature of the situation, it is possible that the developmental implications of a common experience cannot be adequately defined apart from the particular kind of person undergoing this experience. Similarly, common behaviors may have very different meanings in terms of their developmental implications, depending on the existing characteristics of the individual and the situation in which they occur.

Another implication of the ongoing interchange between the individual and the environment is that the individual's selection of and subsequent exposure to different kinds of situations would both express significant aspects of individuality and affect the nature of individual development. In a number of ways, the differential characteristics of the composite prototypes illustrated the importance of situational selection. The existence and developmental importance of situational selection has a number of rather interesting implications. One of these implications is that certain differential characteristics might exert a control over the situations entered into by the members of a composite prototype and so affect the future course of individual development. Consistent selection of situations would lead to a consistent pattern of differential characteristics, although those characteristics might be expressed in different ways at different points in the individual's life. It should be noted that these preponderant controls or salience effects were not always positive in nature. As might be expected, salience effects were capable of distorting the normative relationships between standard differential constructs. This point is illustrated by the fact that, although substantial intellectual ability would lead to the normative expectation that the Competent Nurturers would be quite successful in their jobs, this expectation was not borne out in the data, due to prototype members' focus on nurturant activities rather than occupational success. Interestingly, for a given composite prototype, the composite summary description associated with the relevant preponderant control tended to produce an unusually large number of significant coefficients in the within-prototype correlational analyses. This phenomenon may be seen in the tendency of the Traditional Social Adjustment dimension to produce a large number of significant coefficients within the Unscathed Adjusters prototype. Not all of the composite prototypes exhibited salience effects of this sort, and different composite prototypes did not share common preponderant controls.

Although the salience effects exhibited by a composite prototype in the selection of situations appeared to be of some importance with respect to the nature of individual development, it was possible for the situations that individuals enter to result in marked changes in the nature of this differential behavior when coupled with the other characteristics of prototype members. Any substantial modification in the overall pattern of the composite prototypes' differential characteristics would occur in a fashion that was systematically related to past behaviors and experiences as well as existing differential characteristics.

Because the individual's interchange with the surrounding environment is likely to be a multifaceted event, it is possible that different kinds of individuals will express even a common underlying characteristic in different ways in a common environment due to the operation of a number of other differential characteristics. In other words, it is possible that the complex and selective nature of human individuality and this ongoing interchange may lead to a selective expression of common differential characteristics. An excellent illustration of this selective expression phenomenon may be found in our earlier discussions of achievement motivation and desire for approval.

If it is granted that individuals develop and express their differential characteristics in relation to the broader environment and its component situations, then the existence of the ongoing interchange between the individual and the environment has some further important implications. Clearly, individuals are not exposed to a common set of situational influences over the course of their development, and these differences in situational exposure are not only a matter of degree but may also be a matter of kind. A case in point may be found in fraternity or sorority involvement, which is capable of exerting a profound effect on the developmental pathways followed by the member of certain composite prototypes and which entails an absolute distinction in the sense that the individual either is or is not a member of a fraternity or sorority. Because individuals may be exposed to different situations, and individuality develops through interchange with these situations, it is quite possible that qualitative differences will emerge among individuals in the course of their development. The existence of these qualitative differences was amply demonstrated in the differential characteristics of the composite prototypes, as well as in the within-prototypes correlation analyses discussed earlier.

An additional implication of the influence of this ongoing interchange and the nature of individual development pertains to the uniqueness of individuals and the frequency with which individuals follow alternative developmental paths. Obviously, no two individuals come into the world with identical characteristics, nor will they ever be exposed to an identical set of situations. Thus, in an absolute sense, it is clear that each individual is unique by virtue of the organism–environment interchange and its role in individual development. On the other hand, it is also true that situations do not occur in a random fashion but are structured by society and the broader environment and that occurrence of one situation produces the occurrence of other situations. Moreover, some situations and situational experiences are more likely to occur than others. When this systematic aspect of situational exposure is coupled with the importance of situational interchange in the course of individual development, then it could be expected that, despite their uniqueness, some individuals would be more similar to each other than they are to other individuals, due to their exposure to a common or similar set of situations. This would result in an alternative set of developmental paths. Due to the fact that some situational sequences are more likely to occur than others, some of these paths should be followed more frequently than others. These hypotheses, in turn, explain why multiple composite prototypes were obtained in the present investigation, and why the size of the prototypes displayed a close correspondence to the nature of the sample being examined in the present investigation.

Although the differential characteristics of the composite prototypes point to the importance of the organism environment in understanding the nature of individuality and individual development, the differential characteristics of the composite prototypes also had some implications for our conceptions of the nature of this interchange. A review of the differential characteristics of the composite prototypes indicated that individuality and individual development as it is manifest in this interchange is a complex event that occurs at a variety of levels. The importance of passive organism–environment interchanges for individual development may be seen during adolescence in the differential characteristics of those individuals raised in bad family environment. Here, the presence of a negative family environment led to a general social withdrawal that was no longer apparent when prototype members had been removed from this environment. Reactive interchanges with the environment also appeared to have some effects on the development and experiences of human individuality. An excellent illustration of this form of interchange may be found in the differential characteristics of the Religious Copers. Exposure to a more complex environment in college than the Religious Copers could handle, given their simplicity and intellectual limitations, led to a retreat into organized religion that was maintained in later years, due to the continuing complexity of their environments.

In addition to the influence of these rather simplistic forms of interchange, it was also found that the more complex, active, and interactive forms of interchange could influence the nature of the differential characteristics expressed by the composite prototypes. Interactive interchanges, where the individual and the environment effect each other simultaneously, were manifest in the differential characteristics of nearly all of the composite prototypes. However, the differential characteristics of the Unscathed Adjusters provide a particularly effective illustration of the phenomenon. The Unscathed Adjusters tended to conform to and exploit the traditional feminine role. Yet this prepared them to change and led to changes in a number of differential behaviors as age-graded sex-role expectations changed. These behaviors subsequently led to changes in various aspects of their environment, such as their orientation towards home and family rather than their jobs after marriage, along with the concommittant behavioral changes.

Finally, the importance of the individual's active interchange with the environment in order to obtain specific goals was amply illustrated in the differential characteristics of the composite prototypes. For instance, the Fortunate Approval Seekers actively sought fraternity membership to satisfy their desires for social approval, and once admitted, they actively conformed to the requirements of these organizations by dating and exercising to insure that they obtained approval. Exposure to this aspect of the college environment and the resulting change in their behavior, in time, led to dramatic changes in their differential characteristics, influencing their later course of development. In sum, it appears that these active and interactive forms of interchange, particularly when coupled with a structured environment, can exert a profound effect in the course of individual development.

Emergence of Individuality

The preceding section has elaborated on the importance, complexity, and implications of the ongoing organism–environment interchange for the understanding of individuality and individual development. However, this discussion has not focused to any great extent on the ongoing nature of this interchange, in part because this leads to a concern with the emergence of individuality over time. Because the composite prototypes contain a description of individuality over time and in a number of developmental periods, it should be possible to construct the differential characteristics of the composite prototypes as they emerge over time in order to draw some conclusions concerning the nature of human development. In the ensuing discussion, an attempt is made to lay out some of the developmental implications of the composite prototypes.

One of the most clear-cut implications of the differential characteristics of the composite prototypes was that individual development appeared to be an ongoing phenomenon that did not cease in adolescence or at the time of college graduation. Even a cursory review of the differential characteristics of the composite prototypes indicated that individuals continued to change in response to changing environmental demands, as might be expected given the fundamental importance and the ongoing nature of the organism–environment interchange on individual development. For instance, both the Constrained Careerists and the Upwardly Mobile Individuals exhibited some pronounced changes in their pattern of differential behaviors and experiences between college and young adulthood. It is of note that nearly all of the composite prototypes displayed at least a few fundamental changes in their pattern of differential behaviors and experiences during the course of the present study.

As was noted earlier, the age-grading of behavior and experiences imposed upon the individual by the broader culture leads to changes in the nature of the situations that the individual is likely to be exposed to, the behavior that is required in these situations, and the situations that the individual can feasibly decide to enter. Thus, culturally imposed shifts may lead to the emergence of distinct developmental periods in the course of individuals' lives. Substantial support for this hypotheses may be obtained simply by examining the nature of the shifts occurring in the differential characteristics of the composite prototypes in the different assessments. For instance, the Constrained Careerists dropped their collegiate rebellion and began to concentrate on their jobs during the postcollege years. Of course, this example also suggests that, although there may be some distinct periods in the course of individuals' lives, the particular nature of any changes they induce and the individuals' behavior in them are likely to depend on the broader pattern of the individuals' past behavior and experiences.

Another phenomenon that was observed in reviewing the differential characteristics of the composite prototypes was that, during a given developmental period, certain experiences could lead to a common set of outcomes for all individuals who were the members of the prototypes that were exposed to these experiences. This was illustrated by the fact that members of all the composite prototypes exposed to a bad family environment displayed signs of social withdrawal, social ineffectiveness, and poor adjustment during adolescence. However, when removed from this environment, these trends might or might not be continued, depending on the broader characteristics of the composite prototypes and their later experiences in the college environment. This phenomenon was illustrated by the sociality of the Constrained Careerists and Unconventional Successes during their college years, along with the continued social ineffectiveness and poor adjustment of the Ineffectual Authoritarians. This implies that, although certain environmental influences may lead to some unitary effects in certain developmental periods, the resulting differential characteristics are not necessarily constant over time.

In examining the differential characteristics of the composite prototypes who displayed a substantial involvement with religion, another interesting finding emerged. This analyses indicated that religious involvement had a very different meaning for members of the composite prototypes, depending on the particular developmental period in which it emerged. Among the composite prototypes who had not displayed signs of religious involvement prior to college entry and became highly involved with religion during college, such as the Religious Copers and the Ineffectual Authoritarians, this form of behavior seemed to reflect a mechanism for coping with a complex and ambivalent college environment, which they were ill-prepared to deal with, rather than some set of intrinsic religious values. In later years, this trend might or might not be maintained, depending on whether or not religion continued to serve as an effective coping mechanism for the individuals. On the other hand, the members of composite prototypes who were involved with religion during adolescence and came from religious families tended to manifest religious values and maintain their religious values throughout their lives. When it is borne in mind that the collegiate religious behavior of both these groups of individual prototypes was identical in college, this suggests that the meaning and developmental importance of differential behavior may vary with the period and conditions in which it emerged.

The existence of this trend is closely related to another developmental phenomenon that was identified in reviewing the differential characteristics of the composite prototypes. As was noted earlier, both the Virile Extraverts and the Fortunate Approval Seekers displayed a nearly identical pattern of differential behavior and experiences during their college years that was oriented around the classic fraternity stereotype. Nevertheless, these two composite prototypes displayed very different patterns of antecedent and consequent behaviors and experiences as may be seen in the adolescent withdrawal of the Fortunate Approval Seekers and the adolescent sociability of the Virile Extraverts. These differential antecedents and consequents of collegiate fraternity involvement indicate that their common behavior during the college years had markedly different meanings. This phenomenon entailing the expression of a common pattern of behavior and experiences in one developmental period but not over time has been labeled *local convergence*. The existence of this local convergence phenomenon suggests that it may only be possible to formulate a fully adequate description of individuality on a cross time or developmental basis because it may well be impossible to discriminate between certain individuals on the basis of information gathered at a single point in time.

A corollary of the local convergence phenomenon may be found in the potential divergence of the members of a composite prototype with respect to their likeness and experiences at a single point in time. Their local divergence might be attributed to the fact that a given developmental period may provide multiple answers for the expression of an underlying set of differential characteristics all of which have similar implications for later development. Alternatively, local divergence might arise as a result of the fact that certain behaviors and experiences occurring in a developmental period might be of little importance with respect to the emergence of or change in the individuals broader pattern of differential characteristics. One implication of this local divergence is that the members of a composite prototype would tend to display sample typical behaviors during a developmental period of this sort. An example of this trend may be found in the differential characteristics of the Analytical Adapters during their college years. Earlier, it was pointed out that these individuals were well differentiated from the sample as a whole during adolescence and young adulthood but tended to display sample typical behaviors and experiences during the college years. This result might be traced to the observation that, due to their occupational focus and the multiple ways in which their orientation towards independent thought could be expressed in a college environment, prototype members entered a period of local divergence. Of course, the existence of this local divergence phenomenon, like the local convergence phenomenon, suggests that an adequate definition of individuality can only be formulated on a cross-time basis. However, it should also be noted that the nature and existence of local divergence suggests that the behavior and experiences occuring in certain developmental periods may be more important in shaping the consistencies in individuals lives than those occurring in other developmental periods for a certain kind of individual.

Another interesting observation arose in the course of contrasting the composite prototypes differential characteristics in different developmental periods. Apparently, across the composite prototypes, common differential characteristics did not necessarily emerge in a constant fashion or with similar timing. For instance, achievement motivation appeared to emerge in college among members of the Expansive Compensators, Orphaned Adaptors, and Unconventional Successes prototypes, yet the same characteristic had emerged by the time of adolescence among the members of composite prototypes such as the Channelled Concrete Achievers and the Virile Extraverts. Similarly, it was found that the Social Manipulators and the Virile Extraverts, among others, manifested substantial social skills in adolescence, whereas the Orphaned Adapters and the Fortunate Approval Seekers did not display these skills until their college years. Thus, it appears that common differential characteristics may arise in different developmental periods among different individuals. This variability in the development of differential characteristics seems to be due to the fact that the differing backgrounds of the members of the composite prototypes demanded different processes to arrive at the same end state and so different experiences, most likely to occur in different developmental periods, were required to spur the emergence of these differential characteristics. Some support for this hypothesis may be found in the nature of the factors underlying the variable emergence of achievement motivation. Composite prototypes from a bad family background could not develop achievement motivation through parental warmth, independence training and reinforcement; rather it necessarily arose through a different set of experiences occuring at a later point in time. Thus, it was possible for composite prototypes from a good family background to express achievement motivation in adolescence, whereas individuals from a bad family environment could express this characteristic only after they had been removed from this environment and compensation could occur. If one grants the validity of this hypothesis, then suggests that an individual's failure to express a given differential characteristic at one point in their lives may or may not have salient implications for later behaviors and experiences. Obviously, this is a consideration that should be given some consideration in studies of developmental change because a lack of prediction may reflect little more than variable timing in the emergence of differential characteristics.

A phenomenon closely related to variable timing in the development of differential characteristics may be found in the overall rate of individual development. Of course any discussion of rate must be oriented around some common end point, and in the discussion the acceptance of adult social roles serves as the end point. Typically, it was found that the members of composite prototypes, such as the Premature Conformists and the Insecure Bohemians, who for one reason or another rapidly moved into adult social roles, did not fare well in young adulthood. Apparently, this speeded maturation did not allow these individuals sufficient time to develop the skills they would need to handle the necessary complexity and difficulty of these roles. On the other hand, slow maturation, such as that exhibited by the Upwardly Mobile Individuals, did not necessarily lead to good or bad outcomes. These results may be taken as providing some support for the foregoing hypotheses in the sense that slow maturation might provide the requisite skills although failure to conform to age grading might also lead to some difficulties. Although slow maturation did not necessarily lead to poor outcomes for the individual, it was found that the members of composite prototypes whose developmental pattern of behaviors and experiences conformed with the timing and sequence of age typical sex-role expectations in the different developmental periods generally fared better than those individuals whose development did not conform to these expectations in terms of overall adjustment.

Comparison of the differential characteristics of the composite prototypes also lead to the identification of another phenomenon bound up in the emergence of individuality over time. It appeared that the previous differential behaviors and experiences of certain composite prototypes made developmental change far more likely for the members of some prototypes than others during certain developmental periods. An example of this phenomenon may be obtained by examining the impact of college life in the developmental paths followed by the composite prototypes. Those composite prototypes who came from bad family environments and had been through a difficult, withdrawn adolescence such as the Unconventional Successes, Orphaned Adapters, Constrained Careerists, and Fortunate Approval Seekers, all displayed a marked departure from the pattern of adolescent behavior and experiences during their college years. Although the particular nature of this change from a socially withdrawn pattern of behavior might entail either rebellion or traditional social involvement, depending on the background of the particular prototype at hand, it appears that the members of composite prototypes coming from these negative backgrounds were especially likely to change during college years. Regardless of the specific reasons for the significance of this period, these results suggest that certain developmental periods are likely to constitute sensitive periods for individuals with certain backgrounds in which interchange with the environment is capable of inducing marked shifts in the general pattern of an individual's differential characteristics.

The preceeding discussion of sensitive periods points to another important aspect of individual development that emerged in our review of the composite prototypes differential characteristics. Here we refer to the fact that individual development appears to be a cumulative phenomenon. This statement is intended to imply the fact that individual development and developmental change does not occur in a random fashion but is systematically related to the individual's prior characteristics. The foregoing discussion of sensitive periods provides an excellent illustration of this principle. Although the events occurring in this sensitive period were capable of inducing a marked change in the pattern of the differential characteristics exhibited by certain composite prototypes, the timing of these sensitive periods, the events likely to induce change and the nature of the observed change were all internally tied to the individual's developmental history.

The cumulative nature of individual development suggests that individuals change and develop in relation to their prior pattern of differential behavior and experiences, yet it does not follow from this statement that individual development is necessarily a uniformly progressive phenomenon. Rather, a review of the differential characteristics of the composite prototypes suggested that individual development involved both gains and losses. One example of this postulate may be found in the differential characteristics of the Fortunate Approval Seekers. These males were somewhat intellectually oriented during their adolescence, were socially withdrawn and displayed little interest in athletics. However, their conformity to the demands of the collegiate fraternity environment led them to develop themselves physically and display an overt interest in sports, yet at the same time, they dropped their earlier interests in intellectual pursuits. In their later lives they continued to display an interest in sports, but not intellectual pursuits. Thus, their collegiate development involved both gains and losses.

Not only did the differential characteristics of the composite prototypes suggest that individual development involved certain gains and losses, they also suggested that individual development involved a simultaneous process of self-limitation and self-expansion. The composite prototypes generally did not engage in all those activities they might profit by in a given developmental period; instead they appeared to reject certain feasible activities and behaviors while engaging in others. The operation of this self-limitation phenomenon was manifest in the differential characteristics of the Competent Nurturers who appeared to reject occupational success in favor of home and family. Similarly, members of the composite prototype labeled Female Eunuchs tended to reject activities traditionally reserved for males despite their interest in them. Although other examples of the importance of self-limitation in individual development could be cited, the foregoing examples serve to illustrate certain points. First, self-limitation may be either beneficial or detrimental with respect to its developmental outcomes, depending on the nature of both the individual and the situation that was rejected. Second, the particular kind of self-limitation exhibited by an individual is likely to be highly dependent on the nature of his or her past behaviors and experiences. Finally, some form of self-limitation seems to be necessary in individual development because individuals have neither the time nor resources to engage in all possible activities. Thus, the nature of these self-limiting chances may reflect an important component of individuality.

On the other hand, there can be little doubt that development requires individuals to enter a variety of novel situations. Hence, it is not especially surprising that self-expansion would also appear to be of some importance in individual development. An excellent example of the ben-

eficial effects of self-expansion may be found in the differential characteristics of the Expansive Compensators who dramatically expanded the
number of different activities they engaged in during their college years
to their later advantage. However, the self-expansion apparent in the
Premature Conformists' early marriage serves to suggest that inappropriate expansion may have disasterous consequence. Although these
examples suggest that self-expansion may have both good and bad effects, they also suggest that self-expansion is most likely to be beneficial
when the individual has had adequate preparation.

There are four additional points with respect to self-limitation and
self-expansion that should be noted. First, both self-limitation and self-
expansion appear to be systematic processes in the sense that the particular forms of limitation and expansion exhibited by a composite prototype
appeared to be linked to the previous pattern of differential behavior
and experiences. Thus, self-limitation and self-expansion represent aspects of the cumulative nature of development. Second, optimal developmental outcomes appeared to be tied to appropriate self-limitation
and self-expansion with respect to the broader pattern of the composite
prototype differential characteristics. Third, the nature of favorable or
unfavorable self-limitation and self-expansion varied with the particular
developmental period under consideration along with the demands it
made and the opportunities it presented for a particular kind of individual. Finally, although there is no evidence in this regard, it seems
likely that these two processes must be carefully balanced for optimal
individual development.

Underlying self-limitation and self-expansion is a selection of the
kinds of situations in which an individual will engage. Earlier, it was
pointed out that the individual's choice of situations can play an important role in individual development. However, when individuality is explicitly considered in a developmental context, it becomes apparent that
this situational selection does not occur in an unrestrained fashion. The
situations an individual may enter at different points in their lives are
restricted by the age grading of behavior. This constraint is likely to
channel the course of individual development and, when coupled with
developmental discontinuities in the situations individuals are exposed
to, it may lead to dramatic shifts in the individual's overt behavior and
experiences. Then hypotheses finds some support in the shifts on differential behavior and experiences exhibited by the composite prototypes as
they moved across developmental periods. However, due to the cumulative nature of development, and the availability of at least some alternatives, these changes were also systematically related to the individual's
past behaviors and experiences.

Of course, the foregoing paragraph suggests that individual development over time is channelled by society, and it is also clear that heredity exerts some influence in this channelling process and the nature of individual development. In the context of this study, the source of evidence pointing to the impact of these social and biological structuring influences may be found by contrasting the differential characteristics of the male and female composite prototypes because these sex differences are a likely reflection of both biological and social functions acting to structure the nature of individual development. Comparisons of the male and female composite prototypes' characteristic developmental paths in fact underscored the importance of structuring influences of this sort. On a general level it was apparent that, although a larger number of female developmental paths were identified, most of the female members of the longitudinal sample were flowing through a smaller number of very large composite prototypes than was the case in the male sample. Generally, the high-flow composite prototypes identified in the female sample reflected variations on a traditional sex role orientation, whereas the low-flow composite prototypes tended to reflect a nontraditional role orientation. These results seem to reflect a structuring of female development by social sex-role expectations, and it is of note that the male composite prototypes did not appear to be free of this phenomenon, although its effects were less readily apparent. On a more microscopic level it was found that the male composite prototypes were somewhat more likely to be differentiated from each other on the basis of occupational and educational considerations, whereas the female composite prototypes were somewhat more likely to be differentiated from each other in terms of social behavior and family concerns. Again this result seems to reflect a social or biological structuring of the developmental paths that may be followed by individuals. It is interesting to note in this regard that the differential characteristics of the composite prototypes indicated that other variables of this sort, such as parental socioeconomic status, could exert a similar structuring effect under certain conditions, although their influence appeared far less pervasive.

One background characteristic that was also found to have a profound impact on the course of individual development was found in the individual's early family environment. The impact of family background on the ontogeny of the composite prototypes' differential characteristics was demonstrated in the earlier discussion of achievement motivation and adolescent adjustment. However, in a qualitative sense, family background appeared to have a much wider and more diffuse effect on the course of individual development. Although the effects of these experiences was complicated and diluted by the ongoing interchange between the individual and the environment, they could often impinge upon the individual's later behavior and experience. For instance, the Paternal

Reactives' marriages appeared markedly effected by the nature of the relationship between these females and their fathers, whereas the Orphaned Adapters' career choices seemed closely tied to the nature of their family background. Moreover, the Ineffectual Authoritarians highly authoritarian lifestyles and the Competent Nurturers' focus on achievement in the nurturant activities of home, family, community, and religion appeared to be rooted in the tendency of their parents to display similar characteristics and their apparent identification with the same-sex parent. Although it is difficult to specify the mechanisms leading to these effects, it appears that family background can have a critical, although a complex and diffuse, effect on the course of individual development.

Examination of the impact of family background on the course of individual development revealed another phenomenon that is noteworthy in any attempt to understand individuality and human development. This phenomenon was manifest in the relationship between marital satisfaction and identification with the cross-sex parent. Member of composite prototypes, such as the Paternal Reactives and the Withdrawn Effeminates, who identified with their cross-sex parent, were less likely than most to marry and were more likely than most to be dissatisfied with their marriages. This suggests that these early experiences could have a marked effect on later social relationships in young adulthood. Interestingly, in the intervening years no clear cut consequents of their background emerged that generalized beyond a given composite prototype. Thus, it appears that some early experiences among certain kinds of individuals may exhibit a sleeper effect of sorts. Differential characteristics developed in earlier periods of an individual's life lie dormant until the individual is faced with a characteristic-relevant situation in later years, and at this time this characteristic and background influence might suddenly exert a profound effect on the course of individual development. More generally, the potential existence of these sleeper effects, like many of the other phenomena discussed earlier, suggests that predictive relationships may vary in a complex fashion across developmental periods as well as across composite prototypes.

Continuity and Change

Historically, one of the most important issues in studies concerned with human development and the emergence of individuality over time has been the nature, level, and amount of consistency or change exhibited by individuals as they moved through their lives. Although the concept of consistency is not necessarily synonymous with stability, over the years a great deal of attention has been devoted to establishing the degree of stability exhibited by various differential characteristics. Typically, stability studies have attempted to establish the extent to which the same individuals manifest a given quality to the same degree across developmental periods. Given the fact that each assessment utilized a different set of age-specific indicators, it was difficult to address this issue in any direct fashion within the context of the present study. Nevertheless, it was possible to gather some indirect information in this regard by reviewing differential indicators, such as those associated with religious involvement, which were included in all three assessments.

Even a cursory inspection of scores on these common indicators indicated that the stability of differential characteristics was a limited phenomenon specific to the composite prototype under consideration. A case in point was found in the religious involvement of the Competent Nurturers, the Religious Copers, and the Ineffectual Authoritarians. The Competent Nurturers displayed a high degree of religious involvement in all of the assessments and appeared to come from a religious family. On the other hand, the Religious Copers and the Ineffectual Authoritarians expressed heightened religious involvement during their college years despite the fact that their family background were not especially religious. In the later assessments, the Religious Copers continued to display a high degree of religious involvement while the Ineffectual Authoritarians became somewhat less religious than was typical of the sample as a whole.

The foregoing examples indicate that the stability of differential *behavioral* characteristics is highly dependent on both the quality being examined and the particular kind of individual under consideration. Moreover, when the interpretation applied to the developmental paths followed by these composite prototypes is recalled, it becomes apparent that whether or not stability was observed was dependent on the broader pattern of the composite prototype's differential characteristics and its implications within the ongoing organism-environment interchange.

Of course, this suggests that the stability of differential behavioral characteristics is not a simple all or none phenomenon, but instead represents a highly complex manifestation of a particular form of individuality. The importance of environmental interchange in guiding the nature of the differential characteristics expressed for a composite was illustrated in a rather nebulous result which emerged in contrasting the differential characteristics of the composite prototypes. That is, in all instances in which the composite prototypes exhibited marked changes, it was found that the changes were the result of some change in the nature of the situations to which individuals were exposed. The situations were such that they constituted an empirically compelling impetus for change among the members of certain composite prototypes. One implication of this conclusion is that individuals do not actually change themselves by mere will but change only in relation to situational demands. Hence, individuals cannot exert direct control over the nature of developmental change, although they may exert some indirect control over the nature of the change by virtue of their ability to select the situations they will enter. The second implication of this conclusion is more problematic. If it is granted that individuals change and develop through interchange with various aspects of their environment, and it is recognized that the situations any environment presents to the individual vary considerably from time to time, then it is difficult to see how there could be any stability or consistency in differential behavior.

This brings to fore the question of the source, nature, and kind of consistency that was observed in the emergence of the composite prototypes' differential behaviors and experience over time. It is important to note in this regard that although the composite prototypes' differential characteristics did not display a high degree of phenotypic consistency or overt behavioral stability, they did display a substantial amount of genotypic or predictive consistency. The existence and importance of these complex yet systematic predictive relationships has been readily illustrated in the foregoing discussion. For instance, the impact of identification with the cross-sex parent on marital success and satisfaction provides one example of the existence and significance of these genotypic predictive relationships. Another example pointing to the significance of these genotypic consistencies may be found in the differential characteristics of the Social Manipulators where their concern with social control was expressed through their occupation in young adulthood, whereas during adolescence it was expressed through sociability and social leadership. Finally, the movement of the Fortunate Approval Seekers into fraternities represented a form of consistency despite the change induced in the sense that it was tied to their previous desire for approval. Thus, it appears that the differential behavior of the composite prototypes might be unstable, but through its linkage to past behaviors and experiences, it gave rise to systematic genotypic consistencies. However, the nature of these genotypic consistencies was often quite specific to the particular composite prototype under consideration.

In reviewing the differential characteristics of the composite prototypes it was found that genotypic consistencies appeared to emerge as a result of a two-part process. First, the cumulative nature of individual development and the individual's past behavior and experiences tended to condition the individual's preferences, desires, needs, understandings, and capacities. Characteristics of this sort appeared to condition the individual's selection of situations, perceptions of situations, and their feasible behavior within them. Second, subsequent interaction with these situations was channelled by these constraints, and so development was channelled in a systematic fashion. The fundamental importance of these processes in the emergence of genotypic consistencies was readily apparent in the differential characteristics of the composite prototypes.

Although it appears that this process and the genotypic consistencies it gave rise to provided some continuity in individual development despite changing situations, it is obvious that these genotypic consistencies were quite complex. When this observation is coupled with the substantial instability apparent in the composite prototypes' overt behavior in different developmental periods, it becomes difficult to determine how a label capable of summarizing the composite prototypes' differential characteristics over a relatively long period of time could be formulated. In part, this result seems to stem from the tendency of the composite prototypes' differential characteristics to organize themselves into a cohesive pattern that appeared to reflect a general adaptive style. For instance, the Unscathed Adjusters appeared to organize their differential behavior and experiences around age-typical sex role expectations that their background and personal characteristics had prepared them to accept and exploit. On the other hand, the Religious Copers were uncomplicated, intellectually limited individuals who appeared to organize their behavior and experiences around religion as a means for adapting to a complex social world. Because an adaptive style incorporated a variety of discrete behaviors and appeared intimately tied to the individual's selection of situations, it was not surprising that they emerged in their clearest form only when data were examined from a developmental perspective.

The utility of these adaptive styles in summarizing the composite prototypes' differential characteristics was enhanced by their tendency to be relatively stable once they had formed. In this sense, these adaptive styles represented a stable developmental trajectory around which behavioral and experiential variability occurred.

Despite the apparent stability of adaptive styles, which may be linked to their self-propagating nature derived from their tendency to direct situational selection and future interchange, many of the postulates discussed here would tend to suggest that these styles may not be absolutely immutable. Nevertheless, their tendency to control and in part be expressed through situational selection suggests that they will tend to remain stable once formed unless the individual is faced with a pervasive environmental change in which the exerting adaptive style is grossly inappropriate. Inspection of the composite prototypes' differential characteristics suggested that these adaptive styles tended to crystallize or take a self-propagating form rather early in an individual's life (Mumford, Wesley, & Shaffer, 1987). For many composite prototypes, such as Virile Extraverts, the Channelled Concrete Achievers, the Unscathed Adjusters, Competent Nurturers and the Social Manipulators, their characteristics adaptive styles appear to have crystallized by the time of adolescence. Unfortunately, the time frame employed in the present investigation did not allow for detailed examination of earlier periods and so prohibited an exact specification of the time of crystallization. The adaptive styles of all of the remaining prototypes had crystallized by the time of college graduation. Interestingly, those composite prototypes whose adaptive styles tended to crystallize relatively late, such as the Expansive Compensators, Fortunate Approval Seekers, Social Copers, and Unconventional Successes, all come from bad family environments where early crystallization of an adaptive style would have been detrimental. Moreover, with the exception of the Adaptive Successes, those members of the composite prototypes who were raised in a "bad" family environment and whose adaptive style crystallized relatively early while they remained in their environment tended to have a number of difficulties in later years. Some examples of this phenomenon may be found in the differential characteristics of the Ineffectual Authoritarians and the Disgruntled Male Dependents. It should be pointed out that Valliant (1977) and Valliant and McArthur (1972) have reached similar conclusions in a review of the life history of males between the ages of 18 and 50. Additionally, the patterns and potential consequences of crystallization within the composite prototypes suggests that, although complex and highly diffuse, the individual's early experiences in his or her immediate family may have profound consequences for the course of individual development.

CONCLUSION

The preceding sections have reviewed a number of observations and conclusions that emerged in comparing the differential characteristics of the composite prototypes with each other over four distinct developmental periods. Although the reader is well advised to bear in mind the selective nature of these comparisons, it seems fair to say that this effort did yield some important results. Perhaps the most significant conclusion to be drawn in the course of this comparative effort was that individual development is a highly complex phenomenon that is the product of a complex process. The process of individual development seems to continue throughout the individual's life, and it appears to be driven by an ongoing interchange between the organism and various aspects of the environmental surround. Moreover, because the content and outcome of this interchange appears to be dependent on the nature of the individual, individual development represents a cumulative and systematic phenomenon reflected in a complex set of genotypic consistencies rather than phenotypic consistencies in overt behavior.

In reviewing the differential characteristics of the composite prototypes, a number of somewhat less general conclusions emerged that are worthy of mention. For instance, it was found that similar bits of differential behavior may have very different meanings and identical experiences may have very different outcomes associated with them for different kinds of individuals. Further, it appeared that the individual's selection of situations played an important role in guiding development, but that developmental change was always tied to situational experiences. There also appeared to be distinct sensitive periods for certain kinds of individuals where change was especially likely to occur. Finally, it appeared that there were multiple qualitatively different developmental courses that might be followed by individuals in keeping with the principle of multipotentiality.

Although this chapter has covered a great deal of ground, there can be little doubt that further examination of the composite prototypes' differential characteristics would yield even more findings. Yet at this juncture it should be clear that the observations discussed in the preceeding paragraph have a number of implications for our conceptions of individuality as a natural phenomenon and for the technical strategies we employ in attempts to summarize and predict differential behavior and experiences. Thus, the following chapters attempt to draw out these implications and elaborate their practical importance for psychological research and theory.

Theoretical Implications: A General View of Human Individuality

In chapter 11, comparison of the composite prototypes' differential characteristics led to a number of conclusions concerning the nature of human individuality and individual development. These theoretical implications seem especially important because it appears that our more traditional conceptualizations of individual development may have difficulty in accounting for many of the observations that were laid out in the preceeding discussion. The ensuing discussion is an attempt to sketch out a general view of individuality and individual development that appears to be capable of subsuming the specific results obtained in examining the differential characteristics of the composite prototypes.

Despite the substantial support that was offered in previous chapters for the use of the composite prototypes in theory construction, there are some subtle problems associated with formulating a general theoretical view of individuality and individual development on the basis of the differential information obtained from the composite prototypes. One difficulty derives from our rather selective review of the results obtained in contrasting the composite prototypes' differential characteristics. Although this selectivity seemed necessary, given the sheer volume of the data base and the number of potential comparisons, it can also be argued that this selectivity could bias the conclusions drawn. Yet, to the extent that the composite prototypes provided a valid description of individuality, then it seems that even these selective results should be subject to explanation within an effective theoretical system.

A second problem with this approach involves the breadth of descriptive information being employed in theory development. Obviously, it is open to question whether the results obtained in a study examining only a limited range of differential behaviors and experiences over a limited portion of the individual's life span can provide a groundwork of sufficient breadth for a general theory construction effort. Despite the appropriateness of the criticism, it should be recognized that a concerted effort was made to employ a set of indicators capable of examining a wide variety of significant behaviors and experiences in multiple developmental periods. Further, it should be recognized that there has never been a point in the history of any science where all potentially relevant information could be considered in theory development. This theoretical effort should be viewed as one more attempt to enhance our understanding of individuality.

The composite prototypes provide one of the most general and valid summary descriptions of individuality and individual development available in the literature while incorporating the antecedent–consequent information that is critical in theory development. Additionally, a preliminary conception of human individuality based on this sound framework might have some value as a guide for future research. The following sections present a general theoretical view of individuality and individual development that appears to be capable of explaining the results obtained in reviewing the comparative data, as well as the differential characteristics of the composite prototypes.

A CONCEPTUAL VIEW OF INDIVIDUALITY

General Principles

The question, "Why does individuality exist?" is perhaps the most basic question that must be addressed in any attempt to formulate a general theory of individual development. Inherent in this question is a concern with the function of individuality in the broadest possible sense. Any attempt to answer a question of this scope is likely to be based on a variety of complex issues. Yet overriding these varied and complex issues is the simple fact that individuals are biological organisms and, like all biological organisms, must alternately be concerned with the survival of the species. Hence, if individuality actually serves some practical purposes, it seems reasonable to conclude that, in some way, it must help insure individual adaptation and the survival of the species as a whole.

It has long been recognized that individuality or individual differences may exist as one means for enhancing the adaptation of the species. In fact, individual differences among the members of a species provide a requisite background for evaluation and continual adaptation, because it is only through the existence of these differences that there is some basis for the operation of natural selection. Some indirect support for this hypothesis may be found in the very origination of individual existence. Fertilization in nearly all complex organisms is dependent on an exchange of parents' chromosomes, and the generality of this process seems linked to its ability to insure diversity as well as the value of diversity within a species under changing conditions and continued natural selection.

However, it should also be borne in mind that, unlike many single organisms, mankind is a species that exists in a social world where the survival of the individual and the evolution of the species are intrinsically tied to the survival of the groups or societies to which the individual belongs. As a result, it seems germane to ask whether individual differences have any substantial adaptive value for human society. Although many social planners may dolefully have wished that individuality did not exist, it is also clear that individual differences play an important role in the day to day workings of human society. The efficiency and mere existence of human social organizations is closely tied to an effective division of labor among the individuals participating in various social organizations. To the extent that the division of labor can capitalize on existing individual differences, then the efficiency of human social organizations would be enhanced.

Although individual differences may serve society in a variety of ways, it should be recognized that society and human individuality coexist in an ongoing state of tension. Although social organizations require individual differences for maximum efficiency, it is also true that the effective operation of social organizations requires a certain degree of conformity. More often than not the problem seems to be handled by the systematic channelling of individuality into those forms deemed acceptable by and necessary to society as a whole. It should also be noted that this social channelling does not occur in a manner that is completely independent of biological influences. Instead, it appears that through various mechanisms, including the age-grading of behavior and experiences, social and biological influences interact to produce an integrated pattern of individual development and human individuality.

Even bearing the foregoing caveats in mind, it appears that, on both a biological and social level, individuality serves the fundamental biological function of enhancing the adaptation of the species. If individuality serves as a basic biological function of this sort, then it seems reasonable to expect that the development and expression of human individuality would be subject to hereditary influences. There can be little doubt that hereditary influences play an important and pervasive role in the emergence of human individuality. The mechanism by which the species is propogated insures that each individual will draw genetic material from two sources and so express some unique characteristics. Moreover, it appears that this genetic background serves to establish certain salient differential characteristics, the personal resources and limitations available to the individual, as well as the general course of individual development between conception and adolescence where biological pre-programming plays a critical, and perhaps central, role.

Although heredity is likely to be an important influence on the expression of individuality and the course of individual development, it should not be assumed that human individuality and individual development are under complete hereditary control. Humans live in a wide range of environments and adaptation to, as well as survival in, their varied environments can not be insured through a complete pre-programming of behavior. Rather, the individual behavior and differential characteristics must be fine-tuned to environmental demands. Moreover, the variability of the human environment forces individuals to attempt to adapt to a number of novel situations over the course of their lives, and effective adaptation in these new situations can not be effectively insured through hereditary pre-programming only. Evolution appears to have handled these difficulties by building into mankind's heredity a high degree of flexability and a relatively slow process of maturation that permits behavior and differential characteristics to be shaped and fine-tuned by immediate environmental demands and permits developmental change with ongoing experience. As a result, environmental feedback must play an important role in determining the nature and expression of human individuality. Further, it seems likely that social influences will constitute an important aspect of this environmental feedback and that these and other environmental influences will interact with hereditary resources and limitations in determining the course of individual development.

The specific focus of the interaction bertween heredity and the environment may be found in the dynamic organism—environment interchange. When examining individuality and individual development in terms of the individual's behavior and experiences, it is obvious that hereditary influences can express themselves only as pre-existing characteristics that effect the individual's actions in any given situation. This interchange with the surrounding environment, in turn, will tend to modify both the characteristics of the individual and the characteristics of the situation. This interchange is a complex phenomena that may occur on a variety of levels, including: (a) passive interchange, or a simple oscillation of behavior in relation to environmental demands; (b) reactive interchange, or a change in the nature of expressed behavior in relation to environmental demands; (c) interactive interchange, or a joint change in the nature of both the individual and the situation due to individual action and environmental demands, and (d) active interchange, when the individual seeks certain goals and, in doing so, affects both personal characteristics and the environment. All of these forms of interchange will occur in an ongoing fashion and will result in systematic modifications in the individual's characteristics that are tied to the nature of the environment and the environment's adaptive demands. Thus, the process will modify and fine-tune the individual's existing characteristics to environmental demands. The fundamental importance of this ongoing organism–environment interchange and some of its many implications for the course of individual development were outlined in our earlier discussion of the results obtained in contrasting the differential characteristics of the composite prototypes. As a result, these areas are not elaborated here at any length, although there are three concepts of this ongoing interchange that are worthy of further attention.

One of these issues is concerned with the active component of the interchange. Not all of human behavior is purposeful or under the control of our conscious thought processes. Yet, it is also true that the effective adaptation of the individual to the environmental surround is a nontrivial process that is often subject to conscious control for certain fundamental reasons. In attempting to adapt to any environment, individuals must attain certain goals, and there are severe constraints on the time and energy that an individual may take to reach these goals and continue to display an effective pattern of adaptation. Further, in any given environment, a variety of subenvironments or alternative interactions are likely to be available, which the individual might or might not enter. Due to the pre-existing characteristics of the individual, the demands of some of these subenvironments are more likely to be in line with personal resources and limitations than are others, and so are more likely to result in goal attainment. As a result, efficient goal attainment and adaptation is likely to place a high premium on the appropriate and effective selection of situations or subenvironments, because the individual's time and energy are limited, and not all situations will be of equal value. Of course, once the individual has entered a situation, interchange with it may effect the fundamental manner in which individuality is expressed. By extension, this implies an important but often overlooked fact: A developmental change occurs only as a consequence of situational exposure, despite the fact that the individual's conscious selection of situations may provide an indirect basis for this change. More directly, individuals change only through situational exposure and selection not simply by willing change.

Another aspect of the organism–environment interchange is the manner in which the subenvironment and the individual's interchange with it influences the nature and expression of human individuality and the eventual course of individual development. One major outcome of an individual's exposure to situations and whether or not his or her actions lead to goal attainment is that it will provide a basis for learning. It is worthy of note that the learning or knowledge acquisition may occur through a variety of mechanisms, including operant, Pavlovian, observational, and vicarious learning, and that much of the learning process will be distinctively social in nature. However, it can be expected that what is learned and the manner in which it is learned will be conditional on past learning, the individual's existing differential characteristics, and heredity, species-wide characteristics of human mental functioning that may well vary with the individual's mental stage of development during the early years of life. Additionally, the best available evidence suggests that the hereditary aspects of the human mind and cognitive functioning will act to insure that similar bits of knowledge are organized into systematic categories that may be tied to the individual's current stage of development. These categories will, in turn, be systematically interrelated, and these categories and category interrelationships will result in the systematic understandings that will be used by the individual in understanding the surrounding world and employing general problem-solving processes.

In acting on any existing situation, it can be expected that the expression of differential behavior will be controlled by whether or not its manipulation results in desired outcomes. Further, individuals can be expected to select those behaviors that are most likely to result in desired outcomes with respect to their own capacities. Thus, to some extent, the differential behavior of the individual will be under the control of operant learning and situational influences. Within the general learning process, there may be some generally desirable outcomes; however, it can also be expected that individuals will display some differences with respect to the particular nature of the outcomes that they consider desirable. In other words, individuals may differ in terms of exactly what constitutes reinforcement, and this can lead to marked differences in the course of individual development when combined with the ongoing organism–environment interchange. Additionally, it is likely that, over time, individuals will build up a knowledge of the kind of behaviors that lead to reinforcement in different situations and the kind of situation most likely to provide those outcomes that they find desirable. In turn, this knowledge, or generalized understanding, is likely to have a substantial impact on the individual's selection of situations and the future course of development.

The third issue arising from the centrality of this organism–environment interchange revolves around the cumulative nature of individual development and the importance of prior behavior and experiences in conditioning the nature of individual development. Obviously, past learning and the individual's form of understanding the surrounding world will be likely to condition the individual's responses to and perceptions of novel situations. Moreover, the evaluation of alternative situations must clearly be learned on the basis of the individual's generalization from past experiences and an assessment of the outcomes and behaviors that resulted. Choices between alternative situations are likely to entail an approval of the relative value of these outcomes, given the content and nature of past experiences and the individual's general understandings. Thus, situational influences will modify the individual, and the individual's developmental path will be closely tied to his or her past behaviors and experiences. However, due to discontinuities in situational exposure as well as the ongoing nature of the organism–environment interchange, this cumulative process may not result in point-to-point phenotype consistence. Instead, what is expected is a systematic set of transformations over time, or a pattern of genotypic consistencies.

THE EMERGENCE OF INDIVIDUALITY

Having laid out these general principles, it now seems appropriate to examine the manner in which individuality and individual developmental paths may emerge over the course of a person's life, and some of the operations and concerns that might influence the general nature of the process. At birth, the individual comes into the world with a highly refined set of genetically controlled behavioral and physical characteristics. Additionally, heredity and biological maturation to this point will also have provided the individual certain special predispositions or differential characteristics in terms of temperament and abilities that will constitute either resources or limitations relative to certain situations and environments. The principal subenvironment that the individual will be interacting with from birth through the first few years of life is that of a family, and it can be expected that this early family environment will provide the primary basis for the organism–environment interchange during the first few years of life. Of course, the principal elements in this environment that will influence the individual's development are the child's parents.

Although there is some evidence available that indicates that, even at birth, an infant is capable of active interchange with the environment, due to restrictions on environmental control and physical capacity, it can be expected that the majority of these interchanges will be directed to the immediate family environment and will predominately rely on the passive, reactive, and interactive models of interchange. Nevertheless, these actual interchanges will begin the complex learning processes that play such a crucial role in individual development. Perhaps the most important outcomes of these initial interchanges is that they will provide the foundation for the emergence of the child's initial schema and his or her understanding of the world. Concommittantly, these interchanges will encourage the development of new differential characteristics, such as values, goal, or preferred reinforcements, along with the refinement of hereditary predispositions such that they are brought into line with the demands of this family environment.

Obviously, the general framework that was just sketched out is likely to be moderated by a number of other influences. Although any list of these potential moderators is likely to be too large for adequate coverage in the present discussion, there are a few that should be given at least limited attention. First, it seems likely that the nature and degree of learning that takes place during these initial interchanges will tend to be moderated by the child's current stage of maturation. This implies that the learning that takes place and the specific effects of any form of interchange may vary with the developmental phase of the child and his or her particular capacities at this point in time. Second, the nature and consequence of the primary parent–child interchange may be modified by other characteristics of the family environment and the opportunities for contact that it provides with various objects or other individuals. Indeed, it should be noted that the "subjective" emotional content of these interchanges, as well as their objective components, may play an important role in individual development. Finally, the nature of all these interchanges must be viewed as a complex, systematic phenomenon associated with a variety of influences on outcomes, in the sense that the behavior of parents or other family members may be influenced by external social factors, which will, in turn, influence the child's experiences and parents' reactions to the child's behavior.

The net outcomes of these initial interchanges is that they provide the child with a set of differential characteristics that are well integrated with respect to the initial family environment, as well as a particular set of schema for understanding the broader world. As a child grows older, he or she will be faced with the central problem of finding ways of adapting to this broader world. At first, these interchanges with people and things outside the immediate family will be highly circumscribed and will occur in rather standard settings provided by school, playmates, and the surrounding physical and social environment. By virtue of the fact that the environment provided by parents is likely to be clearly aligned with the broader social environment, the child's initial differential characteristics and understandings shall have been somewhat channelled for successful contact with this broader world. However, the child's interchange with the novel situations provided by the broader environment are likely to result in new understandings, and ongoing development is likely to result in a more refined set of catagories and category interrelationships for these new understandings. Similarly, these interchanges are likely to serve to concentrate or modify the individual's limited differential characteristics. For instance, in a bright, motivated child, schooling may serve to further accentuate these characteristics relative to peers through positive feedback, whereas an insecure child's contact with larger, bullying friends may lead to the emergence of introversion. Finally, the differential feedback from the broader world that occurs in these initial extrafamilial interchanges is likely to gain an understanding of the kinds of situations he or she can obtain and the kinds of outcomes they desire.

At the time of adolescence, background maturation is more or less complete, and society suddenly presents the individual with a larger number of options. Concommittantly, external structuring of the individual's activities decreases, and society encourages the individual to begin exploring the world as an independent entity. This change in the individual's general environment is typically marked by junior or senior high school entry, and it may continue through college. The individual is presented with a unique problem at this time in that he or she must now choose certain activities or select certain situations that will result in desired outcomes. The individual will, of course, bring to these selections his or her past history, the understandings it has resulted in, his or her desires, and some knowledge of the kind of outcomes most likely to satisfy these desires. On the basis of his or her background, the individual will decide to engage in certain activities or situations to the exclusion of others. These activities will themselves result in an interchange by which the individual and the situation modify each other. Typically, successful patterns of interchange can be expected to reinforce the differential characteristics that led to the initial selection of these activities and to refine or strengthen the individual's differential capacities for exploiting this sort of situation. Obviously, this differential development, guided by exposure to certain kinds of situations, will encourage similar choices in the future and increase the individual's capacity for exploiting them. On the other hand, choices that have failed to yield desirable outcomes will have a more erratic effort in the sense that they are likely to lead to the development or modification of existing differential characteristics, particularly those that influenced the initial choice, while at the same time they are likely to diminish the individual's likelihood of entering similar situations in the future.

These choices of activities or situations are not likely to occur in isolation from each other, in part because they are all bound up in a broader adaptive process. In selecting and interacting in certain situations, individuals will be developing certain differential characteristics. When this is coupled with the fact that individuals must obtain a pattern of outcomes with limited time and resources through these characteristics, this suggests that maximum adaptation and efficiency of action demands that these changes occur in an integrated fashion so that the differential characteristics emerging in one kind of activity will be complimentary to those required for desirable outcomes in other situations. This phenomenon will be supplemented by the individual's tendency to select situations on the basis of his or her total pattern of past behavior and experiences, which themselves reflect a systematic phenomenon. As a result of these considerations, various discrete activities will be selected in a systematic and integrated fashion that will subsequently influence the selection of future activities and the course of individual development leading to a maintenance of this systematic pattern.

In essence, then, adaptive demands and the nature of individual development will force the individual to create a niche for himself or herself that would incorporate a variety of specific situations in an integrated fashion. The acquisition of this niche, to some extent, will be based on and guided by the individual's prior history and existing differential characteristics. However, in acquiring this niche, the nature of the niche and the situational interchanges occurring within it are likely to refine and modify the individual's characteristics in such a way that they are better able to meet the adaptive demands made by the niche as a whole. This implies that the characteristics developed by the individual in the organism—environment interchange are likely to be those of some general value in the total niche, rather than those that are highly specific to a particular situation. Additionally, it is quite possible that the individual may perform poorly in some situations incorporated in the niche, yet be well adapted to the niche as a whole.

By defining a niche for himself or herself, the individual will enter into a highly channelled pattern of development. The niche itself will insure the development of those differential characteristics in the individual required for local adaptation. Further, by virtue of those characteristics, the individual is likely to enter analogous or comparable situations in the future. Thus, the course of individual development is likely to fall into a stable trajectory, and the stability of the trajectory is likely to be reinforced by two additional phenomena. First, the niche itself will commonly, although not always, insure that the new situations that are presented to the individual by the broader environment are, to some extent, conjoint with those already incorporated in the niche. More directly, once individuals have created a niche, they will predominately came into contact with niche-relevant situations, due to the systematic structuring of the broader environment, and, in fact, the social environment itself may directly limit the feasibility of entering disjoint or noncongruent situations. Second, because stable expansion into new situations is likely to improve successful engagement in those situations, the niche's influence on the emergence of the differential characteristics that are required for success in the niche will tend to insure entry into congruent situations in the future, while the individual's own actions in new situations may lead to the creation of congruent situations where they did not exist before.

The combination of the individual's needs and existing differential characteristics might be viewed as an adaptive complex, or style, guiding the course of later development. As described previously, both the niche and the adaptive complex as a whole may have a rather static flavor to them. Hence, it should be noted that, in real life, these phenomena will reflect a dynamic process that is analogous to the flow of a river. This dynamism is bound up in the individual's ability to affect the nature of a situation through his or her actions in it, as well as the fact that ongoing interchange with the integrated set of situations incorporated in a niche will assure an ongoing, yet consistent, pattern of individual development and change. The foregoing discussion may also have led to the impression that adaptive complexes and niches are common across individuals. This is not the case. In the course of their development, different individuals will have been provided with differing degrees of certain characteristics as well as different kinds of situational exposures in different sequences. When this is coupled with the staggering number of discrete situations presented to an individual from birth onward, it suggests that, in some ultimate sense, each individual is unique and qualitatively different from every other individual. However, because heredity is a highly structured influence and the social environment both restricts and organizes the situations to which an individual can be exposed, the number and kind of adaptive styles that can be employed in a given culture is likely to be limited to some finite number. As a result, individuals are likely to move into the most appropriate of the available niches, and individuals entering a common niche are likely to display certain commonalities in their future pattern of development that could serve to differentiate them from individuals entering other niches. Finally, because some combination of situations and pre-existing characteristics are more likely to occur than others within a given culture, some adaptive styles are likely to be expressed more frequently than others, although differences in the prior history of individuals expressing a style may lead to some residual variation.

In creating and occupying any given niche what will emerge is a crystallized pattern of differential behavior and experiences that will tend to remain stable for the period of time that the individual is capable of maintaining the niche (Mumford, Wesley, & Shaffer, 1987). This crystallization and the concommittent emergence of a stable adaptive style will necessarily involve both gains and losses, in the sense that certain differential characteristics that are irrelevant to adaptation in the niche will be diminished, whereas those that are facilitative of adaptation to the niche are likely to be enhanced. Moreover, because individuals will select the situations that initially define their niche on the basis of their ability to provide outcomes that the person holds to be desirable, these crystallized patterns and adaptive styles are most likely to form when the individual is placed in a general environment that provides some opportunities for satisfying these desires. If the environment that confronts the individual is such that satisfaction is not possible, then crystallization of an adaptive style is not likely to occur, and the individual will be likely to withdraw and continue to search for an appropriate niche.

The preceeding paragraph suggests that the adaptive style adopted by an individual will, for that individual, always be adaptive at the time of crystallization. However, it is not necessarily the case that a crystallized adaptive style will lead to favorable developmental outcomes. An adaptive style that crystallizes in an environment that is dangerous, threatening pathologically, or bears little resemblance or relevance to the situational demands may have disastrous outcomes for the individual, because it would not tend to facilitate adaptation in these later environments. Additionally, the individual's understandings or desires may be unrealistic or incapable of satisfaction and could lead to the emergence of an ineffective adaptive style with respect to later outcomes. A number of other difficulties may also arise for the individual's construction of an adaptive style. Two of these may be found in the phenomena of over-specialization and over-expansion. In the hope of enhancing efficiency to the greatest extent possible, the individual may construct a highly restricted niche, consisting of a set of highly similar activities. Consequently, the individual will not be prepared to adopt and exploit any new situations, leading to poor outcomes. On the other hand, an over-expanded niche, incorporating a number of highly diverse elements, may prevent the development of an integrated set of characteristics and optimal utilization of time and energy in attaining desired outcomes. Thus, there seems to be a trade-off between over-specialization and over-expansion, and optimal developmental outcomes may depend on the individual's ability to construct a niche that balances these trends. Finally, it should be pointed out that problems may arise when an individual enters a niche and formulates an adaptive style that either justifiability or unjustifiabilty is denigrated by the culture as a whole.

Social Influences

At a number of points in the foregoing discussion, the potential impact of society on the nature and content of the adaptive styles formulated by an individual was noted. Unfortunately, those brief, tangential references were not, in any way, sufficient to give the reader an adequate grasp of the importance of social influences in determining the course of individual development. For society or culture to be able to operate in an effective manner, the individual must be carefully integrated into a limited set of social roles, and, as a result, society exerts a profound, albeit often indirect, control over the nature of individual development and the emergence of an adaptive system.

One of the more important social influences on the expression and formation of adaptive styles is cultural control over the situations to which an individual is exposed, and the nature of the interrelationships among these situations. Thus, society exerts a profound influence over the kind of niche that it is feasible for an individual to create for himself or herself. A common manifestation of this form of cultural control may be found in the phenomenon of social roles. Social roles, as manifest in being a homemaker, a singer, or a psychologist, all present the individual with an organized set of situations that he or she is expected to respond to in a certain way under the pressure of social sanctions. As may be seen in the scientific focus of the Analytical Adapters, as well as the effects of early movement into adult social roles on the lives of the Premature Conformists, acceptance of and movement into adult social roles can have a profound effect on the course of individual development. In fact, the roles may sometimes constitute initial elements of the individual's niche and adaptive style.

Typically, it can be expected that, in forming a niche and an adaptive style, the individual will select those social roles that are most likely to facilitate adaptation in accordance with the general principles sketched out previously. The role itself is of some importance in this regard. Society does not generally allow the individual to completely immerse himself or herself in any single role; instead, it forces the individual to accept and play multiple roles at any given time. For instance, an individual may be required to be a wife, mother, and personnel adminstrator. The tendency of society to force multiple roles on the individual helps insure individual adaptation, in the sense that it will tend to operate against the over-specialization of niches and adaptive styles, insuring some breadth in the process of individual development. Nevertheless, society does not attempt to force multiple roles on individuals in a random or unsystematic fashion. Rather, elaborate rules exist for interrelating these roles within any given developmental period, and the individual's occupancy of any one role, in conjunction with this social structuring of role interrelationships, determine what other roles the individual may or may not enter. Further structuring may be provided by the individual, because many roles include some room for individual latitude, and then the individual may choose to emphasize or de-emphasize certain aspects of any role.

Another way in which society structures the individual pattern of development may be found in the age-grading of behavior and experiences. As has often been noted, society deems that certain behaviors or experiences are appropriate for individuals at certain ages or at certain phases of their development. To some extent, the social age-grading of behavior and experiences takes into account biological or hereditary aspects of maturation; prosaically speaking, no culture currently in existence requires toddlers to accomplish heavy manual labor. However, outside these extreme instances, there is not necessarily a point-to-point correspondence between biological maturation and social age-grading. Generally, this age-grading is a rather pensive social influence based on normative expectations and subtle sanctions that determine permissable behavior and experiences as well as the social roles that will be open to individual at that point in their lives. Further, societies often induce sharp discontinuities in the behavior, experiences, and roles considered legitimate for individuals of different ages, resulting in distinctive, albeit culturally determined, developmental periods.

This age-grading of behavior and experiences has some important implications for the general view of individuality and individual development sketched out earlier. Perhaps the most obvious of these implications is that, as individuals move across developmental periods, they may be exposed to a markedly different set of situational alternatives and behavioral expectations. Consequently, the situation entered by an individual, and the resulting behavior, will be subject to change and shifts in meaning, resulting in substantial discontinuities in overt differential behavioral characteristics or traits. It is also possible that, by virtue of changes in the nature of behavioral expectations, situational exposure, and the available roles, the basic content of the individual's niche and adaptive style may change as well. Obviously, then, one outcome of the age-grading of behavior and experiences will be a certain degree of instability in the overt manifestation of individuality and the course of individual development, which, to some extent, might affect the self-perpetuating nature of an adaptive style and serve to supplement the instability induced by the ongoing interchange between the organism and the environment.

Despite the phenotypic instability and the possibility of major developmental change, the existence of age-grading and a shifting social environment does not necessarily imply genotypic instability or demand major shifts in the general outline and nature of an individual's adaptive style. Although the age-grading of behavior and experiences may be highly rigid in certain instances, at no time in the course of an individual's life will the structuring be so severe that the individual will not be required to make a number of choices with respect to these activities that will be most likely to enhance his or her adaptation. As was the case with the incorporation of new situations and the extension of an existing adaptive style, these choices are likely to be made in a systematic fashion, based on the individual's previous pattern of development and his or her existing adaptive style. The need for these selective choices is based on the fact that individuals must engage in that subset of activities that will maximize adaptation, given a limited amount of time and energy. Thus, in moving into new developmental periods, the individual will tend to recreate his or her original niche and adaptive style by employing his or her understandings, differential characteristics, and desires to select a new set of age-appropriate activities. As a result, a high degree of genotypic consistency may be observed as individuals move across developmental periods with respect to their adaptive style, although the specific elements incorporated in a niche and overt behavior and experiences may vary. Further, the underlying genotypic stability may lead to some phenotypic stability in certain kinds of differential characteristics and for certain kinds of individuals. However, it can generally be expected that the self-perpetuating adaptive style will display greater stability than discrete patterns of differential behavior as individuals move across developmental periods.

Although the self-perpetuating nature of adaptive styles argues for some genotypic consistencies in differential behavior and experiences, as individuals progress through their lives, change is not impossible or necessarily unlikely. It is possible that an adaptive style constructed by individuals in an earlier phase of their lives may not be applicable in a novel environment forced on them by developmental discontinuities or other situations, such as war. As a result, for individuals displaying a particular adaptive style, this phase of their lives may constitute a sensitive period where marked underlying changes in their pattern of differential characteristics are possible as they attempt to construct a new adaptive style that will allow them to function in a new environment. It can be expected that this construction of a new adaptive style will involve a restructuring of past understandings and values, along with exploration of alternative activities, values, and understandings, as well as anticipation of the outcomes associated with alternative activities. However, it should be noted that, although the anticipating process may be necessary in order to insure efficiency, it is likely to be less than wholly effective, due to the breakdown of the existing adaptive complex, and the limited relevance and stability of existing understandings. Thus, existing differential characteristics, situational exposure, and situational outcomes are likely to play a premier role in the process. Moreover, because the individual's personal history and existing characteristics will play an important role in generating the search for new activities and obtaining the outcomes associated with the activities and their value to the individual, it can be expected that the new adaptive style will still be closely tied to the individual's past history, thus maintaining the cumulative nature of development and some genotypic consistencies.

Another potential cause of drastic shifts may be found in the individual's failure to successfully define a niche and adaptive style in the preceeding developmental period. In this case, one can again expect exposure to a new environment to create a sensitive period in which the individual attempts to define and construct an effective niche and an appropriate adaptive style. Again, the developmental timing and the nature of the adaptive style formulated in this sensitive period can be expected to be tied in some loose fashion to the individual's past history, although it can also be expected that the search will be less stressful and more directed than is likely to be true in the preceeding case, by virtue of the fact that the collapse of an existing adaptive style was not involved.

Before proceeding with the present discussion, there are four important implications of the preceeding discussion that should be given some attention. First, individuals who crystallize an adaptive style that has limited general effectiveness across developmental periods or crystallize the style in a pathological environment, and who fail to change this style during a sensitive period, are likely to show signs of maladjustment in later years. Second, the fundamental impact of the organism–environment interchange and the existence of these developmental discontinuities imply that different sorts of differential characteristics may emerge in different developmental periods. Third, because the nature of these emergent differential characteristics will be tied to the individual's adaptive complex niche, and situational exposure, it is quite possible that there will be individual differences in the timing of the emergence of true differential characteristics. Thus, a set of differential behavioral continuities on traits must be viewed not as absolute, molecular entities. Fourth, variation arising from developmental discontinuities and sensitive periods may be complex, yet the structural nature of the social environment and the choices it presents insures some additional genotypic consistency beyond that attributable to the individual's differential characteristics.

To this point, two critical principles concerning the nature of human individuality and individual development have been adroitly sidestepped, primarily because they are rather difficult to elaborate and understand outside the social context. One obvious implication of the foregoing discussion is that individuals must not only select situations that are likely to facilitate their adaptation but, in the face of systematic changes in their environment that are to some extent predictable, maximum efficiency in adaptive efforts is likely to be facilitated by the individual's active preparation to exploit certain situations and roles that are likely to emerge at a later date. Thus, individuality will incorporate an important purposive and proactive preparatory component intended to facilitate future adaptation. In the course of development, this preparatory activity will entail the use of schema and understandings of the general physical and social environments to project future situations. These future situations will be appraised in terms of the individual's existing differential characteristics, projected situational demands, likely outcomes, and the desirability of these outcomes to determine what situations or roles should be sought after. Further, the individual is then likely to determine exactly what outcomes he or she should take immediately or in the near future in order to prepare himself or herself to exploit these situations or roles. Subsequently, the individual will tend to extend his or her current niche to incorporate those activities that he or she believes will serve as preparation to exploit later situations or roles. These decisions are all likely to be based on prior learning and generalization from past behaviors and experiences, and they are likely to be well integrated with the individual's current niche and adaptive style. Yet, regardless of the particular decision made by the individual, it is clear that, through the anticipatory activity and the consequent extension of the existing niche and adaptive style, the individual will be creating a niche and an adaptive style that is oriented not only to immediate adaptation but also to future adaptation.

The existence of this proactive component has a number of implications for the nature of human individuality. Perhaps the most obvious of these is that, through its future orientation, the proactive aspect of individuality induces a certain amount of genotypic consistency in differential behavior and experiences. The nature of this proactive component also suggests that the schema that an individual employs in understanding the world, as well as generalizing to future outcomes, may exert a profound influence on the course of individual development by channelling it in a certain direction. Interestingly, this suggests that, by virtue of their powerful impact in the definition of schema and desirable outcomes, it is possible that early parent–child interactions may have a pervasive, although somewhat diffuse, influence on a child's developmental trajectory. Another implication of the nature of the proactive component is that it will tend to involve both some expansion and some limitation of the individual's niche by leading the individual to adopt certain preparatory activities to the exclusion of other activities. The nature of the proactive component also suggests that the individual's self-understandings and understanding of the environmental surround may play an important role in individual development, and a lack of understanding may lead to disasterous outcomes. Individuals are likely to spend a certain amount of their time and energy acquiring information about the future environmental surround and projecting its likely implications as well as their likely actions and outcomes. This scouting, or anticipatory activity, will clearly play an important role in individual development, and in fact it may well be tied to play, daydreaming, and various forms of entertainment.

It appears that this scouting activity is likely to occur more frequently in some developmental periods than others. Generally, scouting will be most likely to occur when the individual anticipates major changes in environmental demands in the near future. The age-grading of behavior and cultural expectations impose upon individuals in adolescence and young adulthood the need to prepare for certain pervasive social roles. As a result, the period through adolescence and young adulthood is likely to involve a high degree of scouting activity, and the individual's effectiveness in scouting is likely to be of great importance for the future course of individual development.

This scouting component embedded in the proactive aspect of individuality is related to two additional phenomena. First, it is possible that individuals will enter and subjugate themselves to situations or activities that do not provide desirable outcomes or have a low relative value if, through scouting, they come to believe that this situational entanglement will serve to prepare them to successfully exploit their future environment. This phenomenon is most likely to occur when perceived future benefits outweigh current inconvenience, and it may involve a degree of rationalization of post hoc explanation. Second, when this anticipatory activity is lost sight of and it is linked to the ongoing interchange with an unfavorable situation, this process may lead to maladaptation. In this regard, it seems plausible to speculate that the phenomenon might underlie the crystallization of adaptive styles in an unfavorable environment.

Society may structure the nature of individuality and individual development by capitalizing on their scouting activity and the proactive nature of development. One of the more obvious characteristics of the age-grading of behavior and experiences is that it makes the individual aware of the fact that, at certain ages, society will impose upon the individual the need to select and enter certain kinds of social roles. The adequate adaptation of individuals to the demands of these roles, as well as maximum utilization of individuals in these roles, demands some pre-existing conceptions of their relevant strengths and weaknesses and the roles they are best suited to, along with some relevant experience in role relevant situations. As a result, scouting and the proactive nature of development may benefit society by preparing individuals for later roles, and so it is not surprising that society encourages this activity through a variety of institutions, such as high-school extra-curricular activities. The preparatory nature of these proactive activities and society's tendency to provide opportunities for preparation in accordance with the age-grading of behavior and experience provide an explanation for another intriguing finding. If the frequency hypothesis held true, then it would be expected that individuals who entered major social roles ahead of schedule would have less preparation and so might have some difficulty in adapting to these roles.

Due to its need to insure an adequate division of labor, society often presents the individual with a choice among pervasive, incompatible roles that require very different characteristics for preparation and adaptation. This forces the individual to make certain mutually exclusive choices about the course of their future lives. Although the proactive nature of individuality and scouting will tend to minimize inappropriate selections, the proactive activity itself will give rise to differential characteristics that reflect these contrasting situational demands, resulting in systematic qualitative differences among individuals in their behavior and experiences that will tend to display some stability due to their proactive nature. Moreover, the nature and stability of these qualitative differences will tend to be reinforced by qualitative differences in background as they affect activity selection as well as the tendency of the niche to organize other elements of experiences with these non-common elements.

From the perspective of society, scouting, proactive activities, and systematic qualitative differences are of some tangible value. Consequently, social institutions are likely to provide individuals with differential feedback concerning these activities via general rewards, such as acknowledgment or money. When linked to the operant learning process and its implications for individual development, this feedback is likely to channel individuals into different roles and kinds of activities. Quite often, it can be expected that the social reinforcement will occur relative to other individuals as a form of proactive feedback, which tends to reward and provide for the further development of the individual in those areas that are valued by society and where the individual has shown greater-than-average potential. Thus, to increase an adequate "labor" supply, society may choose to emphasize or de-emphasize certain characteristics in a particular individual or a number of individuals. By this differential channelling of individuals, society is likely to insure a maximum return on its investment and an optimal division of labor. However, in certain instances, society is likely to supplement this naturally occurring process in two ways. First, because individuals will display differences in the outcomes they consider desirable, society may offer different kinds of rewards for entry into different kinds of roles or niches as one means of insuring the desired division of labor. Second, in certain instances, society may attempt to supplement these naturally occurring processes by the overt selection of individuals for certain roles. This phenomenon is particularly likely to occur where role requirements are demanding and social costs are high.

Although the dynamic nature of individual development, as well as the pervasive nature of individual differences and socially controlled differential feedback, tend to insure an adequate division of labor, it should be noted that this slow process will not always be sufficient. At any time, in any society, there are likely to be certain pervasive roles, such as certain occupations, some of which are generally perceived as being more desirable than others across individuals. As a result, this phenomenon is likely to induce competion among individuals for these roles and the associated niche when there are more aspirants than vacancies. This competition for desirable roles and the associated niches has a number of interesting implications for the course of individual development. One of these is that the differential feedback provided by society in the course of individuals competing for generally desirable roles is likely to constitute an important source of feedback effecting the individual's understanding of the kind of situations that he or she is likely to be effective in. Additionally, failure to attain a desired role of this sort may contribute a powerful impetus for developmental change and, under certain conditions for certain individuals, may be capable of triggering a sensitive period. This competition may also lead to maladaptation when change does not take place after failure or when the individual pursues these generally desirable roles to the exclusion of roles that are more appropriate for his or her niche and adaptive style. Finally, it should be noted that this competition may serve as a central mechanism for allocating high-talent individuals to a limited number of critical social roles when society has ascribed to role occupancy a large number of powerful general reinforcers.

To this point, the present discussion has focused on a set of rather general considerations that are relevant to understanding the emergence of human individuality in a biosocial context. However, it might prove useful to examine a few significant extensions of these concepts into some related area before attempting to evaluate this theoretical position.

Of late, one phenomenon that has received considerable attention in the developmental literature may be found in the influence of historic change on the nature and course of individual development. The general theoretical framework sketched out herein would lead to the expectation that cultural shifts over time might have some influence on the patterns and nature of individual development. Historic change in any culture implies that the situations facing individuals, as well as the available roles and activities, will change. In the course of the organism–environment interchange, the individual's expression of individuality is likely to be modified by those situational changes that lead to historic change in the course of individual development. Moreover, when a number of individuals, living their lives at roughly the same time, are exposed to a common set of situations that are characteristic of a certain historic period, interchange with these situations may result in cohort effects. Some prototypes may be far more sensitive than others to any effects induced by historical change, due to the nature of their niche and adaptive style. For instance, the differential characteristics of the Unconventional Successes suggests that these females would be far more sensitive to changes induced by the expanding role of women than would be members of the Competent Nurturers prototype. Studies of historical change must be sensitive to the nature of the individual understanding this change if historical effects are to be fully understood.

The existence of historical change in the nature of the situations that are presented to an individual suggests a certain degree of historic instability in the differential behavior and experience of the composite prototypes. Although this comment might also be taken to suggest that the adaptive styles and niches that are associated with composite prototype membership will also display instability across historic periods, this conclusion must be approached with some caution. The evidence laid out earlier in comparing Block's (1971) results with those obtained in the present investigation indicated that, even over a 30-year period, there may be substantial stability in the general developmental pathways followed by individuals. This future stability appears to be a result of a number of contributing trends. Niches and adaptive styles are, in part, based on some factors, such as heredity, biological maturation, child-rearing practices, education, and occupations, which change very slowly, and thus should induce some stability in the nature of the composite prototypes. Second, the formation of niches and an adaptive style is likely to be closely tied to the general choices that are presented to an individual in the broader culture, and these choices are likely to change rather slowly in an established social framework. Indeed, many of the changes in situational exposure brought about by historic change may entail little more than extension of existing niches and adaptive styles to incorporate the new element. Consequently, the basic pattern may display some stability even though the elements contained in it have been subject to some change.

If it is granted that there is at least some limited stability on adaptive styles over time and changes in the social environment, then the question comes to fore as to whether there would be some stability in the nature of the developmental paths emerging in different cultures. In one sense, the foregoing discussion and its emphasis on the impact of the ongoing organism–environment interchange suggests that different niches and adaptive styles should emerge in different cultures. However, there are some constant elements in all human cultures, and all cultures present certain types of situations to individuals at certain points in their lives. Because heredity and biological maturation also play an important role in individual development, then it does not seem unreasonable to speculate that certain common archetypes might exist across cultures. Further, such archetypes might have a hereditary basis if they are intimately tied to the effective adaptation of social groups through the division of labor. Of course, this is clearly a highly speculative hypothesis. Even if archetypes exist, it seems likely that they would represent little more than hereditary patterns of differential characteristics subject to modification through interchange with the environment. Nevertheless, the potential existence of these archetypes is an intriguing possibility that should not be disregarded until adequate evidence along these lines has been obtained.

Of course, the upshot of the foregoing discussion for cultural differences is similar to that presented in our discussion of historical change; that is that there will be some underlying stability and a great deal of surface variability. Surface variability will be pervasive because, unlike many forms of historical change, cultural differences often impact on the most basic aspects of individual development, such as a child-rearing practices. Thus, it seems likely that different kinds of prototypes may arise under different cultural conditions, and that these cultural differences may lead to differences in the frequency with which individuals follow shared developmental pathways. These former outcomes are more likely to occur in the face of massive cultural differences, whereas the latter is more likely to characterize subculture differences, such as those found between the United States and England, and among American ethnic groups. On the other hand, due to the existence of these underlying commonalities, the number of potential prototypes across cultures is likely to be a finite, although sizable, number, because there are only a limited number of ways of adapting to the human condition.

One place where society, biological demands, and heredity all converge to affect the developmental paths followed by individuals may be found in sexual activity. Biology forces upon males and females an overlapping but not identical set of developmental demands to insure the propagation of the species. Of course, these biological influences are not absolutely restrictive, because multiple, divergent adaptive styles may be effectively employed by both males and females. However, it appears that, in response to these biological differences and the need for an effective division of labor, society exposes males and females to very different situations from the onset of life and has rather different expectations as to what constitutes appropriate behavior in these situations. As a result of these differences and the cumulative aspect of the organism–environment interchange, different niches and adaptive styles are likely to be entered by males and females. These differences in niches and adaptive styles will lead to differences in the meaning and developmental implications of certain behaviors and experiences. Due to these differences, it appears necessary to examine differential developmental pathways within a sex group. However, individual males and females may take rather different attitudes towards these sex-role expectations. Some individuals, including members of the Virile Extraverts and Unscathed Adjusters composite prototypes, appear to employ sex-role expectations as a central aspect of their niches and adaptive styles, whereas other individuals, including members of the Orphaned Adapters and Burgeois Outliers composite prototypes, do not seem readily characterized in terms of sex-role expectations. This observation points to the fact that even broad-based influences on individual development, such as sex, may be modified in meaning by the individual's prior history.

Before concluding this section, it seems germane to ask how this theoretical model can be applied to differential characteristics such as intelligence and spatial ability, which have been shown to display some stability and to have a strong hereditary basis. Differential characteristics that are subject to marked hereditary control constitute a relative resource or limitation that the individual brings to the world at the time of birth. In the environment in which the individual is initially placed, these characteristics will either facilitate or hinder adaptation. In turn, the individual is likely to select situations in which their resource characteristics will be of some adaptive value while rejecting situations involving limiting characteristics. In essence, the environment provides a positive feedback mechanism for enhancing the development and differentiation of these characteristics, explaining their correlational stability, the increasing differentiation observed in them over the course of development, and the reason why it is difficult to measure these constraints in a culture-free setting.

The foregoing analyses suggest that the developmental processes that underlie the emergence of these characteristics is not markedly different than those that underlie individual development as a general phenomenon. It is also true that aptitudes and abilities, such as intelligence and spatial orientation, have displayed a far greater degree of stability than other differential characteristics, such as honesty. However, these differences may be traced to the fact that most stable ability and aptitude characteristics have a more pronounced hereditary component. Moreover, their general value to adaptation in a wide variety of situations insures that they are likely to be associated with pervasive feedback. Because of their general value, society may attempt to facilitate the emergence of these aptitudes and abilities in all individuals, resulting in a common set of developmental experiences. On the other hand, differential characteristics such as religiosity may lead to valued outcomes only in certain situations for certain individuals, resulting in a lack of uniform, consistent feedback and less stability.

If it is granted that the development of aptitudes and abilities might occur in accordance with this framework, there are a number of interesting implications. One of these is that, even when an individual has the requisite hereditary resource background, an ability or an aptitude may not develop to a noticeable extent if its application will not further immediate or further adaptation. Second, these characteristics may be expressed in different ways in different developmental periods, due to differing adaptive demands and situational exposure. Thus, infant intelligence may not be directly analogous to adult intelligence. Third, even when the individual pursues these characteristics, he or she may or may not choose to employ them, depending on his or her general adaptive style and the situation at hand. An excellent example of this phenomenon may be found in the differential characteristics of the Competent Nurturers' use of academic ability.

SUPPORTING EVIDENCE

Having provided the broad conceptual overview of the nature of human individuality and individual development, it now seems germane to ask just how well this theoretical perspective itself accounts for actual phenomena observed in the assessment of human individuality and individual development. Validation of any theory, particularly one as broad as the one presented herein, is a difficult task that is subject to a variety of ambiguities. These ambiguities are so numerous and pervasive that it will always be impossible to fully establish the validity of any theoretical perspective. However, it is possible to pose two questions. First, it might be asked how well the theory accounts for the results obtained in other studies and how well it is aligned with alternative conceptions of the phenomena. Second, it might be asked how well this theory accounts for the differential characteristics of the composite prototypes and the comparative results that were laid out earlier. In the ensuing discussion, an attempt is made to address both of these questions.

Internal Support

At various points, this discussion has touched on the ability of this theoretical perspective to account for the comparative results presented in chapter 11. Perhaps the more important result obtained in contrasting the differential characteristics of the composite prototypes was that common differential behavior and experiences did not appear to have common meaning for different prototypes. These are hardly surprising findings within the present theoretical system, because it could be expected that differing backgrounds would lead to different forms of interchange with a constant stimulus set and that common behaviors could serve markedly different purposes for individuals who employ different adaptive styles. For instance, fraternity involvement may serve as a coping mechanism for some individuals, whereas it may serve as a means of social contact for others. These different purposes could, in turn, lead to different developmental outcomes and meanings. These effects and the complications of ongoing interchange within the model also provide an attractive explanation for the local convergence/local divergence phenomenon. More specifically, local convergence may reflect common responses to a given subenvironment that have different antecedents and consequents due to the differing adaptive styles of prototype members, whereas local divergence may reflect a temporary modification of an adaptive style where this style permits the expansion into a variety of conjoint situations.

Comparison of the composite prototypes' differential characteristics also suggested that common behaviors or experiences might have very different meanings and developmental implications in different developmental periods. However, as individuals move across developmental periods, the situations to which they are exposed change along with their differential characteristics. As a result, the implications of behavior and experiences may shift as well, due to either the changing nature of the environment or the influence of ongoing development. This phenomenon is related to the explanation of an additional observation; even though common experiences may have uniting effects in one developmental period, these effects may not be maintained in later developmental periods, and the eventual outcome may depend on the nature of the individual at hand. When the individual is placed in a new environment due to movement across developmental periods, whether or not a developmental outcome is maintained will depend on future interchanges.

The model also appears to have some value in explaining the diffuse, yet fundamental, importance of parental behavior in shaping the course of individual development. Early interchanges between a child and his or her parents are likely to strongly influence the basic understandings and categories that the individual employs in understanding the world, as well as the value that the individual places on certain outcomes. These factors will exert a pervasive influence on the individual's selection of situations. Thus, parental behavior may influence future development, despite its distal nature. Along similar lines, it is clear that the sleeper effect identified for certain kinds of emergent differential characteristics, such as the impact of cross-sex-role identification on marital happiness, is also a possible outcome within this theoretical framework. Differential characteristics developed in earlier situations may remain dormant if they are of little importance in adapting to the individual's current environment due to the cumulative nature of individual development. However, if these same characteristics have relevance to the individual's understanding, evaluation of, or preparation for certain situations and roles presented later on, their influences on the course of individual development may suddenly become apparent.

Because individuals are exposed to different situations in the course of their development, and the timing of these exposures may vary as well as their implications for different developmental periods, this theory makes it possible to account for three additional phenomena observed in the earlier comparative effort. First, because the specific situations that are likely to facilitate the emergence of differential characteristics depend on an individual's background, and the individual's background and differences in the social timing may lead to a non-constant timing of the requisite situational exposure, it is quite possible that similar differential characteristics will emerge in different developmental periods. Second, because some patterns of experiences and personal history are more likely to occur than others in a given culture, it is not especially surprising that some developmental pathways should be followed more frequently than others. Third, because these experiences occur systematically within a given environment, are sometimes a matter of kind rather than degree, and sometimes involve mutually exclusive choices, the ongoing organism–environment interchange and its impact on the emergence of differential characteristics suggests that there might be qualitative difference in the adaptive styles employed by different prototypes.

The model's emphasis on the social age-grading of behavior and experiences, as well as the proactive element in individuality that this gives us, allows the model to explain two additional comparative phenomena. Through the age-grading of behavior and experiences, society is capable of preparing the individual to enter and exploit certain roles, and it can be expected that society will structure this age-grading so as to maximize preparation of the individual for certain general roles. Consequently, when the individual enters these complex social roles prematurely, he or she will not have developed the requisite characteristics, possibly leading to negative developmental outcomes. Further, the proactive aspect of individuality suggests that individuals are capable of consciously preparing themselves for entry into desirable future roles.

One of the more interesting observations to emerge in the course of the comparative effort was that it was quite possible for individuals to change overt behavior as they moved across developmental periods while maintaining their characteristic adaptive style, thus giving rise to genotypic consistency along with overt phenotypic inconsistency. Despite the contradiction that is apparent in this statement, it does seem that the model can provide an adequate explanation for both of these phenomena. As individuals move across developmental periods, by virtue of the age-grading of behavior and experiences, they will be presented with new situations and new demands for adaptation that lead to changes in overt behavior. However, individuals will tend to select certain aspects of the new environment for engagement on the basis of their personal history, and they will initially attempt to adapt to these situations through their existing differential characteristics. Further, through proactive engagement in certain situations, they will have prepared themselves to enter these situations through past interchanges. These trends should lead to a maintenance of the individual's basic niche and adaptive style and some genotypic consistency, despite the existence of overt phenotypic inconsistency.

The existence of genotypic consistency and phenotypic inconsistency leads to some interesting issues concerning the when, where, and how of developmental change. As outlined earlier, the model clearly suggests that a change in either overt behavior or an adaptive style can occur only under the impetus of situational change. Although it can be argued that, by changing goals, schema, values, or understandings, individuals may change themselves without direct external stimulation, it should be noted that these qualities were also developed through the organism–environment interchange and that change in them is also likely to be tied to situational change. This statement is not intended to imply that individuals have no control over the course of their development; rather, they have a great deal of control through the proactive aspect of individuality and the active selection of situations. When the importance of the situation in triggering change is considered along with the fact that the timing of situational exposure is controlled by society through the age-grading of behavior and experience, then it is quite possible that certain developmental periods are especially likely to present a change-producing situation for certain individuals, leading to the emergence of prototype-specific sensitive periods in the course of an individual's development.

Taken as a whole, the preceding discussion appears to indicate that the general model of individuality and individual development laid out herein can account for a number of the phenomena observed in con-strasting the differential characteristics of the composite prototypes. Given the validity, generality, and stability of the summary descriptions of individuality incorporated in the composite prototypes, this, in turn, suggests that this theoretical model might have some value in attempts to understand the nature and ontogeny of human individuality and differential development. The potential value of this general theoretical perspective is underscored by the models' ability to account for a wide range of highly diverse and apparently contradictory phenomena.

External Support

An additional source of evidence bearing on the validity of the theoretical model presented earlier may be found in the results obtained and interpretations employed in other studies of individuality and individual development. Of course, in any effort along these lines, it will not be possible to examine all of the research studies that have been conducted in the field of differential psychology. However, a selective review might provide sufficient evidence to allow the reader to place some confidence in the theoretical framework.

One of the more interesting findings in the individual differences literature is concerned with the ontogeny of vocational interests. Dunkleberger and Tyler (1961) have found that high-ability individuals often take longer to develop vocational interests than do individuals of lower ability. These investigators have attributed the phenomenon to the relatively constant practice feedback provided to high-ability individuals for engagement in vocation-related endeavors. This finding and the associated explanation appear to be in line with the theoretical position sketched out earlier. As the individual creates a niche and attempts to prepare himself or herself for later roles in the occupational world through scouting activity and the proactive extension of a niche, uniform positive feedback would make it difficult for the individual to determine what kind of activities are more likely to be adaptive. That, in turn, would make it difficult for the individual to express differential interest in any particular occupational role.

Two related findings in the vocational interest literature are also readily incorporated within the theoretical framework. First, Ekehammar (1977) has provided evidence that suggests that vocational choice is related to the perceived costs and benefits associated with occupational entry and the likelihood of the individual having the differential characteristics required for occupational success. By emphasizing the conscious selection of activities in terms of likely outcomes and the individuals perceived evaluation of these outcomes, Ekehammar's results would seem to be in accordance with theoretical expectations. Second, Holland and Gottfredson (1975) and Mumford and Owens (1984) have found that the background behavior and experiences that lead to the emergence of differential characteristics relevant to personally satisfying engagement in vocationally relevant activities are directly related to vocational interests, and Super (1957) has found that knowledge of personal capacities and job demands influence vocational choice. Again, both of these results would be predicted under the present theoretical system, due to the importance of scouting and the proactive aspect of individuality in situational selection.

Another rather problematic finding in the individual differences literature may be found in the ontogeny of understanding occupational achievement. Earlier, it was pointed out that Lehman (1953) has found that major occupational contributions are most likely to occur during young adulthood, whereas minor contributions are most likely to occur in middle age. Mumford (1984) has argued that these findings can not be accounted for by any of the more traditional explanatory propositions, but are instead accounted for by the adaptive demands placed on young adults and the middle-aged and their influence on the emergence of characteristics that are likely to facilitate major and minor contributions, respectively. Because this explanation rests on the individual's attempt to adapt to the environmental surround and the emergence of differential characteristics in relation to these demands, these observations seem to be in line with the present theory.

Unlike young adulthood, which focuses on integration, the primary focus in adolescence seems to be on the assimilation of information and explanation (Haan, 1981). Within the context of the present theoretical system, the existence of this pervasive developmental trend is not especially surprising. In most outcomes, adolescence may be viewed as a preparatory period prior to the individual selection of and entry into adult social roles. Thus, at this time in an individual's life, it could be expected that proactive activity and the exploration of alternative niche-relevant situations would be especially frequent, central to the individual's future well-being, and encouraged by society, thus giving rise to a general developmental stage geared in this direction. Moreover, under the present theoretical system, a lack of proactive activity at this time should lead to poor later outcomes, due to inadequate preparation and niche definition. Haan (1981) has provided some evidence that suggests that this expectation holds true. The same set of principles can be readily extended to account for negative long-term outcomes Livson and Peskin (1967) found to be associated with early maturation. Thus, adolescent exploration may have been limited by social demands for early movement into adult roles, forcing early maturers into a limited—perhaps inappropriate—role. Both of these trends would tend to lead to later difficulties.

In arguing for the social channelling of individual development and the selective expression of differential characteristics due to environmental interchange, this theory finds substantial support in Crandall's (1972) work with the Fels Institute data. In this study, a reanalysis of the Kagan and Moss data on achievement motivation indicated that differential environmental feedback led to the selective expression of achievement needs during adolescence and an apparent breakdown in the earlier stability of general achievement motivation. However, due to the age-grading of behavior and experiences, as well as society's tendency to encourage role preparation and niche definition during this period, it could be expected that, during this time, achievement motivation would come to be expressed in a manner that is appropriate for the individual's niche and general adaptive style. Another investigation that falls rather neatly into the foregoing conceptual framework may be found in Lerner's (1980) study of adjustment. In this investigation, she found that adjustment was better among individuals whose temperamental characteristics were in line with the situation in which they had been placed. This result might have been expected on the basis of the foregoing arguments that both adaptation and psychological health were closely tied to the individual's ability to exploit a situation, given his or her background characteristics. Additionally, the finding that the individual's perception of alignment with the environment was a better predictor of adjustment than actual measured alignment may be attributed to the fundamental importance of the situation as experienced and understood by the individuals within the system.

A well-known and often remarked on phenomenon in the individual differences literature may be found in the inverted pear. Broadly speaking, the inverted pear phenomenon implies that it will be easier to predict pathological outcomes than nonpathological outcomes. The phenomenon is often observed in personnel selection and situational testing, where we found that our tests are more effective in predicting true negatives than true positives. Within the present theoretical framework, this result might be attributed to the fact that different individuals may adapt to a given subenvironment's demands through any one of a number of alternate avenues, depending on the particular adaptive style. For instance, collegiate success may be brought about by rather high motivation or substantial intellectual powers. On the other hand, maladaptation is likely to arise from a rather limited number of sources related to common elements of individuality that generalize across adaptive styles and niches, such as a lack of preparation or a lack of the requisite differential characteristics. Thus, failure should be more easily predicted than success. This observation, in turn, leads to an explanation for one of the fundamental postulates of clinical psychology. Here, we refer to the old truism that the prognosis for recovery and the effectiveness of any given treatment will depend on the individual's pre-breakdown history of behavior and experiences. This result would not be surprising when it is borne in mind that, in the case of nonbiological disorders, the present theory would suggest that the individual's prior pattern of differential characteristics in relation to environmental demands and situational exposure would have led to the emergence of the disorder in the first place. The developmental pathways followed by individuals exposed to bad family environments support this hypothesis and suggest that enduring difficulties may often be related to the crystallization of an adaptive style in a pathological environment.

To this point, our discussion of the relationship between this theory and the broader literature has tended to focus on a rather narrow set of investigations and relatively specific findings. However, by showing that the theory sketched out previously is capable of incorporating and explaining this diverse set of often anomalous findings, it appears that some evidence has been generated for the meaningfulness and explanatory power of this conceptualization of human individuality and individual development. Consequently, it now seems appropriate to ask whether some support for this conceptual framework may be obtained from other, more general attempts to describe and account for individual development.

One relatively direct source of support for this conceptualization may be found in Vaillant's (1977) attempt to come to grips with the results obtained in the Harvard Longitudinal Study. In the course of this effort, Vaillant came to the conclusion that the development pathways followed by members of the Harvard group were best conceived of in terms of the individuals' attempts to adapt to the situations they were placed in within the constraints set by their previous developmental history and the resulting differential limitations. Moreover, Vaillant concluded that this adaptive effort and background influences led to an organized set of behavior and experiences, along with a characteristic adaptive style. Although differences in nomenclature abound, and the foregoing statements represent a rather cursory summarization of Vaillant's impressive and extensive study, this degree of overlap with the conclusion drawn in the present effort seems to argue for their validity.

Some additional support for this perspective may be found in Holland's (1966) attempt to account for the ontogeny of vocational activities. Holland has argued that vocational choice and interests can only be understood as part and parcel of the individual's more general attempts to adapt to life. Moreover, in accordance with the present theoretical perspective, he has argued that these adaptive efforts fall into certain qualitatively different patterns that are organized around the individual's total set of prior behaviors and experiences. As was the case in the present effort, these considerations led Holland to argue for the ability of a typological approach in the description of human individuality.

On a more global level, Riegel (1975) has argued that, as a general phenomenon, human development can only be understood by conceiving of the emergence of behavior over time as a result of an ongoing interchange between the organism and the environment. The same conclusion was reached in the present study, and the ongoing interchange, in fact, play a pivotal role in the derivative theoretical framework. A number of recent theorists have attempted to extend Riegel's conclusion, and, typically, these extensions have been in line with the foregoing theoretical system. For instance, Tobach (1981) has underscored the importance of adaptation as the fundamental driving force underlying this dynamic interchange. Moreover, Lerner and Busch-Rossnagel (1981), Bem and Funder (1978), and Haan (1981) have all provided compelling arguments that indicate the importance of social factors, such as the age-grading of behavior, in guiding this purposeful interchange while suggesting that the individual's own activities may make an important contribution to the content of this interchange and the course of individual development. Again, these concepts all converge in the theoretical framework derived in the present effort.

Earlier, it was pointed out that Block's (1971) investigation bears a greater degree of similarity to the present study than any other piece of research that appears in the literature. Although there are a variety of differences between Block's approach to the interpretation of his prototypes and the interpretation applied to the prototypes obtained in the present study, certain central concepts appeared in the interpretations applied to the prototypes obtained in both these investigations. For instance, both studies note the importance of prior behavior and experience in determining the course of individual development while emphasizing the special role of early family experiences in this process. Additionally, each of these investigations acknowledges the existence of genotypic consistency as well as phenotypic instability. Finally, the potential impact of social influences on social functioning and the ongoing nature of individual development is given considerable attention in each of these efforts. There appears to be some convergence between the explicit theoretical framework that has been formulated in the present investigation and the one that is implicit in Block's study.

Before concluding this discussion, the similarity between the theoretical framework derived in the course of the present investigation and those provided by two individuals whose work was a major impetus to the current effort should be noted. First, Allport (see Allport & Vernon, 1930) has argued that individual development may give rise to complex qualitative differences among individuals and that the individual can only be understood in terms of the total pattern of his or her prior behavior and experiences, rather than through discrete behavioral traits. The theoretical framework laid out in the foregoing discussion leads to much the same conclusion. Second, Tyler (1964) has argued that the *interaction* between heredity and the environment, along with the individual's active conscious selection of situations, may constitute the primary driving force in individual development. Both of these concepts are central elements in the present theoretical system. Thus, it appears that the present theoretical system finds some support in this early work, and it is our belief that the results obtained in this effort and the conceptions it gave rise to point to the insight of these scientists.

CONCLUSIONS

Taken as a whole, the discussion laid out in the preceding section seems to indicate that this theoretical perspective finds some support in other attempts to conceptualize the nature of human individuality and individual development. Moreover, it appears that this theoretical framework is capable of explaining the results obtained in other investigations. The explanatory power of this theory seems especially impressive, because it can provide explanation for results in such diverse areas as vocational interests and psychological adjustment. In light of the internal support obtained for this theoretical framework, it seems reasonable to conclude that this conceptualization has substantial humanistic value.

Nevertheless, it is clear that the present theoretical framework represents little more than an initial exploratory attempt with respect to a highly complex phenomenon. Thus, at present, total confidence can not be placed in this theory, and follow-up investigations will be needed to fully establish many of the postulates incorporated in this perspective. Yet, despite these reservations, it appears that this conceptual framework might have substantial value, and in the following chapters, an attempt is made to link this theory and its technical and practical implications.

13

Technical Implications: Methodological Considerations in the Description of Human Individuality

The description and assessment of human individuality has always presented psychologists with a number of methodological problems. Over the years, a number of paradigms for the assessment and summary description of human individuality have been employed in attempts to address these issues. Although it is difficult and, perhaps, inappropriate to state that any one of these techniques is necessarily superior to another, it is also true that any methodology employed in the summary description of human individuality should be sensitive to the nature of the phenomenon under consideration. When the techniques employed in the summary description of human individuality are inappropriate, then little faith can be placed in the accuracy of the resulting summary descriptions and the conclusions that flow from them.

In the preceding discussion, it was argued that one way in which psychology may obtain some understanding of individuality is by carefully examining the relationships between antecedents and consequents in the unfolding of individuality over time. A similar argument has been presented by Fiske (1979), and the results obtained in a number of investigations have indicated that the examination of these antecedent–consequent relationships may provide a viable tool for generating an understanding of individuality and individual development (Holland & Gottfredson, 1975; Mumford & Owens, 1984).

At the outset of this book, it was pointed out that four primary methodological paradigms have traditionally been employed in psychology's attempts to construct summary descriptions of human individuality. These paradigms were described as the trait, type, experimental, and idiographic models. However, the present study has, at least to some extent, succeeded in establishing the utility of the prototype model in constructing summary descriptions of human individuality. As a result, it seems appropriate to examine the technical implications that emerge from the differential characteristics of the composite prototypes as they pertain to the validity and generality of the summary description produced by each of these models. In the ensuing discussion, an attempt is made to evaluate the appropriateness of each of these models with respect to the understanding provided by the composite prototypes. However, before proceeding to this topic, there are certain more general methodological implications associated with the differential characteristics of the composite prototypes that should be mentioned.

SPECIFIC METHODOLOGICAL IMPLICATIONS

General Laws

Psychologists have long held that, as a science, psychology entails a search for general laws of human behavior. In a global sense, it is difficult to dispute the appropriateness of this statement. Nevertheless, the results obtained in the present investigation bring to question the strategies that psychologists commonly employ in their attempts to formulate these general laws. Typically, in constructing what commonly pass for general laws among psychologists, some variant on the following strategy is employed. Initially, the investigator obtains a relatively small sample of 20 to 150 individuals. Subsequently, the co-occurrence of two sets of behaviors or the co-occurrence of behavior with an intervening experimental manipulation is observed among sample members. Finally, the significance of these co-occurrences is established through some set of statistical tests applied to the sample as a whole. Although the magnitude of the relationships obtained in these analyses is often rather weak, statistically significant relationships are used to construct general laws that state that behaviors A and B will co-occur for all individuals or that all individuals will react in the same way in response to a given experimental manipulation.

The flaw in this logic derives in part from the weak magnitude of the effects obtained in most psychological studies and in part from the nature of the results obtained in the present investigation. Whenever the results obtained in studies of the sort just described cannot account for the total (or even a sizable portion) of the variability in behavior, it is quite possible that a significant result may be obtained, but that the results will not reflect a general law. For instance, if six different prototypes are contained in a sample, and the members of the four largest prototypes behave way X in the presence of some manipulation, but the members of the two smaller prototypes behave in way Y or do not change as a result of the manipulation, then it is quite possible that a significant effect indicating that the manipulation will lead to behavior X is likely to be observed. However, this significant result cannot be said to constitute a general law in the sense that it applies to all individuals, only in the sense that it is likely to apply to most individuals.

Unfortunately, even those relationships that apply to most individuals cannot be taken as providing sufficient evidence for the existence of a general law, because the primary concern of psychological theory is the exploration of individual behavior, and these "usually applicable" rules could be grossly misleading in the individual case. This point might be illustrated by reconsidering the foregoing example. Here, the members of the less populous prototypes might behave in a contradictory fashion relative to the members of the larger prototypes (e.g., one set of prototypes becomes passive while the other set becomes aggressive), yet a significant result might still be obtained that indicates that most individuals exhibited behavior X in response to an experimental manipulation, given the smaller prototype's limited relative sizes. Clearly, in this case, an attempt to formulate a general law on the basis of these aggregate findings would lead to misleading descriptions of the behavior of the members of the smaller prototypes. Not only can this aggregate strategy lead to inappropriate conclusions with respect to the individual, it can also lead to inappropriate theoretical conclusions. Quite often, attempts to sort out competing hypotheses are carried out by employing aggregate analyses and determining which of the alternative theoretical perspectives best accounts for the observed data; yet, this strategy may lead the investigator to rule out legitimate explanations that apply to only a limited number of individuals, thus limiting the explanatory power of the resulting theoretical system. This phenomenon was illustrated in the differential characteristics of the composite prototypes. Earlier, it was pointed out that the members of 12 composite prototypes, such as the Virile Extraverts and the Channelled Concrete Achievers, displayed substantial achievement motivation, apparently as a result of the commonly accepted developmental influences, including parental warmth, reinforcement for achievement, and independence training. However, four of the smaller composite prototypes, including the Expansive Compensators and the Orphaned Adapters, appeared to develop substantial achievement motivation as a result of Adlerian compensation. Under these conditions, an aggregate study conducted on a collegiate sample would indicate that the Adlerian hypothesis should be rejected in favor of the traditional developmental formula, despite the fact that the Adlerian model applies in certain subpopulations. As a result, a legitimate explanation would be rejected in this test of competing hypotheses, and an incomplete and inaccurate theoretical framework would be developed.

Of course, the preceding paragraph suggests that relationships that apply to most individuals cannot be held to constitute general laws because they may not apply to all individuals. As a result, it appears that such aggregate studies should be considered exploratory efforts and that investigators should carefully consider the highly approximate nature of the aggregate findings when constructing theoretical systems and general laws. Further, it should be recognized that these commonly applicable relationships may not constitute a sufficient basis for eliminating alternative hypotheses, due to their approximate nature, as was illustrated by the existence of alternative pathways in the emergence of achievement motivations.

The question that comes to fore at this point is exactly how general laws of human behavior might be adequately established. Obviously, the most direct and satisfying answer to this question would entail studying sizable samples of individuals at an individual level and subsequently establishing general laws by identifying those relationships that consistently replicate across individuals. Unfortunately, this would be an extremely expensive and time-consuming effort that would tend to inhibit the progress of psychological science. As an alternative, researchers might consider employing a strategy that is similar to the one that has long been used by laboratory psychologists in the attempt to address this issue. Quite simply, one might attempt to identify homogeneous groups of individuals and establish the relationships that hold within the homogeneous subgroups. These relationships, which were replicated across the different groups, might then be used to constitute general laws. The composite prototypes provide an excellent vehicle for efforts along these lines, because they were explicitly designed to reflect groups of individuals displaying similar behavior and experiences at various points in their lives. Moreover, because only a limited number of prototypes would need to be examined, this approach appears to provide a reasonably economical basis for establishing general laws.

Application of the composite prototypes in attempts to establish general laws offers a number of additional benefits that should also be mentioned. First, by conducting studies within these controlled domains of people, there should be an accompanying restriction in error ratio, resulting in more powerful effects within a given composite prototype. Second, by linking relationships to composite prototype status and a detailed knowledge of the individual's background, it should be feasible to formulate a better conceptual understanding of the meaning of any observed relationship. Third, in building up to general laws by replicating studies across composite prototypes, it should be possible to identify significant, yet less common, developmental pathways or sets of relationships. This, in turn, will allow investigators to determine whether different kinds of relationships hold for different kinds of individuals and whether one or more of a set of competing hypotheses are legitimate but, in fact, hold for different kinds of individuals under different circumstances. Fourth, by identifying these limited general laws or relationships and linking them to the individual's past behavior and experiences, it should be possible to formulate a more accurate and sophisticated theoretical understanding of individual behavior. In sum, it appears that the construction of general laws by building them up after examining multiple groups of similar individuals will provide a stronger base for the development of theory and general laws on the social sciences than is presently available.

Constancy

A methodological issue that is clearly related to the development of general laws within aggregate level samples may be found in the constant behavior or constant situation assumption that is commonly employed by psychologists. This assumption appears to have derived from the operational movement of the 1930s and 1940s. Broadly speaking, the constancy assumption holds that individuals who exhibit the same operationally defined behavior are exhibiting a behavior of similar meaning, and individuals who are exposed to identical situations as operationally defined as being exposed to an identical situation or experience of constant meaning. In essence, then, the constancy assumption holds that behavior or experience may be defined apart from the individual on the basis of overt physical similarity, and that there are no qualitative differences in the meaning of behavior and experiences across individuals.

Both the theory laid out in chapter 12 and the results obtained in constrasting the differential characteristics of the composite prototypes suggest that the assumption of situational constancy may not hold. It has been pointed out that individuals bring a great deal of baggage to any situation as a result of the cumulative nature of individual development. Moreover, individuals will employ this background in interpreting and reacting to any objectively identical situations, and when there are qualitative differences in the nature of the individual's developmental background, this may lead to qualitative differences in the meaning of even one objectively identical stimulus situation. This phenomenon was illustrated in our earlier discussion of collegiate fraternity involvement and how it might have very different effects on the developmental paths followed by the Virile Extraverts and the Fortunate Approval Seekers. Fraternity involvement had little effect on the Virile Extraverts' differential characteristics, but it induced a marked change in the differential characteristics and developmental path followed by the Fortunate Approval Seekers. Frazier (1971) has found that the meaning of various projective stimuli also appears to be markedly influenced by the individual's past history. Taken as a whole, this evidence suggests that objectively identical stimulus situations may have different, yet nonrandom, meanings for different individuals due to systematic differences in their developmental histories.

Because objectively identical situations may not have identical meanings, it is clear that application of the consistency assumption may lead to some serious technical problems. If individuals respond in a qualitatively different but nonrandom fashion to the same experimental manipulations or test items, and constancy is assumed, then an overt confound will be operating in the descriptive system. The operation of this confound will result in increased error, less powerful effects, and some difficulty in interpreting the meaning of any significant relationships that did emerge. Aggregate level studies would be especially problematic, because there would not be any way for the investigation to sort out, define, and analyze the differences. In fact, significant effects at the individual level could be lost in an aggregate level analysis, because even when a situation effects behavior, it might have different and offsetting effects for different kinds of individuals. Regardless of the particular strategy employed in attempts to control for these meaning differences, a failure to employ such controls whenever the constancy assumption does not hold is likely to result in poor description and diminished prediction. Further, given the pervasive differences in the developmental paths followed by different individuals in the present study, it seems that the constant stimulus model should be abandoned as a rule of thumb. Instead, the assumption should be employed only when the investigator can provide some evidence that it holds for the particular effort at hand.

Developmental Effects

One implication that tends to flow from the existence of the variable meaning of behavior or situations is that the techniques employed in the assessment of human individuality may have to take into account the nature and implications of individual development, and that these developmental or temporal effects may have a number of implications for the techniques that may be appropriately employed in the description and assessment of human individuality. This expectation was borne out on the results obtained in the present investigation. Perhaps the most interesting of these implications concerns the particular nature of the information that will be required in order to obtain an optimal definition of individuality. Earlier, it was pointed out that composite prototypes that were well differentiated when the behavior and experiences were examined over time might, for very different reasons, display effectively identical patterns of behavior and experience at a single point in their lives. This phenomenon was labled *local convergence*. The existence of this local convergence phenomenon indicates that individuals who are well differentiated over time might not be adequately discriminated at a single point in their lives. A fully adequate definition of individuality, therefore, can be obtained only by examining individual behavior and experience over time.

This conclusion finds some support in a supplemental phenomenon that emerged in evaluating the results obtained in the present study, which has been labelled *local divergence*. Local divergence arises from the potential for individuals who are quite similar over time to engage in a variety of different activities and behaviors without markedly affecting their pattern of differential development. This phenomena was illustrated by the weak differentiation of certain composite prototypes during a single developmental period along with the tendency of certain composite prototypes to distribute themselves among multiple cross-sectional prototypes during a single developmental period. Again, the existence of the local convergence phenomenon suggests that individuality can only be adequately defined on a cross-time basis, because individuals who follow a common developmental path might diverge at a single point in their lives for rather superficial reasons.

When an attempt is made to describe and understand individuality on a cross-time basis, investigators must show some sensitivity to the complex considerations that influence the expression of individuality at different points in the course of an individual's life. Along these lines, one of the more important implications of individual development may be found in variations in the timing of the development of certain differential characteristics. Earlier, it was pointed out that different individuals may develop similar characteristics at different points in their lives due to qualitative differences in their developmental backgrounds. For instance, individuals who develop achievement motivation through parental warmth, independence training, and reinforcement for achievement are likely to display these characteristics in adolescence, whereas individuals who develop these characteristics through compensation may not display this characteristic until their college years.

The existence of this variable timing and the emergence of certain differential characteristics have three important implications for the procedures that psychologists employ in the description of human individuality. First, it can not be assumed that all differential characteristics will be expressed at all points in an individual's life. Any attempt to assess these characteristics before they have had a chance to emerge in a particular individual is likely to result in poor description and prediction. Thus, investigators should pay careful attention to when a particular characteristic may be appropriately assessed in a particular kind of individual, as has often been noted in the vocational interest and intelligence literature (Muchinsky & Hoyt, 1974; Tyler 1964). Second, because the life history of individuals may lead them to develop certain differential characteristics at different rates, it is quite possible that an individual's failure to express a characteristic at one point in his or her life may not have any valid implications for later behavior and experience, relative to other individuals. Third, when individuals whose developmental characteristics have led to the slow emergence of a given differential characteristic are contrasted with individuals who have developed these characteristics, comparing these incomparable groups on a common metric will lead to inaccurate description and poor prediction. Typically, the consequences will be apparent near the mean or the lower end of the measurement continuum where individuals who have developed the characteristics to a limited or moderate degree are compared with individuals who have not yet developed the characteristic. Just as this situation will limit the accuracy of description and prediction, it may also lead to poor definition of a construct and gravely misleading conclusions concerning individuals' behaviors. Of course, all these considerations suggest that investigators should either devise and employ techniques for insuring that individuals have had the relevant developmental experience before attempting to apply a common set of measures to individuals or carry out measurement within controlled domains of people with respect to their known developmental history.

Both the theory laid out earlier and the results obtained in contrasting the differential characteristics of the composite prototypes suggested that different bits of behavior and different experiences might have very different implications for later development, depending on exactly when they occurred. Of course, the existence of this phenomenon may be traced to the cumulative nature of individual development, yet it also suggests that an adequate index of an underlying differential characteristic is likely to be formulated only by employing age-appropriate indicators. As Ferguson (1967) has pointed out, a failure to employ these age-appropriate indicators is likely to result in diminished prediction. On a somewhat more subtle level, however, it should be recognized that the existence of these differences suggests that the same measures can not be arbitrarily applied to individuals at different points in the course of their lives and be assumed to have identical meanings and be subject to common interpretations. Unfortunately, because many investigations of age differences in the expression of differential characteristics have failed to consider this possibility, it seems that the results obtained in such efforts must be approached with some caution. All of these considerations suggest that attempts to describe, predict, and understand human individuality must be more closely tied to a clearly delimited developmental framework than has been the case in most previous studies of individuality and individual development.

One of the most cherished axioms of psychological measurement is that the best predictor of future behavior is past behavior. Given the emphasis in the foregoing discussion on the cumulative nature of individual development, this postulate does not appear to be inappropriate. However, this statement has often been taken as implying that identical bits of past behavior will be the best predictor of identical bits of future behavior, and both the theory and the comparative findings laid out earlier suggest that this will not hold true. It has been pointed out that the ongoing, organism—environment interchange leads to changes in the nature of both the individual and the situation, and that it may induce changes in the meaning or developmental impact of differential behavior and experience over time. This implies that identical bits of past behavior may not be related to identical bits of current behavior in any direct fashion. Although these shifts are most likely to occur when individuals have moved into a qualitatively different developmental period where new adaptive demands are placed on the individual by society and a novel set of situations, it is also possible that these shifts will occur in a more subtle fashion with ongoing development. As a result, it can not be assumed that certain prior behavior will necessarily predict objectively similar bits of future behavior. Rather, in attempts to predict the individual's future differential characteristics, investigators must search for prior behavior and experiences that are a likely sign for the future behavior of interest. In such efforts, it seems likely that the more distant the time frame under consideration, the more highly divergent these signs for behavior and experiences will be from the actual target or criterion behaviors. Further, as these signs become less and less similar in overt content from the behavior and experiences targeted for prediction, investigators are likely to find a purely rational strategy for the definition of predictions to become less effective, and so adequate prediction is most likely to be obtained by employing an empirical approach in the definition of predictors.

Of course, this limitation on the ability of past behavior to predict identical bits of future behavior is closely related to the issue of phenotypic and genotypic consistencies in the course of individual development. Generally, it can not be expected that overt behavioral characteristics will manifest a high degree of point-to-point stability over time, because the individual's interaction with new situations and ongoing development are likely to lead to some change in the differential behavior and experiences of the individual, as well as changes in the meaning of these differential characteristics. Moreover, even when a relatively "stable" underlying characteristic is under consideration, the manner in which it is expressed in the individual's overt behavior and experiences may change over the course of an individual's life as a result of ongoing interaction with the environment and further development.

Although it can not be expected that stability or overt consistency in differential characteristics will be the rule, it should be recognized that a limited form of stability may arise in certain instances. Earlier, it was noted that, for certain individuals, certain differential characteristics may exhibit substantial stability for a period of time. These stable characteristics are likely to be those that exert a preponderant control over the individual's future selection of situations or those that are closely aligned with the particular strategy that the individual employs in carrying out a niche and adaptive style. For instance, the stability of the Religious Copers' religious involvement seems to be tied to the fact that, across developmental periods, religion provided these individuals with a mechanism for adapting to a complex social world that they were ill-prepared to deal with in a direct fashion. Additionally, it can be expected that differential characteristics subject to a high degree of hereditary control and positive environmental feedback that reinforces existing differences are likely to exhibit a high degree of stability across individuals. Nevertheless, even in these instances, stability may not be permanent, and the degree or duration of the stability is likely to depend on the particular kind of individual at hand and the situations to which he or she is exposed. Thus, although there may be some stability in the individual's differential characteristics, it should be viewed as a limited, circumscribed phenomenon, rather than the general case.

If phenotypic stability is not the general case, then it seems germane to ask exactly what investigators should search for in their attempts to summarize and predict differential behavior and experience over the course of an individual's life. The answer to this question was alluded to in the foregoing discussion via an emphasis on empirical predictive relationships; that is, in attempts to summarize and predict individuality over time, investigators will generally be searching for a set of genotypic consistencies. These genotypic consistencies reflect systematic transformations of individuality in relation to changing situational demands and are brought about by the individual's tendency to select and react to situations on the basis of prior history and existing differential characteristics. Although this suggests that the individual's differential characteristics may change with ongoing development, due to the individual's construction of a systematic niche and adaptive style in an organized social environment, individual development is likely to proceed in an organized fashion and be characterized by a pattern of systematic tranformation. Thus, it can be expected that prediction will be obtained by relating the individual's existing differential characteristics to future situational demands. Obviously, this also suggests that the predictive relationships identified at one point in the life of a particular individual may not generalize over time or to other individuals. More directly, because individuals exhibit qualitative differences in their prior behavior and experiences, the complex nature of genotypic consistencies and their basis in the pattern of individual development suggest that the behavior and experiences that are predictive of a given outcome for one individual may not be so for another. In this case, attempts to establish genotypic relationships on an aggregate sample will tend to be ineffective and result in poor prediction. Instead, these genotypic consistencies are most likely to be established at the individual level or by only studying groups of individuals having similar developmental histories. Although the specificity of these genotypic consistencies to a certain kind of individual indicates that they will be somewhat troublesome to establish, the nature of these consistencies in individual development are likely to be clearly tied to these constructs that influence the individual's selection of situations and his or her outcome in a variety of situations. Thus, broad constructs, such as interests, intelligence, extraversion, social class, or educational level, may be of substantial general value in identifying these genotypic consistencies, despite the fact that the particular nature of the observed relationships may be specific to a certain individual or composite prototype.

Person Effects

At a number of points in the foregoing discussion, it was noted that the nature and implications of certain developmental influences may vary with the particular kind of individual at hand. It should also be obvious that the earlier discussion of general laws and the assumed constancy in the meaning of behavior and experiences was clearly tied to the potential existence of qualitative differences among individuals in their expression of differential behavior in experiences. However, the technical implications of these systematic qualitative differences among individuals on these person effects deserve some attention in their own right. Hence, an attempt is made in the following section to lay out some of the more salient conclusions that may be drawn in this regard, given the results obtained in the present study.

One obvious implication of person effects is that overtly similar behavior and experiences may not have the same meaning for different individuals. Because any attempt to formulate general statements concerning individual behavior or experiences will be of limited accuracy and predictive power under these conditions, it can generally be expected that summarization will have to be carried out within homogeneous groups of individuals in terms of their developmental histories, or at the level of the individual.

Another interesting implication of person effects may be found in the potential specificity of differential characteristics. Psychologists have long assumed that a common set of differential characteristics may be employed in describing all individuals. However, the existence of person effects implies that not all individuals may express the same differential characteristics because they might not have been exposed to the relevant developmental experiences. Differences among individuals in the absolute possession of certain differential characteristics are likely to constitute an important manifestation of human individuality, and by not considering the differences in describing and defining individuality, a significant aspect of the phenomenon may be lost, resulting in a system of limited descriptive accuracy and predictive power. When the possibility of differential possession is ignored and all individuals are assessed on a common set of characteristics, then individuals lacking a characteristic are likely to be scored at the mean or the lower end of the scaling continuum. As was the case in the variable timing of the emergence of differential characteristics, this will result in a confounding of a limited and average amount of the quantity with a lack of the quantity and results in poor description, prediction, and understanding. Again, this might be controlled for by employing possession-specific indicators and working at the individual level or within groups of individuals having similar developmental histories. Additionally, the potential existence of differential possession suggests that, when a measure is being employed to describe an individual, some evidence should be presented that indicates that they are likely to possess the characteristics under consideration, given this developmental history.

In the area of person effects, a phenomenon that is closely related to differential possession may be found in salience effects. In the case of salience effects, the individual's developmental background will have led certain differential characteristics to exert a preponderant controlling influence over the individual's later differential behavior and experience. An example of this phenomenon may be found in the Social Manipulators' focus on social control and the Competent Nurturers' focus on nurturant activities. A number of salient technical issues are associated with the nature and mere existence of these salience effects. It could be expected that salient variables would moderate the relationship between other characteristics of the individual and their typical developmental outcomes. For instance, on the basis of their intellectual ability and motivation, one would expect that the Competent Nurturers would be highly successful at their jobs. However, their focus on nurturant activities apparently lead them to de-emphasize their occupational role and exhibit only a moderate degree of occupational achievement. Of course, this suggests that one way that prediction might be enhanced is by controlling moderator effects of this sort, because they constitute a likely source of false positives and false negatives in a general predictive system. Moreover, because these salience effects exert a preponderant control over the later behavior and experience of certain individuals, it appears that they might be an important source of genotypic consistency. Thus, by identifying potential salience effects and developing measures of the relevant characteristics, an especially effective set of predictors might be formulated.

Another type of moderator effects also emerged in the course of contrasting the differential characteristics of the composite prototypes, which has some bearing on the general issue of person effects. It was found that the predictive relationship between differential characteristics might be moderated by the broader pattern of an individual's differential characteristics, despite the fact that there were no obvious salience effects in operation. For instance, the adolescent social isolation and family background of the Unconventional Successes would lead one to expect that they would have some difficulty during their college years. Yet these expectations were not borne out, apparently because their verbal ability, intellectual interests, and tendermindedness facilitated the adoption of a rather bohemian, intellectual lifestyle that moderated this trend during their college years. This complex moderation of discrete antecedent–consequent relationships due to the individual's broader pattern of differential characteristics might have been expected, given the theoretical portion outlined earlier, because it suggests that individuals select activities and develop differential characteristics on the basis of their adaptive style and niche, which constitute an integrated pattern of behavior and experience. The existence of these moderator effects suggests that description and prediction will generally be improved by examining the individual's prototype status and a wide variety of differential characteristics.

Psychometricians have long been interested in moderator effects, hoping that, by identifying and measuring these effects, they might be able to improve their ability to predict certain criterion behaviors. As a general rule of thumb, however, the approach has not shown a great deal of promise. Typically, studies have failed to identify moderator effects of any substantial predictive value and replicability. Yet these findings should not be taken as indicating that moderator effects do not exist or are of limited significance. One of the most important characteristics of the moderator effects laid out in the preceding paragraphs was that they were highly specific to the particular kind of individual under consideration. No two composite prototypes displayed the same salience effects, and moderation by virtue of the composite prototype's broader pattern of differential characteristics was closely linked to the highly specific and well-organized pattern of differential behavior and experience that defined a single composite prototype. Under these conditions, a given moderator effect is likely to apply only to a limited number of individuals. In fact, it is quite possible that highly significant moderator effects would be lost in aggregate analyses, because contradictory moderator effects might be exhibited by the members of different prototypes. This, of course, suggests that moderator effects are most likely to be identified by employing the composite prototype as a control variable.

It can be argued that efforts of the sort that have been recommended here will be unduly expensive, because they suggest that different kinds of moderators must be established for different composite prototypes in an extensive series of studies. On the other hand, it can be argued that, under certain conditions, a failure to identify and control these moderator effects may have negative consequences. For instance, it is commonly argued that the number of individuals capable of succeeding in executive positions is limited and so a failure to identify as many good fits as possible might be quite expensive with respect to organizational performance. When these utility considerations are replicated over the thousands of decisions that must be made and their potential importance to the individual, it would seem that the payoff in improved prediction and description may well be worth the effort.

Person effects have two other interesting implications that should be broached before concluding this section. One of these implications is concerned with the complex nature of the predictive situation. Individual selection of situations, the individual's behavior in these situations, and the resulting outcomes are likely to be tied to the individual's total pattern of differential behavior and experience. This suggests that there are likely to be a variety of factors that contribute to the prediction of differential performance in even a relatively simple criterion situation. As the complexity of the criterion increases, a larger number of factors will become relevant to prediction. Although some of these predictions may well generalize across composite prototypes, the existence of person effects and specific moderators suggests that some of the predictions will have value only for certain individuals. Consequently, a number of significant predictors can be expected to emerge in most analyses, and it may not be desirable to limit the predictor set to the indices that make significant independent contributions in an aggregate level analysis, due to the highly approximate nature of aggregate data and the existence of these specific moderators.

Another implication is that it may not be desirable to employ the same predictors or the same indicators of even a common underlying characteristic in description and prediction for a number of different individuals. Because individuals are exposed to—and develop their characteristics in—different situations, the same predictors may not be useful for different individuals. Moreover, even when a common underlying characteristic is being considered, it may not be expressed through the same behavior and experience. An example of this phenomenon may be found in the differential characteristics of those composite prototypes who developed achievement motivation through parental warmth, independence training, and reinforcement for achievement. Even though the same characteristic is under consideration, due to differences in their broader pattern of differential characteristics and selective feedback from the broader social environment, the members of different composite prototypes seemed to express the characteristic in a qualitatively different fashion during adolescence. In cases such as these, very different indicators may be needed to accurately assess the achievement motivation of the members of different composite prototypes. Moreover, a failure to employ these prototype specific indicators may limit the accuracy and prediction obtained from the resulting summary descriptions. As a result, it appears that investigators should make some attempt to employ indicators that are appropriate to a particular kind of individual in their attempts to assess various differential characteristics, particularly because qualitative differences in the manner in which an underlying characteristic is expressed may, in themselves, constitute an important expression of individuality.

Situational Effects

At various points in our review of temporal and person effects, the fundamental importance of interchange between the individual and the situation has been enunciated. Yet, apart from these issues, the nature of the situations to which an individual is exposed has a number of important implications for the kind of strategies that may be effectively employed in the summary description of individuality and individual development. Because individuality develops, and is expressed, in relation to situational demands, three central conclusions are apparent. First, any predictive statement to be made about an individual's later differential characteristics must always be contingent on exposure to a certain situation or sequence of situations. Second, because there will always be a certain degree of uniqueness in the nature of the individual's exposure to various situations, to some extent, each individual is likely to express some unique differential characteristics. As a result, all summary descriptions, regardless of whether or not they are carried out at the aggregate or the prototype level, will provide only an approximate description of the individual. Third, because the situations presented to individuals over the course of their lives will never be completely predictable, despite the systematic nature of individual development, there will always be some upper limit to the predictive efficiency of any descriptive system. Thus, in our attempt to understand a particular individual, psychologists will always be faced with a certain degree of uncertainty that should be carefully considered before a decision is made for the individual on the basis of the information provided by any descriptive system.

Although the existence of these situational influences sets an upper limit on prediction and induces a certain instability in behavior, it should be recognized that the individual interchange with the situation constitutes an important source of genotypic consistency. It has been noted that individuals actively select situations on the basis of their prior history in such ways as to maximize overall adaptation. Thus, the individual's selection of situations and interchange with them constitutes an important expression of individuality. Indicators of the individual's selection, perception, and manipulation of alternative situations may provide particularly powerful indicators of individuality that will be especially useful in predicting future behavior and experiences. Unfortunately, the importance of the individual's selective interchange with situations has received relatively little attention in studies of human individuality, because measurement specialists focus almost exclusively on overt behavior, whereas experimentalists prefer to control situational experiences. By paying little attention to the systematic selection of situations over time, it seems likely that psychology has implicitly ignored an important component of individuality and that this has limited the accuracy and predictive power of the resulting descriptions of human individuality.

In examining situational influences and their impact on the developmental expression of human individuality, investigators not only ignore the selective aspects of this process, they also tend to ignore the fact that the situations can not be defined independently of the individual experiencing it. As a result of the dynamic interchange between overt situational influences and the characteristics of the individual experiencing them, the meaning of objectively identical stimulus situations may vary with the particular individual at hand. This phenomenon was illustrated by the different antecedents and consequents associated with fraternity membership among members of the Virile Extraverts and the Fortunate Approval Seekers. These influences limit the power and clarity of the conclusions that may be drawn in experimental studies, and so it appears desirable to control for these influences on the meaning of experimental manipulations. This may be accomplished in a variety of ways, although the most promising approach appears to entail carrying out experimental studies within a composite prototype and constructing general laws on the basis of those relationships that hold across composite prototypes.

In holding that differential behavior is dependent on the individual's interchange with a situation and that individuals will engage these situations in a manner that will further adaptation, a number of other conclusions may be reached concerning the conduct of studies on individuality and individual development. For instance, the adaptive, controlled nature of the interchange suggests that individuals will not express differential characteristics in a haphazard fashion, but rather that they will express them in relation to situational demands and their prior history. Then it is quite possible for a differential characteristic to remain dormant in individual development until the individual is faced with a relevant situation. When the existence of sleeper effects is considered in light of the fact that psychology will never be able to expose individuals to all feasible situations, it is clear that, in a strictly observational sense, the full range of an individual's differential characteristics can never be established. Moreover, different situations may be required to elicit a common behavior for different individuals, because differences in the meaning of a situation may lead to differences in the conditions under which a common differential characteristic will be expressed.

In stating that differential characteristics will be selectively expressed by the individual, it becomes apparent that even a common underlying characteristic may be expressed in different ways in different situations. It may be necessary to tailor the indicators being employed in the assessment of individuality to the particular situation confronting the individual. When a common differential characteristic is experienced differently in one situation, as opposed to another, and a common set of indicators is in use, the accuracy of description is likely to suffer. Thus, changes in the situations presented to the individual across developmental periods, due to cultural age-grading, may necessitate different kinds of indicators. Further, to the extent that the meaning of the situation varies with the individual, it may be necessary to tailor these indicators to a particular kind of individual. This also suggests that the predictive power of various measures of individuality may change with situational demands. However, this need not always be the case, because validity generalization will be possible whenever different situations have similar meanings and make similar demands on the individual. Nevertheless, the potential existence of this situational variability indicates that validity generalization should be proved, rather than assumed, and that the reasons for this generality should be clearly stated in relation to the measures in each case and the situations under consideration. One final implication of the selective expression of differential characteristics in relation to the situation derives from the potential interaction between the individual and the situation. Even when a given situation makes a constant set of demands and has similar meaning for different individuals, it is possible that individuals may employ different characteristics to arrive at a common outcome. Thus, individuals may arrive at a common end point via different avenues, and so the prediction of their performance may require a different set of descriptors.

Because individuals change in response to situational influences and because their own actions induce a number of changes in the situation, it seems reasonable to conclude that the individual will be in a constant flux. On the surface, this ongoing state of change might seem to imply that attempts to predict future behavior and experiences represent an exercise in futility. When the manner in which individuals actually live their lives is considered, this pessimistic conclusion does not appear to hold true. By selectively entering situations and expressing differential characteristics in relation to these situations, individual change will be highly systematic. This systematic process will itself generate the genotypic consistencies that make prediction possible. Although situational influences do not preclude prediction, the existence of predictability should not lead to the conclusion that individuality represents a static system. Rather, it appears that individuality is a dynamic system that is driven by the ebb and flow of events over the course of an individual's life. Moreover, this ebb and flow is likely to be systematic and tied to the individual's prior developmental history and adaptive style, generating a complex set of genotypic consistencies and a certain degree of predictability, regardless of situational change.

Despite the existence of these powerful genotypic consistencies and the self-perpetuating nature of an adaptive style, situational variation constitutes an important source of change in the nature of human individuality. When the ongoing nature of individual development is considered in relation to changes in the situation over time, then it could be expected that the strength of the relationship between past behavior and experiences and later behaviors and experiences will diminish with time, especially when the individual has little control over situational exposure and the alternative situations are associated with a limited range of acceptable responses. Of course, this suggests that traditional experimental paradigms may, in effect, operate to maximize change, because they intentionally limit situational selection and response options. On the whole, however, such change can be expected to be a slow process under normal conditions, and patterns of genotypic consistencies can be expected to be reasonably enduring.

The preceding statements should not be taken as implying that change in the pattern of an individual's general pattern of differential characteristics can not occur as a result of situational influences that arise in the normal course of human development. It has been pointed out that, whenever marked changes were observed in the pattern of the composite prototypes' differential characteristics, they were found to be linked to a marked change in the nature of the individual's broader environment and the opportunities it presented. This observation suggests that, in any attempt to change individuals, the situation must first be changed so that it encourages successful engagement. However, due to the fact that the meaning of situations is tied to the individual's prior history and existing differential characteristics, it seems likely that the environmental and situational changes required to induce a particular kind of change will be specific to a certain kind of individual. Due to the cumulative nature of development and the systematic timing of situational exposure in the broader social environment, it is quite possible that sensitive periods will occur where the situations and experiences required to induce a marked change in the pattern of an individual's differential characteristics are especially likely. By identifying these sensitive periods and the relevant situational influences that will induce certain changes in the members of different prototypes, it might be possible for psychologists to exert far more control over individual development and to develop more effective treatments than has previously been possible.

CONCEPTUAL IMPLICATIONS

To this point, examination of the technical issues embedded in the assessment of individuality and individual development has focused on these discrete conclusions that flow from the differential characteristics of the composite prototypes. Yet, investigators do not approach the many decisions that must be made in formulating a summary description of individuality as a discrete set of methodological issues. Instead, investigators typically employ one of the general technical models as a framework for guiding the many technical decisions that must be made. These general models have been labelled the trait, experimental, idiographic, and typological models, and each has played an important role in the definition of summary descriptions. As a result, the technical implications of the results obtained in the present study, with respect to each of these alternative models, are examined.

The Trait Model

As defined in the most rigid sense, the trait model holds that individuals possess certain underlying qualities, called *traits,* which are capable of summarizing differences in a variety of behaviors and experiences with constant meaning and accuracy across time, persons, and situations. Typically, these traits are defined by classifying differential behaviors into a set of relatively homogeneous entities. Differences in the frequency with which individuals express indicative behaviors relative to the mean of all individuals are then employed as a basis for defining the individual's status on this characteristic. Summarization is accomplished by assuming that the individual will express this trait to roughly the same degree on another set of trait-relevant indicators. Moreover, these summary descriptions may be used to summarize other forms of differential behavior by establishing the predictive relationships between the individual's status on the trait measure and other indicators of interest. Essentially, then, the trait model formulates summary descriptions by classifying behavior and experience, establishing the extent to which the individual expresses these behaviors or experiences, and generalizing this description to other relevant indicators of behavior or experience.

Before proceeding to the implications of the present study, with respect to general application of the trait model, there are certain additional characteristics of the trait approach that should be mentioned. First, application of the trait model is based on a nomothetic strategy. Second, by assuming that all individuals share a common set of traits and by attempting to establish predictive relationships among these traits, the model is tied to a search for general laws of differential behaviors and experiences in the population as a whole. Third, the ability of the trait model to generate meaningful summary description of individuality is grounded in the existence of a constant set of interrelationships among the differential behaviors and experiences of various individuals, as well as the assumption that identical behaviors and experiences have identical meaning for different people with respect to their predictive implications. Fourth, parsimony is induced in the model through the assumption that the same traits may be employed in the same way in attempts to describe individuality in different situations or at different points in the course of an individual's life.

The apparent parsimony and simplicity associated with describing all individuals on a limited number of homogeneous dimensions, or traits, that could be applied across the board was one of the factors that lead to initial acceptance of the model. Unfortunately, the results obtained in the present study, along with the conclusions that flow from them, can not yield both a legitimate and a parsimonious description of human individuality. Earlier, it was pointed out that the meaning of differential behavior and experience, as well as the interrelationships among them, will change as a result of variation in the nature of the situation. Thus, to obtain a fully adequate description of human individuality in different situations, it may be necessary to employ different traits or different indicators of even a constant underlying trait. Further, traits, as manifest in homogeneous sets of behavior and experience, will not be especially stable descriptions of the individual, due to situational variation and the influence of the ongoing organism–environment interchange on the course of individual development. This suggests that a given trait, or the individual's status on a trait measure, can not be arbitrarily assumed to be capable of accurately describing an individual's later behavior and experiences.

When employing the trait model, failure to take temporal and situational variation into account will tend to restrict the accuracy of description and the power of any predictive statements. Measurement specialists have been aware of these difficulties for some time and have devised modified procedures for implementation of the trait model in the hope of eliminating these difficulties. For instance, professional guidelines hold that, in applying trait measures, investigators must establish their predictive validity over a specified period of time and in a specified situation before any confidence can be placed in their results. Further, careful attention has been given to establishing the situations and demographic groups to which any given trait measure can be appropriately applied. Although these steps, along with a number of other strategies, can be effectively employed to alleviate difficulties with the trait model induced by the existence of temporal or situational effects, they also further underscore the failure of the trait model to provide the promised parsimony. Additionally, the existence of these temporal and situational effects indicate that, even under the best of circumstances, traits can not be viewed as enduring, general characteristics of human individuality. Instead, it appears that they must be viewed as temporary aggregates of similar behavior or experience that may sometimes be used to predict certain later aggregates of behavior or experience in certain situations.

Although the limitations placed on the efficiency and generality of trait descriptions by the existence of temporal and situational effects on the development of human individuality are important, they do not constitute the central argument against application of the trait model as a general framework for the summary description and conceptualization of human individuality. Trait measures implicitly assume that person effects do not exist, and that it is possible to formulate a general nomothetic description of individuality. Even a cursory review of the foregoing discussion reveals that this assumption is not accurate. Certain additional considerations compound this limitation. First, because differential characteristics develop at different rates, and not all individuals share the same characteristics, application of the trait model and a common set of differential characteristics may fail to adequately describe certain individuals while yielding poor description and prediction at the individual level. Second, it has been shown in the preceding discussion of achievement motivation that even a common underlying characteristic may be expressed in different ways by different individuals, and this suggests that qualitatively different kinds of indicators may be required in order to obtain an accurate description of the individual. However, application of the trait model demands a common set of indicators to insure comparability in scores, and the resulting classification is likely to yield summary descriptions of limited accuracy.

Although the existence of person effects implies that the trait model will not provide a fully adequate, general framework for the summary description of human individuality, the model may have some legitimate value under certain conditions. First, temporary, approximate descriptions of human individuality provide a kind of shorthand for describing discrete behavior and relationships that may have some communication value even when the assumptions of this model do not hold. Second, when a given kind of differential behavior has arisen out of a common developmental background and/or is subject to marked hereditary control coupled with punitive environmental feedback, then person effects and differences among individuals in the meaning of behavior and experience are likely to be minimized. As a result, the trait model could be legitimately employed in this limited domain, subject to modification or control for temporal and situational effects. The influence of common educational experiences on the expression of certain scholastic aptitudes represents a case in point, and it seems reasonable to conclude that the trait model may be legitimately employed in this area. Third, under certain conditions, certain situations in which the prediction of differential performance is of interest may make a common set of behavioral demands on all individuals. When these behavioral aggregates being employed in prediction are also associated with constant meaning for different individuals, then it is possible that trait measure will be found to be highly effective predictors in this particular situation. Thus, it appears that, although the trait model cannot provide a general vehicle for the summary description of human individuality, it may provide a highly useful adjunct strategy under certain conditions.

The Experimental Model

Another strategy that has often been employed in attempts to formulate a summary description of human individuality may be found in the experimental model. Broadly speaking, the use of experimentation in attempts to formulate summary descriptions of human individuality is predicated on theory. Clearly, experimentation employs a nomothetic strategy and entails a search for general laws. In theory testing and summarization, it is also assumed that only one set of general laws will be required to describe individual behaviors and experiences. Further, in implementing the experimental model, it is commonly assumed that a given manipulation and the relevant behaviors or experiences have the same meaning for all individuals. Finally, it is held that the effects observed on an aggregate level sample can be extended to the descriptions of a particular individual.

When this model is reviewed in relation to the technical implications laid out earlier and the differential characteristics of the composite prototype, certain problems become evident. Perhaps the most important of these problems lies in the assumption that a given manipulation will have constant meaning for all individuals. The experimental model's failure to recognize the inaccuracy of this assumption has led to weak effects and an incomplete model for the description and understanding of human individuality. Of course, in an animal laboratory, where all individuals have been exposed to a relatively constant developmental background, this may constitute a somewhat less serious difficulty, but in studies of human individuality, these meaning differences constitute a serious threat to the effectiveness of experimentation, because nearly all individuals will have been socialized under uncontrolled and widely divergent conditions, giving rise to pervasive and highly significant differences in the meaning of stimulus situations.

The effect of these meaning differences becomes especially pernicious because of the particular summarization strategy employed in experimental efforts. Summarization occurs through theoretical extensions of existing observations concerning the effects of various events, and, generally speaking, it is held that only one theory may be legitimately employed in describing the phenomenon at hand. However, these effects and theories are established at an aggregate level, and so it is possible that different kinds of individuals will respond in a significantly different fashion to a given manipulation but that these differences will be ignored in the overall descriptive system. In this case, multiple theories that are specific to a certain kind of individual would be needed to account for the observed effects, yet the data obtained in an experimental study would often tend to support a single theory. Although the existence of these person effects in the individual's reaction to a situation suggests that the experimental model, as rigidly defined, will not provide a fully adequate summarization model for the description of individuality, these problems might be handled by incorporating summary descriptions of individuality into experimental studies as a control variable.

Although the presence of person effects suggests that application of the experimental model may not provide an ideal vehicle for the summary description of human individuality, the general utility of experimentation is likely to be limited by certain additional considerations. The most obvious of these is that the effectiveness of experimentation in the summary description of human individuality is linked to our ability to manipulate events and induce change. However, many aspects of human individuality may not be easily manipulated, due to both the nature of the phenomenon and ethical considerations. The existence of this problem constituted a major roadblock to use of the experimental model as a general framework for the description of individuality and individual development (Fiske, 1979).

A second limitation on the feasibility of employing the experimental model derives from the fact that, in experimentation, only a limited number of events may be manipulated at any one time as a result of the need for economy and the tendency of causal inferences to become more ambiguous as the complexity of the manipulation increases. However, a great deal of evidence has been presented that suggests that individuality is a complex and highly integrated phenomenon, and it is difficult to see how a limited number of tightly controlled manipulations can capture this integrated pattern. This difficulty is compounded by the fact that experimental manipulations can only be administered over a limited period of time in most settings. Yet the preceding discussion has indicated that individuality emerges in a complex fashion over time and that the effect of any given experience is likely to be quite diffuse and may not be immediately apparent. Finally, even the most realistic experimental setting can provide the individual with only a limited number of alternative courses of action, and, commonly, individuals are exposed to a highly structured setting that forces a particular course of action in order to insure control and effective manipulation. As a result, the experimental model does not provide an especially effective strategy for examining the individual's systematic selection and rejection of activities over time, and so may ignore what appears to be an important factor in generating genotypic consistencies in individual development. When all these effects are considered, it is clear that, in the search for effective manipulation, the experimental model may fail to take into account significant elements in the expression of human individuality, and so it may not provide an adequate strategy for constructing general summary descriptions. Moreover, by failing to take these considerations into account, it seems likely that the summary descriptions produced by the experimental model will display limited accuracy and prediction power.

Although the preceding discussion suggests that the experimental model will not provide a fully adequate strategy for constructing general summary descriptions of individuality and individual development, this statement should not be taken to imply that the model has no value in describing and understanding human individuality. The experimental approach may prove highly useful in addressing discrete issues, particularly when the behavior and experiences under consideration are not subject to person effects. Moreover, when combined with adequate control for individual differences, the information derived from experimental studies may allow for the refinement and extension of preliminary hypotheses in a wide variety of areas. Thus, the experimental technique may provide a useful supplemental device, even though it is incapable of generating a truly general summary description of individuality and individual development.

The Idiographic Model

Unlike the trait and experimental models, the idiographic model does not attempt to construct general laws in aggregate level samples. Generally speaking, the idiographic model employs expert judgment and detailed clinical observations in attempts to construct an extensive and highly accurate description of a single individual. In carrying out these observations, investigators typically consider the individual's current behavior and experiences along with his or her prior history, and the information is used to construct a theory that summarizes and explains *the individual's* behavior and experiences over some period of time. Summarization is carried out on the basis of the investigator's understanding of the particular individual. General laws may be formulated by replicating observations of relationships over a number of individuals, although descriptive accuracy, rather than well-established general laws, is the primary concern of this model, and there is no requirement that any given law or set of relationships will apply across individuals.

This rather brief description of the idiographic approach points to certain characteristics of the model that should be touched on before examining its efficacy as a general model for the summary description of human individuality. First, it is clear that the primary focus of this model is on the description and understanding of a particular individual. Second, within this model, the summarization of differential behavior and experiences is carried out at the level of the individual via expert understanding. Third, variation in the individual's differential characteristics with changes in the situations or ongoing development may or may not be postulated, although they commonly are. Fourth, the replication of relationships across individuals and the definition of even limited laws applying to some subset of the population is limited by the difficulties entailed in objectively replicating qualitative understandings.

As described earlier, the idiographic model displays a number of positive characteristics with respect to the technical implications discussed thus far. By carrying out summarization at the level of the individual, the idiographic model can easily capture person effects or qualitative differences among individuals. The model can also be sensitive to the complex systematic nature of human individuality. Further, this intensive individual analysis does not require the investigator to assume that behavior and experience will have the same meaning for all individuals, thus eliminating the questionable assumption of constancy. Finally, by extending observations over time and examining the individual's behavior in a variety of situations, the idiographic model can usually incorporate many of the critical phenomena noted earlier, including the expression of individuality in situational selections, the modification of individuality with ongoing development, the selective expression of differential characteristics, and differences in the possession and rate of development of differential characteristics.

Although these considerations argue for the potential utility of the idiographic approach, there are certain disadvantages associated with its use as a general model for the summary description of human individuality. On a rather prosaic level, the general ability of the idiographic model is limited by the expense entailed in having professional personnel study a single individual for prolonged periods of time. Human individuality, as it was manifest in the differential characteristics of the composite prototypes, was an enormously complex phenomenon, and it is open to question whether even the most sophisticated observer can completely capture and comprehend the nature of individuality without resorting to comparative statistical data. This is particularly likely to be true, because observational periods will be limited, and a large number of interacting influences guide the expression of human individuality. This difficulty would be compounded by the tendency of human observers to force observations into some pre-existing model as a means for coping with the complexity. Finally, by considering each individual a unique entity, the idiographic model prohibits the formation of common principles and a science of human individuality.

In the complex interactive network of behavior and experiences that constitute human individuality, it can be expected that, in some way, every individual will be unique. However, this does not preclude the possibility that some individuals will be more similar to each other than they are to other individuals, and that the replication of relationships across these groups of similar individuals might provide a basis for the development of truly general and more limited laws. Without these laws and at least some demonstrated replicability of observations, it is difficult to see how an understanding of human development can be formulated. Although the idiographic model does not provide an ideal vehicle for formulating general summary descriptions and a science of human individuality, the approach may have substantial value when the problem at hand requires a thorough understanding of a particular individual.

The Typological Model

As traditionally formulated, the typological model represents something of a compromise between extreme nomothetic and extreme idiographic positions. Historically, implementation of the typological model has required the identification of groups of similar individuals whose characteristic behavior and experiences differ in some systematic fashion from the members of other groups. Thus, the crux of the typological model lies in the specification of groups of similar individuals. Investigations have commonly employed one of two basic strategies for defining these types or groups: (a) the definition of types on the basis of qualitative observations and theoretical considerations, and (b) the definition of types on the basis of pre-existing social groups of some pragmatic interest. Regardless of the particular procedures employed in defining the types, once they have been established, all implementations of the typological model will attempt to determine how the members of a given type differ from the members of other types. This information may then be used for describing, predicting, and summarizing the individual's differential characteristics by ascribing to the individual all known characteristics of the particular type to which he or she is assigned.

Clearly, the typological model is based on a classification of persons, rather than a classification of behaviors. When this strategy is employed, it permits each type to constitute a law unto itself with respect to the development and experiences of differential characteristics, so that different types can display qualitative differences. Nevertheless, general laws may be formulated by determining the relationships that apply across types, and limited laws may be formulated by determining the relationships that hold for one or more types. Finally, in applying the typological model, it is commonly assumed that an individual will be a member of a single type and that the differential characteristics of an individual and the type to which he or she is assigned to will be stable across time and situations.

The assumption of the typlogical model that type assignments and the differential characteristics of type members will be stable across time and situations is made to induce some parsimony in the model, because instability in this regard would require the perpetual reassignment of individuals and the need to establish the differential characteristics of type members at different points in their lives and in a variety of different situations. Unfortunately, the differential characteristics of the composite prototypes suggest that this is not an appropriate assumption, and failure to control for these temporal and situational influences is likely to limit the accuracy of the summary descriptions produced by the typological model, as well as its predictive power. Of course, with some loss in parsimony, these difficulties may be readily handled, simply by establishing the differential characteristics of type members in different situations and at different points in their lives and by periodically updating type assignments while allowing for the existence of overlapping cases.

Despite the importance of these issues, the major problem entailed in employing the typological model as it has traditionally been implemented in constructing general summary descriptions centers on the manner in which these groups of similar individuals are defined. When qualitative observations or theoretical considerations have been used to define the types, there is no assurance that the definitions of the types will be truly generalizable. Instead, they are more likely to be a reflection of the investigator's particular concerns. On the other hand, when types are defined on the basis of pre-existing social groups, such as age, sex, socioeconomic status, or job success, it is clear that only a limited number of factors will be reflected in type status. These characteristics of the typological model may prove quite advantageous when the investigator's primary concern is the prediction of membership within the socially defined categories. However, this advantage in addressing specific concerns becomes a disadvantage when an attempt is to be made to formulate a general summary description of human individuality. As Meehl (1967) has noted, the number of social categories available for type definition is relatively small, and the legitimate indicators of type status often lack a firm behavioral foundation. As a result, it is unlikely that such groups can provide a general framework for the summary description of human individuality. Thus, the utility of the typological model in constructing general summary descriptions is limited by the inability to find a satisfactory general framework for defining groups of similar individuals.

It is unfortunate that this fundamental definitional difficulty prohibits application of the typological model as a basis for constructing general summary descriptions of individuality, because the model has a number of advantages. First, by summarizing and describing individuality directly on the basis of the similarities and differences among individuals, the typological model addresses the fundamental concern at hand in a direct fashion. Second, the typological model is capable of incorporating person effects simply by allowing the individuals assigned to different types to display qualitative differences in the meaning of behavior and experience. Third, this model provides for the possibility of general laws, while allowing the accurate description of a particular individual. These advantages suggest that the typological model might provide a viable strategy for the construction of general summary descriptions if the basic definitional problem can be resolved.

The Prototype Model

In fact, one of the principal concerns of the present investigation entailed determining whether the prototype variation on the typological theme might provide an adequate basis for constructing a general summary description of human individuality. Essentially, the prototype model attempts to identify groups of individuals who are more similar to each other, in terms of their behavior and experiences, than they are to other individuals through the use of empirical clustering techniques. The groups of similar individuals identified in this analysis are then held to constitute a set of prototypes that may be conceived of as a set of modal patterns of individuality and individual development. Subsequently, the differential behavior and experiences of these prototypes are established on a variety of indicators, and summarization is carried out by ascribing to the individual all known characteristics of the prototypes to which he or she is assigned.

The prototype model has a number of salient characteristics. First, behaviors or experiences are not assumed to have constant meaning for all individuals, although they are assumed to have constant meaning for individuals assigned to a particular prototype. Second, like the typological model, the prototype model is capable of capturing some of the more complex manifestations of person effects, such as the differential possession of certain characteristics, the selective expression of common differential characteristics, and differences in the organization of behavior and experiences. Third, the prototype model represents an appealing compromise between the extreme nomothetic and the extreme idiographic positions, so that truly general laws may be established by specifying the relationships that hold across all composite prototypes while incorporating more specific relationships into the definitions of individuality incorporated within the composite prototype. Thus, the prototype model represents an appealing compromise between demands for descriptive accuracy and the need to establish general laws.

These considerations suggest that a properly designed implementation of the prototype model may be capable of producing a general summary description of human individuality. In light of the fact that the generality of the trait and the experimental models is limited by their inability to capture person effects and the more complex aspects of the individual's ongoing interchange with the environment, it appears that a properly implemented developmental extension of the prototype model provides a better technique for the construction of general summary descriptions than do either of these alternatives. Moreover, the prototype model avoids the fundamental difficulty that is associated with traditional implementations of the typological model by empirically defining prototypes on the basis of the manifest similarities and differences among individuals, and by allowing prototypes to be constructed on the basis of a broad set of indicators that explicitly examine significant behaviors and experiences that occur at various points in the course of an individual's life. Finally, the developmental extension of the prototype model appears to provide a more viable foundation for the summary description of human individuality than does the idiographic model by virtue of the prototype model's ability to capture at least the person effects and qualitative differences that replicate themselves among the individuals assigned to a given prototype.

Taken as a whole, these considerations indicate that the prototype model appears to provide the best available paradigm for the construction of general summary descriptions of human individuality. Although the results obtained in the present study provide a great deal of support for this conclusion, this does not imply that the composite prototypes formulated in this investigation will provide the ultimate, general summary description of human individuality. These prototypes describe individuality only over a limited time period and on a limited segment of the human population. Thus, before a fully general summary description can be said to have been formulated, new prototypes will necessarily be added to this taxonomic system, and data that describe individuals during the later portions of their lives will have to be collected. Nevertheless, the evidence obtained in the present study argues for the effectiveness of the approach and appears to provide a sound framework for future extensions of the approach in the construction of general summary descriptions.

CONCLUSION

In this chapter, the technical implications of the composite prototypes and their differential characteristics were reviewed in some detail. At the outset of this discussion, an attempt was made to delineate some of the more specific conclusions that flow from the differential characteristics of the composite prototypes. These conclusions indicated that psychologists must be far more cautious about exactly what constitutes a general law than they have been in the past and that this definition of general laws and the assessment of alternative theoretical systems can only be adequately carried out within controlled domains of people. This discussion also noted that the assumption that overtly identical behavior and experiences necessarily have identical meaning cannot be maintained. Individuality can only be adequately defined and described in a developmental or a cross-time context that allows for the manifestations of person and situational effects, and failure to take these considerations into account will lead to poor description and prediction.

The second part of this chapter reviewed the major models for the summary description of human individuality in relation to these technical conclusions. It was concluded that none of the traditional models were capable of producing a fully adequate general summary description of human individuality, although the composite or cross-time extension of the prototype model appeared to have substantial value in this regard. When these considerations were coupled with the data presented earlier, pertaining to the validity and robustness of the composite prototypes, it led to the conclusion that the prototype model would provide a sound vehicle for the construction of general summary descriptions of individuality and individual development.

Practical Implementation Strategies for Applying the Prototype Model

Having reviewed the technical implications of the composite prototypes differential characteristics and concluded that the cross-time extension of the prototype's approach might provide an adequate model for constructing general summary descriptions of human individuality, it now seems appropriate to examine some of the techniques that might be employed in applying this model to various practical problems. Of course, in the sense that the prototype model represents a generalization of the trait model and is closely related to the typological model, there can be little doubt that the approach has already seen wide application. However, the principles involved in applying the prototype model are somewhat different than those entailed in application of the trait and type models.

Perhaps the first question that must be addressed in any discussion concerned with practical implementation of a descriptive model is whether or not there is any justification for the model's application. More directly, it seems germane to ask whether the model will have any unique value in solving the problems that currently face researchers and practitioners. One justification for application of the prototype model, especially in its more general form, was laid out in chapter 13. Broadly speaking, when the general summary descriptions that are obtained from the composite prototypes are linked to the results that are obtained in more traditional implementations of the experimental, trait, and idiographic models, it might provide a basis not only for enriching our understanding of the composite prototypes, but also for interpreting the findings obtained through these divergent models. This integration should enhance the efficiency of research efforts by allowing investigators in different areas to capitalize on each other's efforts.

A second justification for employing the prototype model is bound up in the differential characteristics of the composite prototypes and the nature of the alternative models that are available for the summary description of human individuality. Examinations of the composite prototypes' differential characteristics indicated that individuality and individual development are reflected in a variety of phenomena that can not be readily incorporated within the more traditional models, including the nonconstant expression of differential characteristics and variations in the meaning of behavior and experiences. When these phenomena are operating in a particular assessment situation, a failure to employ a model that is capable of capturing them will lead to less accurate descriptions of individuality and limited predictions. Thus, it appears that the prototype model's ability to capture a greater range of the phenomena that are relevant to the development and expression of human individuality may argue for its application in certain situations.

A third issue that justifies application of the composite prototypes may be found in the nature of the criteria to be predicted. In a variety of situations, there appears to be some need to consider noncognitive characteristics in making predictive statements for an individual. Unfortunately, few of the existing measures of noncognitive characteristics have shown any substantial predictive value in applied settings. On the other hand, a variety of evidence that was presented in chapter 13 has indicated that the composite prototypes are capable of capturing significant aspects of traditional noncognitive constructs while producing sizable predictive validity coefficients against such nebulous criteria as job and marital satisfaction. In lieu of adequate alternatives, the need to assess noncognitive influences on differential performance may provide a compelling argument for application of the composite prototype.

The issue of complex, rare events and moderators provides a fourth argument for application of the composite prototypes. Because the experimental and trait models employ an approach in which relationships are established in an aggregate sample, it is difficult for these models to identify individuals who will be exceptions to the general rule. Yet, by employing composite prototype status as a second-order predictor in general regression equations, it should prove possible to identify these individuals and to adjust decision rules so the number of false negatives and false positives will be reduced. Similarly, by virtue of their nomothetic approach, attempts to establish discrete general relationships require sizable samples to implement the trait and experimental models, and only a limited number of variables are likely to be considered in predictive equations. However, in many situations, the prediction of complex, rare events is a critical concern that may have great utility for both researchers and practitioners. It appears that, due to their reliance on probability statements tied to a particular kind of individual and their ability to incorporate a great deal of potentially predictive descriptive information, the composite prototypes may provide an adequate basis for the prediction of complex rare events and, thus, widen the boundaries of psychological research.

An excellent justification for application of the general summary description provided by the prototype model may be found in the issue of economy. By providing a general summary description of human individuality, the composite prototypes are likely to produce adequate prediction of a wide variety of criteria. Hence, rather than constructing different predictions for each criterion of interest, the investigators might employ the composite prototype as a set of general predictions. The enhanced economy associated with the use of a single set of predictions is especially likely to be of value when the individual must be evaluated with respect to a variety of discrete criteria occurring at different points in the course of his or her life. Moreover, because the composite prototypes provide a general prediction set, they may provide the integrative decision base required when multiple competing criteria must be considered in making decisions about individuals.

A final justification for application of the cross-time extensions of the prototype model may be found in its ability to enhance our understanding of the differential phenomena under consideration. One of the most powerful constraints on the field's prediction, control, and understanding of human individuality has been our inability to establish unambivalent causal relationships. However, because the composite prototypes can capture antecedent developmental paths and link them to their behavioral or experiential consequences in a given setting, application of the composite prototypes will provide the antecedent–consequent information required to construct at least a preliminary understanding of differential phenomena. This understanding may then be used as a basis for guiding future research efforts and targeting treatments and predictions on the particular kind of individual at hand.

In the ensuing discussion, some of the more salient applications of the prototype model are illuminated, along with some of the major issues that must be addressed in implementation of the model. First, it is necessary to describe the basic equation that must be employed when the composite prototypes are used to predict individual performance.

THE PREDICTIVE SYSTEM

Absolute Prediction

When the composite prototypes are being employed to predict individual performance on any given criterion, there are two basic components that must be considered. The first is the individual's probability of membership in any given composite prototype. The second is the probability that an individual will express the criterion behavior of interest, given a knowledge of composite prototype membership. Given the assumption made in applying the prototype model that the characteristics of the prototype as a whole may be ascribed to any single member of a prototype, the foregoing statements suggest that the probability of an individual expressing a certain criterion behavior of interest will be a joint function of the probability of the prototype member displaying the criterion behavior and the probability of the individual's membership in the composite prototype. In a formal sense, the relationship may be expressed in the following equation:

$$Pbj = Psi \cdot Pbj \mid si \qquad (1)$$

where

Pbj = the probability of the individual displaying certain behaviors

Psi = the probability of the individual's membership in prototype

$Pbj \mid si$ = the probability of a prototype member of prototype i displaying criterion behavior j

Of course, the fundamental limitations inherent in applying Equation 1 is that it implicitly assumes that an individual is a member of a single prototype. However, it is quite possible that the individual for whom the predictive statement must be made is an overlapping case who could legitimately be assigned to two or more prototypes. This problem can be readily handled because the individual's cumulative probability of membership in all of the composite prototypes can be no greater than one. This may be accomplished by extending Equation 1 so that the individual's probability of membership in each alternative prototype is considered in establishing the probability of the individual displaying the criterion behavior, using the following equation:

$$Pbj = \left(\sum_{1}^{i} Psi \cdot Pbj \mid si \right) \qquad (2)$$

where

i = each alternative prototype from 1 to i.

This equation entails little more than multiplying the joint probability of the individual's membership in each prototype by the probability of the prototype member displaying the criterion behavior of interest and summarizing these joint probabilities for each prototype in order to obtain an overall estimate of the probability of the individual displaying the criterion behavior of interest.

Equation 2 presents the fundamental operations that must be carried out in order to employ prototype status as a basis for making individual predictive statements. A brief inspection of this equation indicates that it will reduce to Equation 1 if the individual has a probability of one of belonging to a single composite prototype and a 0 probability of belonging to all other prototypes. Moreover, it should be clear that the maximum value for Pbj is 1 and the minimum value is 0. Of course, the first term in Equation 2 may be obtained simply by applying the discriminant function used in assigning individuals to each of the prototypes on the basis of the relevant indicators and obtaining the aposteriori probabilities reflecting the likelihood of an individual's membership in each of the alternative prototypes. The second term, reflecting the probability of the members of each composite prototype displaying the criterion behavior of interest must be empirically established in an appropriate set of field studies.

Quite often in employing this descriptive system in an attempt to make predictive statements about an individual, the investigator may wish to assess the individual's likely performance on a variety of discrete criteria. This concern is especially likely to occur when decisions will be made about an individual given his or her likely performance in a variety of different areas. For instance, in the personnel setting, an organization may wish to consider the probability of an individual remaining in a job as well as his or her probability of job success. One of the advantages of employing the prototype model is that, by providing a general summary description of human individuality, the resulting consistency in the descriptive system being employed makes it relatively easy to extend Equation 2 to incorporate multiple criteria. Equation 3 presents this extension:

$$Pbt = \left(\sum_1^i Psi \cdot \left(\frac{\left(\sum_1^j Pbj \mid si \cdot Wj \right)}{Nj \cdot \left(\sum_1^j \frac{Wj}{Nj} \right)} \right) \right) \tag{3}$$

where

Pbt = the aggregate probability of the individual displaying each criterion behavior of interest

Wj = the importance weight assigned to each criterion behavior

Nj = the number of criteria

j = the criterion behavior from 1 to j

As may be seen in Equation 3, this extension requires little more than taking a weighted sum of the prototype's probability of displaying each criterion behavior of interest and multiplying this value by the individual's probability of prototype membership. Again, summarizing these values over all prototypes will result in an index that reflects the probability of an individual displaying the criterion behavior of interest. The weighting item Wj is included to reflect the relative importance of each criterion. These weights may be obtained through either judgmental or empirical procedures, and they need not be used if each criterion is held to be of equal importance.

Differential Prediction

All of the foregoing equations were concerned with absolute prediction and may be applied in those cases where the investigator is only interested in establishing the individual's overall level of performance. However, in such cases as the assignment of an individual to the best available job, the investigator will be concerned not only with establishing overall levels of performance, but also with determining whether the individual will perform relatively more effectively in one situation or under one treatment condition than in another. Again, the basic principles delineated in Equation 2 may be extended so that problems in differential predictions may be approached through the prototype model. In employing the prototype model in differential predictions, the two base lines that must be established are the base rate with which prototype members will display the criterion behavior of interest across alternative conditions and the probability of prototype members displaying the criterion behavior of interest in each alternative condition. To establish the prototype's differential probability of displaying the criterion behavior of interest in a given condition, it is necessary to correct the conditional probability for the base rate. This is a relatively simple extension of Equation 2 that would take the following form:

$$Pbd \mid ck = \sum_{1}^{i} Psi \cdot (Pbj \mid si \mid Ck \cdot Pbj \mid si) \qquad (4)$$

where

$$Ck = \text{a given alternative treatment condition from 1 to } k$$

$$Pbj \mid si \mid Ck = \text{the probability of the members of a given proto-}$$
$$\text{type displaying the criterion behavior of interest}$$
$$\text{under condition } k$$

$$Pbj \mid si = \text{the probability of the member of a given proto-}$$
$$\text{type displaying the criterion behavior of interest}$$
$$\text{across all conditions or the base rate}$$

$$Pbd \mid Ck = \text{the differential probability of prototype mem-}$$
$$\text{bers displaying the criterion behavior of interest}$$
$$\text{in condition } k$$

Of course, Equation 4 can also be extended to incorporate multiple criteria, as shown in Equation 5:

$$Pbtd \mid Ck = \sum_{j}^{i} Psi \cdot \left(\frac{\left(\sum_{1}^{i} (Pbj \mid si \mid Ck \cdot Pbj \mid si) \cdot Wj \right)}{Nj \cdot \left(\sum_{1}^{j} \frac{Wj}{Nj} \right)} \right) \tag{5}$$

where

$$Pbtd \mid ck = \text{the aggregate probability of the individual display-}$$
$$\text{ing each of the criterion behaviors of interest}$$
$$\text{under condition } k$$

The reader should note that the sum of the $Pbj \mid si \mid ck$ multiplied by the $Pbj \mid si$ terms over all conditions will equal the base rate across conditions. Then it may be seen that Equations 4 and 5 can be reduced to Equations 2 and 3 by ignoring condition differences. Further, the only new information required to implement these equations are empirical estimates of the probabilities of prototype members displaying adequate performance on the criteria in each condition under consideration. Again, it appears that the information will have to be obtained through appropriate and well-conducted field studies. In applying either Equation 4 or Equation 5 to make predictive statements for an individual, the term Pbd or Pbtd would be calculated for each alternative condition. The condition yielding the highest overall probability would then be the one most likely to maximize individual performance. In a system without constraint, the individual should be assigned to the condition that yields the highest joint probability, because it would maximize overall utility.

When the assignment of individuals to conditions has been placed under constraints, the assignment of individuals to the condition that yields the highest Pbd or Pbtd values may not necessarily yield maximum utility, because maximum utility can be obtained only by considering the individual's likely performance in relation to various system's characteristics. For instance, in placing individuals in alternate occupational categories, it is necessary to consider not only how well the individual is likely to perform in a given condition or a given job, but also factors such as the importance of filling openings for a given position, the absolute number of openings, and the likelihood of finding an individual who expresses a certain pattern of characteristics. Aside from these rather concrete considerations, investigators might also find it necessary to consider such constraints as the cost of assigning an individual to a given condition. In a clinical setting, an "objectively" optimal assignment may be rejected due to disproportionately high costs relative to the increase in the likelihood of improvement. Thus, to maximize utility, it may be necessary to adjust these basic descriptive probabilities via appropriate weighting schemes to control for the operation of system influences.

METHODOLOGICAL ISSUES

Aside from recognizing that the optimal absolute and differential prediction produced by the foregoing equations may not necessarily maximize utility, there are certain other methodological issues associated with application of these equations that should be mentioned. As may be seen in these equations, the likelihood of adequate outcome performance need not be established on a sample of individuals for whom predictive statements will be made; rather, it is established for prototype members as a separate, unique entity. Because accuracy in the description of a prototype is of some concern in this case, probabilities should be established by employing those who have high probabilities ($p \geq .90$) of belonging to a single prototype. The use of this rather specific sample in establishing the criterion performance of the members of a composite prototype is predicated on the fact that optimal absolute or differential prediction will only be obtained by having an unambivalent definition of the criterion performance of the members of different prototypes. This requirement might perhaps be better understood by considering the ambiguities that will arise by including overlapping cases in the definition of a prototype's typical criterion performance. Because these individuals would be assigned to two or more prototypes, their inclusion in the definition of performance probabilities will confuse the characteristics of two or more prototypes, and, therefore, reduce the clarity, accuracy, and predictive statements that can be made on the basis of a single prototype's differential characteristics.

A second implication of establishing criterion performance with respect to a prototype, rather than a particular individual, pertains to the flexibility of the system in predicting future events. Traditionally, one of the major considerations limiting psychology's ability to predict future behavior and experiences has been the need to follow a substantial number of individuals for long periods of time, and the availability of subjects, subject loss, time limitations, and resource limitations have all placed severe constraints on the length of these follow-ups. However, because the present system defines probabilities of performance for the prototype as a whole, a quasilongitudinal approach may be employed in which the known characteristics of other prototype members at a later time may be ascribed to the individual on the basis of his or her current probabilities of prototype membership. Thus, prototypes are described, rather than tracking the lives of particular individuals, and the characteristics of any set of prototype members—even those later in their careers—may be ascribed to the individual. For instance, the performance of prototype members currently employed in a higher-level job to which new individuals might be promoted could be established in a separate sample at the same time as these probabilities of performance were being established on a lower-level job. Both of these sets of probabilities could be considered in assessing a new individual's likely performance over a period of time. Thus, the quasilongitudinal strategy that focuses on the description of prototypes may allow distal events to be predicted with less effort and at a lower cost than has been possible in the past.

This quasilongitudinal strategy and the focus on description of a prototype makes it easier to address the prediction of rare events. In more traditional systems, it is difficult to predict rare events because development of the relevant equations requires a sizable sample, and, by definition, rare events occur to only a few individuals. As a result, the prediction of rare events in traditional systems is often prohibited by the need for extremely large samples. However, within the present predictive system, it would be legitimate to identify all individuals undergoing such events along with their prototype status and criterion performance. Once a sufficient number of prototype members undergoing this event had been identified, their probabilities of displaying adequate criterion performance could be used to describe the prototype and make predictive statements for many individuals on the basis of their prototype status. Moreover, this information could be accumulated over time as more and more individuals undergo the event, thus making it possible to address many rare events and obtain sizable samples of prototype members for the definition of performance probabilities.

Another advantage of carrying out predictions with respect to prototype status and the general summary descriptions contained in them is that it allows the use of a common predictive system for multiple divergent criterion performance. By virtue of this common predictive system, a variety of different criteria may be considered in making a decision about the individual, given a knowledge of his or her probability of membership in each prototype and the known performance of prototype members on each criterion of interest. The use of the common predictor base seems especially appropriate when the prototypes have been constructed to provide a general summary description of individuality. This characteristic of the system is likely to have its greatest value when resources are limited and a number of discrete criterion performances must be considered.

The ability of the present predictive system to incorporate a diverse set of criteria may prove especially valuable in addressing classification or placement problems. In certain instances, where it is necessary to evaluate and predict performance in alternative conditions, it is neither possible nor legitimate to employ a common set of criterion measure. For example, in evaluating the performance of individuals in different job categories, it is often necessary to employ different kinds of criterion measures. However, because individuals are evaluated in terms of prototype status, and the probability of prototype members displaying adequate performance under different conditions may be established in any set of criteria of interest (provided the $Pbj \mid si$ term reflects the average of these different performance probabilities), there is no need to employ a common criterion set or differential prediction efforts. This enhances both the sensitivity and the flexibility of the system with respect to classification efforts.

A final advantage of this predictive system is that it relies on simple probability statements. It has often been pointed out that probabilities stabilize relatively rapidly. As a result, it can be expected that no more than 10 to 20 prototype members will have to be obtained in order to acquire adequate stability in the probabilities of adequate performance for a prototype. Further, if a Bayesian approach is employed and investigators are willing to accumulate data over time, this predictive system could be implemented with very small samples, and more stable probability estimates could be built over time. The feasibility of implementing this predictive system on the basis of relatively small samples makes it possible to employ it in a variety of problem areas, further enhancing the overall utility of this approach.

IMPLEMENTATION

To this point, the discussion has focused on the basic predictive equations that would be employed in implementing the prototype model, rather than the specific steps that must be carried out to obtain the descriptive information. Consequently, an attempt is made in the ensuing discussion to address some of the issues that must be considered in establishing and employing prototypical descriptions of individuality within this predictive system. Although a discussion of this scope can not cover all of the issues that are relevant to such an effort, an attempt is made to examine some of the more critical issues.

Perhaps the most basic decision that must be made in any attempt to implement the prototype model concerns the nature of the indicators that will be employed in defining the prototypes. When the primary concern of the investigation is establishing a summary description of individuality for general predictive and descriptive purposes, background data indicators that describe a variety of significant behaviors and experiences over the relevant developmental period would seem to provide an appropriate vehicle. However, under certain conditions, the investigator may be concerned with predicting a more limited set of behaviors and experiences, and so it may be appropriate to employ a more limited set of indicators that are relevant to the specific problem.

If an attempt is to be made to formulate a general summary description, some decision must be made as to whether the indicators will be localized to a particular developmental period or whether they will be designed to extend across periods. Due to the fact that it is difficult to obtain a fairly adequate definition of individuality by examining indicators gathered at a single point in time, the best available description will be obtained by developing indicators that are capable of capturing the individual's behavior and experiences at various points in time. On the other hand, when the intent of the descriptive system is to describe and predict differential behaviors and experiences during a particular developmental period, then it may be appropriate to employ indicators that are specific to the developmental period. Although this strategy may reduce the costs entailed in prototype development, there will also be some loss in descriptive accuracy. Such cross-sectional prototypes might provide the initial building blocks for a later cross-time system to be constructed when data pertaining to later developmental periods becomes available.

Once an adequate set of indicators has been constructed, it will then be possible to formulate the prototypes that will be used in implementation. The first step in this regard entails obtaining a sample that provides an adequate representation of the target population. These individuals would then be administered the relevant indicators at the appropriate times. Once a set of prototypes has been formulated, the members of each prototype should be described in terms of their differential performance on various indicators. In deciding the differential characteristics of the prototypes, the widest range of available information, including that available in organizational records, should be considered in order to enhance the breadth of characterizations.

There are certain salient points concerning the general framework for the construction of prototypical summary descriptions that should be mentioned. First, under certain conditions, investigators may wish to employ the prototypical descriptions constructed in earlier investigations. When existing prototypical summary descriptions are in use, the foregoing developmental steps may be dropped, reducing costs and enhancing efficiency. Second, when a general summary description is desired and background data items are being employed, the retrospective nature of background data items may be used to develop indicators that are capable of capturing significant behavioral experiences that occur in earlier developmental periods. This expansion on the breadth of the developmental period under consideration should enhance descriptive accuracy and predictive power. Finally, in all instances, discriminant functions employing the relevant indicators or indicator summarizations as predictors of prototype status should be obtained so that this information may be used in deriving new individuals' probabilities of prototype membership.

Once these prototypical summary descriptions have been formulated, the next step in implementation entails establishing the probabilities of prototype member's displaying the criterion behavior of interest. Consequently, it will be necessary to obtain or construct accurate and meaningful indicators as measures of each criterion behavior. Subsequently, a sample of 10 or more individuals who have probabilities of membership in a specific prototype in excess of .90 should be obtained for each prototype, and the probabilities of prototype members displaying adequate criterion performance should be established. In establishing these probabilities, the same basic strategy would be employed in all efforts, in the sense that the definition of these probabilities will always be accomplished by observing the criterion performances of a sample of prototype members. However, it may be necessary to employ very different methodological designs in obtaining these observations, depending on the nature of the criterion. Further, in all cases, an attempt should be made to demonstrate the accuracy and meaningfulness of the methodology if any confidence is to be placed in the resulting predictive statements.

Aside from these rather general issues, there are certain specific points that should be considered in establishing these probability statements. In order to maximize accuracy in the description of prototype members, it is critical that these probabilities be established using only those individuals who may be assigned to a single component prototype. Further, ongoing changes in the nature of the environment or the predictive situation will require a periodic updating of the probability estimates. When the prototypes are being employed in field studies or for predictive purposes in operational organizations, the investigator may not be able to identify a sufficient number of prototype members who have been placed in the relevant predictive situation to allow confidence to be placed in the adequacy of the resulting probabilities. This situation may be handled by employing the population mean until the criterion performance of a sufficient number of prototype members has been observed.

In fact, the ability of investigators to accumulate descriptive data over time for the members of each composite prototype constitutes one of the major advantages of this approach. Once the prototypes have been established, all individuals entering an organization or set of conditions can be described in terms of their prototype status, and any individual entering a given condition can be assessed in terms of his or her performance on the relevant criteria. When this information has been accumulated over time, it should provide a sizable sample for formulating the probabilities that reflect the likelihood of prototype members displaying adequate criterion performance. Additionally, by accumulating this descriptive information on a ongoing basis, periodically updating the probability of adequate performance will require little effort. Finally, by collecting this descriptive information on an ongoing basis, it becomes relatively easy to extend the descriptive system to new criteria in new predictive situations. Quite simply, once the change had been made, all individuals placed in the predictive situation would be assessed in terms of their performance, and the data could be linked to their known probabilities of prototype membership to establish new performance probabilities. Thus, by accumulating descriptive data over time and describing all individuals in terms of their prototype status and criterion performance, it becomes relatively easy to extend this predictive system into new domains.

The preceding discussion of the advantages of collecting descriptive information concerning prototype members on an ongoing basis has necessarily touched on an important issue that is likely to arise when composite, rather than cross-sectional, prototypical summary descriptions are employed. When cross-sectional descriptions are in use, it will generally be possible to administer all relevant indicators prior to establishing the individual's probability of membership in each alternative prototype. As a result, most individuals are likely to have a high probability of membership in a single prototype when a well-constructed classification is in use. However, when composite prototypes are in use, it may be necessary to make predictive statements for individuals before they have completed all of the relevant developmental periods. Consequently, it will be feasible to administer to the individual only those indicators that pertain to their current or earlier developmental periods. Because the composite prototypes will not have been formulated on the basis of the total set of indicators, it can be expected that the individual will have lower overall probabilities of membership in the various prototypes.

The potential existence of these lower or deflated probabilities may initially seem detrimental to implementation of the descriptive system. However, this does not appear to be the case when certain additional considerations are taken into account. First, when a given form of behavior or experience develops over a long period of time, and the individual has not undergone all of the relevant developmental experiences, then it is obvious that the precision of the statements that can be made about the individual will be limited and that this should be reflected in an adequate descriptive system. Second, it should be borne in mind that changes in an individual's probabilities over time might be of some interest in their own right. For instance, if an individual has a .40 probability of membership in composite prototype 1 and .40 probability of membership in composite prototype 2, and it is found after a certain experience or set of experiences that the individual has a .80 probability of membership in composite prototype 1 and a .20 probability of membership in composite prototype 2, then it could reasonably be hypothesized on the basis of the available evidence that these experiences were critical to the individual's development as a member of prototype 1. When relationships of this sort have been replicated over a number of individuals, they should provide a strong basis for identifying the events that influence individual development and managing the process to the individual's benefit.

By employing the individual's probability of membership in the various composite prototypes and the probability of prototype members displaying adequate performance on certain criteria of interest, the descriptive information contained in the composite prototypes should provide a valuable framework for predicting future behavior or experiences. Although the general framework appears to have substantial value, the predictions generated by it will be no better than the classification system and indicators employed in establishing the prototypes. It is essential that investigators make some effort to establish the validity, clarity, power, and robustness of any set of prototypical descriptions. This may be accomplished in accordance with the procedures outlined in chapters 5 and 10 while recognizing that certain modifications may be made in this general appraisal depending on the particular problem at hand. Like any other predictive system, the predictive efficiency of the prototypical descriptions will be influenced by the general criterion problem. Consequently, investigators who wish to employ prototypical summary descriptions in the most effective manner possible should devote substantial effort to establishing accurate, valid, and unbiased measures of the criterion behavior or expression of interest.

APPLICATIONS

Having provided some justification for application of the prototype model and outlined some of the more important issues that must be considered in its implementation, it now seems appropriate to examine some of the specific applications of this descriptive system. Due to the ability of the composite prototypes to provide a general summary description of individuality and individual development in a rather flexible format, application of these prototypical summary descriptions appear to have substantial value in addressing a number of critical problems facing psychologists in a wide variety of content areas. The ensuing discussion highlights some of the potential applications of the prototype model as well as the methodological strategies that might be used in employing it.

Measurement

One area in which these prototypical summary descriptions are likely to prove especially valuable is in the field of measurement and individual differences. One of the most important applications of the cross-time extension of the prototype model is that it provides a general basis for formulating and understanding individuality and individual development. One way in which this enhanced understanding might be used is in the construction of new kinds of measures of human individuality. Earlier, it was pointed out that the differential behavior and experiences of many of the composite prototypes were guided by an apparent salience effect attributable to differential characteristics that seemed to exert a preponderant control over the future behavior and experiences of certain individuals. These salience effects were exhibited in the apparent importance of nurturant activities to the developmental paths followed by the Competent Nurturers and the importance of religion to the developmental path followed by the Religious Copers. Although differential characteristics of this sort have not always received a great deal of attention in the measurement literature, the fact that they may exert a powerful influence over the behavior and experiences of certain individuals suggests that these characteristics might provide a viable set of constructs for guiding the development of new and potentially useful predictions of differential behavior. Further, the use of these new indices as an adjunct to more traditional measures might provide, for certain individuals, some control over salience effects and so enhance the accuracy and predictive power of this resulting summary description.

Although the composite prototypes evidenced little phenotypic stability in their overt behavior and experiences, they displayed a high degree of genotypic stability or systematic predictable transformations. This suggests that the most effective prediction is likely to be obtained from measures that are capable of capturing the genotypic consistencies or measures that are designed to tap critical influences leading to the emergence of these consistencies. As a result, investigators might find it useful to pursue this avenue by employing the differential characteristics of the composite prototypes as a guide. Although it might prove difficult to completely capture these genotypic consistencies within the traditional measurement framework, measures that are capable of identifying the individual's selection of alternatives and valued outcomes, as well as their fundamental educational or social success, would seem likely to provide especially effective prediction. Many of the most effective noncognitive measures, such as the Strong-Campbell Interest Inventory and the Allport Vernon Lindzey Scale of Values, have employed some variation of this strategy, and an understanding of the genotypic consistencies that are apparent in the differential characteristics of the composite prototypes might provide one basis for extending this effort into new areas.

Although it appears that the prototype model and the general understanding it can provide might have some value in guiding the development of new measures, the important application of the composite prototypes is that they will provide a mechanism for the control of person effects, and so enhance the accuracy and predictive power of more traditional measurement procedures. Measures of the individual's differential characteristics during certain developmental periods could be formulated within a given composite prototype, and the validity and reliability of the resulting measures would be assessed with respect to the members of the prototype. In this sense, the composite prototypes would serve as basic elements whose properties, as defined by their differential characteristics, would be determined independently of each other. Application of this strategy would help insure that the measures employed in describing an individual would be appropriate, given his or her life history.

By developing measures within the prototypes provided by this taxonomic system, a number of potentially useful side products are likely to emerge. One of these is that, by defining and constructing the measures that may legitimately be employed for different modal individuals at different periods in the course of their lives, information would have been generated that should prove highly useful in understanding the nature of individuality and individual development. Moreover, generalizability studies concerned with the reliability and validity of these measures could be employed within the standard analytic paradigm simply by extending the analysis of variance strategy so that prototype membership may be used as an additional classification variable. This would allow the investigator to ignore poorly defined classification variables, such as race or sex, when establishing the generalizability or the meaning and accuracy of measures across different individuals. When differences arise in these generalizability studies, they might be linked to the differential characteristics of the composite prototypes and used to draw out their conceptual implications. A dearth of such effects in an adequately defined general classification of persons would provide a reasonably unambivalent demonstration of the generality of the measures. Thus, the generalizability framework, might provide an effective, economical, and quantitatively sound procedure for implementing the taxonomic approach described herein.

In an attempt to control for person effects and enhance the accuracy and predictive power of traditional summary descriptions, another way in which the composite prototypes might be employed entails applying a moderation variable strategy mentioned previously. Here, sample members' current probabilities of membership in each alternative prototype would be employed as second-order predictors when standard psychometric inventories were regressed on some criterion of interest. When any one of the prototype membership variables added significantly to the predictive equation, it would be known that this predictive system must be adjusted before it can apparently be employed to predict the individuals' differential performances. If the information detailed in the analysis was used to adjust the traditional equations for the individuals' probabilities of prototype membership, it would provide a control for person or moderator effects, thereby reducing the number of false positives and false negatives and enhancing the overall predictive power of the system. This approach should prove highly efficient, because it does not require substantial modification of the existing measurement systems, but merely the addition of a new set of control variables to the standard regression equation. However, this information will be neither as detailed nor as sensitive to the significance of person effects as that produced by the foregoing taxonomic strategy, and so it is more likely to be useful in addressing practical, rather than conceptual, issues.

The composite prototypes might also provide measurement specialists with a strategy for addressing one of the perenial problems that plagues the field. Theoretical progress in the field of measurement and individual differences has been stymied by our inability to effectively manipulate human individuality. Although many considerations, both ethical and technical, prohibit manipulation of individuality, the composite prototype provides a vehicle for addressing some of the relevant issues in at least a tentative fashion. The composite prototypes provide a set of modal patterns of individual development, and the likelihood of an individual following any one of these paths, given his or her personal history, will be manifest in the individual's probabilities of membership in each of the alternative prototypes. Thus, if the experiences that occur to an individual after these probabilities have been obtained could be established, any subsequent change in the relative magnitude of these probabilities could be used as evidence that the experiences affected the path taken by that individual. It seems likely that, when replicated on a number of individuals, this strategy would provide a basis for inferring a significant change in the nature of individuality for certain persons on the basis of certain experiences. By identifying naturally occurring experiences rather than conducting overt manipulations, this application of the composite prototypes might provide a groundwork for specifying the experiences that will change individuality in a tangible way at certain points in a person's life.

Industrial/Organizational

Given the content of the foregoing discussion, it could be expected that the composite prototypes might have a variety of potential applications in the industrial setting, where the prediction of differential performance is often a critical concern. One of the fundamental difficulties that is apparent in current selection procedures is that, to optimize prediction, the organization must construct and validate new measures for each job category in which selection decisions are being made, using a sizable sample. This makes personnel selection an inordinately costly effort and effectively prohibits it in many smaller job categories. However, because the composite prototypes provide a general summary description of individuality, and application of the necessary equations is based on sample probability estimates, the prototypes may be used to construct a selection system in a far more economic fashion than has been possible in the past.

Aside from the issue of enhanced efficiency, the composite prototypes offer a number of additional advantages when employed in personnel selection. First, the field's ability to predict organizationally relevant criteria has been restricted by the inability of traditional systems to predict distinctly noncognitive criteria, such as tenure, satisfaction, and honesty. By providing a general summary description of individuality and individual development, the composite prototypes appear to be capable of capturing these noncognitive influences. Second, although interviews have not been found to be valid selection devices, organizations continue to employ them in the hope of obtaining some understanding of the individual in making a hiring decision. Yet the summary descriptions incorporated in the component prototypes will provide much the same information in a far more valid fashion, particularly when the behavior and experiences of prototype members have been assessed on a variety of organizationally relevant criteria, and in this case they will provide a sound information base for assessing the individual's likely career in the organization. Third, by employing the moderator variable strategy sketched out earlier when standard aptitude and ability measures are being used in personnel selection, prediction may be improved and the number of correct decisions increased by adjusting the decision system to incorporate qualitative differences among individuals. Fourth, these increments in prediction are likely to prove especially valuable when the rejection of certain classes of individuals, such as potential organizational leaders or effective minority group members, may have a disproportionate impact on later organizational effectiveness. Because the prototypes that are most likely to yield these individuals can be established by determining the prototypes that these individuals have come from in the past, it is a relatively simple matter to adjust decision weights to that the existing predictive system will capture these individuals. Finally, because the probabilities of prototype members displaying adequate performance can be readily established on a variety of criteria incorporated in a number of different jobs that the individual might be placed in over the course of his or her career, the composite prototypes appear to provide a far more general and comprehensive basis for personnel selection.

The many advantages associated with employing the composite prototypes in personnel selection would lead one to expect that they might also have substantial value in personnel placement. Although many of the advantages associated with use of the prototype model in the selection situation also apply in the placement situation, the composite prototypes offer a number of additional advantages in placement. Because the individual's probability of membership in the different composite prototypes is effectively independent, the difference score problem and the resulting increase in error variance that has plagued many previous classification efforts is minimized, and so a more effective set of classification decisions is likely to result. Additionally, the composite prototypes provide a general description of individuality that may be used to predict performance on a variety of different criteria, and the same set of criteria need not be employed in establishing the probability of prototype members displaying adequate performance under different job conditions. As a result, the effectiveness and appropriateness of the system will be little influenced by the fact that different job classifications may require qualitatively different criteria to accurately assess performance. Thus, a classification system based on the composite prototypes will be substantially more flexible and accurate than the differential regression line procedure that requires a limited number of constant criteria.

The summary descriptions incorporated into composite prototypes might also have a number of applications in the area of personnel administration. Personnel administrators carry out a number of policy actions in the hope of enhancing employee satisfaction and productivity. Unfortunately, due to the lack of an efficient general strategy for the summary description of human individuality, organizations have found it difficult to consider how individuals might react to these experiences and tailor their actions to the needs of the individual. As a result, many of their policy actions have not been effective, because individual differences were not considered. The composite prototypes could provide a vehicle for tailoring organizational actions to the needs of the individual.

One way in which an organization attempts to insure productivity is by providing individuals with a variety of rewards for adequate or high performance. The composite prototypes could be used to enhance the effectiveness of such rewards by allowing them to be tailored to the individuals. Managers could be provided with information regarding the individual's current prototype status and encouraged to provide the individual with those rewards preferred by the members of the composite prototypes that he or she occupies. This should result in more powerful reinforcement for performance at the individual level and higher performance and productivity at the aggregate level. In addition, because the prior history of individuals, including their reward and activity preferences, will be incorporated in prototype descriptions, this information might be employed in conjunction with manpower needs to guide recruiting efforts and devise advertising or incentives that are likely to attract individuals who would perform well in areas where the organization is likely to have openings.

Another potential application of the composite prototypes may be found in attempts to enhance the efficiency of industrial training programs. Many organizations invest immense sums in elaborate training programs. Although instructional systems developers have long argued that training should be tailored to the needs and characteristics of the individual, in practice it has proved difficult to implement this strategy, due to the field's inability to define exactly what contributes to effective training for a particular kind of individual, as well as the need to develop training programs for a large group of individuals. However, it would not be difficult to establish the training strategies most likely to facilitate the performance of the members of the different prototypes. Training programs could be applied to all individuals who had a high probability of prototype membership. Because only a limited number of prototypes would be require training that is relevant to any particular job, it seems likely that learning might be maximized with the development of only three or four alternative programs.

A primary determinant of productivity in any organization is the manner in which individuals work together. Although managers have long recognized that, other things being equal, the productivity of work groups could be markedly effected by different combinations of individuals, it has been difficult for researchers to provide managers with any guidelines for mixing and matching individuals to enhance work groups' productivity. The composite prototypes might provide a basis for enhancing work group productivity. Field or laboratory studies could be conducted on which a number of different composite prototypes are assigned to a common task within a given task category. Any observed differences in the performance of work groups containing different combinations of prototype members could be used to suggest the kinds of individuals who should be assigned together in order to maximize work group performance on a given task.

In recent years, organizations have become increasingly willing to make long-term employment commitments, and, as a result, they have become sensitive to the need to formulate systematic career development programs. The composite prototypes provide a nearly ideal vehicle for formulating systematic career development programs that are cognizant of the needs of the individual. For instance, by establishing the typical criterion performance of prototype members at different positions in an organizational hierarchy, along with the number of prototype members entering each position, each prototype's likely career in the organization could be empirically defined. This basic descriptive information would have established value in providing both the individual and the organization with realistic expectations concerning the course of an individual's likely career when linked to his or her prototype status while suggesting potentially useful developmental experiences. Further, once the high- and low-performing members of each composite prototype have been identified through field studies or retrospective organizational records, the experiences that are likely to enhance prototype member's expected performance could be identified. The information could then be used to construct a systematic career development program for the members of each composite prototype. Moreover, when the composite prototypes are in use and individuals are in the initial phases of their career, it might be possible to identify those experiences occurring in the work place that would enhance the individual's likelihood of ending up in a composite prototype that is highly valued by the organization. Subsequently, all this information could be synthesized for a particular individual on the basis of his or her current probabilities of prototype membership, presented to the individual, and when coupled with guidance provided by professional staff, it could be used to formulate a systematic career development program that was cognizant of both organizational and individual needs.

Taken as a whole, the discussion suggests that the prototype model seems likely to enhance the performance of individuals, work groups, and the organization as a whole while encouraging the development of personnel policies that are sensitive to the needs of the individual. This is particularly likely to be true when general cross-time descriptions of individuality are formulated through the prototype model, and when the composite prototypes are described in terms of their behaviors and experiences on a variety of organizationally relevant variables. In sum, it appears that the prototype model might have substantial practical value in the organizational setting.

Counseling

As the foregoing discussion of career development would lead one to expect, it also appears that the prototype model might have substantial value in the counseling area. On a rather prosaic level, it seems that assessment of the individual's prototype status prior to the outset of formal counseling would provide the counselor with a reasonably complete and extensive developmental history describing the individual's past behavior and experiences as well as his or her adaptive style. This information could then be used in guiding the initial phase of the counseling effort and in developing a global understanding of the individual.

When the differential characteristics of this composite prototype have been systematically tied to the problem area of interest, such as drug use, irrational behavior, or marital unhappiness, this approach might prove to be especially valuable. Experimental or field studies could be conducted to provide information reflecting the kind of individual that is most likely to manifest certain difficulties at different points in their lives. Such information would provide counselors with knowledge of the kinds of life histories that lead individuals to enter counseling and the likely timing of difficulties. The information would also serve to help counselors identify those individuals whose problems represent transitory phenomena associated with their current developmental phase and those individuals for whom the problem represents a chronic condition. It could then be expected that more extensive counseling efforts will be required to solve the problems of those individuals who are the members of chronic prototypes, whereas shorter-term, remedial efforts might suffice to solve the problems of the members of transitory prototypes. Knowledge of the individual's characteristic adaptive style in situations in his or her current environment is likely to prove valuable, because the theoretical position sketched out earlier suggests that many difficulties may arise from an individual's inappropriate use of an adaptive style in a particular environmental context.

In addition to these advantages of the prototype model with respect to diagnosis and understanding, the composite prototypes might also provide an appropriate background for the development of individualized treatment programs. Here, members of the various composite prototypes who display certain problems of interest might be identified. Subsequently, these individuals could be subjected to alternative kinds of treatment, and the effects on their later behavior and experiences would be assessed. This information might then be used to identify the treatments or treatment strategies that are most likely to benefit the members of a certain composite prototype displaying a certain problem. The "cookbook" of good and bad treatments that resulted from the effort would provide a systematic validated system for the selection of treatment strategies.

Beyond these rather general applications of the prototype model, it should be recognized that the prototype model might also have a number of specific applications. For instance, in the marriage counseling literature, it has long been argued that the outcome of marriages is heavily dependent on the prior developmental histories of both partners. As a result, the composite prototypes could be used for the assessment of marital compatibility. Here, field studies of married couples might be conducted to identify the particular combinations of male and female prototypes who have happy and unhappy married lives. This criterion information could be employed in the general predictive system that was discussed earlier. Moreover, field studies could also be conducted to specify the behaviors and experiences that are likely to make good marriages bad and bad marriages good. This information might be used to develop specific treatment strategies and recommendations as well as to provide some understanding of the dynamics of marital adjustment.

In the area of vocational counseling, the composite prototypes might serve a number of purposes. One of these is that the differential characteristics of the composite prototypes might be reviewed to identify those individuals who were dissatisfied with their jobs regardless of job content, and this information might subsequently be used to modify normative recommendations for change in particular careers. Second, in making recommendations, counselors might review the adaptive style characteristics of one composite prototype to which an individual is likely to be assigned in relation to the generic requirements of certain kinds of jobs. This information might then be used to provide a groundwork for recommendations to enter a certain kind of vocation. Finally, the differential characteristics of the composite prototypes and the theory laid out earlier suggest that individuals are most likely to be successful when they have been prepared to exploit certain situations and have engaged in relevant preparatory activities. As a result, counselors might employ these principles in discovering developmental experiences for an individual, given a knowledge of his or her prototype status, developmental stage, and job requirements.

Clinical

The fact that the composite prototypes appear to have some value in addressing problems in the counseling area suggests that they might have substantial value in addressing various practical issues in the area of clinical psychology. Nevertheless, these two areas do not represent identical applications, because counseling often focuses on a troubled but fundamentally normal individual, whereas clinical efforts often focus on an abnormal, pathological population. Use of the prototype model in the clinical area may require a set of prototypes that are specific to the population. Historically, clinicians have recognized this in their reliance on a medical model that employs qualitatively defined types of syndromes as a basis for integration, diagnosis, and treatment. However, it has long been recognized that these qualitatively defined typologies provide less than optimal descriptive or predictive systems.

The essential step required for implementing the prototype model in the clinical setting would entail defining a set of prototypes that is capable of capturing the life history of individuals manifesting mental disease. The basic descriptive information required to establish these prototypes might be obtained by administering background data indicators to patients or knowledgeable external observers. These indicators should cover a variety of significant behaviors and experiences occurring in multiple developmental periods, and they could be used to construct a set of clinical prototypes once the indicators had been applied to a sufficient number of individuals. The resulting prototypes would define a set of modal clinical cases whose later behaviors and experiences could be described on a variety of indicators, including those reflecting progress, recovery, and traditional clinical diagnosis.

Once defined, these clinical prototypes might serve a number of purposes. Perhaps the most important of these is that they would provide a set of objectively defined clinical categories for diagnosis and treatment. These prototypical descriptions might also be employed as a basis for integrating the literature. Individuals could be assigned to categories in a reasonably objective fashion through their assessed life histories, rather than on the basis of general subjective judgments, thus enhancing the accuracy and objectivity of diagnosis. The descriptive information incorporated in the composite prototypes would also provide the clinician with the descriptive life-history data that is so often sought after in the clinical setting, in a highly economical fashion. This background information should help provide the clinician with the critical understanding of the individual required to select treatments and diagnose the individual's difficulty.

In addition to these rather straightforward applications of the prototype model in the clinical setting, it seems likely that some simple extensions of this basic descriptive information might also enhance clinical theory and practice. For instance, when the differential characteristics of the clinical prototypes are reviewed in relation to the individual's prototype status and developmental history, the information could be used to support alternative treatments. Moreover, information obtained from field or experimental studies examining the effects of alternative treatments on later behaviors and experiences of prototype members could determine treatments that were especially effective for a particular set of individuals. Clinicians might then employ this information as a basis for designing a treatment sequence of known validity for a particular individual, given a knowledge of his or her probability of membership in alternative clinical prototypes. Moreover, this information could be fed back into the initial characterization of the clinical prototypes and used to enhance understanding of their implications for prototype status.

Another way in which the information obtained from the clinical prototypes might be employed may be found in establishing the linkages between the clinical prototypes and composite prototypes providing a description of individuality and individual development in the general nonclinical populations. This linkage could be accomplished by administering both clinical and nonclinical indicators to a clinical sample or to knowledgeable external observers. Alternatively, a large sample of normal individuals might be followed for some period of time, and the clinical prototypes, if any, entered by the members of a given composite prototype might be established. Clinicians could specify the relationship between normal patterns of development and clinical pathologies. This information would, in time, enhance psychologists' understanding of the ontogeny of clinical disorders. When the likelihood of a normal prototype member entering a clinical prototype is considered as criterion data, the information could be used in conjunction with the equations outlined earlier to predict the individual's likelihood of displaying any given clinical syndrome. Assuming that the individual for whom these predictive statements were being made had not manifested overt signs of abnormality, but had a high chance of entering one or more of the clinical prototypes, he or she might be considered to be a high-risk case. The resulting prediction system could be extended to develop preventive steps to be taken for high-risk individuals.

Results obtained in the earlier phase of the present research effort suggest that any of the treatments required as either preventive or corrective must be capable of changing or influencing the individual's basic adaptive style. Changes of this sort will not be made easily, due to the self-perpetuating nature of adaptive styles. Additionally, given the biological basis of some clinical syndromes, it is likely that, in many cases, effective treatment will require both psychological and physiological manipulations. Even having these caveats in mind, it appears that the general approach laid out heretofore will provide an integrated and meaningful basis for clinical diagnosis and treatment. Application of this prototype model would allow clinicians to extend their activities into the relatively uncharted, yet critical, area of prevention.

Social

Despite the wide gulf that separates modern clinical and modern social psychology, it appears that application of the prototype model in the experimental setting of social psychology might yield some substantive benefits. Earlier, it was pointed out that one of the major problems associated with applications of the experimental model as it is applied in social psychology is that a given experimental manipulation may have nonconstant but systematically different meanings for individuals with different developmental histories. This assumptional violation will tend to restrict the magnitude of the effects obtained in various experimental studies and limit the effectiveness of attempts to contrast alternative, competing hypotheses and establish general laws. More directly, the existence of systematic person effects or qualitative differences may limit the feasibility and effectiveness of human experimentation in the social area.

Although it is difficult to control for person effects within the traditional experimental model, the composite prototypes provide one technique for controlling such effects. By conducting social psychological experiments within a controlled domain of people or a single composite prototype, the influence of those qualitatively different developmental effects may be controlled. However, a general law could only be established by demonstrating that a given experimental effect replicates itself across prototypes. Despite the expense entailed in this strategy, it is clear that it provides a stronger basis for the definition of general laws. It also will allow investigators to determine whether different laws or competing hypotheses hold in different subpopulations, thus providing for a more refined and accurate set of laws.

Development

Human development is closely tied to various social influences, and so it is not surprising that the prototype model might also have a number of implications for developmental psychology. The single most important application of the prototype model in developmental psychology may be found in the fact that it provides a strategy for describing individuality that is congruent with general models of individual development. In the broadest sense, these models typically postulate that individual development proceeds as a result of an ongoing interchange between the organism and the environment, which leads to systematic changes in the nature of the individual and the situation. This model makes it quite possible for individuals to display qualitative differences and for individuality to be markedly influenced by temporal and situational effects. Because alternative models, such as the trait and experimental approaches, are incapable of capturing the more complex manifestations of individuality that arise as a result of this interchange, it appears that the prototype model provides the best available approach for describing individual development as a general phenomenon.

Even given this consideration, it is not inappropriate to ask what developmental psychologists might gain by employing the prototype model in their studies of human development. Some of these potential gains were tracked in a rather tangential fashion in the foregoing discussion. For instance, it has been noted that new phenomena might be identified by employing the general summary descriptions incorporated in the composite prototype. Illustrations of this application may be found in the present study's demonstration of salience effects and sensitive periods. Additionally, the composite prototypes might provide a basis for integrating competing notions about how individual development occurs. Finally, the composite prototypes might provide basic descriptive information that can be employed in gaining at least a preliminary understanding of individual development by examination of the derivative antecedent–consequent relationships incorporated in the composite prototypes.

CONCLUSION

The foregoing discussion has covered a great deal of ground with respect to application of the prototype model. Broadly speaking, it appears that application of this model is readily justified on the basis of both theoretical considerations and the varied practical applications associated with employing a general summary description of human individuality. This justification for application of the prototype model finds some support in these additional considerations. First, the equations required to implement the prototype model are relatively straightforward and can be implemented in such a way as to capture a variety of complex considerations, such as rare events. Second, the methodological steps entailed in implementing the prototype model are not overly complex or expensive, particularly when the many and varied practical applications of this approach are considered and the relevant descriptive information is accumulated on an ongoing basis.

Despite the ease with which this model can be implemented, it would be of limited value if it could not help solve problems currently being faced in psychological practice and research. However, the preceding discussion has served to demonstrate that implementation of the prototype model may help investigators solve existing problems in such diverse areas as psychological measurement and counseling psychology. It also appears that application of this model will serve to expand the resources and capabilities of psychological science. Yet, even bearing in mind the ability of the prototype model and the general summary descriptions incorporated in the composite prototypes to produce valuable products, perhaps the most important contribution of this model is that it will provide a basis for integration and an enhanced understanding of individuality and individual development.

15

Retrospective and Parting Comments

Broadly speaking, the study at hand concerns what is perhaps the most fundamental topic in all of psychology and one of the more important issues in social science; that is, the nature, content, and description of human individuality. At the outset, it was noted that human individuality is an enormously complex phenomenon that provide the fundamental groundwork for all psychological theory, regardless of the particular content area. The present study represents an initial, exploratory attempt to construct a general model for the summary description of individuality and individual development. Having examined the theoretical, technical, and practical implications of the prototype model, we now turn to the limitations that are inherent in the effort and suggest some steps that might be taken in future research efforts to eliminate these difficulties.

DESIGN FLAWS

To the authors' knowledge, a large-scale research study has never been conducted that was not subject to a number of methodological and conceptual flaws. Even in research, perfection is a matter for God's, rather than mankind's efforts. Although it is always difficult to delineate the conceptual errors that one has made, it is much easier to delineate the methodological limitations that appear in any piece of work. At various points in the course of this study, an attempt was made to minimize these difficulties. Nevertheless, in evaluating the worth of this effort and the

479

conclusions that flow from it, the reader should carefully consider these limitations.

Perhaps the most severe methodological limitations that are apparent in the present study can be traced to the size and characteristics of the sample in use. The sample employed in the present study clearly does not provides a truly random representation of the general American population, and it certainly does not examine individuals raised in different cultures. The most straightforward implication of this restricted sample is that it indicates that the composite and cross-situational prototypes identified in the present study probably do not represent an exhaustive listing of all the prototypes that may exist. Hence, it seems likely that a broader sampling of the American population, especially one that taps the lower socioeconomic brackets, may result in the identification of some additional prototypes. A number of additional prototypes would be identified when individuality in other cultures is examined.

Although these observations indicate that the present study has not provided the definitive list of prototypes, it should be borne in mind that this reflects a tangible limitation, rather than a devastating flaw. Apparently, the composite prototypes identified in the present investigation were of sufficient generality to allow them to replicate the prototypical descriptions obtained by Block (1971) in a separate study employing another middle-class American sample. Regardless of whether or not other prototypes might be identified in other samples, this does not, in any way, invalidate the conclusions drawn on the basis of the differential characteristics of the prototypes identified in the present study. To the extent that these phenomena exist in any given set of prototypes and have been found to be replicable, they provide an appropriate basis for identifying phenomena manifest in the course of individual development and questioning the appropriateness of the more traditional paradigm for summary descriptions.

Another problem that arises from the nature of the sample in use is concerned with the various sampling problems that may arise in any longitudinal study. More specifically, it is possible that the selective survival of individuals in the university setting may have biased the results obtained. This issue was given considerable attention at the outset of the present effort. Here, it was found that the characteristics of the members of the longitudinal samples were effectively identical to the characteristics of the members of the CEI and PCEI samples on a variety of indicators during each developmental period. However, it was found that members of the CEI, PCEI, and longitudinal samples were a somewhat more select group with respect to academic performance than were the members of the initial BQ sample. Although this observation indicates some bias, it should be pointed out that the magnitude of those effects was weak, less than one quarter of a standard deviation, and that the degree of bias did not appear to be sufficient to grossly distort the conclusions drawn in the course of the present efforts.

The issue closely related to these sampling influences may be found in potential historical, temporal limitations on the generality of the conclusions drawn in the present study. Here, then, is the possibility that the modal patterns of individual development might change with changing historical conditions, thus limiting the stability of these summary dimensions and the generality of the conclusions that may be drawn from them. At a theoretical level, there can be little doubt that the nature and content of these modal patterns of individual development will change with ongoing changes in the broader culture. Nevertheless, at least over the limited time frame examined in the present study, neither cohort nor cohort-by-time effects yielded any significant results or set any overt limits on the generality of the derivative conclusions. Further, the results obtained in comparing Block's prototypes with the prototypes obtained in the present study suggest that this stability is likely to hold over relatively long periods of time. Thus, it seems reasonable to conclude that although prototypical description will not represent permanent entities, what change does occur happens slowly and will probably be tied to rather basic shifts in the pattern of broader culture.

A second temporal issue that must be considered in evaluating the results obtained in the present effort pertains to the limited developmental time frame examined for constructing the composite prototypes. Obviously, the time frame of the present investigation did not permit the composite prototypes to be formulated on the basis of sample member's differential characteristics throughout their life spans. Although data of this sort would provide a nearly ideal basis for differentiation of the composite prototypes, the information will not become available for many years, given the current age of sample members. Thus, it seems that the summary descriptions of individuality incorporated in the composite prototypes must be considered to be fully applicable only during a limited portion of the individuals' lives. Further, it is open to question whether an identical set of composite prototypes would be identified if a more extensive portion of the individual's life span was examined. It is quite possible that ongoing development would lead to the emergence of new prototypes with further differentiation. On the other hand, it was also true that the self-perpetuating nature of the adaptive style characteristics of the composite prototypes in young adulthood might lead to substantial stability in the observed composite prototypes, even over longer developmental periods, provided that the prototypes have been described in one or more developmental periods following crystallization. Of course, this issue can only be resolved through further research.

Yet, it should be borne in mind that the conclusions reached in the initial comparison of the composite prototypes' differential characteristics still will represent legitimate phenomena that may be used in evaluating alternative models and drawing some preliminary conclusions concerning the nature of individuality and individual development.

Another problem that was apparent in the methodology employed in the present investigation derives from the overall size of the sample available for definition and description of the composite prototypes. Although the initial sample obtained for use in this study was unusually large with respect to most psychological research efforts, containing some 10,000 males and females, selective survival and limited, though sizable, response rates to the mailout surveys combined to reduce the sample available for definition of the composite prototypes to 417 males and 358 females. Although this is still a sizable sample, relative to those employed in most research efforts, it remains true that a larger sample would have been desirable. The relatively small sample implies that a certain degree of error was likely to arise in defining the composite prototypes' differential characteristics.

Although it should be recognized that this error constitutes one limitation in the conclusions that may be drawn in the present study and that any single discrete relationship, particularly within the smaller prototypes, should be approached with some caution, it should also be recognized that a number of steps were taken to minimize these problems. First, a highly conservative significance criterion was employed in ascribing differential characteristics to the composite prototypes. Second, this data was supplemented by the correlational analyses relating the individuals' probabilities of prototype membership to indicator scores within the male and female samples. Because this strategy allowed the initial sample to be examined in establishing the prototypes' differential characteristics, it, to some extent, provided a means for remediating this difficulty. However, due to the inclusion of overlaps, this technique provided a somewhat less-than-optimal strategy for definition of the composite prototypes' differential characteristics, and it could not solve the multiple comparisons problem. Finally, an attempt was made to base all major interpretations on the general pattern of the results obtained for a given composite prototype, rather than any single significant relationship. Taken as a whole, although some confidence can be placed in the general conclusions derived in the course of this investigation, any single relationship should not be overinterpreted or be considered absolutely definitive.

The final potential limitation in the conclusions that may be drawn from the present investigation originates in the results that emerged in comparing the differential characteristics of the composite prototypes and the procedure employed in formulating the prototypes. In surveying the differential characteristics of the composite prototypes, as well as the results obtained in the within-prototype correlational analyses, it was apparent that there were qualitative differences among the prototypes in the organization of behavior and experiences. This implies that any attempt to describe the members of different prototypes in terms of their performance on a set of general summary dimensions is likely to yield a highly appropriate aggregate description of the individual. In time, this would induce some error in definition of the composite prototypes. Moreover, it seems that the prototypes are best defined in terms of their behavior and experiences on a set of type-specific indicators. Unfortunately, limitations in computer capabilities required that the prototypes be defined in terms of their scores on a limited set of summary dimensions rather than individual indicators. Although this might have been handled by an algorithm attempting the simultaneous definition of summary dimensions and prototypes, no effective clustering algorithms of this sort are currently available. Given these considerations, it was somewhat surprising that the aposteriori probabilities of prototype membership indicated that the clarity of the classification was not markedly affected by this error, and so it appears that this effect did not distort the resulting descriptions in any significant way. Further, any distortion that did occur would act only to decrease the clarity of the classification structure and the magnitude of the observed effects.

In sum, it appears that, like any other research effort, particularly exploratory efforts, there are a certain number of flaws in the methodology that must be considered in evaluating the derivative conclusions. Nevertheless, the power of these influences does not appear sufficient to invalidate the results obtained in this effort and the conclusions that flow from them. However, one must remain cautious in making statements concerning the generality of the composite prototypes with respect to markedly different samples and later developmental data until the appropriate studies have been conducted.

FUTURE RESEARCH

The limitations placed on the conclusions that may be drawn in the present study indicate a need for future research concerned with the characteristics of the prototype model and the general summary description incorporated in the composite prototypes. A number of potential applications and theoretical or technical implications of the composite prototypes' differential characteristics have been mentioned. Yet, before the promises that are implicit in many of these statements can be fulfilled, it is apparent that more detailed, problem-specific investigations will be required. Although it would be impossible to comprehensively examine each of these potential research topics in the present chapter, it seems appropriate to review some of the more fundamental topics and issues that must be addressed in future research efforts.

Perhaps the most obvious task of future research pertains to extension of the existing data base. Here, two strategies appear to be especially useful. First, data should be collected describing another sample of individuals on the indicators employed in the present study and over a similar developmental period. This data might then be used to cross-validate the summary descriptions incorporated in the composite prototypes formulated in the present investigation. Second, new sets of indicators describing significant behaviors and experiences during the early part of middle age should be formulated and administered to the members of the longitudinal sample. Subsequently, a new set of composite prototypes describing this and the preceding developmental periods should be formulated and compared with the existing prototypical summary descriptions in order to assess their generality with respect to later developmental periods, as well as the stability of the existing composite prototypes and the summary descriptions contained in them. These two extensions of the present efforts should prove useful in addressing some of the questions that are left unanswered by the present study.

A second area of future research would entail extending the prototype model into new and more representative samples. For the composite prototypes to yield maximum benefits as a tool for prediction and integration in psychological research, a set of composite prototypes describing individuality and individual development between adolescence and old age in the general American population should be formulated. Thus, a representative sample of the population should be obtained and an attempt made to follow these individuals from adolescence onward in order to generate a timely, comprehensive set of composite prototypes. Additionally, it would be useful to begin carrying out efforts to establish cross-sectional and composite prototypes in other cultures. The nature of the differences and similarities between the prototypes obtained in these cross-cultural studies and the prototypes obtained in the present study might then be used to determine whether they are, in fact, archetypes or underlying commonalities in the prototypes obtained in various cultures. Any new prototypes identified in either of these investigations that produced significant improvements in the accuracy of the classification above and beyond that obtained from the existing prototypes might be added to the comprehensive list of prototypes.

A third area where research is desperately needed is in the development and refinement of methodological procedures. One important issue that should be addressed in this area concerns the identification and construction of potentially significant indicators for use in defining general prototypical summary descriptions. Here, research is needed delineating the significant behavior and experiences occurring to individuals throughout their life spans. Further research should address the issue of how this information may be uniformly and systematically translated into a set of background measures. Another important methodological issue pertains to the particular procedures employed in assessing the similarities and differences among individuals. As was noted earlier, one profitable avenue of investigation in this area might involve attempts to construct efficient and effective algorithms that are capable of the simultaneous clustering of indicators and persons. Along these lines, there would be substantial value in explicitly contrasting alternative similarity matrices and clustering algorithms with respect to the classification of persons. Finally, there might be some value in attempts to link clustering algorithms with more formal mathematical models, such as those employed in discriminant and factor analyses. Although it is clear that there are many similarities among these techniques, teasing out a formal mathematical model for the application of clustering procedures may represent an enormous and rather difficult undertaking.

The extension of the prototype model into more discrete problem areas constitutes a fourth important area of further research. Earlier, a variety of area-specific applications of the prototype model were laid out in detail. Yet, to date, little progress has been made towards the implementation of the prototype model in these discrete content areas. One of the more important projects in this area would entail an attempt to establish a set of clinical prototypes and investigate the ability of the prototype model in attempts to improve treatment and diagnosis. Another project in this area might involve implementation of the prototype model in the industrial setting and investigating its applications to problems in career development, personnel selection, and personnel classification. Finally, there is a compelling need for research that addresses the issue of when and in what content area use of the prototype model to control for moderator effects would be desirable in terms of either increased prediction or better-defined laws with respect to a particular individual.

Of course, there are a wide variety of other research topics that might be addressed with respect to the development and application of the prototype model. Actually, the preceding discussion represents little more than the authors' own highly selective views of some of the more fundamental issues at hand. As a new approach to the definition and description of individuality and individual development, it seems likely that research concerned with the prototype model will develop in a number of directions, many of which can not be anticipated in this early stage. Thus, it is our hope that the preceding section has served to stimulate curiosity and thought.

A RETURN TO THE UNDERGROUND

Having reviewed some of the limitations and potential future extensions of the present research effort, it seems appropriate to return to a theme that was presented at the outset of the discussion. In chapter 1, it was pointed out that, even within professional circles, the trait model has been subjected to enormous criticism. This has given rise to what might be regarded as an underground literature that has attempted to develop alternative strategies for assessing the nature of individuality and individual development in the hope of developing a more varied picture of the individual as a human being. Broadly speaking, there are certain common themes that run through this literature that argue that individuality can only be adequately described as it emerges over time, that it involves a variety of highly complex moderator effects, that it may be reflected in complex qualitative differences among individual which prohibits simple nomothetic understanding, and that it can only be adequately assessed by describing the situational context in which it emerges.

In the present study, a variety of evidence was obtained that provides compelling support for these basic tenets of the underground literature. For instance, it was found that individual development is an ongoing phenomenon that does not suddenly halt at the time of adolescence, but continues to be driven by interchange with the environmental surround. Further, it appeared that the individual's conscious and active selection of situations plays a critical role in generating genotypic consistencies in the course of individual development. The differential characteristics of the composite prototypes also suggested that there are a variety of highly significant qualitative differences among individuals with respect to their organization of behavior and experiences, the meaning of differential behaviors and experiences, and the basic processes underlying the development of even common differential characteristics. Moreover, it appears that these complex qualitative differences may give rise to a variety of complex, person-specific moderator effects that limit the value of simple nomothetic laws in the description of a particular person.

Although all of these observations tend to support the criticisms of the trait model found in the underground literature, as well as those applied to the major alternative strategies, perhaps the most central criticism that the underground literature has leveled against the trait model and its competitors is that they fail to capture the complex manifestations of human individuality as it emerges over the course of an individual's life. Concerns of this sort seem to underlie Tyler's (1965) comment that the trait model does not feel right. Similarly, Allport's (1937) persuasive argument for a conception of individuality that goes beyond simple nomothetic laws seem bound up in a similar revulsion concerning a psychology that has lost sight of the individual in a desire to treat human beings as a simple response function. Given the stature of these commentators and the many years that have passed since they originally made these comments, as well as the support for this position obtained in the present study, one must wonder why so little progress has been made in remediating these difficulties and rethinking our general approach to the definition and description of human individuality.

In a broad sense, this lack of progress may be tied to psychology's inordinate, almost pathological, preoccupation with becoming a science in accordance with the model laid down by Newtonian physics. This preoccupation and the traditions inherited from it have led to an assumption that parsimony was as important, if not more so, than accuracy of description. Moreover, acceptance of this mode led psychologists to a misguided belief in the adequacy of operational definitions and a rather simplistic belief that the observable was the measure of a person. Finally, acceptance of this model holds out the promise, which is clearly inappropriate, that phenomena as complex as individual differences can be described and predicted through a mechanistic model that ignores purpose and interest while conceiving of the individual as little more than the weighted sum of linear dependencies among a set of invariant particles often called *traits*.

All of these influences led psychologists to prefer a simplistic, mechanistic conception of human behavior in general and individuality in particular. Unfortunately, the results obtained in the present investigation suggest that these simple mechanical principles have not been—and will not be—sufficient to provide an adequate summary description of human individuality except under very limited conditions. Moreover, even in those areas where the mechanistic model can be successfully employed, it is open to question whether its application can provide a true understanding of individuality and individual development.

Broadly speaking, both the underground literature and the results obtained in the present study seem to argue that, if any real progress is to be made in psychology, a more sophisticated view of individuality and individual development must be formulated. A first step along this path would be made by discarding simplistic physical models. It must also be recognized that the individual does not exist as a steady state element, but is subject to modification and change throughout his or her life. This malleability does not imply randomness, because change will occur within an ongoing stream of behavior. Further, in making these adjustments, it must be recognized that no situation has an existence apart from the individual experiencing it, and all behavior will, to some extent, be determined by the situation. The operational definitions of behavior and experiences, as such, probably represent little more than convenient fiction. Another convenient fiction that must be done away with is that general laws of the relationship among behavioral and experimental elements are the sole legitimate goal of psychological science and can be established simply by establishing those relationships that hold for *most* individuals. This strategy implicitly downgrades the fundamental importance of the individual and ignores the fact, which has been well established in the present study, that different laws may hold for different kinds of individuals. A failure to devise strategies that take this phenomenon into account will restrict the accuracy of description and prediction and will trivialize psychological research.

The foregoing discussion suggests that psychologists must recognize that they are trying to understand, describe, and predict a highly complex natural phenomenon. In our attempts to achieve these goals, it can be expected that progress will be slow and that our precepts, concepts, and methods must display similar complexity and sophistication. These conclusions also suggest that, prior to attempts to establish general laws, there must be far more emphasis placed on naturalistic description and prediction if we are to avoid the mistakes of the past. In devising models for these descriptions, an attempt should be made to formulate strategies that are sufficiently flexible to be capable of capturing the many manifestations of the highly complex phenomenon that has been labeled *human individuality*. More so than anything else, the present study reported an initial, preliminary attempt to construct a more general and flexible model for the summary descriptions of human individuality that would allow psychologists to accurately describe the gritty realities of differential behavior and experiences as they emerge from the soil of human development.

References

Alker, H. A. (1972). Is personality situationally specific or intra-psychically consistent? *Journal of Personality, 40,* 1–16.

Allport, G. W. (1937). *Personality: A psychological interpretation.* New York: Holt, Rinehart & Winston.

Allport, G. W., & Vernon, P. E. (1930). The field of personality. *Psychological Bulletin, 27,* 677–730.

Allport, G. W., Vernon, P. E., & Lindzey, G. (1960). *Study of values* (3rd ed.). Boston: Houghton-Mifflin.

Anastasi, A. (1934). Practice and variability: A study in psychological method. *Psychological Monograph, 45,* 1–31.

Anderberg, J. (1972). *Clustering algorithms.* New York: Academic Press.

Anderson, B. B. (1973). An interinstitutional comparison on dimensions of student development: A step toward the goal of a comprehensive developmental-integrative model of human behavior (Doctoral dissertation, University of Georgia, 1972). *Dissertation Abstracts International, 33,* 4558B. (University Microfilms No. 73-5638, 87)

Asher, J. J. (1972). The biographical item: Can it be improved? *Personnel Psychology, 25,* 251–269.

Atkinson, J. W. (1981). Studying personality in the context of an advanced motivational psychology. *American Psychologist, 36,* 117–128.

Baltes, P. B. (1968). Longitudinal and cross sectional sequences in the study of age and generation effects. *Human Development, 11,* 145–171.

Baltes, P. B., & Nesselroade, J. R. (1972). Cultural change and adolescent personality development. *Developmental Psychology, 7,* 244–256.

Baltes, P. B., & Nesselroade, J. R. (1973). The developmental analysis of individual differences on multiple measures. In J. R. Nesselroade & H. W. Reese (Eds.), *Life-span developmental psychology: Methodological issues* (pp. 219–252). New York: Academic Press.

Baltes, P. B., & Schaie, W. K. (1973). On life-span developmental research paradigms: Retrospects and prospects. In P. B. Baltes & W. K. Schaie (Eds.), *Life-span developmental psychology: Personality and socialization* (pp. 366–432). New York: Academic Press.

Bayley, N. (1949). Consistency and variability in the growth of intelligence from birth to eighteen years. *Journal of Genetic Psychology, 75,* 165–196.

Bayley, N. (1957). Data on the growth of IQ between 16 and 21 years, as measured by the Wechsler Bellevue Scale. *Journal of Genetic Psychology, 90,* 3–15.

Bayley, N. (1965). Research in child development: A longitudinal perspective. *Merrill-Palmer Quarterly, 11,* 183–208.

Bayley, N. (1968). Behavioral correlates of mental growth: Birth to thirty-six years. *American Psychologist, 23,* 1–17.

Bayley, N., & Jones, H. E. (1937). Environmental correlates of mental and motor development: A cumulative study from infancy to six years. *Child Development, 8,* 329–341.

Bayley, N., & Oden, M. H. (1955). The maintenance of intellectual ability in gifted adults. *Journal of Gerontology, 10,* 91–107.

Bell, D. E. (1974). *Life history antecedents and attitudes towards death.* Unpublished master's thesis, University of Georgia, Athens.

Bell, R. Q. (1960). Retrospective and prospective views of personality and development. *Merrill-Palmer Quarterly, 6,* 131–141.

Belsky, J., & Tolan, W. (1981). Infants as producers of their own development: An ecological analysis. In R. M. Lerner & N. A. Busch-Rossnagel (Eds.), *Individuals as producers of their own development: A life span perspective* (pp. 87–116). New York: Academic Press.

Bem, D. J. (1972). Constructing cross sectional consistencies in behavior: Some thoughts on Alker. *Journal of Personality, 40,* 17–26.

Bem, D. J., & Allen, A. (1974). On predicting some of the people some of the time. *Psychological Review, 81,* 506–520.

Bem, D. J., & Funder, J. (1978). Predicting more of the people more of the time. *Psychological Review, 85,* 485–501.

Benedict, R. (1938). Continuities and discontinuities in cultural conditioning. *Psychiatry, 1,* 161–167.

Bergman, L. R. (1972). Inferential aspects of longitudinal data in studying developmental problems. *Human Development, 15,* 287–293.

Binet, A., & Simon, T. (1905). New methods for the diagnosis of the intellectual level of subnormals. *Anee Psychology, 11,* 191–244.

Blashfield, R. (1981). Reply to Lorr and reanalyses. *Applied Psychological Measurement, 5,* 75–76.

Blashfield, R., & Morey, J. (1980). A comparison of four clustering methods using MMPI Monte Carlo data. *Applied Psychological Measurement, 4,* 57–64.

Block, J. (1971). *Lives through time.* Monterey, CA: Bancroft Books.

Block, J., & Turula, E. (1963). Identification, ego control and adjustment. *Child Development, 34,* 945–953.

Boardman, W. K., Calhoun, L. G., & Schiel, J. H. (1974). Life experience patterns and the development of college leadership roles. *Psychological Reports, 31,* 333–334.

Bray, D., Campbell, R. J., & Grant, D. L. (1974). *Formative years in business.* New York: Wiley.

Brisson, G. R., LaBarre, R., Lavallee, H., Rajic, M., Beaucage, C., & Jequier, J. (1974). "Training effect" in the design of a longitudinal study. *Perceptual and Motor Skills, 39,* 693–694.

Brogden, H. E. (1949). When testing pays off. *Personnel Psychology, 2,* 171–183.

Bronson, W. C., Katten, E. X., & Livson, N. (1959). Patterns of authority and affection in two generations. *Journal of Abnormal and Social Psychology, 58,* 143–152.

Brooks, J. D., & Elliott, D. M. (1971). Prediction of psychological adjustment at the age of 30 from leisure time activities and satisfaction in childhood. *Human Development, 14,* 51–61.

Brush, D. H. (1974). *Predicting major field of college concentration with biographical and voca-*

tional interest data: A longitudinal study. Unpublished master's thesis, University of Georgia, Athens.

Buhler, C. (1968). The course of human life as a psychological problem. *Human Development, 11,* 184–200.

Cascio, W. F. (1975). The accuracy of verifiable biographical information blank responses. *Journal of Applied Psychology, 60,* 767–769.

Cattell, J. McK. (1890). Mental tests and measurements. *Mind, 15,* 373–380.

Cattell, R. B. (1982). *Personality and learning theory.* New York: Springer Publishing Company.

Chaney, F. B., & Owens, W. A. (1964). Life history antecedents of sales, research and general engineering interests. *Journal of Applied Psychology, 48,* 101–105.

Crandall, V. C. (1972). The Fels Study: Some considerations to personality development in childhood and adulthood. *Seminars in Psychiatry, 4,* 383–397.

Cronbach, L. J. (1954). Report on the psychometric mission to clinicia. *Psychometrica, 16,* 221–230.

Cronbach, L. J. (1957a, August). *A measure of profile similarity.* Paper presented at the meetings of the American Psychological Association, Chicago, IL.

Cronbach, L. J. (1957b). Two disciplines of scientific psychology. *American Psychologist, 12,* 671–684.

Cronbach, L. J. (1971). Test validation. In E. K. Thorndike (Ed.), *Educational testing* (pp. 703–824). New York: American Council on Education.

Cronbach, L. J., & Snow, R. E. (1977). *Aptitudes and instructional methods.* New York: Irvington Publishers, Inc.

Damon, A. (1965). Discrepancies between findings of longitudinal and cross sectional studies in adult life: Physique and physiology. *Human Development, 8,* 16–22.

Dennis, W. (1956). Age and achievement: A critique. *Journal of Gerontology, 11,* 331–333.

Dennis, W. (1958). The age development in scientific achievement. *American Psychologist, 13,* 457–460.

Dennis, W. (1966). Creativity between the ages of 20 and 80. *Journal of Gerontology, 21,* 1–8.

Dunkleberger, C. J., & Tyler, L. E. (1961). Interest stability and personality traits. *Journal of Counseling Psychology, 8,* 70–74.

Dunnette, M. D. (1966). *Personnel selection and placement.* Monterey, CA: Brooks/Cole.

Eberhard, C., & Owens, W. A. (1975). Word association as a function of biodata subgrouping. *Developmental Psychology, 11,* 159–164.

Eberhardt, B. J., & Muchinsky, P. M. (1982). An empirical investigation of the factor stability of Owens' Biographical Questionnaire. *Journal of Applied Psychology, 67,* 138–145.

Eichorn, D. H. (1973). The Berkeley Longitudinal Studies: Continuities and correlates of behavior. *Canadian Journal of Behavioral Science, 5,* 297–320.

Ekehammar, B. (1977). Test of a psychological cost-benefit model for career choice. *Journal of Vocational Behavior, 10,* 245–260.

Elkind, D. (1964). Ambiguous pictures for the study of perceptual development and learning. *Child Development, 35,* 1391–1396.

Evans, L., & Bartholemew, J. (1981). *Must success cost so much?* New York: Free Press.

Feild, H. S. (1975). Subgroup and individual differences in the quasi-actuarial assessment of behavior: A longitudinal study (Doctoral dissertation, University of Georgia, 1973). *Dissertation Abstracts International, 35,* 4240B. (University Microfilms no. 75-2590, 338)

Feild, H. S., Lissitz, R. W., & Schoenfeldt, L. F. (1975). The utility of homogeneous subgroups and individual information in prediction. *Multivariate Behavioral Research, 10,* 449–462.

Ferguson, L. W. (1967). Economic maturity. *Personnel Journal, 46,* 22–26.

Fiske, D. W. (1971). *Measuring the concepts of personality*. Chicago: Alding.

Fiske, D. W. (1979). Two worlds of psychological phenomena. *American Psychologist, 34,* 733–739.

Fleishman, E. I., & Parker, J. F. (1962). Factors in the retention and relearning of perceptual-motor skill. *Journal of Experimental Psychology, 64,* 215–226.

Fleishman, E. A., & Quaintance, M. K. (1984). *Taxonomies of human performance: The description of human tasks*. New York: Academic Press.

Frazier, R. W. (1971). *Differential perception of individuals subgrouped on the basis of biodata responses*. Unpublished doctoral dissertation, University of Georgia, Athens.

French, N. R. (1974). *Biographical correlates of writing ability*. Unpublished master's thesis, University of Georgia, Athens.

French, N. R., Lewis, M. A., & Long, R. E. (1976, March). *Development and validation of a methodology to assess social desirability responding in a multiple choice biographical questionnaire*. Paper presented at the meeting of the Southeastern Psychological Association, New Orleans, LA.

Galton, F. (1883). *Inquiries into human faculty and its development*. New York: Macmillan.

Geisinger, K. F. (1974). *Prayer, biographical background and college students*. Unpublished manuscript, University of Georgia, Institute for Behavioral Research, Athens.

Geisinger, K. F. (1977). *Differential self-concepts among prior experience subgroups*. Unpublished master's thesis, University of Georgia, Athens.

Gist, N. P., & Clark, C. D. (1938). Intelligence as a selective factor in rural–urban migration. *American Journal of Sociology, 44,* 36–58.

Goldstein, I. L. (1971). The application blank: How honest are the responses? *Journal of Applied Psychology, 55,* 491–492.

Golembiewski, R. T., Billingsley, K., & Munzenrider, R. (1970). *Electoral choice and individual characteristics: Towards a biodata approach*. Unpublished manuscript, University of Georgia, Institute for Behavioral Research, Athens.

Gordon, S. M. (1976). *Logical incongruities contained within the biographical inventory blank*. Unpublished master's thesis, University of Georgia, Athens.

Gough, H. G. (1957). *Manual for the California Psychological Inventory*. Palo Alto, CA: Consulting Psychologists Press.

Gould, R. L. (1978). *Transformations: Growth and change in adult life*. New York: Simon and Schuster.

Guilford, J. P. (1954). *Psychometric methods*. New York: McGraw-Hill.

Guthrie, E. R. (1944). Personality in terms of associative learning. In J. McV. Hunt (Ed.), *Personality and behavior disorders* (Vol. 1, pp. 49–68). New York: Ronald Press.

Haan, N. (1981). Adolescents and young adults as producers of their own development. In R. M. Lerner & N. A. Busch-Rossnagel (Eds.), *Individuals as producers of their own development: A life span perspective* (pp. 155–182). New York: Academic Press.

Halpin, W. G. (1973). A study of the life histories and creative abilities of potential teachers (Doctoral dissertation, University of Georgia, 1972). *Dissertation Abstracts International, 33,* 3382A. (University Microfilms No. 72-34, 146)

Hamer, R. M., & Cunningham, J. W. (1981). Cluster analyzing profile data confounded with interrater differences: A comparison of profile association measures. *Applied Psychological Measurement, 5,* 63–72.

Hartshorne, H., & May, I. (1928). *Studies in deceit*. New York: Macmillan.

Hatcher, J. C. (1973). Differential persuasibility: Subgrouping on the basis of experiential data (Doctoral dissertation, University of Georgia, 1970). *Dissertation Abstracts International, 34,* 2932B. (University Microfilms No. 73-31, 141)

Havighurst, R. J. (1971). Social class perspectives on the life cycle. *Human Development, 14,* 110–124.

Helms, W. (1972). *Biodata subgroup differences in recall and clustering of interest area stimulus words.* Unpublished master's thesis, University of Georgia, Athens.

Hilden, A. H. (1949). A longitudinal study of intellectual development. *Journal of Psychology, 28,* 187–214.

Hindley, C. B. (1962). Social class influences on the development of ability in the first five years. *Proceedings of the XIV International Congress of Applied Psychology, 3,* 29–41.

Holland, J. L. (1966). *The psychology of vocational choice.* Waltham, MA: Blaisdell.

Holland, J. L., & Gottsfredson, G. B. (1975). Predictive value and psychological meaning of vocational aspirations. *Journal of Vocational Behavior, 6,* 349–363.

Honzick, M. P. (1967). Review of J. Hogan and H. Moses' *Birth to Maturity. Merrill-Palmer Quarterly, 11,* 77–88.

Howe, A. (1982). Biographical evidence and the development of outstanding individuals. *American Psychologist, 37,* 1071–1081.

Hughes, M. J. (1971). Biodata subgroup differences in serial verbal learning (Doctoral dissertation, University of Georgia, 1970). *Dissertation Abstracts International, 31,* 5026B. (University Microfilms No. 71-3741, 121)

Jones, E. L. (1970). *The affinity of biodata subgroups for vocational interest.* Unpublished manuscript, Institute for Behavioral Research, University of Georgia, Athens.

Jones, E. L. (1971). *The relationships among biographical similarity, perceived similarity and attraction in the roommate situation.* Unpublished master's thesis, University of Georgia, Athens.

Jones, H. E. (1958). Consistency and change in early maturity. *Human Development, 1,* 43–51.

Jones, H. E., & Conrad, H. W. (1933). The growth and decline of intelligence. *Genetic Psychology Monographs, 13,* 223–298.

Jung, C. G. (1923). *Psychological types.* London: Routledge, Kegan & Paul.

Kagan, J. (1964). American longitudinal research on psychological development. *Child Development, 35,* 1–32.

Kagan, J., & Moss, H. (1961). The stability of passive and dependent behaviors from childhood through adulthood. *Child Development, 31,* 577–581.

Kagan, J., & Moss, H. (1962). *Birth to maturity.* New York: John Wiley & Sons.

Kagan, J., & Pankove, E. (1972). Creative ability over a five-year span. *Child Development, 43,* 427–442.

Kagan, J., Sontag, L. W., Baker, C. T., & Nelson, V. L. (1958). Personality and IQ change. *Journal of Abnormal and Social Psychology, 56,* 261–266.

Kangus, J. (1971). Intelligence at middle age: A 36-year follow up. *Developmental Psychology, 5,* 333–337.

Kelly, L. E. (1955). Consistency of adult personality. *American Psychologist, 10,* 659–681.

Kerlinger, F. N. (1973). *Foundations of behavioral research.* New York: Holt, Rinehart and Winston.

Klein, H. A. (1973). Personality characteristics of discrepant academic achievers (Doctoral dissertation, University of Georgia, 1972). *Dissertation Abstracts International, 33,* 3387A. (University Microfilms No. 72-34, 105)

Kluckhohn, C., & Murray, H. A. (1949). *Personality in nature, society and culture.* New York: Knopf.

Koch, S. (1981). The nature and limits of psychological knowledge: Lessons of a century qua "science". *American Psychologist, 36,* 257–270.

Kuder, G. F., & Richardson, M. W. (1937). The theory of the estimation of test reliability. *Psychometrica, 2,* 151-160.

Kuhlen, R. G. (1963). Age and intelligence: The significance of cultural change in longitudinal vs. cross sectional findings. *Vita Humana, 6,* 113–124.

Kuhn, T. S. (1970). *The structure of scientific revolutions.* Chicago: University of Chicago Press.

Kupke, T. E. (1974). *Interpersonal attraction as a function of emitted verbal reinforcement, physical attractiveness, and background similarity.* Unpublished master's thesis, University of Georgia, Athens.

Labouvie, E. W., Bartsch, T. V., Nesselroade, J. R., & Baltes, P. B. (1974). On the internal and external validity of simple longitudinal designs. *Child Development, 45,* 282–290.

Lamiell, J. (1981). Toward an idiothetic psychology of personality. *American Psychologist, 36,* 276–289.

Lautenschlager, G. J., & Shaffer, G. S. (1987). A re-examination of the component stability of Owens's Biographical Questionnaire. *Journal of Applied Psychology, 72,* 149–152.

Lefkowitz, J. E. (1972). Comparison of the Strong Vocational Interest Blank and the Kuder Occupational Interest Survey scoring procedure. *Journal of Counseling Psychology, 17,* 357–363.

Lehman, H. C. (1953). *Age and achievement.* Princeton, NJ: Princeton University Press.

Lehman, H. C. (1960). The age decrement in outstanding scientific creativity. *American Psychologist, 15,* 128–134.

Lehman, H. C. (1966). The most creative years of engineers and other technologists. *Journal of Genetic Psychology, 108,* 263–270.

Leifer, E. F. (1971). *An investigation of the validity of subjective frames of references on a life history questionnaire.* Unpublished doctoral dissertation, University of Georgia, Athens.

Lerner, J. V. (1980). *The role congruence between temperament and school demands in school children's academic performance, personal adjustment and social relations.* Unpublished doctoral dissertation, Pennsylvania State University, University Park.

Lerner, R. M. (1978). Dialectics and development. *Human Development, 21,* 1–20.

Lerner, R. M., & Busch-Rossnagel, N. A. (1981). Individuals as producers of their development: Conceptual and empirical bases. In R. M. Lerner & N. A. Busch-Rossnagel (Eds.), *Individuals as producers of their own development: A life span perspective* (pp. 1–36). New York: Academic Press.

Levenson, J. (1978). *The seasons of man.* New York: Wiley.

Lewis, M. A. (1973). *Life experience characteristics of homosexual-activitists.* Unpublished master's thesis, University of Georgia, Athens.

Lewis, P., Hornsby, L., & Brady, P. (1973). *Behavioral correlates of biodata subgroup membership.* Unpublished manuscript, University of Georgia, Institute for Behavioral Research, Athens.

Lewontin, R. C., & Levens, R. (1982). Evolution. *Encyclopedia Einudi, 5,* 30–41.

Lissitz, R. W., & Schoenfeldt, L. F. (1974). Moderator subgroups for the estimation of education performance: A comparison of prediction models. *American Educational Research Journal, 11,* 63–75.

Livson, N. (1965, June). Developmental dimensions of personality: A longitudinal analysis. In R. C. Tryon (Chair), *Personality dimensions and typologies revealed by modern cluster analysis.* Symposium conducted at the meeting of the Western Psychological Association, Honolulu, HA.

Livson, N. (1973). Developmental dimensions of personality. In P. B. Baltes & W. K. Schaie (Eds.), *Life span developmental psychology: Personality and socialization* (pp. 98–122). New York: Academic Press.

Livson, N., & Peskin, H. (1967). The prediction of adult psychological health in a longitudinal study. *Journal of Abnormal Psychology, 72,* 509–518.

Long, R. E. (1975). *Birth order differences on developmental interest factors.* Unpublished master's thesis, University of Georgia.

Long, R. E. (1976). *Individual differences in mood-mediated helping.* Unpublished manuscript, University of Georgia, Athens.

Lord, F. (1980). *Application of item response theory to practical problems in tests.* Hillsdale, NJ: Lawrence Erlbaum Associates.

Maas, R. H. (1968). Preadolescent peer relations and adult intimacy. *Psychiatry, 31,* 161–171.

MacKinnon, D. (1948). *The assessment of men.* New York: Holt, Rinehart and Winston.

Markos, V. (1976). *Self-reported personality differences among female subgroups with similar biographical profiles.* Unpublished master's thesis, University of Georgia, Athens.

Meehl, P. E. (1967). Theory testing in psychology and physics: A methodological paradox. *Philosophy of Science, 38,* 103–115.

Mendoza, M. (1972). *Emotional response and biodata subgroup.* Unpublished master's thesis, University of Georgia, Athens.

Messick, S. (1980). Test validity and the ethics of assessment. *American Psychologist, 35,* 1012–1027.

Miller, N. E., & Dollard, J. (1941). *Social learning and imitation.* New Haven, CT: Yale University Press.

Milner, G. D. (1970). *Biodata correlates of decision making.* Unpublished master's thesis, University of Georgia, Athens.

Mischel, W. (1969). Continuity and change in personality. *American Psychologist, 24,* 1012–1018.

Mosel, J. N., & Cozan, C. W. (1952). The accuracy of application blank work histories. *Journal of Applied Psychology, 36,* 365–369.

Moss, H., & Kagan, J. (1961). Stability of achievement and recognition seeking behaviors from early childhood through adulthood. *Journal of Abnormal and Social Psychology, 62,* 504–513.

Muchinsky, P. M., & Hoyt, D. P. (1974). Predicting vocational performance of engineers from selected vocational interest, personality, and scholastic aptitude variables. *Journal of Vocational Behavior, 5,* 115–123.

Mumford, M. D. (1983). *Prototype prediction of freshman grade point average.* Unpublished manuscript.

Mumford, M. D. (1984). Age and outstanding occupational achievement: Lehman revisited. *Journal of Vocational Behavior, 25,* 225–244.

Mumford, M. D., & Owens, W. A. (1982). Life history and vocational interests. *Journal of Vocational Behavior, 21,* 330–348.

Mumford, M. D., & Owens, W. A. (1984). Individuality in a developmental context: Some empirical and theoretical considerations. *Human Development, 27,* 84–108.

Mumford, M. D., & Stokes, G. (1981, March). *Developmental correlates of positive and negative emotionality.* Paper presented at the meeting of the Southeastern Psychological Association, Atlanta, GA.

Mumford, M. D., Wesley, S., & Shaffer, G. S. (1987). Individuality in a development context: II. The crystallization of developmental trajectories. *Human Development, 30,* 291–321.

Mussen, P. H., & Jones, M. C. (1958). The behaviorally inferred motivations of late and early maturing boys. *Child Development, 29,* 61–67.

Neugarten, B. L. (1964). *Personality in middle and adult life.* New York: Atherton Press.

Neugarten, B. L. (1966). Adult personality: A developmental view. *Human Development, 9,* 61–73.

Newman, H. H., Freeman, F. N., & Holzinger, K. J. (1937). *Twins: A study of heredity and environment.* Chicago: University of Chicago Press.

Newstad, J. H., & Schuster, J. A. (1958). *Predictive measures for the achievement of training success in Air Force technical training.* Patterson, OH: Wright-Patterson Air Force Base.

Nutt, J. J. (1975). *An examination of student attrition using life experience subgroups.* Unpublished master's thesis, University of Georgia, Athens.

O'Neill, P. (1973). Stylistic differences in human maze learning (Doctoral dissertation, University of Georgia, 1973). *Dissertation Abstracts International, 34,* 3152A. (University Microfilms No. 73-31, 114)

Owens, W. A. (1953). Age and mental abilities: A longitudinal study. *Genetic Psychology Monographs, 48,* 3–54.

Owens, W. A. (1976). Background data. In M. D. Dunnette (Ed.), *Handbook of industrial and organizational psychology* (pp. 609–644). Chicago: Rand-McNally.

Owens, W. A. (1978). Moderators and subgroups. *Personnel Psychology, 31,* 243–247.

Owens, W. A., & Henry, E. R. (1966). *Biographical data in industrial psychology: A review and evaluation.* Greensboro, NC: Creativity Research Institute of the Richardson Foundation.

Owens, W. A., & Schoenfeldt, L. F. (1979). Toward a classification of persons. *Journal of Applied Psychology, 65,* 569–607.

Pace, L. A. (1974). *Prior experience as a mediating variable in the reproduction of random shapes in the presence and absence of verbal labels.* Unpublished master's thesis, University of Georgia, Athens.

Precker, J. A. (1952). Similarity of valuings as a factor in selection of peers and near authority figures. *Journal of Abnormal and Social Psychology, 47,* 406–414.

Peskin, H. (1967). Pubertal onset and ego functioning: A psychoanalytic approach. *Journal of Abnormal Psychology, 72,* 1–15.

Piacentini, J. J. (1974). *Physical correlates of prior behavior pattern.* Unpublished master's thesis, University of Georgia, Athens.

Reichard, S., Livson, N., & Peterson, P. (1962). *Aging and personality.* New York: Wiley.

Reilly, R. R., & Chao, G. T. (1982). Validity and fairness of some alternative employee selection procedures. *Personnel Psychology, 35,* 1–62.

Riegel, K. F. (1975). Toward a dialectical theory of development. *Human Development, 18,* 50–64.

Riegel, K. F., Riegel, R. M., & Meyers, G. (1967). A study of dropout rate in longitudinal research on aging and prediction of death. *Journal of Personality and Social Psychology, 5,* 342–348.

Roadheaver, D., & Datan, N. (1981). Making it: The dialectics of middle age. In R. M. Lerner & N. A. Busch-Rossnagel (Eds.), *Individuals as producers of their own development: A life span perspective* (pp. 183–196). New York: Academic Press.

Robbins, M. D. (1975). *Biographical correlates of job changing behavior.* Unpublished manuscript, University of Georgia, Athens.

Roe, A. (1956). *The psychology of occupations.* New York: Wiley.

Rose, C. L. (1965). Representativeness of volunteer subjects in a longitudinal study. *Human Development, 8,* 152–156.

Rosow, I. (1978). What is a cohort and why. *Human Development, 21,* 65–75.

Rychlack, J. R. (1972). *Introduction to personality theory and psychotherapy.* Boston: Houghton Mifflin.

Scandura, J. M. (1977). *Problem solving.* New York: Academic Press.

Schaie, W. K. (1972). Limitations on the generalizability of growth curves of intelligence. *Human Development, 15,* 141–152.

Schaie, W. K., & Parham, I. A. (1977). Cohort-sequential analysis of adult intellectual development. *Developmental Psychology, 13,* 649–653.

Schmidt, F. L., & Hunter, J. E. (1977). Development of a general solution to the problem of validity generalization. *Journal of Applied Psychology, 62,* 524–540.

Schmidt, F. L., Hunter, J. E., McKenzie, R., & Muldrow, T. (1979). The impact of valid selection procedures on work force productivity. *Journal of Applied Psychology, 64,* 609–626.

Schoenfeldt, L. F. (1974). Utilization of manpower: Development and evaluation of an assessment-classification model for matching individuals with jobs. *Journal of Applied Psychology, 59,* 583–595.

Schrader, A. D., & Osburn, H. G. (1977). Biodata faking: Effects of induced subtlety and position specificity. *Personnel Psychology, 30,* 395–404.

Schwartz, E. M., & Cohen, A. S. (1975). IQ and the myth of stability: A 16-year longitudinal study of variation in intelligence test performance. *Journal of Clinical Psychology, 31,* 687–694.

Sears, R. (1977). Sources of life satisfaction in Terman's Gifted Group. *American Psychologist, 32,* 119–128.

Sechrest, L. (1974). Personality measurement. In E. F. Borgatta & W. W. Lambert (Eds.), *Handbook of personality theory and research* (pp. 529–628). Chicago: Rand-McNally.

Shaffer, D. R. (1988). *Social and personality development.* Monterey, CA: Brooks/Cole.

Shaffer, G. S., Saunders, V., & Owens, W. A. (1986). Additional evidence for the accuracy of biographical data: Long-term retest and observer ratings. *Personnel Psychology, 39,* 781–809.

Sheldon, H. M., Stevens, S. S., & Tucker, W. B. (1940). *The varieties of human physique.* New York: Harper and Row.

Shien, E. H. (1980). *Career dynamics: Matching individual and organizational needs.* Reading, MA: Addison-Wesley.

Sontag, L. W. (1971). The history of longitudinal research: Implications for the future. *Child Development, 42,* 987–1002.

Speed, A. A. (1970). *Differential influence of monetary incentives upon performance on the College Qualifications Test.* Unpublished master's thesis, University of Georgia, Athens.

Spool, M. D. (1973). *Life experience differences between black and white college students as assessed with a biographical questionnaire.* Unpublished master's thesis, University of Georgia, Athens.

Staats, A. W. (1969). Experimental demand characteristics and the classical conditioning of attitudes. *Journal of Personality and Social Psychology, 11,* 187–192.

Sternberg, R. J. (1982). A componential approach to intellectual development. In R. J. Sternberg (Ed.), *Advances in the psychology of human intelligence.* Hillsdale, NJ: Lawrence Erlbaum Associates.

Strimbu, J. J. (1973). *A quasi-actuarial approach to the identification of college student drug users.* Unpublished doctoral dissertation, University of Georgia, Athens.

Strimbu, J. J., & Schoenfeldt, L. F. (1973). Life history subgroups in the prediction of drug usage patterns and attitudes. *JSAS Catalog of Selected Documents in Psychology, 3,* 83. (Ms. No. 412).

Strong, E. K. (1943). *The vocational interests of men and women.* Palo Alto, CA: Stanford University Press.

Super, D. E. (1957). *The psychology of careers.* New York: Harper & Row.

Terman, L. M. (1916). *The measurement of intelligence.* Boston: Houghton Mifflin Company.

Terman, L. M. (1925). *Genetic studies of geniuses: Mental and physical traits of 1000 gifted children.* Stanford, CA: Stanford University Press.

Terman, L. M. (1947). *Genetic studies of geniuses: The gifted child grows up.* Stanford, CA: Stanford University Press.

Terman, L. M. (1959). *The gifted group at mid-life.* Stanford, CA: Stanford University Press.

Thomae, H. (1965). Objective socialization variables and personality development: Findings from a longitudinal study. *Human Development, 8,* 87–116.

Thomas, A., & Chess, S. (1972). Development in middle childhood. *Seminars in Psychiatry, 4,* 321–341.

Thomas, A., & Chess, S. (1977). *Temperament and development.* New York: Brunner/Mazel.

Thomas, A., & Chess, S. (1981). The role of temperament in the contributions of individuals to their development. In R. M. Lerner & N. A. Busch-Rossnagel (Eds.), *Individuals as producers of their own development.* New York: Academic Press.

Thorndike, R. L. (1949). *Personnel selection.* New York: Wiley.

Thurstone, L. L. (1931). Multiple factor analysis. *Psychological Review, 38,* 406–427.

Tobach, E. (1981). Evolutionary aspects of the activity of the organism and its development. In R. M. Lerner & N. A. Busch-Rossnagel (Eds.), *Individuals as producers of their own development* (pp. 37–68). New York: Academic Press.

Toops, H. A. (1948). The use of addends in experimental control, social census and managerial research. *Psychological Bulletin, 45,* 41–74.

Toops, H. A. (1959). A research utopia in industrial psychology. *Personnel Psychology, 12,* 189–225.

Torrance, E. P. (1972). Career patterns and peak creative achievements of creative high school students 12 years later. *Gifted Child Quarterly, 16,* 75–88.

Tuddenham, R. D. (1959). The consistency of personnel ratings over two decades. *Genetic Psychology Monographs, 60,* 3–29.

Tyler, L. E. (1959). Toward a workable psychology of individuality. *American Psychologist, 14,* 75–81.

Tyler, L. E. (1964). The antecedents of two varieties of interest patterns. *Genetic Psychological Monographs, 70,* 177–227.

Tyler, L. E. (1965). *The psychology of human differences.* Englewood Cliffs, NJ: Prentice-Hall.

Tyler, L. E. (1974). *Individual differences in abilities and motivational directions.* Englewood Cliffs, NJ: Prentice-Hall.

Vaillant, G. L. (1977). *Adaption to life.* New York: Wiley.

Vaillant, G. L., & McArthur, C. L. (1972). Natural history and male psychological health in the adult life cycle from 18 to 50. *Seminars in Psychiatry, 4,* 415–427.

Vale, J. R., & Vale, C. A. (1969). Individual differences and general laws in psychology: A reconciliation. *American Psychologist, 24,* 1093–1108.

Vincent, D. F. (1952). The linear relationship between age and score of adults in intelligence tests. *Occupational Psychology, 26,* 243–249.

Wagner, M. A. (1947). Preliminary study of the significance of measures of autonomic balance. *Psychosomatic Medicine, 9,* 301–309.

Walton, B. E. (1976). *Prediction of individual and subgroup behavior via quasi-actuarial assessment: A cross-validation.* Unpublished master's thesis, University of Georgia, Athens.

Ward, J. H., & Hook, M. E. (1963). Application of a hierarchical grouping procedure to the problem of grouping profiles. *Educational and Psychological Measurement, 23,* 69–81.

White, C. B. (1974). Moral judgment in college students: The development of an objective measure and its relationship to life experience dimensions (Doctoral dissertation, University of Georgia, 1973). *Dissertation Abstracts International, 34,* 3480B. (University Microfilms No. 73-31, 191)

Witkin, H., Goodenough, D. R., & Karp, S. A. (1967). Stability of cognitive style from childhood to young adulthood. *Journal of Personality and Social Psychology, 7,* 219–300.

Wright, R. B. (1973). *Some biodata subgroup differences in reading comprehension.* Unpublished master's thesis, University of Georgia, Athens.

Yarrow, L. J., & Yarrow, M. R. (1964). Personality continuity and change in the family context. In P. Worchel & D. Bryne (Eds.), *Personality change* (pp. 489–523). New York: Wiley.

Zimmerman, R., Jacobs, R., & Farr, J. (1982). A comparison of the accuracy of four methods of clustering jobs. *Applied Psychological Measurement, 6,* 353–366.

Author Index

Subject Index